Anthropology

The Basics

Anthropology

The Basics

Christopher R. DeCorse
Syracuse University

Raymond Scupin
Lindenwood University

PEARSON

Boston Columbus Indianapolis New York San Francisco Amsterdam
Cape Town Dubai London Madrid Milan Munich Paris Montréal Toronto
Delhi Mexico City São Paulo Sydney Hong Kong Seoul Singapore Taipei Tokyo

Editorial Director: Dickson Musslewhite
Publisher: Charlyce Jones-Owen
Editorial Assistant: Maureen Diana
Program Manager: Rob DeGeorge
Project Manager: Richard DeLorenzo
Procurement Specialist: Mary Ann Gloriande
Permissions Specialist: Brooks Hill-Whilton
Image Permissions Specialist: Jen Simmons/Lumina Datamatics, Inc.
Cover Art Director: Maria Lange
Cover image: Shutterstock
Director, Digital Studio: Sacha Laustein
Media Product Manager: David Alick
Media Project Manager: Amanda Smith
Full-Service Project Management and Composition: Tracy Duff/Lumina Datamatics, Inc.

Credits and acknowledgments borrowed from other sources and reproduced with permission appear in the appropriate Credits sections at the end of the book.

Library of Congress Cataloging-in-Publication Data is available on request from the Library of Congress

10 9 8 7 6 5 4 3 2 1

Student Edition
ISBN-10: 0-13-401286-0
ISBN-13: 978-0-13-401286-5

Instructor's Review Copy:
ISBN-10: 0-13-416122-X
ISBN-13: 978-0-13-416122-8

Á La Carte
ISBN-10: 0-13-402907-0
ISBN-13: 978-0-13-402907-8

Brief Contents

Contents

Boxes

Anthropologists at Work

Critical Perspectives

Preface

Human origins, ancient civilizations, different cultures; what is more exciting than the study of anthropology? Anthropology spans the biological and cultural diversity of human societies in the past and present, making it uniquely relevant to the modern world. The Internet, international trade, geopolitical events, and ease of travel have brought people from different cultures into more intimate contact than ever before, forcing this generation of students to become more knowledgeable about societies other than their own. The holistic perspective that anthropology provides is a key means of leading students to an appreciation of both the similarities and diversity of humans throughout the world, which is essential in the interconnected world of the twenty-first century. The subfields of anthropology help liberate students from narrow, parochial views and enable them to appreciate the full sweep of the human condition. Anthropology stands apart from other disciplines because it combines four subfields that bridge the natural sciences, the social sciences, and the humanities. These four subfields—biological anthropology, archaeology, linguistic anthropology, and cultural anthropology—constitute a broad approach to the study of humanity the world over, both past and present. The concluding chapter of this volume ties together these different subfields and specifically confronts anthropology's relevance to the modern world in applied anthropology.

Educational Goals

Anthropology: The Basics provides a concise introduction to the subfields of anthropology, including the key concepts, methods, and some of the central questions that anthropologists have grappled with in their research. It is aimed at anthropologists who might prefer a less comprehensive textbook that provides an introduction to key concepts, to which they can add supplementary case studies and readings.

The anthropological perspective, which stresses critical thinking, the evaluation of competing hypotheses, and the skills to generalize from specific data, is fundamental to a well-rounded education. This textbook engages readers in anthropology by delving into both classic and current research. It reflects a commitment to anthropology's holistic and integrative approach, clearly illustrating how the subfields of anthropology, together, yield a comprehensive understanding of humanity. Perspectives from each of the subfields are woven together to reveal how anthropologists unlock the workings of a particular society or the threads that unite human societies, both past and present.

The comparative approach, another cornerstone of anthropology, is highlighted throughout the textbook. When anthropologists assess fossil evidence, artifacts, languages, or cultural beliefs, they weigh the evidence from a comparative perspective, even as they acknowledge the unique elements of each case, society, or culture. Anthropologists draw on examples from across both time and space. Consequently, the text casts an inquiring eye on materials from numerous geographical regions and historical eras to enrich students' understanding. In evaluating human evolution, past human societies, language divergence, or developments in social structure, anthropologists must rely on a diachronic approach, and draw on models that accommodate change through time. Exploring interactions between anthropology and other fields further underscores anthropology's unique, holistic perspective that sparks the critical imagination that brings learning to life.

Three Unifying Themes of This Text

This textbook has three unifying themes that structures the material presented. These are: 1) The need to understand and appreciate the *diversity of human societies* and cultural patterns the world over; 2) The *similarities that make all humans fundamentally alike*, and 3) A *synthetic-complementary approach* that underscores the interconnections between the sciences and humanities within anthropology. To achieve these objectives, we pay as much attention to universal human characteristics as we do to individual cultural contexts and conditions.

Drawing on a *synthetic-complementary approach*, we view the scientific method and the methods in the humanities as complementary and suggest that one is incomplete without the other. It has sometimes been suggested that the scientific approach is not suitable for assessing and interpreting human behavior and culture, just as it has been suggested that the humanistic approach is not appropriate for developing general cross-cultural and causal explanations about human behavior and culture. We feel that this is not the case. In this book, we highlight how an interpretive-humanistic perspective is complementary to both perspectives. This view resonates with an observation made by the late Eric Wolf. In an anthropology textbook published decades ago, Wolf emphasized that anthropology has always had one foot in the sciences and one foot in the humanities. This observation is evermore true today. Wolf said, "Anthropology is both the most scientific of the humanities and the most humanistic of the sciences" (1964, 88). An interpretive-humanistic perspective provides insight into the specifics of human behavior within different cultures, whereas the scientific approach offers a method to test causal explanations that allow for insight into universal aspects of human behavior.

Boxes

Throughout the textbook, Critical Perspectives boxes and Anthropologists at Work boxes are used to highlight particular aspects of anthropological research. They provide more detailed illustration of the kinds of research that anthropologists undertake, and serve as a basis for further discussions of anthropological research and questions that are not explored in detail in the chapters.

Critical Perspectives boxes are designed to stimulate independent reasoning and judgment. Students are placed in the role of an anthropologist and engaged in the analysis of specific questions using anthropological research. Critical Perspectives boxes encourage students to use rigorous standards of evidence when evaluating assumptions and hypotheses regarding scientific and philosophical issues that often have no easy answers. By probing beneath the surface of various assumptions and hypotheses in these exercises, students discover the excitement and challenge of anthropological investigation.

Anthropologists at Work boxes feature anthropologists working in a variety of areas of biological anthropology, cultural anthropology, archaeology, linguistics, and applied anthropology. They profile work by leading anthropologists and humanize many of the issues dealt with in the chapters. The anthropologists whose work is highlighted are involved in topics ranging from unraveling the puzzle of human origins and development issues in various countries, to the challenges of saving languages that are becoming extinct.

Pedagogical Aids

Each chapter opens with a list of *Learning Objectives* that will help students focus on important concepts introduced in the chapter. Summaries of these learning objectives at the end of each chapter provide succinct reviews of the material to aid students' comprehension of the text they have read. *Key Terms*, which deal with particularly important concepts, are highlighted in the relevant discussions throughout the book. These terms are listed at the end of each chapter. A *Glossary* at the end of the book provides definitions of each of these terms.

Supplementary Materials

Instructor's Manual with Tests For each chapter in the text, the Instructor's Manual contains a detailed Chapter Outline, Learning Objectives from the text, Lecture and Discussion Topics, Classroom Activities, and Research and Writing Topics. The Test Bank contains questions in multiple-choice, true/false, and essay formats. For easy access, this manual is available for download at www.pearsonhighered.com/irc.

MyTest This computerized software allows instructors to create their own personalized exams, edit any or all of the existing test questions, and add new questions. Other special features of the program include random generation of test questions, creation of alternate versions of the same test, scrambling question sequence, and test preview before printing. For easy access, this software is available for download at www.pearsonhighered.com/irc.

PowerPoint Presentation These PowerPoint slides combine text and graphics for each chapter to help instructors convey anthropology principles in a clear and engaging way. For easy access, they are available for download at www.pearsonhighered.com/irc.

Acknowledgments

A textbook like this one requires the enormous effort of many people. First, we would like to offer thanks to colleague Christina Dames, who is a recent graduate of the University of Missouri-Columbia's anthropology program and a faculty member at Lindenwood University. She provided in-depth research assistance on the production of this textbook, helping to update material in many areas of this book.

We also extend thanks to all colleagues who sent us photos and information for use in the biography boxes. We are grateful for the unwavering support given to this project by Pearson. Without the moral support and encouragement of our acquisition editor, Charlyce Jones-Owen, publisher, Rob DeGeorge, program manager, and Richard DeLorenzo, project manager, this project would have been much harder to complete. We would also like to thank the copyeditor Barry Wilkinson for his valuable comments in preparation for this Basics edition.

Our warmest appreciation goes to our families, whose emotional support and patience throughout the production of this textbook has been very helpful.

Anyone with comments, suggestions, or recommendations regarding this text is welcome to send e-mail messages to the following addresses: **rscupin@lindenwood.edu** or **crdecors@maxwell.syr.edu**.

Christopher R. DeCorse

Raymond Scupin

REVEL™

Educational technology designed for the way today's students read, think, and learn

When students are engaged deeply, they learn more effectively and perform better in their courses. This simple fact inspired the creation of REVEL: an immersive learning experience designed for the way today's students read, think, and learn. Built in collaboration with educators and students nationwide, REVEL is the newest, fully digital way to deliver respected pearson content.

REVEL enlivens course content with media interactives and assessments—integrated directly within the authors' narrative—that provide opportunities for students to read about and practice course material in tandem. This immersive educational technology boosts student engagement, which leads to better understanding of concepts and improved performance throughout the course.

Learn more about REVEL: www.pearsonhighered.com/REVEL

About the Authors

Christopher R. DeCorse received his B.A. in anthropology and a minor in history from the University of New Hampshire, before completing his M.A. and Ph.D. degrees in archaeology at the University of California–Los Angeles. His theoretical interests include the interpretation of ethnicity and culture change in the archaeological record, archaeology and popular culture, and general anthropology. Dr. DeCorse has excavated a variety of prehistoric and historic period sites in the United States, the Caribbean, and Africa, but his primary area of research has been in the archaeology, history, and ethnography of West Africa. Dr. DeCorse has taught archaeology and general anthropology in undergraduate and graduate programs at the University of Ghana, Indiana University of Pennsylvania, and Syracuse University, where he is currently professor and past chairman of the Department of Anthropology. His academic honors and awards include: the Daniel Patrick Moynihan Award for Outstanding Teaching, Research and Service; the William Wasserstrom Award for Excellence in Graduate Teaching; and the Syracuse University Excellence in Graduate Education Faculty Recognition Award.

Dr. DeCorse is particularly interested in making archaeology more accessible to general audiences. In addition to the single-authored physical anthropology and archaeology textbook *The Record of the Past: An Introduction to Physical Anthropology and Archaeology*, DeCorse coauthored with Brian Fagan the eleventh edition of *In the Beginning: An Introduction to Archaeology*, both published by Prentice Hall. Dr. DeCorse's published academic works include more than 60 articles, book chapters, and research notes in a variety of publications, including *The African Archaeological Review*, *Historical New Hampshire*, *Historical Archaeology*, the *Journal of African Archaeology*, and *Slavery and Abolition*. A volume on his work in Ghana, *An Archaeology of Elmina: Africans and Europeans on the Gold Coast 1400–1900*, and an edited volume, *West Africa during the Atlantic Slave Trade: Archaeological Perspectives*, were published in 2001. His most recent book (2008), *Small Worlds: Method, Meaning, and Narrative in Microhistory*, coedited with James F. Brooks and John Walton, deals with the interpretation of the past through the lens of microhistory.

Raymond Scupin is Professor of Anthropology and International Studies at Lindenwood University. He is currently the Director at the Center for International and Global Studies at Lindenwood. He received his B.A. degree in history and Asian studies, and anthropology, from the University of California–Los Angeles. He completed his M.A. and Ph.D. degrees in anthropology at the University of California–Santa Barbara. Dr. Scupin is truly a four-field anthropologist. During graduate school, he conducted archaeological and ethnohistorical research on Native Americans in the Santa Barbara region. He did extensive ethnographic fieldwork in Thailand with a focus on understanding the ethnic and religious movements among the Muslim minority. In addition, Dr. Scupin taught linguistics and conducted linguistic research while based at a Thai university.

Dr. Scupin has been teaching undergraduate and graduate courses in anthropology for more than 30 years at a variety of academic institutions, including community colleges, research universities, and a four-year liberal arts university. He has taught a broad spectrum of undergraduate students. Through his teaching experience, Dr. Scupin was prompted to write this textbook, which would help a wide range of undergraduate students to understand the holistic and global perspectives of the four-field approach in anthropology. In 1999, he received the Missouri Governor's Award for Teaching Excellence. In 2007, Dr. Scupin received the Distinguished Scholars Award at Lindenwood University.

Dr. Scupin has published many studies based on his ethnographic research in Thailand. He returned to Thailand and other countries of Southeast Asia to update his ethnographic data on Islamic trends in that area, an increasingly important topic in the post-9/11 world. He is a member of many professional associations, including the American Anthropological Association, the Asian Studies Association, and the Council of Thai Studies. Dr. Scupin has recently authored *Religion and Culture: An Anthropological Focus; Race and Ethnicity: The United States and the World;* and *Peoples and Cultures of Asia*, all published by Pearson Prentice Hall.

Chapter 1
Introduction to Anthropology

Chapter Outline

Learning Objectives

After reading this chapter you should be able to:

1.1 Compare and contrast the four major subfields of anthropology.

1.2 Describe how the field of anthropology is holistic, interdisciplinary, and global.

1.3 Explain how the scientific method is used in anthropological explanations.

1.4 Discuss how the field of anthropology bridges both the sciences and the humanities.

1.5 Describe why any student should study anthropology.

First contact. To science-fiction writers, *first contact* refers to the first meeting between humans and extraterrestrial beings. To anthropologists, the phrase refers to the initial encounters between peoples of different societies. For thousands of years, people throughout the world have had first contacts with each other. Today, "first contacts" are happening at every moment—through e-mail, smartphones, and the Web; as well as by the ease of international travel. What do we observe at these "first contacts"? How do we understand diverse peoples of the world? How can we explain human behavior? In a globalized world, these questions are growing more and more important. As we shall see in this chapter, anthropology incorporates four major subfields that seek to understand different aspects of humanity in much the same way that future space travelers might investigate extraterrestrials.

Anthropologists use a variety of field methods, techniques, and theoretical approaches to conduct their investigations, which have two major goals: to understand the *uniqueness and diversity* of human behavior and human societies around the world and to discover the *fundamental similarities* that connect human beings throughout the world in both the past and the present. To accomplish these goals, anthropologists undertake systematic case studies of human populations across the globe.

These studies have broadened our understanding of humanity, from the beginning of human societies to the present. This chapter introduces the distinctive approaches used in anthropology to achieve these goals.

Anthropology: The Four Subfields

1.1 Compare and contrast the four major subfields of anthropology.

The word *anthropology* is derived from the Greek words *anthropo*, meaning "human beings" or "humankind," and *logia*, translated as "knowledge of" or "the study of." Thus, we can define **anthropology** as the study of humankind. This definition in itself, however, does not distinguish anthropology from other disciplines. After all, historians, psychologists, economists, sociologists, and scholars in many other fields systematically study humankind in one way or another. Anthropology stands apart because it combines four subfields that bridge the natural sciences, the social sciences, and the humanities. These four subfields—biological anthropology, archaeology, linguistic anthropology, and cultural anthropology—constitute a broad approach to the study of humanity the world over, both past and present. Figure 1.1 shows these subfields and the various specializations that make up each one. A discussion of these subfields and some of the key specializations in each follows.

The subfields of anthropology initially emerged in Western society in an attempt to understand non-Western peoples. When Europeans began exploring and colonizing the world in the fifteenth century, they encountered native peoples in the Americas, Africa, the Middle East, and Asia. European travelers, missionaries, and government officials described these non-Western cultures, providing a record of their physical appearances, customs, and beliefs. By the nineteenth century, anthropology had developed into the primary discipline for understanding these non-Western societies and cultures. The major questions that these nineteenth-century anthropologists sought to answer dealt with the basic differences and similarities of human societies and cultures, and with the physical variation found in peoples throughout the world. Today, anthropologists do not solely focus their attention on non-Western cultures: They are just as likely to examine cultural practices in an urban setting in the United States as to conduct fieldwork in some far-off place. However, anthropologists continue to grapple with the basic questions of human diversity and similarities through systematic research within the four subfields described below.

Figure 1.1 The four core subfields of anthropology and applied anthropology.

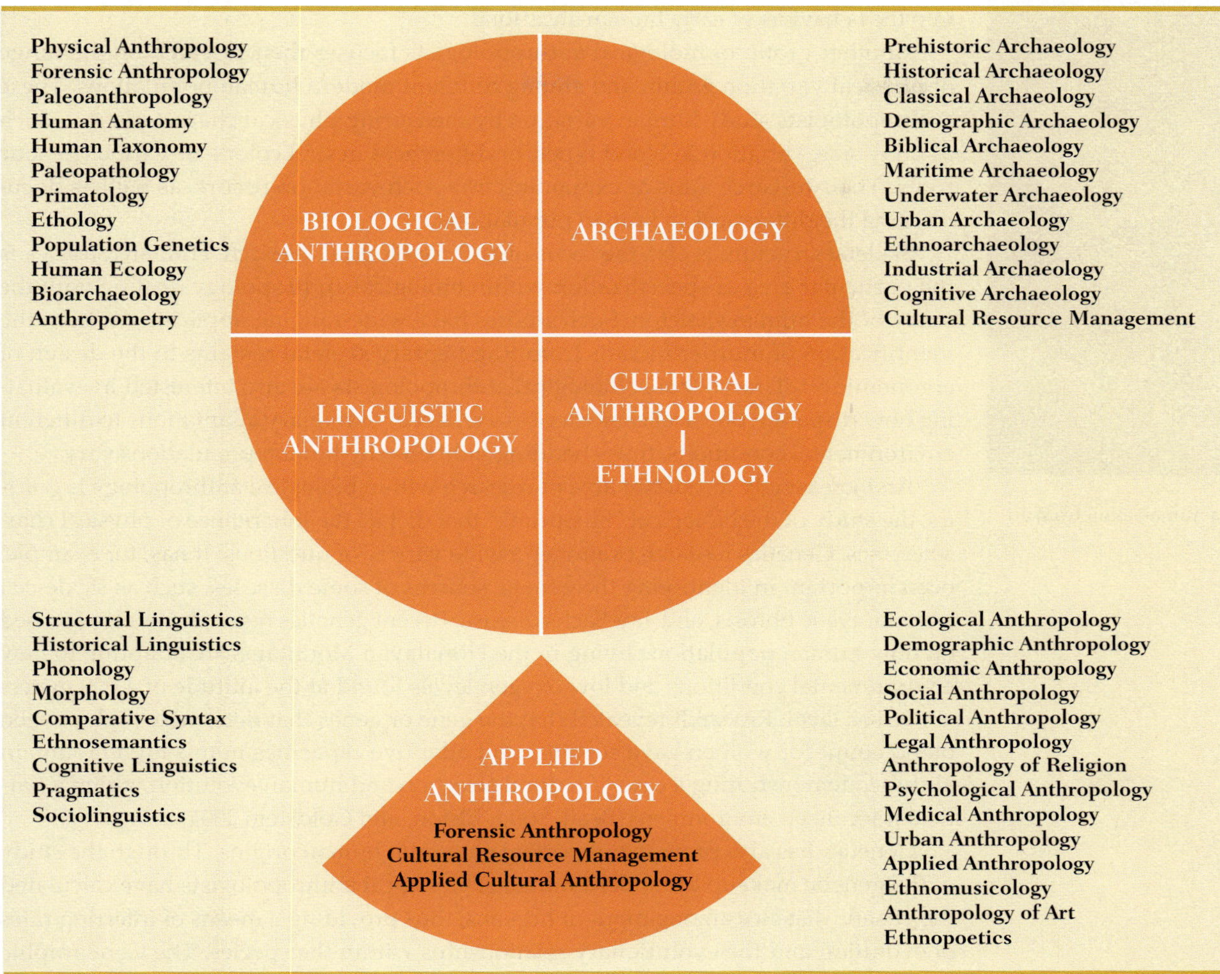

Biological Anthropology

Biological anthropology (also referred to as physical anthropology) is the branch of anthropology concerned with humans as a biological species. As such, it is the subfield most closely related to the natural sciences. Biological anthropologists conduct research in two major areas: human evolution and modern human variation. The investigation of human evolution presents one of the most tantalizing areas of anthropological study. Research has now traced the African origins of humanity back over six million years, while fieldwork in other world areas has traced the expansion of early human ancestors throughout the world. Much of the evidence for human origins consists of **fossils**, the fragmentary remains of bones and living materials preserved from earlier periods. The study of human evolution through analysis of fossils is called **paleoanthropology** (the prefix *paleo-* from the Greek word *palaios,* means "old" or "ancient"). Paleoanthropologists use a variety of scientific techniques to date, classify, and compare fossilized bones to determine the links between modern humans and their biological ancestors. These paleoanthropologists may work closely with archaeologists when studying ancient tools and activity areas to learn about the behavior of early human ancestors.

Other biological anthropologists explore human evolution through **primatology**, the study of primates. **Primates** are a diverse order of mammals that share an evolutionary history with humans and, therefore, have many physical characteristics in common with us. Many primatologists observe primates such as chimpanzees, gorillas, gibbons, and

Excavation of a human skull from an ancient burial

orangutans in their natural habitats to ascertain the similarities and differences between these other primates and humans. These observations of living primates provide insight into the behaviors of early human ancestors.

Another group of biological anthropologists focuses their research on the range of physical variation within and among different modern human populations. These anthropologists study human variation by measuring physical characteristics—such as body size, variation in blood types, or differences in skin color—or various genetic traits. Their research aims at explaining *why* such variation occurs, as well as documenting the differences in human populations.

Skeletal structure is also the focus of anthropological research. Human *osteology* is the particular area of specialization within biological anthropology dealing with the study of the human skeleton. Such studies have wide-ranging applications, from the identification of murder victims from fragmentary skeletal remains to the design of ergonomic airplane cockpits. Biological anthropologists are also interested in evaluating how disparate physical characteristics reflect evolutionary adaptations to different environmental conditions, thus shedding light on why human populations vary.

An increasingly important area of research within biological anthropology is *genetics*, the study of the biological "blueprints" that dictate the inheritance of physical characteristics. Genetics research examines a wide variety of questions. It has, for example, been important in identifying the genetic sources of some diseases, such as sickle-cell anemia, cystic fibrosis, and Tay-Sachs disease. Recent genetics research has also focused on how human populations living in the Himalayan Mountains are adapting to new environmental conditions and low oxygen levels found at the altitude of 4,000 meters above sea level. Research revealed that the gene or genes that determine high-oxygen blood count for women gave survival and adaptive capacities in this high mountain altitude, demonstrating a case of natural selection and human evolution within a particular localized environment (Beall, Song, Elston, and Goldstein 2004).

Genetics has also provided important clues into human origins. Through the study of the genetic makeup of modern humans, biological anthropologists have calculated the genetic distance among modern humans, thus providing a means of inferring rates of evolution and the evolutionary relationships within the species. The Genographic Project is gathering samples of DNA from populations throughout the world to trace human evolution. Labs analyzing DNA have been established in different regions of the world by the Genographic Project. As DNA is transmitted from parents to offspring, most of the genetic material is recombined and mutated. However, some mutated DNA remains fairly stable over the course of generations. This stable mutated DNA can serve as "genetic markers" that are passed on to each generation and create populations with distinctive sets of DNA. These genetic markers distinguish ancient lineages of DNA. By following the pathways of these genetic markers, genetic paleoanthropologists can blend archaeology, prehistoric, and linguistic data with paleoanthropological data to trace human evolution. The Genographic Project traces both mitochondrial DNA (passed from mother to offspring in long lineages of maternal descent) and the Y chromosome

Children of different nationalities and cultures

Anthropologists at Work

JOHN HAWKS, Biological Anthropologist

John Hawks

John Hawks is a biological anthropologist who works on the border between paleoanthropology and genetics. He got his start teaching evolution in his home state of Kansas, followed by doctoral training and teaching in Michigan, Utah, and his current home, the University of Wisconsin. He studies the relationships between the genes of living and ancient people, to discover the ways that natural selection has affected them. In 2007, Hawks and co-workers scanned the genome, finding evidence for widespread selection on new, advantageous mutations during the last 40,000 years (Hawks et al. 2007). The breadth of this selection across the genome indicated that human evolution actually accelerated as larger populations and new agricultural subsistence exerted strong pressures on ancient people. Far from slowing down our evolution, culture had created new opportunities for adaptive change in the human population.

Hawks made substantial contributions examining the Neandertal genome. The availability of genetic evidence from ancient bones has transformed the way we study these ancient people. By comparing Neandertal genes with humans and chimpanzees, it will become possible to expand our knowledge of evolution beyond the skeletal record, finding signs from the immune system, digestion, and pigmentation, to traits like hearing and, ultimately, the brain itself.

Hawks is probably most widely known for his blog, which is visited by several thousand readers every day. Describing new research from an expert's perspective, he has shown the power of public outreach as an element of the scientific process. This element of his work has made him a leader in the "open science" movement, trying to expand public accessibility to scientific research and open access to scientific data. On his blog, Hawks writes:

What does it mean to be a paleoanthropologist? To use evidence from the fossil record, we must be trained in human anatomy—especially *bone* anatomy, or osteology. We have to know the anatomical comparisons between humans and other primates, and the way these anatomies relate to habitual behaviors. The social and ecological behaviors of primates vary extensively in response to their unique ecological circumstances. Understanding the relationship of anatomy, behavior, and environment gives us a way to interpret ancient fossils and place them in their environmental context. My scientific work hasn't been limited to genetics and fossils. Lately, I have become more and more interested in the problems of cultural transmission and information theory. This is part of my "first principles" approach to problems in prehistory—I think that we have to build an account of the origins of culture that is based in the simplest rules of information transfer.

Hawks welcomes everyone who is interested in human evolution based on a scientific approach to go to his blog at http://johnhawks.net/weblog/hawks/hawks.html.

(passed from father to son). These data have helped provide independent evidence for the African origins of the modern human species and human ancestors. This evidence will be discussed in later chapters on the evolution of modern humans. Individuals can join the project and submit samples of their own DNA to trace their genetic linkage to ancient populations at https://genographic.nationalgeographic.com.

Archaeology

Archaeology, the branch of anthropology that examines the material traces of past societies, informs us about the culture of those societies—the shared way of life of a group of people that includes their values, beliefs, and norms. **Artifacts**, the material products of former societies, provide clues to the past. Some archaeological sites reveal spectacular jewelry like that found by the film character Indiana Jones or in the treasures of a pharaoh's tomb. Most artifacts, however, are not so spectacular. Despite the popular image of archaeology as an adventurous, even romantic, pursuit, it usually consists of methodical, time-consuming, and—sometimes—somewhat tedious research. Archaeologists often spend hours sorting through ancient trash piles, or **middens**, to discover how members of past societies ate their meals, what tools they used in their households and in their work, and what beliefs gave meaning to their lives. They collect and carefully analyze the broken fragments of pottery, stone, glass, and other materials. It may take them months, or even years, to fully complete

Archaeologists digging at the site of Elmina in coastal Ghana.

the study of an excavation. Unlike fictional archaeologists, who experience glorified adventures, real-world archaeologists thrive on the intellectually challenging adventure of systematic, scientific research that enlarges our understanding of the past. While excavation, or "scientific digging," and fieldwork remain the key means of gathering archaeological data, a host of new techniques are available to help archaeologists locate and study archaeological sites. One innovative approach increasingly used in archaeology employs the GIS (Geographic Information Systems), a tool that is also increasingly used by environmental scientists and geologists, as well as geographers. Archaeologists can use the GIS linked to satellites to plot the locations of ancient settlements, transportation routes, and even the distribution of individual objects, allowing them to study the patterns and changes represented (Tripcevich and Wenke 2010).

Archaeologists have examined sites the world over, from campsites of the earliest humans to modern landfills. Some archaeologists investigate past societies whose history is primarily told by the archaeological record. Known as *prehistoric archaeologists*, they study the artifacts of groups such as the ancient inhabitants of Europe and the first humans to arrive in the Americas. Because these researchers have no written documents or oral traditions to help interpret the sites they examine and the artifacts they recover, the archaeological record provides the primary source of information for their interpretations of the past. *Historical archaeologists*, on the other hand, work with historians in investigating the societies of the more recent past. For example, some historical archaeologists have probed the remains of plantations in the southern United States to gain an understanding of the lifestyles of enslaved Africans and slave owners during the nineteenth century. Other archaeologists, called *classical archaeologists*, conduct research on ancient civilizations such as in Egypt, Greece, and Rome.

There are many more areas of specialization within archaeology that reflect the geographic area, topic, or time period on which the archaeologist works (see Figure 1.1). Examples of these specializations include industrial archaeology, biblical archaeology,

Anthropologists at Work

KELLEY HAYS-GILPIN, Archaeologist

Kelley Hays-Gilpin

Conservation of the past, the deciphering of gender in the ar-chaeological record, and the meaning of rock art are just a few of the intriguing topics that Kelley Hays-Gilpin has addressed in more than two decades of research. Hays-Gilpin is an archaeologist with a research focus on the prehistoric American Southwest, particularly the history and archaeology of the Pueblo peoples. Like many modern archaeologists, her career has included work in both cultural resource management and university teaching (See Chapter 10). Her doctoral work focused on early decorated ceramics in the Four Corners region in the Southwest, and she began her career with the Navajo Nation Archaeology Department in Flagstaff, Arizona. Hays-Gilpin worked on collections salvaged from archaeological sites destroyed by development projects or threatened by construction. Currently, she teaches archaeology, ceramic analysis, and rock art courses at Northern Arizona University in Flagstaff, located just hours from the Petrified Forest National Park and significant rock art sites.

Although concerned with the interpretation of past technology and adept at ceramic classification, Hays-Gilpin has consistently sought to push the interpretation of archaeological data to extract deeper meaning than archaeologists usually propose. Beginning with her doctoral work, she became increasingly interested in the study of ideology, symbols, and gender in the archaeological record. Through the comparative study of pottery, textiles, and rock art, she used ancient art as a means of understanding cultural continuity and change. This research furthered her understanding of modern Native American perceptions of and concerns about the past. For Hays-Gilpin, the significance of ancient objects to contemporary indigenous people—having conversations about ancestors and making connections between the past and present—is of crucial importance. It is about being able to glean messages from the past that help us live better lives in the present, including such matters as how to grow food in the desert and how to help others understand and appreciate their heritage.

Hays-Gilpin co-authored an interdisciplinary study of *Prehistoric Sandals from Northeastern Arizona: The Earl H. Morris and Ann Axtell Morris Research*, published in 1998. It draws on the research of three generations of women engaged in the study of essentially the same group of archaeological materials from sites in northeastern Arizona. While it provides a detailed examination of a particular collection, the study also affords insight into changing perceptions of archaeological interpretation. Also published in 1998 was Hays-Gilpin's co-edited volume, *Reader in Gender Archaeology*, which helped establish the legitimacy of gendered approaches to the study of the archaeological record.

For archaeologists, rock art—paintings and engravings—provides a unique source of information, offering clues to prehistoric subsistence, ideology, and religion. Yet the interpretation of these prehistoric creations is challenging, and they have often received less attention than they deserve. Hays-Gilpin's *Ambiguous Images: Gender and Rock Art* (2004), which won the Society for American Archaeology's 2005 book prize, provides a significant contribution to the relatively unexplored field of gender in rock art. Hays-Gilpin demonstrates that rock art is one of the best lines of evidence available to understand the ritual practices, gender roles, and ideological constructs of prehistoric peoples.

In addition to her current academic position, Hays-Gilpin holds the Edward Bridge Danson Chair of Anthropology at the Museum of Northern Arizona, where she is director of the Hopi Iconography Project. This project, a collaborative effort between the museum and the Hopi Tribe's cultural preservation office, explores Hopi cultural continuity over centuries, if not millennia, through pottery, rock art, mural painting, baskets, and textiles. More important, the project is exploring ways in which Hopi traditions can help shape a sustainable future for Hopi communities through subsistence farming, craft production, public health programs, and cultural revitalization.

For Hays-Gilpin, the study of archaeology must emphasize teamwork and reward team players. She feels that archaeologists are not in competition with one another, but rather in competition with the forces that are destroying the archaeological record faster than it can be studied. Her research and career epitomize this approach to archaeology. Hays-Gilpin advocates monitoring and reporting on sites that have been threatened with destruction, and she continues work on many collections that have resided in museums for as much as a century. Her work has led her to collaborate with a network of archaeologists, cultural anthropologists, art historians, linguistic anthropologists, and Hopi artists. Her interdisciplinary approach to the past exemplifies modern archaeology's holistic and inclusive requirements—quite a contrast to its more narrowly specialized traditions. With this new approach, Hays-Gilpin has helped to redefine the discipline of archaeology.

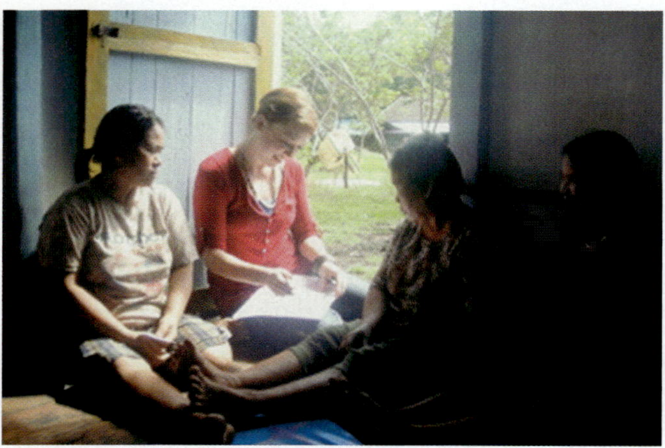

Christina Dames doing linguistic anthropological research in West Kalimantan, Borneo, Indonesia

medieval and postmedieval archaeology, and Islamic archaeology. Underwater archaeologists are unique in being distinguished from other archaeologists by the distinctive equipment, methods, and procedures needed to excavate under water. They investigate a wide range of time periods and sites throughout the world, ranging from sunken cities to shipwrecks. Another field of archaeology is called ethnoarchaeology. **Ethnoarchaeology** is the study of artifacts and material record of modern peoples to understand the use and symbolic meaning of those artifacts.

In another novel approach, still other archaeologists have turned their attention to the very recent past. For example, in 1972, William L. Rathje began a study of modern garbage as an assignment for the students in his introductory anthropology class. Even he was surprised at the number of people who took an interest in the findings. A careful study of garbage provides insights about modern society that cannot be ferreted out in any other way. Whereas questionnaires and interviews depend upon the cooperation and interpretation of respondents, garbage provides an unbiased physical record of human activity. Rathje's pioneering "garbology project" is still in progress and, combined with information from respondents, offers a unique look at patterns of waste management, consumption, and alcohol use in contemporary U.S. society (Rathje 1992).

Linguistic Anthropology

Linguistics, the study of language, has a long history that dovetails with the discipline of philosophy, but is also one of the integral subfields of anthropology. **Linguistic anthropology** focuses on the relationship between language and culture, how language is used within society, and how the human brain acquires and uses language. Linguistic anthropologists seek to discover the ways in which languages are different from one another, as well as how they are similar. Two wide-ranging areas of research in linguistic anthropology are structural linguistics and historical linguistics.

Structural linguistics explores how language works. Structural linguists compare grammatical patterns or other linguistic elements to learn how contemporary languages mirror and differ from one another. Structural linguistics has also uncovered some intriguing relationships between language and thought patterns among different groups of people. Do people who speak different languages with distinct grammatical structures think and perceive the world differently from each other? Do native Chinese speakers think or view the world and life experiences differently from native English speakers? Structural linguists are attempting to answer this type of question.

Linguistic anthropologists also examine the connections between language and social behavior in different cultures. This specialty is called **sociolinguistics**. Sociolinguists are interested both in how language is used to define social groups and in how belonging to a particular group leads to specialized kinds of language use. In Thailand, for example, there are 13 forms of the pronoun *I*. One form is used with equals, other forms come into play with people of higher status, and some forms are used when males address females (Scupin 1988).

Another area of research that has interested linguistic anthropologists is historical linguistics. **Historical linguistics** concentrates on the comparison and classification of different languages to discern the historical links among languages. By examining and analyzing grammatical structures and sounds of languages, researchers are able to discover rules for how languages change over time, as well as which languages are related to one another historically. This type of historical linguistic research is

Anthropologists at Work

BONNIE URCIUOLI, Linguistic Anthropologist

Bonnie Urciuoli

Bonnie Urciuoli completed her B.A. in English at Syracuse University. She completed her M.A. and Ph.D. at the University of Chicago. Her doctorate combined the study of both anthropology and linguistics. She has done research in New York City as a linguistic consultant on a Columbia University-sponsored project with Puerto Rican and African-American teenagers, and, with grants from the Ford Foundation and the Spencer Foundation. In this project she studied Puerto Rican families in Manhattan and the Bronx, examining patterns of Spanish-English bilinguals and related language ideologies. She has taught linguistics and anthropology at Indiana University and, since 1988, at Hamilton College in Clinton, New York. Based on her research on Puerto Rican bilingualism in New York City, Urciuoli began examining the intersection of race, class and linguistic identity, which resulted in several articles and a 1996 book recently reissued and titled *Exposing Prejudice: Puerto Rican Experiences of Language, Race, and Class*. In this book, Urciuoli describes how Puerto Rican migrants struggle to adjust to the mainly English-speaking majority. She discusses the history and relationship of the United States and Puerto Rico, in which Puerto Rico has often been referred to as a 'backward' and 'undeveloped' society. These negative characterizations have consequences for the Puerto Rican migrants who come to the United States and find themselves as a discriminated racial underclass. With Urciuoli's focus on language, she notes how Puerto Rican English is often described as 'broken' or 'ungrammatical' and how prejudice connects to language and influences discrimination in obtaining jobs and achievements in education. The Puerto Rican migrants are urged to get rid of their accent in order to succeed in business and in education. When Puerto Rican migrants do speak English with teachers, employers, and others, their experience is often fraught with fear and anxiety. Urciuoli studies how "accents," "pronunciation," "tone," and "word choice" are perceived by people of various ethnic backgrounds, including Puerto Ricans. Her book indicates that language prejudices are prevalent in the United States and have a definite influence on how ethnic minorities are treated.

Urciuoli's current research began when she met Latino students from working-class backgrounds at the rural and the largely white affluent student population at Hamilton College in upstate New York. These Latino students were very similar to the Puerto Rican teenagers that she encountered in New York City, who were the topic of her book *Exposing Prejudice*. Urciuoli has been publishing articles about how colleges market *multiculturalism* and *diversity* as part of their image, while the Latino students and those of other minority groups who provide that diversity often experience social and academic struggles. At times, these Latino students are categorized and diagnosed as having "language interference"' or "learning disorders" (Urciuoli 2003). Currently, Urciuoli is conducting in-depth interviews with these Latino students about their educational experiences, which will become her new book on this topic.

Urciuoli has also contributed some unique linguistic anthropological research of the Internet. In an essay titled "Skills and Selves in the New Workplace" published in the *American Ethnologist*, Urciuoli analyzes the language of Internet corporate Web sites that market skills-related services. She investigates the language that the corporate world uses in which students or workers have to position themselves when seeking and performing their jobs. Corporations include key terms such as *skills*, *communication*, *team*, and *leadership* in their advertisements, workshops, and literature on the Internet. Urciuoli seeks to understand how students and workers are supposed to manage their "selves" in the corporate environment. The corporate world presents "skills" as quantifiable, testable, and subject to ratings. In the early days of the industrial revolution, "skills" were related to the tasks that were needed to perform in the factory. However, currently, the corporate language used tends to construct diverse "soft skills" as easily assessed and unproblematic for evaluating the market value of one's own self in relation to leadership, teamwork, or other management performance criteria. Educational institutions in the United States. have been influenced by what the corporate world deems important for skill development. Students and workers have to market themselves as having a "bundle of skills" in order to become successful. Corporate websites and workshops emphasize how students and workers are responsible for developing these 'soft skills'. However, in reality, these diverse skills are not as easily tested and assessed as presented in these corporate advertisements and literature. It is important to realize that this essay was published in 2008, just as the American economy was entering a devastating recession. Since that time, many students have been striving to market themselves for the American economy by developing and presenting these "bundles of skills" for success. Urciuoli has contributed toward an understanding of this process with her linguistic anthropological analysis of the Internet.

particularly useful in tracing the migration routes of various societies through time by offering multiple lines of evidence—archaeological, paleoanthropological, and linguistic. For example, through historical linguistic research, anthropologists have corroborated the Asian origins of many Native American populations.

Cultural Anthropology

Cultural anthropology is the subfield of anthropology that examines contemporary societies and cultures throughout the world. Cultural anthropologists do research all over the world, from the tropical rainforests of the Democratic Republic of the Congo and Brazil to the Arctic regions of Canada, from the deserts of the Middle East to the urban areas of China. The first professional cultural anthropologists conducted research on non-Western or remote cultures in Africa, Asia, the Middle East, Latin America, and the Pacific Islands and on the Native American populations in the United States. Today, however, many cultural anthropologists have turned to research on their own cultures in order to gain a better understanding of their institutions and cultural values.

Cultural anthropologists (sometimes the terms *sociocultural anthropologist* and *ethnographer* are used interchangeably with *cultural anthropologist*) use a unique research strategy in conducting their fieldwork in different settings. This research strategy is referred to as **participant observation** because cultural anthropologists learn the language and culture of the group being studied by participating in the group's daily activities. Through this intensive participation, they become deeply familiar with the group and can understand and explain the society and culture of the group as insiders. We discuss the methods and techniques of cultural anthropologists at greater length in Chapter 9.

The results of the fieldwork of the cultural anthropologist are written up as an **ethnography**, a description of a society. A typical ethnography reports on the environmental setting, economic patterns, social organization, political system, and religious rituals and beliefs of the society under study. This description is based on what anthropologists call *ethnographic data*. The gathering of ethnographic data in a systematic manner is the specific research goal of the cultural anthropologist. Technically, **ethnology** refers to anthropologists who focus on the cross-cultural aspects of the various ethnographic studies done by the cultural anthropologists. Ethnologists analyze the data that are produced by the individual ethnographic studies to produce cross-cultural generalizations about humanity and cultures. Many cultural anthropologists use ethnological methods to compare their research from their ethnographic fieldwork with the research findings from societies throughout the world.

Applied Anthropology

The four subfields of anthropology (biological anthropology, archaeology, linguistic anthropology, and cultural anthropology) are well established. However, anthropologists also recognize a fifth subfield. **Applied anthropology** is the use of anthropological data from the other subfields to address modern problems and concerns. These problems may be environmental, technological, economic, social, political, or cultural. Anthropologists have played an increasing role in the development of government policies and legislation, the planning of development projects, and the implementation of marketing strategies. Although anthropologists are typically trained in one of the major subfields, an increasing number are finding employment outside of universities and museums. Although many anthropologists see at least some aspects of their work as applied, it is the application of anthropological data that is the central part of some researchers' careers. Indeed, approximately half of the people with doctorates in anthropology currently find careers outside of academic institutions.

Anthropologists at Work

SCOTT ATRAN, Cultural Anthropologist

Scott Atran

Born in 1952 in New York City, Scott Atran went to Columbia University as a Westinghouse mathematics scholar. At a student demonstration against the Vietnam War in 1970, he met the famous anthropologist Margaret Mead and she invited him to work as her assistant at the American Museum of National History. In 1970, Atran also traveled to the Middle East for the first time, conducting fieldwork in Palestinian villages. As a graduate student in 1974, Atran organized a famous debate at the Abbaye de Royaumont in France on the nature of universals in human thought and society, with the participation of some well-known scholars such as the linguist Noam Chomsky, psychologist Jean Piaget, anthropologists Claude Lévi-Strauss and Gregory Bateson, and biologists François Jacob and Jacques Monod, a conference which many consider a milestone in the development of the field known as cognitive science.

Atran continued observing societies as he traveled overland from Portugal to China, via Afghanistan and Pakistan. Landing again in the Middle East, he conducted ethnographic research on kinship and social ties, land tenure, and political economy among the Druze, a religious group in Israel and Lebanon. Later, Atran became a pioneer in the study of the foundations of biological thinking in Western science and other Native American Indian groups such as the Itzá Maya in Mexico. This research became the basis of his well-known books *Cognitive Foundations of Natural History: Towards an Anthropology of Science*, *The Native Mind and the Cultural Construction of Nature*, and *Plants of the Petén Itzá Maya*, which illustrate how people throughout the world classified biological species of plants and animals in very similar ways.

Later, Atran began an investigation of the cognitive and evolutionary foundations of religion, which resulted in his widely acclaimed book *In Gods We Trust: The Evolutionary Landscape of Religion*. In this book, Atran explores the psychological foundations of religion and how it has become a universal feature of all human societies. He has also contributed toward an understanding of the characteristics associated with suicide bombers and political and religious terrorism in different areas of the world. Atran has been funded by the National Science Foundation and other agencies to study the phenomena of terrorism: This has included fieldwork and interviews with al-Quaeda associates and other militant groups, as well as with political leaders in conflict zones in Europe, the Middle East, Central and Southeast Asia, and North Africa. His recent book *Talking to the Enemy: Faith, Brotherhood and the (Un)Making of Terrorists* is based on this long-term research. In March 2010, Atran testified before the Senate Armed Services Subcommittee on Emerging Threats and Capabilities today on "Pathways to and from Violent Extremism: The Case for Science-Based Field Research."

Atran has taught at Cambridge University, Hebrew University in Jerusalem, and the École des hautes études en sciences sociales (School for the Advanced Studies of the Social Sciences) in Paris. He is currently a research director in anthropology at the Centre national de la recherche scientifique (The Center for Scientific Research, CNRS) based in Paris and is a member of the Jean Nicod Institute at the École normale supérieure. He is also visiting professor of psychology and public policy at the University of Michigan, presidential scholar in sociology at the John Jay College of Criminal Justice in New York City, and co-founder of ARTIS Research and Risk Modeling. Most recently Atran has become Senior Fellow and co-founder of the Centre for the Resolution of Intractable Conflicts at Harris Manchester College and the Department of Social Anthropology, Oxford University.

Atran's broadly interdisciplinary scientific studies on human reasoning processes and cultural management of the environment, and on religion and terrorism, have been featured around the world in science publications, such as *Science*, *Nature*, *Proceedings of the National Academy of Sciences USA*, and *Brain and Behavioral Sciences*, as well as the popular press, including features stories with BBC television and radio, National Public Radio, *The Wall Street Journal* and *Newsweek*. He has been the subject of a cover story in *The New York Times Magazine* ("Darwin's God," 2007) and has written numerous op-eds for *The New York Times* and the magazine *Foreign Policy*.

Atran has teamed up with psychologists and political scientists, including Douglas Medin and Robert Axelrod, to experiment extensively on the ways scientists and lay people categorize and reason about nature, on the cognitive and evolutionary psychology of religion, and on the role of sacred values in political and cultural conflict. Based on recent fieldwork, he has testified before the U.S. Congress and has repeatedly briefed National Security Council staff at the White House on paths to violent extremism among youth in Southeast and South Asia, the Middle East, North Africa, and Europe. Atran has utilized his knowledge and research as a cultural anthropologist to help understand some of the basic questions of human life and also to contribute to solving some of our current problems with globally sponsored political and religious terrorism.

Each of the four major subfields of anthropology has applied aspects. Biological anthropologists, for example, sometimes play a crucial role in police investigations, using their knowledge of the human body to reconstruct the appearance of murder victims on the basis of fragmentary skeletal remains or helping police determine the mechanisms of death. Archaeologists deal with the impact of development on the archaeological record, working to document or preserve archaeological sites threatened by the construction of housing, roads, and dams. Some linguistic anthropologists work with government agencies and indigenous peoples to document disappearing languages or work in business to help develop marketing strategies. Cultural anthropologists, such as A. Peter Castro (see "Anthropologists at Work: A. Peter Castro, Applied Anthropologist"), have played a key role in the planning of government programs so that they take peoples' cultural beliefs and needs into consideration. These applied aspects of anthropological research are highlighted in Chapter 10.

Anthropologists at Work

A. PETER CASTRO, Applied Anthropologist

Peter Castro with Darfur people

Conflict over use of the environment is a theme that unites A. Peter Castro's work as an applied cultural anthropologist, including his more than two decades of service as a consultant for the Near East Foundation, the Food and Agriculture Organization of the United Nations (FAO), the United States Agency for International Development (USAID), the United Nations Development Program (UNDP), CARE, and other organizations. Conflict is a ubiquitous aspect of human existence. While disputes may be an important means for people to assert their rights, interests, and needs, conflicts can escalate into violence that threatens both lives and livelihoods. Castro has used his perspective, skills, and knowledge as a cultural anthropologist to address issues related to understanding and dealing with environmental conflicts in participatory and peaceful ways. Besides his ongoing work as a consultant, he incorporates conflict issues into his classes in the anthropology department of the Maxwell School of Citizenship and Public Affairs at Syracuse University, where he is an associate professor.

Castro's interest in environmental conflicts reflects his rural California upbringing, where farm worker unionization struggles, debates about offshore oil development, and conflicts over housing and commercial expansion were everyday occurrences. He credits his professors at the University of California, Santa Barbara, where he obtained his undergraduate and graduate degrees, with giving him the inspiration and training to use cultural anthropology to address pressing social and environmental issues. As an undergraduate, Castro was a research assistant on a number of applied anthropology projects. In classes and through long discussions outside of class, he learned invaluable lessons about issues in health care and agricultural programs and about the importance of linking local, national, and global dimensions of human and environmental crises. Castro's Ph.D. advisor, David Brokensha, has a distinguished record as an applied anthropologist and was instrumental in providing opportunities for Castro to develop contacts in international agencies. Brokensha was one of the founders of the Institute for Development Anthropology, a nonprofit research and educational organization dedicated to applying anthropological theories and methods to improve the condition of the world's poor.

Castro's early work as an applied anthropologist for international organizations focused on practical aspects of planning, managing, and evaluating community forestry programs and projects. Although conflict between communities and public forest administrators often propelled the rise of such programs and projects, conflict itself was not initially seen by officials and technical officers as a topic of concern. Nonetheless, Castro found that, whether carrying out applied ethnographic fieldwork on deforestation in Kenya for the USAID or preparing a literature-based review of indigenous forest management practices for the FAO, one needed to take such issues into account. For example, it was apparent that conservation efforts in Kenya could not be understood without relating them to long struggles involving different rural groups, government agencies, commercial interests, and other stakeholders. In addition, Castro discovered through ethnographic interviews and archival research that conflicting parties had sometimes in the past negotiated agreements calling for their co-management of local resources that still had relevance today (for example, see Castro's book *Facing Kirinyaga: A Social History of Forest Commons in Southern Mount Kenya*, 1995). Castro's concern with integrating historical analysis, as well as conflict analysis, into international development planning is illustrated in his edited collection of articles on the theme "Historical Consciousness and Development Planning" in the interdisciplinary journal *World Development* (1998).

The importance of dealing with environmental conflicts became starkly clear when Castro was asked by UNDP in 1992 to serve as team leader for the midterm evaluation of Bangladesh's Social Forestry Project, a countrywide effort being implemented at a cost of $46 million. The project was supposed to create the capacity for Bangladesh's Forestry Department to engage in community-oriented training, tree planting, and resource protection. While the project had many accomplishments, it also had severe problems in many areas due to lack of public participation. Sadly, a project meant to address long-standing conflicts served to intensify them. The evaluation mission identified these issues, but because the UNDP could not compel changes, it terminated the project early in some tribal areas where conflict was becoming particularly intense.

Castro worked as a consultant for FAO, writing and editing a number of publications aimed at providing information and practical training on natural resource conflict management. He co-edited a useful book with Antonio Engel called *Negotiation and Mediation Techniques for Natural Resource Management* in 2007. Most recently, Castro is a consultant for the Near East Foundation. He served as lead trainer for workshops on collaborative natural resource conflict management in Zalingei, Central Darfur State, Sudan (in August-September 2012) and in Sévaré, Mopti Region, Mali, in September 2013. Both areas have suffered from conflict. For more than a decade, Darfur has suffered from large-scale violence and instability. National political instability and violence in Mali's North and West have had a severe impact on Mopti, including its world-renowned tourist areas at Djenné and in the Dogon area. The Near East Foundation has projects aimed at contributing to livelihood restoration and peace building. Trainees at the workshop included local members of the Near East Foundation staff, as well as members from local partner organizations and other NGOs. The Near East Foundation has reported that this training has already directly contributed to several successfully mediated and negotiated agreements in local land conflicts.

Castro is also involved in research on climate change. His research culminated in the coauthored book *Climate Change and Threatened Communities: Vulnerability, Capacity and Action*, edited by A. Peter Castro, Dan Taylor and David W. Brokensha. The book presents 15 case studies from different regions, including 2 that Castro wrote on highland Ethiopia and on central Darfur (coauthored by Yassir Hassan Satti). Castro's work as an applied anthropologist has been recognized throughout the world.

Holistic Anthropology, Interdisciplinary Research, and the Global Perspective

1.2 Describe how the field of anthropology is holistic, interdisciplinary, and global.

Anthropology is an interdisciplinary, holistic field. Most anthropologists receive some training in each of four subfields of anthropology. However, because of the huge amount of research undertaken in these different subfields—more than 300 journals and hundreds of books are published every year—no one individual can keep abreast of all the developments across the discipline. Consequently, anthropologists usually specialize in one of the four subfields. Nevertheless, most anthropologists are firmly committed to a **holistic** approach to understanding humankind—a broad, comprehensive account that draws on all four subfields under the umbrella of anthropology. This holistic approach integrates the analyses of biological, environmental, psychological, economic, historical, social, and cultural conditions of humanity. In other words, anthropologists study the physical characteristics of humans, including their genetic endowment, as well as their prehistoric, historic, and social and cultural environments. Through collaborative studies among the various specialists in the four subfields, anthropologists can ask broadly framed questions about humanity.

Anthropology does not limit itself to its own four subfields to realize its research agenda. Although it stands as a distinct discipline, anthropology has strong links to other social sciences. Cultural anthropology, for instance, is closely related to sociology. In the past, cultural anthropologists examined the traditional societies of the world, whereas sociologists focused on modern societies. Today, cultural anthropologists and sociologists explore many of the same societies using similar research approaches. For example, both rely on statistical and nonstatistical data whenever appropriate in their studies of different types of societies.

As we shall discover in later chapters, cultural anthropology also overlaps the fields of psychology, economics, and political science. Cultural anthropologists draw on psychology when they assess the behavior of people in other societies. Psychological questions bearing on perception, learning, and motivation all figure in ethnographic fieldwork. Additionally, cultural anthropologists or ethnologists probe the economic and political behavior and thoughts of people in various societies, using these data for comparative purposes.

Finally, anthropology dovetails considerably with the field of history, which, like anthropology, investigates the human past. Every human event that has ever taken place in the world is a potential topic for both historians and anthropologists. Historians describe and explain human events that have occurred throughout the world; anthropologists place their biological, archaeological, linguistic, and ethnographic data in the context of these historical developments. An important area of anthropological research that overlaps with history is the field of ethnohistory. **Ethnohistory** is the study of the history of a particular ethnic group. Ethnohistory may be based on written historical documents, or more often oral narratives that are recorded by ethnographers working in various regions of the world.

Through the four subfields and the interdisciplinary approach, anthropologists have emphasized a *global perspective*. The global perspective enables anthropologists to consider the biological, environmental, psychological, economic, historical, social, and cultural conditions of humans at all times and in all places. Anthropologists do not limit themselves to understanding a particular society or set of societies, but attempt to go beyond specific or local conditions and demonstrate the interconnections among societies throughout the world. This global perspective is used throughout this text to show how anthropologists situate their findings in the interconnecting worldwide context.

Anthropological Explanations

1.3 Explain how the scientific method is used in anthropological explanations.

A fundamental question faced by anthropologists is how to evaluate the particular social, cultural, or biological data they gather. Human knowledge is rooted in personal experience, as well as in the beliefs, traditions, and norms maintained by the societies in which people live. This includes such basic assumptions as putting on warm clothing in cold weather and bringing an umbrella if it is going to rain, for example. Yet, it also includes notions about how food should be prepared, what constitutes "appropriate" behavior, and what the appropriate social and cultural roles are for men and women.

Religion constitutes another source of human knowledge. Religious beliefs and faith are most often derived from sacred texts, such as the Bible, Qur'an, and Talmud, but they are also based on intuitions, dreams, visions, and extrasensory perceptions. Most religious beliefs are cast in highly personal terms and, like personal knowledge, span a wide and diverse range. People who do not accept these culturally coded assumptions may be perceived as different, abnormal, or nonconformist by other members of their society. Yet, ethnographic and cross-cultural research in anthropology demonstrates that such culturally constituted knowledge is not as general as we might think. This research indicates that as humans, we are not born with this knowledge. Such knowledge tends to vary both among different societies and among different groups within the same society.

Popular perceptions about other cultures have often been based on ethnocentric attitudes. **Ethnocentrism** is the practice of judging another society by the values and standards of one's own society. To some degree, ethnocentrism is a universal phenomenon. As humans learn the basic values, beliefs, and norms of their society, they tend to think of their own culture as preferable, and as what is normal, while ranking other cultures as less desirable. Members of a society may be so committed to their own cultural traditions that they cannot conceive of any other way of life. They often view other cultural traditions as strange or alien, perhaps even inferior, crazy, or immoral.

Such deeply ingrained perceptions are difficult to escape, even for anthropologists. Nineteenth-century anthropologists, for example, often reinforced ethnocentric beliefs about other societies. The twentieth century saw the co-opting of anthropological data to serve specific political and social ends. As the twentieth century progressed, however, anthropologists increasingly began to recognize the biases that prevented the interpretation of other cultures in more valid, systematic ways.

The Scientific Method

Given the preceding concerns, it is critical to understand how anthropological interpretations are evaluated. In contrast to personal knowledge and religious faith, anthropological knowledge is not based on traditional wisdom or revelations. Rather, anthropologists employ the **scientific method**, a system of logic used to evaluate data derived from systematic observation. Researchers rely upon the scientific method to investigate both the natural and the social worlds because the approach allows them to make claims about knowledge and to verify those claims with systematic, logical reasoning. Through critical thinking and skeptical thought, scientists strive to suspend judgment about any claim for knowledge until it has been verified.

Testability and *verifiability* lie at the core of the scientific method. There are two ways of developing testable propositions: the inductive method and the deductive method. In the **inductive method**, the scientist first makes observations and collects data (see Figure 1.2).

The data collected are referred to as variables. A **variable** is any piece of data that changes from case to case. For example, a person's height, weight, age, and sex all constitute variables. Researchers use the observations about different variables to develop hypotheses about the data. A **hypothesis** is a testable proposition concerning the relationship between particular sets of variables in the collected data. The practice of testing hypotheses is the major focus of the scientific method, as scientists test one another's hypotheses to confirm or refute them. If a hypothesis is found to be valid, it may be woven together with other hypotheses into a more general theory.

Theories are statements that explain hypotheses and observations about natural or social phenomena. Because of their explanatory nature, theories often encompass a variety of hypotheses and observations. One of the most comprehensive theories in anthropology is the theory of evolution (see Chapter 2). This theory explains diverse hypotheses about biological and natural phenomena, as well as discoveries by paleoanthropologists and geneticists.

In contrast to the inductive method, the **deductive method** of scientific research begins with a general theory from which scientists develop testable hypotheses. Data are then collected to evaluate these hypotheses. Initial hypotheses are sometimes referred to as "guesstimates" because they may be based on guesswork by the scientist. These hypotheses are tested through experimentation and replication. As with the inductive method, scientists test and retest hypotheses and theories to ensure the reliability of observations made.

Through these methods, researchers do not arrive at absolute truths. Theories may be invalidated or falsified by contradictory observations. Yet, even if numerous observations and

Figure 1.2 Deductive and inductive research methods

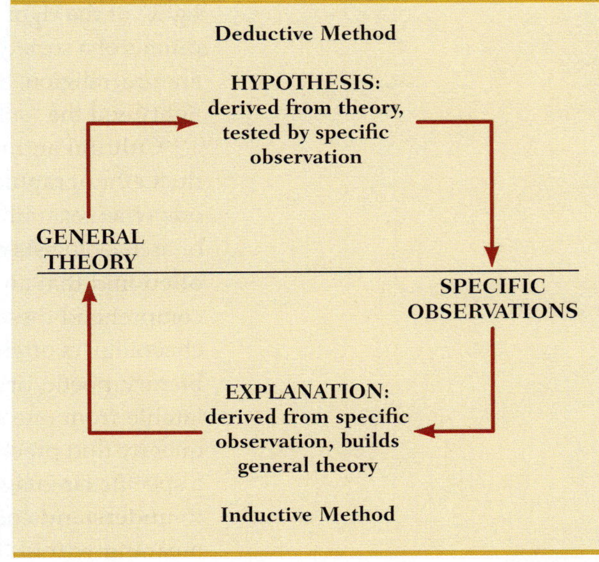

hypotheses suggest that a particular theory is true, the theory always remains open to further testing and evaluation. The systematic evaluation of hypotheses and theories enables scientists to state their conclusions with a certainty that cannot be applied to personal and culturally construed knowledge.

Despite the thoroughness and verification that characterize the research, anthropological explanations have limitations. Anthropologists must grapple with a myriad of complex, interwoven variables that influence human society and biological processes. The complexities of the phenomena being studied make it difficult to assess all of the potential variables, and disagreements about interpretations are common. Consequently, conclusions are frequently presented as tentative and hypothetical. The point here, however, is not that progress is impossible. Anthropological evidence can be verified or discarded by making assumptions explicit and weeding out contradictory, subjective knowledge. Inadequate hypotheses are rejected and replaced by better explanations. Explanations can be made stronger by drawing on independent lines of evidence to support and evaluate theories. This process makes the scientific method much more effective than other means of acquiring knowledge.

Humanistic Interpretive Approaches in Anthropology

1.4 Discuss how the field of anthropology bridges both the sciences and the humanities.

The scientific method is not the only means used by anthropologists to study different societies and cultures. Anthropologists also employ a more humanistic-interpretive approach as they study cultures. Think of this analogy: When botanists examine a flower, they attempt to understand the different components of the plant within a scientific framework; they analyze the biochemical and physical aspects of the flower. However, when painters, poets, or novelists perceive a flower, they understand the plant from an aesthetic standpoint. They might interpret the flower as a symbolic phenomenon that represents nature. The scientist and the humanist use different approaches and perspectives when examining the natural world. Anthropologists employ a humanistic-interpretive approach in many circumstances.

James Peacock uses another type of analogy to discuss the difference between the scientific and the humanistic-interpretive approaches in anthropology (1986). Peacock draws from the field of photography to construct his analogy. He discusses the "harsh light" of the rigor of scientific analysis, used to study the biological and material conditions of a society, versus the "soft focus" used when interpreting the symbols, art, literature, religion, or music of different societies. Peacock concludes that both the "harsh light" and the "soft focus" are vital ingredients of the anthropological perspective.

Cultural anthropologists utilize the humanistic-interpretive method as they conduct ethnographic research. However, archaeologists also employ these same methods when examining artifacts from ancient societies. When cultural anthropologists or archaeologists examine various practices and institutions in different societies, they often find that an outsider cannot easily comprehend these phenomena. In order to comprehend these different practices and institutions, cultural anthropologists or archaeologists often have to interpret these phenomena, just as one might interpret a literary, poetic, or religious text. Cultural beliefs and practices may not be easily translatable from one society to another. Cultural anthropologists or archaeologists frequently find practices and institutions that have meaning and significance only within a specific language and culture. Cultural anthropologists or archaeologists endeavor to understand cultural practices or institutions that may have rich, deep, localized meaning within the society being examined, but that are not easily converted into transcultural or cross-cultural meaning. We focus more thoroughly on this humanistic-interpretive approach in Chapter 8 on anthropological explanations.

Thus, in addition to its interconnections with the natural and social sciences, the discipline of anthropology is aligned with the humanistic fields of inquiry. This is particularly true with respect to the field of cultural anthropology, as these researchers are involved in the study of different contemporary cultures. When participating in the life and experience of people in various societies, ethnographers must confront a multitude of different behaviors and values that may have to be translated and interpreted. As mentioned above, archaeologists also confront this type of problem when studying past cultures and civilizations from different regions of the world. Similar issues confront linguistic anthropologists as they translate and understand various languages.

Many anthropologists explore the creative cultural dimensions of humanity, such as myth, folklore, poetry, art, music, and mythology. **Ethnopoetics** is the study of poetry and how it relates to the experiences of people in different societies; for example, a provocative study of the poetry of a nomadic tribe of Bedouins in the Middle East has yielded new insights into the concepts of honor and shame in this society (Abu-Lughod 1987). Another related field, **ethnomusicology**, is devoted to the study of musical traditions in various societies throughout the world. Ethnomusicologists record and analyze music and the traditions that give rise to musical expression, exploring similarities and differences in musical performance and composition. Ethnomusicologist Dale Olsen completed a fascinating study of Japanese music in South America. There are Japanese minority populations in the countries of Peru, Brazil, Argentina, Paraguay, and Bolivia. Olsen has studied the musical forms, both popular and classical, of these Japanese minorities and how they reflect the maintenance of ethnicity and culture in South America (2004). Other anthropologists study the art of particular societies, such as pottery styles among Native American groups.

Studies of fine art conducted by anthropologists have contributed to a more richly hued, global portrait of humankind. Artistic traditions spring up in all societies, and anthropologists have shed light on the music, myths, poetry, literature, and art of non-Western and other remote peoples. As a result, we now have a keener appreciation of the diverse creative abilities exhibited by humans throughout the world. As anthropologists analyze these humanistic and artistic traditions, they broaden our understanding of the economic, social, political, and religious conditions that prevail within these societies.

One fundamental difference exists between the scientific and the humanistic-interpretive aspects of anthropology. This difference pertains to the amount of progress one can achieve within these two different but complementary enterprises. Science has produced a cumulative increase in its knowledge base through its methodology. Thus, in the fields of astronomy, physics, chemistry, biology, and anthropology, there has been significant progress in the accumulation of knowledge; we know much more about these fields of science than our ancestors knew in the fifteenth or event the nineteenth century. As a result of scientific discoveries and developments, the scientific knowledge in these areas has definitely become more effective in offering explanations regarding the natural and social worlds. As we shall see in Chapter 8 on anthropological explanations, anthropologists today have a much better understanding of human behavior and culture than did anthropologists in the nineteenth century. Through the use of the scientific method, anthropology has been able to make strides in assessing human behavior and cultural developments.

In contrast, one cannot discuss the progress in the humanities in the same manner. Myth, literature, music, and poetry have not progressed in the way that scientific explanations have. One certainly cannot say that the literature or music of the twenty-first century has progressed beyond that of the time periods of Sophocles, Shakespeare, Dante, Bach, or Beethoven. As we shall see, the various humanistic endeavors involving beliefs, myths, and artistic expression in small-scale and ancient

This photo shows three blind Yalunka musicians from Sierra Leone in West Africa. Ethnomusicologists study musical traditions from every area of the world.

civilizations are extremely sophisticated and symbolically complex, and one cannot assess modern societies as "superior" or more "progressive" in those domains.

The essence of anthropology consists of understanding and explaining human behavior and culture with endeavors monopolized by no single approach. Such an enlarged perspective within anthropology requires peaceful coexistence between scientism and humanism, despite their differences. In a recent discussion of this issue within anthropology, Anne Campbell and Patricia Rice suggest that many anthropologists do not agree with one another's assumptions from either a humanistic or a scientific perspective because of their philosophical commitments to one or the other area (Campbell and Rice 2003). However, anthropologists recognize these differences among themselves, and this is helpful, to a great degree, in making progress in our field because we continue to criticize and challenge one another's assumptions and orientations, which results in a better understanding of both the scientific explanations and the humanistic understandings within our field.

What we are going to find in this textbook is that the many great syntheses of anthropological knowledge require the fusion of both the scientific and the humanistic perspectives. When the archaeologist studies the precision and beauty embodied in the 4,500-year-old pyramids of the Egyptian civilization, he (or she) finds that their inspiration came partly from the mathematics of numbers considered sacred and divine and partly from the emulation of nature. Both scientific and humanistic approaches enable anthropologists to study the sacred and the mundane aspects of nature and culture. When anthropologists combine the scientific and humanistic approaches, they can discover what is transcultural and universal and what is unique to specific societies. This is the major goal of anthropological research to determine the similarity and differences of humans in the past and the present.

Why Study Anthropology?

1.5 Describe why any student should study anthropology.

Students sometimes question the practical benefits of their educational experience. Hence, you might ask, "Why study anthropology?" First, anthropology contributes to a general liberal arts education, which helps students develop intellectually and personally, as well as professionally. Studies indicate that a well-rounded education contributes to a person's success in any chosen career, and because of its broad interdisciplinary nature, anthropology is especially well suited to this purpose (Briller and Goldmacher 2008). Because students of anthropology can see the "whole picture," they may be able to generate creative solutions to the problems that face humanity today. Anthropology students have diverse and widely applicable skill sets that include research, critical thinking, speaking foreign languages, and an understanding of law, politics, history, biology and economics, just to name a few. Further, anthropology students understand fundamental aspects of what it means to be human—an understanding that can be applied to multiple areas of life.

Critical Thinking and Global Awareness

In the context of a liberal arts education, anthropology and anthropological research cultivate critical thinking skills. As we noted earlier, the scientific method relies on constant evaluation of, and critical thinking about, data collected in the field. By being exposed to the cultures and lifestyles of unfamiliar societies, students may adopt a more critical and analytical stance toward conditions in their own society. Critical thinking skills enhance the reasoning abilities of students wherever life takes them.

Anthropology also creates an expanding global awareness and an appreciation for cultures other than our own. In this age of rapid communication, worldwide travel, and increasing economic interconnections, young people preparing for careers in the twenty-first century must recognize and show sensitivity toward the cultural differences among peoples, while understanding the fundamental similarities that make us all distinctly human. In this age of cultural diversity and increasing internationalization, sustaining this dual perception of underlying similar human characteristics and outward cultural differences has both practical and moral benefits. Nationalistic, ethnic, and racial bigotry are rife today in many parts of the world, yet our continuing survival and happiness depend upon greater mutual understanding. Anthropology promotes a cross-cultural perspective that allows us to see ourselves as part of one human family in the midst of tremendous diversity. Our society needs not just citizens of some local region or group but also, and more importantly, world citizens who can work cooperatively in an inescapably multicultural and multinational world to solve our most pressing problems of bigotry, poverty, and violence.

In addition, an anthropology course gives students a chance to delve into a discipline whose roots lie in both the sciences and the humanities. As we have seen, anthropology brings to bear rigorous scientific methods and models in examining the causes of human evolution, behavior, and social relationships. But anthropologists also try to achieve a humanistic understanding of other societies in all their rich cultural complexity. Anthropology casts a wide net, seeking an understanding of ancient and contemporary peoples, biological and societal developments, and human diversity and similarities throughout the world.

Viewing life from the anthropological perspective, students will also gain a greater understanding of their personal lives in the context of the long period of human evolution and development. In learning about behavior patterns and cultural values in distant societies, students question and acquire new insights into their own behavior. Thus, anthropology nurtures personal enlightenment and self-awareness, which are fundamental goals of education.

While these general goals are laudable, the study of anthropology also offers more pragmatic applications (Omohundro 1998). As seen in the discussion of applied anthropology, all of the traditional subfields of anthropology have areas of study with direct relevance to modern life. Many students have found it useful to combine an anthropology minor or major with another major. For example, given the increasingly multicultural and international focus of today's world, students preparing for careers in business, management, marketing, or public service may find it advantageous to have some anthropology courses on their résumés. The concepts and knowledge gleaned from anthropology may enable students to find practical applications for dealing with issues of cultural and ethnic diversity and multiculturalism on a daily basis. Similarly, policymakers in federal, state, and local governments may find it useful to have an understanding of historic preservation issues and cultural resource management concerns. In education, various aspects of anthropology—including the study of evolution, the human past, and non-European cultures and the interpretation of cultural and social phenomena—are increasingly being integrated into elementary and secondary school curricula. Education majors preparing for the classroom can draw on their background in anthropology to provide a more insightful context for some of these issues.

Summary and Review of Learning Objectives

1.1 Compare and contrast the four major subfields of anthropology.

Anthropology consists of four subfields: biological anthropology, archaeology, linguistic anthropology, and cultural anthropology or ethnology. Each of these subfields uses distinctive methods to examine humanity in the past and in all areas of the world today. Biological anthropologists investigate human evolution and the physical variation of modern human populations throughout the world. Archaeologists study the past by analyzing artifacts (material remains) of past societies. Linguistic anthropologists focus their studies on languages, seeking out historical relationships among languages, pursuing clues to the evolution of particular languages, and comparing one language with another to determine differences and similarities. Cultural anthropologists conduct fieldwork in human societies to examine people's lifestyles. They describe these societies in written studies called ethnographies, which highlight behavior and thought patterns characteristic of the people studied. In examining societies, cultural anthropologists use systematic research methods and strategies, primarily participant observation, which involves participating in the daily activities of the people they are studying.

1.2 Describe how the field of anthropology is holistic, interdisciplinary, and global.

Through the combination of the four subfields in anthropology, many different variables are investigated ranging from biological factors such as genetics to material artifacts, language, and culture to provide a holistic view of humankind. Anthropology is inherently interdisciplinary and connects with other fields of research such as biology, psychology, economics, history, political science, and sociology, as well as the fine arts and humanities. By its nature, anthropology takes a global approach with its studies of humanity everywhere throughout the world, both past and present.

1.3 Discuss how the scientific method is used to assess and verify anthropological explanations.

Central to anthropological inquiry is the systematic collection and evaluation of data. This includes employing both inductive and deductive methods to evaluate hypotheses and develop theories. Theories explain natural or social phenomena. The conclusions reached are always open to reevaluation and further testing in light of new data. In this way, faulty interpretations and theories are discarded.

1.4 Discuss how the field of anthropology bridges both the sciences and the humanities.

Anthropologists draw on the scientific method to investigate humanity, while recognizing the limitations of science in grasping the subtleties of human affairs. Yet, anthropology is also a humanistic discipline that focuses on such cultural elements as art, music, and religion. By bridging the sciences and the humanities, anthropology enables us to look at humanity's biological and cultural heritage with a broad perspective.

1.5 Describe why any student should study anthropology.

For students, anthropology creates a global awareness and a deep appreciation of humanity past and present. By evaluating anthropological data, students develop critical thinking skills. And the process of anthropological inquiry—exploring other cultures and comparing them to one's own—sheds light on one's personal situation as a human being in a particular time and place.

Key Terms

anthropology, p. 2
applied anthropology, p. 10
archaeology, p. 5
artifacts, p. 5
biological anthropology, p. 3
cultural anthropology, p. 10
deductive method, p. 15
ethnoarchaeology, p. 8
ethnocentrism, p. 14
ethnography, p. 10
ethnohistory, p. 14
ethnology, p. 10
ethnomusicology, p. 17
ethnopoetics, p. 17
fossils, p. 3
historical linguistics, p. 8
holistic, p. 13
hypothesis, p. 15
inductive method, p. 15
linguistic anthropology, p. 8
linguistics, p. 8
middens, p. 5
paleoanthropology, p. 3
participant observation, p. 10
primates, p. 3
primatology, p. 3
scientific method, p. 15
sociolinguistics, p. 8
structural linguistics, p. 8
theories, p. 15
variable, p. 15

Chapter 2
Evolution

Chapter Outline

Learning Objectives

After reading this chapter you should be able to:

2.1 Explain how cosmologies regarding human origins differ from scientific views of evolution.

2.2 Discuss how the scientific revolution provided the context for the theory of evolution.

2.3 Explain how Darwin's views of natural selection and evolution differed from those of earlier scientists.

2.4 Discuss Gregor Johann Mendel's principles of inheritance.

2.5 Discuss how Mendel's principles of inheritance have changed in light of a better understanding of molecular genetics.

2.6 Define and discuss how evolution takes place.

2.7 Discuss how and why new species arise.

2.8 Briefly outline the evidence for the evolution of life on Earth and how evolutionary relationships are evaluated.

2.9 Discuss primate characteristics and the basis for primate classification.

One of the major questions anthropologists grapple with is the origins of humankind. The fossil record preserves evidence of past life on Earth, tracing a progression of simple one-celled organisms to increasingly diverse forms. A small portion of the fossil record relevant to human evolution is discussed in Chapters 4 and 5. How did these different forms of life emerge and new species arise? The biological explanations for this process is the focus of this chapter.

Theories concerning the evolution of life date back to the ancient Greeks, but it was only during the nineteenth century that the first comprehensive theories of evolution were developed. They were made possible through discoveries in many different areas. The acceptance of evolutionary theory is based on research in many fields. Indeed, the value of evolutionary theory is its utility as a unifying explanation for a wide variety of phenomena. Before examining the scientific basis for our understanding of evolution, it is useful to consider other explanations of human origins.

Cosmologies and Human Origins

2.1 Explain how cosmologies regarding human origins differ from scientific views of evolution.

The most profound questions are the ones that perplex us the most. Where did we come from? Why are we here? What is our place in the universe? These questions have been shared by many people throughout history. Most cultures have developed explanations that provide answers to these fundamental questions. **Cosmologies** are conceptual frameworks that present the universe (the *cosmos*) as an orderly system. They often include answers to these basic questions about human origins and the place of humankind in the universe, usually considered the most sacred of all cosmological conceptions.

Cosmologies account for the ways in which supernatural beings or forces formed human beings and the planet we live on. These beliefs are transmitted from generation to generation through ritual, education, laws, art, and language. For example, the Navajo people of the southwestern United States believe that the Holy People, supernatural and sacred, lived below ground in 12 lower worlds. A massive underground flood forced the Holy People to crawl through a hollow reed to the surface of the Earth, where they created the universe. A deity named Changing Woman gave birth to the Hero Twins, called Monster Slayer and Child of the Waters. Human mortals, called Earth Surface People, emerged, and First Man and First Woman were formed from the ears of white and yellow corn.

In the tradition of Taoism, male and female principles known as *yin* and *yang* are the spiritual and material sources for the origins of humans and other living forms. Yin is considered the passive, negative, feminine force or principle in the universe, the source of cold and darkness, whereas yang is the active, positive, masculine force or principle, the source of heat and light. Taoists believe that the interaction of these two opposite principles brought forth the universe and all living forms out of chaos. These examples illustrate just two of the highly varied origin traditions held by different people around the world.

Western Traditions of Origins

In Western cultural traditions, the ancient Greeks had various mythological explanations for human origins. One early view was that Prometheus fashioned humans out of water and earth. Another had Zeus ordering Pyrrha, the inventor of fire, to throw stones behind his back, which in turn became men and women. Later Greek views considered biological evolution. The Greek philosopher Thales of Miletus (c. 636–546 B.C.) attempted to understand the origin and the existence of the world without reference to mythology. He argued that life originated in the sea and that humans initially were fishlike, eventually moving onto dry land and evolving into mammals.

This painting by Michelangelo in the Sistine Chapel represents the idea of spiritual creation, the dominant worldview in Western cosmology for centuries.

The most important cosmological tradition affecting Western views of creation is recounted in the biblical Book of Genesis, which is found in Greek texts dating back to the third century B.C. This Judaic tradition describes how God created the cosmos. It begins with "In the beginning God created the heaven and the earth" and describes how creation took six days during which light, heaven, Earth, vegetation, Sun, Moon, stars, birds, fish, animals, and humans originated. Yahweh, the Creator, made man, Adam, from "dust" and placed him in the Garden of Eden. Woman, Eve, was created from Adam's rib. Later, as Christianity spread throughout Europe, this tradition became the dominant cosmological explanation of human origins.

In Europe before the Renaissance, the Judeo-Christian view of creation provided the only framework for understanding humanity's position in the universe. The versions of creation discussed in the biblical text fostered a specific concept of time: a linear, nonrepetitive, unique historical framework that began with divine creation. These events were chronicled in the Bible; there was no concept of an ancient past stretching far back in time before human memory. This view led some theologians to attempt to calculate the precise age of the Earth on the basis of information in the Bible, such as references to births and deaths and the number of generations mentioned. One of the best known of these calculations was done by Archbishop James Ussher of Ireland (1581–1656). By calculating the number of generations mentioned in the Bible and drawing of classical writers, Ussher dated the beginning of the universe to the year 4004 B.C. Thus, according to Bishop Ussher's estimate, the Earth was approximately 6,000 years old.

The biblical account of creation led to a static, fixed view of plant and animal species and the age of the Earth. Because the Bible recounted the creation of the world and everything on it in six days, medieval theologians reasoned that the various species of plants and animals must be fixed in nature. God had created plant and animal species to fit perfectly within specific environments and did not intend for them to change. They had been unaltered since the time of the divine creation, and no new species had emerged. This idea regarding the permanence of species influenced the thinking of many early scholars and theologians.

The Scientific Revolution

2.2 Discuss how the scientific revolution provided the context for the theory of evolution.

In Europe during the Renaissance (after c. 1450 A.D.), scientific discoveries began to challenge conceptions about both the age of the Earth and humanity's relationship to the rest of the universe. Copernicus and Galileo presented the then-novel idea that the Earth was not circled by the celestial bodies, but rather was just one of several planets revolving around the sun. As this idea became accepted, humans could no longer view themselves and their planet as the center of the universe, which had been the traditional belief. This shift in cosmological thinking set the stage for entirely new views of humanity's links to the rest of the natural world. New developments in the geological sciences began to radically revise the estimates of the age of the Earth, which contradicted a literal reading of the biblical account of creation. These and other scientific discoveries in astronomy, biology, chemistry, physics, and mathematics dramatically transformed Western thought, including ideas about humankind (Henry 2002).

Among the most dramatic ideas to result from the scientific revolution was the theory of evolution, which sees plant and animal species originating through a gradual process of development from earlier forms. Although it is not intended to contradict cosmologies, it is based on a different kind of knowledge. Cosmological explanations frequently involve divine or supernatural forces that are, by their nature, impossible for human beings to observe. We accept and believe in them on the basis of faith. Scientific theories of evolution, in contrast, are derived from the belief that the universe operates according to regular processes that can be observed. The scientific method is not a rigid framework that provides indisputable answers. Instead, scientific theories are propositions that can be evaluated by testing and observation. Acceptance of the theory of evolution is based on observations in many areas of geology, paleontology, and biology.

Catastrophism versus Uniformitarianism

The pre-Renaissance view of a static universe and of an Earth a few thousand years old with unchanging species posed problems for early geologists and naturalists (a term used at that time to refer to biologists), who were beginning to study the thick layers of stone that cover the earth and the fossilized remains they contained. Many of the forms of life represented in these fossils were unlike any living species. How long had it taken to form these thick deposits of soil and stone? How old were the remains of the strange creatures represented in the fossil remains? The geological record did not fit within the time frame that a literal reading of the biblical account of creation allowed.

As evidence for the great antiquity of the Earth and for many extinct animal species accumulated, some scholars proposed theories that attempted to reconcile the geological and fossil records with the biblical account of Genesis. One interpretation was presented by Georges Chrétien Léopold Frédéric Dagobert Cuvier (1769–1832), a French naturalist who is sometimes called the father of zoology (Rudwick 1997). Georges Cuvier, as he is more commonly known, studied the fossil record, including the remains of extinct, prehistoric elephant-like animals called *mammoths* in the vicinity of Paris. He also noted the successive replacement of fossil species through time. However, he saw species as fixed and unchanging. He proposed the geological theory known as **catastrophism**, which reasoned that the Earth had been created and destroyed multiple times. The extinct species represented in the fossil record had disappeared through a series of catastrophes of divine origin. Some species of animals might survive these events, just as the account of creation in the Book of Genesis recounted that animals collected by Noah and taken aboard the ark survived the biblical flood. The new species of animals that appeared in the following layers represented a new creation event. Catastrophism became the best-known geological explanation consistent with the literal interpretation of the biblical account of creation.

Other geologists challenged catastrophism and the rigidity of nature through scientific studies. They noted evidence that suggested the Earth changed through gradual, natural processes that were still observable. This view, which provided the basis for later geological interpretations, became known as **uniformitarianism** (Repcheck

2003). One of the first proponents of this perspective was the French naturalist and keeper of the king's gardens, Georges-Louis Leclerc, the Comte de Buffon (1707–1788). In 1774, Buffon theorized that the Earth changed through gradual, natural processes that were still observable. He proposed that rivers had created canyons, waves had changed shorelines, and other forces had transformed the features of the Earth. After being criticized by theologians, Buffon attempted to coordinate his views with biblical beliefs. He suggested that the six days of creation described in the Bible should not be interpreted literally. Buffon rather suggested that these passages actually refer to six *epochs* representing a gradual period of creation rather than 24-hour days. Each epoch consisted of thousands of years in which the Earth and different species of life were transformed. Although Buffon's interpretation allowed more time for geological changes in the Earth's past, there was no geological evidence for the six epochs of gradual creation.

As information on the geological record accumulated, the uniformitarian view eventually became the mainstream position in geology. In 1795, James Hutton, in his landmark book *Theory of the Earth*, explained how natural processes of erosion and deposition of sediments had formed the various geological strata of the Earth. Hutton observed that these natural processes must have taken thousands of years. In his book, he estimated that the Earth was at least several million years old. In 1833, the English scholar Charles Lyell (1797–1875), noted by some as the father of modern geology, reinforced the uniformitarian view. In his *Principles of Geology*, Lyell discussed natural processes, such as volcanoes, earthquakes, glaciers, erosion, and decomposition that shaped the geological landscape. More importantly, in a readable and comprehensive way, he observed that these processes were still observable and had been constant—uniform—over time. He also argued that scientists could deduce the age of the Earth from the rate at which sediments are deposited and by measuring the thickness of rocks. Through these measurements, Lyell also concluded that the Earth was millions of years old.

Modern geologists have a far better understanding of geological processes and much more sophisticated means of dating the Earth. As will be discussed later, the age of the Earth is now estimated to be billions, rather than millions, of years, divided into five major ages and many other periods and epochs (see page 44). Although many of the views of Buffon, Hutton, and Lyell have been superseded, they were historically important in challenging traditional views of a static universe with fixed species. Their fundamental points concerning the consistent and ongoing natural processes that have shaped the geological landscape have been reaffirmed by modern research. The uniformitarian view thus set the stage for an entirely new way of envisioning the universe, the Earth, and the living forms on the planet.

Theory of Evolution

2.3 Explain how Darwin's views of natural selection and evolution differed from those of earlier scientists.

The scientific revolution also led to changing perspectives regarding the origin of species and humankind's place in nature. There were discoveries of archaeological remains and contacts with the non-Western populations that were unmentioned in any written records, including the Bible and classical Greek and Roman writings. Where did the Native American Indians come from? Were they one of the lost tribes of Israel referred to in the Bible, or were they created separately and without souls, as some sixteenth-century scholars suggested (Adovasio and Page 2002, 5)? Antiquarians—as collectors of artifacts and curiosities of the past were sometimes called—of the eighteenth and nineteenth centuries increasingly began to recognize archaeological materials that predated written history. The relative ages of both fossils and archaeological materials could be dated by their stratigraphic positions (see relative dating methods in Chapter 3), suggesting periods older than the historically known Greek and Roman civilizations. There were also many discoveries of fossil remains clearly unlike any living species. Scholars, including many clergy, documented systematic change through time in the fossil species represented (see discussion of faunal succession in Chapter 3). How were these finds to be explained? Scholars started to question the fixity of species and a literal interpretation of the biblical account of creation. They suggested that plants and animals had evolved—changed through time—through natural processes.

Evolution refers to the process of change in the genetic makeup of a species over time. It is used to explain the emergence of new species. Evolutionary theory holds that existing species of plants and animals have emerged over millions of years from simple organisms. Although the theory of evolution is usually associated with Charles Darwin, the idea that modern plants and animals could change was posited by a number of scholars prior to the mid-1800s. Georges-Louis Leclerc, the Comte de Buffon (1707–1788), who had argued that the Earth changed through gradual, natural processes, also underscored the changing nature of species and their ability to adapt to local environmental conditions. Erasmus Darwin (1731–1802), an eighteenth-century physician and Charles Darwin's grandfather, also suggested evolutionary concepts. However, none of these early theorists suggested a unified theory that *explained* evolution. They proposed no reasonable mechanism for evolution and, consequently, most people could not accept these ideas.

A more comprehensive early theory that attempted to explain evolution was posited by a French chemist and biologist, Jean-Baptiste Pierre Antoine de Monet, Chevalier de Lamarck (1744–1829). Lamarck proposed that species could change as a result of dynamic interactions with their environment. As a result of changing environmental conditions, behavioral patterns of a species would alter, increasing or decreasing the use of some physical structures. As a result of these changing physical needs, the *besoin* (the force for change within organisms) would be directed to these areas, modifying the appropriate structures and enabling the animal to adapt to their new environmental circumstances. In other words, if a particular animal needed specialized organs to help in adaptation, these organs would evolve accordingly. In turn, because the characteristics made the animal better suited to its environment, these new structures would be passed on to their offspring (Mayr 1982).

The most famous example used by Lamarck was the long necks of giraffes. He suggested that this distinctive feature evolved when a short-necked ancestor took to browsing on the leaves of trees instead of on grass. Lamarck speculated that the ancestral giraffe, in reaching up, stretched its neck. The force for change was directed to the giraffe's neck, and it was increased in length. This physical characteristic was passed on to the giraffe's offspring. The offspring of this ancestral giraffe stretched still further. As this process repeated itself from generation to generation, the present long neck of the giraffe was eventually achieved.

Because evolution takes place as a result of physical characteristics acquired in the course of a creature's lifetime, Lamarck's theory is referred to as the *inheritance of acquired characteristics* or *use-disuse theory*. Variations of Lamarck's view of inheritance were used by many nineteenth-century scientists to explain how physical characteristics originated and were passed on. Today, however, this theory is rejected for several reasons. First, Lamarck overestimated the ability of a plant or an animal to adapt or change to meet new environmental conditions. In addition, we now know that physical traits acquired during an organism's lifetime cannot be inherited by the organism's offspring. In order for traits to be passed on, they must be encoded in genetic information contained within the sex cells (see later discussion). For example, a weightlifter's musculature, an acquired characteristic, will not be passed on to his or her children. Nevertheless, Lamarck's ideas illustrate early theories that attempted to explain evolutionary change. His work is notable in proposing a unified theory of how evolution takes place and also because of the emphasis it placed on the interaction between organisms and their environments.

Charles Darwin (1809–1882). Darwin is known for identifying natural selection as a key evolutionary process.

Darwin, Wallace, and Natural Selection

Two individuals strongly influenced by the scientific revolution were Charles Robert Darwin (1809–1882) and Alfred Russel Wallace (1823–1913), nineteenth-century British naturalists. Through their careful observations and their identification of a plausible mechanism for evolutionary change, they transformed perspectives of the origin of species. Impressed by the variation in living species and their interaction with the environment, Darwin and Wallace independently developed an explanation of why this variation occurs and the basic mechanism of evolution. This mechanism is known as **natural selection**, which can be defined as genetic change in a population resulting from differential reproductive success. This is now recognized as one of the four principal evolutionary processes.

Beginning in 1831, Darwin traveled for five years aboard the British shipHMS *Beagle* on a voyage around the world. During this journey, he collected numerous plant and animal species from many different environments. In the 1840s and 1850s, Wallace observed different species of plants and animals during an expedition to the Amazon and later continued his observations in Southeast Asia and on the islands off Malaysia. Darwin and Wallace arrived at the theory of natural selection independently, but Darwin went on to present a thorough and completely documented statement of the theory in his book *On the Origin of Species*, published in 1859. The volume's full title gives a fair idea of its focus: *On the Origin of Species by Means of Natural Selection, or the Preservation of Favored Races in the Struggle for Life*.

In their theory of natural selection, Darwin and Wallace emphasized the enormous variation that exists in all plant and animal species. They combined these observations with those of Thomas Malthus (1766–1834), a nineteenth-century English clergyman and political economist whose work focused on human populations. Malthus was concerned with population growth and the constraints that limited food supplies had on population size. Darwin and Wallace realized that similar pressures operate in nature. Living creatures produce more offspring than can generally be expected to survive and reproduce. For example, for the thousands of tadpoles that hatch from eggs, few live to maturity. Similarly, only a small number of the seeds from a maple tree germinate and grow into trees. In recognizing the validity of this fact, Darwin and Wallace realized that there would be *selection* in which organisms survived. What factors would determine their survival?

HMS *Beagle* in South America. Charles Darwin's trip around the world on the *Beagle* gave him the opportunity to study many different animals in varied environments.

Variation within species and reproductive success are the basis of natural selection. Darwin and Wallace reasoned that certain individuals in a species may be born with particular characteristics or traits that make them better able to survive. For example, certain plants within a species may naturally produce more seeds than others, or some frogs in a single population may have coloring that blends in with the environment better than others, making them less likely to be eaten by predators. With these advantageous characteristics, certain members of a species are more likely to reproduce and, subsequently, pass on these traits to their offspring. Darwin and Wallace called this process *natural selection*

The photos of different dogs, a Cockapoo, Dachshund, and German Shepard, exhibit the wide variation in physical characteristics that may be found within the same species.
Source: Courtesy of Rodney Livingston (left), C. R. DeCorse (center), and Shutterstock (Right).

because nature, or the demands of the environment, actually determines which individuals (and, therefore, which traits) survive. This process, repeated countless times over millions of years, is the means by which species change or evolve over time.

Examples of Natural Selection

One problem Darwin faced in writing *On the Origin of Species* was a lack of well-documented examples of natural selection at work. Most major changes in nature take place over thousands or millions of years. As a result, the process of natural selection is often too slow to be documented in a researcher's lifetime. However, when animals or plants are exposed to rapid changes in their environment, we can actually observe natural selection in action.

A classic case of natural selection is illustrated by the finches of the Galapagos Islands, located about 500 miles off the coast of South America. These birds were studied by Charles Darwin when he visited the islands during his travels on the HMS *Beagle*. Volcanic in origin and cut off from the South American mainland, the Galapagos have a diversity of species related to, but distinct from, those of South America. Darwin was struck by how the geographic isolation of a small population could expose its members to new environmental conditions where different adaptive features might be favored. Darwin described the variation in the islands' finches. In general, the birds have rather dull plumage and are quite similar, except in the size and shape of their beaks—a feature that is closely related to the ways in which the birds obtain their food. Some species of finch, for example, have short, thick beaks that they use to eat seeds, buds, and fruits, while others have long, straight beaks and subsist primarily on nectar from flowers.

The finches of the island of Daphne Major in Galapagos were the focus of a long-term research project by Peter and Rosemary Grant, beginning in 1973 (Grant 1999; Weiner 1994). The island is small enough to allow researchers to study the island's flora and fauna intensively and provide an unambiguous demonstration of natural selection in operation. The Grants and their students focused on two species of finch—the medium ground finch and the cactus finch. Over time, every finch on the island was captured, carefully measured and weighed, and also tagged so that each bird could be identified in the field. The diet of the birds was documented and the availability of food resources charted. A dramatic change in the finches' food resources occurred between mid-1976 and early 1978 as a result of a drought. The lack of rainfall led to a decrease in the food supplies favored by smaller-beaked finches. The remaining food consisted of larger, harder seeds that were difficult for finches with small beaks to break open. On the other hand, finches with larger, heavier beaks were able to more easily crack and extract food from hard-shelled seeds. Not surprisingly, many of the finches with smaller beaks died of starvation during the drought.

The variation in beak size is a good illustration of how natural selection may act on different species, but it also illustrates the significance of variation within individual species. Of the more than 1,000 medium ground finches found on the island at the beginning of the Grants' study, only 180 remained after the drought. Notably, the finches that survived had a larger average beak size than that of the population prior to the drought. As beak size is an inherited characteristic, the new generations of birds born after the drought also had a larger average beak size. This case study illustrates how natural selection can eliminate maladaptive traits from a population and select for features that help ensure survival and, ultimately, reproductive success for some members of a species. Many modern scientists believe that new species emerge when small populations become isolated from the parent group and encounter new selective pressures that may favor different characteristics.

Natural selection is currently viewed as one of four major forces in the evolution of species. It enabled Darwin to explain the mechanisms of biological evolution, and it remains a powerful explanation for the development of living species of plants and animals. Before turning to the other processes that influence evolution, we will consider the way traits are passed on from one generation to the next.

Principles of Inheritance

2.4 Discuss Gregor Johann Mendel's principles of inheritance.

Darwin contributed to the modern understanding of biological evolution by thoroughly documenting the *variation* of living forms and by identifying the key process of natural selection. Like most nineteenth-century scientists, however, he did not understand *heredity*, or how specific traits are passed on from one generation to the next. Darwin reasoned that during the reproductive process, the parental substances are mixed to produce new traits in the parents' offspring. These conclusions were based in part on his experiments with plants and animals, in which he had observed that the offspring often had characteristics from both parents. Darwin was unclear about how these traits were transmitted, but he reasoned that as with metal alloys, such as bronze, which is a mixture of tin and copper, the traits of an offspring represented a blending of parental substances. Today, we know that inherited characteristics are not a mixture of parental substances, such as with the mixing of fluids or metal alloys. Rather, traits are passed from parents to offspring in individual "particles" or packages—what we now refer to as genes.

Mendel and Modern Genetics

Modern understanding of heredity emerged through the studies of an Austrian monk named Gregor Johann Mendel (1822–1884). During the 1860s, Mendel began a series of breeding experiments with pea plants that revolutionized biological thought. Although his findings were not recognized until the twentieth century, Mendel laid the groundwork for what is today known as the science of *genetics*, the biological subfield that deals with heredity. In compiling his rules of heredity, Mendel discredited earlier theories of inheritance. He was the first to conclusively demonstrate that traits are inherited in discrete packages of information that were not mixed during reproduction. The principles he laid out as a result of this work are useful in understanding inheritance in humans, as well as all other biological organisms.

Mendel's most important experiments involved the crossbreeding of pea plants. In order to discern patterns of inheritance, Mendel focused on traits that could each be expressed in only one of two ways. Height and seed color are two examples: He studied plants that were either tall *or* dwarf or plants that produced either green *or* yellow peas. He initially focused his experiments on one characteristic or trait at a time,

Figure 2.1 The finches of the Galapagos Islands provide an excellent example of natural selection at work. The beaks of the various species of finch are used for exploiting different kinds of foods. If environmental conditions suddenly change, some characteristics may be more favored than others.

carefully cross-pollinating *purebred* plants, plants that were similar with regard to one of his traits. Mendel crossed purebred tall pea plants with purebred dwarf, or short plants. In this way, he was able to study the traits that appeared in *hybrids*, the offspring resulting from tall and dwarf plants. He could then evaluate the proportion of characteristics found in successive generations. Mendel drew several important conclusions from these experiments.

Mendel's Principle of Segregation By following the results of cross-pollination through several generations, Mendel discovered a distinct pattern of reproduction. The first generation of hybrid plants—that is plants produced by parents having purebred tall and purebred dwarf characteristics—were all tall. However, when he crossbred these hybrid plants, the next generation contained both tall and dwarf plants. Thus, the dwarf variety that seemed to disappear in the first generation of hybrids reappeared in the second generation (see Figure 2.2).

Significantly, the ratio of tall to dwarf plants in the second hybrid generation was always approximately 3 to 1 (three tall plants to one dwarf plant). Mendel conducted similar experiments focusing on other characteristics and obtained similar results. This led Mendel to reject the earlier notions of inheritance, such as blending. None of the pea plants exhibited mixed characteristics: all of the plants were either tall or short; all of the peas were either green or yellow.

The fact that the 3 to 1 ratio reappeared consistently convinced Mendel that the key to heredity lay deep within the pea plant seeds. Mendel correctly concluded that the particles responsible for passing traits from parents to offspring occurred in pairs, each offspring receiving half of a pair from each parent. During fertilization, the particles of heredity, what we now call genes, from each parent are combined. The observation that units of heredity (or genes) occur in pairs and that offspring receive half of a pair from each parent is the basis of the *principle of segregation*, Mendel's first principle of inheritance.

Gregor Johann Mendel (1822–1884). Through his study of pea plants, Mendel laid the foundation for the understanding of heredity.

Dominant and Recessive Traits Mendel also observed that certain traits prevailed over others. He labeled the prevailing traits **dominant**. In contrast, he labeled as **recessive** those traits that were unexpressed in one generation but expressed in following generations. In pea plants, he found that tall was dominant and dwarf was recessive.

Figure 2.2 illustrates why recessive traits can disappear in one generation and appear in the next. In the first generation, a purebred tall plant and a purebred dwarf plant are crossbred. The pairs of genetic information in the purebred tall plants only contain genetic material for tallness (*TT*), and the purebred dwarf plants only contain information for the dwarf trait (*tt*). When these purebred plants are crossbred, the offspring receive genetic material from each parent (*Tt*). Only the tall trait appears in the offspring because tall is the dominant trait and the dwarf characteristic is recessive. However, when these hybrid plants are crossbred, the recessive trait reappears. As Figure 2.2 illustrates, the crossing of two hybrid parents (*Tt*) produces four possible combinations: one *TT*, two *Tt*, and one *tt*. The single offspring that only has the tall characteristic (*TT*) as well as those that inherited both tall and dwarf characteristics (*Tt*) appear

Figure 2.2 In one of his experiments, Mendel crossbred plants that were purebred (homozygous) for particular traits, as illustrated here by the tall and dwarf pea plants. As tallness is a dominant trait, all the offspring of this cross were tall. In the third generation, however, the recessive traits reappear, or segregate.

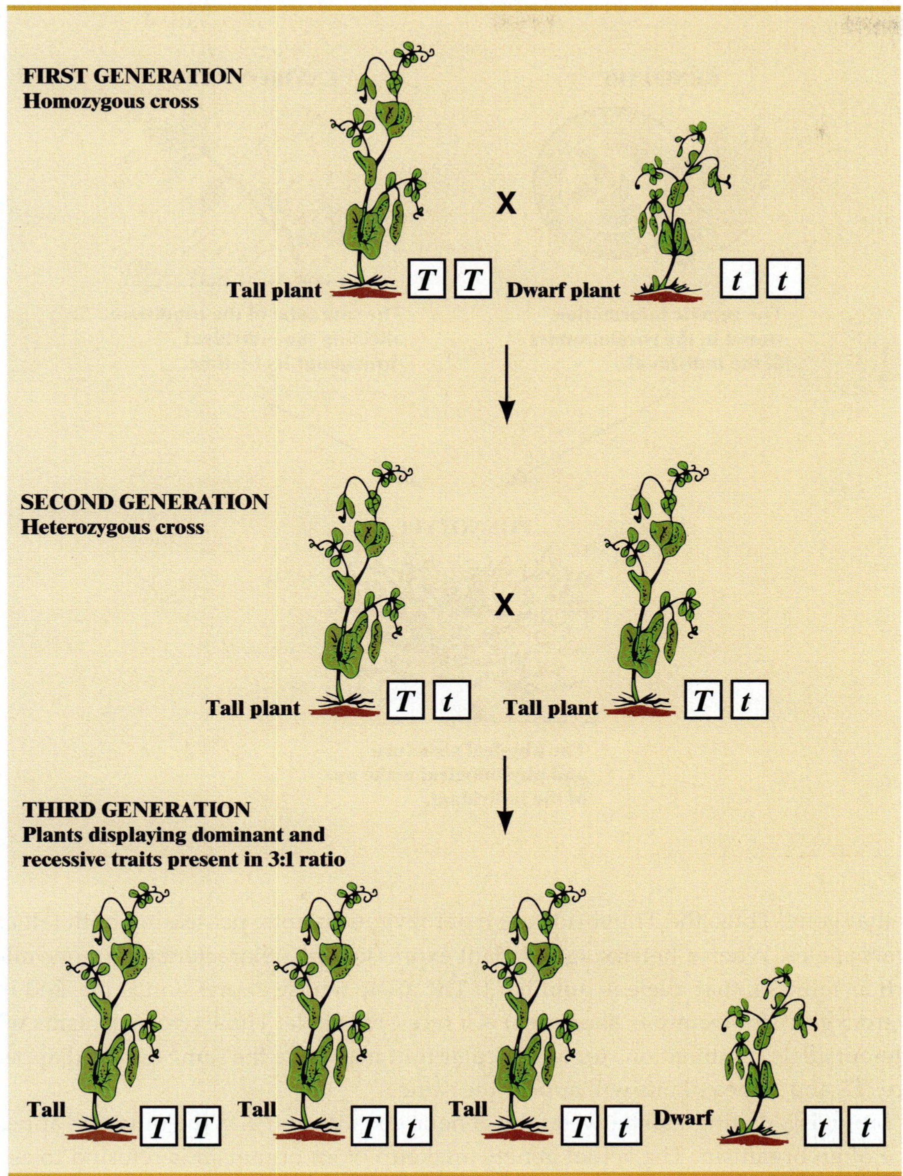

tall, the dwarf characteristic being recessive. The offspring that inherit two recessive particles (*tt*) exhibit the recessive trait. This accounts for the 3 to 1 ratio that Mendel observed in the offspring of two hybrid plants. Mendel concluded that the particle containing the recessive trait, which is masked by the dominant trait in one generation, can reappear if it occurs in both parents. Mendel's theory explained how hybrid parents expressing only the dominant trait could produce offspring exhibiting the recessive trait. Purebred parents could pass on only the dominant or recessive trait, whereas hybrid parents could pass on either one.

The alternate forms of the same genes, such as "tall" or "dwarf," are referred to as **alleles**. When an organism has two of the same kinds of alleles, it is referred to as **homozygous** for that gene. Thus, homozygous tall plants are *TT* (purebred dominant for tallness), whereas homozygous dwarf plants are *tt* (purebred recessive for shortness). In contrast, when an organism has two different alleles, it is **heterozygous**

Figure 2.3 The genotype interacts with the external environment to produce the phenotype.

Source: From *The Illustrated Origin of Species* by Charles Darwin, abridged by Richard Leakey (Rainbird/Faber & Faber, 1979). Reprinted by permission of the Robert Harding Picture Library.

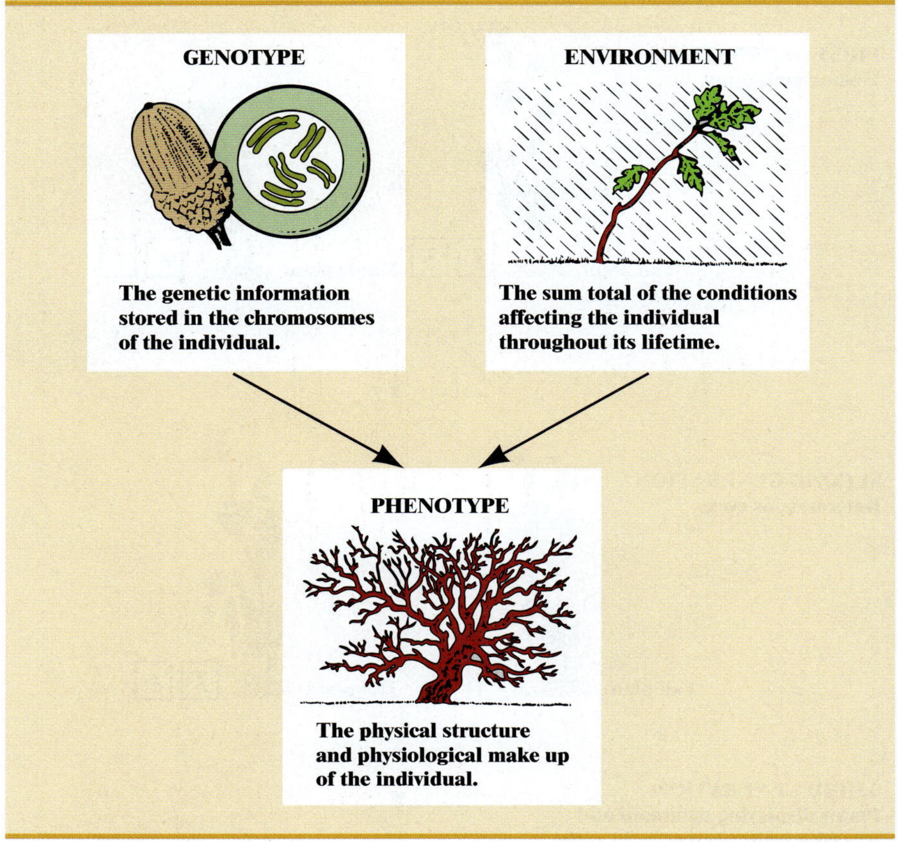

for that gene. Thus, the *Tt* hybrids are heterozygous plants, possessing both tall and dwarf alleles. When a heterozygous plant expresses only characteristics of one allele such as tallness, that allele is dominant. The allele whose expression is masked in a heterozygote (for example, shortness) is a recessive allele. Thus, two organisms with different allele combinations for a particular trait may have the same outward appearance: *TT* and *Tt* pea plants will appear the same.

Biologists distinguish between the genetic constitution and the outward appearance of an organism. The actual genetic makeup of an organism is referred to as its **genotype**; the external, observable characteristics of that organism that are shaped in part by the organism's genetic makeup, as well as its unique life history, are called its **phenotype**. Genotype and phenotype are illustrated in Figure 2.3.

Principle of Independent Assortment The preceding experiments all focused on one physical trait. In subsequent studies, Mendel investigated the outcomes of fertilization between pea plants that differed in two ways, such as in both plant height and color of the pea, in order to evaluate whether the two characteristics were linked. As in the previous experiments, the offspring of purebred (homozygous) parents exhibited only the dominant characteristics. When Mendel cross-fertilized these hybrids, however, the offspring displayed the characteristics present in the purebred generation in a ratio of 9:3:3:1, as illustrated in Figure 2.4.

This experiment indicated that no two traits are always passed on together. Mendel concluded that during the reproductive process, the particles determining different traits separate from one another and then *recombine* to create variation in

Figure 2.4 This diagram, referred to as an extended Punnett square, demonstrates the principle of independent assortment discovered by Mendel. When two heterozygous pea plants are cross-fertilized, the alleles that determine two different traits sort independently of each other, creating the phenotypic ratio of 9:3:3:1.

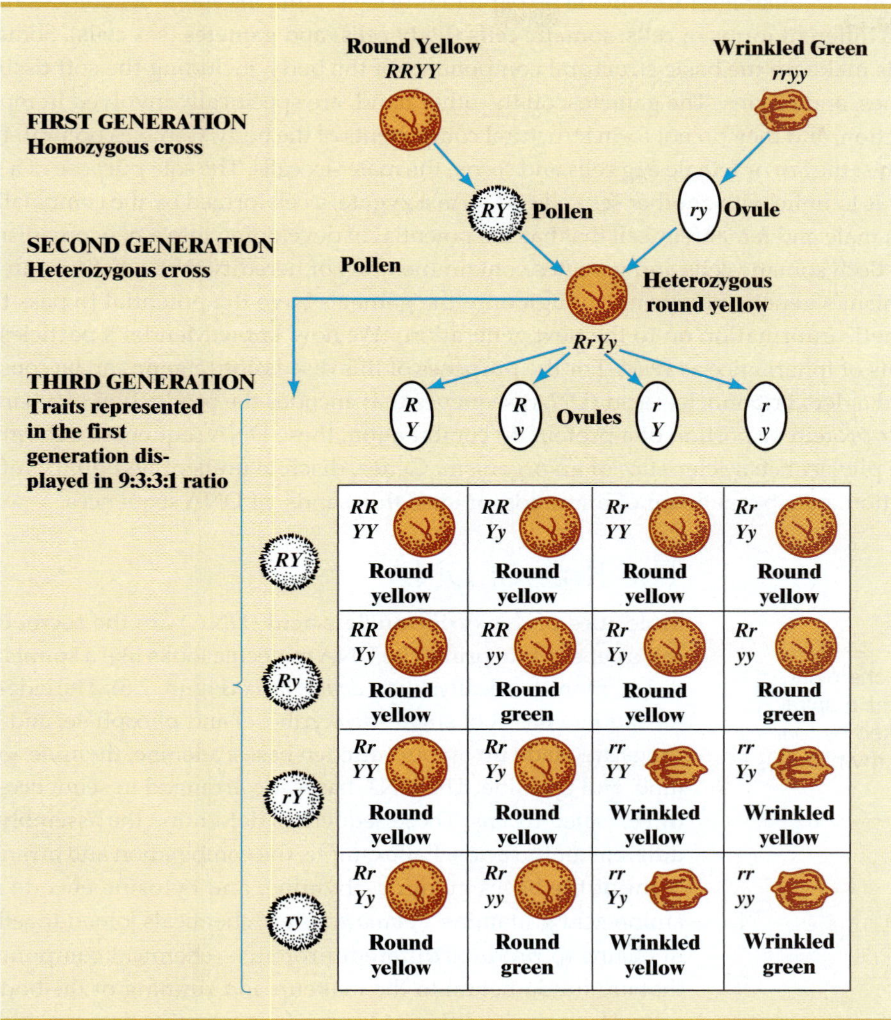

the next generation. Thus, in the experiments by Mendel discussed above, plants produced peas that were yellow and round, yellow and wrinkled, green and wrinkled, and green and round. Mendel referred to the fact that individual traits (such as height or color) occur independently of one another as the *principle of independent assortment*.

Inheritance and Molecular Genetics

2.5 Discuss how Mendel's principles of inheritance have changed in light of a better understanding of molecular genetics.

Mendel's principles of segregation and independent assortment and the concepts of recessive and dominant traits are still viewed as key mechanisms of heredity. However, because Mendel did not have the advanced technology needed to investigate cellular biology, he did not know the inner workings of the units of inheritance. Modern scientists have a better understanding than did Mendel of the dynamics of heredity at the cellular level.

Cells and Genes

Heredity is encoded in cells, which are the building blocks of all living things. Bacteria and amoebas are examples of single-celled organisms; in contrast, plants and animals are multicellular life-forms made up of billions of cells. Humans and other animals have two different forms of cells: **somatic cells** (body cells) and **gametes** (sex cells). Somatic cells make up the basic structural components of the body, including the soft tissues, bones, and organs. The gametes, on the other hand, are specifically involved in reproduction, and they do not form structural components of the body. Gametes occur in two forms: the *ova* or female egg cells and *sperm*, the male sex cells. The sole purpose of a sex cell is to unite with another sex cell and form a **zygote**, a cell formed by the combination of a male and female sex cell that has the potential of developing into a new organism.

Both somatic cells and gametes contain the units of heredity that constitute an organism's genetic blueprint (though only the gametes have the potential to pass this genetic information on to the next generation). We now know Mendel's particles or units of inheritance as *genes*. For the purposes of this discussion, a **gene** can be considered a deoxyribonucleic acid (DNA) sequence that encodes the production of a particular protein or portion of a protein. In combination, these DNA sequences determine the physical characteristics of an organism. Genes, discrete units of hereditary information, may be made up of hundreds, or even thousands, of DNA sequences.

The Role of DNA

Molecules of **deoxyribonucleic acid** (DNA) are the secret of a cell's genetic blueprint. The DNA molecule looks like a spiral ladder or, more poetically, like a *double helix* (Figure 2.5). The sides of the ladder consist of sugar (deoxyribose) and phosphate, and the rungs are made up of four nitrogen bases: adenine, thymine, guanine, and cytosine. The DNA bases are arranged in sequences of three, called *codons*. These sequences determine the assembly of different amino acids. For example, the combination and arrangement of the bases guanine, thymine, and cytosine encode the amino acid glutamine. *Amino acids* are chemicals joined together in chains to produce different proteins—chemical compounds that are fundamental to the makeup and running of the body's cells. There are 20 different kinds of amino acids that can, in differing combinations and amounts, produce millions of different proteins basic to life.

Figure 2.5 This illustration shows the chemical structure of DNA. The DNA molecule forms a spiral ladder of sugar (S) and phosphate (P) linked by four nitrogen bases: adenine (A), guanine (G), thymine (T), and cytosine (C).

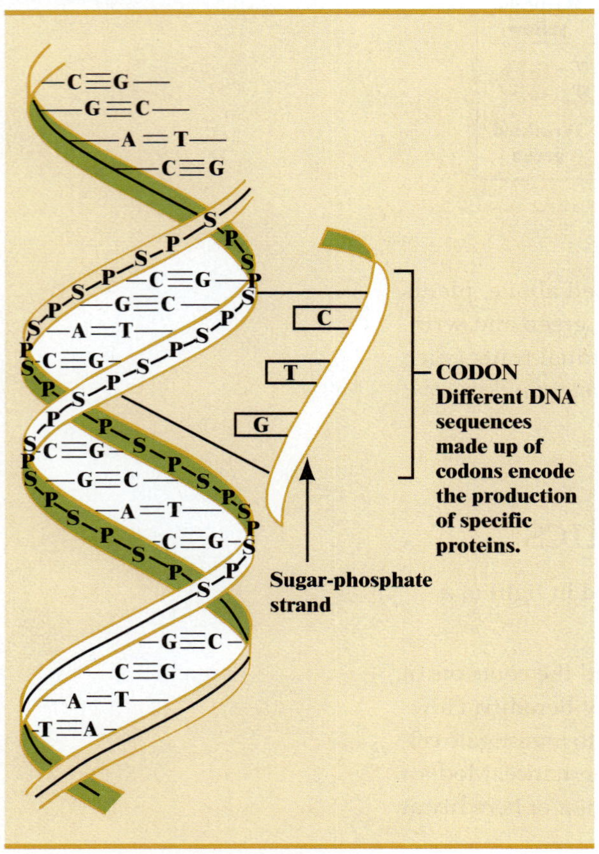

Mitosis and Meiosis

At certain times, cells divide to form new cells. Gametes and somatic cells divide in different ways, a fact that is very significant in terms of their differing roles. Strands of DNA containing heredity information are contained in each living cell, but while both kinds of cells contain an organism's genetic code, only the gametes provide a means of passing this information on to an offspring through reproduction. Normally, the DNA molecules exist as single, uncoiled, thread-like strands within each cell. The minute DNA threads contained within each human somatic cell are estimated to be as much as 6 feet long. During cell division the DNA becomes tightly coiled and forms discrete structures called *chromosomes*. The single DNA threads replicate by forming a double strand, one strand being an exact copy of the original. Each species has a specific number of chromosomes that make up their somatic cells. Humans have 23 pairs of chromosomes or 46 chromosomes in all.

When somatic cells divide to produce new cells—a process biologists call **mitosis**—they replicate themselves to produce identical cells. Somatic cells have complete pairs of chromosomes. Mitosis is simply a process for making identical cells within a single individual. In contrast, sex cells, or gametes, are produced through the process of **meiosis**—two successive cell divisions that produce cells with only *half* the number of chromosomes (23 in the case of humans). Meiosis reduces the amount of genetic material to half to prepare for sexual reproduction. During fertilization, when two sex cells are joined together, they reproduce a new organism with a complete complement of chromosomes (46 in humans).

The process of meiosis is very important in terms of evolution because it necessitates genetic recombination. Offspring of sexually reproducing species are not identical copies of their parents, but rather unique individuals who have received contributions of genetic material from each parent. It is during meiosis and sexual reproduction that Mendel's principles of segregation and independent assortment operate. This reshuffling of genetic material does not change allele frequencies by itself. It ensures, however, that the entire range of traits present in a species is produced and can subsequently be acted on by evolutionary forces.

Polygenic Inheritance

Mendel's experiments with pea plants discussed above focused on the investigation of physical traits that were controlled by alleles at one genetic locus and had phenotypic expressions that were distinct: Plants were either tall or dwarf; the peas either green or yellow. There were no plants of varying height or of mixed green and yellow color. Today these are called *Mendelian traits* or *traits of simple inheritance*. More than 4,500 human traits are inherited in this manner. The A, B, and O blood types in humans are an example. Individuals have one or another of these blood groups; they do not have a mixture.

While some human characteristics are inherited as discrete traits, the majority are passed on in a more complicated fashion. In contrast to Mendelian traits, many physical characteristics in humans have phenotypic expressions that form a gradation and are influenced by alleles at more than one genetic locus. Traits that display a graded series determined by genes at multiple genetic loci are referred to as *polygenic* or *continuous traits*. They include many of the most visible aspects of human features, such as height, skin color, and hair color; consequently, they were often used as the basis for racial classifications. None of these traits fall into perfectly bounded categories. Unlike pea plants, humans occur in a variety of heights (and sizes) and have a wide range of natural hair colors.

Epigenetic Factors

To complicate matters further, genes and their expression are influenced by many other factors (Jablonka and Lamb 2006). Although DNA provides the fundamental genetic blueprint, other factors influence the expression of genetic traits. In some cases, the genetic directions provided by genes may be turned "on" or "off," modifying the effect the genes have without modifying the DNA sequence. For example, skin, muscle, and brain cells all contain the same DNA; they have same genetic blueprint, but appear different because their genes are turned on or off in varied ways. These modifications that are external to the DNA sequence are referred to as **epigenetic**, which literally means "above" or "on top of" genes. The complex interaction of DNA with these varied factors during cellular development makes it impossible to predict what a person will be like solely by mapping the sequences of their DNA.

Population Genetics and Evolution

2.6 Define and discuss how evolution takes place.

To understand the process of evolution fully, we cannot focus on individuals. A person's genetic makeup, fixed during conception, remains with that individual throughout his or her lifetime. Although people mature and change in appearance, they do not *evolve* in a biological sense.

Evolution refers to change in the genetic makeup of a *population* of organisms. A **population** here refers to a group of individuals who can potentially interbreed. To understand evolution, a scientist must consider all the genes in a population. This assortment of genes is known as the **gene pool**. Any particular gene pool consists of different allele frequencies, the relative amounts of the alternate forms of genes that are present.

In terms of genetics, evolution can be defined as the process of change in allele frequencies between one generation and the next. Alteration of the gene pool of a population is influenced by four evolutionary processes, one of which, natural selection, has already been discussed in relation to the work of Charles Darwin and Alfred Wallace. The other three processes are mutation, gene flow, and genetic drift. In addition, cultural, behavioral and epigenetic factors also influence the genetic makeup of a population and thus are potential sources of evolutionary change. These various factors are discussed in the following paragraphs.

Mutations

Mutations are alterations of genetic material at the cellular level. They can occur spontaneously during the cell replication process, or they can be induced by environmental factors such as radiation. Although we frequently think of mutations as harmful, they introduce variation into the gene pool and may create new, advantageous characteristics. Mutation serves as the primary force behind evolution because it is the *only* source of new genetic variation. The other evolutionary processes act on the genetic variation introduced through mutation. Maladaptive characteristics introduced by mutation are quickly eliminated by natural selection.

The role of mutation was only recognized during the twentieth century with better understanding of molecular genetics. Most mutations occur in the somatic cells of organisms. These types of mutations are not heritable. When the organism dies, the mutation dies with it. Some mutations, however, alter the DNA in reproductive cells. In this case, even change in a single DNA base, or a *point mutation*, may produce observable phenotypic change, for example, differences in blood chemistry. A mutation occurring in this instance will be passed on to the offspring.

Generally, the rates of mutations are relatively stable. If we make the conservative estimate that humans have approximately 20,000 to 25,000 genes with hundreds of DNA bases, then each of us clearly holds great potential for carrying new mutant genes. When the size of the human population is considered, it is evident that the mutation process provides a large source of variability. It would, however, be unlikely for evolution to occur solely as a result of a single mutation. The rate of mutation of a particular trait within a specific population as a whole is likely to be relatively low—perhaps present only in one individual out of 10,000. Hence, mutation alone would be unlikely to effect great change in allele frequencies within the population. In addition, some mutations may have no adaptive consequences. Yet, if mutations are acted on by natural selection and other evolutionary processes, they become a potentially important source of evolutionary change.

Gene Flow

Gene flow is the exchange of alleles between populations as a result of interbreeding. When this exchange occurs, new genetic material may be introduced, changing the allele frequencies in a population. The process of gene flow has affected most human societies. Migrants from one society enter a new region and intermarry with the local population. Through reproduction, they transmit new genes into the population. In this way, new mutations arising in one population can be transmitted to other members of the species.

In addition to providing a mechanism for introducing new genetic material, gene flow can act to decrease variation between populations. If two distinct populations continue to interbreed, they will become progressively similar genetically. Migration and connections between different populations have long been a feature of human societies and among early human ancestors. This genetic interconnectedness explains why new human species have not emerged: There has been sufficient gene flow between populations to prevent the creation of substantial genetic distance.

With the development of modern transportation, gene flow occurs on a worldwide scale. In this context, however, it is useful to remember that many cultural or social factors play a role in gene flow in human populations. Religious practices, socioeconomic status, and ethnicity may all influence the selection of mates (see discussion of cultural and behavioral factors below and in Chapter 5).

Genetic Drift

Genetic drift is evolutionary change resulting from random sampling phenomena that eliminate or maintain certain alleles in a gene pool. It includes the influence of chance events that may affect evolutionary change that are in no way influenced by individuals' genetic makeup. For example, in any population, only a small sample of the potential array of genetic material is passed on from one generation to the next. Every human being produces hundreds of thousands of gametes, each representing a different genetic combination, yet people produce only a few offspring. The chance selection of genetic material that occurs during reproduction results in minor changes in allele frequencies from one generation to the next. Chance events, such as death by disease or accident, also bring about change in allele frequencies. For example, if only ten individuals within a population carry a particular genetic trait and all of them die as a result of accident or disease, this genetic characteristic will not be passed on to the next generation.

Because evolution occurs in populations, change resulting from genetic drift is influenced by the size of the population as well as the relative allele frequencies represented. In larger populations, random events, such as accidental deaths, are unlikely to have as significant an effect on the population's gene pool. In smaller populations, however, such events can substantially alter the genetic variation present. A particular kind of genetic drift, known as the **founder effect**, results when only a small number of individuals in a population pass on their genes to the following generation. Such a situation might result when a famine decimates a large group or when a small migrant population moves away and establishes a new settlement in an isolated area. In these instances, the founding members of the succeeding generation will have only a portion—a sample—of the full range of the genetic material that was present in the original population. Because early human ancestors and human populations lived in small bands of people, perhaps consisting of family groups, genetic drift was likely an important evolutionary force.

Natural Selection

Natural selection provides the key to evolution. It can be defined as genetic change in a population, as reflected in allele frequencies and as a result of differential reproductive success. The other evolutionary forces already discussed are important in creating variation in allele frequencies within and between populations, but they provide no direction.

As illustrated in the case of Darwin's finches on the Galapagos Islands, certain alleles (as expressed in particular physical traits such as long or short beaks) may be selected for by environmental factors. They may enable an organism to resist disease better, obtain food more efficiently, or avoid predators more effectively. Individuals with such advantages will, on average, be more successful in reproducing and will thereby pass on their genes to the next generation at higher rates. Evolutionary "success" can be evaluated in relative terms; if the environment changes, natural selection pressures also change.

In the case of the finches, the larger- and smaller-beaked varieties were initially equally successful (or "fit"), but as food resources were depleted by drought, the individuals with heavier beaks were favored. This shift in allele frequencies in response to changing environmental conditions is called **adaptation**. Through evolution, species develop characteristics that allow them to survive and reproduce successfully in particular environmental settings. The specific environmental conditions to which a species is adapted is referred to as its **ecological niche**.

Cultural, Behavioral, and Epigenetic Factors

Mutations, gene flow, genetic drift, and natural selection have long been regarded as the primary evolutionary processes; they influence the genetic material present, its exchange, and distribution. However, other cultural, behavioral, and epigenetic factors interact with these processes and so influence the genetic makeup of a population and thus are potential sources of evolutionary change. One factor is an organism's interactions with its surroundings. Plant and animal species may alter their environment, something that may affect their adaptability and influence natural selection. For example, through grazing or predation, a species may change the distribution of other plant or animal species, changing the types of species represented and the availability of food resources. As these changes alter the environment, they also alter the characteristics that are being selected for by natural selection, and thus the direction of evolutionary change. The process by which organisms modify their environment is referred to *niche construction*. These modifications are not necessarily in the best interest of the species.

More than any other species, human societies dramatically impact the environments in which they live. Activities such as the hunting and gathering of food resources, land clearing, and water control modify the distribution of previously occurring plant and animal species. For example, as land is cleared for farming, plant species better suited to these changing conditions become more common. This, in turn, may lead to further changes in plant distribution and morphology. Significantly, these changes are unintentional, unplanned consequences of these activities.

In modern societies, industrialization, urbanization and pollution have dramatic implications for human health and reproduction. Overcrowding, combined with poor knowledge of sanitation, food storage, and personal hygiene has contributed to nutritional deficiencies, the spread of infectious disease, reduced growth rates, and decline in reproductive success, all of which have implications in evolutionary terms. In some instances, human cultural practices influence evolutionary processes even more directly, inhibiting gene flow and so contribute to genetic drift within a population. For example, restrictive marriage practices and laws prohibiting marriage between people of certain groups restrict the exchange of genes within a population. These factors are further discussed in Chapter 5.

Epigenetic Factors and Evolution As discussed previously, epigenetic changes refer to modifications of the genetic code that are external to DNA sequences. As in the case of mutations, most epigenetic changes occur in the somatic cells of organisms or, in sperm and egg cells, are erased when the two combine to form a fertilized egg.

Consequently, those changes are not heritable. However, it is possible that epigenetic changes in parents' sperm and egg cells may be passed on to the next generation. While epigenetic inheritance has not been demonstrated in human populations, a strong case can be made for it having played a role in evolution (Jablonka and Lamb 2006).

How Do New Species Originate?

2.7 Discuss how and why new species arise.

Evolutionary change is a dynamic, complex process. Although it is useful to discuss the preceding processes and factors as distinct variables, they all interact to affect evolutionary change. Mutation provides the ultimate source of new genetic variants, whereas gene flow, genetic drift, and natural selection alter the frequency of the new allele. Behavior and cultural factors further influence its distribution. The key consideration is the changes in the genetic characteristics of a population from one generation to the next. Over time, these changes may produce major differences among populations that were originally very similar. Ultimately these changes result in the origin of new species.

Measuring Evolutionary Change

To measure evolutionary change, researchers find it useful to evaluate evolutionary processes operating on a population by comparing allele frequencies for a particular trait to an idealized, mathematical model known as the **Hardy-Weinberg theory of genetic equilibrium**. This model, developed independently by G. H. Hardy and W. Weinberg, sets hypothetical conditions under which none of the evolutionary processes is acting and no evolution is taking place. The model makes several important assumptions. It presumes that no mutation is taking place (there are no new alleles); there is no gene flow (no migration or movement in or out of the population); no genetic drift (a large enough population is represented that there is no variation in allele frequencies due to sampling); and that natural selection is not operating on any of the alleles represented. The model also assumes that mating is randomized within the population so that all individuals have equal potential of mating with all other individuals of the opposite sex.

Given these assumptions, there will be no change in allele frequencies from one generation to the next. If examination of genotype frequencies within a population matches the idealized model, no evolution is taking place, and the population is said to be in Hardy-Weinberg equilibrium. If study suggests the genotype frequencies are not the same as the predicted model, then we know that at least one of the assumptions must be incorrect. Further research can then be undertaken to identify what the source of evolutionary change is. In practice, determining which evolutionary processes are acting on a population is challenging. Different evolutionary processes may act against one another, giving the appearance that none is operating. Small amounts of change may also go unrecognized. Nevertheless, the Hardy-Weinberg theory provides a starting point for evaluating evolutionary change.

A characteristic of a species is that its members can successfully interbreed only with one another. The mule is the offspring of a female horse and a male donkey, two clearly distinct species. As mules are always sterile, however, the reproductive isolation of the two species is maintained.

Speciation

One of the most interesting areas of research in evolutionary theory is how, why, and when new species arise. This is known as the study of **speciation**. Generally, biologists define a **species** as a group of organisms that have similar physical characteristics, can potentially interbreed with one another to produce fertile offspring, and who are reproductively isolated from other populations.

Phyletic Gradualism According to this perspective of evolution, speciation occurs when there is an interruption in gene flow between populations that formerly were one species but became isolated by geographic barriers. In geographic isolation, these populations may reside in different types of environments, and natural selection, mutation, or genetic drift may lead to increasingly different allele frequencies. Eventually, through evolutionary change, these two populations become so different genetically that they are no longer the same species. Darwin hypothesized that speciation was a gradual process of evolution occurring very slowly as different populations became isolated. This view is called *gradualism*, or **phyletic gradualism**.

Punctuated Equilibrium Beginning in the early twentieth century, some scientists challenged the gradualistic interpretation of speciation, arguing that new species might appear rapidly. Paleontologists (fossil specialists) Stephen Jay Gould and Niles Eldredge (1972) proposed a theory known as **punctuated equilibrium**. When examining ancient fossil beds, paleontologists discovered that some plants or animals seemed to exhibit little change over millions of years. These creatures appeared to remain in a state of equilibrium with their habitats for long geological periods, which were interrupted by major changes, or punctuations, leading to rapid speciation.

Punctuated equilibrium and gradualism (see Figure 2.6) present extreme perspectives of the rate at which evolution occurs, but the two views are not incompatible. Indeed, neither Darwin nor Gould and Eldredge suggested particular rates that were the same in all cases (Gingerich 1984). The fossil record provides examples of both cases (Brown and Rose 1987; Levinton 1988). The particular rate of change in a particular species depends on its specific adaptive features and the surrounding environmental conditions. Most paleontologists, biologists, and anthropologists agree that both types of evolution have occurred under different circumstances during different geological epochs. As our understanding of the fossil record increases, we will be better able to specify when and where speciation and evolution occurred rapidly and when and where they occurred gradually.

Figure 2.6 An illustration of two models of evolution. Gradualism implies a gradual, steady rate of speciation, while punctuated equilibrium suggests evolutionary change as a series of stops and starts. The two perspectives are not inconsistent with each other and the fossil record provides evidence of both.

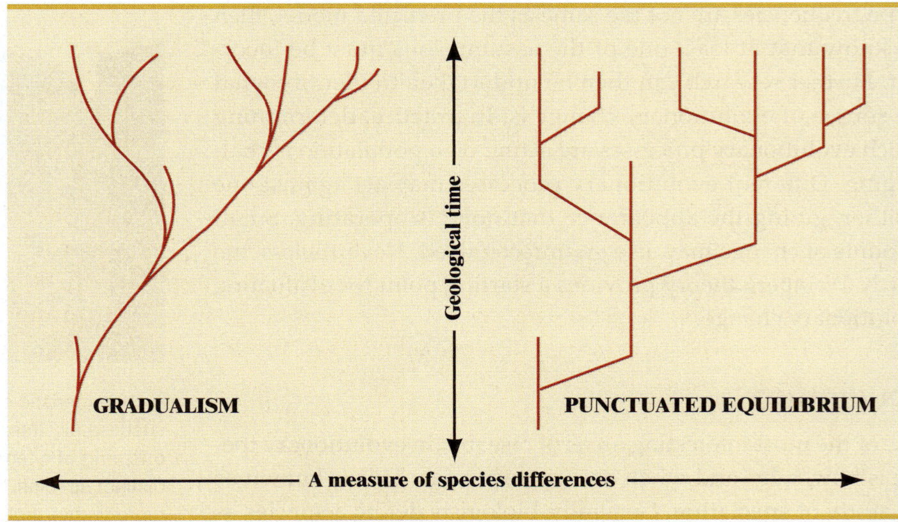

Adaptive Radiation

Adaptive radiation is the rapid diversification and adaptation of an evolving population into new ecological niches. It provides a useful illustration of the evolutionary process and the factors that influence rates of evolutionary change. As we have seen, organisms have tremendous reproductive potential, yet this potential is generally limited by the availability of food, shelter, and space in the environment. Competition with other organisms and natural selection limit the number of offspring that live. Eventually, organisms may utilize all the resources available in a particular ecological niche, making competition for food and other resources intense. Some individuals in a population may move into new environmental niches or explore new territories where resources are more available and chances for survival greater. In these new environments, with limited competition and abundant food, they may expand rapidly.

The creatures of the Galapagos Islands, discussed earlier with regard to Darwin's studies, provide an illustration of adaptive radiation. Located 500 miles off the coast of South America, the islands present an amazing diversity of flora and fauna. The islands species are similar to those found on the South American mainland where they originated. Yet, while similar, they are also distinct in many respects. Darwin reasoned that the island was initially colonized by a few representatives of the mainland species. The newly formed volcanic islands had no life-forms and the arriving, mainland colonists, unfettered by competition, quickly expanded in the new niche. Because the various environments of the islands were different from those of the mainland, the descendants of the original arrivals evolved traits favorable to the exploitation of the new conditions and, therefore, increased chances of reproductive success.

The adaptive radiation of many species is recorded in the fossil record. For example, at the beginning of the Mesozoic Era when reptiles first adapted to land environments, they were able to expand into a vast array of ecological niches with little competition. Environmental change may also create conditions favorable for the adaptive radiation of some species. Even natural disasters that lead to the extinction of many species may provide opportunity for others, as described in the box on Planetary-Level Extinctions. Such conditions favor species that have the ability to exploit the changing conditions, and this likely explains the expansion of the placental mammals at the beginning of the Cenozoic Era Evolutionary processes acting on the expanding population may produce many new varieties and species adapted to ecological niches different from the parent population, ultimately leading to new species.

The Evolution of Life

2.8 Briefly outline the evidence for the evolution of life on Earth and how evolutionary relationships are evaluated.

Modern scientific findings indicate that the universe as we know it began to develop between 13 billion and 20 billion years ago. At approximately 4.6 billion years ago, the sun and Earth formed, and about a billion years later, the first life appeared in the sea. Through evolution, living forms developed adaptive characteristics, survived, and reproduced. Geological forces and environmental changes, bringing about both gradual and rapid changes, led to new forms of life.

From studying the fossilized bones and teeth of different creatures, paleontologists have tracked the evolution of living forms throughout the world. They document the fossil record according to geological time, which is divided into *eras*, which are subdivided into *periods*, which in turn are composed of *epochs* (see page 44).

Analogy and Homology

How do paleontologists determine evolutionary relationships? Two useful concepts in discussing the divergence and differentiation of living forms are homology and analogy. **Homology** refers to traits that have resulted from a common evolutionary origin, though they may differ in form and function. For example, a human hand bears little resemblance to a whale's fin. Humans and whales live in very different environments, and the hand and fin perform in very different ways. Careful examination of human and whale skeletons, however, reveals many structural similarities that can be explained by a common, albeit distant, evolutionary relationship. Thus, the hand and the fin are referred to as homologous. To understand the evolutionary relatedness of different species, researchers focus on homologous features.

Yet, not all features result from shared evolutionary origins. **Analogy** refers to similarities in organisms that have no evolutionary relationship. Analogous forms result from *convergent evolution*, the process by which two unrelated types of organisms develop similar physical characteristics. These resemblances emerge when unrelated organisms adapt to similar environmental niches. For example, hummingbirds and hummingbird moths resemble each other physically and have common behavioral characteristics. However, they share no direct evolutionary descent.

Blood Chemistry and DNA

The majority of information on the evolution of life and human origin is provided by the information found in the fossil record. In recent years, however, studies of the genetic makeup of living organisms have received increasing attention. It is striking to note that despite the tremendous diversity of life, the DNA codes for the production of proteins—with few exceptions—dictate the joining of the same amino acids in all organisms, from the simplest one-celled plants and animals to humans. This semblance of genetic building blocks provides additional evidence for the common origin of all life.

Study of the differences and similarities in the arrangement of genetic material for living animals provides important insights into evolutionary relationships. Similarities in the DNA of different species indicate that they inherited genetic blueprints (with minor modifications) from a common ancestor. In most instances, this information has provided independent confirmation of conclusions about evolutionary relationships based on the study of skeletal characteristics and fossil remains. In some instances, however, physical characteristics may be confused because of convergent evolution. Study of genetic information and blood chemistry helps to avoid this confusion.

Genetic material of living animals has also been used to estimate when different species diverged. A technique known as *molecular dating* was developed by Vincent Sarich and Allan Wilson of the University of California, Berkeley (1967). The technique involves comparing amino acid sequences or, more recently, using what is called *DNA hybridization* to compare DNA material itself. As a result, Sarich and Wilson provided useful insights into the genetic relationship of humans to other species and estimates regarding when species may have separated. Molecular dating is based on two key assumptions: (1) Molecular evolution proceeds at a fairly constant rate over time, and (2) The greater the similarity between animals in biochemical terms, the more likely it is that they share a close evolutionary relationship. Research based on these concepts has been applied to the interpretation of human and primate evolution (see Chapter 4).

While providing a relative measure, the reliability of this technique as a dating tool has been widely debated. Some scientists have challenged the assumption that molecular evolution is constant over time. Rather, they believe that variation in mutation rates and the disparate generation lengths of different species skew the measurements of the "molecular clock" (Lovejoy and Meindl 1972; Goodman, Baba and Darga 1983; Li and Tanimura 1987; Langergraber et al 2012). Other researchers feel that the technique remains useful if the potential limitations are taken into consideration. Future work may help to resolve these issues.

The Paleontological Record

The Precambrian and Paleozoic Eras The fossil evidence shows that by the end of the Precambrian, simple forms of life resembling modern bacteria, including some species that may have been able to *photosynthesize*, had emerged. Apparently, the predominant organisms during this era were various kinds of algae (see Table 2.1). Beginning with the Paleozoic, which dates from 541 million to 252 million years ago, deposits of fossils became more abundant, enabling paleontologists to follow the adaptive radiation of jellyfish, worms, fish, amphibians, and early reptiles.

The Mesozoic Era The Mesozoic (252 million to 65 million years ago) marks the adaptive radiation of reptiles. This era is divided into the Triassic, Jurassic, and Cretaceous periods. The Mesozoic is known as the Age of Reptiles. Unlike earlier forms of life, reptiles could exist entirely outside water. They were the first successful land animals and reigned as the dominant species in this new environment. Many of the snakes, lizards, and turtles found in Mesozoic formations are similar to contemporary species. Of all the species that lived during the Mesozoic, the dinosaurs are the most well known today. They included the giant carnivore (meat eater) *Tyrannosaurus*; larger, plant-eating creatures such as the *Brachiosaurus*; and numerous other species, both large and small.

Although reptiles were the dominant animals of the Mesozoic, paleontologists have found fossils of many other organisms from this same era. For example, bird fossils, some even showing the outlines of feathers, have been preserved from the Jurassic period. The paleontological record demonstrates beyond a doubt that a direct evolutionary relationship exists between reptiles and birds. One classic fossil example is *Archaeopteryx*, an animal about the size of a crow, with small wings, teeth, and a long, reptilian tail.

Near the end of the Cretaceous period, many animals became extinct. Changing climatic conditions, competition from newly evolving mammals, and, possibly, extraterrestrial episodes led to the demise of many reptile species, including the dinosaurs, as well as many other organisms.

The Cenozoic Era The Cenozoic Era (65 million years ago to the present), or the Age of Mammals, was characterized by the dominance and adaptive radiation of mammals. This era is divided into two periods, the Tertiary, which encompassed 63 million years, and the Quaternary, which covers the last two million years. During the Cenozoic, various species of mammals came to occupy every environmental niche. Some, such as whales and dolphins, adapted to the sea. Others, such as bats, took to the air. Most mammals, however, are represented by a diverse array of land animals, including dogs, horses, rats, bears, rabbits, apes, and humans. One of the major evolutionary advantages that enabled mammals to radiate so rapidly was their reproductive efficiency. In contrast to reptiles, which lay eggs that are vulnerable to predators, most mammals retain their eggs internally within the female. The eggs are thus protected and nourished until they reach an advanced stage of growth. Consequently, a much higher percentage of the young survive into adulthood, when they can reproduce. It is the early Cenozoic period that witnessed the evolution of earliest primates, the order of which humans are part.

Table 2.1 A Record of Geologic Time

Era	Period	Epoch	Millions of Years Ago	Geological Conditions and Evolutionary Development
Cenozoic (Age of Mammals)	Quaternary	Holocene	0.0117	End of last Ice Age; warmer climate. Decline of woody plants; rise of herbaceous plants. Age of *Homo sapiens.*
		Pleistocene	2.6	Four Ice Ages; glaciers in Northern hemisphere; uplift of Sierras. Extinction of many large mammals and other species. Emergence of genus *Homo*.
	Tertiary	Pliocene	5.3	Uplift and mountain building; volcanoes; climate much cooler. Development of grasslands and flowering plants; decline of forests. Large carnivores; many grazing mammals; australopithecines appear.
		Miocene	23	Major continents in approximately their current locations; mountain formation. Climate drier, cooler. Flowering plants continue to diversify. Many forms of mammals; anthropoid primates flourish; earliest hominoid primates.
		Oligocene	33	Rise of Alps and Himalayas; most land low; volcanic activity in Rockies. Spread of forests and flowering plants; rise of monocotyledons. All present mammal families represented; anthropoid primates evolve.
		Eocene	56	Climate warmer. Gymnosperms and flowering plants dominant. Modern birds; first true primates appear.
		Paleocene	65	Climate mild to cool; continental seas disappear; North America and Europe still joined. Age of Mammals begins; likely emergence of the first primate ancestors.
Mesozoic (Age of Reptiles)	Cretaceous		145	Continents start to separate; formation of Rockies; swamps. Rise of flowering plants; gymnosperms decline. Dinosaurs peak, then become extinct; toothed birds become extinct; first modern birds; primitive mammals.
		Jurassic	201	Climate mild; continents low; inland seas; mountains form; continental drift continues. Gymnosperms common. Large, specialized dinosaurs; first toothed birds; insectivorous marsupials.
		Triassic	252	Many mountains and deserts form; continental drift begins. Gymnosperms.
Paleozoic (Age of Ancient Life)	Permian		298	Continents merge as Pangaea; glaciers; formation of Appalachians. Conifers diversify; cycads evolve. Modern insects appear; mammal-like reptiles; extinction of many Paleozoic invertebrates.
	Carboniferous		358	Lands low; great coal swamps; climate warm and humid, then cooler. Forests of ferns, club mosses, horsetails, and gymnosperms. First reptiles; spread of ancient amphibians; many insect forms; ancient sharks abundant.
	Devonian		419	Glaciers; inland seas. Terrestrial plants well established; first forests; gymnosperms and bryophytes appear. Age of Fishes; amphibians and wingless insects appear; many trilobites.
	Silurian		443	Continents mainly flat. Vascular plants appear; algae dominant in aquatic environment. Fish evolve; terrestrial arthropods.
	Ordovician		485	Sea covers continents; climate warm. Marine algae dominant; terrestrial plants appear. Invertebrates dominant; fish appear.
	Cambrian		541	Climate mild; lands low; oldest rocks with abundant fossils. Algae dominant in aquatic environment. Age of Marine Invertebrates; most modern phyla represented.
Precambrian	Proterozoic		2,500	Planet cooled; glaciers; Earth's crust forms; mountains form. First multicellular forms of life appear; primitive algae and fungi, marine protozoans; marine invertebrates appear toward end of period.
Origin of the Earth; Origin of the Universe			4 billion 13 to 14 billion	Evidence of first prokaryotic cells.

Critical Perspectives

Creationism, Intelligent Design, and Evolution

Despite the increasing scientific evidence supporting evolution, not all segments of American and Western society have accepted the geological, genetic, and fossil data that are the basis of evolutionary theory (Petto and Godfrey 2007; Young and Largent 2007). Various versions of creation that rely on literal interpretations of the Bible are taught by some Christian, Jewish, and Islamic groups, as well as other religious denominations. For example, many members of the Old Order Amish (discussed in Chapter 5) accept an extreme literal reading of the biblical passage that refers to "four corners of the Earth held up by angels" and believe that the Earth is a two-dimensional flat plane. Members of the International Flat Earth Society have similar beliefs about a flat Earth (Scott 2004). These views reflect the ancient Hebrew description in the biblical passages referring to the Earth as a flat disk floating on water with the heavens held up by a dome (or firmament) with the sun, moon, and stars attached to it.

In the nineteenth century, some individuals attempted to reconcile a literal reading of the account of creation in Genesis 1:22 by translating the Hebrew term *day* as periods of time thousands or millions of years long, rather than 24-hour days (Sedley 2007). Some contemporary creationists' teachings expose similar views; they are sometimes referred to as "day-age" creationists. However, the vast majority of activists in the campaign against teaching evolution call themselves "progressive creationists." The progressive creationists accept the modern scientific view of the Big Bang and that the Earth is billions of years old, but do not accept the theory of evolution. They believe that God not only created the Big Bang, but also created separate "kinds" of plants and animals with genetic variations that resulted in the development of contemporary species of living organisms.

A group of creationists that have actively campaigned against the teaching of evolution call themselves "scientific creationists," represented by the Institute for Creation Research. This group proposes a biblically based explanation for the origins of the universe and of life. They reject modern physics, chemistry, and geology concerning the age of the Earth. They argue that the entire universe was created within a period of six days, based on the account in Genesis 1:2. They believe that the universe was spontaneously created by divine fiat 6,000 to 10,000 years ago, challenging evidence for billions of years of geological history and fossil evidence. These creationists explain the existence of fossilized remains of ancient life by referring to a universal flood that covered the entire Earth for 40 days. Surviving creatures were saved by being taken aboard Noah's ark. Creatures that did not survive this flood, such as dinosaurs, became extinct. This creationist view is taught in some of the more fundamentalist denominations of Protestantism, Judaism, and Islam.

Scientific creationists read the texts and theories presented by biologists, geologists, and paleontologists and then present their arguments against the evolutionary views. They do very little, if any, direct biological or geological research to refute evolutionary hypotheses (Rennie 2002). Their arguments are based on biblical sources mixed with misinterpretations of scientific data and evolutionary hypotheses. The cosmological framework espoused by the scientific creationists is not based on any empirical findings. For example, scientists around the world find no physical evidence of a universal flood. Local floods did occur in the Near East and may be related to the story of Noah that appears in the Bible (and in earlier Babylonian texts). But to date, no evidence exists for a universal flood that had the potential to wipe out human populations worldwide or to cause the extinction of creatures such as dinosaurs (Isaak 2007).

A more recent form of creationism has been referred to as "intelligent design creationism" (Gross and Forest 2004; Petto and Godfrey 2007). The historical roots of this conceptual stance go back to philosophers such as Plato and Aristotle in the Greek tradition, who suggested that a spiritual force structured the universe and society. These ideas were Christianized by Saint Thomas Aquinas (1225–1274) and European scholars during the medieval period. In the nineteenth century, theologian William Paley (1743–1805) argued that one could see proof of God's existence by examining the Earth and the remarkable adaptations of living organisms to their environments, using the famous analogy that if we found a watch, we would have to assume that there was a watchmaker—we can see God's plan as we observe the natural world (1803). Two contemporary theorists who support this position are Lehigh University's biochemist Michael Behe, author of *Darwin's Black Box* (1996), and philosopher and mathematician William Dembski, professor of science and theology at Southern Seminary in Louisville, author of the book *Intelligent Design* (1999).

Debates between intelligent design proponents and other researchers have been extensive and, at times, quite spirited (Rennie 2002; Shanks 2004; Shanks and Joplin 1999). Critics of intelligent design creationism note that Behe, Dembski, and their followers concede that microevolution and macroevolution has occurred, but contend that some biological phenomena and the complexity of life cannot be explained by modern science and that this complexity itself is proof that there must be an intelligent supernatural designer. Although most scientists would not rule out the possibility of supernatural creation, they do require evidence. In this respect, intelligent design has failed to provide a more compelling argument of human origins than evolutionary theory.

Given these diverse perspectives, is there any common ground between religious explanations of human origins and scientific theories? Surveys indicate that a surprising number of Americans assume that the creation-evolution controversy is based on a dichotomy between believers in God and

(*continued*)

secular atheists who are antireligious. This is incorrect. There are many varieties of both religious perspectives and evolutionary explanations, many of them compatible. Scientists and others who accept evolution are not necessarily atheists (Pennock 2003; Scott 2004). One major view of evolution is known as *theistic evolution*, which promotes the view that God creates through the evolutionary processes. Supporters of this perspective accept the modern scientific findings in astronomy, biology, genetics, and fossil and geological evidence, but see God as intervening in how evolution takes place. Theistic evolution is the official view accepted by the Roman Catholic Church; it was recently reiterated by Pope John Paul II in 1996. In this statement, John Paul II emphasized that evolution was not just "theory," but was based on an enormous amount of empirical evidence, or "facts." The Roman Catholic theological position is that although humans may indeed be descended from earlier forms of life, God created the human soul. Other contemporary mainstream Protestant, Jewish, Muslim, Hindu, and Buddhist scientists also accept theistic evolution. This position sees no conflict between religion and science and reflects a continuum between the creationist and evolutionary views.

Another view of evolution is sometimes referred to as *materialist evolutionism* or *philosophical materialism*. Scientists and philosophers who hold this view believe that the scientific evidence for evolution results in a proof of atheism. Charles Darwin recorded in his memoirs how he vacillated between muddled religious faith, atheism, and what he later accepted as agnosticism (the belief that one cannot know as humans whether God exists or not) (Desmond and Moore 1991). Survey polls demonstrate that most Americans believe materialist evolutionism is the dominant view among scientists, despite the fact that this is not the case. Because it challenges religious interpretations, it is one of the primary reasons why some fundamentalist religious-based groups have opposed the teaching of evolution in public schools in the United States.

In actuality, there are scientists who accept theistic evolution or other spiritual views along with scientific theories. For example, one of the leading critics of intelligent design creationism is the practicing Roman Catholic biologist at Williams College, Kenneth Miller. Miller has authored a book called *Finding Darwin's God: A Scientist's Search for Common Ground between God and Evolution* (2000). In this book, Miller draws on biology, genetics, and evolutionary data to challenge intelligent design proponents' claims that the complexity of life demonstrates an intelligent designer. Paul Davies, a Protestant theologian and philosopher who authored the book *The Fifth Miracle* (2000) about faith and the evolution of life, is also critical of the intelligent design creationist model and relies on the empirical findings in science and evolution to refute their claims.

These individuals and other scientists accept theistic views of evolution, but emphasize that scientific understanding of the universe and life must be based on the methods of *naturalism*. This *methodological naturalism* requires the scientist to rely on "natural" or "materialist" (biological and physical) explanations rather than spiritual or theological explanations for examining the universe and evolution, *but it does not compel one to accept atheism*. In fact, many major philosophers and scientists, such as anthropologist Eugenie Scott (director of the National Center for Science Education) and the famed Albert Einstein, argued that one cannot prove or disprove the existence of God through the use of science. Methodological naturalism does not result in a conflict between faith and science. Rather, faith and science are viewed as two separate spheres and modes of understanding the world. This method of naturalism coincides with the teachings of the Roman Catholic position and many mainstream Protestant, Jewish, Muslim, Hindu, and Buddhist traditions.

Evolutionary explanations and other scientific theories often fail to satisfy our deep spiritual questions and moral concerns. While science can give us some basic answers about the universe and life, it cannot reveal spiritual insights. And yet, a scientific perspective does tend to leave us in a state of "spiritual awe" as described by Darwin in the famous closing passage of the *Origin of Species*: "There is grandeur in this view of life."

Points to Ponder

1. How can accounts of creation such as that found in Genesis 1:2 be evaluated empirically?
2. Have any of the scientific creationist claims convinced you of the falsity of evolution?
3. Do you think that faith and science are compatible when assessing the scientific record regarding evolution?

The Primates

2.9 Discuss primate characteristics and the basis for primate classification.

Humans are members of the mammalian order **Primates**, a diverse group of animals that also includes monkeys, prosimians, and apes. While a diverse group, primates share a number of key characteristics, such as large brain size, keen vision, dexterous hands, and a generalized skeleton that allows for great physical agility. Primates also tend to have smaller litters than other animals, devoting more care and attention to the rearing of their offspring. These traits are more prominent in some primates, while hardly evident in others. Similar features can also be found in many nonprimates. For example, the lion has very efficient eyesight, and the tree squirrel is exceedingly agile.

Figure 2.7 Examples of primate hands. Although they vary in form, they share a high degree of manual dexterity.

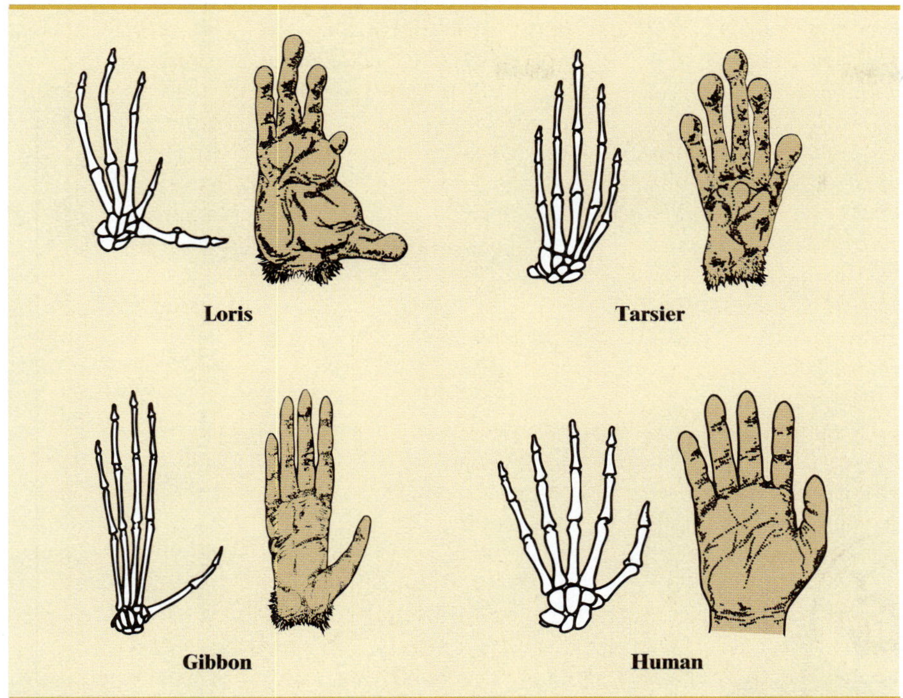

However, the unique *combination* of traits found in the primates distinguishes them from other animals.

As humans are primates, examination of both living and fossil primate species is key to understanding human origins. We can trace the striking similarities among primates to a series of shared evolutionary relationships. Many people hold a common misconception about human evolution—the mistaken belief that humans descended from modern apes such as the gorilla and chimpanzee. This is a highly inaccurate understanding of Charles Darwin's thesis and contemporary scientific theories of human evolution, as well as the available fossil evidence. Gorillas and chimpanzees are not human ancestors. Rather, like humans, the gorilla and chimpanzee represent the end points of their own distinct evolutionary lineages (see Figure 2.8). As primates, however, they share a distant common ancestor (now extinct) with other primates.

Primate Classification

Primates are placed in a distinct group on the basis of their shared physical characteristics. Individual species—groups of individuals that can potentially interbreed and are reproductively isolated from other populations—share even more specific traits. These categories are useful to researchers. **Taxonomy**, the science of classification, gives scientists a convenient way of referring to, and comparing, living and extinct organisms. Modern taxonomy is based on the work of the Swedish scientist Carl von Linnace, also known as Carolus Linnaeus (1707–1778). Linnaeus created a system of Latin names to categorize plants and animals based on their similarities. The Linnaean system follows a hierarchical pattern (see Table 2.2), ranging from large categories, such as *kingdoms* that encompass creatures sharing overarching characteristics, to small groups, or *species*, whose members can all potentially interbreed.

Human beings belong to the kingdom Animalia, one of several major divisions of nature. Members of this kingdom are mobile, complex organisms that sustain

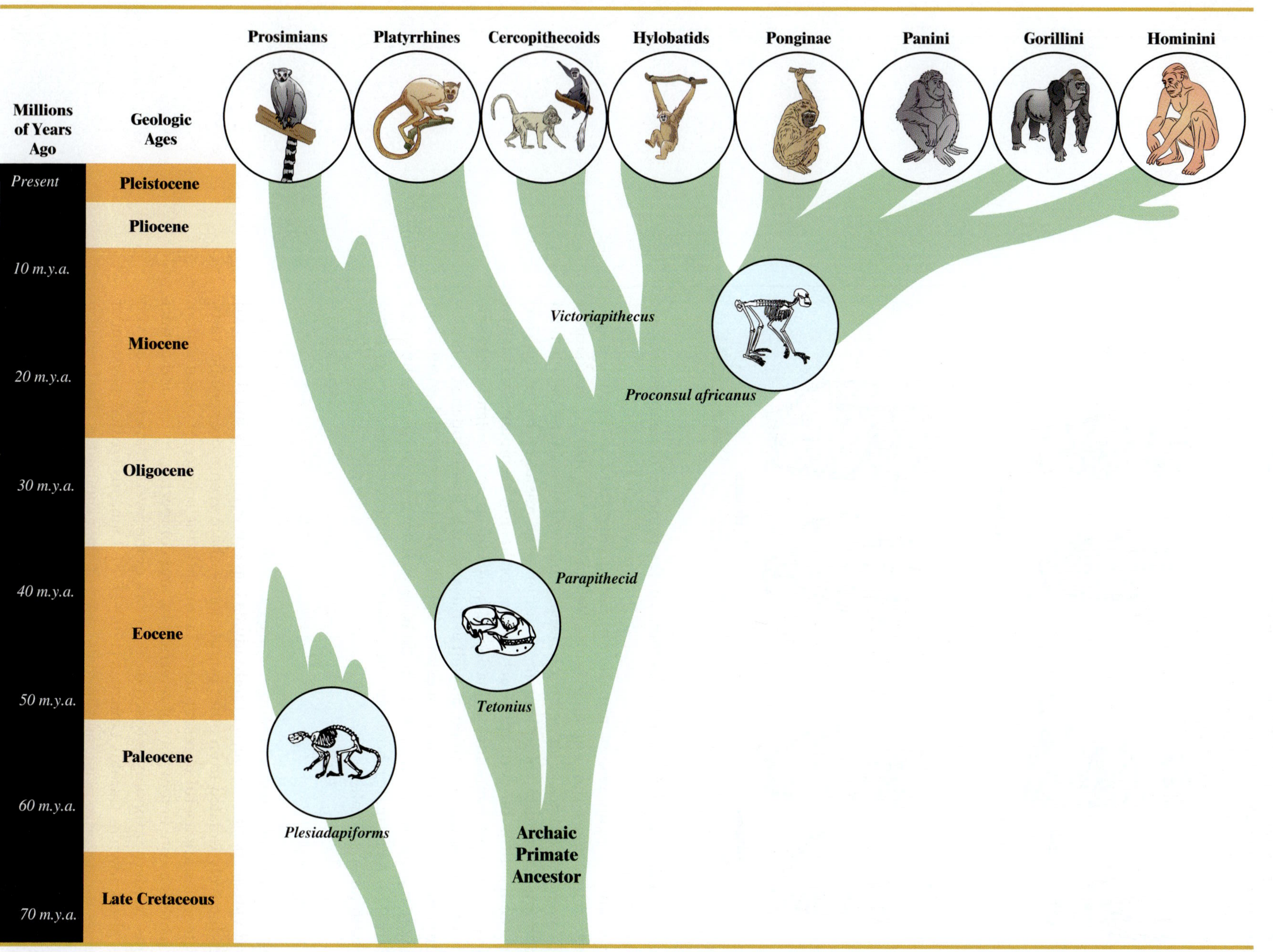

Figure 2.8 One interpretation of primate evolutionary relationships.

Table 2.2 Classification Relevant to Human Ancestry
The classification of living organisms is hierarchical: Membership in a kingdom is determined by very basic characteristics; Classification into other categories is based on increasingly specific criteria. The words *primate*, *anthropoid*, *hominoid*, and *hominid* are used to refer to members of the categories Primates, Anthropoidea, Hominoidea, and Hominidae. Superfamily names generally end in *-idae*, family names in *idae*, and subfamily names in *-inae*.

Category	Taxon	Common Description
Kingdom	Animalia	Animals
Phylum	Chordata	Animals with notochords
Subphylum	Vertebrata	Animals with backbones
Superclass	Tetrapoda	Four-footed vertebrates
Class	Mammalia	Vertebrates with body hair and mammary glands
Order	Primates	All prosimians, monkeys, apes, and humans
Suborder	Anthropoidea	All monkeys, apes, and humans
Infraorder	Catarrhini	Old World anthropoids
Superfamily	Hominoidea	Apes and humans
Family	Hominidae	Orangutans, chimpanzees, gorillas, and humans
Subfamily	Homininae	Chimpanzees, gorillas, and humans
Tribe	Hominini	Bipedal apes including humans
Genus	*Homo*	Humans and their immediate ancestors
Species	*Homo sapiens*	Modern humans

themselves by eating plants and other animals. Other categories, or *taxa*, are based on more specific criteria. For example, humans have backbones, a feature that places them in the subphylum Vertebrata, while the presence of body hair and mammary glands further identifies them as members of the class Mammalia (mammals). Classes are subdivided into a number of orders; humans belong to the order Primates. Like other mammals, primates are warm-blooded animals that possess hair for insulation and nourish their young with milk from mammary glands. However, primates' refined visual sense, manual dexterity, distinctive skeletal structure, and large brain size differentiate them from other mammals.

Although all primates share certain basic characteristics, there is a great deal of variation among species. There is some disagreement among primatologists about how particular species are related to one another and how the order should be divided. When Linnaeus developed his classification system to facilitate the comparison of organisms, Darwin had not yet introduced his theory of evolution. However, after Darwin's publication of *On the Origin of Species* in 1859, biologists increasingly applied theories of evolution to systems of classification, giving rise to a number of scientific disputes about the basis of classification. Scientists initially focused on physical similarities among species, traits that most likely emerged as evolutionary adaptations to specific environments. More recently, the actual genetic links can be determined through the study of DNA. With increasing research into the genetic codes of living primates, genetic relatedness has become more important in taxonomy (see the box "What's in a Name?").

The Human Primate

As members of the order Primates, humans share many physical and anatomical similarities, as well as some behavioral characteristics, with other primate species. Like other primates, modern humans can rotate their arms fully, grasp branches, and stand

What's in a Name?

Primate Classification and Taxonomy

Scientists have traditionally used physical characteristics that reflect shared adaptive histories in classifying primates into various families, genera, and species (see Table 2.2, Figure 2.8). However, the unraveling of genetic codes has revealed the specific genetic links between living species. While the two approaches have yielded similar, if not identical divisions, they are not always the same.

Let's consider the classification of humans, chimpanzees, gorillas, and orangutans. On the one hand, the African apes (chimpanzees and gorillas) and orangutans, which have certain physical traits in common, were traditionally placed in their own family, Pongidae; the pongids. Humans, on the other hand, followed another evolutionary line, making them distinct in appearance, distinctive in terms of their upright posture, and very different in terms of their behavioral adaptations. In contrast to other primates, humans have larger brains and lack the thick body hair found in other species. Humans also have developed a complex culture—material objects and nonmaterial concepts—that they use to interact with the environment. For this reason, scientists placed humans and their immediate ancestors in the family Hominidea; the hominids. The separation of the hominids from the pongids makes sense both in light of their distinct evolutionary histories.

However, molecular studies of genetic material of living primates, as well as the careful study of ape and human anatomy, indicate that in actuality, humans and the African apes are more closely related than either group is to the orangutans (Andrews and Martin 1987). As a result, a variety of new classification schemes emerged over the past two decades that attempt to represent the close genetic relatedness between humans and their closest living relatives, and the implications that this has for the understanding of evolutionary relationships.

One solution has been to place the orangutans, chimpanzees, and gorillas, as well as humans and their ancestors into family Hominidae, which is further divided into two subfamilies: Subfamily Ponginae is used to refer to the orangutans, while subfamily Homininae includes gorillas, chimpanzees, and humans, a grouping that reflects their close genetic relatedness. Humans and their ancestors are then placed in their own tribe, Hominini (hominins) to denote their unique characteristics.

This classification schema has significant implications for the discussion of human evolution. The classification more accurately reflects the genetic relatedness of the different species, and for that reason is used in this book. However, the new terminology is more cumbersome and potentially confusing as previously used terms have different meanings in the new scheme. The term *hominid* had been used to denote the split of the human family from the rest of the apes. In the revised classification, Hominidae includes both humans and the African apes with humans, gorillas, and chimpanzees each making up their own tribe within the subfamily.

Points to Ponder

1. Review the different approaches to primate classification. Outline how and why these perspectives differ.
2. A key objective taxonomy is to facilitate comparison. Discuss how the revision of taxonomic systems is, or is not, useful.

Order	Suborder	Infraorder	Superfamily	Family	Subfamily	Tribe	Common Term
PRIMATES	*Prosimii*						Loris Lemur Tarsier
	Anthropoidea	*Platyrrhini*					New World monkey
		Catarrhini	*Cercopithecoidea*				Old World monkey
			Hominoidea	*Hylobatidae*			Gibbon
				Hominidae	*Ponginae*		Orangutan
					Homininae	*Gorillini*	Gorilla
						Panini	Chimpanzee Bonobo
						Hominini	Human

erect. Humans' sensory organs also bear a striking similarity to those of some of the other primates. Humans, as well as apes and monkeys, have keen visual acuity, including stereoscopic, binocular, and color vision. They also have diminished olfactory abilities compared to other animals. Thus, humans, apes, and monkeys all appear to perceive the external world in much the same way. The striking resemblance between the skeletons of a chimpanzee and a human being clearly identifies humans and chimpanzees as fellow primates. Yet, humans also possess physical and mental abilities that make them unique.

One of the most striking differences between humans and other primates is the human ability to walk upright on two legs. Chimps, gorillas, and orangutans may stand upright for short periods, but only humans maintain a completely erect posture and consistently walk upright on two legs. The human pelvis, legs, and feet provide the balance and coordination that make this type of movement possible. Because human hands are not needed for locomotion, they have evolved into highly precise organs for the manipulation of objects. Human hands have short finger bones (or phalanges) compared with other primates (see Figure 2.7). This trait further enhances humans' manual dexterity. We examine the adaptive aspects of *bipedalism* (walking on two legs) and the implications these physical abilities had for the behavior of early human ancestors in Chapter 4.

Another distinctive human characteristic is their brain size. Although all primates have large brains relative to body size, the human brain is three times as large as we would expect for a primate of this size and build (Passingham 1982). The human cerebrum, referred to in common usage as the "gray matter," and its outer covering, the neocortex (the section that controls higher brain functions), are far more highly developed than those of other primates. These features have important implications for a human's ability to engage in complex learning, abstract thought, and the storing and processing of information.

Human social organization also likely had important implications for human evolution. As seen above, most primates congregate in social groups and this was likely true for early human ancestors. Living in groups confers many advantages, including greater opportunities for social learning. The protracted period of dependence and maturation characteristic of humans—longer than any other primate—make this aspect of human behavior particularly important. This extended period of dependency provides extended opportunity for social learning and passing information such as strategies for obtaining food, how to avoid predators, and tool manufacture. The size and complexity of the human brain, together with the long period of maturation, stand as the most significant differences between humans and other primates. These features are expressed in a human's extraordinary capacity to learn, to their imaginative social interactions, and to their facility—unique among all life-forms—to use and produce symbols, language, and culture.

Summary and Review of Learning Objectives

2.1 Explain how cosmologies regarding human origins differ from scientific views of evolution.

Cosmologies are conceptual frameworks that present the universe (the *cosmos*) as an orderly system. They often include explanations of human origins and the place of humankind in the universe. Cosmological explanations frequently involve divine or supernatural forces that are, by their nature, impossible for human beings to observe. We accept them and believe in them, on the basis of faith. Scientific theories of evolution, in contrast, are derived from the belief that the universe operates according to regular processes that can be observed. The scientific method is not a rigid framework that provides indisputable answers. Instead, scientific theories are propositions that can be evaluated by future testing and observation. Acceptance of the theory of evolution is based on observations in many areas of geology, paleontology, and biology.

2.2 Discuss how the scientific revolution provided the context for the theory of evolution.

In Europe during the Renaissance (after c. 1450 A.D.), scientific discoveries began to challenge conceptions about both the age of the Earth and humanity's relationship to the rest of the universe. Astronomers such as Copernicus and Galileo discovered that the earth was not the center of the universe and along with other planets revolved around the sun. Geologists initiated research that demonstrated that the age of the earth was much older than described in religious texts such as the Bible. These findings provided the historical context for the development of the theory of evolution.

2.3 Explain how Darwin's views of natural selection and evolution differed from those of earlier scientists.

Evolution refers to the process of change in the genetic makeup of a species over time. It is used to explain the emergence of new species. Theories regarding the evolution of plants and animal species were proposed by a number of scholars prior to the mid-1800s. However, none of these early theorists suggested a unified theory that *explained* evolution and, consequently, most people could not accept these ideas. Research by Charles Robert Darwin (1809–1882) and Alfred Russel Wallace (1823–1913) independently identified natural selection as a key mechanism for explaining change in a species over time. Natural selection is now recognized as one of the four principal evolutionary processes.

2.4 Discuss Gregor Johann Mendel's principles of inheritance.

Principles of Inheritance refer to how specific traits are passed on from one generation to the next. Modern understanding of heredity emerged through the studies of an Austrian monk named Gregor Johann Mendel (1822–1884). Through the study of successive generations of pea plants, Mendel made several important observations. He demonstrated that traits are inherited in discrete packages of information that are not mixed during reproduction. The observation that units of heredity (or genes) occur in pairs and that offspring receive half of a pair from each parent is the basis of the *principle of segregation.* Mendel also observed that certain traits prevailed over others. He labeled the prevailing traits "dominant" and those traits that were unexpressed in one generation but expressed in following generations "recessive." Mendel referred to the fact that individual traits occur independently of one another as the principle of independent assortment.

2.5 Discuss how Mendel's principles of inheritance have changed in light of a better understanding of molecular genetics.

Mendel's principles of segregation and independent assortment and the concepts of recessive and dominant traits are still viewed as important aspects of heredity. However, using more advanced technology, modern scientists have a better understanding of the dynamics of heredity at the cellular level. Mendel's experiments focused on the investigation of physical traits in pea plants that were controlled by alleles at one genetic locus and had phenotypic expressions that were distinct: Plants were either tall or dwarf; the peas either green or yellow. There were no plants of varying height or of mixed green and yellow color. Today these are called *Mendelian traits* or *traits of simple inheritance*. While some human characteristics are inherited as discrete traits, the majority are passed on in a more complicated fashion. In contrast to Mendelian traits, many physical characteristics in humans have phenotypic expressions that form a gradation and are influenced by alleles at more than one genetic locus. Traits that display a graded series determined by genes at multiple genetic loci are referred to as *polygenic* or *continuous traits*. They include many of the most visible aspects of human features, such as height, skin, color, and hair color.

2.6 Define and discuss how evolution takes place.

Evolution refers to the process of change in the genetic makeup of a species over time. It is used to explain the emergence of new species. Alteration of the gene pool of a population is influenced by four evolutionary processes: mutation, gene flow, genetic drift and natural selection. In addition, cultural, behavioral and epigenetic factors may further influence the genetic makeup of a *population* and thus are potential sources of evolutionary change. Evolutionary change is a dynamic, complex process. Although it is useful to discuss the preceding processes and factors as distinct variables, they all interact to affect evolutionary change. The key consideration is change in the genetic characteristics of a population from one generation to the next. Over time, this change may produce major differences among populations that were originally very similar.

2.7 Discuss how and why new species arise.

The study of speciation, or how and why new species arise, is one of the most interesting areas of research in evolutionary theory. A species is a group of organisms that have similar physical characteristics, can potentially interbreed with one another to produce fertile offspring, and who are reproductively isolated from other populations. Punctuated equilibrium and gradualism present extreme perspectives of the rate at which evolution and the process of speciation occur. According to phyletic gradualism, speciation occurs when there is an interruption in gene flow between populations that formerly were one species but became isolated. Gradually, through evolutionary change, these two populations become so different genetically that they became separate species. In contrast, **punctuated equilibrium** views evolution as occurring at variable rates; some species remaining in a state of equilibrium with their habitats for long geological periods, which were then interrupted by major changes, or punctuations, leading to rapid speciation. The fossil record provides examples of both and most scientists agree that both types of evolution have occurred.

2.8 Briefly outline the evidence for the evolution of life on Earth and how evolutionary relationships are evaluated.

From studying the fossilized remains of different creatures, paleontologists have tracked the evolution of living forms throughout the world. They document the fossil record according to geological time, which is divided into *eras*, which are subdivided into *periods*, which in turn are composed of *epochs*. Paleontologists and anthropologists determine evolutionary relationships using both the fossil evidence and the genetic make-up of modern organisms. Prior to the advent of modern genetic studies, evolutionary relationships were inferred on the basis of organisms' physical characteristics. A useful concept in discussing the evolutionary relationships of living forms is homology. Homology refers to traits that have resulted from a common evolutionary origin, though they may differ in form and function. For example, a human hand bears little resemblance to a whale's fin. Careful examination of human and whale skeletons, however, reveals many structural similarities that can be explained by a common, albeit distant, evolutionary relationship. The majority of information on the evolution of life and human origin is provided by the information found in the fossil record. In recent years, however, studies of the genetic make-up of living organisms have received increasing attention. Study of the differences and similarities in the arrangement of genetic material for living animals provides important insights into evolutionary relationships. Similarities in the DNA of different species indicate that they inherited genetic blueprints (with minor modifications) from a common ancestor. Through the use of molecular dating, the genetic material of living animals has also been used to estimate when different species diverged. In most instances, this information has provided independent confirmation of conclusions about evolutionary relationships based on the study of skeletal characteristics and fossil remains.

2.9 Discuss primate characteristics and the basis for primate classification.

Primates are a diverse group of animals that includes prosimians, monkeys, apes, and humans. While a diverse group, primates share a number of key characteristics, including large brain size, keen vision, dexterous hands, and a generalized skeleton that allows for great physical agility. **Taxonomy,** the science of classification, gives scientists a convenient way of referring to, and comparing, living and extinct organisms. Modern taxonomy is based on the work of the Swedish scientist Carolus Linnaeus (1707–1778). The Linnaean system follows a hierarchical pattern, ranging from large categories, such as *kingdoms* that encompass creatures sharing overarching characteristics, to smaller groups that share more specific traits. The smallest categories consist of species—groups of individuals that can potentially interbreed and are reproductively isolated from other populations. Members of individual species share the most features. Primates, including humans, are placed into groups on the basis of their shared physical characteristics and evolutionary relatedness. Linnaean classification was originally based on visible physical similarities and differences between species. However, with increasing research into the genetic codes of living primates, genetic relatedness has become a more important basis for taxonomy.

Key Terms

adaptation, p. 38
adaptive radiation, p. 41
alleles, p. 31
analogy, p. 42
catastrophism, p. 24
continental drift, p. 44
cosmologies, p. 22
deoxyribonucleic acid (DNA), p. 34
dominant, p. 30
ecological niche, p. 38
epigenetic, p. 35
evolution, p. 26
founder effect, p. 37
gametes, p. 34
gene, p. 34
gene flow, p. 36
gene pool, p. 36
genetic drift, p. 37
genotype, p. 32
Hardy-Weinberg theory of genetic equilibrium, p. 39
heterozygous, p. 31
homology, p. 42
homozygous, p. 31
meiosis, p. 35
mitosis, p. 35
mutations, p. 36
natural selection, p. 27
phenotype, p. 32
phyletic gradualism, p. 40
population, p. 36
punctuated equilibrium, p. 40
recessive, p. 30
somatic cells, p. 34
speciation, p. 39
species, p. 39
uniformitarianism, p. 24
zygote, p. 34

Chapter 3
The Record of the Past

Chapter Outline

Learning Objectives

After reading this chapter you should be able to:

3.1 Define paleoanthropology and discuss what we can learn about the past from fossil evidence.

3.2 Discuss what the archaeological record can tell us about past societies.

3.3 Discuss the basic techniques used to locate archaeological sites and fossil localities.

3.4 Discuss the basic techniques of archaeological excavation.

3.5 Compare and contrast how archaeologists and paleoanthropologists date their discoveries.

3.6 Discuss the challenges of interpreting the past and how these are overcome.

Why study the human past? During the early history of anthropology, the answer to this question was straightforward. The study of fossils and artifacts of the past sprang out of a curiosity about the world and the desire to collect and organize objects. This curiosity was, in part, a reflection of the increasing interest in the natural world that arose with the Western scientific revolution beginning in the fifteenth century (see Chapter 2). For early collectors, however, the object was often an end in itself. Items were placed on shelves to look at, with little or no interest expressed in where the fossils might have come from or what the artifacts and their associated materials might tell about the people that produced them. Collectors of this kind are called **antiquaries**.

Early antiquarian collections often incorporated many different items in addition to fossils and archaeological materials. For example, the museum of Olaus Wormius, a seventeenth-century Danish scholar, included uniquely shaped stones, seashells, ethnographic objects, and curiosities from around the world, in addition to fossils and ancient stone tools. While these objects were sometimes described and illustrated with great care, they were not analyzed or interpreted to shed light on the evolution of life or on the lifeways of ancient humans. Of course, ancient coins, metal artifacts, and jewelry were recognized for what they were, but stone tools and even ancient pottery were generally regarded as naturally occurring objects or the work of trolls, elves, and fairies (Stiebing 1994).

By the late eighteenth century, scholars started to move beyond the simple description of objects to an increasing appreciation of the significance of fossil remains and the material traces of ancient human societies. This appreciation fell within the context of a host of new observations in the natural sciences, including many about the geological record and the age of the Earth. In 1797, an English country gentleman named John Frere published an account of some stone tools he had found in a gravel quarry in Suffolk. Although brief, the description is tantalizing in terms of the changing attitude toward traces of the past. Fossilized bones of extinct animals and stone tools—actually Paleolithic hand axes—were found at a depth of more than 12 feet in a layer of soil that appeared undisturbed by more recent materials. Frere correctly surmised that the tools were "from a very remote period indeed, even beyond that of the present world" (Daniel 1981:39). This was a recognition of prehistoric archaeology.

The nineteenth century saw the first fossil finds of ancient human ancestors. They included the bones found in the Neanderthal Valley of Germany in 1856, now recognized as an archaic human species, *Homo neanderthalensis*, or Neandertal man (see Chapter 4). Although this was a historic discovery, the significance of the fossils was not realized at the time. The initial interpretations were diverse. Some scholars correctly interpreted the finds as an early human ancestor, but others variously dismissed the bones as those of a Cossack soldier, an elderly Dutchman, a powerfully built Celt, or a pathological idiot (Trinkaus and Shipman 1993)! Information continued to accumulate, however, and by the end of the nineteenth century, the roots of modern archaeological and paleoanthropological study were well established.

This chapter examines the material record of the past and some of the techniques used by modern anthropologists to locate, recover, and date their discoveries. On one hand, this includes the bones and preserved remains used by paleoanthropologists to trace human origins. On the other hand, it deals with the material traces of human behavior that archaeologists focus on to interpret past cultures. In reality, the subdisciplines are often intertwined. Paleoanthropologists use excavation and surveying techniques similar to those used by archaeologists—or they rely on archaeologists—to locate and recover their finds. As to be discussed in Chapter 10, archaeological methods have also played an important role in forensic anthropology.

This book provides an overview of some of the techniques used by paleoanthropologists and archaeologists in their research. It also deals with some of the major questions that have been addressed by anthropologists, including the evolution of the human species, the human settlement of the world, the origins of agriculture, and the rise of complex societies and the state. In reading these discussions, it is important to remember that interpretations are constantly being revised. New fossils are constantly uncovered and archaeological sites exposed. Improved methods also modify the amount and kind of information available to researchers. Each of these discoveries adds to the amount of information available to interpret the past—and to evaluate and revise existing interpretations.

Answering Questions

Few modern archaeologists or paleoanthropologists would deny the thrill of finding a well-preserved fossil, an intact arrow point, or the sealed tomb of a king, but the romance of discovery is not the primary driving force for these scientists. In contrast to popular movie images, modern researchers are likely to spend more time in a laboratory or in front of a computer than looking for fossils or exploring lost cities. Their most fundamental desire is to reach back in time to understand our past more fully.

Although anthropologists make an effort to document the record of bygone ages as completely as possible, they clearly cannot locate every fossil, document every archaeological site, or even record every piece of information about each artifact recovered. Despite decades of research, only a minute portion of such important fossil localities as those in the Fayum Depression in Egypt and Olduvai Gorge in Tanzania have been studied (see Chapters 4 and 5). In examining an archaeological site or even a particular artifact, many different avenues of research might be pursued (see the box "Engendering Archaeology: The Role of Women in Aztec Mexico" on page 57). For example, when investigating pottery from a particular archaeological site, some archaeologists might concentrate on the technical attributes of the clay and the manufacturing process (Rice 1987). Others might focus on the decorative motifs on the pottery and how they relate to the myths and religious beliefs of the people who created them. Still other researchers might be most interested in the pottery's distribution (where it was found) and what this conveys about ancient trade patterns.

Research is guided by the questions about the past that the anthropologists want to answer. In order to formulate these, the researcher reviews existing data that help place their research in wider context. The anthropologist also begins by being well-grounded in the different theoretical perspectives of anthropology that shape their questions. With this background, the anthropologist plans a research project. This is done in a systematic way, as outlined in the discussion of the scientific method in Chapter 1. To ensure that the data recovered are relevant to their questions, paleoanthropologists and archaeologists begin a project by preparing a **research design** in which the objectives of the project are set out and the strategy for recovering the relevant data is outlined. The research design must take into account the types of data that will be collected and how those data relate to existing anthropological knowledge. Within the research design, the anthropologist specifies what types of methods will be used for the investigation, what regions will be surveyed, how much of a site will be excavated, and how the artifacts will be analyzed. Generally, the research design is then reviewed by other anthropologists, who recommend it for funding by various governments or private research.

Critical Perspectives

Engendering Archaeology: The Role of Women in Aztec Mexico

Aztec codex showing women weaving.

The interpretation of the material record poses a challenge to archaeologists. It provides excellent evidence on some subjects—ancient technology, diet, hunting techniques, and the plan of an ancient settlement—but some topics are more difficult to address. What were the marriage customs, the political system, or the religious beliefs of the ancient inhabitants of a site? These factors are by nature nonmaterial and are not directly preserved archaeologically. Even documentary records may offer only limited insight on some topics.

In a fascinating study of gender among the Aztec of ancient Mexico, archaeologist Elizabeth Brumfiel utilized both the archaeological and the documentary record to provide new insights into the past (Brumfiel 1991, 2005). The Aztec civilization was flourishing in central Mexico when the Spanish reached the Americas. It had emerged as the principal state in the region by the fifteenth century, eventually dominating an area stretching from the Valley of Mexico to modern-day Guatemala, some 500 miles to the southwest. The capital, Tenochtitlán, was an impressive religious center built on an island in Lake Texcoco. The city's population numbered tens of thousands when the Aztec leader, Montezuma, was killed during fighting with Spanish conquistadors led by Hernán Cortés in 1520. Within decades of the first Spanish contact, the traces of the Aztec empire had crumbled and been swept aside by European colonization.

Records of the Aztec civilization survive in documentary accounts recorded by the Spanish. The most comprehensive is a monumental treatise on Aztec life, from the raising of children to religious beliefs, written by Fray Bernardino de Sahagun (Brumfiel 1991). It is the most exhaustive record of a Native American culture from the earliest years of European contact. For this reason, it has been a primary source of information about Aztec life and culture.

Brumfiel was particularly interested in reconstructing the roles of women in Aztec society. Sahagun's description of women focuses on weaving and food preparation. Regrettably, as Brumfiel points out, his work offers little insight into how these endeavors were tied to other economic, political, and religious activities. In addition, Sahagun does not comment on some of his own illustrations that show women involved in such undertakings as healing and marketing. Interpretations based solely on Sahagun's descriptions seemed to marginalize women's roles in production as non-dynamic and of no importance in the study of culture change.

To obtain a more holistic view of women in Aztec society, Brumfiel turned to other sources. The Aztecs also possessed their own records. Although most of them were sought out and burned by the zealous Spanish priests, some Aztec codices survive. These sources indicate that textiles were essential as tribute, religious offerings, and exchange. Many illustrations also depict women in food production activities. In addition to various categories of food, the codices show the griddles, pots, and implements used in food preparation.

Independent information on these activities is provided by the archaeological record. For example, the relative importance of weaving can be assessed by the number and types of spindle whorls (perforated ceramic disks used to weight the spindle during spinning) that are found in large numbers on archaeological sites. Archaeological indications of dietary practices can be inferred from ceramic griddles, cooking pots, jars, and stone tools used in the gathering and preparation of food.

Brumfiel notes that the most interesting aspect of archaeological data on both weaving and food preparation is the variation. Given the static model of women's roles seen in the documentary records, a uniform pattern might be expected in the archaeological data. In fact, precisely the opposite is true. Evidence for weaving and cooking activities varies in different sites and over time. Brumfiel suggests that the performance of these activities was influenced by a number of variables, including environmental zones, proximity to urban markets, social status, and intensified agricultural production.

Food preparation, essential to the household, was also integral to the tenfold increase in the population of the Valley of Mexico during the four centuries preceding Spanish rule. As population expanded during the later Aztec period, archaeological evidence indicates that there was intensified food production in the immediate hinterland of Tenochtitlán. Conversely, the evidence for weaving decreases, indicating that women shifted from weaving to market-oriented food

(*continued*)

production. These observations are not borne out at sites farther away from the Aztec capital, though. In more distant sites, women intensified the production of tribute cloth with which the Aztec empire transacted business.

Brumfiel's research provides insights into the past that neither archaeological nor documentary information can supply on its own. She was fortunate to have independent sources of information that she could draw on to interpret and evaluate her conclusions. Her interpretation of Aztec life provides a much more dynamic view of women's roles. The observations are also consistent with the view of the household as a flexible social institution that varies with the presented opportunities and constraints. Brumfiel's work underscores the importance of considering both women's and men's roles as part of an interconnected, dynamic system.

Points to Ponder

1. In the absence of any documentary or ethnographic information, how can archaeologists examine gender in past societies?
2. Can we automatically associate some artifacts with men or with women?
3. Would interpretations vary in different cultural settings?

Paleoanthropological Study

3.1 Define paleoanthropology and discuss what we can learn about the past from fossil evidence.

As discussed in Chapter 1, paleoanthropology is the field within biological anthropology that focuses on human evolution and the behavior of early human ancestors. As will be discussed in Chapter 5, the behavior, diet, and activities of these early humans were very different from those of modern humans. Determining their behavior, as well as the age of the finds and the environment in which early humans lived, is dependent on an array of specialized skills and techniques. Understanding depends on the holistic, interdisciplinary approach that characterizes anthropology.

As in all anthropological research, a paleoanthropological project begins with a research design outlining the objectives of the project and the methodology to be employed. This would include a description of the region and the time period to be examined, the data that will be recovered, and an explanation of how the proposed research would contribute to existing knowledge. For example, researchers might target geological deposits of a specific location and age for examination because of the potential to discover the origins of the common ancestors of humans and apes (see Chapter 4), the earliest branches on the human lineage, or the fossil record of the first modern humans (see Chapter 5).

The initial survey work for a paleoanthropological project often relies on paleontologists and geologists, who provide an assessment of the age of the deposits within the region to be studied and the likely conditions that contributed to their formation. Clues about the age may be determined through the identification of distinctive geological deposits and associated floral and faunal remains (see the discussion of dating methods and faunal correlation later in this chapter). Such information also helps in the reconstruction of the paleoecology of the region and, hence, the environment in which early human ancestors lived. **Paleoecology** (*paleo*, from the Greek, meaning "old," and *ecology*, meaning "study of environment") is the study of ancient environments.

Based on the information provided by paleontologists and geologists, more detailed survey work is undertaken to locate traces of early humans. Looking for such traces has been likened to looking for a needle in a haystack, except in this case the "looking" involves the scrutiny of geological deposits and the careful excavation of buried skeletal remains and associated material. This stage of the research may draw on the skills of the archaeologist, who is trained to examine the material remains of past societies (see later discussion of "Archaeological Excavation").

Figure 3.1 Only a small number of the creatures that have lived are preserved as fossils. After death, predators, scavengers, and natural processes destroy many remains, frequently leaving only fragmentary traces for researchers to uncover.

Fossils and Fossil Localities

Much of paleoanthropological research focuses on the locating and study of fossil remains. Fossils are the preserved remains, impressions, or traces of living creatures from past ages. They form when an organism dies and is buried by soft mud, sand, or silt (Figure 3.1). Over time this sediment hardens, preserving the remains of the creature within. Occasionally, conditions may be such that actual portions of an organism are preserved—fragments of shells, teeth, or bones. But most fossils have been altered in some way, the decayed parts of bone or shell having been replaced by minerals or surrounding sediment. Even in cases in which fragments of bone or shell are present, they have often been broken or deformed and need to be carefully reconstructed. The challenge faced by paleoanthropologists is what criteria to use to distinguish species from a number of closely related taxa on the basis of fragmentary skeletal remains. The unraveling of the genetic codes of living species has also led to debate over the classification. Despite the imperfection of the fossil record, a striking history of life on Earth has survived.

Paleoanthropologists refer to places where fossils are found as **fossil localities**. These are spots where predators dropped animals they had killed, places where creatures were naturally covered by sediments, or sites where early humans lived. Of particular importance in interpreting fossil localities is the **taphonomy** of the site—the study of the variety of natural and behavioral processes that led to the formation of the deposits uncovered. As seen in Figure 3.2, the taphonomy of an individual fossil locality may be complex and the unraveling of the history that contributed to its formation very challenging indeed (Blumenschine 1995; Lyman 2010). The fossil locality may include traces of the activities of early humans—the artifacts resulting from their behavior, tool manufacture, and discarded food remains, as well as the remains of the early humans themselves. On the other hand, these traces may have been altered by

Figure 3.2 A variety of different activities and events contribute to the formation of an individual fossil locality. These include the activities of early human ancestors, but also such natural processes as decomposition and decay, erosion by wind and rain, and movement of bones and artifacts by animals. Paleoanthropologists must try to decipher these different factors in interpreting the behavior of early human ancestors.

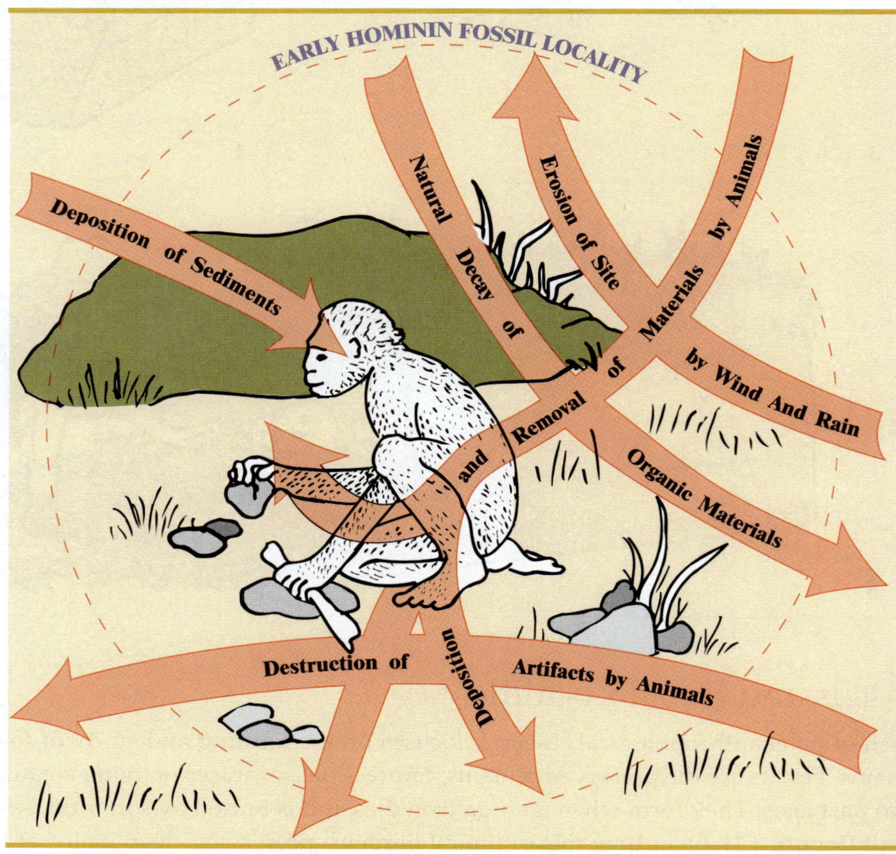

a host of disturbances, including erosion by wind and rain, as well as destruction and movement by wild animals.

Only a small number of the once-living creatures are preserved in the fossil record. After death, few animals are left to lie peacefully, waiting to be covered by layers of sediment and preserved as fossils. Many are killed by predators that scatter the bones. Scavengers may carry away parts of the carcass, and insects, bacteria, and weather quickly destroy many of the remains that are left. As a result, individual fossil finds are often incomplete. Some areas might not have had the right conditions to fossilize and preserve remains, or the remains of early human ancestors that may be present might be so fragmentary and mixed with deposits of other ages that they are of limited use. Another consideration is the accessibility of fossil deposits. Fossils may be found in many areas, but they often lie buried under deep deposits that make it impossible for researchers to study them and assess their age and condition. In other instances, however, erosion by wind or water exposes underlying layers of rock that contain fossils, thus providing the paleoanthropologist the chance to discover them—even as they are weathering away.

Once a fossil locality is found, systematic excavations are undertaken to reveal buried deposits. In excavating, paleoanthropologists take great pains to record a fossil's context. **Context** refers to a fossil's or artifact's exact position in relation to the surrounding sediments and any associated materials. Only if the precise location and associations are known can a fossil be accurately dated and any associated archaeological and paleontological materials be fully interpreted.

After fossils have been removed from the ground, the detailed analysis of the finds begins. This starts with the careful cleaning of fossil remains and associated materials. Fossils are generally preserved in a hardened, mineralized deposit, and cleaning may be tedious and time-consuming. Careful study of fine-grained sediments sometimes reveals the preservation of minute fossils of shellfish, algae, and pollen. Improved techniques, such as computer and electronic scanning equipment, have revealed that images of the delicate structure in bones or the interior of a skull may be preserved in a fossil. Artifacts and faunal remains from the excavations are labeled and carefully described and any fossil remains of early humans are reconstructed.

Drawing on all of the geological, paleontological, archaeological, and physical anthropological information, the paleoanthropologist then attempts to place the discoveries in the context of other discoveries and interpretations. The anatomical characteristics of the fossils of the early humans will be compared with other fossils to try to assess their evolutionary relationship, and the other data will be brought to bear on the reconstruction of the ancient environment and models of the way they lived. As more evidence is uncovered, the original interpretation may be confirmed, reinterpreted, or declared false in light of the new findings.

Archaeological Research

3.2 Discuss what the archaeological record can tell us about past societies.

As seen in Chapter 1, archaeology is the subdiscipline of anthropology that deals with the study of past human cultures through the material traces they left behind. Culture is a fundamental concept in the discipline of anthropology. In popular use, most people use the word *culture* to refer to "high culture": Shakespeare's works, Beethoven's symphonies, Michelangelo's sculptures, gourmet cooking, imported wines, and so on. Anthropologists, however, use the term in a much broader sense. **Culture** is a shared way of life that includes the material products and nonmaterial products (values, beliefs, and norms) that are transmitted within a particular society from generation to generation. This view of culture includes agricultural practices, social organization, religion, political systems, science, and sports. Culture encompasses all aspects of human activity, from the fine arts to popular entertainment, from everyday behavior to the most deeply rooted religious beliefs. Culture contains the plans, rules, techniques, and designs for living.

In seeking to understand past cultures through their physical traces, archaeologists face an inherent difficulty. By its very nature, culture is *nonmaterial*—that is, it refers to intangible products of human society (such as values, beliefs, religion, and norms) that are not preserved archaeologically. Hence, archaeologists must rely on the artifacts—the physical remains of past societies. This residue of the past is called material culture. **Material culture** consists of the physical products of human society (ranging from weapons to clothing). The earliest traces of material culture are stone tools dating back more than two-and-a-half million years: simple choppers, scrapers, and flakes. Modern material culture consists of all the physical objects that a contemporary society produces or retains from the past, such as tools, streets, buildings, homes, toys, medicines, and automobiles. Archaeologists investigate these material traces of societies to examine the values, beliefs, and norms that represent the patterned ways of thinking and acting within past societies. In the study of the more recent past, archaeologist may be able to draw on observations of contemporary peoples, written records or oral traditions to aid in their interpretation of the archaeological materials found (see the Box "Historical Archaeology").

Critical Perspectives

Historical Archaeology

Archaeologist Merrick Posnansky interviewing the chief of the town of Hani, Ghana in 1983. Researchers can use knowledge gathered from living informants to help interpret archaeological finds.

Source: Courtesy errick Posnansky, UCLA.

Some archaeologists have the luxury of written records and oral histories to help them locate and interpret their finds. Researchers delving into ancient Egyptian sites, the ancient Near East, Greek and Roman sites, Chinese civilization, Mayan temples, Aztec cities, Islamic sites, biblical archaeology, and the settlements of medieval Europe can all refer to written sources ranging from religious texts to explorers' accounts and tax records.

Why dig for archaeological materials if written records or oral traditions can tell the story? Although such sources may provide a tremendous amount of information, they do not furnish a complete record (Deetz 1996; Noel Hume 1983; Orser 2004). Whereas the life story of a head of state, records of trade contacts, or the date of a temple's construction may be preserved, the lives of many people and the minutiae of everyday life were seldom written down. In addition, documentary sources are often biased by the writer's personal or cultural perspective. For example, much of the written history of Native Americans, sub-Saharan Africans, Australian Aborigines, and many other indigenous peoples were recorded by European missionaries, traders, and administrators, who frequently provided only incomplete accounts viewed in terms of their own interests and beliefs.

Information from living informants and oral traditions may also provide important information about some populations, particularly societies with limited written records. In recognizing the significance of such nonwritten sources, however, it is also necessary to recognize their distinct limitations. The specific roles oral traditions played (and continue to play) varied in different cultural settings. Just as early European chroniclers viewed events with reference to their own cultural traditions, so oral histories are shaped by the worldviews, histories, and beliefs of the various cultures that employ them. Interpreting such material may be challenging for individuals outside the originating cultures. The study of the archaeological record may provide a great deal of information not found in other sources and provide an independent means of evaluating conclusions drawn on the basis of other sources of information (see the box "Engendering Archaeology: The Role of Women in Aztec Mexico"). For example, it has proven particularly useful in assessing change and continuity in indigenous populations during the past 500 years (DeCorse 2001; Lightfoot 2005).

In the Americas, during the past several decades, an increasing amount of work has concentrated on the history of immigrants who arrived in the last 500 years from Europe, Asia, Africa, and other world areas. Archaeological studies have proven of great help in interpreting historical sites and past lifeways, as well as culture change, sociopolitical developments, and past economic systems. Among the most significant areas of study is the archaeology of slavery (Ferguson 1992; Singleton 1999). Although living in literate societies, slaves were prohibited from writing, were often illiterate, and thus left a very limited documentary record of their own. Archaeological data have been used to provide a much more complete picture of plantation life and slave society.

Points to Ponder

1. What are some different sources of "historical" information—written and orally preserved accounts—that you can think of? How are these different from one another in terms of the details they might provide?
2. Consider a particular activity or behavior important to you (for example, going to school, participating in a sport, or pursuing a hobby). How would evidence of the activity be presented in written accounts, oral histories, and the archaeological record?

Archaeological interpretation has historically been strongly influenced by cultural anthropology theory (Lamberg-Karlovsky 1989; Trigger 2006). *Cultural anthropology*—the study of modern human populations—helps archaeologists understand how cultural systems work and how the archaeological record might reflect portions of these systems. On the other hand, archaeology offers cultural anthropology a time depth that cannot be obtained through observations of living populations. The archaeological record provides a record of past human behavior. Clearly, it furnishes important insights into past technology, providing answers to such questions as "When did people learn to make pottery?" and "How was iron smelted?" However, artifacts also offer clues to past ideals and belief systems. Consider, for example, what meanings and beliefs are conveyed by such artifacts as a Christian cross, a Jewish menorah, or a Hopi kachina figure. Other artifacts convey cultural beliefs in more subtle ways. Everyday items, such as the knife, fork, spoon, and plate used in Americans' meals, are not the only utensils suitable for the task; indeed, food preference itself is a culturally influenced choice.

The objectives of archaeological research vary tremendously in terms of the time periods, geographical areas, and research questions considered. Many researchers have examined the themes dealt with in this book: the behavior of early human ancestors, the initial settlement of the Americas, the origins of agriculture, and the emergence of complex political systems. However, other archaeologists have turned their attention to the more recent past and have examined the archaeological record of European colonization over the past 500 years and nineteenth-century American society; they have even shed light on modern society by sifting through garbage bags and landfills.

The Archaeological Record

The preservation of archaeological materials varies (Lucas 2012; Schiffer 1987). Look at the objects that surround you. How long would these artifacts survive if left uncared for and exposed to the elements? As is the case with the fossil record, the archaeological past is a well-worn and fragmentary cloth rather than a complete tapestry. Stone artifacts endure very well, and thus it is not surprising that much of our knowledge of early human lifeways is based on stone tools. Ceramics and glass may also survive very well, but iron and copper corrode, and organic materials, such as bone, cloth, paper, and wood, generally disappear quickly.

Anthropologists at Work

GEORGE FLETCHER BASS: Underwater Archaeologist

Dr. George Bass, after a dive

George Fletcher Bass is one of the pioneers of underwater archaeology—a field that he actually did not set out to study and, indeed, a field that was virtually unrecognized as a discipline when he entered it. Although he was always fascinated with the sea and diving, Bass began his career working on land sites, earning a master's degree in Near Eastern archaeology at Johns Hopkins University in 1955. He then attended the American School of Classical Studies at Athens and excavated at the sites of Lerna, Greece, and Gordion, Turkey. Following military service in Korea, Bass began his doctoral studies in classical archaeology at the University of Pennsylvania. It was there, in 1960, that he was asked by Professor Rodney S. Young if he would learn to scuba dive in order to direct the excavation of a Bronze Age shipwreck discovered off Cape Geldonya, Turkey. Bass's excavations of this site marked the first time an ancient shipwreck was excavated in its entirety under the water.

During the 1960s, Bass went on to excavate two Byzantine shipwrecks off Yassi Ada, Turkey. At these sites he developed a variety of specialized methods for underwater excavation, including new mapping techniques, a submersible decompression chamber, and a two-person submarine. In 1967, his team was the first to locate an ancient shipwreck using side-scan sonar. In addition to setting standards for underwater archaeological research, these excavations captured popular imagination and revealed shipwrecks as time capsules containing a spectacular array of artifacts, many unrecovered from terrestrial sites (Throckmorton 1962; Bass 1963, 1973).

After completing his doctorate in 1964, Bass joined the faculty at the University of Pennsylvania. He remained there until 1973, when he left to found the Institute of Nautical Archaeology (INA), which has been affiliated with Texas A&M University since 1976. Under his guidance, the INA has become one of the world's premier programs in underwater archaeology. The institute has conducted research throughout the world on shipwrecks and sites of a diversity of time periods. Bass has continued to focus on shipwrecks in Turkey, where he is an honorary citizen of the town of Bodrum. Some of his more recent projects include a fourteenth-century B.C. wreck with a cargo of copper, ivory, tin, glass, and ebony, and a medieval ship with a large cargo of Islamic glass (Bass et al. 2004). Bass has written or edited more than a dozen books and is the author of more than 100 articles. Through his publications, he has introduced both archaeologists and the wider public to the potential and excitement of underwater archaeology.

Because of his unique contribution to underwater archaeology, Bass has been widely recognized and has received awards from the National Geographic Society, the Explorers' Club, the Archaeological Institute of America, and the Society for Historical Archaeology. President George W. Bush presented him with the National Medal for Science in 2002.

In some cases, environmental conditions that limit insect and microbial action and protect a site from exposure to the elements may allow for the striking preservation of archaeological materials. Some of the most amazing cases are those in which items have been rapidly frozen. An illustration of this kind of preservation is provided by the discovery in 1991 of the 5,300-year-old frozen remains of a Bronze Age man by hikers in Italy's Tyrol Mountains (Fowler 2000). With the body were a wooden backpack, a wooden bow, fourteen bone-tipped arrows, and fragments of clothing. In other instances, underwater sites, waterlogged environments, very dry climate, or rapid burial may create conditions for excellent preservation. Such unique instances provide archaeologists with a much more complete record than is usually found.

Places of past human activity that are preserved in the ground are called **archaeological sites**. Sites reflect the breadth of human endeavor. Some are settlements that may have been occupied for a considerable time—for example, a Native American village or an abandoned gold-mining town in the American West. Other sites reflect specialized activities—for instance, a ceremonial center, a burial ground, or a place where ancient hunters killed and butchered an animal.

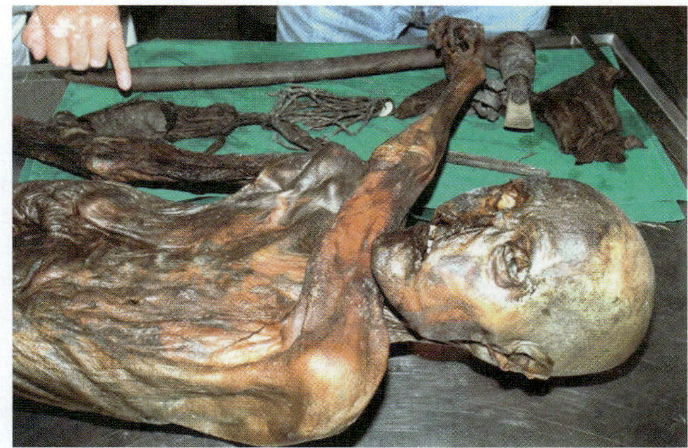

In some cases, environmental conditions may allow for amazing preservation, as illustrated by the 4,000-year-old naturally mummified remains of a woman discovered in the arid hills near the Chinese city of Ürümqi (left) and the 5,300-year-old frozen remains of a man found in Italy's Tyrol mountains (right).

Much of the archaeologist's time is devoted to the study of artifacts—any object made or modified by humans. They include everything from chipped stone tools and pottery to plastic bottles and computers. Nonmovable artifacts, such as an ancient fire hearth, a pit dug in the ground, or a wall, are called **features**. In addition to artifacts and features, archaeologists examine items recovered from archaeological sites that were not produced by humans, but nevertheless provide important insights into the past. Animal bones, shells, and plant remains recovered from an archaeological site furnish information on both the past climatic conditions and the diet of the early inhabitants. The soil of a site is also an important record of past activities and the natural processes that affected a site's formation. Fires, floods, and erosion all leave traces in the earth for the archaeologist to discover. All of these data may yield important information about the age, organization, and function of the site being examined. These nonartifactual organic and environmental remains are referred to as **ecofacts**.

As is the case with the recovery of fossils, the archaeologist takes special care to record the *contexts* in which archaeological materials are found: the artifacts' specific location in the ground, and associated materials. Without a context, an artifact offers only a limited amount of information. By itself, a pot may be identified as something similar to other finds from a specific area and time period, but it provides no new information. If, however, it and similar pots are found to contain offerings of a particular kind and are associated with female burials, a whole range of other inferences may be made about the past. By removing artifacts from sites, laypersons unwittingly cause irreparable damage to the archaeological record.

Locating Sites and Fossil Localities

3.3 Discuss the basic techniques used to locate archaeological sites and fossil localities.

In 1940, schoolboys retrieving their dog from a hole in a hillside near Montignac, France, found themselves in an underground cavern. The walls were covered with delicate black and red paintings of bison, horses, and deer. The boys had discovered Lascaux Cave, one of the finest known examples of Paleolithic cave art. Chance findings such as this sometimes play a role in the discovery of archaeological remains, as well as paleoanthropological research, but researchers generally have to undertake a systematic examination, or **survey**, of a particular area, region, or country to locate archaeological sites or fossil localities. They will usually begin by examining previous descriptions, maps, and reports of the area for references to archaeological sites.

Critical Perspectives

Underwater Archaeology

Remains of the *Mary Rose*.

Sunken ships, submerged settlements, and flooded towns: This wide variety of sites of different time periods in different world areas shares the need for specialized techniques to locate, excavate, and study them (Bass 2005; Menotti 2004). Although efforts were occasionally made in the past to recover cargoes from sunken ships, it was only with the invention and increasing accessibility of underwater breathing equipment during the twentieth century that the systematic investigation of underwater sites became feasible. Often artifacts from underwater sites are better preserved and so present a wider range of materials than those from land. Even more important, underwater sites are immune to the continued disturbances associated with human activity that are typical of most land sites. Shipwrecks can be compared to time capsules, containing a selection of artifacts that were in use in a certain context at a specific time. Archaeologists working on land seldom have such clearly sealed archaeological deposits.

A tantalizing example of an underwater archaeological project is the excavation and raising of the preserved remains of the *Mary Rose*, the pride of the young English Navy and the flower of King Henry VIII's fleet. The 700-ton warship, which was probably the first English warship designed to carry a battery of guns between its decks, foundered and sank in Portsmouth harbor on a warm July afternoon in 1545. Henry VIII, camped with his army at Southsea Castle, is said to have witnessed the disaster and heard the cries of the crew. In the 1970s, the site of the *Mary Rose* was rediscovered and was systematically explored by volunteer divers from around the world. The ship produced a spectacular array of over 14,000 artifacts, ranging from massive cannons to musical instruments, famed English longbows, and navigational equipment. Finds from the *Mary Rose* and the preserved portions of the hull can be seen at the Mary Rose Ship Hall and Exhibition at the Her Majesty's Naval Base, Portsmouth, England (Marsden 2003, 2009).

Most people associate underwater archaeology with sunken ships and this, in fact, represents an important part of the subdiscipline. However, rising sea levels or natural disasters may also submerge cities and towns. Research on settlements now under water is providing increasing insight into early human settlement (Bass 2005; Menotti 2004). As in the case of shipwrecks, the lack of oxygen and the sealed nature of the archaeological materials present special challenges in excavation, but also remarkable preservation. Such is the case of Port Royal, Jamaica, a flourishing trade center and infamous gathering place for pirates during the seventeenth century. In 1692, a violent earthquake and tidal wave submerged or buried portions of the city, preserving a record for future archaeologists. Excavations at the site spanning the last three decades have recovered a wealth of materials from seventeenth-century life (Hamilton and Woodward 1984).

Points to Ponder

1. Archaeological excavation on land is a meticulous and careful process. Discuss how excavation and recording methods would have to be modified to conduct archaeological research underneath the water.
2. Given the unique location and preservation found at underwater sites, why might they be more appropriate or important than land sites for considering certain types of research questions?

Informants who live and work in the area may also be of great help in directing archaeologists to discoveries.

Of course, some archaeological sites are more easily located than others: the great pyramids near Cairo, Egypt; Stonehenge in southern England; and the Parthenon of Athens have never been lost. Though interpretations of their precise use may differ, their impressive remains are difficult to miss. Unfortunately, many sites, particularly some of the more ancient, are more difficult to locate. The settlements occupied by early humans were usually small, and only ephemeral traces are preserved in the ground. In many instances, they may be covered under many feet of sediment. Fossils are also often deeply buried, resting beneath layers of sediment. Examination of the ground surface may reveal scatters of artifacts, discolorations in the soil, or exposed fossils which provide clues to buried deposits. Sometimes nature inadvertently helps researchers, as erosion by wind or rain may expose sites. Archaeologists can also examine road cuts, building projects, and freshly plowed land for archaeological materials. Fossils are often deeply buried, resting beneath layers of sediment, making locating them especially difficult. For this reason, paleoanthropologists often cannot employ many of the techniques archaeologists use to locate shallower archaeological deposits.

In the field, the researcher defines what areas will be targeted for survey. These areas will be determined by the research design, but also by environmental and topographical considerations, as well as the practical constraints of time and money. Surveys can be divided into *systematic* and *unsystematic* approaches (Renfrew and Bahn 2012). The latter is easier as the researcher simply walks over trails, riverbanks, and plowed fields in the survey area and takes note of any archaeological material. In a similar way, paleoanthropologists searching for fossils may examine places where buried sediments have been exposed by erosion, This approach avoids the problem of climbing through thick vegetation or rugged terrain. Unfortunately, it may also produce a biased sample of the archaeological remains present; ancient land uses might have little correspondence with modern trails or plowed fields.

Researchers use many different methods to ensure more systematic results. In some instances, a region, valley, or site is divided into a *grid*, which is then walked systematically. In other instances, transects may provide useful information, particularly where vegetation is thick. In this case, a straight line, or *transect*, is laid out through the area to be surveyed. Fieldworkers then walk along this line, noting changes in topography, vegetation, and artifacts.

Subsurface Archaeological Testing and Survey

Because many archaeological sites are buried in the ground, many surveys incorporate some kind of subsurface testing. This may involve digging auger holes or shovel test pits at regular intervals in the survey, the soil from which is examined for any traces of archaeological material. This technique may provide important information on the location of an archaeological site, its extent, and the type of material represented.

Today, many different technological innovations allow the archaeologist to prospect for buried sites without lifting a spade. The utility of these tools can be illustrated by the magnetometer and resistivity meter. The **proton magnetometer** is a sensor that can detect differences in the soil's magnetic field caused by buried features and artifacts. A buried foundation will give a different reading than an ancient road, both being different from the surrounding undisturbed soil. As the magnetometer is systematically moved over an area, a plan of buried features can be created.

Electrical **resistivity** provides similar information, though it is based on a different concept. A resistivity meter is used to measure the electrical current passing between electrodes that are

Electrical resistivity survey directed by Matthew Johnson underway at Bodiam Castle, East Sussex, England. Photograph taken by Dr. David Underhill.

placed in the ground. Variation in electrical current indicates differences in the soil's moisture content, which in turn reflects buried ditches, foundations, or walls that retain moisture to varying degrees.

Although at times yielding spectacular results, techniques such as magnetometer and resistivity surveys are not without their limitations. Buried metal at a site may confuse the magnetic readings of other materials, and a leaking hose wreaks havoc with a resistivity meter. Both techniques may produce confusing patterns as a result of shallowly buried geological features such as bedrock.

Remote Sensing

An archaeologist was once heard to say that "one ought to be a bird to be a field archaeologist," and indeed, the perspective provided by **aerial photography**, sometimes called "aerial archaeology," has been a boon to archaeologists. Experiments with aerial photography occurred prior to World War I, but it was during the war that its potential importance to archaeological surveys was recognized (Daniel 1981:165). Pilots noticed that some sites, invisible on the ground, were seen dramatically from the air. The rich organic soils found in archaeological sites, subtle depressions in the ground surface, or slight differences in vegetation resulting from buried features may be dramatically illustrated in aerial photographs. More recent technological innovations, such as the use of infrared, false color photography, help identify differences in vegetation and make abandoned settlements and patterns of past land use more apparent. Aerial photography has proven very important in locating sites, but it is also of particular use in mapping and interpretation (Brophy and Cowley 2005; Kruckman 1987).

Of increasing use to archaeologists are photographs or images taken from extremely high altitudes by satellites or space shuttles. The scale of these pictures sometimes limits their use and their cost sometimes make them beyond the reach of many researchers (Madry 2003; Madry et al. 2003). The potential application of such sophisticated techniques, however, has been well demonstrated. National Aeronautics and Space Administration (NASA) scientists, working with archaeologists, have been able to identify ancient Mesopotamian and Mayan settlements and farmlands that had not been located with other techniques. *Space imaging radar*, which can detect features buried under 6 feet of sand, proved helpful in identifying ancient caravan routes on the Arabian Peninsula. These routes enabled researchers to locate the lost city of Ubar, a trade center that was destroyed around 100 A.D., and the city of Saffara on the Indian

Aerial photography often allows the identification of archaeological sites that may be invisible on the ground. This aerial photograph of a recently plowed cornfield in Perry County, southern Illinois, led to the discovery of the Grier Site. Subsequent excavation revealed that the site had been occupied from the Archaic to the Mississippian; the burials date to about 1000 B.C.
Source: Courtesy of Larry Kruckman, Indiana University of Pennsylvania.

Anthropologist at Work

SCOTT MADRY: Google Earth and Armchair Archaeology

NASA photo from the international space station showing the pyramids at Dashur, Egypt

The value of aerial photography and high-tech satellite imagery in archaeology is well demonstrated, but the cost of such resources has often placed them beyond the reach of most archaeologists. But this situation is changing. Once the purview of governments and space programs, high-altitude images are becoming both more common and of more general interest, and archaeologists are reaping the benefits.

A case in point is Google Earth, a popular desktop program that provides satellite imagery, allowing the user to zoom in on specific locales and even track their own movements. The program is useful in getting directions and checking out vacation spots, as well as an aid in planning for a variety of nonprofit and public benefit organizations. Archaeologist Scott Madry became curious about the potential use of Google Earth in his long-term research on the archaeology of Burgundy, France (Madry 2007). Madry is interested in the application of aerial photography, remote sensing, and geographic information systems technology to understand the interaction between the different cultures and the physical environment over the past 2,000 years. While he found that the images available on Google Earth were of limited use in his research area, the data available for a neighboring region that shared a similar environment and culture history provided dramatic images of archaeological sites. Although many of these sites had been previously identified, the results demonstrated the potential of Google Earth as an archaeological research tool.

Google Earth is not the perfect solution for every research situation. The coverage is dependent of the images available and is of variable quality. Consequently, it is of limited use for some areas. Even in cases where good images are available, thick vegetation and tree cover may limit the use of both satellite images and aerial photography. Finally, while the images provided by Google Earth may help in locating and mapping sites, archaeologists still need to excavate.

Ocean (Clapp 1998). As this technology becomes both more refined and more affordable, it will provide an increasingly important resource for archaeologists (see box "Anthropologists At Work: Scott Madry").

Archaeological Excavation

3.4 Discuss the basic techniques of archaeological excavation.

Archaeological surveys provide invaluable information about the past. The distribution of sites on the landscape offers knowledge about the use of natural resources, trade patterns, and political organization. Surveys also help define the extent of specific sites and allow for a preliminary assessment of their age and function. These data are invaluable in interpreting regional developments and how individual sites form part of a larger picture. For example, changes in settlement patterns have been used to assess the development of sociopolitical complexity and state level societies.

Figure 3.3 Excavation, archaeological plan, and artist's reconstruction of an eighteenth-century slave cabin at Seville Plantation, St. Anne's, Jamaica. The meticulous recording of excavated artifacts and features allows archaeologists to reconstruct the appearance of past settlements. In this case, eighteenth-century illustrations and written descriptions helped the artist add features, such as the roof, that were not preserved archaeologically.

Source: Courtesy of Douglas V. Armstrong, Syracuse University.

However, depending on the project's research objectives, an archaeologist may want more detailed information about individual sites. Once an archaeological site has been located, it may be targeted for systematic archaeological excavation (Figure 3.3).

Excavation is costly, time-consuming, and also destructive. Once dug up, an archaeological site is gone forever; it can be "reassembled" only through the notes

Archaeologists taking notes from an excavation.

kept by the archaeologist. For this reason, archaeological excavation is undertaken with great care. Although picks and shovels, or even bulldozers, may occasionally come into play, the tools used most commonly are the trowel, whisk broom, and dustpan. Different techniques may be required for different kinds of sites. For example, more care might be taken in excavating the remains of a small hunting camp than a nineteenth-century house in an urban setting covered with tons of modern debris. On underwater sites, researchers must contend with recording finds using specialized techniques while wearing special breathing apparatus (see the boxes "Underwater Archaeology" and "George Fletcher Bass: Underwater Archaeologist"). Nevertheless, whatever the site, the archaeologist carefully records the context of each artifact uncovered, each feature exposed, and any changes in surrounding soil.

Work usually begins with the clearing of the site and the preparation of a detailed site plan. A grid is placed over the site. This is usually fixed to a **datum point**, some permanent feature or marker that can be used as a reference point and will allow the excavation's exact position to be relocated. As in the case of other facets of the research project, the research design determines the areas to be excavated. Excavations of *midden* deposits, or ancient trash piles, often provide insights into the range of artifacts at a site, but excavation of dwellings might provide more information into past social organization, political organization, and socioeconomic status.

Excavation of a burial in Warszawa, Poland.
Source: Courtesy of Marek E. Jasinski, Institute of Historical Studies, Archaeology Programme Norwegian University of Science and Technology.

A question often asked of archaeologists is how deep they have to dig to "find something." The answer is, "Well, that depends." The depth of any given archaeological deposit is contingent upon a wide range of variables, including the type of site, how long it was occupied, the types of soil represented, and the environmental history of the area. In some cases, artifacts thousands or even hundreds of thousands of years old may lie exposed on the surface. In other cases, flooding, burial, or cultural activities may cover sites with thick layers of soil. A clear illustration of this is seen in *tells* (settlement mounds) in the Near East, which sometimes consist of archaeological deposits covering more than 100 square acres hundreds of feet deep.

Dating Methods

3.5 Compare and contrast how archaeologists and paleoanthropologists date their discoveries.

How old is it? This simple question is fundamental to the study of the past. Without the ability to temporally order fossils, archaeological sites, and artifacts, there is no way to assess evolutionary change, cultural developments, or technological innovations. Paleoanthropologists and archaeologists employ many different dating techniques. Some of these are basic to the interpretation of both the fossil record and archaeological sites. Others are more appropriate for objects of certain ages or for particular kinds of materials (for example, volcanic stone, as opposed to organic material). Hence, certain techniques are more typically associated with archaeological research than paleoanthropological research, and vice versa. In any given project, several different dating techniques are used in conjunction with one another to independently validate the age of the materials being examined. Dating methods can be divided into two broad categories that incorporate a variety of specific dating techniques: relative dating and numerical dating. Accurate dating of discoveries depends upon both methods. The following discussion is not exhaustive, but rather intended to illustrate the different kinds of dating methods that have been employed.

Relative Dating

Relative dating refers to dating methods that determine whether one particular fossil, artifact, fossil locality, or site dates before or after another. Relative dating methods do not provide an actual date, just an age relative to something else. The most basic relative dating method is **stratigraphic dating**, a technique pioneered by the seventeenth-century Danish scientist Niels Stensen (1638–1687). Today, Stensen is better known by the latinized version of his name, Nicholas Steno. Steno was the first person to suggest that the hard rock where fossils are found had once been soft sediments that had gradually solidified. Because sediments had been deposited in layers, or *strata*, Steno argued that each successive layer was younger than the layers underneath. Steno's **law of supraposition** states that in any succession of rock layers, the lowest rocks have been there the longest and the upper rocks have been in place for progressively shorter periods. This assumption forms the basis of stratigraphic dating.

Steno was concerned with the study of geological deposits, but stratigraphic dating is also of key importance in dating archaeological materials (Figure 3.4). An archaeological site presents a complex layer cake of stratigraphic levels representing the accumulation of cultural material, such as trash and housing debris, as well as natural strata resulting from flooding, the decomposition of organic material, and the like. Layers associated with human occupation often accumulate to striking depths.

Like all relative dating methods, stratigraphic dating does not allow researchers to assign an actual numerical age to a fossil or artifact. Rather, it indicates only whether one fossil is older or younger than another within the same stratigraphic sequence. This technique is essential to paleoanthropological and archaeological interpretation because it allows researchers to evaluate change through time. However, researchers

Figure 3.4 Archaeological materials and the remnants of human occupation often accumulate to striking depths. This hypothetical profile illustrates the potentially complex nature of the archaeological record and how different techniques might be combined to date discoveries.

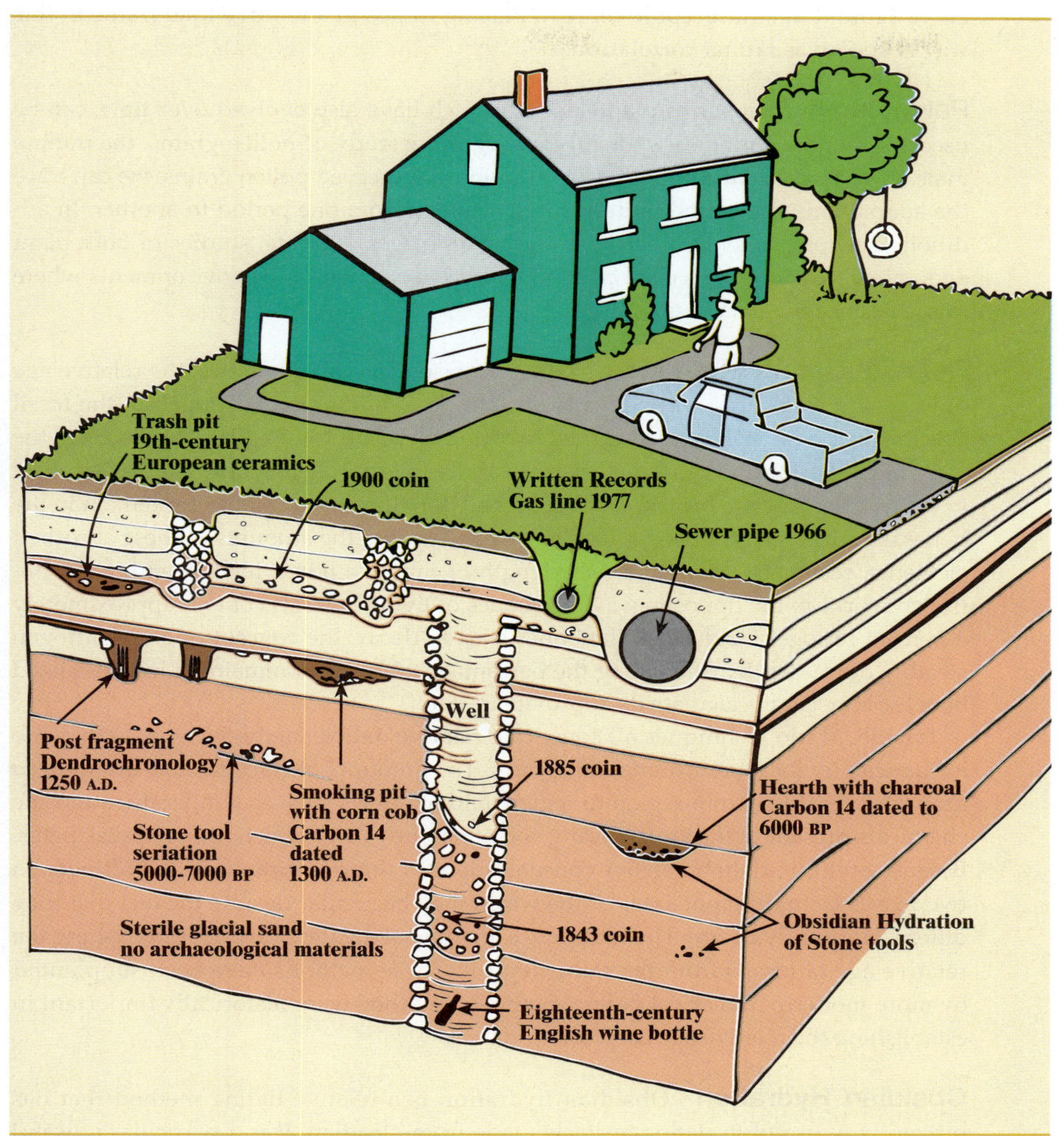

must take notice of any disturbances that may have destroyed the order of geological or archaeological deposits. Disturbances in the Earth's crust, such as earthquakes and volcanoes, can shift or disrupt stratigraphic layers. Archaeological sites may be ravaged by erosion, burrowing animals, and human activity.

Faunal Succession One of the first people to record the location of fossils systematically was William Smith (1769–1839), the "father" of English geology (Winchester 2002). An engineer at a time when England was being transformed by the construction of railway lines and canals, Smith noticed that as rock layers were exposed by the construction, distinct fossils occurred in the same relative order again and again. He soon found that he could arrange rock samples from different areas in the correct stratigraphic order solely on the basis of the fossils they contained. Smith had discovered the principle of **faunal succession** (literally, "animal" succession). A significant scientific milestone, Smith's observations were made 60 years before Darwin proposed his evolutionary theories to explain how and why life-forms changed through time.

Since Smith's era, paleontologists have studied hundreds of thousands of fossil localities around the world. Fossils from these sites provides a means of correlating the relative ages of different fossil localities and also casts light on the dating of fossils that are not found in stratigraphic context. Placing fossils in a relative time frame in this way is known as **faunal correlation**.

Palynology Remains of plant species, which have also evolved over time, can be used for relative dating as well. **Palynology** is the study of pollen grains, the minute male reproductive parts of plants. By examining preserved pollen grains, we can trace the adaptations vegetation underwent in a region from one period to another. In addition to helping scientists establish the relative ages of strata, studies of both plant and animal fossils offer crucial clues to the reconstruction of the environments where humans and human ancestors lived.

Relative Dating Methods of Bones Scientists can determine the relative age of bones by measuring the elements of fluorine, uranium, and nitrogen in the fossil specimens. These tests, which can be used together, are sometimes referred to as the *FUN trio*. Fluorine and uranium occur naturally in groundwater and gradually collect in bones after they are buried. Once absorbed, the fluorine and uranium remain in the bones, steadily accumulating over time. By measuring the amounts of these absorbed elements, scientists can estimate the length of time the bones have been buried. Nitrogen works in the opposite way. The bones of living animals contain approximately 4 percent nitrogen, and when the bones start to decay, the concentration of nitrogen steadily decreases. By calculating the percentage of nitrogen remaining in a fossilized bone, scientists can calculate its approximate age.

The FUN trio techniques all constitute relative dating methods because they are influenced by local environmental factors. The amounts of fluorine and uranium in groundwater differ from region to region, and variables such as temperature and the chemicals present in the surrounding soil affect the rate at which nitrogen dissipates. Because of this variation, relative concentrations of fluorine, uranium, and nitrogen in two fossils from different areas of the world may be similar despite the fact that they differ significantly in age. The techniques are thus of greatest value in establishing the relative age of fossils from the same deposit. These methods have been supplanted by more modern, numerical dating methods, but they were historically important in establishing the relative ages of fossil finds.

Obsidian Hydration **Obsidian hydration** is a relative dating method that has proven very useful in dating artifacts made from obsidian. It is a particularly useful technique as it provides dates on actual artifacts, as opposed to associated materials. Obsidian, sometimes referred to as volcanic glass, is a naturally occurring stone that is common in some world areas. It flakes very regularly and so was used to produce beautiful stone tools such as knives, spear points and scrapers. Obsidian hydration dating is based on the rate at which hydration layers accumulate on the surface of tools made from obsidian. When an obsidian artifact is made, the old, weathered surface is flaked off, exposing the un-weathered interior of the stone. This newly exposed surface contains little water. However, over time, the surface absorbs water, forming a rind, or layers, that can be measured using a high-powered microscope. As the water is absorbed at a regular rate, the thickness of the hydration layers provides an indication of the relative ages of obsidian artifacts within an archaeological site.

Obsidian hydration is a relative dating method because the rate at which the hydration layers form is influenced by the local environmental conditions in which the obsidian artifacts are found. For example, the thickness of the hydrated surface layers on artifacts from a very dry region would be thinner than those on artifacts recovered from a waterlogged site, despite the fact that the sites might be of the same age. Obsidian hydration can, however, be used as a numerical dating method if the site conditions and chronologies are well understood. For example, if obsidian hydration rates from a specific site can be tied to a well-established chronology based on radiocarbon dating, they would provide quite accurate numerical dates.

Seriation Unlike the methods discussed thus far that utilize geological, chemical, or paleontological principles, seriation is a relative dating method based on the study of archaeological materials. Simply stated, **seriation** is a dating technique based on the assumption that any particular artifact, attribute, or style will appear, gradually increase in popularity until it reaches a peak, and then progressively decrease. Systematic change in style can be seen in a wide range of material culture, ranging from stone tools to clothing fashions and automobile designs. Archaeologists measure changes in artifact types by comparing the relative percentages of certain attributes or styles in different stratigraphic levels in a site or across different sites. Using the principle of increasing and decreasing popularity of attributes, archaeologists are then able to place the artifacts in a relative chronological order. Seriation was particularly important for chronologically ordering ceramics and stone tools before the advent of many of the numerical dating techniques discussed later

The principles of seriation can be illustrated by examining stylistic changes in New England gravestones of the seventeenth, eighteenth, and nineteenth centuries. Unlike many artifacts, gravestones can be closely dated, and so can be used to evaluate the principle of seriation. Archaeologist James Deetz charted how designs on dated colonial gravestones changed through time (Deetz 1996). His study of gravestones in Stoneham Cemetery, Massachusetts, as illustrated in Figure 3.5, demonstrates the validity of the method. In the course of a century, death's head motifs were gradually replaced by cherub designs, which in turn were replaced by urn and willow decorations. The study also illustrates how local variation in beliefs and trade patterns may influence the popularity of an attribute.

Figure 3.5 The seriation of gravestones in a New England cemetery by archaeologist James Deetz illustrates the growth and gradual decline in popularity of a closely dated series of decorative motifs.

Source: From *In Small Things Forgotten* by James Deetz. Copyright © 1996 by James Deetz. Used by permission of Doubleday, a division of Random House, Inc.

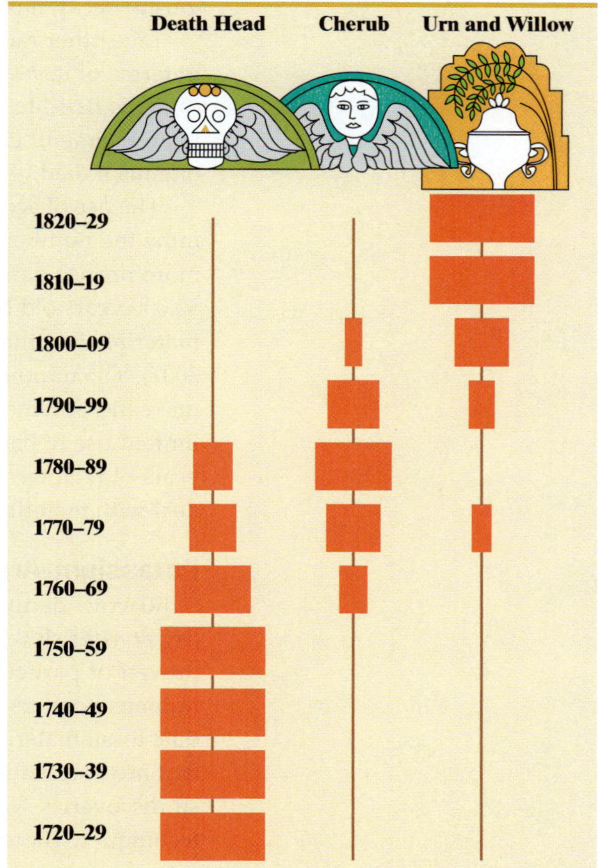

Numerical or Absolute Dating

In contrast to relative dating techniques, numerical dating methods (sometimes also referred to as "absolute" or "chronometric" methods) provide actual ages. For recent time periods, historical sources such as calendars and dating systems that were used by ancient peoples provide numerical dates. Mayan and Egyptian sites, for example, can often be dated by inscriptions carved into the monuments themselves. However, such written records only extend back a few thousand years and these sources are not available for many regions. Researchers have consequently explored a variety of methods to establish the age of fossil finds and archaeological discoveries.

During the nineteenth century, scientists experimented with many methods designed to pinpoint the numerical age of the Earth itself. A number of these methods were based on observations of the physical world. Studies of erosion rates, for instance, indicated that it had taken millions of years to cut clefts in the earth like the Grand Canyon in the United States. Other strategies were based on the rates at which salt had accumulated in the oceans, the Earth had cooled, and geological sediments had formed (Prothero 1989). By observing current conditions and assuming a standard rate at which these processes had occurred, scientists calculated the amount of time represented. These early approaches were flawed by a limited understanding of the complexity of natural processes involved and the range of local conditions. Therefore, these techniques at best provide only crude relative dating methods. In contrast to these early researchers, today's scientists have a wide variety of highly precise methods of dating paleontological and archaeological finds (Aitken 1990; Brothwell and Pollard 2001).

Several of the most important numerical dating techniques used today are based on *radioactive decay*, a process in which *radioisotopes*, unstable atoms of certain elements, break down or decay by throwing off subatomic particles and energy over time. These changes can produce either a different isotope of the same element or another element entirely. In terms of dating, the significance of radioactive decay is that it occurs at a set rate regardless of environmental conditions, such as temperature fluctuations, amount of groundwater, or the depth below surface. The amount of decay that has taken place can be measured with a device called a *mass spectrometer*. Hence, by calculating how much decay has occurred in a geological specimen or an artifact, scientists can assign a numerical age to it.

Radiocarbon Dating Radiocarbon dating, also known as carbon-14 dating, is perhaps the best known and most common numerical dating technique used by archaeologists. It is of particular importance because it can be used to date any organic matter that contains carbon, including fragments of ancient wooden tools, charcoal from ancient fires, and skeletal material. The technique of using radioactive decay as a dating tool was pioneered by Willard Libby, who received the 1960 Nobel Prize in chemistry for his work on radiocarbon dating.

Radiocarbon dating, as its name implies, is based on the decay of carbon-14 (^{14}C), a radioactive (unstable) isotope of carbon that eventually decays into nitrogen. The concentration of carbon-144 in a living organism is comparable to that of the surrounding atmosphere and is absorbed by the organism as carbon dioxide (CO_2). When the organism dies, the intake of CO_2 ends. Thus, as the carbon-14 in the organism begins to decay, it is not replaced by additional radiocarbon from the atmosphere.

Like other radioisotopes, carbon-14 decays at a known rate that can be expressed in terms of its *half-life*, the interval of time required for half of the radioisotope to decay. The half-life of carbon-14 is 5,730 years. By measuring the quantity of carbon-14 in a specimen, scientists can determine the amount of time that has elapsed since the organism died.

The use of accelerator mass spectrometry (AMS), which makes it possible to determine the number of individual atoms of ^{14}C remaining in a sample, has allowed for more precise dating and also for the dating of much smaller samples. Dates of up to 80,000 years old have been obtained, but the technique is generally limited to dating materials less than about 60,000 years old (Plastino et al. 2001; Taylor and Southon 2007). The minuscule amounts of radiocarbon remaining in materials older than this make measurement difficult. Because of the time period represented, radiocarbon is of limited use to paleoanthropologists who may be dealing with fossil finds millions of years old. However, radiocarbon dating is of great importance to archaeologists who deal with materials of more recent age.

Potassium-Argon and Fission-Track Dating Several isotopes that exhibit radioactive decay are present in rocks of volcanic origin. Some of these isotopes decay at very slow rates over billions of years. Two radiometric techniques that have proven of particular help to paleoanthropologists and archaeologists studying early human ancestors are potassium-argon and fission-track dating. These methods do not date fossil material itself. Rather, they can be used to date volcanic ash and lava flows that are associated with fossil finds. Fortunately, many areas that have produced fossil discoveries were volcanically active in the past and can be dated by using these techniques. These methods have been employed at such fossil localities as the Fayum

Depression in Egypt (see Chapter 4), Olduvai Gorge in Tanzania and Hadar, Ethiopia (see Chapter 5).

In **potassium-argon dating**, scientists measure the decay of a radioisotope of potassium, known as potassium-40 (^{40}K), into an inert gas, argon (^{40}Ar). During the intense heat of a volcanic eruption, any argon present in a mineral is released, leaving only the potassium. As the rock cools, the potassium-40 begins to decay into argon. Because the half-life of ^{40}K is 1.3 billion years, the potassium-argon method can be used to date very ancient finds, and has thus been important in dating early of early human ancestors fossils. Although this technique has been used to date volcanic rocks a few thousand years old, the amount of argon is so small that it is more commonly used on samples dating over 100,000 years (McDougall and Harrison 1999).

Fission-track dating is based on the decay of a radioactive isotope of uranium (^{238}U) that releases energy at a regular rate. In certain minerals, microscopic scars, or tracks, from the spontaneous splitting of ^{238}U are produced. By counting the number of tracks in a sample, scientists can estimate fairly accurately when the rocks were formed. Fission-track dating is used to determine the age of geological samples between 300,000 and 4.5 billion years old, and thus it can provide independent confirmation on the age of strata using potassium-argon dating. Although this is generally a technique of more use to paleoanthropologists, it may also be used on manufactured glasses. Dates have been obtained on glass and pottery glazes less than 2,000 years old, and so it presents a technique of potential help to archaeologists studying the more recent past (Aitken 1990).

Thermoluminescence Dating This dating method is also based on radioactive decay, but the technique operates slightly differently than the methods discussed above. It is based on the number of electrons trapped in crystalline minerals. The electrons are primarily produced by the decay of three elements present in varying amounts in geological deposits: uranium, thorium, and a radioactive isotope of potassium (^{40}K). Hence, for accuracy, thermoluminescence dates should include an evaluation of the radioactivity in the surrounding soil so that the background radiation present in the deposit can be included in the calculations. As these elements decay, electrons are trapped in the crystals of the surrounding matrix. In order to be dated using the technique, artifacts must have been heated, as in the case of the firing of ceramics. Heating releases any trapped electrons; decay subsequently begins again and electrons once again start to accumulate in the crystal matrix of the object. By calculating the rate at which electrons have accumulated and measuring the number of electrons trapped in a sample, the age can be determined.

The importance of thermoluminescence dating lies in the fact that it can be used to date artifacts themselves, as opposed to associated stratigraphic deposits, as with potassium-argon dating. **Thermoluminescence dating** has been particularly useful in dating ceramics—one of the most common artifacts found on sites dating to the last 10,000 years. It has, however, also been used in cases where stone tools have been heated during their manufacture or time of use (some stone becomes easier to work with if heated). Similarly, it has been used in cases where the clay or stone of a hearth has been heated; the key once again is that the sample has been heated at the time of use or manufacture to set the amount of accumulated electrons to zero. Dates of tens or hundreds of thousands of years have been obtained on stone tools (Aitken et al. 1993). The method has also proven very useful in differentiating modern fakes from ancient ceramic objects.

Dendrochronology **Dendrochronology** is a unique type of numerical dating based on the annual growth rings found in some species of trees (Figure 3.6). Because a ring corresponds to a single year, the age of a tree can be determined by counting the number of rings. This principle was recognized as early as the late eighteenth century

Figure 3.6 Dendrochronology is based on the careful examination of distinct patterns of thin and thick growth rings that preserve a record of a region's environmental history. As illustrated here, samples of wood from different contexts may be pieced together to provide a master dendrochronology. Fragments of wood from archaeological sites can then be compared to this dendrochronology to determine the period in which the tree lived.

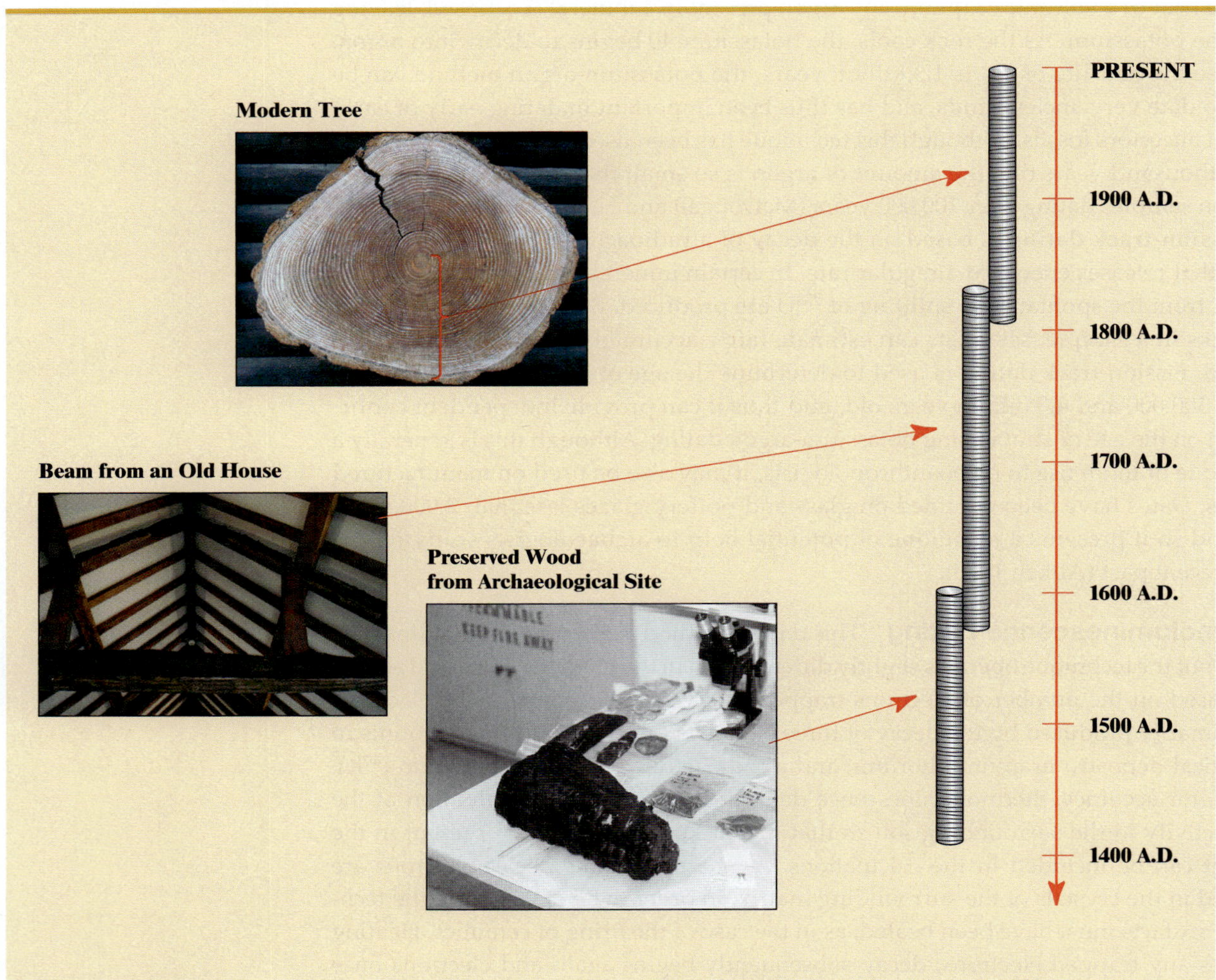

by the Reverend Manasseh Cutler, who used it to infer that a Native American mound site in Ohio was at least 463 years old. The modern science of dendrochronology was pioneered in the early twentieth century by A. E. Douglass using well-preserved wood from the American Southwest.

Today tree-ring dating is a great deal more sophisticated than counting tree rings. In addition to recording annual growth, tree rings also preserve a record of environmental history: thick rings represent years when the tree received ample rain; thin rings denote dry spells. In more temperate regions, the temperature and the amount of sunlight may affect the thickness of the rings. Trees of the same species in a localized area will generally show a similar pattern of thick and thin rings. This pattern can then be overlapped with patterns from successively older trees to build up a master dendrochronology sequence. In the American Southwest, a sequence using the bristlecone pine has now been extended to almost 9,000 years ago. Work on oak sequences in Ireland and Germany has been used to create a master dendrochronology sequence dating back over 10,000 years.

The importance of this method is manifest. Dendrochronology has proven of great significance in areas such as the American Southwest, where the dry conditions often preserve wood. The growth rings in fragments of wood from archaeological

Critical Perspectives

The Piltdown Fraud

One of the most bizarre stories in the history of paleoanthropology involves the fossil known as "Piltdown man." Widely discussed and debated for several decades, this discovery was eventually exposed as an elaborate fraud. Although it does not figure in current theories of hominin evolution, we examine the Piltdown man controversy because the alleged specimen was accepted as a legitimate human ancestor during the early decades of the twentieth century and influenced interpretations of human evolution (Weiner 1955; Blinderman 1986). This cautionary tale illustrates the efficiency of modern scientific techniques, but also serves as a warning about how scientists can be swayed by their own preconceived ideas.

Piltdown man was "discovered" in 1912 in a gravel quarry near Sussex, England, by a lawyer and amateur geologist named Charles Dawson. The quarry had previously produced the bones of extinct animals dating to the early Pleistocene (approximately 1.8 million years ago). The supposed hominin remains uncovered there consisted of the upper portion of the cranium and jaw. The skull was very large, with a cranial capacity of about 1,400 cc, which placed it within the range of modern humans. However, the lower jaw was apelike, the canine teeth large and pointed. This picture of early hominins mirrored popular early twentieth-century notions of the unique intellectual capabilities of humanity. Humans, so the interpretation went, evolved their large brains first, with other characteristics appearing later. In fact, available fossil evidence points to just the opposite evolutionary pattern.

Piltdown man was officially classified as *Eoanthropus dawsoni* ("Dawson's dawn man") and accepted by the scientific community as the earliest known representative of humans found in western Europe. A number of paleoanthropologists in France, Germany, and the United States remained skeptical about the findings, but they were unable to disprove the consensus of the English scientific community. As time went by, however, more hominin fossils were discovered, and none of them exhibited the combination of an apelike jaw and a large, humanlike cranium seen in the Piltdown find.

With contradictory evidence mounting, skepticism grew in the paleoanthropological community concerning the legitimacy of the Piltdown fossils. Finally, in the early 1950s, scientists completed a detailed re-examination of the Piltdown material. Using fluorine analysis (see Chapter 2), they discovered that the skull and jaw were of relatively recent vintage; the jaw, in fact, was younger than the skull. In reality, the Piltdown fossil consisted of a human skull from a grave a few thousand years old attached to the jaw of a recently deceased adolescent orangutan. The apelike teeth embedded in the jaw had been filed down to resemble human teeth. The place where the jaw joined the skull was also broken away so that it would not be immediately evident that the jaw and skull did not go together. To complete the ruse, the jaw was stained with a chemical to match the color of the skull.

Clearly, whoever perpetrated the Piltdown hoax had some knowledge of paleoanthropology. By the time the hoax was unmasked, most of the people who could have been implicated had died (Blinderman 1986). Putting aside the question of who was responsible for the hoax, we now recognize that paleoanthropological research between 1912 and the 1950s was definitely harmed by the Piltdown find, because the scientific community pursued a false path in hominin research. The initial acceptance of the Piltdown fraud as legitimate may partially explain why Taung child, one of the most startling hominin fossil discoveries of the early twentieth century, was relegated to relative obscurity for so many years.

Points to Ponder

1. What lessons does the Piltdown fraud provide for the way paleoanthropological research should proceed and how findings should be validated?
2. The recovery methods and the limited information on the context of the find clearly contributed to the success of the Piltdown fraud. Contrast the details of the Piltdown discovery with more recent finds at Olduvai Gorge, Tanzania, or Hadar, Ethiopia.
3. Can you think of other cases in which researchers' theoretical perspectives have affected their interpretation of the evidence?

sites can be compared to the master dendrochronology sequence, and the date the tree was cut down can be calculated. Even more important, dendrochronology provides an independent means of evaluating radiocarbon dating. Fragments dated by both techniques confirm the importance of radiocarbon as a dating method. However, wood dated by both techniques indicates that carbon-14 dates more than 3,000 years old are increasingly younger than their actual age. The reason for this lies in the amount of carbon-14 in the Earth's atmosphere. Willard Libby's initial radiocarbon dating calculations were based on the assumption that the concentration was constant over time, but we now know that it has varied. Dendrochronologies have allowed scientists to correct, or calibrate, radiocarbon dates, rendering them more accurate.

Interpretations About the Past

3.6 Discuss the challenges of interpreting the past and how these are overcome.

Views of the past are, unavoidably, tied to the present. As we discussed in Chapter 1, anthropologists try to validate their observations by being explicit about their assumptions. Prevailing social and economic conditions, political pressures, and theoretical perspectives all may affect interpretation. During the early twentieth century, bits and pieces of physical anthropology, archaeology, and linguistic information were muddled together to support the myth of a superior German race (Pringle 2006). Gustav Kossina, initially trained as a philologist, distorted archaeological interpretations to bolster chronologies that showed development starting in Germany and spreading outward to other parts of Europe.

Archaeological and historical information was also used to validate racist apartheid rule in South Africa. South African textbooks often proffered the idea that black, Bantu-speaking farmers migrating from the north, and white and Dutch-speaking settlers coming from the southwest arrived in the South African hinterland at the same time. This interpretation had clear relevance to the present: Both groups had equal claim to the land. However, archaeological evidence knocked out the foundations of this contrived history (Hall 1988). Archaeological evidence indicates that the ancestors of the black South Africans had moved into the region by 200 A.D., 1,500 years before the initial European settlement.

In these cases, versions of the past were constructed with dangerous effects on the present. More commonly, errors in interpretation are less intentional and more subtle. All researchers carry their own personal and cultural bias with them. Human societies are complex, and how this complexity is manifested archaeologically varies. These factors make the evaluation of interpretations challenging, and differences of opinion frequently occur.

Although there is no formula that can be used to evaluate all paleoanthropological and archaeological materials, there are useful guidelines. As seen in the preceding chapter, a key aspect of anthropological research is a systematic, scientific approach to data. Outmoded, incorrect interpretations can be revealed through new observations and the testing of hypotheses. The validity of a particular interpretation can be strengthened by the use of independent lines of evidence; if they lead to similar conclusions, the validity of the interpretation is strengthened. Academic books and articles submitted for publication are reviewed by other researchers, and authors are challenged to clarify points and strengthen observations. In many cases the evaluation of a particular theory or hypothesis must await the accumulation of data. Many regions of the world and different aspects of the past are virtually unstudied. Therefore, any theories about these areas or developments must remain tentative and subject to reevaluation.

Summary and Review of Learning Objectives

3.1 Define paleoanthropology and discuss what we can learn about the past from fossil evidence.

Paleoanthropologists often use fossils, the preserved traces of past life. Places where fossils are found are termed *fossil localities*. The fossil record is far from complete; only a small portion of the creatures that have lived are preserved. Nevertheless, an impressive record of past life has survived. Careful study and improved technology reveal minute fossils of shellfish, algae, and pollen and images of the delicate structure in bones. On one hand, this information allows for the reconstruction of the environments in which early human ancestors lived. On the other hand, fossils of human ancestors are used to trace human origins and evolution.

3.2 Discuss what the archaeological record can tell us about past societies.

The archaeological record encompasses all the material traces of past cultures. Places of past human activity that are preserved in the ground are called *archaeological sites*. Sites contain artifacts (objects made or modified by humans), as well as other traces of past human activity and a record of the environmental conditions that affected the site. In studying archaeological materials, archaeologists are particularly interested in the context, the specific location of finds and associated materials. Understanding the context is of key importance in determining the age, uses, and meanings of archaeological materials.

3.3 Discuss the basic techniques used to locate archaeological sites and fossil localities.

Archaeological sites and fossil localities provide important information about the past. They may be located in many different ways. Often traces of a site may survive on the ground, and local informants, maps, and previous archaeological reports may be of help. To discover sites, archaeologists may survey large areas, looking for any indications of archaeological remains. Technological aids, such as aerial photographs and satellite imagery may help locate sites. Surface examinations may be supplemented by subsurface testing, as well as tools such as the magnetometer or resistivity meter to help archaeologists identify artifacts and features beneath the ground. Fossils are often deeply buried, resting beneath layers of sediment, making locating them especially difficult. For this reason, paleoanthropologists often cannot employ many of the techniques archaeologists use to locate shallower archaeological deposits.

3.4 Discuss the basic techniques of archaeological excavation.

Depending on a project's objectives, archaeological sites may be targeted for excavation, which can be thought of as "scientific digging." Excavation is always undertaken with great care, and the material recovered carefully recorded. Although picks and shovels may sometimes be used, hand trowels and dust brooms remain the most important tools. Before excavation, a site is divided into a grid, which allows for the context of each artifact to be carefully noted. The depth of an excavation depends on a number of variables, including the type of site, the length of occupation, the soils present, and the area's environmental history.

3.5 Compare and contrast how archaeologists and paleoanthropologists date their discoveries.

Dating of fossils and archaeological materials is of key importance in the interpretation of the past. Without the ability to place finds in their relative ages, there is no way of assessing evolutionary change, technological innovations, or cultural developments. Paleoanthropologists and archaeologists use many different dating techniques that can be classified as either relative or absolute dating methods. Methods such as stratigraphic dating, faunal succession, and obsidian hydration provide only relative ages for finds in the same deposits. In contrast, numerical dating techniques like radiocarbon dating, potassium-argon dating, and dendrochronology can be used to assign actual numerical ages to finds.

3.6 Discuss the challenges of interpreting the past and how these are overcome.

Interpretations of the past are inevitably influenced by the present. At times, interpretations about the past have been used to support political ends, as seen in Nazi Germany and the apartheid policies of South Africa. Researchers try to avoid biases by employing systematic, scientific methodology. Theories can be revealed as false through testing and replaced by more convincing arguments. These, in turn, can be negated or strengthened by exploring new lines of evidence. Archaeological theories, often derived from cultural anthropology, help archaeologists conceptualize how cultures work and what aspects of a past culture might be preserved archaeologically. Ultimately, this reflection provides a more complete explanation of the dynamics of past cultures and culture change.

Key Terms

Chapter 4
The Hominins

Chapter Outline

Learning Objectives

After reading this chapter you should be able to:

4.1 Explain the principal trends in hominin evolution and within genus *Homo*.

4.2 Describe the fossil evidence for early hominin evolution.

4.3 Discuss the challenges paleoanthropologists face in interpreting the fossil record and explain why their interpretations sometimes change.

4.4 Describe and discuss the different models for the emergence of anatomically modern humans.

4.5 Describe how new genomic research and molecular dating have helped anthropologists interpret human evolution.

4.6 Discuss the different theories regarding the relationship of *Homo sapiens neanderthalensis* and *Homo sapiens*.

4.7 Define and describe the principal tool industries of the Lower Paleolithic.

4.8 Describe the changes in the archaeological record that distinguish the Upper Paleolithic from the preceding periods.

The evolution of primates in the Miocene and Pliocene epochs serves as a backdrop for the emergence of early human ancestors. By the Miocene epoch (23 million to 5 million years ago), primates in various forms—the precursors of modern prosimians, monkeys, and apes—proliferated in many geographic regions. Sometime in the late Miocene or early Pliocene, new and distinct forms of primates of the subfamily Hominidae emerged. Classified as members of the tribe hominini or **hominins** (see the box "What's in a Name?" in Chapter 2), these varied species present a range of distinctive features in their teeth, jaws, and brains that represent adaptations to varying environments. However, they all share the structural anatomy needed for **bipedalism**—the ability to walk upright on two legs. It is this characteristic that separates the hominins from other primates and collectively identifies them as the species most directly related to modern humans.

Paleoanthropologists have advanced numerous interpretations of hominin evolution over the past century. Although opinions diverge on the proper naming and classification of individual fossil specimens, paleoanthropologists are in broad agreement about the evolution of the human species from a small-brained bipedal ape, the Hominini lineage branching off from the other primates approximately six to ten million years ago. For the purposes of this discussion, we primarily focus on two genera of hominins: *Australopithecus*, which emerged first, and genus *Homo*. Both of these groups include a number of different species, some of which have at times been placed in separate genera. Going back over six million years, the australopithecines are the older group, and they are only known from African fossil finds. The earliest representatives of the species are *A. anamensis* and *A. afarensis*. Australopithecine fossils date from roughly six million to one million years ago. After that, there is no trace of this genus in the fossil record, leading paleoanthropologists to conclude that they became extinct at about that time.

The first representatives of genus *Homo*, the genus that includes modern humans, first appear in the fossil record just over two million years ago. There is a consensus among anthropologists that genus *Homo* evolved from the australopithecines, though interpretations vary as to which australopithecine species gave rise to the new genus. The earliest members of the *Homo* line to be identified in the fossil record are the species *H. habilis* and *H. rudolfensis*, dating between 2.2 million and 1.6 million years ago. What distinguishes the first representatives of genus *Homo* from the australopithecines is a trend toward larger brain size. *H. habilis* is followed in the fossil record by *H. erectus* (including finds sometimes designated *H. ergaster*), which is known from finds in Africa dating 1.8 million years old. *Homo erectus*, in turn, evolved into *H. sapiens*, the species that encompasses modern humans, during the past 400,000 years. Members of genus *Homo* coexisted with some of the later australopithecine species between 2.2 million and 1 million years ago.

Trends in Hominin Evolution

4.1 Explain the principal trends in hominin evolution and within genus *Homo*.

The hominins are members of the order primates. As such, they share the basic primate characteristics including a generalized skeleton, a high degree of manual dexterity, and prolonged infant dependency. But the hominins evolved with distinctive, derived characteristics. As noted, the first and most significant of these is bipedalism, a feature found in all hominins. Other distinctive features include the reduction of face, jaw, and anterior teeth and a trend toward increasing cranial capacity in genus *Homo*. Changes in these attributes are preserved in the fossil remains of early hominins, and the evolutionary relationships of different species are traced on the basis of the similarities and differences present in individual finds. These characteristics are exemplified in modern humans and least pronounced in earlier hominin species.

The evolution of certain physical, social, and cultural characteristics of hominins is difficult to trace because the characteristics are not preserved in the fossil record. For example, unlike other surviving primates, modern humans are not completely covered with hair. Loss of body hair, as well as characteristics such as skin color and the prevalence of sweat glands, might be a relatively recent phenomenon (see the discussion in Chapter 5), but we can find no indication of these developments in fossilized remains. Other trends, such as degrees of social complexity and the origins of human culture, are also of great importance, but such features cannot be directly inferred from fossil remains. Rather, they are evaluated on the basis of archaeological information on early hominins' tools, food remains, and living sites, topics examined in the discussion of "The Life and Times of Genus *Homo*" below.

Bipedalism

Hominins are the only primates that are fully bipedal. Although gorillas, chimpanzees, orangutans and other primates can stand upright, they spend most of their time on all fours. As with other types of locomotion, bipedalism is reflected in skeletal structure and so its evolution can be traced in the fossil record. For example, the hips and knees of hominins differ markedly from those of knuckle walkers like the chimpanzee (Lovejoy 1981, 1988; Steudel 1994; Richmond et al. 2001). Paleoanthropologists also focus a great deal of attention on the **foramen magnum**, the opening in the base of the skull through which the spinal cord passes. In quadrupedal animals, this aperture is at the back of the skull, which allows the head to extend out in front of the body. In contrast, the foramen magnum in bipedal creatures is on the bottom of the skull, sitting squarely above the body. Structures of the skull associated with bipedalism are especially important because the postcranial bones of many fossil hominins have not been preserved.

Bipedalism stands as the earliest and most important trend in hominin evolution. Initially, many paleoanthropologists believed that the earliest hominins, the australopithecines, were not proficient at bipedalism, perhaps moving with a swinging, slouched gait like that of chimpanzees or gorillas. These interpretations were based on limited fossil finds and have not been supported by more recent studies. Fossil remains of the oldest known hominins, in fact, indicate that these creatures walked as well as modern humans. Our best scientific guess places the appearance of bipedalism in hominins sometime between six million and ten million years ago, a period of time that is unfortunately poorly represented in the fossil record.

Why Bipedalism? Although bipedal posture can be clearly inferred on the basis of skeletal remains, it is more difficult to reconstruct the behavior of early hominins and thus evaluate how upright posture may have been beneficial. The adaptive aspects of bipedalism—how it may have enhanced the survival and reproductive success of early

Figure 4.1 Drawing of Lucy's knee bones and hips compared with those of humans and apes. Lucy's skeletal structure is almost identical to that of modern humans, indicating that, like humans, *A. afarensis* was fully bipedal.

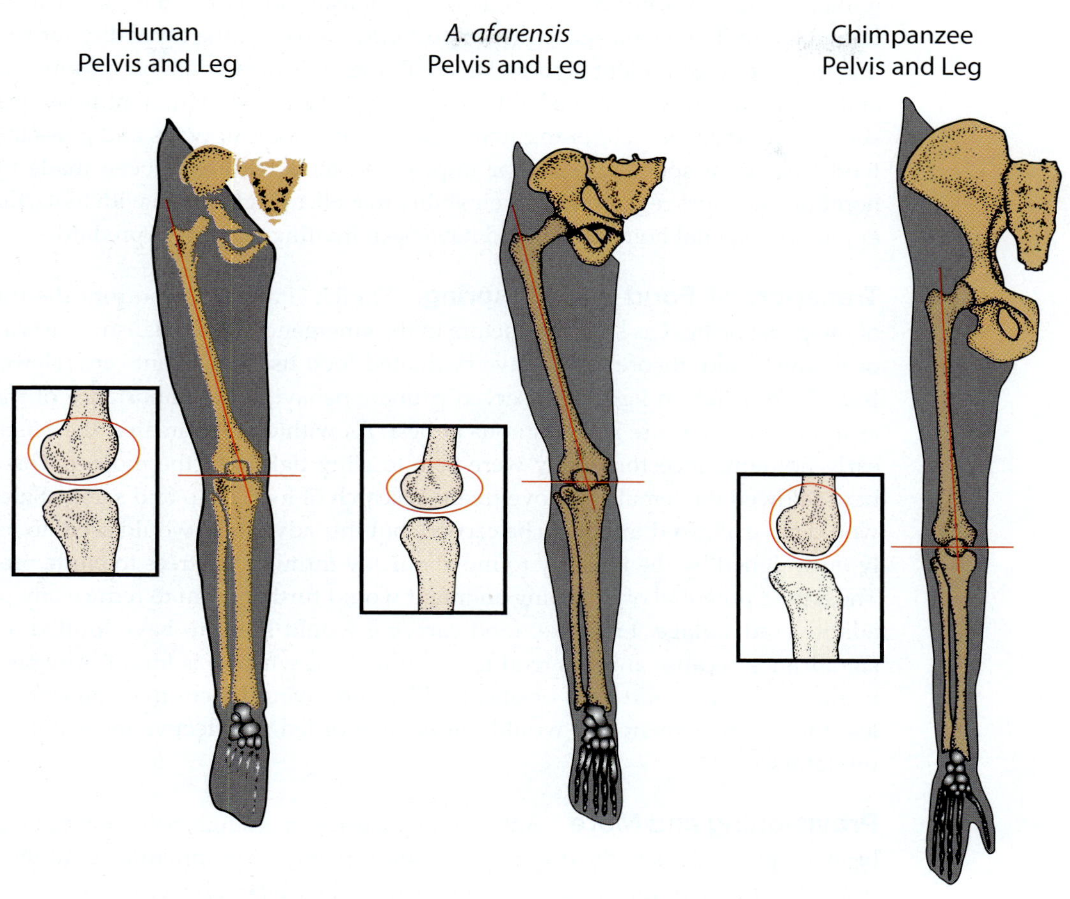

hominins—are not immediately apparent. Bipedalism, for example, is a relatively slow means of locomotion. Nor does the skeletal and muscle structure needed for bipedalism provide the most effective way of climbing or moving through trees—clearly, disadvantages in terms of avoiding predators. Upright posture also places added stress on the lower back, hips, and legs and makes it more difficult to supply the brain with blood. In light of these seeming disadvantages, there has been a great deal of debate regarding how this feature was adaptive, and why was it selected for in early hominins.

While there is ongoing debate about the origins of bipedalism, two overarching points can be made. First, bipedal locomotion probably evolved as a result of a confluence of factors rather than a single adaptive characteristic. As discussed later, thermoregulation models may provide the most plausible explanation for the origins of bipedalism. Perspectives, however, vary and researchers have suggested different views of how walking upright may have been adaptive. Secondly, bipedalism clearly had important social, as well as behavioral, consequences. Once developed, this type of locomotion served early hominins well in a variety of ways by freeing their hands for such tasks as tool use, transporting food, and carrying infants. These activities, in turn, would have facilitated a number of important social and cultural innovations.

Tool Use One of the early theories regarding the origins of bipedalism suggested that it evolved because it freed the hands to make tools. Because early hominins lacked sharp teeth and strong jaws, the ability to use tools would have given them access to a greater variety of food sources, thus ensuring increased survival and ultimate reproductive success (Washburn 1960; Pilbeam 1972; Shipman 1984). This would have been an important adaptive advantage. Unfortunately, the existing evidence does not support this hypothesis. The earliest tools, simple stone choppers, date just over 2.6 million years ago, whereas the origin of bipedalism can be traced back at least six million to ten million years ago. More importantly, however, the capability for tool manufacture is not dependent on bipedalism. Rather, it is dependent on cognitive abilities and the manual dexterity needed to manipulate objects. Modern nonhuman primates, such as chimpanzees and orangutans, make simple tools of twigs and grass to extract food from tight spots, and similar improvised tools may have been made by early hominin ancestors regardless of their ability to walk upright. Even with tools, the slower moving bipedal hominins would have been inviting targets for predators.

Transport of Food and Offspring Similar limitations confront the transport of offspring or food as selective factors in the emergence of bipedalism. Carrying food or infants could, theoretically, have facilitated food use and infant care (Hewes 1961; Isaac 1978a). Yet, in light of observed primate behavior, the importance of transport as a selective pressure is ambiguous at best. As with other primates, the offspring of early hominin ancestors likely were able to cling tightly to the mother. This would have allowed the female to move freely in search of food or to find safety. Bipedalism would have allowed infants to be carried, but this advantage would seem to be greatly outweighed by the inability to move quickly through the trees to elude predators. The added potential of dropping an infant would further seem to reduce any possible adaptive advantage. Likewise, food carrying would seem to have limited adaptive significance because animals tend to consume food where it is found. Any benefits of being able to transport food or offspring by hand would seem to be offset by slower, less mobile movement that would not have afforded an effective means of avoiding predators.

Provisioning and More Rather than focusing on a single behavior that may have been adaptive, clues to the origins of bipedalism may lie in thinking about the unique *combination* of activities and social interactions that bipedalism may imply. Paleoanthropologist Owen Lovejoy (1981, 1984) suggested that the evolution of bipedalism turned on more than merely the ability to carry objects or use tools. Because it involved the modification of a wide range of biological and behavioral traits, it must have conferred some adaptive advantage on early hominins, even before they had fully developed the physical capabilities for bipedalism. Lovejoy posits that the crucial advantage may have been the ability to transport food back to a mate by walking upright and using simple implements, such as broad leaves, to maximize the amount of food that could be carried. Provisioning by the male would have allowed the female to increase the quality and quantity of time devoted to infant care. This intensification of parental attention, in turn, would have promoted the survival of infants and, therefore, the species. Taking the theory a step further, Lovejoy asserts that food sharing and the cooperation that underlies this behavior may have produced a reproductive strategy that favored sexual fidelity and close, long-term relations between a male and a female. While plausible, assessing Lovejoy's interpretations concerning early hominin behavior on the basis of fragmentary fossils remains difficult indeed, and many researchers have critiqued his suggestions. A major criticism is that there is no evidence that early hominins favored sexual fidelity or close, long-term male-female relations, things that by nature are difficult to assess on the basis of the fossil record.

Thermoregulation Models More recent theories have considered the unique adaptive advantages that bipedal locomotion may have conferred in the environment in which early hominins evolved—possibly the semi-open savannas and mixed woodlands of East and Central Africa, regions that have produced many of the early hominin fossil finds (Wheeler 1991). Food resources in this mixed savanna-woodland environment would have been scattered and selection would have favored endurance, rather than speed, in locomotion. A combination of attributes in humans makes us very efficient at bipedal locomotion, particularly with regard to endurance running or jogging (Bramble and Lieberman 2004; Lieberman et al. 2007). Less heat is generated in the legs of bipeds. In addition, the ligaments in the legs and feet (the Achilles tendon, for example) allow humans to release energy like a spring as they move forward. Our flexible chests and anatomy also makes for stable bipedal movement.

An interrelated aspect of the thermodynamic model also considers the possible benefits of sweat glands and the loss of body hair (Wheeler 1992, 1994). Sweat cools the body; less body hair and more exposed skin would have further facilitated cooling. These features would have provided an adaptive advantage to movement under the hot equatorial sun, and so may have been selected for in early hominins. Early hominins may have been able to move during the hottest times of the day, times when predators such as lions rest. Modern humans have substantially less body hair than other primates and also sweat more than any other animal. Modern apes such as the chimpanzees and gorillas sweat, though not as much as humans, and it is likely that early hominins sweated.

As a consequence of these varied attributes, bipedal hominins, while slower moving than some four-legged (quadrupedal) animals over short distances, would have moved more efficiently over *longer* distances, something that would have allowed them to travel greater distances in search of food. Humans are not simply able to walk upright; we excel at walking. In fact, Daniel Lieberman and Dennis Bramble (2007) have observed that with our steady pace, humans can outdistance almost all other mammals over long distances, particularly when it is hot. Indeed, it has been noted that the modern San people of southern Africa sometimes employ persistence hunting; literally chasing animals until they collapse (Liebenberg 2006). These interrelated traits may have conferred important adaptive advantages on early hominins; their bipedal stature, combined with efficient vision, would also have facilitated their ability to identify food resources.

While these interpretations are plausible, and they may explain why bipedalism emerged, the movements of early hominins across the savanna and their behaviors are difficult, if not impossible, to assess on the basis of the archaeological record. Nor does the fossil provide a record of features such as body hair and sweat glands, so it is unknown how sweaty or hairy early hominins might have been. It is, therefore, difficult to fully evaluate the thermoregulation model. Sorting out all of the variables and which ones played the most prominent roles in the development of bipedalism continues to challenge anthropologists.

Reduction of the Face, Teeth, and Jaws

We also see in hominin evolution a series of interrelated changes primarily associated with diet and food-processing requirements. The oldest fossil hominins have a protruding, or *prognathic*, face, the jaw extending out further than in modern humans. In addition, the canine teeth of early hominins, while smaller than those of other apes, are large compared with those of humans. In this respect, they can be seen as transitional between earlier species and later human ancestors. To accommodate these larger canines, which extend beyond the other teeth, there are gaps between the teeth of the opposing jaw. This feature, called *diastema*, is characteristic of the early hominins, as well as living apes and monkeys such as the gorilla and baboon, but absent in humans. Finally, the teeth of early hominins are arranged in a U-shape pattern, and the teeth on opposite sides of the mouth are parallel. This arrangement is similar to that found in modern gorillas, orangutans, and chimps. In contrast, in the human jaw the teeth are not parallel, but flare away from each other at the back of the mouth.

Approximately 2 million years ago, these characteristics started to become less pronounced in hominins. Primate teeth, including those of hominin species, can generally handle an omnivorous diet with ease. However, hominin teeth, with flat molar crowns and thick tooth enamel, are highly specialized for grinding. Early primates, as well as living prosimians and anthropoids, had large canine and incisor teeth that are well suited to cutting and slicing. In contrast, the size of these teeth is greatly reduced in later hominin species. Early representatives of the genus *Homo* have smaller canines, and the gaps associated with larger canine teeth disappear. In humans, the canine teeth retain a distinctive shape, but they are almost the same size as the other teeth. Of all the hominins, the faces of modern humans are the least protruding.

Some of the other hominin species have teeth and cranial structures that suggest adaptations to specialized diets. In particular, the robust australopithecines (*A. robustus*, *A. boisei* and *A. aethiopicus*, discussed later) developed massive chewing muscles and extremely large molars compared with those of modern humans. This strong dentition earned one species, *Australopithecus boisei*, the nickname "nutcracker man." Scientists believe that these features most likely evolved in response to a diet of coarse, fibrous vegetation. Paleoanthropologists cite several key skeletal structures in the jaw and the cranium as evidence of this creature's powerful chewing capacity. Thick, enlarged jaws and cheekbones provided attachments for these huge muscles. Some australopithecine fossil specimens have a **sagittal crest**, a bony ridge along the top of the skull that grows larger as more chewing muscles reach up along the midline of the cranium.

In contrast to the australopithecines, evolving *Homo* species may have consumed a more varied diet based on gathering vegetation, hunting animals, and scavenging. This theory corresponds with the size and contour of their molars—similar to those of modern humans—and the absence of such features as sagittal crests, which accompany specialized chewing muscles.

Increase in Cranial Capacity

The defining characteristic of genus *Homo* is a tendency toward increased cranial capacity and the complexity of the brain. Like the changes in dentition, growth in cranial capacity first appears in hominins dating from about two million years ago. Before that, the size and organization of the hominin brain underwent comparatively little change. Early australopithecines such as *A. afarensis* (which lived some three million to four million years ago) had a cranium about the size of a softball, barely surpassing that of a modern chimpanzee. Hominin cranial capacity remained fairly constant at this size for two million years, averaging just over 400 cubic centimeters (cc). Then, sometime after two million years ago, members of the genus *Homo* began to show a steady increase in cranial size. The cranial capacity of *H. habilis*, the first representative of the genus, was over 600 cc. The brain in *Homo erectus* averaged 1,000 cc, and the modern human brain measures, on average, 1,350 cc, a threefold increase from the australopithecines. Significantly, this constitutes an increase in both *relative* and *absolute* size. Even taking into account that modern humans are substantially larger than australopithecines, the relative size of the hominin brain more than doubled in the last two million years (McHenry 1982).

Changes in the cranial capacity of early hominins undoubtedly influenced physical and social developments, which are less easily studied through fossil remains. For instance, increasing brain size almost certainly prompted numerous modifications in hominin diet, the use of tools, the evolution of language, and the intricacies of social organization. Greater sophistication in any of these areas may have improved early hominins' chances of survival.

Fossil Evidence for Hominin Evolution

4.2 Describe the fossil evidence for early hominin evolution.

In *On the Origin of Species*, Charles Darwin devoted relatively little attention to human evolution, noting simply, "Much light will be thrown on the origin of man and his history" (Darwin 1859). In the mid-nineteenth century, when Darwin was writing his treatise, scientists had scant fossil evidence for hominin origins. Since Darwin's time, however, thousands of hominin fossils have been recovered, most of them in Africa. The Hominid Vault of the Kenya National Museum alone contains hundreds of hominin specimens from Kenya and Tanzania, and more than 1,500 other specimens have been recovered from South African sites. Specimens range from isolated teeth to nearly complete skeletons. Although paleoanthropologists have uncovered many spectacular finds, some discoveries merit special attention because they prompted anthropologists to modify theories of human evolution. In this section, we examine several of the most important fossil finds, beginning with the first hominin ancestors. The locations of some of these key discoveries are illustrated in Figure 4.2.

The Oldest Hominins

Fossil evidence for the evolution of the first hominins—from the period between six million and ten million years ago when the transition to bipedalism first

Figure 4.2 Map of African fossil finds.

Source: Figure, "Map of African fossil finds," from Roger Lewin, *In the Age of Mankind: A Smithsonian Book of Human Evolution*, Smithsonian Books, 1988, p. 71. (Art by Phil Jordan and Julie Scheiber). Reprinted by permission of Phil Jordan and Associates, Inc.

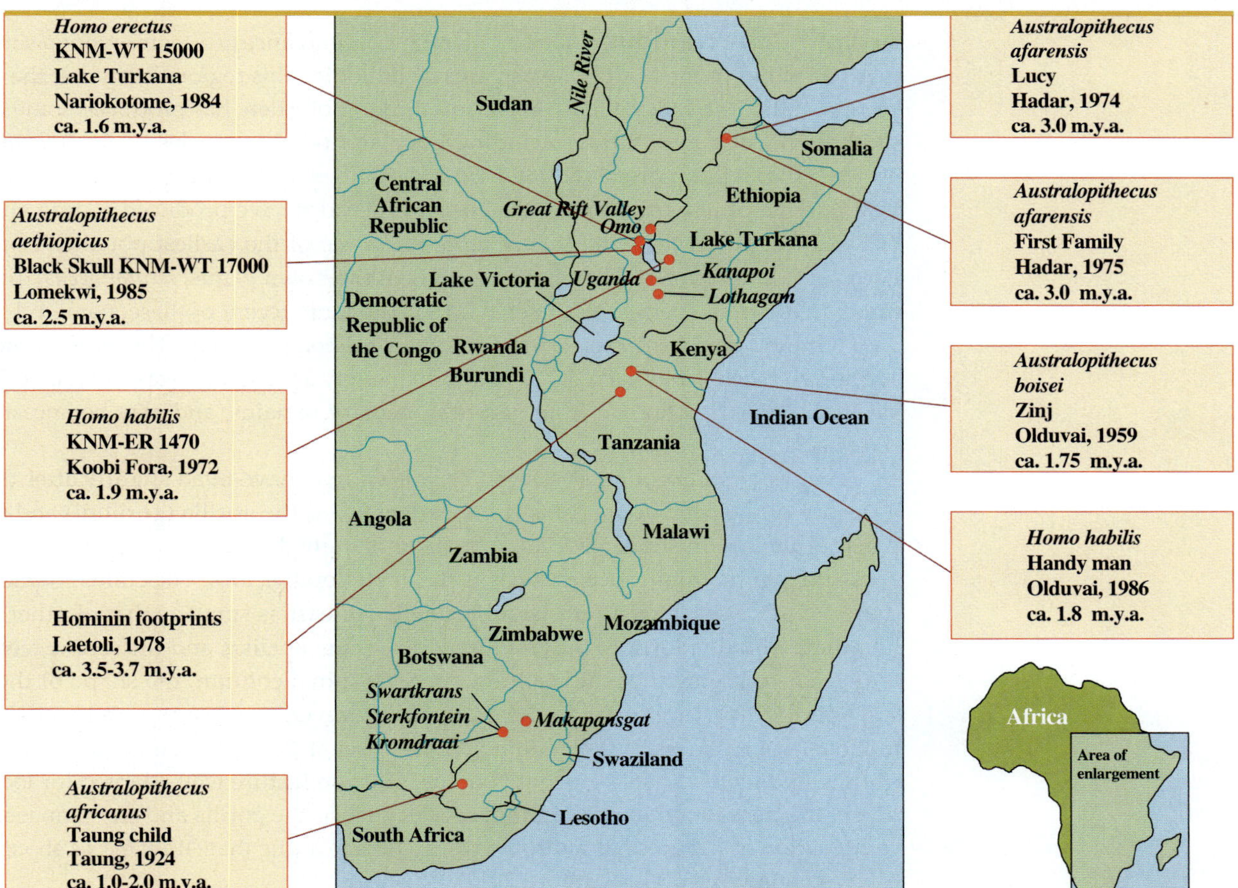

occurred—remains very incomplete. The classification of these discoveries and their relationship to later species are uncertain, though some intriguing finds have been discovered. Among the most promising locales are a series of sites in Kenya, particularly the areas around Lake Turkana, Lake Baringo, and the Tugen Hills in the Rift Valley region. The Middle Awash area of Ethiopia also has great potential. Geological deposits in each of these areas span the relevant time periods, and well-preserved fossil deposits are represented. Notably, several exciting discoveries have also been made in Chad in Central Africa, a region that had not previously produced hominin remains.

Sahelanthropus tchadensis The Chad discoveries are especially notable because they occur some 1,500 miles farther west than any other early hominin find. This specimen, named *Sahelanthropus tchadensis*, consists of a complete, though distorted, cranium dated to approximately six million to seven million years ago, making it the oldest possible hominin (Brunet et al. 2002; Wolpoff et al. 2006). The dentition and cranium possess features that are a mixture of ape and hominin characteristics. In particular, the teeth are smaller than those of apes and do not extend below the other teeth, making it more comparable to later hominins. The limited information on the post-cranial skeleton prevents the full assessment of how *S. tchadensis* may have moved. However, the shape and orientation of the foramen magnum suggests the ability to walk upright. Until more information becomes available, the evolutionary relationship of *Sahelanthropus tchadensis* to species will remain uncertain. Nevertheless, this fossil discovery from Chad has important implications regarding the evolution of the early hominins as it affords insight into the distribution and diversity of species present when hominin species were emerging.

Ardipithecus ramidus Other potential hominin ancestors come from a series of fossil localities in the Middle Awash area of Ethiopia. This region, located at the intersection of the Rift Valley, the Red Sea, and the Gulf of Aden, has produced some of the most spectacular fossil finds, including Lucy and other examples of *Australopithecus afarensis* that will be discussed later. Fossil localities in the Middle Awash excavated by a number of researchers over the past two decades have produced a large number of fossil fragments that collectively represent some of the earliest potential hominin ancestors yet recovered. They have been given their own genus, *Ardipithecus*, divided into two different species (White et al 2009). The more recent of these, named *A. ramidus* ("Ground ape at the root"), lived about 4.4 million years ago. The older of the two species, *A. kadabba*, has been dated to approximately 5.6 million years old (Haile-Selassie et al. 2004). It is known from very fragmentary remains, and may be ancestral to *A. ramidus*.

A. ramidus is of particular interest because it may have lived slightly after the divergence of the tribe hominini and the African apes; the gorilla (gorillini) and chimpanzee (panini). In some respects, *A. ramidus* is quite different from both the African apes and later hominin species, such as the australopithecines. The cranial capacity of these Middle Awash creatures is quite small—at least as small as that of other early hominins—but the form of the cranium is also more apelike, and the canine teeth are larger. The placement of the cranium over the spinal column, the shape of the pelvis, and the structure of the limb bones are, however, consistent with bipedal locomotion—the hallmark of the hominins (Lovejoy et al. 2009). Yet unlike other hominin species, *Ardipithecus* had a grasping big toe. This is a feature well adapted for locomotion in the trees found in nonhominin species such as the gorilla and chimpanzee. This combination of features has led some researchers to argue that *Ardipithecus* should not be given hominin status (Stanford 2012).

Australopithecus anamensis: Early Hominins from Lake Turkana

The region around Lake Turkana in northern Kenya has also yielded a host of important fossil finds, including the discoveries of *Australopithecus aethiopicus*, *Homo habilis*, and *Homo erectus* (discussed below). Some of the earliest widely recognized hominin remains are represented by a number of finds made over the past 30 years at Kanapoi, southwest of Lake Turkana, and Allia Bay, on the eastern side of Lake Turkana, including the remains of a species designated *Australopithecus anamensis* (Leakey et al. 1995).

The fossils of *A. anamensis* are fragmentary, including teeth and jaw fragments and some postcranial bones. The age of the finds is placed between 3.9 million and 4.2 million years ago. The leg bones are consistent with bipedal— hominin—posture, but the finds also present some distinctive attributes. Like *Ardipithecus*, the skull and the teeth are quite primitive. The external ear openings are also unlike more recent hominins. However, in contrast to the *Ardipithecus* remains, the molar enamel on the teeth of these specimens is thick and, thus, more analogous to more recent hominin species. Hence, the finds may represent a transitional link between species such as early *Ardipithecus* and the australopithecines. Because of their similarity to later finds, they have been placed in genus *Australopithecus* but have been assigned a new species designation, *A. anamensis*, in recognition of their distinctive attributes. The relationship of these finds to *Australopithecus afarensis* is still being evaluated, but most researchers place them near the base of the branches leading to genus *Homo* and the later australopithecines.

Australopithecus afarensis

During the 1970s, a joint American–French team of paleoanthropologists led by Donald Johanson and Maurice Taieb made several exciting hominin finds in the well-preserved geological beds near the Great Rift Valley in the Hadar area of the Afar region of Ethiopia (Johanson et al. 1982). This valley has experienced extensive mountain-building and volcanic activity over the last several million years, and erosion has brought many fossils to the surface where they await discovery by researchers.

The *Australopithecus afarensis* fossils discovered at Hadar and Laetoli (see discussion below) have been dated between 3 million and 4 million years ago, making these some of the earliest well-described hominin remains. The fossils are remarkably primitive in comparison to later australopithecines; from the neck up, including the cranium and jaw, *A. afarensis* is definitely apelike. The upper body also has features, such as curved fingers, that would have made it well adapted for climbing and moving through an arboreal environment. However, the abundant lower limb bones and the pelvic orientation, as well as the position of the hips and knees, indicate that *A. afarensis* was a fully erect, bipedal creature (Lovejoy 1988). This mélange of postcranial features has led researchers to debate whether *A. afarensis* was ground dwelling or still spent a great deal of time in the trees. Such interpretive disagreements underscore the challenges researchers face in analyzing fragmentary remains of nonliving species.

Lucy Among the most spectacular finds made by Johanson's team at Hadar was a fossilized skeleton of an ancient hominin that was almost 40 percent intact, making it among the earliest and most complete fossil hominins recovered. This find, scientifically designated *Australopithecus afarensis*, became popularly known as "Lucy" (named after a Beatles song, "Lucy in the Sky with Diamonds"). Lucy had a small cranium (440 cc) and large canine teeth. In fact, Lucy's skull resembles that of a modern chimpanzee. However, below the neck the anatomy of the spine, pelvis, hips, thigh bones, and feet clearly shows that Lucy walked on two feet (Lovejoy 1988). Lucy was a fairly small creature, weighing approximately 75 pounds, and she stood about 3.5 to 4 feet tall.

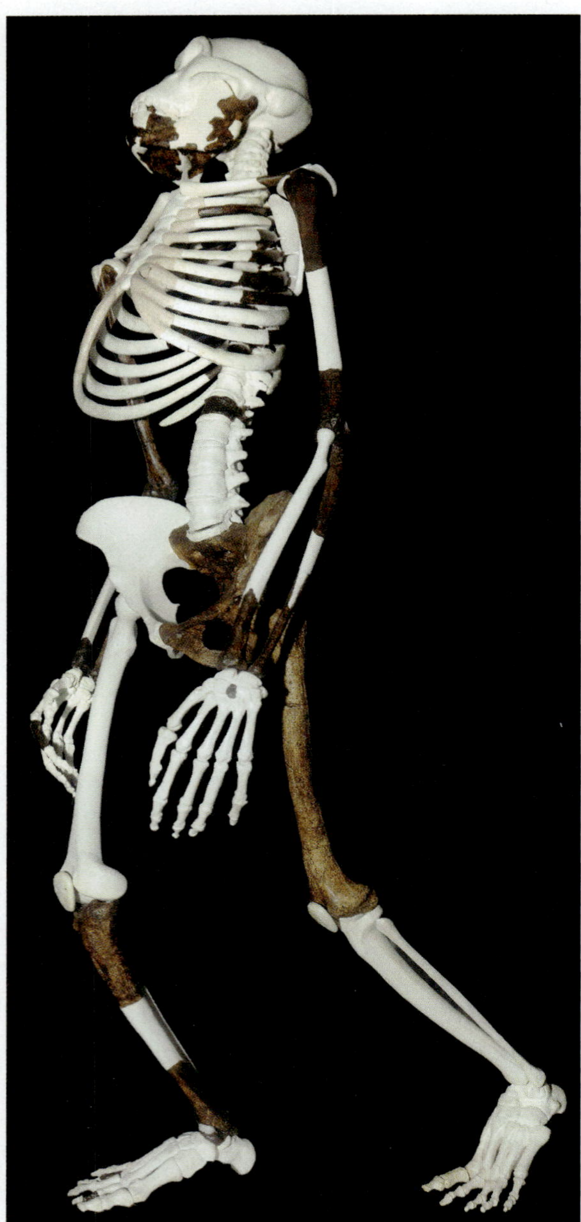

Reconstruction of *Australopithecus afarensis* based on skeletal remains recovered by Donald Johanson at Hadar, Ethiopia, in 1974.

The Dikika Baby Another fascinating find from Hadar is the popularly named "Dikika baby" or "Lucy's baby." Excavated by paleoanthropologist Zeresenay Alemseged in 1999 at a site called Dikika, just a couple of miles from where the Lucy find was discovered, the fossil remains were encased in stone and took five years of careful excavation to extract. Like the Lucy discovery, the Dikika find is the well-preserved remains of an *A. afarensis*, but whereas Lucy was an adult, the Dikika fossil is of a 3-year-old child (Alemseged et al. 2006). The find consists of an almost complete skull, the entire torso, much of the legs, and parts of the arms. The young age of the Dikika baby and the completeness of the find afford unique insight into the growth and development of the species, as well as the physical attributes of the species, which includes features, such as the shoulder blades, that have been poorly preserved in other *A. afarensis* finds. While just an infant, the Dikika baby possesses the definitely bipedal features that characterize adult examples such as Lucy. In addition, the structure of the bones of the hands and shoulder blades may suggest *A. afarensis* was well suited to an arboreal environment. The arm sockets in particular are oriented upward, more like those of a gorilla than those of later hominins and humans. This would support interpretations that have underscored the species' adaptation to an arboreal environment.

The Laetoli Footprints

The site of Laetoli, some 30 miles south of Olduvai Gorge in northern Tanzania, has produced a number of fossil finds, including possible examples of *Australopithecus afarensis*, the fossil species described at Hadar. However, the site is best known for the remarkable discovery of fossilized footprints. Thousands of footprints of various species of ancient animals are preserved in an ancient layer of mud covered with volcanic ash. However, a remarkable finding by Mary Leakey in 1978 revealed footprints clearly left by fully bipedal creatures approximately 3.5 million years ago (Leakey and Hay 1979). The evidence consists of a trail more than 75 feet long made by three hominins. Studies of these footprints have revealed that the mode of locomotion for these early hominins was fully bipedal and comparable to that of modern humans. The presence of bipedal species at this time period had been well established on the basis of fossil evidence. However, the Laetoli footprints provide independent, and indisputable, evidence of the existence of a bipedal creature 3.5 million years ago.

Australopithecus africanus

Australopithecus africanus is primarily known from fossil finds in southern Africa dating between 2 million and 3 million years ago. The species lived after those discussed in the preceding sections. However, it possessed a smaller cranial capacity than more recent examples of genus *Homo*. An adult *A. africanus* had a cranial capacity that averaged around 450 cc, probably weighed between 40 and 60 pounds, and was between 3.5 and 4.75 feet tall. Although the age of the South African finds are challenging to date, these gracile australopithecines are dated to between 3 million and 2 million years ago on the basis of fossils of extinct animals of known age found in the same deposits.

Taung child *A. africanus* is memorable as the first described example of an australopithecine. The Taung child, found in 1924, was named *Australopithecus africanus*, the "southern ape of Africa," by its discoverer. The discovery was a remarkable combination of coincidence and luck. The man responsible for the find was Raymond Dart, an Australian-born anatomist living in South Africa. In 1924, Dart was given a box of fossils from the rubble of a limestone quarry near the town of Taung, South Africa. The rubble included the front of a skull, a jaw, and an endocranial cast of a bipedal creature that was clearly very different than modern humans. On the basis of the teeth, Dart judged the creature to have been quite young at death, and he called his discovery the "Taung child" (Dart 1925, 1967). Today, the individual is estimated to have been between three and four years old at the time of death.

Although *A. africanus* had certain apelike features, it also exhibited a number of unique characteristics. For example, the foramen magnum was farther forward in the Taung child than in modern apes, indicating that this creature's head was balanced above the spine. In other words, it moved with the upright posture characteristic of a biped—a key hominin characteristic. The brain of the Taung child was very small, hardly larger than that of a chimpanzee. Its structure, however, differed from that of apes and was more highly developed in some regions. The canine teeth were much closer in size to a human child's than to an infant ape's, and lacked the diastema found in apes' teeth. Dart astounded the scientific world by announcing that the Taung child was a hominin, an intermediate link between humans and earlier primates.

A hominin footprint fossilized in volcanic ash at Laetoli, Tanzania, is shown next to a modern foot. Dated at over 3.5 million years, the trail of footprints at the site provides dramatic evidence that early hominins such as *Australopithecus afarensis* were fully bipedal.

Other A. africanus Finds At the time of its discovery, many paleoanthropologists challenged Dart's conclusions, arguing that the Taung child was really an ape. Contemporary evolutionary theories suggested that large cranial capacity was the critical characteristic of hominin evolution, and critics pointed out that the cranial capacity of Dart's find was too small for it to have been ancestral to humans. But Dart's critics were proven wrong. In the decades following the discovery of the Taung child, a number of similar finds were made in South Africa. During the 1940s, Dart excavated additional fossils from Makapansgat Cave. Scottish paleontologist Robert Broom (1938) also came upon a number of similar fossils at Sterkfontein. Some of these new finds were adult specimens of creatures like the Taung child. With their humanlike dentition, bipedal capabilities, and small cranial capacity, they were unquestionably hominins. These discoveries clearly established the Taung child as a hominin and *Australopithecus* as a valid genus.

The Robust Australopithecines: Branches on the Family Tree

While a number of fossil finds present possible, albeit debated, ancestors of modern humans, a variety of discoveries have revealed creatures decidedly unlike us who likely represent side branches on the human family tree. These include several species that have been collectively classed as robust australopithecines. They include three different species, *A. robustus*, *A. boisei*, and *A. aethiopicus*, dated between 2.7 million and 1 million years ago. Their specific taxonomic designations, however, have been widely debated and an increasing number of researchers place them in a separate species, *Paranthropus* (Tattersall 1998; Stringer and Andrews 2005). *Paranthropus* translates as "alongside humans," a name that signals their distinct ancestry from modern humans. Nevertheless, while possessing a number of distinct features, they are also clearly bipedal and are, therefore, closely related to hominin species that were ancestral to humans. The identification of robust australopithecine species presents an increasingly complex picture of evolution that emphasizes diversity within the hominins and what paleoanthropologists emphasize as "bushiness." That is, instead of a neat, ladder-like, unidirectional evolution of bipedal hominins from an early ancestor to modern humans, multiple species of hominins—some of them not ancestral to modern humans—roamed Africa at the same time. The fact that many of these species became extinct raises questions about the selective pressures that led to their demise and what ensured the adaptive success of human ancestors.

Robust Australopithecines from South Africa The first remains of robust species of australopithecine were found in South Africa, following the discovery of the Taung child. In addition to the Taung child and adult examples of *Australopithecus africanus*, the South African cave sites produced distinct hominin remains more recent in age (Broom 1938, 1949). These specimens have a large, broad face and enormous teeth and jaws. Because of this variation, Dart, Broom, and other researchers gave these discoveries a number of new genus and species designations, placing then in the genus *Paranthropus*. Although differences of opinion still exist about their exact relationship to other species, for convenience they are here referred to as *Australopithecus robustus* to distinguish them from the more delicate, or gracile, *A. africanus*.

South African examples of *A. robustus* are poorly dated, but available evidence suggests that they are more recent than *A. africanus*, perhaps dating between 2 million and 1 million years ago. *A. robustus* was not necessarily taller or heavier than *A. africanus*. In fact, the body sizes of the gracile *A. africanus* and robust forms may have been similar (McHenry 1988). Rather, the term *robust* refers to the distinctive features of the skull and heavy dentition of *A. robustus*. A particularly distinct feature found in *A. robustus* but absent in *A. africanus* is a sagittal crest, a bony ridge running along the top of the skull that is associated with the species massive chewing muscles. Collectively these features indicate that *A. robustus* likely relied heavily on a diet of tough, fibrous foods.

***Australopithecus boisei:* The "Nutcracker Man"** Following the initial discovery of hominin fossils in South Africa, many additional finds came to light. One of the most exciting of these, called *Australopithecus boisei*, was the first of many discoveries made in eastern Africa by paleoanthropologists Louis and Mary Leakey. *Australopithecus boisei* was found in the Olduvai Gorge, a 30-mile canyon stretching across the Serengeti Plain of Tanzania. In 1959, Mary Leakey recovered an almost complete fossil skull from the gorge. The find was a robust australopithecine, but a species that was even more robust than the examples known from South Africa. The teeth of *A. boisei* were distinctly hominin in form, but were much larger than those of any other hominin species, a feature that earned *A. boisei* the nickname "Nutcracker Man" (Leakey 1959).

Australopithecine skulls. The example at the left is a robust form; a gracile form is at right

At the time of its discovery in the 1950s, Zinj was a particularly exciting find because it increased the range and number of potential human ancestors that had existed, revealing the complex history of hominin evolution. However, what made the find especially notable was that it was the first early hominin find to be well dated using a numerical dating technique: potassium-argon. The earlier hominin fossil finds from South Africa had been difficult to date. Scientists could not precisely determine the conditions that formed the different fossil localities represented.

The South African cave deposits had been eroded and disturbed by nature, mixing fossils of varying ages. In contrast, the fossil deposits at Olduvai Gorge lie in undisturbed strata, occupying the same relative positions in which they were originally deposited. In addition, the area around Olduvai Gorge was volcanically active in the past. As a result, deposits of *tuff*, a porous rock formed from volcanic ash, created distinct layers within the Olduvai deposits. These volcanic layers can be dated by using the potassium-argon method (see Chapter 3). Potassium-argon dates on tuffs above and below Zinj placed the fossil's age at approximately 1.75 million years old. This date, and additional dates on other fossil finds, revolutionized paleoanthropology by finally providing numerical ages for specific fossil specimens.

***Australopithecus aethiopicus:* The "Black Skull"** The incomplete puzzle of hominin ancestry was filled in with one more piece in 1985, this one dug out of the fossil beds west of Lake Turkana, Kenya, at a fossil locality known as Lomekwi I. The find consists of the fragments of an australopithecine dating to approximately 2.5 million years ago. Because the fossil had been stained blue-black by manganese in the soil, it became known as the "Black Skull," or, by its Kenya National Museum catalogue number, KNM-WT 17000 (Walker et al. 1986). Another example of the same species may be represented by more incomplete remains found earlier in the Omo River valley of Ethiopia.

The Black Skull is a robust australopithecine, but of a type far more robust than *A. robustus* and *A. boisei*, which are more recent in age. It also has some features resembling the older australopithecines, such as *A. afarensis*, but absent in more recent robust australopithecines. For example, the cranium of the Black Skull is small, comparable in size and shape to that of the older *A. afarensis* fossils. The movement of the *A. aethiopicus* jaw is also similar to that of *A. afarensis*. Yet the face is large, prognathic, and very robust, boasting massive teeth and a pronounced sagittal crest. This suggests a different evolutionary lineage from the other robust australopithecines and, thus, presents a more complex picture of the hominin family tree. Because of its distinct combination of features, some researchers place it in a separate genus, *Paranthropus aethiopicus* (Stringer and Andrews 2005).

The Origins of Genus *Homo*

If the robust australopithecines are shirttail relations in the human family tree, what species present the most likely precursors of genus *Homo*? Our earliest ancestors are represented by a number of tantalizing finds that suggest the earliest members of our own species first emerged over 2 million years ago. The earliest known accepted representatives of the genus include two species, *Homo habilis* and *Homo rudolfensis*, distinguished from the australopithecines by their larger cranial capacity. The first representatives of these species came to light at Olduvai Gorge in the 1960s, with more recent discoveries coming from Koobi Fora, Kenya, (Simons 1989b; Leakey et al. 2012). The various *H. habilis* remains from Olduvai and Koobi Fora date from between 2.3 million and 1.4 million years ago, while the best dated example of *H. rudolfensis* dates to between 1.8 million and 1.9 million years ago. Hence, the temporal range of these hominins overlap with each other, as well as those of the robust australopithecines and the earliest *Homo erectus* finds, making it difficult to infer their evolutionary relationships. *Homo habilis* and *H. rudolfensis* may represent distinct evolutionary lineages separate from those leading to modern humans. Yet, their larger cranial capacity clearly separates them from the australopithecines.

***Homo habilis:* "The Handyman"** Fragmentary finds of *H. habilis* were first made by Louis and Mary Leakey at Olduvai Gorge in the 1960s. Between 1960 and 1964, the Leakeys and their colleagues excavated the fragmentary remains of approximately 20 fossil hominins (Leakey 1961). Some were clearly *Homo erectus* (discussed below);

others appeared comparable to the Zinj find. However, still other fossils pointed to the existence of a creature dating more than two million years old that was unlike any of the known australopithecines or more recent representatives of genus *Homo*. The distinguishing characteristic of the new species was its cranial capacity, which Louis Leakey estimated at close to 640 cc, significantly larger than that of any australopithecines, but still substantially smaller than that of *H. erectus*. The Leakeys named the creature *Homo habilis*, or "handyman," feeling that it was this species that must be responsible for the simple Oldowan stone tools that had been recovered at Olduvai Gorge. Oldowan tools, however, have been found in contexts predating the appearance of *H. habilis* in the fossil record and also in association with other hominin species. Hence, these earliest known representatives of genus *Homo* cannot be credited with the earliest known use of stone tools. Nonetheless, *H. habilis* remains notable for its larger cranial capacity, the hallmark of genus *Homo*.

Homo rudolfensis: KNM-ER 1470 The Leakeys' son, Richard, made a series of exciting discoveries at Koobi Fora on the eastern shores of Lake Turkana, Kenya. Excavations produced several specimens that have been classified as *Homo habilis*. Among the finds, however, was a relatively complete skull that has been classified with the new species name *Homo rudolfensis*. Discovered in 1972 by Bernard Ngene and dated between 1.8 million and 1.9 million years ago, the fossil is known by its Kenya National Museum catalogue number, KNM-ER 1470. The skull has a cranial capacity of 775 cc, at the upper range of the known *H. habilis* fossils. It also possesses a flatter and broader face with thickly enameled cheek teeth. On the basis of these differences, the 1470 skull and related finds have been designated as a different species *H. habilis*: *Homo rudolfensis* (Leakey et al 2012). Some researchers have, however, questioned this classification and so far no reliable postcranial remains have been found for *H. rudolfensis*. Thus, further evidence will be needed to determine the actual connection between *H. habilis* and *H. rudolfensis*.

Homo erectus

H. habilis and *Homo rudolfensis* are followed in the fossil record by *Homo erectus* (including finds labeled *H. ergaster*), which in turn is followed by *H. sapiens*, the species that encompasses modern humans. *Homo erectus* was a highly successful and widely dispersed species. Well-dated fossil finds identified as *H. erectus* range in age between 1.9 million and 140,000 years ago. However, dates obtained on *H. erectus* fossils and associated animal bones from the sites of Ngandong and Sambungmacan, Java, suggest that pockets of *H. erectus* populations may have existed as recently as 40,000 to 70,000 years ago, though the depositional histories of these fossil localities are uncertain and the direct dating of the fossils is problematic (Yokoyama et al. 2008). Fossil finds bearing *H. erectus* features have been recovered from Kenya, Tanzania, Zambia, Algeria, Morocco, Georgia in southeastern Europe, China, and Indonesia, indicating that the species had the widest distribution of any hominin species with the exception of *Homo sapiens*.

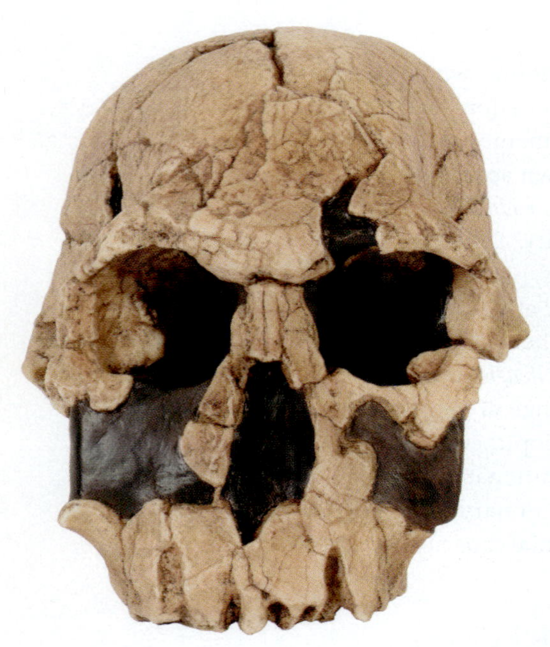

Homo rudolfensis, the KNM-ER 1470 skull. Found at Lake Turkana in 1972 it is one of the oldest representatives of genus Homo.

Many of the discoveries now regarded as representatives of *H. erectus* were initially known by a variety of other genus and species names, including *Pithecanthropus erectus* and *Sinanthropus pekinensis*. However, more recent consensus has recognized the majority of the variation represented in the different finds as within the range that occurs in a single species. Some of the examples of *H. erectus* share many similarities with modern humans, illustrating both the interrelatedness of the species with *H. sapiens* and the challenges of classification. Some researchers have argued that the finds possessing the more modern characteristics should be designated by a separate species name, *H. ergaster*, including very early finds from Africa such as the Turkana Boy. Other researchers have argued that some of more recent *H. erectus* fossils should simply be regarded as archaic *H. sapiens*.

Turkana Boy The oldest remains of *H. erectus* have been found in Africa. One of the most complete finds, known as "Turkana Boy," was recovered at the Nariokotome site near Lake Turkana in Kenya. This discovery consists of the relatively complete skeleton of an eight-year-old boy about 5 feet tall. The skeleton indicates that, below the neck, Turkana Boy was physically comparable to modern humans. The cranium has a brain capacity of about 900 cc, which falls into the range of other *H. erectus* finds (Stringer and Andrews 2005). More recently, fossils that may date from the same period as Nariokotome have been found outside Africa. For example, fossil evidence from Dmanisi in the southeastern European nation of Georgia has been dated at 1.7 million years ago (Balter and Gibbons 2000; Vekua et al. 2002). A relatively complete skull from Dmanisi indicates a brain size of only 600 cc and other characteristics, which overlap with those of the earlier hominin species *H. habilis or H. rudolfensis*. This suggests a possible transitional creature between earlier *Homo* and *H. erectus*.

Finds from Indonesia: Java Man The first examples of fossils now generally categorized as *H. erectus* were made in Asia, discovered in 1891 by the Dutch doctor Eugene Dubois. At the time, this was the first bona fide discovery of a pre-*Homo sapiens* hominin. Digging near Trinil in northern Java (an Indonesian island), Dubois found a leg bone, two molars, and the top of a hominin cranium. The leg was indistinguishable from that of a modern human, but the cranium was small and flat, and had heavy brow ridges compared with modern humans. Dubois named his find *Pithecanthropus erectus* ("erect ape-man"), but today the species is classified as *Homo erectus*.

Dubois (1894) viewed his find as a missing link between humans and modern apes, but this view betrayed faulty understanding of Darwin's theory of evolution. Darwin's "missing link" referred to a common ancestor of the human and ape lineages; he never proposed a direct link between modern humans and apes, which represent the end points of distinct evolutionary lines. Other scientists correctly placed *Pithecanthropus* as an intermediary form on the evolutionary track between *Homo sapiens* and an earlier hominin ancestor.

Other *Homo erectus* Finds Following Dubois' discoveries, information about similar creatures accumulated at an increasing rate during the first decades of the twentieth century. Many of the most important finds came from Zhoukoudian, about 30 miles southwest of Beijing (then spelled Peking in English transliteration), China. In 1929, a team of researchers led by Chinese geologist W. C. Pei found a skull embedded in limestone during an excavation. Pei showed the skull to Davidson Black, a Canadian anatomist, who concluded that the skull represented an early form of human. Black labeled the creature *Sinanthropus pekinensis*, commonly known as "Peking Man."

In addition to more finds in China, discoveries were made in other areas. Forty years after Dubois' excavations in Java, anthropologist G. H. R. Koenigswald uncovered the remains of comparable early hominins in the same area. Initially, scientists, working with few finds and lacking comparative specimens, speculated that each of these discoveries constituted a new evolutionary branch. We now know that, despite their disparate locations, these early discoveries are all representatives of a single genus and species, today classified as *Homo erectus*. In many respects, *Homo erectus* is identical to modern humans, although the postcranial skeleton is generally heavier and more robust. What most sets this species apart from *Homo sapiens* is the cranium, which lacks the high, vaulted appearance of that of modern humans and has a smaller average brain capacity.

Interpreting the Fossil Record

4.3 Discuss the challenges paleoanthropologists face in interpreting the fossil record and explain why their interpretations sometimes change.

Several sources of evidence indicate that the earliest human ancestors evolved in Africa. The oldest hominin species, as well as the earliest fossil evidence for anatomically modern humans, are from Africa. Climatic conditions on the African continent during the Pliocene and Pleistocene were warm, and they would have been well suited to evolving hominins. Our closest genetic relatives, the chimpanzee and gorilla, also come from Africa, suggesting a large primate genetic pool. Finally, the earliest stone tools, represented by the Oldowan tradition, are also known to be from Africa.

While the geographical origins of the hominins may be somewhat clear, it is more challenging to chart the hominin family tree. As illustrated in the preceding discussion of fossil finds, as paleoanthropologists have unearthed increasing numbers of early hominin fossils their interpretations of hominin evolution have become increasingly complex. Initially, scientists drew a straight evolutionary line from *Australopithecus africanus* to *Homo erectus* and on to *Homo sapiens*. But a number of finds clearly demonstrate that in several instances more than one species of hominin roamed the Earth at the same time. How were these different species related, and how do they relate to the evolution of *Homo sapiens*?

Fundamental to tracing hominin evolution is the question of which features should be used to classify genera and species. Because the size and complexity of the brain are the most distinctive physical characteristics of modern humans, increasing cranial capacity is clearly an important feature in examining the evolution of genus *Homo*. Yet, the range of cranial capacities overlaps among hominins, making it difficult to use this as the basis for distinguishing discrete species (Armelagous and van Gerven 2003; Tattersall 1986). Study of modern primate species—including humans—demonstrates that there is, in fact, a great deal of variation within species in features such as cranial capacity, body size, and skeletal structure (Bower 1990).

In the preceding discussion of the fossil evidence for hominin evolution, the names designating specific genera and species are intended to provide a simplified overview of some of the principal discoveries. The names used here are widely accepted appellations used by paleoanthropologists, but they are not universally agreed on. Perspectives of hominin classification lie between two extremes. Some scientists, who can be called *splitters*, argue that some species designations do not reflect all the species represented. For instance, some researchers have argued that the *A. afarensis* finds from Hadar do not constitute a single, sexually dimorphic species, but at least two distinct species. Similar concerns about the differences between the early and late examples of *H. erectus* have led to the reclassification of some of the former as *H. ergaster*. Some researchers have called for further divisions.

At the opposite extreme from the splitters are the *lumpers*, who maintain that current taxonomic designations place too much emphasis on differences among individuals and do not sufficiently consider the variation that might be expected within species. This position is best advocated by C. Loring Brace (Brace and Montagu 1965; Brace 1967, 1989). Brace asserts that the information available on *Homo habilis*, *A. afarensis*, and *A. aethiopicus* is insufficient to categorize each as a distinct species, and he advocates including them with other genus and species. For example, *H. habilis*, *H. ergaster*, and other finds might all be included with *Homo erectus*.

At this point, it is useful to underscore that the different perspectives presented by lumpers and splitters include a great deal of consensus about the differences present in the individual fossil finds. The divergence in opinion is about what the differences in the fossil finds imply about taxonomic classification and the process of speciation. Unfortunately, the ultimate defining aspect of a species, the ability to interbreed, is not something that can be assessed on the basis of fossil evidence.

Changing Views

Many interpretations of hominin evolution have been advanced through the years. Some of these, explored in the following section, are illustrated in Figures 4.3. When they were proposed, they represented valid attempts to explain the available fossil evidence. Like all sciences, paleoanthropology proceeds by formulating hypotheses and then testing them against empirical data. In contrast to most sciences, however, the data from the fossil record cannot be obtained by laboratory experiments. Rather, paleoanthropologists must await the next unpredictable fossil find. As new evidence is uncovered, new hypotheses are developed, and old ones are modified or discarded. As the number of fossil species represented has increased and our understanding of the fossil record has become more refined, the interpretations have had to account for more variation and, thus, have become increasingly complex (see Figures 4.3 and 4.4).

Figure 4.3 Changing interpretations of hominin evolution: (a) Various theories during the 1960s and 1970s placed *A. africanus* in a position ancestral to *Homo* or to both *Homo* and later australopithecines. The robust australopithecines were placed on their own side branch; (b) In 1979, Johanson and White named a new species, *A. afarensis*, which they placed at the base of the hominin family tree leading to both *Australopithecus* and *Homo. A. africanus* was moved to a side branch leading to the robust australopithecines; (c) In 1985, the discovery of *A. aethiopicus* made the picture more complex, suggesting that all of the australopithecines cannot be located on a single side branch. More recent discoveries have led to further revision (see Figure 4.4).

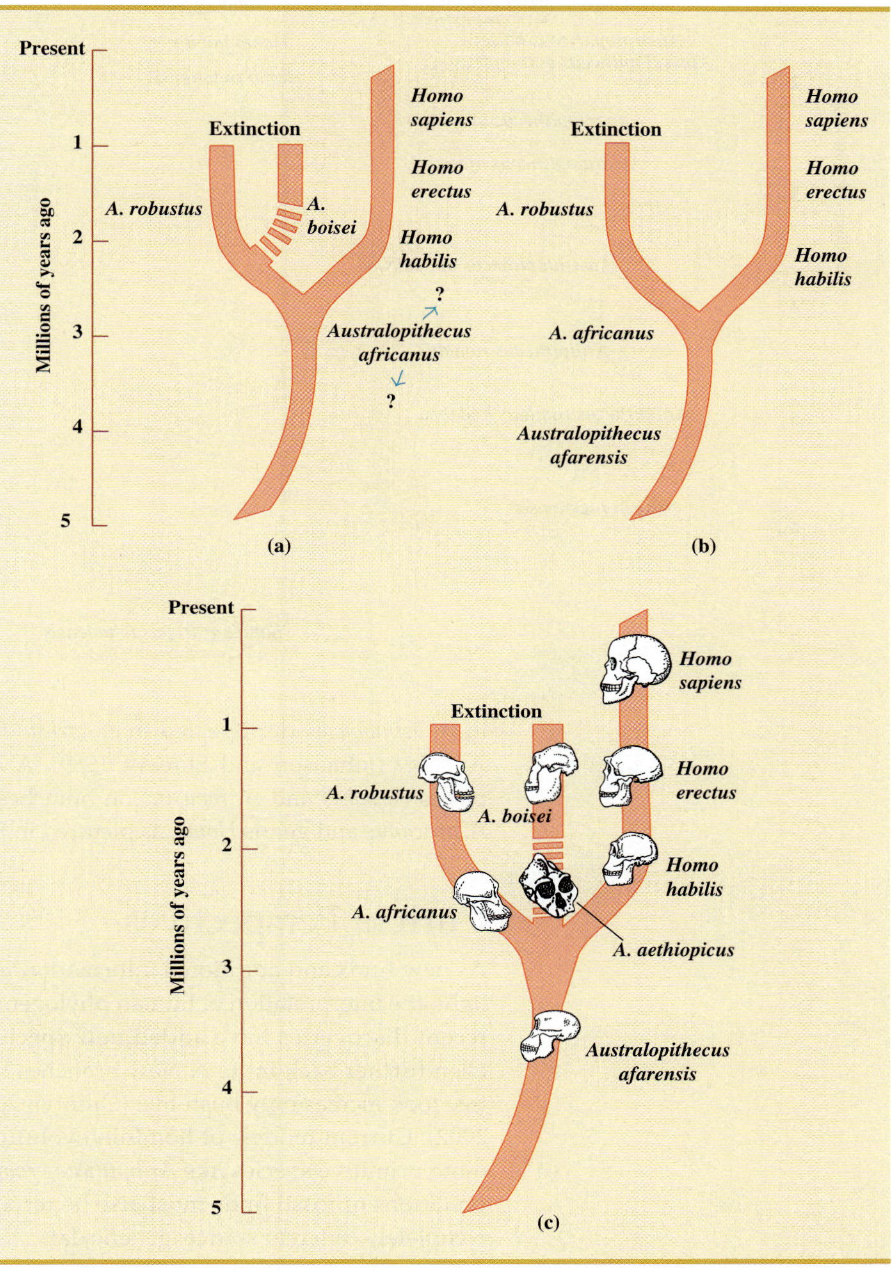

A number of theories propounded in the 1960s and 1970s placed *A. africanus* at the base of the hominin family tree, as illustrated in Figure 4.3(a). These interpretations of evolution basically held that hominins developed along two main branches. As the most sophisticated of the australopithecines, *A. africanus* was considered the most likely to have given rise to the genus *Homo* and was, therefore, placed at the bottom of the branch leading to *Homo habilis*, *Homo erectus*, and ultimately *Homo sapiens*. The robust australopithecines (including various species sometimes classified in genus *Paranthropus*) occupied their own branch, eventually becoming extinct around 1 million years ago. Because of their large teeth and specialized chewing apparatus, the robust australopithecines were not viewed as directly ancestral to *Homo*.

Following the discovery of Lucy and other *A. afarensis* fossils at Hadar in the 1970s, Donald Johanson and Timothy White proposed a new interpretation of hominin evolution, which is illustrated in Figure 4.3(b). Variations of this interpretation were incorporated into many models in the following decade. Johanson and White hypothesized that the genus *Australopithecus* began with *A. afarensis*, dated at about 4 million to 3 million years ago. They contended that *A. afarensis* was the common ancestor of all

Figure 4.4 More recent discoveries have extended the hominin family tree further back in time. New branches have also been added, making the hominin family tree look more like a bush.

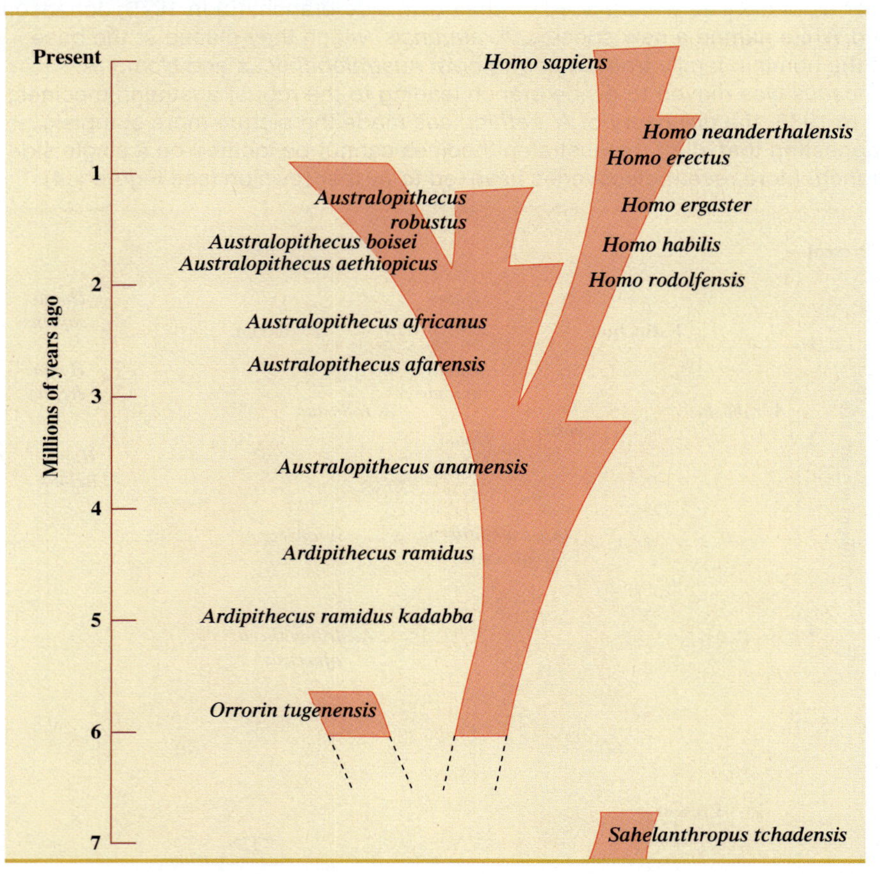

subsequent hominin species. In their scheme, one of the branches from *A. afarensis* leads to *A. africanus* and *A. robustus*. The other major branch leads toward the evolution of *Homo habilis* and succeeding species of genus *Homo*, culminating in modern *Homo sapiens* (Johanson and White 1979). Many paleoanthropologists concurred with this model of hominin evolution until the mid-1980s.

Revised Interpretations Interpretations of the late 1980s and 1990s had to grapple with a new spate of discoveries. With the discovery of the Black Skull in 1985, a relatively neat picture of human evolution grew more clouded and more complex. Johanson and White had placed *A. boisei* at the end of the extinct line of australopithecines, a sort of hyper-robust form of *A. robustus* (Figure 4.3b). This was a logical conclusion, given the available fossil evidence at the time. Unfortunately, *A. aethiopicus* does not fit into this neat picture. It has certain characteristics found in *A. boisei* but not in *A. africanus* and *A. robustus*, yet *A. aethiopicus* is as old as *A. africanus*. Scientists wishing to insert the Black Skull into the Johanson and White evolutionary tree would be hard pressed to explain how certain features appeared in *A. aethiopicus*, disappeared in *A. africanus* and *A. robustus*, and then reappeared in *A. boisei* (Johanson and Shreeve 1989). A more logical and workable interpretation places *A. boisei* and *A. robustus* on branches of their own. Other limbs would lead to *A. africanus* and genus *Homo*, as pictured in Figure 4.3(c).

Current Perspectives

As new finds and additional information relevant to hominin ancestry have come to light, the interpretation of human phylogeny has become ever more challenging. More recent discoveries have added new species and extended the hominin family tree even further back in time. New branches have also been added, making our family tree look increasingly bush-like (Quintyn 2009; White 1995; Wolpoff et al. 2006; Wood 2002). Current models of hominin evolution must now take into account older and more primitive species like *Ardipithecus ramidus* and *Australopithecus anamensis*. Interpretations of fossil finds must also be reconciled with increasing information from a completely different source: genetic data. As discussed later, study of the genetic relatedness of living primate species has implications for both the classification of hominin finds and the interpretation their evolutionary history.

Despite the seemingly confusing array of interpretations, the diversity of finds uncovered provides insight into human origins. While a number of possible hominin ancestors may be represented, the varied fossil finds are nonetheless consistent with a model of human phylogeny that traces the evolution of genus *Homo* from small-brained bipedal apes. No discoveries, for example, have revealed the presence of species with cranial capacities comparable to modern humans living 6 million years ago.

Some additional general observations regarding hominin evolution can also be noted. While species such as *Ardipithecus ramidus* may or may not be the ancestors of later australopithecines, they provide an indication of the types of features and range of species present 4 million to 6 million years ago, from which latter species may have emerged. These early species in the fossil record are followed by the earliest australopithecines, dating just over 4 million years ago to 3 million years ago. They include *A. afarensis* (typified by Lucy) and *A. anamensis*. The early australopithecines are clearly bipedal creatures, but have small brains and prognathic faces. Occurring more recently in the fossil record are more specialized, derived australopithecine species dating roughly between 2.5 million and 1 million years ago; they are known from finds in both east and southern Africa. These include the robust australopithecines, sometimes classified as *Paranthropus*. They have been divided into a number of species, of which there are at least three: *A. aethiopicus*, *A. robustus*, and *A. boisei*. They are characterized by specialized features, such as broad faces, enormous teeth and jaws, and sagittal crests that are associated with massive chewing muscles. Importantly, they do not display an increase in cranial capacity compared to the earlier australopithecines. These features suggest that the robust australopithecines represent a specialized adaptation that makes them unlikely candidates for human ancestors.

Early representatives of the genus *Homo* appear in the fossil record at the same time as the robust australopithecines and, thus, coexisted with them. Most of the known specimens (*H. habilis* and *Homo rudolfensis*) are from East Africa, but possible representatives have also been found in South Africa. This group of fossils has a number of important characteristics—including larger cranial capacity, change in the shape of the cranium, and smaller teeth—that place them as intermediaries between earlier australopithecines and the large-brained *Homo erectus*.

Missing Pieces in the Fossil Record All of the preceding views of hominin evolution are based on excavated fossils. Part of the problem with these interpretations—and the continuing need for revision—lies in the fact that our perception of the fossil record is woefully incomplete. The currently known fossils do not begin to represent the extent and diversity of extinct species. It has been estimated that less than three percent of the primate species that once roamed the Earth have been recognized in the fossil record (Martin 1990). Some scholars have long contended that australopithecines like Lucy emerged after the split between the *Australopithecus* and *Homo* lineages. In other words, the australopithecines represent a separate hominin branch, and the early part of the *Homo* lineage is still poorly known (Shipman 1986a). Given the fact that fossils of hominins dating earlier than 4 million years ago are fragmentary and their ancestry uncertain, any number of scenarios might be posited but cannot currently be evaluated because of the lack of fossil remains.

It is likely that future discoveries will continue to extend the human lineage further back in time and produce an increasingly "bushy" hominin family tree, and models of hominin lineages will continue to be revised. Further research may also lead the search for human ancestry in entirely new directions. This perspective recognizes the inadequacy of the fossil record and the incomplete nature of the available data. Of course, it also lacks explanatory value and, as a result, is a somewhat unsatisfactory conclusion. Despite the limited information, the majority of paleoanthropologists prefer to speculate on the potential relationships of the known fossil species. These reconstructions allow us to think about how the human species may have emerged. While debate regarding interpretation of individual finds and their place in human ancestry will continue, new information is gradually providing greater insight.

Genetic Differences and Hominin Evolution

The preceding discussion of hominin phylogeny has focused on information gleaned from the fossil record—actual traces of early hominins recovered from the ground. During the past several decades, some researchers have increasingly approached the study of human evolution from a completely different direction. As highlighted in the box "What's in a Name?", scientists have studied the similarities and differences in chromosomes and DNA sequencing of living primates and determined the genetic relatedness of individual species. Genetic information has shed new light on hominin evolution, aiding in both the formulation of new hypotheses and their evaluation.

The genetic data on living primates has led to a reassessment of the way in which both living and fossil species are classified. Scientists traditionally placed humans and their immediate ancestors in the family Hominidea—the hominids—because of their upright posture, distinctive appearance, and unique behavioral adaptations. The so-called "Great Apes," including chimpanzees, gorillas and orangutans, were placed in the separate family of Pongidae. However, comparing genetic data from modern humans and nonhuman primates, researchers have demonstrated that the base pairs in the DNA sequences of chimpanzees and humans are 95 percent the same (Britten 2002). There is slightly more distance between humans and gorillas, but genetically the similarities between the two species still approaches 100 percent. This similarity in genetic code indicates a closer evolutionary relationship among chimpanzees, gorillas and humans than there is between any of these species and any of the other primates, including the orangutan. Consequently, taxonomic classification has been revised. Family *Hominidea* (the hominids) now includes both subfamily *Ponginae*, consisting of the orangutan, and subfamily *Homininae*, including the chimpanzee, gorilla and humans (respectively referred to as the tribes *Panini*, *Gorillini*, and *Hominini*). This classification more accurately reflects the genetic relatedness of the different species. Yet, it is somewhat confusing as previously used terms have different meanings.

Drawing upon the genetic data from living primates, researchers have gone a step further and attempted to infer the amount of time it took for evolution to produce the amount of genetic distance between various species. This is based on determining the rate at which mutation and, ultimately, the process of speciation takes place. Genetic research suggests the separation of the human and chimpanzee lineages approximately 5 million to 6 million years ago (Kumar et al. 2005; Yang 2002). The genetic information, therefore, would appear to complement the fossil evidence, which provides evidence of species that lived near the time of the divergence of chimpanzees and humans (*Ardipithecus ramidus* and *kadabba*).

Genetic data provides new and, importantly, independent data that can be used to assess the relative genetic distance between different primate species and the possible times of their evolutionary divergence. Researchers have also used DNA to examine the origins of modern humans and their dispersal out of Africa, as well as the relationship of Neandertals to modern humans (discussed below in "Neandertals and Modern Humans" and "The Denisovians"). Yet, genetic data provides no clues to how ancestral hominins adapted to different environments, their feeding habits, their geographic range, their lifeways, or any of the myriad other questions that concern paleoanthropology. Clues to human origins, therefore, will continue to also depend upon discoveries pried from the fossil record.

From *Homo erectus* to *Homo sapiens*

4.4 Describe and discuss the different models for the emergence of anatomically modern humans.

Scientists cannot pinpoint which selective pressures prompted *H. erectus* to evolve into *H. sapiens*. Fossils of *H. erectus* (including finds designated *H. ergaster*) range in age from 1.9 million to less than 140,000 years old. The longevity of the species is a testament to how well *H. erectus* adapted to different environmental conditions, having ranged across the diverse climates from Africa and southern Europe to Asia. Presumably,

H. sapiens must have had some adaptive advantage over earlier hominin species, but no consensus has emerged about what specific selective pressures were involved. Among the physical changes found in *H. sapiens* are a larger brain and full speech capabilities, which undoubtedly sparked concomitant behavioral consequences. Many of the distinctive characteristics seen in *H. sapiens* stem from cultural factors as well. As will be discussed in the "Life and Times of Genus *Homo*" below (pages 111–117), *H. erectus* made increasing use of socially learned technology to interact with and control the environment. This trend intensifies in later human populations.

Many hominin remains from the period between 400,000 and 200,000 years ago are difficult to classify because they exhibit physical traits characteristic of both *H. erectus* and *H. sapiens*. These hominins, which can be alternately viewed as either advanced *H. erectus* or early *H. sapiens*, can be referred to as **transitional forms**. The discovery of finds that do not fit neatly into taxonomic categories is not surprising. Related species have many similar characteristics that reflect their evolutionary relationships. Transitional forms illustrate these relationships and offer physical evidence of the process of speciation.

Transitional Forms

In examining the transition from *H. erectus* to *H. sapiens*, we need to cast a critical eye on the physical characteristics that distinguish the two species. *Homo erectus* shares many physical features with modern humans; in fact, the postcranial skeletons are essentially the same, except for the generally heavier, more massive structure of *H. erectus* bones. The major differences between the two species appear in the skull. The skulls of *Homo sapiens* are high and vaulted, providing a large cranial capacity. In contrast, the skulls of *H. erectus* feature a **postorbital constriction**, meaning that the front portion of the skull narrows behind the eye sockets and the high forehead of *H. sapiens* is absent. Lacking the high vaulted cranium of *H. sapiens*, the skull of *H. erectus* is widest toward the base.

Other distinctive characteristics of *H. erectus* make scientists believe that these creatures had strong jaw and neck muscles. These traits include a slight ridge at the back of the skull and heavy eyebrow ridges, structural features that have disappeared in modern humans. *Homo erectus* also exhibits a *prognathic* face, the nose and teeth extending toward the front. This is an attribute of early hominins and living, nonhuman primates that is absent in *H. sapiens*. The anterior teeth of *H. erectus* are relatively small compared with those of earlier *Homo* species, but large in comparison to those of modern humans.

Transitional forms bearing various combinations of *H. erectus* and *H. sapiens* features have been discovered in Europe, Asia, and Africa. The mosaic of physical characteristics found in some specimens has sparked debate over how to designate species most appropriately. This debate can be illustrated by the Petralona cranium, uncovered in eastern Greece in 1960 (Day 1986). Scientists have debated the age of the find (claims ranging from 1 million years old to 120,000 have been made), yet the consensus leans toward an age of approximately 350,000 years old. The species designation of this fossil has also been widely contested. The Petralona cranium exhibits many of the classic *H. erectus* characteristics, including thick bones, pronounced brow ridges, and a low cranial vault. However, the cranial capacity is estimated at approximately 1,200 cc, placing it at the uppermost limits of *H. erectus* and within the lower range of the more recent species of genus *Homo*, including both *H. neanderthalensis* and *H. sapiens*.

The Evolution of *Homo sapiens*

Although researchers generally agree that *H. erectus* evolved into *H. sapiens*, there is substantial disagreement about how, where, and when this transition occurred. Early interpretations were based on limited information and often emphasized the uniqueness of individual finds. Currently, there is growing consensus that anatomically modern humans first evolved in Africa and then spread out to other world areas.

A variety of competing interpretations continue to be evaluated. For the purposes of this discussion, two contrasting models are presented: the Multiregional Evolutionary Model and the Replacement Model. Supporting evidence for each of these perspectives has been presented, and the varied models each have their supporters. A third set of interpretations, consisting of Hybridization and Assimilation Models, which attempt to reconcile the two opposing extremes in various ways have also been presented.

Multiregional Evolutionary Model As noted earlier, *Homo erectus* has the widest distribution of any hominin species other than modern humans. According to the **multiregional evolutionary model** of modern human origins, the gradual evolution of *H. erectus* into archaic *H. sapiens* and, finally, modern *H. sapiens* took place concurrently in the various parts of Asia, Africa, and Europe over the past 2.5 million years (as illustrated in Figure 4.5a). In this view, the transition from *H. erectus* to *H. sapiens* was within a single human species. Through natural selective pressures and genetic differences, local *H. erectus* populations developed particular traits that varied from region to region; consequently the variation in physical characteristics noted in modern human populations is deeply rooted in the past (Wolpoff and Caspari 1997). Early variations of this model initially proposed in the early twentieth century, suggested the parallel evolution of *H. sapiens* in different regions. More recent perspectives, however, underscored that *gene flow*—the widespread sharing of genes through interbreeding—between populations in the different regions prevented the evolution of distinct species. The emergence of *H. sapiens* was, therefore, a widespread phenomenon, although different regional populations continued to exhibit distinctive features.

Working from the multiregional evolutionary model, we would expect to see a great deal of regional genetic continuity, meaning that the fossil finds from a particular geographic area should display similarities from the earliest representatives of *H. erectus* to those of modern populations. Supporters of this model argue that such continuities do indeed exist. For example, skeletal remains of early *H. sapiens* from different regions of China, North Africa, and Europe resemble modern populations in those areas in some respects (Bednarik 2011; Smith 1984; Thorne and Wolpoff 1992; Wolpoff and Caspari 2002). Certain distinctive features can be identified in the cranium, dentition, jaws, and particular features of the postcranial skeleton. Researchers favoring this interpretation further note regional continuity in the archaeological records of different world areas.

Replacement Model The **replacement model** or the "recent African origin of modern humans model" has increasingly garnered support among researchers (Liu et al. 2006; Stringer 1985; Stringer and Andrews 2005). It holds that *H. sapiens* evolved in one area of the world first (Africa) and migrated to other regions, as illustrated in Figure 4.5b. It is called the replacement model because it assumes that *H. sapiens* were contemporaries of the earlier *H. erectus* but eventually replaced them without significant interbreeding. According to the replacement hypothesis, *H. sapiens* populations all descended from a single common ancestral group. Thus, although the modern and archaic species overlapped in their spans on Earth, they were highly distinctive, genetically different evolutionary lineages. Consequently, there is minimal diversity among modern humans and the regional differences in modern human populations are relatively recent developments.

Some researchers believe that fossil evidence supporting the replacement hypothesis may be found in the homeland of all hominins: Africa. The earliest known examples of anatomically modern *H. sapiens* come from Ethiopian sites dating 150,000 to 190,000 years ago (McDougall et al. 2005; White et al. 2003). In the replacement view, these remains are evidence of the earliest representatives of modern *H. sapiens*, the species first evolving in Africa and then spreading out of Africa to other areas.

Figure 4.5 Three different interpretations of the emergence of *H. sapiens*. The multiregional evolutionary model (a) suggests regional continuity and the gradual evolution of all *H. erectus* and archaic *H. sapiens* populations into modern humans, gene flow between populations (here represented by horizontal arrows) preventing the emergence of distinct species. In contrast, supporters of the replacement model (b) see modern humans as evolving in Africa and spreading out, replacing earlier hominin populations. Various hybridization and assimilation models (c) allow for varying degrees of gene flow between *Homo sapiens* and earlier populations of archaic *H. sapiens* via gene flow or genetic admixture.

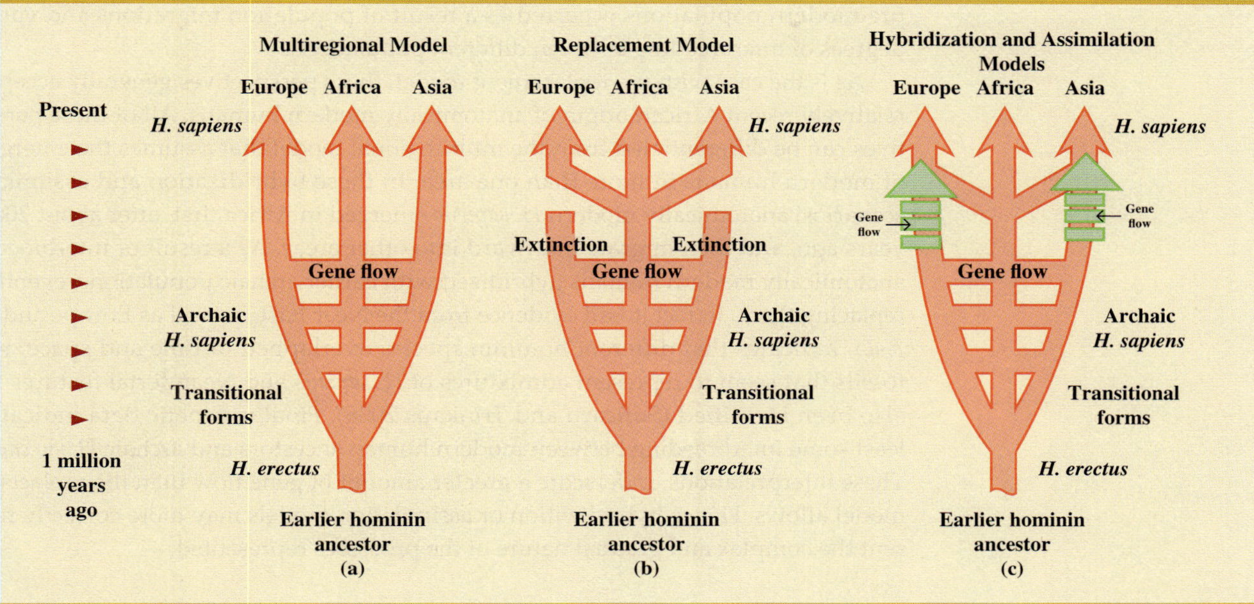

While the preceding scenario remains plausible, the evidence is not without limitations. The fossil evidence from Africa remains fragmentary and a fuller understanding of the distribution of early modern humans is desirable. Genetic data also provides challenges to this perspective. The replacement model was originally given a great deal of support by studies of mitochondrial DNA in modern humans undertaken in the 1980s, which suggested that the maternal line of all living women can be traced to a single female living in Africa about 200,000 years ago. This would clearly support a recent African origin of modern humans. While additional genetic data support an African origin, studies have also suggested that there was at least some interbreeding between anatomically modern *H. sapiens* and earlier archaic species, such as the Neandertals (discussed later), affording a more complex picture of our genetic history.

Hybridization and Assimilation Models It is possible, perhaps likely, that neither of the preceding models for the emergence of anatomically modern humans is completely correct. Neither fully accounts for all of the fossil and genetic evidence. The processes involved in the emergence of modern humans were likely more complex and encompassed more variables than can be neatly wrapped up in either of the two overarching perspectives (Gunz et al. 2009; Lahr and Foley 1994; Stringer 2001). Emergent human populations may have incorporated a great deal of physical diversity—as well as behavioral, social, and linguistic differences. Further, it is unlikely that migrations (out of Africa or elsewhere) were unidirectional affairs involving the movement of homogeneous populations. Many different migrations via different routes, recolonization of previously occupied territories, and gene flow with other populations were more probable. Understanding of such variables provides insight into not only the emergence of modern humans, but also the source of the diversity underlying present-day populations.

A number of more recent interpretations of modern human origins have attempted to reconcile the conflicting aspects of the multiregional and replacement models, as well as the varied factors noted above (Gibbons 2011). These have been referred to by a variety of names. The proposed interpretations can, however, be collectively referred to as **hybridization** and **assimilation models** in that they allow for varying degrees of gene flow between *H. sapiens* and earlier populations of archaic *H. sapiens*. Gene flow or genetic admixture between anatomically modern humans and indigenous pre-modern populations occurred as a result of population migrations and varying degrees of interbreeding between different populations.

As is the case with the replacement model, these perspectives generally accept the relatively recent African origin of anatomically modern humans. All of these perspectives can be differentiated from the multiregional model that assumes the emergence of modern humans in more than one area. In these hybridization and assimilation scenarios, anatomically modern *H. sapiens* emerged in Africa first, after about 200,000 years ago, and then migrated outward into other areas. As a result of interbreeding, anatomically modern humans hybridized with earlier archaic populations, eventually replacing them. In fact, fossil evidence from the Near East, as well as Europe and East Asia, indicates that different hominin species overlapped in time and space, while fossils that seem to represent admixtures of *H. sapiens* and Neandertal features have also been identified (Soficaru and Trinkaus 2006). Finally, genetic data indicates at least some interbreeding between modern human ancestors and archaic *Homo sapiens*. These interpretations underscore a greater amount of gene flow than the replacement model allows. Hence hybridization or assimilation models may more correctly represent the complex and gradual nature of the processes represented.

Genetic Data and Modern Human Origins

4.5 Describe how new genomic research and molecular dating have helped anthropologists interpret human evolution.

As discussed previously with regard to the tracing of primate and earlier hominin ancestry, researchers have also brought biochemical techniques to bear on the question of modern human origins. The genetic research also stands as a good example of the degree of scrutiny—and debate—that new theories attract and the importance of relying on different sources of data (Relethford 2003).

The genetic makeup of modern humans provides a record of the genetic history of our species. When individuals from different groups interbreed, the offspring's DNA is provided by each of the parents (see discussion of DNA in Chapter 2). This admixture of DNA is subsequently passed down through the following generations, all the way to modern humans. The genetic data obtained have increasingly proven consistent with an African origin of *H. sapiens* (Deshpande et al. 2009). Yet in some cases, different kinds of genetic data have been seen as consistent with both the replacement and multiregional models (Ayala 1995; Frayer et al. 1993; Harding et al. 1997; Harris and Hey 1999).

Human genetic variation reflects geographical origins: individuals from one region will, generally, be more genetically similar than individuals from a distant region (see the box on Race and Genetics: The Human Genome Project in Chapter 5). Yet, the study of the genetic makeup of modern humans, as well as the study of DNA extracted from the fossilized bones of archaic humans such as the Neandertals and densovians (discussed below) also provides a record of the complexity of gene flow in ancient populations; populations were never "pure" in a genetic sense. Study of genetic material has also provided clues to gene flow over the more recent past. For example, it may provide a record of Arab and trans-Atlantic slave trades (Hellenthal et al. 2014). Two specific types of genetic markers have been examined with specific regard to the emergence of modern humans: mitochondrial DNA and Y-chromosomal DNA. These are notable in reflecting, respectively, female and male genetic ancestry.

Mitochondrial Eve

Among the genetic studies that have received the most popular media attention is the use of mitochondrial DNA (mtDNA) from modern humans to understand human origins. Working at the University of California, Berkeley in the 1980s, a team of researchers studied the mitochondrial DNA of modern women (Cann et al. 1987; Stoneking et al. 1987; Wilson and Cann 1992). On the basis of the studies, which were widely publicized, they argued that modern humanity could be traced back to a single African female who lived between 200,000 and 130,000 years ago (popularly referred to in the media as "Eve"). This method provided important insights, but interpretation of the data is challenging and remains a source of debate.

The strength of the technique lies in the distinctive characteristics of mtDNA. This type of DNA is located in the portion of the cell that helps convert cellular material into the energy needed for cellular activity. In contrast to nuclear DNA (see Chapter 2), mtDNA is not carried by the (male) sperm when it fertilizes the egg. The genetic code embedded in mtDNA, therefore, is passed on only through the female. Thus, individuals' mtDNA is not altered by recombination during reproduction. Each of us inherits this type of DNA from our mother, our mother's mother, and so on, along a single, maternal genealogical line. The variation present in human female mtDNA is the result of accumulated mutations that have occurred. By determining the rate at which mutations have occurred, the time at which the human lineage diverged from that of earlier human ancestors can be determined. The greater amount of mutation present, the greater amount of time was needed for them to accumulate.

The study by the Berkeley team focused on the mtDNA of 147 women from Africa, Asia, Europe, Australia, and New Guinea (Cann et al. 1987). The accumulation of random mutations in the different populations displayed distinctive patterns. Significantly, the mtDNA of the African women tended to be more diverse, or heterogeneous, suggesting that mutations present had a long time to accumulate. In other populations, the mtDNA was more uniform, or homogeneous, a sign that they had not had as much time to accumulate mutations. Assuming a constant mutation rate, the researchers inferred a maternal line in Africa dating back to between 200,000 and 130,000 years ago. Linking these data to the replacement model of human origins, they further suggested that these anatomically modern humans moved out of Africa, replacing the earlier *H. erectus* populations throughout the world.

Mitochondrial DNA studies provide tantalizing clues to modern human origins. There is still, however, debate about the methods used and the interpretation of the results obtained (Cyran and Kimmel 2010; Mountain 1998; Templeton 1993, 2002). More recent research has demonstrated that mutation rates across the mitochondrial genome vary and that the mutation rate has also varied through time (Henn et al. 2009; Ho et al. 2005; Howell et al. 2003; Soares et al. 2010). Despite the vibrant debate and media hype that at times characterized the mtDNA data, the projected age of a shared female ancestor in the different studies is broadly similar, insofar as they have yielded estimates ranging from 100,000 to 200,000 years ago. The mtDNA data also favors the replacement model, with Africa as the ultimate place of origin of later anatomically human populations. Yet here the likely complexity of the movement of early human populations out of Africa, and their interactions with early hominin populations should again be underscored.

Paternal Genetic Ancestry

Researchers have also studied paternal genetic ancestry through information encoded on the Y chromosome. Humans have two types of sex chromosomes: X and Y. Females have two X chromosomes, while males have an X and a Y. A child's gender depends on whether a father's sperm contains an X or Y chromosome, which combines with an X chromosome from the mother during reproduction (see Chapter 2). Consequently, studies of Y chromosomes provide a genetic record of paternal ancestry. As in the case of mtDNA, the mutation rate of Y chromosomes calculated on the basis of genetic data from modern humans has been used to infer the time when modern humans emerged, as well as the relatedness of different human populations.

Y-chromosomal Adam is the popular name given to the most recent common patrilineal ancestor of all living humans. The mutation rate in Y chromosomes is quite high making assessment of the age of this patrilineal ancestor challenging. Estimates have varied in different studies, some contrasting with the estimated reached in mtDNA studies (Hammer et al. 1998; Hammer and Zegura 2002). However, more recent calibrations of both the mtDNA data and the Y-chromosome data have yielded relatively consistent results (Poznik et al. 2013). Although the estimates of Y-chromosomal Adam range from 100,000 to 200,000 years old, the studies are consistent with the mtDNA data that suggest a relatively recent African origin for modern humans. However, the data also suggest movement back into Africa following the initial expansion of modern humans out of Africa.

Archaic and Anatomically Modern *Homo sapiens*

4.6 Discuss the different theories regarding the relationship of *Homo sapiens neanderthalensis* and *Homo sapiens*.

Although debate continues over the classification of certain hominins dating between 200,000 and 400,000 years ago, there is much more agreement over later finds. For the most part, all hominin fossils dating to the last 200,000 years are classified as *H. sapiens*.

This is not to say that *H. sapiens* populations of 200,000 years ago were identical to modern humans, or that all of the finds represented possess the same physical characteristics. However, the distinctive features noted are all considered within the range of variation found within a single species. To simplify our discussion, hominins of the last 200,000 years can be divided into two categories: **archaic *Homo sapiens*** and **anatomically modern *Homo sapiens***. Archaic *H. sapiens* can be viewed as transitional forms on the evolutionary lineage extending from *H. erectus* to modern *H. sapiens*, possessing features characteristics of both species. Indeed, some finds dating before 200,000 years ago, including the Petralona cranium noted above, have been labeled archaic *H. sapiens*. At the other extreme, hominin fossils with archaic *H. sapiens* features overlap with those of anatomically modern *Homo sapiens*, finds that possess all of the characteristics found in modern humans.

Generally, anatomically modern humans are more delicate than *Homo erectus* and archaic examples of *Homo sapiens*. However, modern humans encompass a great deal of variation and, in some cases, their postcranial anatomy may be quite robust. The major distinguishing features between archaic *Homo sapiens* and anatomically modern *Homo sapiens* are in the skull. In contrast to archaic specimens, anatomically modern *Homo sapiens* have a pronounced forehead, the skull extending upward rather than back from the eyes. The teeth are also somewhat smaller, resulting in a more prominent chin. The earliest examples of anatomically modern humans are known from African finds dating between 190,000 and 160,000 years ago, with the first examples dating as recently as 40,000 years ago in other regions. The oldest African finds consist of two partial skulls and postcranial bones from Omo, Ethiopia, dated to 195,000 years ago. Other early examples are represented by slightly more complete finds excavated at Herto in Ethiopia's Afar Triangle (White et al. 2003). The finds possess some archaic features but were regarded by their discoverers as direct ancestors of modern *Homo sapiens*.

In contrast to the preceding cases, finds possessing features seen in earlier *H. erectus* populations continue to be present, though to a lesser degree. The mosaic of features that characterizes archaic *H. sapiens* takes clear shape in remains unearthed at the

Broken Hill Mine in Kabwe, Zambia. These finds, initially classified as *Homo rhodesiensis* (Rhodesian Man), are now more widely accepted as *Homo heidelbergensis*. The Kabwe finds consist of a cranium and the postcranial bones of three or four individuals, dated to at least 125,000 years ago (Begun 2012; Rightmire 1993). On the one hand, the thickness of the bone, heavy brow ridges, and sloping forehead of the cranium are characteristic of *H. erectus*. Also like *H. erectus*, the Kabwe skull is widest at the base. On the other hand, the cranial capacity is large (1,280 cc), and the postcranial skeleton bears a strong resemblance to *H. sapiens*. Similar remains have been found at other southern African, East African, and North African sites. The Kabwe find once again raises the question of which features best differentiate species, or if separate species designations are justified.

Homo sapiens neanderthalensis

The best-known example of an archaic *H. sapiens* is *H. sapiens neanderthalensis*, also known popularly as "Neandertal Man." Neandertal fossils dating between 200,000 and 30,000 years ago have been discovered in Europe and the Middle East, and it is possible that Neandertals may have coexisted with anatomically modern humans in Europe as recently as 24,000 years ago (Duarte et al. 1999). In the past, climatic conditions in this area spanned a more extreme range than they do today. The southern regions had warmer, milder climates, and the northern regions were partially glaciated and extremely cold.

The Neandertal physique has become the quintessential image of "cave men" in popular culture. They have often been portrayed as second-rate hominins, swept to extinction by quicker-thinking modern humans (Brace 1964; for readable, fictional portrayals, see Auel 1981; Golding 1981). This depiction stems, in part, from an early find of a skeleton of an elderly individual whom scientists later determined had suffered from arthritis. In fact, Neandertals were quite literally thick skulled and had the heavy brow ridges seen in *H. erectus*. In the classic Neandertal, the mid-portion of the face protruded as if the nose and surrounding features were pulled forward (Figure 4.6). The front teeth of Neandertals were larger than those of modern humans. Often, Neandertals' teeth bear evidence of heavy wear (some were actually worn down to stubs), which leads researchers to believe that the teeth may have been used by Neandertals in much the same way as tools.

Yet despite the above features, the image of Neandertals as brutish creatures is misleading. The large Neandertal cranial capacity ranged from 1,200 to 2,000 cc and could accommodate a brain as large as, or even larger than, that of a modern human. Moreover, studies of Neandertal endocasts indicate that the structure and intellectual capacities of the Neandertal brain mirrored those of modern humans (Holloway 1985). Artifacts used by these populations reflect a much more complex range of adaptive skills than do those of pre-*H. sapiens* hominins.

Neandertals and Modern Humans Ever since the first Neandertal skulls were found in the nineteenth century, scientists have pondered the links between Neandertals and modern humans. They have, alternatively, been seen as: a transitional species between *Homo erectus* and modern humans; a distinct branch on the hominin family tree that ended in extinction; and as a subspecies of anatomically modern humans (see Figure 4.7). Early interpretations that viewed Neandertals as an intermediate ancestor between *Homo erectus* and anatomically modern humans have been discarded (Figure 4.7a). Their restricted geographic range (Europe and Middle East) and distinctive physical characteristics make this scenario unlikely. As noted, Neandertals also appear to have coexisted with anatomically modern humans until the relatively recent past.

A growing consensus among anthropologists holds that Neandertals had distinctive physical features that separate them from anatomically modern *H. sapiens*, but no one has come up with a cogent, widely accepted theory to explain which selective pressures produced these features (Trinkaus 2006). Researchers tend to favor the

Figure 4.6 A comparison of the skulls of *H. erectus*, *H. sapiens neanderthalensis*, and modern *H. sapiens*. The most distinctive feature of the latter is the high vaulted forehead and the prominent chin.

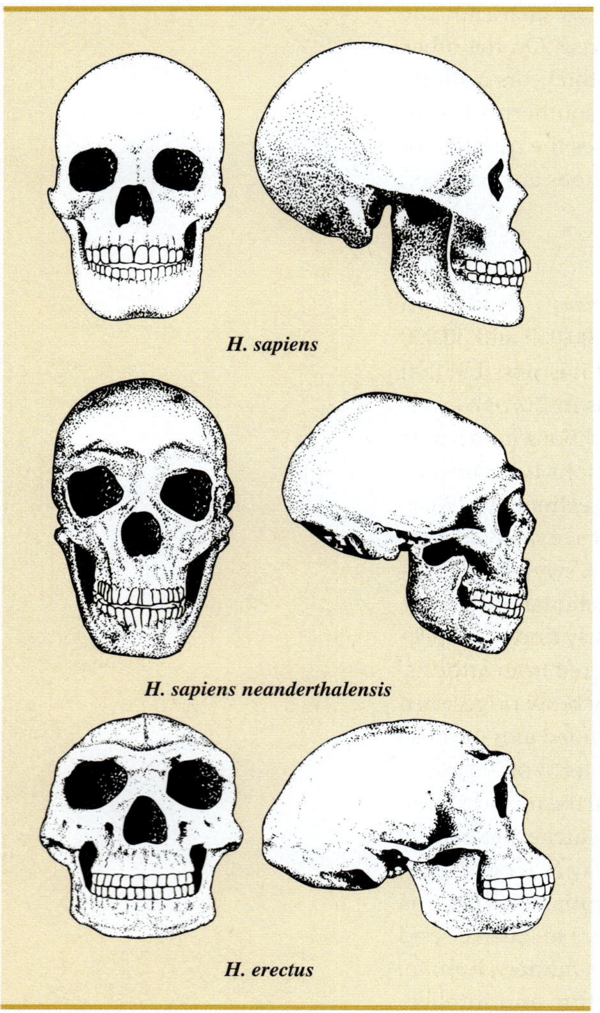

hypothesis that a "pre-Neandertal" population, possibly originating in another region and migrating to the classic Neandertal area, underwent severe natural selection in response to the cold environment of Europe. Fossil finds interpreted as reflecting pre-Neandertal characteristics have been found dating back at least 300,000 years. In this view, natural selection and lack of gene flow with other archaic *H. sapiens* populations produced the distinctive Neandertal characteristics.

In Heidelberg, Germany, some fossil evidence indicates that an early form of Neandertal was evident in Europe. This individual became known as *Homo heidelbergensis* and some paleoanthropologists have hypothesized that this species gave rise to the Neandertals in Europe and in Africa to modern *Homo sapiens* (Stringer and Andrews 2005). *H. heidelbergensis* has smaller teeth and jaws and a very large brain (1300 cc) that differ from *H. erectus*, but larger teeth, jaws, and a prognathic face with large brow ridges make this creature much different than *Homo sapiens* (Rightmire 1997).

The site of Atapuerca in northern Spain has been important in understanding the early Neandertal (Bermúdez de Castro et al. 2004). The Atapuerca site is deep within an extensive cave system that has yielded over 2,500 human fossils. The paleoanthropologists have been divided on how to classify some of the hominin fossils. Some have seen the fossils as a late form of *heidelbergensis*, whereas others perceived them within the category of an early *H. neanderthalensis* (Stringer and Andrews 2005). Nevertheless, these fossils that are dated as early as 300,000 years ago indicate a complex picture of an early "bushy" transitional period of human evolution in Europe.

Clues to the Neandertals' relatedness to modern humans comes from molecular testing of genetic material extracted from Neandertal bones recovered at three sites that indicate substantial differences between the Neandertals and modern humans, while estimates of the separation of the Neandertal and modern human lineages range from 370,000 to 500,000 years ago (Noonan et al. 2006; Green et al. 2010; Hawks 2013). While these data, based on mitochondrial DNA, must be regarded as tentative, they clearly suggest significant genetic distance between humans and Neandertals. Yet, initial findings that indicated Neandertals did not contribute to the mitochondrial DNA pool of modern populations (Krings et al. 1997) has been revaluated in light of the recent work that suggests that Neandertal DNA in non-African modern European populations may range from 1 percent to 4 percent (Green et al. 2010; Hawks 2013). Analysis of mtDNA from a Neandertal tooth discovered in Belgium has further shown that the Neandertals made up a very diverse population (Hodgson et al 2010; Orlando et al. 2006; Hawks 2013).

Figure 4.7 Three interpretations of the evolutionary relationships between Neandertals and modern humans: (a) unilinear evolution, (b) pre-Neandertals, and (c) separate lineages.

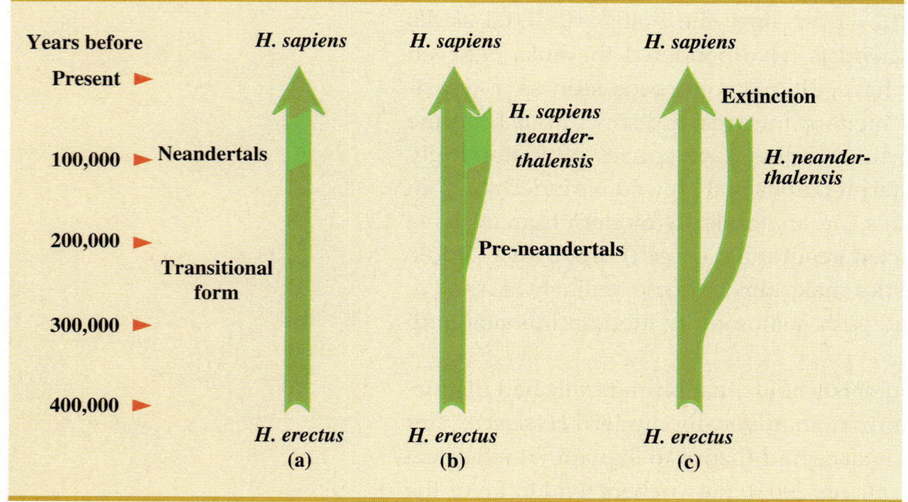

The perceived variation in Neandertal DNA and the inclusion of Neandertal DNA in some modern human populations is particularly significant in light of the previous discussion of hybridization and assimilation models in the emergence of modern humans: Although the distinctiveness of the Neandertal genetic makeup is clear, the evidence for some Neandertal DNA in modern humans suggests some interbreeding (Hawks 2013).

Denisovans or the Denisova Hominins

The intricate picture of the emergence of modern humans and their relationship to archaic human populations has been made all the more complex by the fossil and archaeological evidence that is emerging on the **Denisovans**, or the Denisova hominins, a previously unknown hominin species or subspecies that was contemporaneous with modern humans and Neandertals. The site that the hominin remains are known from is in the Denisova cave in Siberia, Russia. Archaeological data suggests that the site was occupied from over 125,000 years ago up until modern times (Dalton 2010; Krause et al. 2010; Hawks 2013). Archaeological excavations suggest possible occupation by both Neandertals and modern humans. The site is consequently of interest in tracing Neandertal and modern human interactions.

The most tantalizing information was, however, provided by genetic data recovered from bones recovered from the site dating to between 30,000 and 48,000 years ago. Mitochondrial DNA extracted from the bones revealed a pattern unlike either that found in modern human or Neandertals. The mtDNA signature has been described as the "Denisova hominin," apparently an extinct hominin species or subspecies. Additional study of the nuclear genome suggests that the Denisovans share a common origin with Neandertals, and that they interbred with the ancestors of modern-day Melanesians and Australian Aborigines. Additional study of the genomic data, suggests interbreeding with another, unknown human lineage distinct from the Neandertals and modern humans (Pennisi 2013; Hawks 2013). Discoveries such as these begin to hint at the complex history of human interactions and the questions that remain for researchers to answer.

The Life and Times of Genus *Homo*

4.7 Define and describe the principal tool industries of the Lower Paleolithic.

The preceding discussions have focused on the biological evolution of the human species. However, the archaeological record provides an important, indeed, to a large extent *the*, source of information on early hominin behavior. Bipedalism freed hominins' hands for other tasks, such as tool use, food gathering, and infant care. There is no question that tools had important consequences for early hominins, allowing them to exploit a wider range of food, defend themselves more effectively, and generally perform many tasks that they would not have been able to do otherwise. For example, tools would have allowed early hominins to cut through the tough hides of animal carcasses, the meat of which could then be used as food.

Genus Homo, the group that includes human and their closest ancestors, is characterized by greater cranial capacity compared with other hominin species. Physically, the postcranial skeleton of *H. erectus* resembled modern humans, but the species' cranial capacity, while less than modern humans, was greater than that of earlier hominins. In addition, the shape and arrangement of later *H. erectus* skulls (including examples sometimes classified as *H. heidelbergensis*) has led some researchers to believe that these protohumans may have been the first hominins with both the physical and mental capacities for speech (see the box "Could Early Hominins Speak? The Evolution of Language").

These changes in physical characteristics undoubtedly underlaid a myriad of behavioral, social, and cultural developments. A number of innovations in tool

Critical Perspectives

Could Early Hominins Speak? The Evolution of Language

Figure 4.8 The physiology of speech making, which is unique to humans.

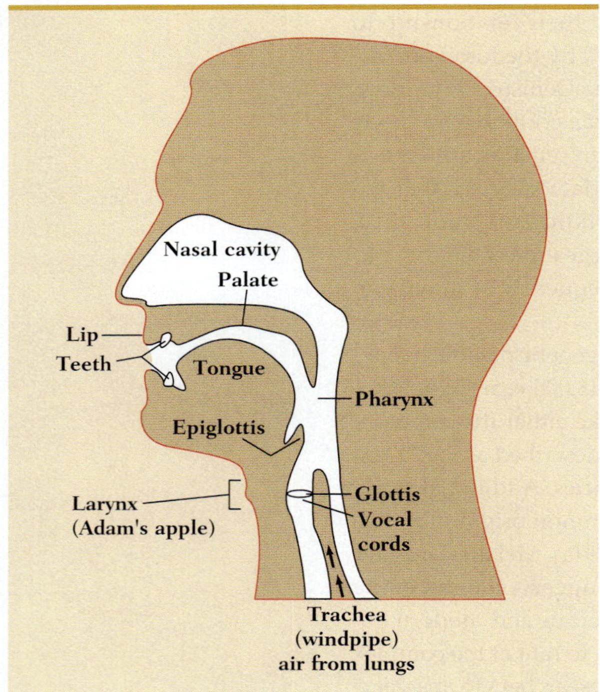

The ability to communicate is a key aspect of human adaptation, and the origin of human speech has been widely debated. Primates, in general, are effective communicators. Apes and monkeys utilize an array of howls, screams, hoots, grunts, and facial gestures that are used to signal one another and other animals (Arbib et al. 2008). The apes most closely related to humans, gorillas and chimpanzees, draw upon an even more highly developed repertoire of communication tools. It is, therefore, likely that early hominins such as *Ardipithecus ramidus* and *Australopithecus anamnesis* were able to communicate in similar ways, but it is unlikely that they were able to speak. While all of the questions are far from addressed, increasing evidence suggests that it may have only been with the emergence of our own species, *Homo sapiens*, that the full range of speaking abilities appeared. Evidence consists of both the cognitive and physical abilities to speak.

Indications of the cognitive abilities of early hominins come from the study of *endocasts*, the casts of the interior of the cranium, which can be likened to a blueprint of the surface of the brain. As discussed earlier, the evolution of hominins was accompanied by increasing cranial capacity (brain size) within the genus *Homo*. It was, however, not solely the increase in cranial capacity that was significant, but also the shape and organization of the brain. Several areas of the brain play important roles in the human capacity for speech. The expansion of the hominin brain corresponded with the increasing size of the cerebral cortex, the outer layer of brain related to higher cerebral functions, such as memory and symbolic capacities. Other areas of the brain particularly related to linguistic abilities are *Broca's area* and *Wernicke's area*, both located in the left hemisphere. Studies of fossil endocasts have suggested that Homo habilis' brains indicate more development in these areas than is found in apes and the australopithecines, and *Homo erectus'* brains are even more developed, being comparable to those of modern humans in shape (Coolidge and Wynn 2009:103-105; Tobias 1998; Wynn 1998; also see Gannon et al. 1998). If this is the case, then it is possible that *H. erectus* had at least some of the cognitive abilities needed for speech, though they lacked the physical capabilities for speech found in modern humans. They may, however, have had pre-adaptations that, in turn, may have resulted in future language capacities (Clegg 2004).

Various anatomical and physiological features also contribute to human speech abilities. Although primates, especially the apes, have lips, mouths, and tongues, no primate other than humans has the full physical anatomy for speech. Human vocal organs form an irregular tube connecting the lungs, windpipe, and *larynx*, the voice box containing the vocal cords. The larynx holds air in the lungs and controls its release. These vocal organs work in conjunction with our tongue, lips, and nose to produce speech. This allows humans to articulate sounds and manipulate their sequence.

Many of the features that are of key importance in human speech, such as the tongue and larynx, are not preserved in fossils. Their development and evolution are, therefore, difficult to assess and the available information is somewhat indirect. One potential source of information that is sometimes preserved in fossil remains is the hyoid bone, a small bone in the throat that is connected to the larynx and the other structures needed for speech. The shape of the human hyoid bones is quite distinct from those of other primates, such as the chimpanzee. A hyoid bone from an *Australopithecus afarensis* appears chimpanzee-like in appearance, suggesting that hominins at this point in time (3 million to 4 million years ago) did not have the physical capabilities for speech. Finds of archaic *Homo sapiens* (*H. heidelbergensis*), however, possess hyoid bones that are human-like in form, possibly suggesting that archaic humans had the physical capability for speech some 530,000 years ago (Martinez et al. 2008).

The capability for speech can also be inferred by the position of the larynx, which is inferred by the shape of the base of the cranium. In humans, the larynx is lower than other animals. This position allows humans to generate a wider array of sounds needed for speech. The low placement of the larynx corresponds with the shape of the base of the cranium, which is curved. In contrast, the bases of the crania of animals with high larynxes, such as modern chimpanzees, are flatter. The cranial bases of the australopithecines are comparable in shape to those of modern apes, suggesting a highly placed larynx and the related lack of range in sound production. The bases of *Homo erectus* skulls are also quite curved. This inferred placement of the *larynx* suggests that the physical capabilities for speech only fully appeared in *Homo sapiens*.

Insight into the genetic basis of human speech was revealed by the recent discovery of the FOXP2 gene that is connected with the embryonic development of the areas of the brain associated with linguistic capacities (Lieberman 2007). The FOXP2 gene is located on human chromosome 7. All normal humans have two copies of chromosome 7 and two copies of FOXP2. In a long-term study of a family, a genetic mutation was identified that leaves them with only one working copy of FOXP2. Individuals within the family have problems with motor control and cognitive deficits. They consequently are unable to control their tongue properly for speaking and have difficulty repeating two-word sequences. FOXP2 is a gene that turns other genes on and off and, consequently, there is no one-to-one correspondence between it and a single trait; it is not a "language" gene. However, it is obvious that the mutation that led to the development of the FOXP2 gene was definitely important in the evolution of the human capacity for language.

In a fascinating new development, anthropologist Svante Pääbo and his colleagues at the Max Planck Institute for Evolutionary Anthropology in Leipzig, Germany, extracted DNA from Neandertal skeletal material and discovered that the Neandertal FOXP2 carries an ancestral form of the same two mutations of amino acids as those carried by modern Homo sapiens (Krause et al. 2007; Maricic et al. 2012; Hawks 2013). This indicates that Neandertal may have been carrying an ancestral form of the FOXP2 mutations prior to modern Homo sapiens, suggesting that Neandertal may have delivered an ancestral form of the language capacity to modern Homo sapiens through interbreeding sometime before the common ancestor of the two species sometime around 300,000 years ago.

With the preceding clues in mind, it remains difficult to identify the critical stage in the evolution of communication from simple vocalizations or a sign-based communication, to complex, symbolic language. Yet, language undoubtedly greatly facilitated human adaptation and creativity. Richard Klein has, in fact, suggested that there was a big-bang scenario for the evolution of language and brain development (2002). He argues that there must have been a sudden alteration in the organization of the *Homo sapiens* brain resulting from a genetic mutation around 50,000 years ago. This organizational change, he suggests, is expressed in the array of cultural innovations that characterize the Upper Paleolithic. Words and grammar facilitated the cultural and technological changes that allowed modern humans to be so successful in adapting to different environments around the world. Klein suggests that more archaic representatives of genus *Homo*, such as the Neandertals, could not have had anything approximating human culture. Examples of Neandertal artifacts like stone tools and jewelry are explained as borrowings from the more advanced *Homo sapiens*. Other researchers disagree, noting the evidence for speech capabilities and the richness of the Middle Paleolithic archaeological record (McBrearty and Brooks 2000).

Although anthropologists may disagree regarding the timing and origins of language capabilities in humans, the capacity for language was probably the last major step in our biological evolution (Klein 2002, Mellars 2006, Mithen 1996; Deacon 1997, Lieberman 2007). Since that time, human history has been dominated by *cultural* rather than *biological* evolution. This cultural evolution and the subsequent developments in adaptation and creativity could not have occurred before a fully evolved language capacity.

Points to Ponder

1. Discuss the evidence that exists for the evolution of both the cognitive and physical abilities for speech. What are some of the challenges faced in interpreting these data?
2. Consider the importance of verbal communication in your life. Examine how and why the abilities for speech may have had dramatic impact on early hominin populations.

technology may be associated with the evolution of genus *Homo*, and these are discussed below. However, perhaps the best indication of the success of the genus is illustrated by the fact that *H. erectus* had the widest distribution of any hominin aside from *Homo sapiens*. Fossil discoveries classified as *H. erectus* range from widely dispersed sites in Africa, to Eurasia, Indonesia, and China, eastern Asia, and the Caucus Mountains of southern Russia (and presumably the areas in between), indicating that these areas had been settled by 1 million years ago. The occupation of Europe was slightly later, with current findings dating later than about 800,000 years ago. Significantly, these areas are not simply widely separated in space, but are also in varied environmental zones ranging from tropical African savannas to cold and temperate forests in Europe and Asia. *H. erectus* was not simply mobile, but equipped with the cognitive abilities to adapt to widely different climates.

The First Tools

Unfortunately, the archaeological evidence relating to the oldest hominins is very limited. The first tools were very likely *unmodified* pieces of wood, stone, bone, or horn that were picked up to perform specific tasks and then discarded soon afterward.

Frustratingly for researchers, artifacts of this kind are unlikely to be preserved or recognized in archaeological contexts. On one hand, wood, bone and horn do not survive as well as stone, and tools of these materials have rarely been recovered in Lower Paleolithic contexts. On the other hand, the simplicity of early tools, as well as their brief periods of use, makes them difficult to identify.

Who made and used the first tools is also a source of debate. Although it is perhaps tempting to associate the manufacture of the first tools with the larger-brained members of our own genus *Homo*, the oldest stone tools clearly predate the earliest representative of the genus. The oldest evidence for stone tool use, albeit limited, comes from cut marks left on two bones recovered in Dikika, Ethiopia, and dated to roughly 3.4 million years ago (McPherron et al. 2010). The oldest well-dated stone tools date back just over 2.6 million years ago (Semaw et al 2003). In contrast, the earliest representative of genus *Homo*, *H. habilis*, does not appear in the fossil record until some 300,000 or 400,000 years later.

During later periods, species that have been interpreted as potential ancestors of genus *Homo* (such as *Australopithecus africanus*) have similarly been identified as the most likely toolmakers. While this may have been the case, other early hominins may have made and used simple tools. In particular, stone tools have been found in association with some of the robust australopithecines, including *A. robustus*, *A. boisei*, and *A. aethiopicus* (Sussman 1994). In this context, it is worthwhile to note that studies of modern chimpanzees have demonstrated that they have the cognitive abilities to manufacture simple stone tools and will use them to obtain food. It would not be surprising that various species of early hominins made similar use of tools.

The Oldowan The oldest, recognizable tools are rudimentary stone implements found at Gona, Ethiopia, dating back almost 2.6 million years ago (de Heinzelin et al. 1999; Semaw et al. 2003). These types of tools were first identified by Louis and Mary Leakey at Olduvai Gorge in Tanzania, East Africa, an area that has also been the site of many important hominin fossil finds. The Leakeys called this stone tool technology the **Oldowan industry** (Toth and Schick 2004). The Oldowan marks the beginning of the Lower Paleolithic. Oldowan tools are basically naturally shaped river cobbles or angular blocks of stone that have intentionally sharpened edges. The cobbles, perhaps measuring 4 or 5 inches across, were sharpened by using another rock as a hammer stone to break off chips or flakes in a process called **percussion flaking** (Figure 4.9a). As flakes were removed, they left behind a sharp edge that could be used for cutting and scraping, producing a crude pebble tool or chopper (Figure 4.9b). The flakes themselves also had sharp edges that could also be used as tools (Potts 1991, 1993). Tools with flaking on one side are termed *unifacial*; those with flaking on two sides are termed *bifacial*.

The Acheulean Industry

In contrast to the scant traces of earlier hominin behavior, the archaeological record after approximately a million and a half years ago is somewhat more substantial and the tools more readily recognizable. Yet, the interpretation of hominin activities still depends on material excavated from relatively few sites, widely scattered in time and space. As is the case with archaeological evidence for earlier hominins' behavior, a principal source of information comes from stone tools.

There were a number of significant changes in stone tool technology during the period of time associated with the evolution of genus *Homo*. After their first appearance 2.6 million years ago, Lower Paleolithic tool traditions changed very slowly. The simple Oldowan pebble tools and flakes remained the characteristic artifacts 1 million years after their first appearance. However, approximately 1.6 million to 1.7 million years ago, some changes began to appear, including tools with more advanced flaking that may have served as drills and proto-bifaces (tools with flaking on two sides somewhat like simple arrowheads). These increasingly sophisticated implements are referred to as the *developed Oldowan*, to distinguish them from the simpler Oldowan tools. Also during this period, a new tool tradition emerged, the **Acheulean industry**. Along with the Oldowan, this is the other major stone tool industry that marks the Lower Paleolithic. These new and varied types of implements would have provided a more varied tool kit.

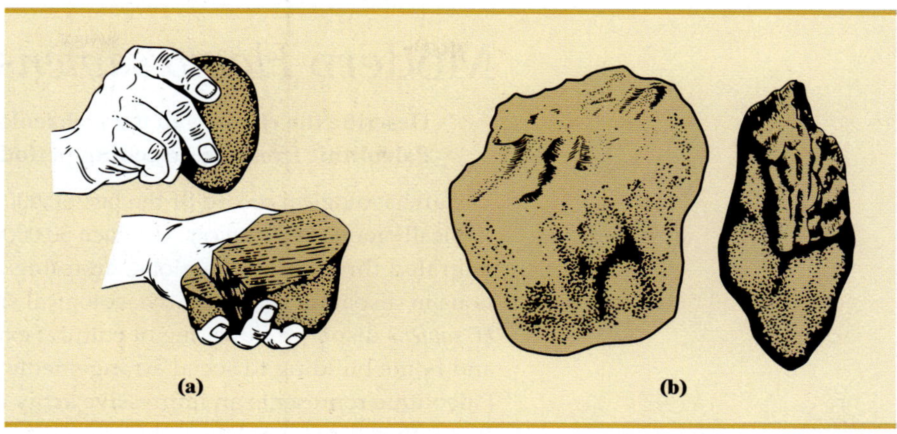

Figure 4.9 Oldowan industry: (a) the percussion flaking method, in which a hammer stone is used to remove flakes from a stone to produce a chopper tool; (b) an Oldowan chopper.

As is the case with the earlier Oldowan finds, the hominins responsible for these technological innovations are uncertain. Acheulean and developed Oldowan tools have been associated with *Homo habilis*, as well as *Homo erectus*. However, the earlier portion of this time period also includes fossil evidence for the robust australopithecines (*A. aethiopicus* and *A. robustus*). Most significantly, both *H. habilis* and *A. boisei* are both associated with both Oldowan and early Acheulean tools at Olduvai Gorge. Later Acheulean tools are found with transitional or archaic forms of *H. sapiens* such as the Neandertals. Given these associations, the resolution of who made and used the tools will remain open (Camps and Chauhan 2009).

Most characteristic of the Acheulean is the *hand axe*, a sharp, bifacially flaked stone tool shaped like a large almond, which would have been effective for a variety of chopping and cutting tasks. Unlike Oldowan pebble tools and flakes, which consisted of irregularly flaked natural cobbles, the hand axe was fashioned by removing many flakes to produce a specific form. In other words, the toolmaker had to be able to picture a specific shape in a stone. This may indicate a significant advance in cognitive abilities (Wynn 1995).

The Middle Paleolithic

The Middle Paleolithic (beginning approximately 300,000 years ago), referred to as the *Middle Stone Age* in Africa, is the period of time associated with archaic *Homo sapiens* and the emergence of anatomically *H. sapiens*. It is followed by the Upper Paleolithic, or *Late Stone Age*, beginning approximately 50,000 years ago. Note, however, that these periods are separated on the basis of variations in tool types and manufacturing techniques; the chronological divisions used here are intended to provide only the crudest of guidelines. The actual appearance of characteristic Middle or Upper Paleolithic tools varies in different world areas and is often defined on the basis of differing characteristics. The earliest dated finds come from Africa, where the earliest dates cluster between 200,000 and 300,000 years ago (McBrearty and Brooks 2000). Yet, even here, dated sites with Middle Stone Age industries have been dated both earlier and later. In contrast to the relatively slow change in the Oldowan and Acheulean tool traditions during the preceding million years, the Middle Paleolithic displays greater complexity and an increasing array of local variation.

The association of specific Middle Paleolithic tool traditions with specific hominin populations has also proven problematic. In some cases, tools defined as Middle Paleolithic have been associated with *H. erectus* remains, while in later contexts identical tools have been found in association with both archaic and modern *H. sapiens* (McBrearty and Brooks 2000). Notably, evidence for the survival of *Homo sapiens neanderthalensis* has been extended up to just 30,000 years ago or less, clearly indicating coexistence with *Homo sapiens* for some time. The overlap of Middle Paleolithic industries with the Acheulean at one end and industries described as Upper Paleolithic on the other, as well as their association with varied hominin species, would appear to be inconsistent with a dramatic, "big bang" model of the emergence of anatomically modern humans and their culture (see the box "Could Early Hominins Speak? The Evolution of Language").

Modern *Homo sapiens* and Their Cultures

4.8 Describe the changes in the archaeological record that distinguish the Upper Paleolithic from the preceding periods.

The archaeological record of the last 50,000 years is principally associated with anatomically modern *H. sapiens*. Between 50,000 and 10,000 years ago, human populations migrated throughout the globe, adapting both physically and culturally to conditions in disparate regions. Archaeological sites associated with anatomically modern *H. sapiens* display a flowering of cultural expressions in everything from tool making and home building to social arrangements and subsistence strategies. If the Middle Paleolithic represents an impressive array of innovations compared with the Lower Paleolithic, the Upper Paleolithic is even more stunning in its appearance. This period also witnessed the expansion of humans into the Americas and Australia, continents that had previously been unoccupied by hominins.

Anatomically modern *H. sapiens* populations crafted increasingly complex tools and developed strategies suited to meet the needs of life in varied environments. These innovations are reflected in an array of different stone tool traditions. Whereas the Lower and Middle Paleolithic can be described in terms of a few tool industries and characteristic tools, Upper Paleolithic industries are represented by a myriad of different local and regional designations that reflect distinct local styles and tool kits. Stone tool production made a major technological advance with increasingly fine techniques for producing *blades* (long, narrow flakes that had all sorts of uses as knives, harpoons, and spear points).

There is no question that Upper Paleolithic peoples also became adept at working with a variety of materials. Upper Paleolithic sites have produced bone needles for sewing clothing, fibers for making rope, evidence of nets, and trapping equipment. This period is also distinguished by the increasing evidence for **composite tools**, implements fashioned from several pieces. For example, consider the harpoon, which might consist of a wooden shaft that is slotted for the insertion of sharp stone flakes, and a detachable point. Spear throwers, or *atlatls*—long, thin pieces of wood or ivory that extended the reach of the hunter's arm—were invented during this period, too. A particularly important innovation, spear throwers enabled Upper Paleolithic hunters to hurl projectiles much faster than they could by hand.

Upper Paleolithic Art

In addition to their other technological accomplishments, Upper Paleolithic peoples created an impressive array of artwork, including paintings, incised carving, three-dimensional sculptures, jewelry, and a variety of non-utilitarian objects. Possible evidence for art has been recovered from earlier Lower and Middle Paleolithic contacts. While tentative, the findings are suggestive of later developments. In particular, beads and other ornaments occur in sites dating back 130,000 years (McBrearty and Brooks 2000:521–528; Cain 2006; Tyron and McBrearty 2002). It is, however, only during the Upper Paleolithic that such items become common and they are sometimes striking in nature. These include sculptures in bone, ivory, and stone found throughout Europe that depict human and animal figures. Among the most notable of these finds are those of female figures, speculatively dubbed "Venus" figurines (see Figure 4.10). Rock paintings, done with mineral pigments such as ochre, also appear. Magnificent abstract and naturalistic renderings of animals and humans dressed in the hides of animals decorate the walls of caves in Spain and France. These murals, or cave paintings, may have been drawn to celebrate a successful hunt or to ensure a better future (Halverson 1987).

Figure 4.10 The archaeological record of the Upper Paleolithic becomes progressively more elaborate, including more sophisticated stone tools and nonutilitarian items such as those pictured here. The large projectile point at left is a Solutrean laurel leaf spear point. The two female figures at top are examples of Venus figurines.

Source: W. J. Sollas, *Ancient Hunters and their Modern Representatives*, Macmillan, 1911.

Summary and Review of Learning Objectives

4.1 Explain the principal trends in hominin evolution and within genus *Homo*.

Hominini (the hominins) is the tribe of order primates that includes modern humans and their immediate ancestors. Although hominin species share certain general features with all primates, they also evince several distinct characteristics. Changes in these attributes are preserved in hominin fossils, and the evolutionary relationships of different species are traced on the basis of the similarities and differences present in individual finds. Bipedalism, the ability to walk upright, is the most important trend in hominin evolution; hominins are the only primates that are fully bipedal. Fossil evidence indicates that bipedalism is the earliest hominin trait, evolving sometime between 6 million and 10 million years ago. Although bipedal posture can be inferred on the basis of skeletal remains, it is more difficult to evaluate why it was selected for in early hominin species. Other trends include a tendency toward the reduction of face, jaw and anterior teeth and, within genus *Homo*, a trend toward increasing cranial capacity. These features appear more recently, primarily during the past 2 million years. These characteristics are exemplified in modern humans and least pronounced in earlier hominin species. Sweat glands and reduction in body hair may also have been selected for in early hominins. However, while these traits are readily apparent in modern humans, they are impossible to assess on the basis of fossil evidence. Some hominin species have teeth and cranial structures that suggest adaptations to specialized diets. In particular, the robust australopithecines developed massive chewing muscles and extremely large molars compared with those of modern humans, suggesting a distinct evolutionary history from more direct human ancestors.

4.2 Describe the fossil evidence for early hominin evolution.

Thousands of hominin fossils have been recovered; all of the earliest remains coming from Africa. There is debate regarding the classification and evolutionary relationships of individual fossil finds. However, the fossil record is consistent with the evolution of the human species from a small-brained bipedal ape, the hominini lineage branching off from the other hominінae primates approximately 6 million to 10 million years ago. Intriguing finds that may represent the oldest hominins have been discovered in Kenya, Ethiopia, and Chad. However, these remains are incomplete and their relationships to later species are still being debated. This discussion has focused on two genera: *Australopithecus*, which includes species that may be ancestral to humans as well as extinct side branches; and genus *Homo*, which includes modern humans and their closest ancestors. Paleoanthropologists believe that *A. anamensis* may be a species that lived close to the base of the hominin family tree, with at least three branches: two branches leading to later australopithecine species, and one to genus *Homo* and modern humans. The first representatives of genus *Homo*, the genus that includes modern humans, first appear in the fossil record just over 2 million years ago. The earliest members of genus *Homo* to be identified in the fossil record are the species *H. habilis* and *H. rudolfensis*, dating between 2.3 million and 1.4 million years ago. Consequently, members of genus *Homo* coexisted with some of the later australopithecine species between 2.2 million and 1 million years ago. What distinguishes the first representatives of genus *Homo* from the australopithecines is a trend toward larger brain size. *H. habilis* is followed in the fossil record by *H. erectus*, known from finds in Africa dating 1.8 million years old. *Homo erectus*, in turn, evolved into *H. sapiens*, the species that encompasses modern humans, during the past 400,000 years.

4.3 Discuss the challenges paleoanthropologists face in interpreting the fossil record and explain why their interpretations sometimes change.

Like all sciences, paleoanthropology proceeds by formulating hypotheses and then testing them against empirical data. In contrast to most sciences, however, the data from the fossil record cannot be obtained by laboratory experiments. Rather, paleoanthropologists must await the next unpredictable fossil find. As new evidence is uncovered, new hypotheses are developed and old ones are modified or discarded. As the number of fossil species represented has increased and our understanding of the fossil record has become more refined, interpretations have had to account for more variation and thus have become increasingly complex. Initially, scientists drew a straight evolutionary line from the earliest known human ancestors to modern humans. A number of finds, however, clearly demonstrate that in several instances more than one species of hominin roamed the Earth at the same time. To account for these discoveries, new branches have been added, making our family tree look increasingly bush-like. New discoveries have also extended the hominin family tree even further back in time. Researchers sometimes disagree about the classifications of individual finds. Splitters argue that some species designations do not reflect all the species represented. At the opposite extreme, lumpers maintain that current taxonomic designations place too much emphasis on differences among individuals and do not sufficiently consider variation within species. To complicate things further, current models of hominin evolution must also be reconciled with increasing information provided by genetic data. Despite this seemingly confusing array of interpretations, the diversity of finds uncovered provides insight into human origins. While a number of possible hominin ancestors may be represented, the varied fossil finds are nonetheless consistent with a model of human phylogeny that traces the evolution of genus *Homo* from small-brained bipedal apes. Future discoveries will continue to extend the human lineage further back in time and models of specific hominin lineages will continue to be revised.

4.4 Describe and discuss the different models for the emergence of anatomically modern humans.

Although researchers agree that *H. erectus* evolved into *H. sapiens*, there is substantial disagreement about how, where, and when this transition occurred. Early interpretations were based on limited information and often emphasized the uniqueness of individual finds. Currently, there is growing consensus that anatomically modern humans first evolved in Africa and then spread out to other world areas. A variety of competing interpretations continue to be evaluated of exactly how this took place. These include two contrasting perspectives referred to as the Multiregional Evolutionary Model and the Replacement Model. A third set of interpretations, consisting of Hybridization and Assimilation Models, that attempt to reconcile the two opposing extremes in various ways have also been presented. Supporting evidence for each of these perspectives has been presented and each have their supporters.

4.5 Describe how new genomic research and molecular dating have helped anthropologists interpret human evolution.

Researchers have increasingly approached the study of human evolution by studying the similarities and differences in the chromosomes and DNA sequencing of living primates and modern humans, as well as genetic material recovered from fossils. The genetic data from living primates led to a reassessment of the way in which both living and fossil species are classified, as illustrated by the change in subfamily *Homininae* to include the chimpanzee, gorilla and humans (respectively referred to as the tribes *Panini*, *Gorillini*, and *Hominini*). This classification more accurately reflects the genetic relatedness of the different species. Researchers have further attempted to infer the amount of time it took for evolution to produce the amount of genetic distance between various species. Genetic research into mutation rates suggests the separation of the human and chimpanzee lineages approximately 5 million to 6 million years ago. Genetic research has also focused on more recent human ancestry. Two specific types of genetic markers have been examined with specific regard to the emergence of modern humans: mitochondrial DNA and Y-chromosomal DNA. These are notable in reflecting, respectively female and male genetic ancestry. While they remain the focus of a great deal of debate, the genetic data obtained have increasingly proven consistent with an African origin of *H. sapiens*. The study of the genetic makeup of modern humans, as well as the study of DNA extracted from the fossilized bones of archaic humans such as the Neandertals and Densovians also provides a record of the complexity of gene flow in ancient populations.

4.6 Discuss the different theories regarding the relationship of *Homo sapiens neanderthalensis* and *Homo sapiens*.

H. sapiens neanderthalensis, popularly known as "Neandertal man," is the best-known example of an archaic *H. sapiens*. Neandertal fossils dating between 200,000 and 30,000 years ago have been discovered in Europe and the Middle East. Ever since their initial discovery, scientists have pondered the links between Neandertals and modern humans. Neandertals have, alternatively, been seen as: a transitional species between *Homo erectus* and modern humans; a distinct branch on the hominin family tree that ended in extinction; and as a subspecies of anatomically modern humans. Early interpretations that viewed Neandertals as an intermediate ancestor between *Homo erectus* and anatomically modern humans have been discarded. The restricted geographic range of the Neandertals (Europe and Middle East) and their distinctive physical characteristics make this scenario unlikely. As noted, Neandertals also appear to have coexisted with anatomically modern humans until the relatively recent past. Current consensus tends to regard Neandertals as an archaic subspecies of *H. sapiens* that disappeared as a result of intensive selective pressures and genetic drift. Some additional clues to the Neandertals' relatedness to modern humans comes from genetic material extracted from Neandertal bones. This indicates substantial differences between the Neandertals and modern humans, while estimates of the separation of the Neandertal and modern human lineages range from 370,000 to 500,000 years ago. Yet research also indicates some interbreeding took place between Neandertals and anatomically modern humans. Estimates of Neandertal DNA in non-African modern European populations range from 1 percent to 4 percent. The inclusion of Neandertal DNA in some modern human populations is particularly significant in light of hybridization and assimilation models of the emergence of modern humans: although the distinctiveness of the Neandertal genetic makeup is clear, the evidence for some Neandertal DNA in modern humans suggests some interbreeding.

4.7 Define and describe the principal tool industries of the Lower Paleolithic.

Researchers refer to the earliest stone tools produced by pre-*Homo sapiens* hominins as Lower Paleolithic, referring to the earliest part of the Old Stone Age. The Lower Paleolithic is dated to roughly between 2.6 million and 300,000 years ago, although the age of tools and their characteristics vary in different world areas. Two distinct stone tool industries characterize the Lower Paleolithic: The Oldowan and the Acheulean. The Oldowan industry marks the beginning of the Lower Paleolithic. The oldest examples of this industry come from a site in Gona, Ethiopia, dating approximately 2.6 million years ago. Oldowan tools are basically naturally shaped river cobbles that have intentionally sharpened edges. The cobbles, perhaps measuring 4 or 5 inches across, were sharpened by using another rock as a hammer stone to break off chips or flakes in a process called percussion flaking. The Acheulean is marked by the appearance of slightly more complicated tools, which first appear in the archaeological record about 1.8 million years ago. The characteristic Acheulean tool is the hand axe, a bifacially flaked tool that could be used for a variety of cutting and chopping tasks. Implements of other materials were also likely used during this period, but they did not survive archaeologically.

4.8 Describe the changes in the archaeological record that distinguish the Upper Paleolithic from the preceding periods.

The Upper Paleolithic is the period of time primarily associated with anatomically modern *Homo sapiens*. It can be dated to between 50,000 and 10,000 years ago, though the distinctive artifacts represented have been dated substantially earlier in some areas, particularly Africa. Upper Paleolithic sites look dramatically different in terms of the richness and diversity of the material culture present and the variety of sites represented. Regional stone tool industries reflect increasingly specialized adaptations to local environmental conditions, but may also hint at ethnic and cultural differences. There is also increased evidence for tools made of bone, ivory and wood, including the first evidence for bone needles. The Upper Paleolithic witnessed a dramatic increase in the amount of non-utilitarian artifacts, such as necklaces, pendants and full development of Paleolithic art. This efficient and varied tool kit facilitated the expansion of humans into the Americas and Australia, continents that had previously been unoccupied by hominins.

Key Terms

anatomically modern *Homo sapiens*, p. 108
archaic *Homo sapiens*, p. 108
bipedalism, p. 83
Denisovans, p. 111
foramen magnum, p. 84
hominids, p. 102
hominins, p. 83
hybridization and assimilation models, p. 106
multiregional evolutionary model, p. 104
postorbital constriction, p. 103
replacement model, p. 109
sagittal crest, p. 88
transitional forms, p. 103

Chapter 5

Human Variation

Chapter Outline

Learning Objectives

After reading this chapter you should be able to:

5.1 Identify the different sources of human variation.

5.2 Provide examples of how physical characteristics in human populations may represent adaptations arising from natural selection.

5.3 Discuss how environmental factors may be sources of evolutionary change.

5.4 Discuss how cultural factors may be sources of evolutionary change.

5.5 Explain the challenges faced in dividing human populations into different races and why modern anthropologists avoid these classifications.

5.6 Discuss how contemporary anthropologists assess the relationship between intelligence and race.

5.7 Discuss current approaches to human variation.

Biological anthropologists study humans as a biological species. As we saw in Chapter 4, *Homo sapiens* populations migrated throughout the world, settling in varied climatic and environmental settings. Yet, despite the fact that modern humans have a wider geographic distribution and live in more diverse environments than any other primate group, we all bear a striking degree of genetic similarity. While human populations are widely distributed and have experienced some reproductive isolation, we are more alike than we are different. Certainly, no population has become so genetically isolated as to constitute a separate species. Rather, modern human populations are the product of a tremendous amount of gene exchange.

Yet, although modern humans represent a single species, we clearly are not all alike. As a species, humans exhibit a great deal of *phenotypic variation*—individuals' external, observable characteristics, which are shaped, in part, by both their genetic makeup and unique life histories (see Chapter 2). Ongoing research into the human genome has provided dramatic insight into the genetic basis of human diversity. It has, however, also underscored the complexity of the processes involved, and the role nongenetic factors play in shaping human evolutionary history (Jablonka and Lamb 2006). The challenge of identifying the sources of human diversity and how this diversity should be viewed are the focus of this chapter. Explaining how and why humans are both similar and different is a major focus of biological anthropology.

Sources of Human Variation

5.1 Identify the different sources of human variation.

Consider the dramatic differences that distinguish human populations. What are the reasons for these variations? Differences in many physical characteristics, including variation in height, skin color, hair texture, and facial features, represent genetically inherited characteristics and are readily discernible. However, we can also note environmental variables that influence variation, such as darker skin color from sun tanning or increase in lung capacity resulting from life at high elevations. Finally, we can think of geographic and cultural factors that might restrict interbreeding and gene flow across different populations, and so influence the genetic makeup of a population. These few examples illustrate how varied factors interact to produce human variation.

To understand variation among human populations, we must consider three primary sources of variation: (1) *evolutionary processes* affecting genetic diversity within and between populations; (2) *environment*—the variation among individuals and populations that springs from their unique life experiences and interactions with the environment; and (3) *culture*—the variation stemming from disparate cultural beliefs and practices inculcated during an individual's formative years and reinforced throughout life. Each of these sources of variation may play a role in long-term evolutionary change in a species, as well as an individual's external, observable characteristics. These sources of variation will be discussed in turn.

Genetics and Evolution

The genetic makeup of modern humans allows for a great deal of potential variation. Genetically determined human traits can frequently be expressed in different ways. As discussed in Chapter 2, a population's total complement of genes is referred to as a *gene pool*. In *Homo sapiens*, as well as in animal populations, genes may have two or more alternate forms (or *alleles*)—a phenomenon called **polymorphism** (literally, "many forms"). These differences are expressed in various physical characteristics, ranging from hair and eye color to less visible differences in blood chemistry. Many of these traits vary in their expression in different world areas. For example, we associate certain hair texture and skin color with populations in specific geographic areas. Species made up of populations that can be distinguished regionally on the basis of discrete physical traits are called **polytypic**.

Four fundamental evolutionary processes have long been recognized and were examined in Chapter 2. They are: mutation, natural selection, gene flow, and genetic drift. *Mutations*, which are random changes in the genetic code, bring about changes in allele frequencies. Mutations may result in evolutionary change only if they occur in the sex cells of individuals, enabling this change to be passed on to succeeding generations. Mutations are important in explaining human variation because they are ultimately the source of all genetic variation. They may be beneficial, detrimental, or neutral in terms of an organism's reproductive success. The evolutionary process that determines which new mutations will enter a population is *natural selection*. Through natural selection, traits that diminish reproductive success will be eliminated, whereas traits enhancing the ability to reproduce will become more widespread.

Although natural selection has favored certain traits in human populations, it does not explain all genetic variation. Some physical characteristics, such as eye color, confer no discernible reproductive advantages. We might therefore expect such neutral traits to be evenly distributed throughout human populations as a result of *gene flow*, the interbreeding of human populations; yet this is not the case. The nonrandom distribution of neutral traits illustrates *genetic drift*, random processes of selection that alter allele frequencies. Genetic drift is particularly useful in explaining differences among genetically isolated populations. Archaeological data suggest that Paleolithic populations may have consisted of small bands of between 30 and 100 individuals, groups in which change arising from genetic drift may have been a particularly important factor.

As discussed in Chapter 2, the study of molecular genetics has revealed that genes and their expression are also influenced by epigenetic factors. While DNA provides the fundamental genetic blueprint, directions provided by genes may be turned "on" or "off," modifying the effect the genes have without modifying the DNA sequence. These modifications that are external to the DNA sequence are referred to as *epigenetic*, which literally means "above" or "on top of" genes.

The Physical Environment

Humans are highly sensitive to changes in their environment and environment is thus an important factor in human variation. Environment may affect the individual during his or her lifetime, as well as cause long-term evolutionary change in populations. The environment influences human variation by promoting or restricting growth and development. Physical differences among humans may arise as a result of how well the requirements for growth are met. We can examine the effects of the physical environment by studying how individuals with similar genetic makeup develop in different environmental settings. If, for example, identical twins were separated at birth and reared in different regions of the world, any physical variation between them could be attributed to their disparate physical environments. Environment also influences human populations. Study of genetic variation in human populations has revealed how natural selection has played a role in adaptations to specific environments.

Culture

Many of the visible features that distinguish human populations are cultural. People differ in the customs and beliefs that guide the way they eat, dress, and build their homes. Such differences are superficial: If a child born in one region of the world is raised in another culture, he or she will learn and embrace the customs and beliefs of the adopted culture. Human behavior and culture may, however, influence human genetic makeup in a variety of ways. As discussed in Chapter 2, plant and animal species alter the environments in which they live, something that may affect their adaptability and influence natural selection. The process by which organisms modify their environment is referred to *niche construction*. These modifications are not necessarily in the best interest of the species. More than any other species, human societies dramatically impact the environments in which they live. Plant and animal domestication, land clearing, and industrialization are human activities that have dramatically affected the environment. Overcrowding, combined with poor knowledge of sanitation, food storage, and personal hygiene has contributed to nutritional deficiencies, the spread of infectious disease, decline in growth rates, and diminished reproductive success, all of which have implications in evolutionary terms. Significantly, these changes are unintentional, unplanned consequences of these activities.

Culture may even more directly influence human genetic variation through religious beliefs, social organization, marriage practices, or prejudices that restrict intermarriage among different groups and thus inhibit gene flow. Many human cultures maintain rules of *endogamy*—that is, marriage to someone within one's own group—thereby restricting gene flow. Cultural beliefs also determine diet, living conditions, and the environment in which people work; these effects, in turn, either promote or hamper human growth and development. As will be seen in our discussion of race, social and cultural factors influence both human variation and our perception of it.

Evaluating Reasons for Variation

Although we know that genetic, environmental, and cultural factors all contribute to human variation, it is often difficult to assess the relative importance of each. All three influences, in combination, yield the characteristics found in an individual, as well as in populations. We can see the intertwined nature of these sources of variation by examining body height. How tall a person grows clearly stems, in part, from his or her genetic makeup. This can be illustrated by certain African, Philippine, and New Guinean populations that have mean heights of less than five feet. This average is much lower than that of most other human populations. Studies indicate that the relatively short stature in these populations is caused by a deficiency in a hormone that stimulates growth, a genetic trend (Shea and Gomez 1988).

At the same time, however, height varies significantly, even among populations that are genetically similar. One way to account for this is to examine variation in environmental factors, such as the amount of sunlight a person is exposed to, the average daily temperature, differences in health and nutrition, and rates of exposure to disease. Consider seasonal changes in growth rates: Children living in temperate climates grow more quickly during the spring and summer than during the fall and winter, while children in tropical climates experience growth spurts during the dry season rather than during the rainy season (Bogin 1978). In both instances, scientists conjecture that more rapid growth correlates with greater exposure to sunlight, although precisely how this works remains unclear. One theory holds that the increased sunlight in certain seasons stimulates the body's production of Vitamin D, which promotes bone growth.

Finally, cultural factors can also affect people's health and, as a consequence, their growth. In some cultures, for example, certain social groups have greater access than others to food, shelter, and protection against childhood diseases, all of which affect growth rates. Underprivileged children whose basic nutritional needs are often unsatisfied will not grow as tall as those born into a society with material abundance.

Because of the complex interrelationships among genetic, environmental, and cultural influences, the relative importance of each of these elements can be deciphered only through detailed analysis of specific human populations.

Adaptive Aspects of Human Variation

5.2 Provide examples of how physical characteristics in human populations may represent adaptations arising from natural selection.

Natural selection has played a key role in the evolution of the human species, as well is in variation among modern humans. As scientists explore human origins, they have posited a variety of ways in which natural selection may have contributed to some of the differences observed in modern human populations. If natural selection promoted these differences, there should be evidence to substantiate this assertion. Unfortunately, since soft tissues are not preserved in the fossil record, the validity of many of these theories can often only be evaluated indirectly. How then do we assess the effects of natural selection? One way is to look at how different physical characteristics enable modern humans to adapt to disparate environmental conditions. In addition, the unraveling of the human genome has provided insight into the genetic basis of human variation and some of the adaptive features represented (see the box "Race and Genetics").

Body Hair and Sweat Glands

One of the striking physical differences between humans and other primates is our lack of body hair. Modern humans are also formidable at sweating, with some 2 million sweat glands spread across our bodies. Our relatively hairless skin is covered with sweat glands, which other primates lack. What led to these differences? The answer may lie in the environments in which our early human ancestors evolved. It is likely that early hominins had relatively light-colored skin covered with hair, much like modern chimpanzees and gorillas, our closest living biological relatives (Mukhopadhyay, Henze, and Moses 2014; Relethford 2013: 385; Jurmain, Kilgore, Trevathan, and Ciochon 2014). Light skin color and thick body hair are well suited to forest and wooded environments. However, as early hominins moved into more open savannas, this would have been a disadvantage. Here human ancestors would have faced higher temperatures, greater energy expenditure to obtain food and, subsequently, increased risk of heat stroke and heat exhaustion. The solution was to sweat more, which cools the body through evaporation (Jablonski and Chaplin 2000; Jablonski 2012; Wheeler 1992, 1994).

Unfortunately, the earliest of our hominin ancestors were likely poor at sweating. As is the case with modern chimpanzees and gorillas, they probably had relatively few sweat glands, which were primarily located on the palms of their hands and the soles of their feet. In some cases, however, individuals may have been born with more than the typical number of sweat glands. The loss of body hair would have further facilitated cooling. These individuals would have been able to sweat more, remain cooler, and thus maximize the time they could spend foraging for food. This, ultimately, better ensured their reproductive success. As seen in the discussion of bipedalism in Chapter 4, the success of our hominin ancestors may partly be a consequence of their ability to search for food and hunt when other creatures could not.

Skin Color

Among the most striking physical differences in modern human populations is skin color, which varies tremendously among individuals, and multiple shades of skin color are found in populations in different world areas. Although human skin color may appear dramatically different in different individuals, it is a physical characteristic that exhibits **continuous variation**; that is, the differences cannot be divided into discrete, readily definable colors, but exhibit a continuous spectrum of variation from one extreme to another. The basis for this variation is complex. Skin color is a *polygenic* trait that is a consequence of variation in the alleles of more than one gene. The specific genetic loci involved, the precise manner of inheritance, and the evolutionary factors that may have contributed to variation in skin color have been the focus of wide-ranging debate (Jablonski and Chaplin 2000).

Differences in Skin Color A number of factors combine to give human skin its color. The most important of these is *melanin*, the dark pigment that primarily determines the lightness or darkness of skin and which is responsible for variations of tan, brown, and black skin color (Parra 2007; Relethford 2013). Melanin is produced by cells known as *melanocytes*, located in the bottom layers of the skin. Interestingly, all modern humans have about the same number of melanocytes. However, their arrangement and the amount of melanin they produce underlie variation in skin color. These factors are, to some extent, genetically controlled (Szabo 1967; Lamason et al. 2005; Relethford 2013). People with lighter skin have less melanin, which allows the white tissues beneath the skin (the *epidermis*) to show through.

A variety of other variables also influence skin color. *Hemoglobin*, a protein that contains iron, gives red blood cells their color. In people with less melanin in their skin, this red color shows through more strongly, tinting their skin pink. *Carotene*, an orange-yellow pigment that confers a yellowish tinge, is contained in certain foods, so people with a large amount of carotene in their diets may have an orange tone in their skin. However, the presence of carotene is not what gives a yellowish cast to the skin of individuals of Asian descent. Rather, this skin tone is the result of a thickening of the exterior layers of skin. Finally, skin color is also directly influenced by the environment. Exposure to the ultraviolet radiation in sunlight stimulates the production of melanin, yielding what we call a tan. Thus, variation in an individual's skin color stems from the interaction of both genetic and environmental factors (Williams-Blangero and Blangero 1992).

Adaptive Aspects of Skin Color While reasons for the variation in skin color are complex, adaptive aspects of light and dark skin color may have played a role in the presence of light and dark skin color in different human populations. Analysis of the distribution of skin pigmentation reveals a distinctive pattern. In most world areas, skin color is generally darker in populations closer to the equator (Birdsell 1981; Relethford 2013; Jablonski 2012). Further north and south of the equatorial zone, skin coloration is progressively lighter (see Figure 5.1). This observation was particularly true before the large population migrations of the last 500 years.

Scientists who have studied the distribution patterns of skin pigmentation hypothesize that natural selection played a decisive role in producing varying shades of skin color. Several adaptive aspects of pigmentation suggest why skin color may have been favored by natural selection. First, darker skin confers advantages in a tropical environment; the regions of Africa where early humans evolved. Melanin provides protection from ultraviolet (UV) radiation in sunlight, which has been shown to have a number of detrimental effects (Relethford 2013; Jablonski 2012). Prolonged exposure to the sun can cause sunburn, sunstroke, and skin cancer. More importantly, it can significantly decrease folate levels (Jablonski and Chaplin 2000; Jablonski 2012). Folate, a member of the Vitamin B complex, is essential for normal fetal development. Low folate levels in mothers have been correlated with embryonic defects, such as spina bifida and anencephaly (the absence of a full brain or spinal cord). Even an hour of exposure to intense sunlight is sufficient to reduce folate levels by half in light-skinned individuals. As *Homo sapiens* evolved in the tropical equatorial zones, darker skin pigmentation was likely highly adaptive.

If the adaptive advantages of darker skin are clear-cut, why do some human populations have light-colored skin? Research suggests that darker skin is not advantageous in all environmental settings. As early humans moved into more temperate

Figure 5.1 Variations in human skin color prior to the major population movements of the past 500 years shows the clustering of darker skin color toward the equator.

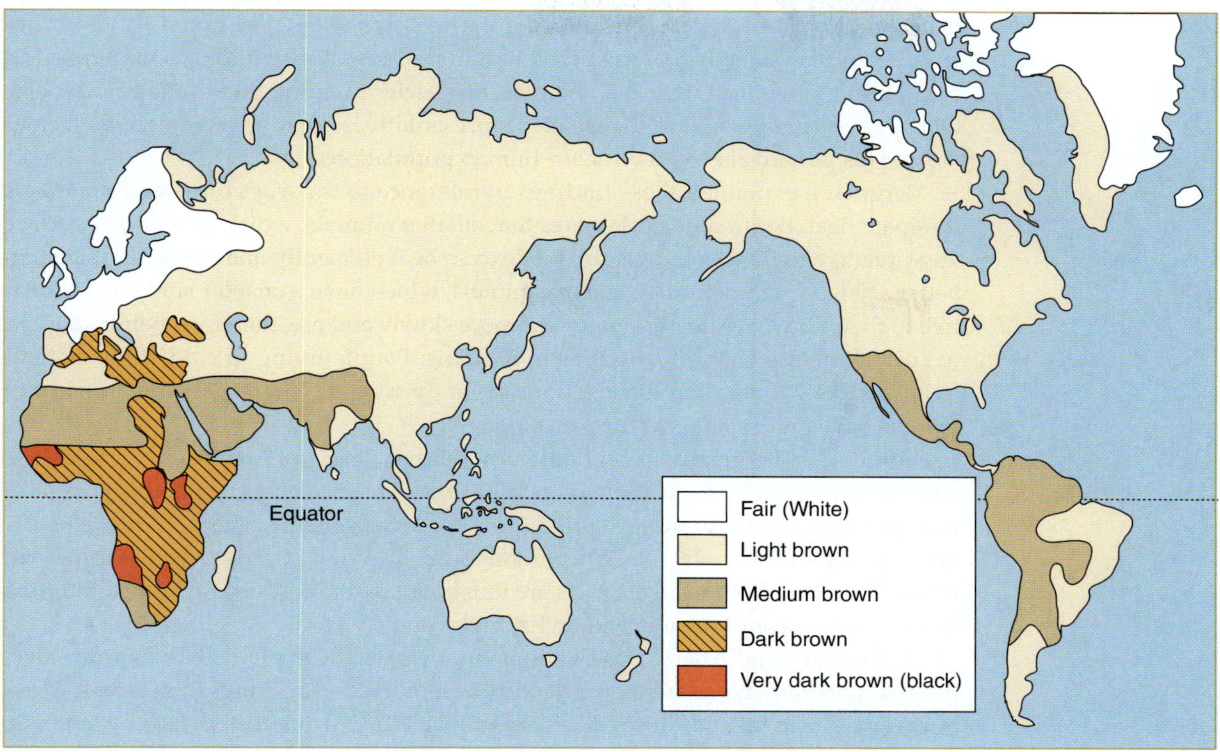

regions with less sunlight, other selective pressures, especially the need for Vitamin D, conferred an adaptive advantage on lighter skin pigmentation. We know today that when human skin is exposed to UV radiation in sunlight, the UV rays stimulate the synthesis of Vitamin D. This is important because insufficient levels of Vitamin D can result in deficiency diseases such as rickets, which is caused by the decalcification of bone. Because of this decalcification, body weight and muscle activity will ultimately deform the bone. Pelvic deformity in women and the associated increase in infant mortality rates would have been a significant adaptive disadvantage. Vitamin D also has other significant functions in regulating thousands of genes that may prevent cancer and provide natural antibiotics (Mukhopadhyay, Henze, and Moses 2014; Relethford 2013; Jurmain et al. 2014). With this in mind, physical anthropologists conjecture that the production of optimal levels of Vitamin D may have had a hand in the distribution of light skin. Lower regional UV levels closely correspond with fairer skin coloration (Jablonski and Chaplin 2000; 2010; Jablonski 2012).

People who inhabited equatorial regions with ample exposure to sunlight evolved darker skin pigmentation to avoid the deleterious effects of UV radiation. In contrast, people who lived in cold, cloudy climates would have increased chances of survival and, ultimately, reproductive success if they had lighter skin that absorbed higher levels of UV radiation and were consequently able to synthesize more Vitamin D. Over time, natural selection favored darker skin in the tropics and lighter skin in regions with lower levels of sunlight and the associated UV radiation (Jablonski 2012).

Recent studies have increasingly revealed the genetic basis of skin color. Research has linked polymorphisms of at least two genes to dark pigmentation in human populations; variations of three other genes are linked to lighter skin in European populations, but not in East Asian groups (Lamason et al. 2005; Norton et al. 2007). This variation in the genes suggests skin color has been acted on by natural selection in varied ways in human populations.

Body Build

The influence of natural selection and environment on human body and limb forms is especially pronounced. These interrelationships were first noted by the nineteenth-century English zoologist Carl Bergmann. He observed that in mammal and bird populations, the larger members of the species predominate in the colder parts of a species range, whereas the smaller representatives are more common in warmer areas. This pattern also holds true for human populations.

Bergmann explained these findings in reference to the ways birds and mammals dissipate heat. Bergmann's rule states that smaller animals, which have larger surface areas relative to their body weight, lose excess heat efficiently and, therefore, function better at higher temperatures. Larger animals, which have a smaller surface area relative to their body weight, dissipate heat more slowly and are, therefore, better adapted to cold climates. The same applies to humans: People living in cold climates tend to have stocky torsos and heavier average body weight, whereas people in warmer regions have more slender frames on average.

Building on Bergmann's observations about heat loss, the American zoologist J. A. Allen did research on protruding parts of the body, particularly arms and legs. Allen's rule maintains that individuals living in colder areas generally have shorter, stockier limbs. Longer limbs, which lose heat more quickly, typify populations in warmer climates. Bergmann's and Allen's rules are illustrated by the contrasting body builds of a Samburu man from Tanzania and an Eskimo woman.

Bergmann's and Allen's observations can be partially explained by natural selection: Certain body types are more adaptive in some climatic settings than others (Mukhopadhyay, Henze, and Moses 2014; Relethford 2013; Jurmain et al. 2014). However, developmental acclimatization also affects body and limb size, according to studies conducted among modern U.S. groups descended from recent migrants from Asia, Africa, and, primarily, Europe (Newman and Munro 1955). Researchers discovered that individuals born in warmer states generally developed longer limbs and more slender body types than did those from colder states. As these developments occurred within such a short time (a few generations at most), they could not be attributed to evolutionary processes. Laboratory experiments with animals produced similar findings. Mice raised in cold conditions developed shorter, stouter limbs than did mice growing up in warmer settings (Riesenfeld 1973; Serrat et al. 2008).

A Samburu warrior from Kenya in East Africa (left) and a Native American Eskimo (right), illustrating how body weight and shape vary according to both Bergmann's rule and Allen's rule.

Cranial and Facial Features

Because the human skull and facial features vary tremendously in shape, numerous theories explaining this variation have been advanced over the centuries. In the nineteenth century, many people embraced *phrenology*, the belief that a careful study of the bumps of the cranium could be used to "read" an individual's personality or mental abilities, or even the future. Other nineteenth-century theories posited a relationship between race, cranial shape, and facial features. For example, nineteenth-century theorists argued that African skulls were smaller than European skulls, ignoring the amount of overlap between the groups or the amount of variation within the groups. None of these beliefs has withstood scientific scrutiny (Mukhopadhyay, Henze, and Moses 2014; Relethford 2013: 385; Jurmain et al. 2014).

Why, then, do skull shapes vary? As with body build, the shape of the skull and face may represent adaptations to the physical environment. By examining hundreds of populations, researchers have found a close correlation between skull shapes and climate. People living in colder climates tend to have rounded heads, which conserve heat better, whereas people in warmer climates tend to have narrow skulls (Beals et al. 1984). Other studies have considered the environmental factors that may have favored specific nose types. Studies indicate that higher, narrower nasal openings have more mucous membranes, surfaces that moisten inhaled air. People living in drier climates tend to have more mucous membranes, regardless of whether the environment is hot or cold. Of course, these observations are generalizations regarding populations; many individual exceptions can also be noted.

Biochemical Characteristics

Research on human variation has revealed less obvious differences among populations than skin color, body build, and facial appearance. Variation occurring in dozens of less visible features—such as blood type, the consistency of ear wax, and other subtle biochemical traits—also illustrates evolutionary processes at work. It is easy to imagine how natural selection may have affected the distribution of some of these features. Consider, for example, resistance to disease. If a lethal illness were introduced into a population, individuals with a natural genetic resistance would have an enhanced chance of survival. With increased odds of reproducing, these individuals' genetic blueprints would quickly spread throughout the population (Motulsky 1971).

History offers many tragic examples of one population inflicting disease on another that had no natural immunity. For example, when Europeans first came in contact with indigenous peoples of the Americas and the South Pacific, they carried with them the germs that cause measles and smallpox. Because these diseases had afflicted European populations for centuries, most Europeans had adapted natural immunities to them. When the diseases were introduced into populations that had never been exposed to them, however, plagues of catastrophic proportions ensued. Many Native American Indian and Polynesian populations were decimated by the spread of diseases brought to their lands by Europeans.

Blood Types Among the most studied biochemical characteristics are blood group systems, particularly the ABO system. This represents the phenotypic expression of three alleles—A, B, and O. A and B are both dominant, whereas O is recessive. These different alleles are a good illustration of polymorphism in a simple genetic trait. They are expressed in four phenotypes: type A (genotypes AA and AO); type B (genotypes BB and BO); type AB (genotype AB); and type O (genotype OO).

The three blood-group alleles are found throughout the world in varying frequencies from population to population. Type O is by far the most common, ranging from over 50 percent in areas of Asia, Australia, Africa, and Europe to 100 percent among some Native American Indian groups. Type A occurs throughout the world, but generally in smaller percentages than does type O. Type B has the lowest frequency. Believed to have been totally absent from native South American groups, type B is most common in Eurasia and can be tracked in a clinal distribution outward into Europe in the west and Asia in the east (see discussion of clines on pages 144–145).

Anthropologists, citing the nonrandom distribution of blood types, conclude that natural selection may have favored certain gene frequencies, keeping the percentage of individual alleles stable in particular populations. This natural selection might have something to do with resistance to disease. Each blood type constitutes a different antigen on the surface of red blood cells. An *antigen* is a substance that promotes the production of *antibodies*, proteins that combat foreign substances entering the body. The presence of these different antigens and antibodies is the reason doctors need to know a person's blood type before giving a blood transfusion. Type A blood has anti-B antibodies, and vice versa. Type O incorporates antibodies that fight against proteins in both type A and type B. People with blood type B (with anti-A antibodies) are better able to fight off diseases such as syphilis, which resemble type A antigens on a biochemical level. Similarly, scientists have posited links between blood types and resistance to many infectious diseases, including bubonic plague, smallpox, and typhoid fever. Before the advent of modern medical technology, natural resistance to these diseases would have conferred critical adaptive advantages.

Sickle-Cell Anemia

By studying population genetics and evolutionary change within populations, scientists have gained important insights into genetic diseases, those diseases arising from lethal genes that cause severe disabilities. One such disease, sickle-cell anemia, produces an abnormal form of *hemoglobin*, the blood molecule that carries oxygen in the bloodstream. In individuals with sickle-cell anemia, the abnormal hemoglobin molecules rupture and collapse into a sickle-like shape, inhibiting the distribution of oxygen. Individuals afflicted with sickle-cell anemia often die in childhood.

If natural selection operates on human characteristics, why did it fail to eliminate such a lethal gene? It did not because under some conditions the sickle-cell gene can confer adaptive advantages, protecting carriers of the gene from malaria, an infectious disease spread by mosquitoes. Researchers discovered a high correlation between the distribution of the sickle-cell gene and regions where malaria is present. In these malarial areas, the gene may be present in up to 40 percent of the population, including portions of Africa, the Mediterranean, the Arabian Peninsula, and India. Malaria is a potentially fatal disease, and individuals without the sickle-cell gene (or access to modern medical treatment) exposed to it tend to die in high numbers. Investigators found, however, that the blood of those who carry the sickle-cell gene is sufficiently inhospitable to the malaria parasite to confer on sickle-cell carriers genetic resistance to the disease. Thus, although sickle-cell carriers may contract malaria, they are less likely to die from it (see Figure 5.2).

It works like this: Recalling from Chapter 2 Mendel's *principle of segregation*, we note that there are three genotypes—homozygous dominant (AA), heterozygous (Aa), and homozygous recessive (aa). Because people who are homozygous for sickle-cell anemia usually die before reproducing (Motulsky 1971), only individuals who are heterozygous for the trait are likely to transmit the disease to the next generation. Two heterozygous parents have a 25 percent chance of having a child who manifests the disease. Although heterozygous individuals are carriers of the sickle-cell trait, they are better able to survive the threat of malaria than are individuals who do not carry the sickle-cell gene. Studies confirm that heterozygous carriers of sickle-cell anemia have higher fertility rates than noncarriers in regions where malaria is common (Mukhopadhyay, Henze, and Moses 2014). Consequently, the survival of those with heterozygous genotypes balances the deaths of those who are homozygous recessive for the trait. The sickle-cell gene, therefore, is transmitted from generation to generation as an evolutionary adaptation in areas where malaria is prevalent.

Balanced Polymorphism In the case of sickle-cell anemia, a lethal recessive gene confers partial protection against malaria. When homozygous and heterozygous genes exist in a state of relative stability, or equilibrium, within a population, this is known as **balanced polymorphism**. In equatorial Africa, 40 percent of the population carries the sickle-cell gene, constituting an evolutionary trade-off. Natural selection has created this balanced polymorphism to protect the African populations, but at a high cost: the deaths of some people.

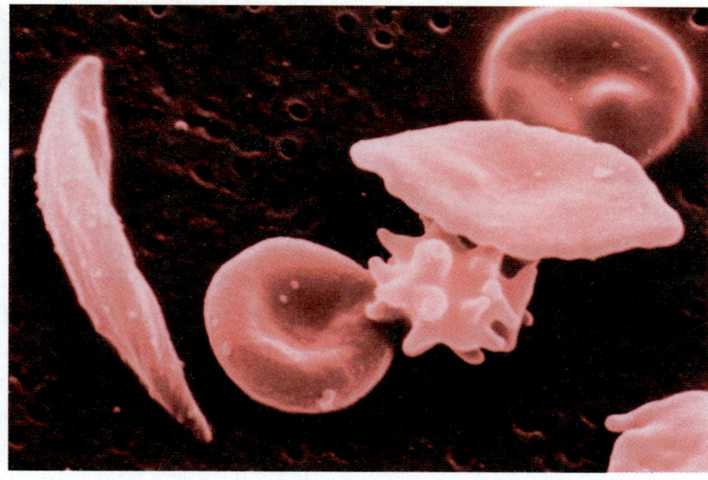

A scanning electron micrograph of a deformed red blood cell (left) in sickle-cell anemia, a hereditary blood disease. To the right of the sickle cell is a normal, biconcave red blood cell.

By examining the sickle-cell gene in regions without malaria, we also see an example of how natural selection acts against a harmful genetic trait. Approximately 2 percent to 6 percent of African-Americans carry the sickle-cell gene—a greater percentage than that found in individuals of non-African origin in the United States, but far lower than incidences of sickle-cell anemia among African populations (Workman et al. 1963). In part, this can be explained by gene flow between African Americans and other populations not affected by the sickle-cell gene. However, statistical studies point to another reason. Unlike Africa, the United States does not have high levels of malarial infection; therefore, the gene represents a severe liability. It is no longer favored by natural selection and is therefore, gradually being eliminated from the gene pool.

Lactase Deficiency

Humans also vary in how well they digest particular foods. Most extensively studied is variation in the production of a digestive enzyme called *lactase*, which is responsible for the digestion of *lactose*, the sugar found in milk. All human infants can digest milk. Milk from domesticated cattle has also been important in many human populations for the last 8,000 years. Yet, the majority of humans lack the genetic coding that continues to produce lactase after about four years of age, a tendency also seen in other mammals. Without lactase, milk ferments in the intestine, causing diarrhea and

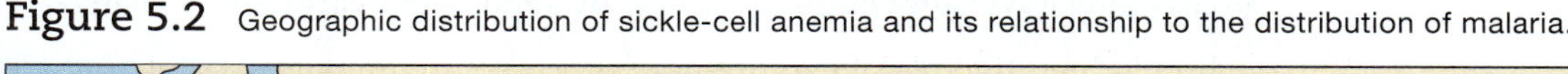

Figure 5.2 Geographic distribution of sickle-cell anemia and its relationship to the distribution of malaria.

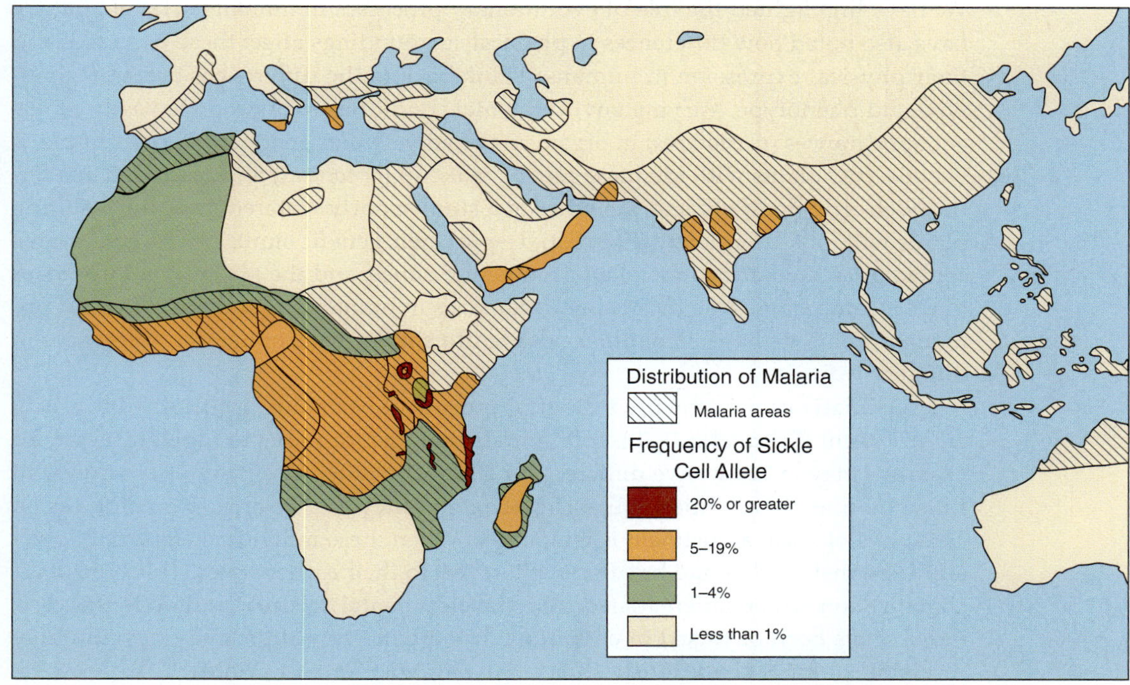

cramps. This condition is referred to as **lactase deficiency**. Contrary to popular advertising, milk is not necessarily good for you, at least not as adults. In fact, for millions of human beings, milk consumption leads to severe discomfort (Hollox 2005). The majority of adults in Asian and African populations do not drink milk because they are not able to digest it properly.

Variation in lactase production among human populations is a result of conditions that favored the ability to digest lactose. The ability to produce lactase is especially common among populations that have a history of *pastoralism*, the reliance on domesticated animals such as cows, sheep, and goats. Such animals provide plenty of milk to drink. In this cultural environment, natural selection favored individuals best able to make use of all available sources of nutrition. Consequently, it is not surprising that populations with long associations with milk-producing, domesticated cattle, are typically more lactose tolerant. African pastoralists such as the Fulani, for example, produce significantly more lactase than do other African populations who do not raise dairy animals (Relethford 2013; Mukhopadhyay, Henze, and Moses 2014).

European populations, among the world's most lactose-tolerant populations, are partly descended from Middle Eastern pastoralists. Milk from domesticated cattle was likely an important food resource in Europe over the past 8,000 years. This long reliance on milk is reflected in the modern populations. Diversity in European cattle milk genes closely mirrors areas that have revealed locations of early European farming sites (more than 5,000 years old) that were likely associated with early cattle raising. This suggests a close correspondence between the domestication of cattle and evolution of lactose tolerance (Beja-Pereira et al. 2003). The presence of this adaptive trait also provides an illustration of how human behavior unintentionally interacts with genetic processes to effect evolutionary change (Jablonka and Lamb 2006: 292-298; Mukhopadhyay, Henze, and Moses 2014; Relethford 2013; Jurmainet al. 2014).

Effects of the Physical Environment

5.3 Discuss how environmental factors may be sources of evolutionary change.

We have highlighted the role of evolutionary processes in human variation, but we have also noted how differences in physical surroundings affect these processes and their physical expression in humans. Think back to the differences between genotype and phenotype. Varying environmental conditions may produce vastly different appearances (*phenotypes*) in organisms of very similar genotypes. For example, if we take two plants with identical genetic makeup (*genotypes*) and plant one in a fertile, well-irrigated field and the other in a stony, poorly watered area, the resulting plants will look completely different, despite their genetic similarity. Humans have settled in an amazing range of environmental zones, and the physical environment plays a comparable role in causing differences in human populations. Notably, human populations have sometimes adapted to similar environmental differences in different ways.

Acclimatization is the physiological process of becoming accustomed to a new environment (Frisancho 1979). Individuals that visit or move to high altitudes, for example, may initially have difficulty breathing, but after living in this environment for some time their bodies will acclimatize and they will be able to breathe easier. This physiological adjustment is temporary: When these individuals return to lower altitudes, their bodies and breathing will revert to their earlier states. This type of acclimatization can be differentiated from **developmental acclimatization**. In this case, individuals born or raised in certain environmental conditions may develop nonreversible physical characteristics, such as larger lungs or body build.

High-Altitude Adaptations

People living in high-altitude environments such as the Himalaya or Andes Mountains provide clear illustrations of acclimatization. Because of the lower barometric pressure at high altitude, people take in less oxygen, making the air feel "thinner." So, at high elevations, most humans experience dizziness and breathing difficulties, which are symptoms of *hypoxia*, or oxygen deficiency (Mukhopadhyay, Henze, and Moses 2014; Relethford 2013: 389; Jurmain et al. 2014: 391; 425-427). Yet, people raised in high-altitude environments, or people who are acclimatized to these environments, do not have these reactions. They have adapted to lower amounts of oxygen in different ways, particularly greater lung capacity, which promotes greater oxygen exchange. We attribute this adaptation to high altitudes to developmental acclimatization, because children born in lowland environments who are raised at higher elevations develop many of the same physical characteristics as those born in the latter environment (Beall 2007).

High-altitude adaptations provide a dramatic example of acclimatization. However, as in some of the other physical characteristics examined, other factors have also been shown to come into play. In some cases, natural selection has played a role in the selection of genes useful to people living in these high-altitude environments. A recent study of Tibetans and Nepalese Sherpa who live at the high altitudes of the Himalayas has shown that they have genes that allow them to maintain relatively low hemoglobin concentrations at high altitude (Jeong et al. 2013). Consequently, Tibetans have a lower risk of complications, such as thrombosis, compared with other humans, something that enhances their ability to thrive at high altitudes. Based on the genetic data from modern populations, researchers have suggested that these genetic adaptations for life at high elevations originated approximately 30,000 years ago in peoples related to modern Sherpa. These genes were subsequently passed on to more recent migrants from lower elevations via interbreeding, and then amplified by natural selection in modern Tibetans.

Native Americans in the Andes Mountains. People raised in high-altitude environments become acclimatized to these conditions in a variety of ways.

Cultural Factors in Human Evolution

5.4 Discuss how cultural factors may be sources of evolutionary change.

While humankind has evolved in a biological sense, humans have increasingly adapted to new conditions using culture, inhabiting the breadth of environmental and ecological zones across the globe. When learned behaviors are passed on from generation to generation, these behaviors inevitably interact with genetic inheritance (Jablonka and Lamb 2006: 292-292). Consequently, social and cultural factors directly influence human variation in a variety of ways.

In some cases, the impact of cultural practices on gene flow and genetic inheritance are quite clear. Although humans can theoretically choose mates from among any potential spouses within geographic limits, culture often circumscribes those choices. In the Middle East, for example, Christians, Jews, and Muslims live in close proximity to one another, yet most marry within their own religious group. Sometimes, these cultural sanctions take on the force of law. For example, at one time both South Africa and certain regions of the United States had laws prohibiting marriage between whites and blacks. Such cultural practices inhibit gene flow and contribute to genetic drift within a population. The Amish, an Anabaptist Christian community in Pennsylvania and the Midwestern United States, provide a dramatic example. The Amish live in a number of closed communities that severely restrict interaction with outsiders and are genetically isolated. As the majority of modern-day Amish are descended from a few hundred eighteenth century founders, genetic disorders that are quite rare in other populations are common in some Amish communities. These include metabolic disorders, dwarfism, and an unusual distribution of blood types (Morton et al. 2003). These are clearly maladaptive traits that can contribute to higher mortality rates.

Humans have also had dramatic impact on the environments in which we live, activities that also affect genetic processes. Lactase deficiency and the inability to digest milk were discussed above with regard to adaptive selection in populations that have a history of pastoralism. In these settings, milk from domesticated animals such as cows, sheep, and goats provided plenty of milk to drink and natural selection favored individuals best able to make use of all available sources of nutrition. The ability to produce lactase, the digestive enzyme needed to digest milk, is a genetically determined characteristic. Consequently, in this cultural setting, selection favored individuals able to take advantage of these additional nutritional resources and lactose tolerance became more common in populations practicing pastoralism. Once developed, the trait also had the benefit of allowing for increased calcium intake, something that helps prevent Vitamin D deficiencies and associated ailments such as rickets (Jablonka and Lamb 2006: 295).

Members of an Amish community. The Amish, a religious community in Pennsylvania and the Midwest, severely restrict interaction with other cultures. Religion, ethnicity, and perceived cultural differences can curb gene flow among human populations.

The point here, however, is that the selective pressures that gave rise to this trait—domestication and associated increase in the availability of milk—were produced by human behavior. In fact, the role of human behavior and lactase production is more complex than simply the association of lactose tolerance and pastoralism. There are also different degrees of lactose tolerance in different populations that historically practiced pastoralism. This variation is also likely the result of cultural preferences. In some cases, cultures such as those in northern Europe favored the use of cattle for their milk and have the highest rates of lactose tolerance. Others cultures such as those in southern Europe consumed milk in the form of cheese, or utilized cattle for their meat. These populations have a lesser ability to digest milk, but it is still greater than in groups that do not practice pastoralism (Jablonka and Lamb 2006: 295).

The example of lactose production in populations associated with pastoralism provides an example of human interaction with the environment that produced an adaptive advantage; the ability to digest milk provided increased nutrition for some populations. The impact of human behaviors on the environment is, however, not always for the best. Sickle-cell anemia, a genetic disorder common in some world areas, was also discussed before in terms of natural selection. Individuals afflicted with sickle-cell anemia often die in childhood. This clearly maladaptive trait was not eliminated from populations because it confers partial protection against malaria, a potentially fatal disease. Yet, while providing a benefit, the case of sickle-cell anemia and malaria also provides a negative example of human behavior in the advent of a genetic trait. In certain parts of Africa, the spread of malaria was the result of the adoption of slash-and-burn agriculture. This agricultural practice, common in many agricultural societies, involves cutting down trees and then burning them. The ashes are left behind to fertilize the land. The deforestation associated with slash-and-burn agriculture created small clearings and pools of water, which in turn attracted mosquitoes and with mosquitoes came malaria. Hence, human agricultural practices provided a partial explanation for the initial spread of malaria in some areas.

Many other examples of the dramatic impacts of human behavior and their potential impact on genetic processes can also be noted. Nowhere is the impact of culture more pronounced than in modern urban societies.

The Impact of Modern Urban Life

Urbanization—the concentration of populations into large urban centers—has altered human lifestyles in dramatic and significant ways. Certain issues must be addressed whenever large numbers of people live together in a small area: How will they be supplied with food and water? How will sanitation needs be met? Will crowded living conditions enhance life or make it barely tolerable? Different cultures have worked through these issues with varying degrees of success. In some cities, overcrowding, combined with poor knowledge of sanitation, food storage, and personal hygiene, has contributed to nutritional deficiencies and the spread of infectious disease and reduced growth rates. Factors such as these explain why archaeological data seems to suggest that health actually declined in some human populations with the advent of food production and the rise of the first cities.

Daily life in modern American cities exposes people to air pollution, contaminated water, high noise levels, and other environmental hazards, all of which aggravate physiological stress. Toxic waste, brought on by the improper disposal of hazardous chemicals, poses a problem of immense proportions in the United States. An example of the threat to human health and development is Love Canal, near Niagara Falls, New York, which was used as a dumping ground for chemical waste between 1940 and 1953 (Vianna and Polan 1984; Paigen et al. 1987). Studies have shown that women who lived close to the dump site gave birth to infants with lower average weights than babies born to women in other areas. Further research demonstrated that children raised near Love Canal were shorter than children of the same age raised elsewhere. This tendency was most pronounced in children who lived near Love Canal for the longest period of time.

Lower birth rates and reduced growth rates may be just the tip of the iceberg. As awareness of the threat of toxic waste increases, links to a host of other health hazards, neurological disorders, and cancer rates are being identified. The long-term implications phenomena such as these have for our long-term genetic history can only be guessed at.

An Ainu elder male. The Ainu, an ethnic group in northern Japan, are generally distinguished from other Japanese by such physical features as lighter skin and higher-bridged noses—attributes frequently associated with European populations. The distribution of characteristics like these confounds attempts at racial classification

The Concept of Race

5.5 Explain the challenges faced in dividing human populations into different races and why modern anthropologists avoid these classifications.

The varied elements of human variation and the complexity of their interpretation are perhaps nowhere highlighted more dramatically than by the differences between popular perceptions and scientific studies of race. Although humans present a diverse bunch, dividing human populations into discrete racial categories or classifications is extremely problematic. Many attempts at racial classifications have been made, but these have failed because they proved too rigid to account for either the tremendous variation found within individual races or the shared similarities between these supposedly different groups. For this reason, modern anthropologists generally avoid using racial classifications, but rather focus on the specific characteristics represented.

The term *race* was likely derived from the Latin root *ratio*, with a meaning similar to "species" or "kind" (of thing). Physical characteristics, such as skin pigmentation, nose shape, and hair texture, have prompted people throughout history to classify humans into different "races." Although the diversity of human populations is undeniable, delineating specific races has little practical or scientific value in studying human variation (MacEachern 2012; Lieberman and Scupin 2012; Templeton 2013). As we shall see, physical characteristics do not divide humans into readily discernible groups or races; clearly bounded, racially distinct populations are not found in the real world.

Further, the word *race* is a loaded term, in part, because people use the word differently in different contexts (MacEachern 2012). Classification of physical characteristics serves only to label particular categories of phenomena arbitrarily selected by the researcher—or the individual. Humans in both the past and present have used various racial classifications to categorize people and have developed stereotypes about the behavior and mental abilities of different "racial categories." Racial categories have subsequently been used as justification for the discrimination against or the marginalization of certain groups. Racial classifications can also be used as self-defined categories in census data or in other contexts to refer to styles of music, dance, or literature.

Perhaps most importantly with regard to the current discussion, racial classifications do not *explain* the reason for the observed variation. In the following discussion, we examine early racial classifications, because incorrect and faulty ideas stemming from some classifications are still widespread. The varied criteria used in these early classifications and the numbers of races identified—ranging from 3 to 30—underscore the limited use of the concept. Table 6.1 summarizes some of these early racial classification systems.

Ancient Classification Systems

Humans have likely always been conscious of the differences between us. Archaeologists have found indications of racial classifications in ancient depictions of people in rock paintings in Europe and other world areas (Jochim 1998). Later civilizations with written texts, including ancient Egypt, Greece, Rome, India, China, and the Near East, used a variety of *folk taxonomies*, informal and unscientific racial classifications, based on skin color or other physical features, as well as cultural characteristics. As early as 3,000 B.C., the ancient Egyptians divided all human populations into one of four categories: red for Egyptians, yellow for people to the east, white for people to the north, and black for Africans to the south. Later, in the biblical book of Genesis, a similar classification scheme appears in a tale chronicling the distribution of the human population:

> *And the sons of Noah that went forth from the ark were Shem, Ham and Japheth: ... these are the three sons of Noah: and of them was the whole earth overspread. (Genesis 9:18–19)*

The descendants of Shem (the Semites) were the ancient Israelites. The descendants of Ham ventured to the south and the east, and the descendants of Japheth

Critical Perspectives

Race and Genetics: The Human Genome Project

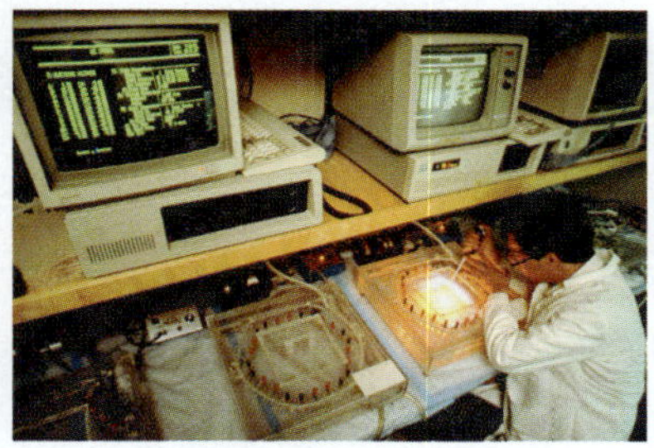

Genome Project lab equipment.

The Human Genome Project, a 13-year study initiated in 1990 and completed in 2003, was a joint effort coordinated by the U.S. Department of Energy and the National Institutes of Health. Its primary objective was the daunting task of mapping the genetic loci of all of the approximately 20,000 to 25,000 human genes and to determine the sequences of the estimated three billion base pairs that make up human DNA. In addition, the project explored the ethical, legal, and social issues of the research, as well as the scientific implications. Although the project has been completed, analysis of the vast amount of information recovered will continue for years to come. The current and potential benefits of the research include applications in the diagnosis of diseases, the creation of new energy sources (biofuels), the monitoring of pollutants, the study of evolution, research into human migration and origins, and the use of genetic information in forensics.

This groundbreaking study of the genetic makeup of modern humans has also dramatically changed the understanding of who we are as a species and the commonality of all human populations. The project research further challenges concepts of "race" and has underscored the limitations of the term in understanding variation in modern human populations. As discussed in this chapter, race is a complicated topic. While in some contexts, the term has been used to indicate physical characteristics, such as skin pigmentation, nose shape, and hair texture, in other settings it may refer to a variety of religious, cultural, social, national, historical, or linguistic criteria. From a scientific perspective, racial classifications fail because they do not account for the tremendous variation within different so-called races, or the shared similarities between these supposedly different groups (Molnar 2006). For these reasons, the majority of anthropologists today find dividing different populations into distinctive racial categories or classifications extremely problematic. The Human Genome Project underscored the shared similarities of human populations and the arbitrary nature of racial classification (Jorde and Wooding 2004; Royal and Dunston 2004).

Criticisms of the concept of race are not new. But the Human Genome Project brings new information to this discussion, which forces the reappraisal of attempts at racial classifications. It makes it clear that human variation is far more nuanced and complex than single traits, such as skin color, suggest. The study does show a correspondence in genetic makeup with shared geographic origin or heredity. Some of these characteristics include features traditionally used in racial classifications. But these correlations are imperfect and genetic variation is distributed in a continuous overlapping fashion across populations. That is, while individuals from the widely separated geographical areas of Europe, Asia, and sub-Saharan Africa may have distinct genetic patterns, such clear differences become blurred as other populations are included. For example, if a South Asian sample is included, there is a significant amount of overlap with the other groups. In addition, individuals within each of the groups also encompass a great deal of variation, frequently possessing some, but not all, of the characteristics shared by other members of the group.

The Human Genome Project and other research indicates that human genetic variation does reflect geographical origins. Individuals from one regional area will, in general, be more genetically similar than individuals from a distant region. However, because of the long history of gene flow between populations, human variation is distributed in a continuous fashion and cannot be partitioned into discrete groups. Populations were never "pure" in a genetic sense, and divisions of race were never neatly bounded.

Points to Ponder

1. Discuss different definitions of race that you have heard or read about. How are these categories different or similar?
2. What are some of the characteristics or features other than genetic differences that explain variation in human populations?
3. What aspects of human ancestry do you think the Human Genome Project will help us understand?

moved north. The word *Ham* originally meant "black" and referred to the black soil of the Nile delta, but its meaning was eventually changed to describe the skin color of Ham's descendants. According to the Bible, Ham had seen his father naked in a drunken sleep and was cursed and sent off to the south to become the father of the black people. At the end of Genesis, the descendants of Ham are condemned to be "servants of servants unto [their] brethren" (Genesis 9:25). During the era of slavery, many Westerners cited this passage as the justification for an entrenched system of racial discrimination (Leach 1988; Braude 1997; Davis 1997).

Table 5.1 How Many Races Are There?

Historically, there have been many attempts to classify races. These classifications are dependent on the criteria selected. The great disagreement among scientists over the number and characteristics of different races is a good indication of the limited usefulness of the concept. Examples of different racial classifications and their basis are contained in the table. Other researchers have suggested completely different races and definitions.

Origin of Theory	Number of Races	Description	Basis of Classification
Ancient Egyptians, 14th century B.C.	4	Egyptians (red), Easterners (yellow), people from the north (white), and people from the south (black)	Skin color
Carolus Linnaeus, 1735	4	Europeans (white), North American Indians (red), Asiatics (yellow), Africans (black)	Skin color
Johann Blumenbach, 1781	5	Caucasian, Ethiopian, Mongolian, Malay, Native American	Skin color, hair color, facial features, and other physical traits
J. Deniker, 1900	29	Adriatic, Ainu, Assyroid, Australian, Berber, Bushman, Dravidian, Ethiopian, Littoral-European, Western-European, Northern-European, Eastern-European, Ibero-Insular, Indo-Afghan, Indonesian, Melanesian, Negrito, Negro, Polynesian, Semite, South American, North American, Central American, Patagonian, Eskimo, Lapp, Ugrian, Turkish, Mongol	Hair color and texture, eye color
William Boyd, 1950	6	European, African, Asiatic, American Indian, Australoid, Early European	Blood groups
Carleton Coon, Stanley Garn, & Joseph Birdsell, 1950	30	Murrayian, Ainu, Alpine, Northwestern European, Northeastern European, Lapp, Forest Negro, Melanesian, Negrito, Bushman Bantu, Sudanese, Carpentarian, Dravidian, Hamite, Hindu, Mediterranean, Nordic, North American Colored, South African Colored, Classic Mongoloid, North Chinese, Southeastern Asiatic, Tibeto-Indonesian, Mongoloid, Turkic, American Indian Marginal, American Indian Central, Ladino, Polynesian, Neo-Hawaiian	Evolutionary trends, body build, and special surface features, such as skin color and facial structure
Stanley Garn, 1961	9	Africans, Amerindian (Native Americans), Asiatics, Australians, Europeans, Indians, Melanesian-Papuans, Micronesians, Polynesians	Geographic boundaries restricting gene flow
Walter Bodmer, 1976	3	Africans, Caucasians, Easterners (including Australians and Pacific Islanders)	Major geographical groups
Current Perspectives	Most modern researchers reject simplistic typological classifications of race and focus their efforts on specific characteristics and explaining why there is variation in particular traits.		

By correlating physical characteristics with cultural differences, ancient classification systems such as these assumed erroneously that populations which shared certain physical traits, especially skin color, also shared other physical characteristics and behaviors. These beliefs gave rise to many popular misconceptions and generalizations concerning the values, traditions, and behaviors of different peoples. Based on contemporary scientific research on DNA, genetics, linguistics, prehistory, historical, and anthropological data, there is no scientific evidence to substantiate the claims of the biblical beliefs about the sons of Noah (Cavalli-Sforza, Menozzi, and Piazza 1994; Brooks, Jackson, and Grinker 2004).

Early "Scientific" Studies of Race

During the 1500s when European explorers began to make contact with different peoples and cultures, various forms of "scientific" classifications began to appear. Earlier ideas based on blood and essential essences influenced these models of scientific racism. In these interpretations, the skin color of the varied peoples in the Americas, Africa, the Middle East, and Asia were associated with particular essences, behaviors, and mental developments. Europeans measured these civilizations in comparison with their own and designated them as "savage" and "barbaric." Europeans began to rank the people they discovered according to differences in skin colors, with nonwhite peoples at the bottom. With this rationale to support them, biased treatment, colonization, and slavery of non-Western peoples could occur freely.

One of the earliest scientific efforts to organize human variation into racial categories was undertaken by the Swedish scientist Carolus Linnaeus, who developed the taxonomic system still used to classify organisms (see the discussion of taxonomy in Chapter 2). Linnaeus's classification of humans, created in 1735, divided *Homo sapiens* into four races based on skin color: *Homo europaeus* (white Europeans), *Homo americanus* (red North American Indians), *Homo asiaticus* (yellow Asians), and *Homo afer* (black Africans). His classification of humans was influenced by ancient and medieval theories, as well as European perceptions of their superiority. For example, he classified the American Indians with reddish skin as choleric, with a need to be regulated by customs. Africans with black skin were relaxed, indolent, negligent, and governed by caprice. In contrast, Europeans with white skin were described as gentle, acute, inventive, and governed by laws (Lieberman and Scupin 2012).

In 1781, a German scientist, Johann Blumenbach, devised a racial classification system that is still sometimes used in popular, unscientific discussions of race. He divided humans into five distinct groups—Caucasian, Mongolian, Malay, Ethiopian, and Native American—corresponding to the colors white, yellow, brown, black, and red, respectively. Blumenbach based his racial typology primarily on skin color as well as geography, but he considered other traits as well, including facial features, chin form, and hair color. Although Blumenbach emphasized the unity of all humanity, his typologies were modified during the nineteenth and early twentieth centuries as the three races of mankind, the Caucasoid, Mongoloid, and Negroid as a means of justifying slavery, colonialism, and racism throughout the world (Lieberman and Scupin 2012; Fluehr-Lobban 2003). Later, a number of physical anthropologists in the United States and Europe, such as Samuel Morton, Ernst Haeckel, Rudolph Virchow, and others, began to assert that the Caucasian race had larger brains and higher intellectual capacities than non-Caucasians (Shipman 1994; Wolpoff and Caspari 1997; Lieberman and Scupin 2012).

Limitations of Early Classification Systems Because early researchers such as Linnaeus and Blumenbach created their typologies before Darwin and Mendel had published their findings, they did not incorporate the modern principles of natural selection, heredity, and population genetics. For example, Mendel's principle of independent assortment holds that physical traits are not linked together in the process of reproduction and transmission of genetic material. In other words, there is no "package" of characteristics that is passed on to members of different "races." Thus, blond hair and blue eyes are not consistently found in tandem, just as a specific skin color and hair texture are not linked to each other. Rather, these traits are independent of one another, leading to varying combinations in different individuals. Variation in the combination of traits makes it impossible to classify races according to well-defined criteria that hold for entire populations.

Continuous Variation and Classification Early scientists, just as modern researchers, encountered another fundamental problem in distinguishing races. Instead of falling into discrete divisions, many characteristics exhibit a spectrum from one extreme to another, a phenomenon called *continuous variation*. Figure 5.3 illustrates this concept by showing the overlap of different skin colors, as measured by reflected light. If skin color is to be used as the primary criterion for determining race, how, then, do we divide the races? Inevitably, any boundaries we draw are entirely arbitrary.

If races constituted fundamental divisions within the human species, such differences would be readily measurable; in fact, they are not. As scientific information has accumulated, the picture has become increasingly complicated and the boundaries

Figure 5.3 Variation in skin color, as measured by the amount of reflected light. The measurements cannot be divided into natural divisions, thus illustrating the arbitrary nature of racial classification.
Source: From *The Human Species: An Introduction to Biological Anthropology* by John Relethford. Copyright ©1990 by Mayfield Publishing Company. Reprinted by permission of the publisher.

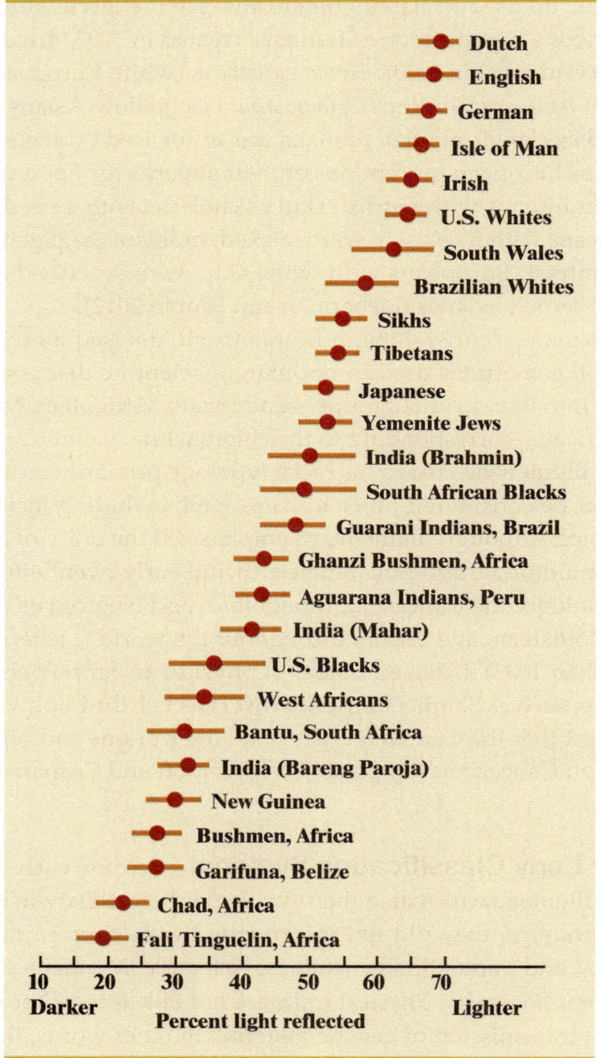

more obscure. Some people have attempted to explain continuous variation as a function of *mongrelization*, or interbreeding. This notion follows the logic that at some point in the past, the races were "pure," but the lines separating one race from another have become blurred by recent interbreeding. Such ideas reveal a naïve understanding of the human past. As has been discussed in Chapters 2 and 4, human history is characterized by a tremendous amount of migration and intermixing that must be accounted for. Although gene flow may have been more restricted in some groups than in others, human populations have always interbred. Consequently, different races would have been impossible to distinguish during any time period.

Geographical Races

By the mid-twentieth century, anthropologists had recognized the arbitrary nature of different racial classifications and took a more biological approach. Unlike earlier theorists, they did not rely on single, arbitrarily defined characteristics, such as skin pigmentation. Instead, in developing classification systems, they focused on the

Critical Perspectives

Joseph Arthur de Gobineau and the Aryan Master Race

The extermination of millions of Jews by the Nazis before and during World War II was justified by unscientific theories of race that had no basis in empirical fact.

At times, racial classifications have been used to justify **racism**, an ideology that advocates the superiority of certain supposed races and the inferiority of others, which leads to prejudice and discrimination against particular populations. Often with limited scientific grounding, such perspectives twist scientific information to meet political and social objectives.

In 1853, racist beliefs coalesced in a four-volume treatise by the French aristocrat Joseph Arthur de Gobineau, titled *Essai sur l'inégalité des races humaines* (*Essay on the Inequality of the Races of Humanity*). In this work, Gobineau described the whole of human history as a struggle among the various "races" of humanity. He argued that each race had its own intellectual capacity, either high or low, and that there were stronger and weaker races. Gobineau promoted the conquest of so-called "weaker races" by allegedly stronger ones.

Gobineau opened his book with the statement that everything great, noble, and fruitful in the works of humanity springs from the Aryan family, the so-called "super race." Just prior to Gobineau's writings, it had been discovered by Western linguists that the languages of the Greeks, Germans, Romans (Latin), and Persians were all related to the ancient Sanskrit "Aryan" language family. Laying a thin foundation on this linguistic classifications, Gobineau argued that a single "super" race of Aryans had led to the development of all the major civilizations of the world. He suggested that the Aryan super race spread out to create, first, the Hindu civilization, then the Egyptian, Assyrian, Greek, Chinese, Roman, German, Mexican, and Peruvian civilizations (Montagu 1997; Banton 1998). Gobineau argued that these civilizations declined because of "racial mixing." Following the biblical narrative about Noah's sons, he argued that the superior Aryan race were the white descendants of Japheth. The Aryans were superior to the sons of Shem, the Semites. The Hamites were the descendants of Ham, an inferior race of blacks residing in Africa.

In the 1930s, drawing on Gobineau's ideas, Nazi racist ideology based on the presumed superiority of a pure "Aryan race" was used to justify the annihilation of millions of Jews and other "non-Aryan" peoples in Europe. Nazi pseudoscientists undertook expeditions across the globe and misconstrued actual scientific data to support the idea of Germany's primary position as a successor to the Aryan civilization. These racist beliefs have no basis in actual fact. Human groups never fit into such neat categories and there was never an Aryan master race. Even staunch advocates of Nazi ideology found it difficult to define precisely which physical characteristics supposedly distinguished one "race" from another. Many Jewish people living in Europe during the Holocaust possessed the same physical features as those associated with so-called "Aryans," Germans, or other Europeans.

Points to Ponder

1. Consider Gobineau's ideas of a master race in light of what you know about modern human variation. What problems do you see with it?
2. Many of the ideas regarding an Aryan master race were clearly fanciful. Why did so many people believe them?
3. Can you think of other cases where pseudoscientific information has been used to foster political aims?

influences evolutionary forces may have had on geographically isolated human populations. Stanley Garn (1971), for example, divided modern humans into what he called *geographical races*, populations isolated from one another by natural barriers such as oceans, mountains, and deserts. He reasoned that because of these barriers most people in each population married within their own gene pool. Garn's taxonomy divided humans into nine geographical races: Amerindian, Polynesian, Micronesian, Melanesian-Papuan, Australian, Asiatic, Indian, European, and African. These were further divided into smaller local races and micro-races that reflected restricted gene flow among smaller populations.

Garn's approach sought to frame the classification of human races in evolutionary terms. However, critics pointed out that even these divisions imply stronger similarities among the races than actually exist. Some of Garn's supposed races exhibit an enormous amount of variation. Consider, for example, the "Mediterranean race," which extends, according to Garn, from Morocco in the far western Mediterranean to the Arabian peninsula thousands of miles to the east. It is difficult to imagine the culturally diverse groups included in this vast area as a discrete breeding population. Even more importantly, the degree of difference between this group and others is no greater than the variation contained within the group itself (Molnar 2006).

Heredity and Intelligence

5.6 Discuss how contemporary anthropologists assess the relationship between intelligence and race.

Before leaving the discussion of race and human variation, one other area of research needs to be examined: the study of intelligence. In no area of study have the varying effects of genes, environment, and culture been more confused. **Intelligence** can be defined as the capacity to process and evaluate information for problem solving. It can be contrasted with **knowledge**—the storage and recall of learned information. Heredity undoubtedly plays a role in intelligence; this is confirmed by the fact that the intelligence of genetically related individuals (for example, parents and their biological children) displays the closest correlation. Yet other environmental, social, and cultural factors also come into play. The interpretation of the varying roles of these different factors has further been confused by the challenges involved in measuring intelligence, and attempts to link these measurements to flawed concepts of races.

Following Darwin's publications on human evolution, many writers grounded allegedly "scientific" racist philosophies on misinterpretations of his theory. Nineteenth-century English thinkers, such as Herbert Spencer and Francis Galton, believed that social evolution worked by allowing superior members of society to rise to the top while inferior ones sank to the bottom. These views reinforced the false belief that particular groups of people, or races, had quantifiably different intellectual capacities.

Problems in Measuring Intelligence

Most scientists agree that intelligence varies among individuals. Yet it has been difficult to measure intelligence objectively because tests inevitably reflect the beliefs and values of a particular cultural group. Nevertheless, a number of devices have been developed to measure intelligence, the most prominent among them being the intelligence quotient (IQ) test, invented by French psychologist Alfred Binet in 1905. Binet's test was brought to the United States and modified to become the Stanford-Binet test. The inventors warned that the test was valid only when the children tested came from similar cultural environments. Yet, the IQ test was used in the late nineteenth century at Ellis Island to weed out undesirables and "mentally deficient" peoples, such as Italians, Poles, Jews, and other Europeans.

These IQ tests are widely used today for tracking students in the U.S. educational system, sparking controversy among educators and social scientists alike. In a controversial book called *The Bell Curve: Intelligence and Class Structure in American Life* (1994), Richard Herrnstein and Charles Murray argue that research supports the conclusion that race is related to intelligence. Utilizing a bell curve statistical distribution, they place the IQ of people with European ancestry at 100. People of East Asian ancestry exceed that standard slightly, averaging 103; people of African descent fall below that standard, with an average IQ of 90. Their findings imply that IQ scores are related to genetic differences among races.

A number of scientists have noted the faulty reasoning used by Herrnstein and Murray, as well as by others who have attributed IQ differences between African-Americans and European Americans to so-called racial groupings. If there truly were IQ score differences between African-Americans and European Americans, then African-Americans with more European ancestry ought to have higher IQ scores than those with less European ancestry. However, in a major IQ study of hundreds of African-Americans whose European ancestry was determined through blood testing, Scarr and Weinberg (1978) found no significant relationship between IQ scores and the degree of European admixture.

These test score disparities indicate that cultural and social patterns are the more significant variables. African-Americans are no less intelligent than other groups, but carrying a legacy of disadvantage, many contend with a cultural environment that discourages self-confidence and achievement. Most anthropological research on this topic indicates that when differences in socioeconomic status and other factors were controlled for, the difference between African-Americans and European Americans was insignificant (Molnar 2006). In Japan, a group of people known as the *burakumin*, who exhibit no major physical differences between themselves and other Japanese people, but who have been subject to prejudice and discrimination for centuries in their society, tend to score lower on IQ tests than other Japanese (Molnar 2006). This indicates the strong influence of socioeconomic factors in measuring IQ. Additional studies show that educational enrichment programs boost IQ scores (Molnar 2006). Much research has determined that IQ scores increase within every generation of every population by three to five points, indicating the profound influence of social and educational conditions on IQ scores. The other major criticism of Herrnstein, Murray, and like-minded theorists is that they reify "race" as if races were based on clear-cut and distinct genetic groups, ignoring the enormous variation within these so-called races (MacEachern 2012; Lieberman and Scupin 2012).

In a recent evaluation of the question of IQ, race, and the environment, psychologist Richard Nisbett of the University of Michigan relies on numerous studies, statistical, historical, and experimental, to refute the notion that IQ is deeply encoded in our genes (2009). In his book *Intelligence and How to Get It* (2009), Nisbett writes about how class differences are much more important than race or heredity in influencing IQ scores. When poor children are adopted into upper-class homes, their IQ scores rise by 12 to 18 points. Nisbett suggests that IQ scores are expandable depending on the enrichment of children's environments. He records an enormous amount of data demonstrating the rapid trend in upward IQ scores. The average IQ score in 1917 would amount to only 73 on today's IQ test, and half the population would be considered mentally retarded by today's measurements. IQ scores have risen remarkably over time, indicating that environmental and educational factors are much more important than heredity in determining intelligence.

Most psychologists agree that intelligence is not a readily definable characteristic like height or hair color. Psychologists view intelligence as a general capacity for "goal-directed adaptive behavior," that is, behavior based on learning from experience, problem solving, and reasoning (Myers 2012). Though this definition of intelligence would be acceptable to most social scientists, we now recognize that some people are talented in mathematics, others in writing, and still others in aesthetic pursuits such as music, art, and dance. Because abilities vary from individual to individual, psychologists such as Howard Gardner question the view of intelligence as a single factor in the human makeup. Based on cross-cultural research, Gardner (2004) has concluded that intelligence does not constitute a single characteristic, but rather, amounts to a mix of many differing faculties. According to Gardner, each of us has distinct aptitudes for making music, for spatially analyzing the visual world, for mastering athletic skills, and for understanding ourselves and others—a type of social intelligence. Not surprisingly, Gardner concludes that no single test can possibly measure what he refers to as "multiple intelligences."

The majority of psychologists and other scientists concur with Gardner's findings that intelligence spans a wide and diverse range of cognitive processes and other capacities. The IQ test ranks people according to their performance of various cognitive tasks, especially those that relate to scholastic or academic problem solving. Yet it cannot predict how successfully a person will adapt to specific environmental situations or even handle a particular job. Throughout the world, people draw on various forms of intelligence to perform inventive and creative tasks, ranging from composing music to developing efficient hunting strategies. Before we call someone "intelligent," we have to know what qualities and abilities are important in that person's environment.

Current Approaches to Human Variation

5.7 Discuss current approaches to human variation.

Taxonomies that classify humans into separate races, even those based on modern scientific observations, fall short because they are too static to encompass the dynamic nature of human interaction and the consequences of varying environmental and evolutionary forces. Any criterion selected as the basis for classification is necessarily arbitrary. The physical characteristics that have historically been used to distinguish one race from another form an extremely small part of a human's total genetic makeup. There is so much variation among individuals within populations that the classification schemes become extremely blurred and break down. For these reasons, the anthropologists studying human variation steer clear of defining race. Instead, they focus on explaining variation in specific traits.

Clinal Distribution

Because many physical traits vary independently of one another, some researchers have found it useful to examine single traits, or unitary variables. In many contemporary studies of biological variation, scientists plot the distribution of individual traits on maps by zones known as **clines**. A map of **clinal distribution** can be likened to a weather map. It traces a continuous, progressive gradation from one geographic region to another. Rather than simply stating whether it is going to be hot or cold, weather maps detail the temperatures in different parts of the country. Lines tracing temperatures identify approaching storm fronts, and special designations indicate areas experiencing heat waves. Weather maps graphically represent the intersection of a range of variables that explain weather patterns beyond the local level. Similarly, plotting the distribution of individual traits in human populations sheds light on the genetic, environmental, and cultural factors that influenced their distribution. Using mathematical models to analyze evolutionary processes in a gene pool, scientists have tracked specific physical traits within a population.

Anthropologist Joseph Birdsell (1981) conducted a classic clinal distribution study of blond, or tawny, hair among Australian Aborigines. While conducting fieldwork, Birdsell noted that the majority of Aborigines had dark brown hair, but some had tawny hair. Significantly, the tawny hair trait was not evenly distributed throughout the Aborigine population, but was concentrated in certain areas. A map of the percentages of tawny-haired individuals in each region revealed the spread of the trait (Figure 5.4). In some areas of the western desert, 100 percent of the people had tawny hair. Farther away from the western desert, fewer tawny-haired people were to be found. Birdsell speculated that a mutation or, more likely, repeated mutations produced light-colored hair in some individuals. In certain areas, the light-colored hair replaced the original dark brown hair color, for reasons that are unclear. Over time, through gene flow with surrounding groups, the new trait spread outward. The clinal distribution of tawny hair offers a graphic illustration of micro-evolutionary change over time within one human population.

Figure 5.4 A clinal distribution map of tawny hair color in Australia. The trait probably originated in the western desert, where it is most common. The percentage of tawny hair decreases in waves spreading out from this area. This is an example of a study focusing on one genetic trait.
Source: From *Human Evolution* by Joseph B. Birdsell. Copyright ©1975, 1981 by Harper & Row, Inc. Reprinted by permission of Addison-Wesley Educational Publishers, Inc.

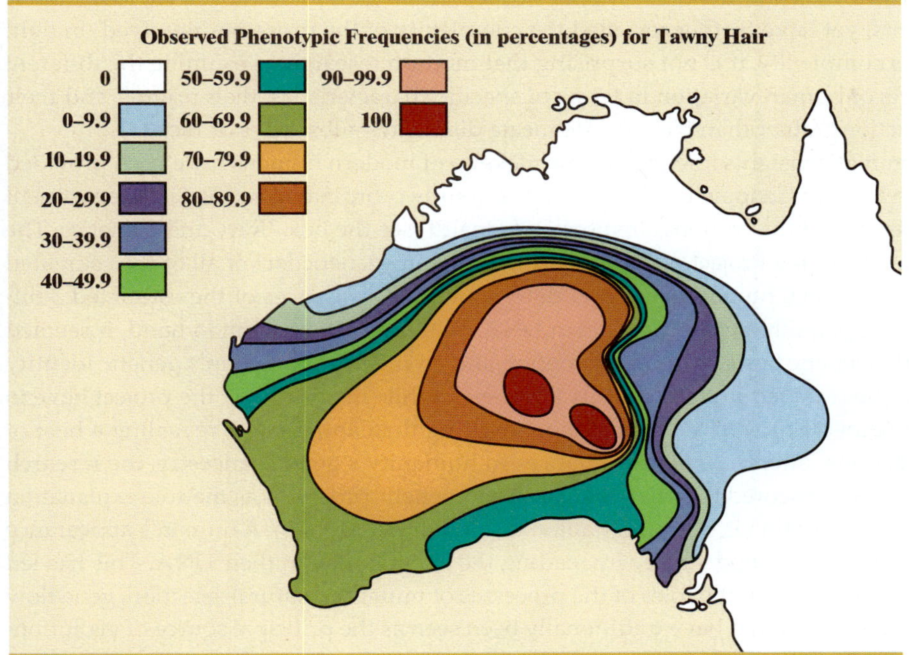

This approach can be used to examine other differences in human populations, but it also further underscores the problems inherent in attempts at the classification of human races. When plotted individually, the varying distribution of physical traits is readily apparent. Notably, the clinal distributions of other physical characteristics in Australian Aborigines differ from that for tawny hair color. This further indicates the limited explanatory value of classifications based on individual or constellations of physical characteristics.

Multivariate Analysis

In addition to univariate approaches that focus on a single trait, **multivariate analysis** examines the interrelationships among a number of different traits. Such studies are extremely complex, and scientists using this approach must decide which physical traits and which variables should be examined. Biologist R. C. Lewontin adopted a multivariate approach in his study of human variation. Lewontin (1972) probed the distribution of physical traits that vary in human populations, including those that have been considered distinctive to certain races, such as skin color and hair texture. In focusing on how the distribution of these traits compares to common divisions by race, he noted that traits used to identify races do not accurately reflect human variation. Observed differences among Africans, Caucasians, Mongoloids, South Asians, Oceanians, Australian Aborigines, and Native Americans (divisions that approximate Garn's geographical races) account for only about 6 percent of the total amount of variation in human populations. Almost 94 percent of human variation of physical traits occurs *within* each of these different "races." Lewontin's genetic findings have been confirmed by many other contemporary studies in biological anthropology that underscore the very limited usefulness of the concept of race ((Mukhopadhyay, Henze, and Moses 2014; Relethford 2013; Jurmain et al. 2014). These observations have been further borne out by recent research such as the mapping of the human genome (see the box "Race and Genetics: The Human Genome Project").

Current Perspectives

Sorting out the varied reasons for variation in human populations is clearly complex. Recent studies and the unwrapping of the human genome have provided dramatic insights, yet have further revealed the complexity of the processes involved. In light of this complexity, it is not surprising that modern researchers examine the different aspects of human variation in terms of specific characteristics, their origins, and their interactions rather than trying to delineate distinctive subspecies or races.

Dramatic insights into the genetic makeup of modern humans have been provided by the Human Genome Project, which was jointly coordinated by the U.S. Department of Energy and the National Institutes of Health (see the box "Race and Genetics: The Human Genome Project"). The project mapped the genetic loci of all of the estimated 20,000 to 25,000 human genes and determined the sequences of the estimated 3 billion base pairs that make up human DNA. With this information in hand, it seemed that the genetic basis of human variation and an individual human's genetic identity would be revealed in their entirety. However, while the results of the project have in some respects proven to be even more exciting than anticipated, revealing a host of connections, intersections and nuances in humanity's genetic ancestry, the research has also underscored that viewing genes and genetic processes as the sole explanation of human variation is not valid (Jablonka and Lamb 2006: 4-8). A human's appearance cannot be understood simply by reading the genetic code in their DNA. This has led to a reassessment of the roles of the processes of mutation, natural selection, gene flow and genetic drift that have traditionally been seen as the principal source of evolutionary change.

This reassessment does not mean that these traditional evolutionary processes are not of great importance and they do provide key mechanisms for evolutionary change. However, researchers are increasingly aware of the important role that human behavior and culture has played in human evolution, and of the dynamic feedback between culture and evolution. This was well illustrated in the cases of sickle-cell anemia and lactose intolerance. As seen in the preceding discussions of the varied genetic, environmental, and behavioral sources of human variation, researchers now increasingly seek to map out the complex interaction of these various sources of variation.

Summary and Review of Learning Objectives

5.1 Identify the different sources of human variation.

Human beings evince tremendous variation. Many of the observable differences are the result of cultural variations and are superficial; individuals taken from one cultural setting and raised in another will adopt the practices and behaviors of the new cultural group. However, humans also exhibit tremendous variation in physical traits, ranging from skin color to body build and a variety of biochemical characteristics. These traits are the products of the dynamic interaction of evolutionary processes affecting genetic diversity within and between populations, the physical environment, and cultural variables. The four principal processes of evolution that influence the genetic makeup of a population are: mutations, natural selection, gene flow, and genetic drift. In addition to these processes, genes and their expression are also influenced by epigenetic factors that are external to the DNA sequence. The physical environment also influences human variation by promoting or restricting growth and development. Humans dramatically impact the environments in which they live, activities that may have evolutionary implications. Culture may even more directly influence human genetic variation through practices that inhibit gene flow. Although we know that all of these factors contribute to human variation, it is challenging to assess their relative importance.

5.2 Provide examples of how physical characteristics in human populations may represent adaptations arising from natural selection.

Studies suggest that many genetically controlled traits may be the result of natural selection. For example, having darker skin may have been an advantage in tropical Africa, where early humans evolved. Melanin, which is found in greater concentration in darker skin, provides protection from ultraviolet (UV) radiation in sunlight, which has been shown to have a number of detrimental effects, including sunburn, sunstroke, and skin cancer. Most importantly, it decreases folate levels, a factor that causes higher numbers of birth defects, and so directly affects reproductive success. As early humans moved into temperate regions with less sunlight, other selective pressures, especially the need for Vitamin D, conferred an adaptive advantage on lighter skin pigmentation. Reduced production of Vitamin D is associated with deficiency diseases such as rickets and increased infant mortality rates. As Vitamin D production is stimulated by UV radiation, people who lived in colder, cloudy climates would have had improved chances of survival if they had lighter skin that absorbed higher levels of UV radiation and, thus, synthesized more Vitamin D. Over time, natural selection favored darker skin in the tropics and lighter skin in regions with less sunlight. The influence of natural selection and the environment can also be seen in human body and limb forms, which in part may relate to thermoregulation. This characteristic can be illustrated by Bergmann's rule that states that smaller animals, which have larger surface areas relative to their body weights, lose excess heat efficiently and, thus, function better at higher temperatures. Larger animals, which have a smaller surface area relative to their body weight, dissipate heat more slowly and so are better adapted to cold climates. The same principle applies to humans: People living in cold climates tend to have stocky torsos and heavier average body weights, whereas people in warmer regions have more slender frames. Adaptive features can also be seen in sweat glands, body hair, cranial and facial features, biochemical characteristics such as blood groups, and lactose tolerance.

5.3 Discuss how environmental factors may be sources of evolutionary change.

Humans are highly sensitive to changes in their physical surroundings, and environment is consequently an important factor in human variation. Environment may affect the individual during his or her lifetime, as well as long-term evolutionary change in populations. Adaptive features resulting from natural selection may arise as a result of how well the requirements for growth are met in certain environments. Acclimatization refers to the physiological process through which humans become accustomed to a new environment. This physiological adjustment is temporary: When these individuals leave the new environment, they revert to their earlier states. This type of acclimatization can be differentiated from developmental acclimatization. In this case, individuals born or raised in certain environmental conditions may develop nonreversible physical characteristics.

5.4 Discuss how cultural factors may be sources of evolutionary change.

Human behavior and culture may also influence human genetic makeup. Species alter the environments in which they live, something that may affect their adaptability and so influence natural selection. The process by which organisms modify their environment is referred to as niche construction. More than any other species, human societies dramatically impact the environments in which they live. Human activities such as plant and animal domestication, land clearing, and industrialization have dramatically impacted the environment. Culture may even more directly influence human genetic variation through religious beliefs, social organization, marriage practices, or prejudices that restrict intermarriage among different groups and, thus, inhibit gene flow. Cultural beliefs also determine diet, living conditions, and the environment in which people work; these effects, in turn, either promote or hamper human growth and development.

5.5 Explain the challenges faced in dividing human populations into different races and why modern anthropologists avoid these classifications.

Physical characteristics, such as skin pigmentation, nose shape, and hair texture, have prompted people throughout history to classify humans into different "races." Although human populations clearly encompass a great deal of diversity, physical characteristics cannot be used to divide humans into readily discernible groups or races. Instead of falling into discrete divisions, many characteristics exhibit a spectrum from one extreme to another, a phenomenon called continuous variation. Different characteristics also sort independently of one another and so do not provide the same divisions. Inevitably, any boundaries we draw are entirely arbitrary. If races constituted fundamental divisions within the human species, such differences would be readily measurable; in fact, they are not. Many attempts at racial classifications have been made, but these have failed because they proved too rigid to account for either the tremendous variation found within individual races or the shared similarities between these supposedly different groups. The varied criteria used in different classifications of human races and the dramatically different numbers of races identified—ranging from 3 to 30—underscore the limited use of the concept. Even more importantly, identifying different races does not explain the reason for the observed variation. The word race is also of limited use because the word is used differently in different contexts. It may be used as justification for the discrimination or the marginalization of certain groups. Racial classifications can also be used as self-defined categories in census data or in other contexts to refer to styles of music, dance, or literature. For these reasons, modern anthropologists avoid using racial classifications, but rather focus on the distribution and study of specific traits and the explanation of the processes that may have produced them.

5.6 Discuss how contemporary anthropologists assess the relationship between intelligence and race.

Another aspect of human variation is intelligence, which can be defined as the capacity to process and evaluate information for problem solving. It can be contrasted with knowledge—the storage and recall of learned information. Although individuals vary in their intelligence, researchers generally agree that environmental and cultural factors influence intelligence much more than hereditary or genetic factors. A consensus among educators and social scientists holds that rather than being a singular trait, intelligence is actually a mix of different faculties that cannot be measured by one culturally coded test. The interpretation of the varying roles of these different factors has further been confused by the challenges involved in measuring intelligence, and attempts to link these measurements to flawed concepts of races.

5.7 Discuss current approaches to human variation.

Modern studies of human variation focus on explaining why such variation occurs. Because many physical traits vary independently of one another, some researchers have found it useful to examine single traits, or unitary variables. Plotting the distribution of individual traits in human populations sheds light on the genetic, environmental, and cultural factors that influenced their distribution. In contrast, multivariate analysis examines the interrelationships among a number of different traits. Such studies are extremely complex, and scientists using this approach must decide which physical traits and which variables should be examined. Dramatic insights into the genetic makeup of modern humans have been provided by the Human Genome Project, which was jointly coordinated by the U.S. Department of Energy and the National Institutes of Health. The project mapped the genetic loci that make up human DNA. The results of the project have revealed a host of connections, intersections, and nuances in humanity's genetic ancestry, as well as the importance of cultural, environmental, cultural, and epigenetic factors in human variation. In light of this complexity, it is not surprising that modern researchers examine the varied aspects of human variation in terms of specific characteristics, their origins, and their interactions rather than trying to delineate distinctive subspecies or races.

Key Terms

acclimatization, p. 132
balanced polymorphism, p. 130
clinal distribution, p. 144
clines, p. 144
continuous variation, p. 125
developmental acclimatization, p. 132
intelligence, p. 142
knowledge, p. 142
lactase deficiency, p. 132
multivariate analysis, p. 145
polymorphism, p. 122
polytypic, p. 123
racism, p. 141

Chapter 6

Culture and Enculturation

Chapter Outline

Learning Objectives

After reading this chapter you should be able to:

6.1 Discuss the basic characteristics and components of *culture* as understood by anthropologists.

6.2 Discuss how humans acquire their culture.

6.3 Discuss how anthropologists understand the sharing of culture.

6.4 Discuss the components of nonmaterial culture studied by anthropologists.

6.5 Describe how culture results in differences among people in various societies.

6.6 Describe how culture leads to universal similarities among people in widely separated societies.

6.7 Discuss the relationship between biology and culture and how anthropologists regard the nature/nurture questions of humanity.

6.8 Describe how anthropologists study enculturation and its relationship to personality formation.

6.9 Discuss what cognitive anthropologists have learned about universals and human thought processes.

6.10 Discuss what anthropologists have discovered about human emotions.

6.11 Discuss the limitations of enculturation in studying human behavior.

The Characteristics of Culture

6.1 Discuss the basic characteristics and components of *culture* as understood by anthropologists.

As mentioned in Chapter 3, culture is a fundamental concept within the discipline of anthropology. E. B. Tylor, the first professional anthropologist, proposed a definition of culture that includes all of human experience:

> *Culture . . . is that complex whole which includes knowledge, belief, arts, morals, law, custom, and any other capabilities and habits acquired by man as a member of society. (1871:1)*

This view suggests that culture includes tools, weapons, fire, agriculture, animal domestication, metallurgy, writing, the steam engine, glasses, airplanes, computers, penicillin, nuclear power, rock and roll, video games, designer jeans, religion, political systems, subsistence patterns, science, sports, and social organizations. As noted in Chapter 3, culture includes all aspects of human activity, from the fine arts to popular entertainment, from everyday behavior to the development of sophisticated technology. It contains the plans, rules, techniques, designs, and policies for living. Tylor was using the term *culture* as a general phenomenon for all of humanity that was different from our physical or biological characteristics. The fundamental aspect of culture recognized by anthropologists today is that it is distinct from our human biological characteristics or genetics.

This nineteenth-century definition of culture has some terminology that would not be acceptable to modern anthropologists. For example, it relies on the word *man* to refer to what we currently would refer to as *humanity*. In addition, nineteenth-century theorists such as Tylor tended to think of "culture" as equivalent to "civilization," which implicitly suggested that there was an increase, accumulation, or growth in "culture" and "civilization" as societies progressed and evolved. This is not the meaning of culture that contemporary anthropologists maintain. Cultures are not evolving in some simplistic manner from early civilizations to modern civilizations as the nineteenth-century anthropologists believed. As we will discuss, humans have had different languages, beliefs, values, dietary habits, and norms or "cultures" that are associated with various regions in the past as well as the present.

Notice that Tylor's definition includes the word *society*. In general terms, society refers to an organized group of animals within a specific territory. In particular, it refers to the patterns of relationships among the animals within that territory. Biologists often refer to certain types of insects, herd animals, and social animals such as monkeys and apes as living in societies.

In the past, anthropologists attempted to make a simple distinction between society and culture. **Society** was said to consist of the patterns of relationships among people within a specified territory, and culture was viewed as the byproducts of those relationships. This view of society as distinguishable from culture was derived from ethnographic studies of small-scale societies. In such societies, people within a specific territory were believed to share a common culture. However, contemporary anthropologists have found this notion of shared culture to be too simplistic and crude. For example, modern anthropologists conduct ethnographic research in complex societies. Within these societies there are many distinctive groups that maintain different cultural traditions. Culture is not a uniform byproduct of society—within societies there are varieties of culture. Even in small-scale societies, the idea that all people share a collective "culture" is also too crude and simplistic. As we shall see in this chapter, this conception of shared culture often resulted in gross stereotypes of and extreme generalizations about groups of people and their behavior.

Many anthropologists adopt the hybrid term *sociocultural system*—a combination of the terms *society* (or *social*) and *culture*—to refer to what used to be called "society" and the byproduct "culture." As we shall see in later chapters, many anthropologists use the term *sociocultural system* as the basic conceptual framework for analyzing ethnographic research.

The young psychologist B.F. Skinner using conditioning to train a pigeon. This is an example of situational learning.

Culture Is Learned

6.2 Discuss how humans acquire their culture.

The unique capacity for culture in the human species depends upon learning. We do not inherit our culture through our genes in the way we inherit our physical characteristics. Instead, we obtain our culture through the process of enculturation. **Enculturation** is the process of social interaction through which people learn and acquire their culture. We will study this process in more detail below. Humans acquire their culture both consciously, through formal learning, and unconsciously, through informal interaction. Anthropologists distinguish among several types of learning. One type is known as **situational learning**, or trial-and-error learning, in which an organism adjusts its behavior on the basis of direct experience. The costs and risks of situational learning can be quite high. Imagine if you only based your decisions about food on trial and error—you might encounter a number of foods that are poisonous or inedible. It would be very risky. Fortunately, humans are capable of learning from one another.

A chimp with a crumpled leaf made to drink water. Chimps learn much through social learning by observing one another.

Learning from one another is called **social learning**. It occurs when one organism observes another organism respond to a stimulus and then adds that response to its own collection of behaviors. Thus, the organism need not have the direct experience; it can observe how others behave and then imitate or avoid those behaviors (Rendell et al. 2010). Obviously, humans learn by observing classmates, teachers, parents, friends, and the media. Within social situations, children and adults can make inferences about what is observed and perceived. Other social animals also learn in this manner. For example, wolves learn hunting strategies by observing pack members. Similarly, chimpanzees observe other chimps fashioning twigs with which to hunt termites and then imitate those behaviors. Recently, some primatologists and anthropologists have suggested that nonhuman primates have "culture" based upon how they learn socially from one another and have variations of behavior from one group to another (Sapolsky 2006; Laland et al. 2009). However, it appears that nonhuman animals, including primates, do not intentionally or deliberately teach one another as humans do (Tomasello et al. 2005). In addition, as we will discuss later and in Chapter 7 on language, these nonhuman primates do not appear to have a core aspect of what most anthropologists view as an important criteria for designating a "culture," and that is the ability to symbolize (Rossano 2010; Konner 2010).

Symbols and Symbolic Learning

Humans do not engage in social learning only through direct observation. Instead, humans can learn about things that are not immediately observable by using symbols. **Symbolic learning** is based on our linguistic capacity and ability to use and understand **symbols**, arbitrary meaningful units or models we use to represent reality. An example of the arbitrary aspects of symbolism would be the colors red, yellow, and green for traffic lights in the United States (Sahlins 1976a). Traffic lights could be other colors in different societies, but in the United States, they take this arbitrary form. Sounds such as "cat," "dog," "tree," "one," "two," and "three" in English are symbolic and arbitrary because, as we know, the sounds that symbolize those words in languages such as Chinese, Navajo, or Russian can be completely different. However, linguistic anthropologists know that symbols do not just refer to items such as animals or numbers. Symbolic communication and language can be used to represent abstract ideas and values. Symbols are the conceptual devices that we use to communicate abstract ideas to one another. We communicate these symbols through language. For example, children can learn to distinguish and name coins such as pennies, nickels, and quarters, and to use this money as a symbolic medium of exchange. The symbols of money in the United States or other societies are embedded within a host of many other symbols. Symbols do not stand in isolation from one another; instead, they are interconnected within linguistic symbol systems that enable us to provide rules and meanings for objects, actions, and abstract thought processes. The linguistic capacity that we are born with gives us the unique ability to make and use symbolic distinctions.

Humans learn most of their behaviors and concepts through symbolic learning. We do not have to depend upon situational learning or observations of others to perceive and understand the world and one another. We have the uniquely human ability to abstract the essence of complex events and patterns, creating images through symbols and bestowing meaning and making inferences about these meanings.

Through the ability to symbolize, humans can learn, create meanings, and infer from those meanings in order to transmit culture. Parents do not have to depend on demonstrations to teach children. As children mature, they can learn abstract rules and concepts involving symbolic communication. Through oral traditions and text humans can transmit this information across vast distances and through time. Symbolic learning has almost infinite possibilities in terms of absorbing and using information in creative ways. Most of our learning as humans is based on this symbolic learning process.

Symbols and Signs Symbols are arbitrary units of meaning, in contrast to **signs**, which are directly associated with concrete physical items or activities. Many nonhuman animals can learn signs. For example, a dog can learn to associate the ringing of

A Vietnamese elder man teaching a child the written language. This is an example of symbolic learning.

a bell (a physical activity) with drinking water. You can teach the dog to drink water when you ring the bell. Hence, both humans and other animals can learn signs and apply them to different sorts of activities or to concrete items.

Symbols are different from signs in that they are not directly associated with any concrete item or physical activity; they are much more abstract. A symbol's meaning is not always obvious. However, many symbols are powerful and often trigger behaviors or emotional states. For example, the designs and colors of the flags of different countries represent symbolic associations with abstract ideas and concepts. In some flags, the color red may symbolize blood; in others, it may symbolize revolution. In many countries, the desecration of the national flag, itself a symbol, is considered a crime. When the symbols associated with particular abstract ideas and concepts that are related to the national destiny of a society are violated, powerful emotions may be aroused.

The ability to symbolize, to create symbols and bestow meaning on them, enhances our learning capacities as humans in comparison with other types of animals. Anthropologist Leslie White maintained that the most distinctive feature of being human is the ability to create symbols:

> *It is impossible for a dog, horse, or even an ape, to have any understanding of the meaning of the sign of the cross to a Christian, or of the fact that black (white among the Chinese) is the color of mourning. No chimpanzee or laboratory rat can appreciate the difference between Holy water and distilled water, or grasp the meaning of Tuesday, 3, or sin.* (1971:23–24)

Symbols and Culture The human capacity for culture is based on our linguistic and cognitive ability to symbolize. Culture is transmitted from generation to generation through symbolic learning and the ability to make inferences regarding our symbols and language (Bloch 2012). (In Chapter 7, we discuss the relationship between language and culture.) Through the transmission of culture, we learn how to subsist, how to socialize, how to govern our society, and what gods to worship. Culture is the historical accumulation of symbolic knowledge that is shared by a society. This symbolic knowledge is transmitted through learning, and it can change rapidly from parents to children and from one generation to the next. Generally, however, people in societies go to great lengths to conserve their cultural and symbolic traditions. The persistence of cultural and symbolic traditions is as widespread as cultural change.

Culture Is Shared

6.3 Discuss how anthropologists understand the sharing of culture.

Culture consists of the shared practices and understandings within a society. To some degree, culture is based on shared meanings that are to some extent "public" and, thus, beyond the mind of any individual (Geertz 1973). Some of this culture exists before the birth of an individual into the society, and it may continue (in some form) beyond the death of any particular individual. These publicly shared meanings provide designs or recipes for surviving and contributing to the society. On the other hand, culture is also within the minds of individuals. For example, we mentioned that children learn the symbolic meanings of the different coins and bills that constitute money. The children figure out the meanings of money by observing practices and learning the various symbols that are public. However, children are not just passive assimilators of that cultural knowledge. Cognitive anthropologists such as Roy D'Andrade and Naomi Quinn emphasize **schemas**, or cultural models that are internalized by individuals and have an influence on decision making and behavior. They emphasize how culture is acquired by and modeled as schemas within individual minds and can motivate, shape, and transform the symbols and meanings (Quinn and Holland 1987; D'Andrade 1989, 1995).

Contemporary anthropologists recognize that cultural understandings are not shared equally by all members of a society (Fox and King 2002; Barth 2002; de Munck 2000). Even in small-scale societies, culture is shared differently by males and females or by young and old. Some individuals in these societies have a great deal of knowledge regarding agriculture, medical practices, or religious beliefs; those beliefs and that knowledge are not equally distributed. In our complex industrialized society, culture consists of a tremendous amount of information and knowledge regarding technology and other aspects of society. Different people learn different aspects of culture, such as repairing cars or television sets, understanding nuclear physics or federal tax regulations, or composing music. Hence, to some extent, culture varies from person to person, from subgroup to subgroup, from region to region, from age group to age group, and from gender to gender. Contemporary anthropologists also note how culture is "contested," referring to how people question and may fundamentally disagree and struggle over the specifics of culture. Yet despite this variation, some common cultural understandings allow members of society to adapt, to communicate, and to interact with one another. Without some of these common understandings, a society could not exist.

One recent anthropological understanding of culture is sometimes referred to as the epidemiological approach pioneered by Dan Sperber and his colleagues (Sperber 1996, Sperber and Hirschfeld 1999, Bloch 2012, Ross 2004). These anthropologists draw on the fields of cognitive science and cognitive psychology to discuss how culture propagates like a contagious disease from one person to another. Thus, religious beliefs, cooking recipes, folktales, and even scientific hypotheses are ideas or representations within the human mind that spread among people in a shared environment. Chains of communication propagate these beliefs or cultural representations within a population. As in the spread of a contagious disease, some representations take hold and are maintained in particular populations, while other beliefs or representations do not resonate with specific groups and become extinct. Also, some beliefs or representations spread and are retained more easily within a population because they are more easily acquired than other beliefs. For example, some folktales or religious narratives are easily maintained within a population in contrast to highly complex abstract mathematical formulae and narratives based on the findings within science.

Aspects of Culture

6.4 Discuss the components of nonmaterial culture studied by anthropologists.

Within a broad and refined understanding, contemporary anthropologists have tried to isolate the key elements that constitute culture. Two of the most basic aspects of culture are material and nonmaterial culture.

Material culture consists of the physical products of human society (ranging from weapons to clothing styles), whereas **nonmaterial culture** refers to the intangible products of human society (values, beliefs, and norms). As we discussed in Chapter 3, the earliest traces of material culture are stone tools associated with early hominins. They consist of a collection of very simple choppers, scrapers, and flakes. Modern material culture consists of all the physical objects that a contemporary society produces or retains from the past, such as tools, streets, buildings, homes, toys, medicines, and automobiles. Cultural anthropologists investigate the material culture of the societies they study, and they also examine the relationship between the material culture and the nonmaterial culture: the values, beliefs, and norms that represent the patterned ways of thinking and acting within a society. Archaeologists, meanwhile, are primarily concerned with interpreting past societies by studying their material remains.

Values

Values are the standards by which members of a society define what is good or bad, holy or unholy, beautiful or ugly. They are assumptions that are widely shared within the society. Values are a central aspect of the nonmaterial culture of a society and are important because they influence the behavior of the members of a society. The predominant values in the United States include individual achievement and success, efficiency, progress, material comfort, equality, freedom, science, rationality, nationalism, and democracy, along with many other assumptions (Williams 1970; Bellah et al. 1985, 2000). Although these values might seem normal to Americans, they are not accepted values in all societies. For instance, just as American society tends to emphasize individualism and self-reliance, other societies, such as the Old Order Amish in the United States, instead stress cooperation and community interest.

Beliefs

Beliefs held by the members of a society are another aspect of nonmaterial culture. Beliefs are cultural conventions that concern true or false assumptions, including specific descriptions of the nature of the universe and humanity's place in it. Values are generalized notions of what is good and bad; beliefs are more specific and, in form at least, have more content. "Education is good" is a fundamental value in American society, whereas "Grading is the best way to evaluate students" is a belief that reflects assumptions about the most appropriate way to determine educational achievement.

Most people in a given society assume that their beliefs are rational and firmly grounded in common sense. As we saw in Chapter 1, however, some beliefs may not necessarily be scientifically accepted. For example, our intuitive and commonsense understandings may lead us to conclude that the Earth is flat and stationary. When we look around us, the plane of the Earth looks flat, and we do not feel as if the Earth is rotating around the Sun. Yet, our cognitive intuitions and commonsense beliefs about these notions are contradicted by the knowledge gained by the scientific method.

Some anthropologists in the past have referred to the worldview of a particular society. A *worldview* was believed to consist of various beliefs about the nature of reality that provided a people with a more or less consistent orientation toward the world. Worldviews were viewed as guides to help people interpret and understand the reality surrounding them. Early anthropologists believed, for example, that the worldviews of the traditional Azande of East Africa and the traditional Navajos of the southwestern region of the United States included meaningful beliefs about witches (Evans-Pritchard 1937; Kluckhohn 1967). In these societies, witchcraft was believed to cause illnesses in some unfortunate individuals. On the other hand, in societies such as that of Canada, medical doctors diagnosed illnesses using the scientific method and believed illnesses were caused by viruses, bacteria, or other material forces. These early anthropologists maintained that such differing beliefs about illness reflected the different worldviews of these societies. However, modern anthropologists remain very skeptical about these notions of worldviews shared by entire cultures. This notion suggested that cultures were very homogeneous. Presently, anthropologists concur that the concept of a people sharing a worldview is highly questionable. Through systematic ethnographic research with different types of people within a society, contemporary anthropologists discover a great deal of variation in cultural beliefs.

In particular circumstances in a society, some beliefs may be combined into an ideology. An **ideology** consists of cultural symbols and beliefs that reflect and support the interests of specific groups within society (Yengoyan 1986; Comaroff and Comaroff 1991:22). Certain groups promote ideologies for their own ends as a means of maintaining and justifying economic and political authority. Different economic and political systems—including capitalism, socialism, communism, democracy, and totalitarianism—are based on differing ideologies. For example, many political leaders in capitalist societies maintain the ideology that individuals should be rewarded monetarily based on their own self-interest. In contrast, leaders in socialist societies have adopted the ideology that the well-being of the community or society takes precedence over individual self-interest.

In some societies, especially complex ones with many different groups, an ideology may produce **cultural hegemony**, the ideological control by one dominant group over values, beliefs, and norms. For example, one dominant ethnic group may impose its cultural beliefs on subordinate groups. In the United States, the dominant ethnic group in the eighteenth and nineteenth centuries, white Anglo-Saxon Protestants, was able to impose its language, cultural beliefs, and practices on the Native Americans in U.S. society. In many areas of the world, minority groups often accept the ideologies of the economically and politically dominant groups through the process of cultural hegemony. Some anthropologists have noted that subordinate groups may accept the ideology of the dominant group even if it is to their disadvantage. For example, in the past some Native Americans or African-Americans accepted the belief that white Americans were superior because they appeared to have many more opportunities to acquire wealth and political power than they did. Thus, the ideological culture of the dominant group becomes the "taken-for-granted" natural order and reality of the minority groups. In other cases of cultural hegemony, subordinate groups begin to resist the ideological foundations of the dominant group. For example, anthropologist Lila Abu-Lughod studied how Bedouin women of the Arab world resisted the imposition of the male-dominated ideologies in Egypt (1990).

Norms

Norms—a society's rules of right and wrong behavior—are another aspect of nonmaterial culture. Norms are shared rules or guidelines that define how people "ought" to behave under certain circumstances. Norms are generally connected to the values, beliefs, and ideologies of a society. For example, we have seen that in U.S. culture, individualism is a basic value that is reflected in the prevailing worldview. It is not surprising, then, that U.S. society has many norms based upon the notion of individual initiative and responsibility. Individuals are admonished to work for their own self-interest and not to become a burden to their families or community. Older Americans, if self-sufficient, are not supposed to live with their children. Likewise, self-sufficient young adults beyond a certain age should not live with their parents. These individualistic norms reflect the values of U.S. society and contrast with norms existing in other societies. In many agricultural societies, it would be considered immoral to allow aging parents to live outside the family. In these populations, the family is a moral community that should not be separated. Rather than individualism, these norms emphasize communal responsibility within the family unit.

Folkways

Norms guiding ordinary usages and conventions of everyday life are known as **folkways**. Members of a society frequently conform to folkways so readily that they are hardly aware these norms exist. For example, if a Chinese anthropologist were to ask an American why Americans eat with knives and forks, why Americans allow dating between single men and women without chaperones, or why American schoolchildren are not allowed to help one another on exams, he or she might get vague and uninformative answers, such as, "Because that's the way it is done," or, "It's the custom," or even, "I don't know." Cultural anthropologists are accustomed to receiving these kinds of answers from the members of the society they are studying. These folkway norms or standards of etiquette are so embedded in the society that they are not noticeable unless they are openly violated.

Folkways help ensure that social life proceeds smoothly by providing guidelines for an individual's behavior and expectations of other people's behavior. At the same time, folkways allow for some flexibility. Although most people conform to folkways most of the time, folkways are sometimes violated, but these violations are not severely punished. Thus, in U.S. society, people who eat with chopsticks rather than with knives and forks or who do not keep their lawns neatly mowed are not considered immoral or depraved, nor are they treated as criminals.

Every society has norms or rules for behavior.

Mores **Mores** (pronounced MOR-ays) are much stronger norms than are folkways. Members of society believe that their mores are crucial for the maintenance of a decent and orderly way of life. People who violate mores are usually severely punished, although punishment for the violation of mores varies from society to society. It may take the form of ostracism, vicious gossip, public ridicule, exile, loss of one's job, physical beating, imprisonment, commitment to a mental asylum, or even execution. For example, in some Islamic societies such as Iran and Saudi Arabia, the manner in which a woman dresses in public is considered morally significant. If a woman violates the dress code in these societies, she may be arrested by religious police and detained. Government and religious regulations control how Saudi women have to dress. They have to wear the *abaya* (a full black cloak), the *hijab* (head scarf), and the *niqab* (face veil). As we shall see later in the text, in hunting-and-gathering societies, individuals who do not share goods or resources with others are often punished by gossip, ridicule, and occasionally ostracism.

Saudi women in full Islamic dress as they are in a public market buying gold jewelry.

Not all norms can be neatly categorized as either folkways or mores. Distinguishing between the two is especially difficult when dealing with societies other than our own. In reality, norms fall at various points on a continuum, depending upon the particular circumstances and the society under consideration. The prohibition of public nudity may be a strong norm in some societies, but it may be only a folkway or pattern of etiquette in others. Even within a society, rules of etiquette may come to have moral significance. For example, as discussed before, the proper form of dress for women in some societies is not just a matter of etiquette, but has moral or religious connotations.

Values, beliefs, and norms are used by many social scientists when referring to nonmaterial culture. However, not all anthropologists agree that there are concise, clear-cut distinctions among these terms. The terms are used only to help us understand the complex symbolic aspects of nonmaterial culture.

Ideal versus Real Culture

When discussing values, beliefs, and norms, cultural anthropologists often distinguish between ideal culture and real culture. **Ideal culture** consists of what people say they do or should do, whereas **real culture** refers to their actual behaviors. Cultural anthropologists have discovered that the ideal culture frequently contrasts with people's actual behavior. For instance, a foreign anthropologist may learn that Americans cherish the value of equal opportunity, yet in observing Americans, the anthropologist might encounter many cases in which people from different economic, class, racial, ethnic, and religious backgrounds are treated in a highly unequal manner. In later chapters, we discuss how some societies are structured around kinship ties and principles of lineage such as patrilineal and matrilineal descent. Anthropologists often discover, however, that these kinship and descent principles are violated by the actual practices of people (Kuper 1988). Thus, in all societies, anthropologists find that there are differences between the ideal and real cultural practices of individuals.

Cultural Diversity

6.5 Describe how culture results in differences among people in various societies.

Throughout history, humans have expressed an interest in cultural diversity. People have recognized differences in values, norms, beliefs, and practices everywhere. Whenever different groups have come into contact with one another, people have compared and contrasted their respective cultural traditions. Societies often differentiated themselves from one another based on these variant cultural patterns. For example, one of the first Western historians, Herodotus, a Greek scholar of the fifth century B.C., wrote about the different forms of behavior and belief in societies, such as that of Egypt. He described how the Egyptians behaved and thought differently from the Greeks.

As we saw in Chapter 1, *ethnocentrism* is the practice of judging another society by the values and standards of one's own society. It appears that ethnocentrism is a universal phenomenon (Brown 2012). As humans learn the basic values, beliefs, and norms of their society, they tend to think of their own group and culture as preferable, ranking other cultures as less desirable. In fact, members of a society become so committed to particular cultural traditions that they cannot conceive of any other way of life. They often view other cultural traditions as strange, alien, inferior, crazy, or immoral.

The study of cultural diversity became one of the principal objectives of anthropology as it developed as a profession in the nineteenth century. But like earlier writers, nineteenth-century anthropologists often reinforced ethnocentric beliefs about other societies (see Chapter 8). In the twentieth century, however, anthropologists began to recognize that ethnocentrism prevents them from viewing other cultures in a scientific manner.

To combat the problem of ethnocentrism, twentieth-century anthropologists developed the concept of cultural relativism. **Cultural relativism** is the view that cultural traditions must be understood within the context of a particular society's responses to problems and opportunities. Cultural relativism is a method or procedure for explaining and interpreting other people's cultures. Because cultural traditions represent unique adaptations and symbolic systems for different societies, these traditions must be understood by anthropologists as objectively as possible. In order to do an ethnographic study, anthropologists must suspend their own judgments and examine the other society in terms of its history and culture. Cultural relativism offers anthropologists a means of investigating other societies without imposing ethnocentric assumptions. Cultural anthropologists attempt to understand the logic of the people they are studying. Perhaps that logic does not make sense from the anthropologists' perspective, but the task is to understand and explain the reasoning of the population studied.

Food and Diversity

To understand the difference between human biological and cultural behaviors, we can simply observe the variety of ways in which different societies satisfy a basic biological drive such as hunger. Although humans are omnivorous animals with the ability to digest many types of plants and animals for nutrition, there are many differences in eating behaviors and food preferences throughout the world. Food is not just a source of nutrition and oral pleasure. It becomes an aesthetic experience, a mechanism of sharing, a center of celebration, and sometimes a statement about one's own ethnic, religious, and cultural identity (Appadurai 1981; Rozin 2010).

In general, American culture labels animals as either edible or inedible. Most Americans would be repulsed by the thought of eating insects and insect larvae, but many societies consider them to be delicacies. American culture also distinguishes between pets, which are not eaten, and farm animals, such as chickens, cows, and pigs, which can be eaten. In the United States, horses are considered pets or work animals, and there are no industries for raising them for human consumption. Yet, horsemeat is a regular part of the continental European diet. The French, Belgians, Dutch, Germans, Italians, Poles, and other Europeans consume significant quantities of horsemeat each year (Harris 1985).

Anthropologists explain differences in dietary preferences in various ways. For example, Mary Douglas offered an explanation of why the Jewish people have prohibitions against eating pork. She described this prohibition in her book *Purity and Danger: An Analysis of the Concepts of Pollution and Taboo* (1966) by suggesting that all societies have symbolic classifications of certain objects or foods that are unclean, tabooed, polluted, or dirty, as well as those that are clean, pure, or undefiled. To illustrate her ideas regarding the classification of matter or foods, Douglas examined the ancient Israelites' classification of animals and taboos against eating certain animals such as pigs and shellfish, as described in Leviticus in the Bible. Douglas argues that like other humans, the ancient Israelites classified reality by placing things into distinguishable "mental boxes." However, some things do not fit neatly into distinguishable mental boxes. Some items are anomalous and ambiguous; thus they fall between the basic categories that are used to define cultural reality. These anomalous items are usually treated as unclean, impure, unholy, polluting, or defiling.

In explaining how these processes influenced the classification of animals among the ancient Israelites, Douglas alludes to the descriptions in the first chapter of the Bible, Genesis, where God creates the animals with specific characteristics: Birds with feathers are soaring in the sky; fish with scales and fins are swimming in the water; and creatures with four feet are walking, hopping, or jumping on the land. However, some animals did not easily fit into the cultural categories used for the classification of animals. Animals that combined elements of different realms were considered ambiguous, and therefore unclean or unholy. For example, terrestrial animals that move by "swarming upon the earth," such as insects, were declared unclean and were prohibited from being eaten. Animals that have cloven hooves and chew cud, such as sheep, goats, and cattle, were considered clean and could be eaten. However, pigs have cloven hooves but do not chew cud and, therefore, failed to fit into the cultural classification of reality accepted by the ancient Israelites. Consequently, pigs were considered unclean and polluting and were prohibited in the ancient Israelite diet. Shellfish and eels were also unclean animals because they swim in the water but lack fins and scales. These anomalous creatures fell outside of the systematic classification of animals. Douglas maintains that the dietary laws of Leviticus represented an ideal construction of reality that represented God's plan of creation, which was based on perfection, order, and holiness. This became integral to the worldview of the ancient Israelites and affected their dietary preferences.

The late anthropologist Marvin Harris hypothesized that cultural dietary preferences frequently have an adaptive significance (1977, 1985). In seeking the origins of the pig taboo, Harris emphasized, as did Douglas, that among the ancient Israelites, pigs were viewed as abominable animals not suited for human consumption. Yet, many societies show no aversion to the consumption of pork. Pigs have been a primary source of protein and fat throughout China and Europe. In some societies in the Pacific Islands, pigs are so highly regarded they are treated as members of the family (but they are also eaten). One medical explanation for the dietary prohibition is that the pig is an unclean animal and that it carries diseases such as trichinosis, which is caused by a type of tapeworm. Harris, however, considered these explanations to be unsatisfactory. Regarding cleanliness, Harris acknowledged that because pigs cannot sweat, in hot, dry climates such as the Middle East they wallow in their excrement to keep cool. He noted, however, that other animals, such as goats and chickens, can also be dirty, but they are eaten. Similarly, Harris emphasized that many other animals, such as cows, which are widely consumed, also carry diseases.

Ultimately, Harris explained the origins of the pig taboo in Judaism (and later Islam) by analyzing the ecological conditions of the Middle East. He maintained that this dietary restriction represented a cultural innovation that helped the societies of this region to adapt. About 1200 B.C., the ancient Israelites had settled in a woodland area that had not been cultivated. As they rapidly cut down trees to convert areas to irrigated agricultural land, they also severely restricted areas suitable for raising pigs on natural forage. Eventually, pigs had to be fed grains as

Chinese man with pig

supplements, which made them extremely costly and direct competitors with humans. Moreover, they required artificial shade and moisture to keep cool. In addition, pigs were not useful for pulling plows, producing milk, or providing hides or wool for clothing.

According to Harris, despite the increasing costs associated with pig raising, people were still tempted to raise them for nutritional reasons. He hypothesized that the pig taboo was established to inhibit this practice through religious authorities and texts that redefined the pig as an unclean animal. Neighbors of the ancient Israelites, such as the Egyptians, began to share the abhorrence of the pig. The pig taboo was later incorporated into the Islamic religious text, the Qur'an, so that today both Muslims and Jews are forbidden to eat pork.

Thus, according to Harris's hypothesis, in the hot, dry regions of the world where pigs are poorly adapted and extremely costly to raise, the meat of the pig came to be forbidden. He emphasized the practical considerations of pig raising, including the fact that they are hard to herd and are not grazing animals like goats, sheep, or cattle. In contrast, in the cooler, wetter areas of the world that are more appropriate for pig raising, such as China and New Guinea, pig taboos are unknown, and pigs are the prized foods in these regions.

Both Douglas and Harris offer insights into the development of the dietary preferences of Jews and Christians. While Douglas explores the important symbolic significance of these preferences, Harris examines the cost effectiveness and practical aspects of these food taboos. Anthropologists such as Harris and others have been studying dietary diversity, such as why some people prohibit the eating of beef, whereas other people have adopted it as an integral aspect of their diet. Food preferences illustrate how humans the world over have universal needs for protein, carbohydrates, minerals, and vitamins but obtain these nutrients in different ways, depending upon the dietary preferences established within their culture. Anthropologists Sidney Mintz and Christine DuBois have summarized how other anthropologists have studied food and eating habits around the world and how these developments are associated with ecological conditions, technological requirements, biological factors, but also with patterns of identity, gender, class differences, and ritual and religious beliefs (2002).

Anthropologists have continued to explore these numerous dimensions of food and eating habits in many different societies. For example, Daniel Fessler and C. D. Naverette looked at a broad cross-cultural sample of food taboos (2003). They found that food taboos are overwhelmingly associated with meat and animal products compared with fruits or vegetables. Animal foods are viewed as much more dangerous than fruits and vegetables with respect to disease or death. The high cost of trial-and-error learning about which animal foods would be harmful would be counterproductive in any cultural tradition; thus food taboos associated with animals tend to become more pervasive than prohibitions against fruits or vegetables. Research on the cultural aspects of food is an important arena for contemporary anthropological research.

Cultural Universals

6.6 Describe how culture leads to universal similarities among people in widely separated societies.

As previously discussed, early anthropologists emphasized the realities of cultural diversity in their research and writings. Some anthropologists, however, began to recognize that humans throughout the world share some fundamental

Donald E. Brown

behavioral characteristics. George Murdock, an anthropologist who devoted himself to cross-cultural analysis, compiled a lengthy list of cultural universals from hundreds of societies. **Cultural universals** are essential behavioral characteristics of societies, and they are found all over the world. Murdock's list of cultural universals includes such basics as language, cooking, family, folklore, games, community organization, decorative art, education, ethics, mythology, food taboos, numerals, personal names, magic, religious rituals, puberty customs, toolmaking, and sexual restrictions. Although the specific content and practices of these universals may vary from society to society, the fact that these cultural universals exist underlies the essential reality that modern humans are of one biological family and one species.

In an influential book titled *Human Universals* (1991), anthropologist Donald E. Brown suggests that in their quest to describe cultural diversity, many anthropologists have overlooked basic similarities in human behavior and culture. This has led to stereotypes and distortions about people in other societies, who are viewed as "exotic," "inscrutable," and "alien."

Following in Murdock's footsteps, Brown describes many human universals. In one imaginative chapter, Brown creates a group of people he refers to as the "Universal People," who have all the traits of any people in any society throughout the world. The Universal People have language with complex grammar to communicate and think abstractly; kinship terms and categories to distinguish relatives and age groupings; gender terms for male and female; facial expressions to show basic emotions; a concept of the self as subject and object; tools, shelter, and fire; patterns for childbirth and training; families and political groupings; conflict; etiquette; morality, religious beliefs, and worldviews; and dance, music, art, and other aesthetic standards. Brown's depiction of the Universal People clearly suggests that these and many other aspects of human behavior result from certain problems that threaten the physical and social survival of all societies. For a society to survive, it must have mechanisms to care for children, adapt to the physical environment, produce and distribute goods and services, maintain order, and provide explanations of the natural and social environments. In addition, many universal behaviors result from fundamental biological characteristics common to all people.

Anthropologists have discovered that culture can be both diverse and universal. The challenge for anthropology is to understand the basis of both this diversity and this universality. To paraphrase the late anthropologist Clyde Kluckhohn: Every human is like all other humans, some other humans, and no other human. The major objective of cultural anthropology is to investigate the validity of this statement.

The Study of Enculturation

When we discussed how culture is learned by individuals above, we discussed the process of enculturation. **Psychological anthropology** is the field that studies the interaction between the individual and culture, or the process of enculturation. Unlike psychologists, who tend to study people within the psychologists' own societies, psychological anthropologists observe people and the process of enculturation in many different types of societies (Henrich, Heine, Norenzayan

2010). Their research findings are then used as the basis of cross-cultural studies to determine how and why behavior, thoughts, and feelings differ and are similar from society to society. Below, we will also discuss the approaches of **cognitive anthropology**, which is the study of cognition and cultural meanings through specific methodologies such as psychological experiments, computer modeling, and other techniques to elicit underlying unconscious factors that structure human-thinking processes.

Psychological anthropologists and cognitive anthropologists study the development of personality characteristics and individual behaviors in a given society and how they are influenced by enculturation. In their studies, anthropologists need to question basic assumptions regarding human nature: Is human nature primarily a matter of biological influences or of cultural factors? In order to study this question, psychological and cognitive anthropologists focus on enculturation and precisely how this process influences personality characteristics, sexual behavior, thinking and cognition, and emotional development.

Biology versus Culture

6.7 Discuss the relationship between biology and culture and how anthropologists regard the nature/nurture questions of humanity.

Before we explore the specific aspects of psychological anthropology, we need to consider some questions. One fundamental concept that anthropologists reflect upon is what is frequently referred to as "human nature." Two questions immediately arise when discussing this concept: If there are basic similarities or universal patterns of human behavior, does that mean that human nature is biologically transmitted through heredity? If this is the case, to what extent can culture or learning change human nature to produce variation in behavior within different societies? These two questions have led to a controversy in anthropology, with some anthropologists emphasizing the biological influences on human behavior and others emphasizing the social or cultural influences on behavior.

Today, however, most anthropologists realize that neither biological nor cultural influences exist in absolute, pure form. Modern anthropologists, therefore, adopt a biocultural or *interactionist perspective*, which combines the effects of biology and culture to explain human behavior. Anthropologists recognize that human behavior depends upon both our biological endowment and what we learn from our society or culture. What interactionists care about is the interrelationship between the biological and the learned factors in any behavior.

Enculturation: Culture and Personality

6.8 Describe how anthropologists study enculturation and its relationship to personality formation.

Enculturation is a lifelong process, and it links individuals with the specific culture to which they are exposed. Immediately after they are born, infants begin to absorb their language and culture—the etiquette, mores, values, beliefs, and practices of their society—through both unconscious and conscious learning—situational, social, and symbolic.

Enculturation is a vital foundation of our humanity. Virtually helpless at birth, an infant needs care and is completely dependent on others for survival. Through the interaction of enculturation with biologically based predispositions, a person acquires his or her **personality**, the fairly stable patterns of thought, feeling, and action associated with a specific person. Personality includes cognitive, emotional, and behavioral components. The cognitive component of personality consists of thought patterns, memory, belief, perception, and other intellectual capacities. The emotional component includes emotions such as love, hate, envy, jealousy, sympathy, anger, and pride. The behavioral component consists of the skills, aptitudes, competence, and other abilities or potentials that are developed throughout the course of a person's life.

Early Studies of Enculturation

During the 1930s and 1940s, a number of anthropologists began to research enculturation to learn about the influence of culture on personality development. At this time, some social scientists suggested that biology and race are the most influential determinants of human behavior. In Germany, for example, social scientists who were members of the Nazi Party promoted the idea that because of biological characteristics, some races are superior to others in respect to behavior and thought. Cultural anthropologists in the United States began to challenge this view of biological or racial determinism through research on enculturation (Boas 1940; Benedict and Weltfish 1943; Degler 1991; Konner 2002). In particular, Ruth Benedict became an important pioneer in early psychological anthropology. She published extensively and became prominent in this area of research. Benedict maintained that each society and culture has a unique history. After studying processes such as child rearing and enculturation, she proposed that every culture is characterized by a dominant personality type. Culture, she argued, is essentially "personality writ large." The field studies Benedict and others did became the basis of what was then called culture-and-personality theory.

Benedict and Culture Types One classic example of the application of culture-and-personality theory is Benedict's analysis of the Plains and Pueblo Native American Indian societies. In an essay titled "Psychological Types in the Cultures of the Southwest" (1928) and in a classic book, *Patterns of Culture* (1934), Benedict classified Pueblo societies as having an Apollonian (named for the Greek god Apollo) culture. The Pueblo cultural ethos stressed gentleness, cooperation, harmony, tranquility, and peacefulness. According to Benedict, these values explain why members of Pueblo societies were "moderate." The Pueblo rarely indulged in violence, and they avoided the use of drugs and alcohol to transcend their senses.

In contrast, Benedict characterized the Plains societies as Dionysian (after the Greek god Dionysius). She described how the values and ethos of the Plains groups were almost the direct opposite of those of the Pueblo. The Plains Indians were involved in warfare and violence, and their ritual behavior included the use of drugs, alcohol, fasting, and physical self-torture and mutilation to induce religious ecstasy. Benedict extended her analysis to such groups as the Kwakiutl Native American peoples and the Dobu of Melanesia. She referred to the Kwakiutl as "megalomaniacs" and the Dobuans as "paranoid," fearing and hating one another. In each case, she claimed that the group's values and ethos had created a distinctive cultural personality. In Benedict's analysis, individual personalities were formed through enculturation and the values, beliefs, and norms of different societies led to variations in culture. In other words, Benedict believed that the culture of a particular society can be studied by investigating the personality of its bearers. She thought that the patterning or configuration of a particular culture is simply reflected in an individual's personality.

The anthropological tradition represented by Ruth Benedict stimulated more careful research regarding personality and culture. Much of the data provided by these early psychological anthropologists was important in understanding the enculturation process. As a result of these early studies, we now have a better understanding of personality formation, thought, behavior, and emotional development within different human societies.

Ruth Benedict with Blackfoot

Childhood Acquisition of Cultural Knowledge

Pioneering female anthropologists such as Ruth Benedict and others were the first to systematically examine the effects of childhood training on personality development. This innovative research has resulted in a much improved understanding of the techniques of childhood training and enculturation throughout the world. Since then, a number of studies of childhood training by psychological anthropologists have contributed to this area of research. Anthropologist Meredith Small in her books *Our Babies, Ourselves: How Biology and Culture Shape the Way We Parent* (1998) and *Kids: How Biology and Culture Shape the Way We Raise Our Children* (2001) summarizes how biological factors interact with learning in enculturation processes in many different societies throughout the world. In these two books, Small emphasizes that biology intersects with culture in infant and child development, but that we are neurologically "unfinished" and brain growth is inextricably connected with social and cultural development.

Japanese Childhood Enculturation Some contemporary ethnographic research projects focus on the type of childhood training and enculturation that influence the learning of basic concepts of a particular culture. One study, conducted by Joy Hendry (1992, 2013), focused on how children in Japan become enculturated. According to the Western stereotype, Japanese society is characterized as "collectivistic," rather than "individualistic." A related stereotype is that Japanese society is a "consensus" or "conformist" society, with everyone submitting to the norms of the group. Hendry's ethnographic research on whether these stereotypes are correct focused on how children learn their initial concepts of Japanese culture and adjust to group behaviors.

Hendry found that small children are extremely important in Japanese culture. Babies are afforded every possible individual attention. For example, many highly educated mothers give up their careers to dedicate themselves to full-time nurturing once a child is born. The child is to be kept in a secure, harmonious household. A tiny child is often strapped to a mother's back or front while the mother works, shops, and performs daily routines. Also, an adult will lie down with a child at bedtime until he or she falls asleep and in some cases, sleeps all night with the child. From an American perspective, it appears that the child is totally indulged, but the child learns a great many routine tasks such as eating, washing, dressing, and toilet training through repetition until the child can do these tasks on his or her own.

During this early phase of enculturation, children learn two basic cultural concepts: *uchi*, or inside of the house, including the people inside, and *soto*, the outside world. Human beings are categorized by these concepts, and various behaviors in a Japanese household, such as removing shoes before entering the house, reinforce the inside/outside dichotomy. *Uchi* is associated with safety, security, and cleanliness. *Soto* is where danger may lurk; big dogs, strangers, or even demons and ghosts may be outside. For the first few years of their lives, children play with siblings and cousins and then gradually with close neighbors. They are allowed to play in the immediate neighborhood from as early as 2 years of age if it is a safe environment, and they begin to build up a new set of "inside" personal relations with neighbors who live nearby.

At the age of 4 or 5, children are introduced to group life with outsiders in a kindergarten or day nursery. At first, the children cry for a while and refuse to join in, but eventually they become involved with the new group of fellow kindergartners, and this becomes a new *uchi* group for them. They learn to cooperate with one another in the group and begin to develop an identity appropriate for group life. However, Hendry emphasized that the children do not lose their individuality. Each child is treated as an individual by the teacher, who obtains a great deal of background knowledge about the child. (Parents fill out forms regarding their child's strengths and weaknesses, likes and dislikes, siblings, and other details.) In addition, the teacher visits each child's home at least once during the academic year. Thus, along with learning to cooperate with their new *uchi* group, these children also become familiar with their own individuality and the individual characteristics of their peers. When engaging in group activities, whether in games, sports, learning activities, or other responsibilities, the children teach each other personal skills and abilities so that the entire group will benefit.

In addition, Hendry notes the intricacies of the interrelation between the inner self (*tatemae* or face) and harmony. Children are taught that group harmony is predicated upon how one presents themselves to others, which is based on the empathic understanding of what it means to feel hurt. These young children learn to empathize with the feelings of others and are taught that selfishness is an "an unrestrained state." Hendry points out that a child's behavior is disapproved of if it stems merely from self-interest (and does not consider either the needs of others or the implications of such behavior on others). This is related to the important interrelation between the inner self (*tatemae* or face) and group harmony.

Hendry concluded that even though Japanese children learn to participate in many group-oriented activities, they do not completely lose their sense of individuality. Although Japanese society does not emphasize individualism in the same way U.S. society does, with its connotations of self-assertion and individual rights, Japanese children develop their own sense of self in respect to their individual talents and abilities. One of the conclusions based on the new types of psychological anthropology studies such as Joy Hendry's is that children are not just passive recipients in the enculturation process. Instead, they are active contributors to the meaning and outcome of interactions with other members of society.

Japanese mother and child

Critical Perspectives: The Anthropology of the "Self"

One topic that is currently inspiring a great deal of cross-cultural research is the issue of the individual, or the concept of the "person" within society. More specifically, many anthropologists are addressing these questions: Do people in different societies view themselves as *individuals*, *selves*, or *persons* who are separate from their social group? If not, can we assume that people in these societies are *self-motivated* or *self-interested* in pursuing various goals? We usually make this assumption to explain our own behaviors and those of other people in our own society, but can we use this assumption to explain the behavior of people in other societies?

In the West, we tend to regard people as individuals who feel free to pursue their self-interests, to marry or not to marry, and to do what they want with their private property. Individualism is stressed through cultural beliefs and ideologies that serve as a basis for our economic, social, political, legal, and religious institutions. But is this sense of individualism a "natural" condition, or is it a byproduct of our distinctive social and historical development? One way of answering this question is through cross-cultural research. If we find that other people do not think in these terms, then we can assume that our thoughts about the self, mind, and individual are conditioned by our historical and cultural circumstances.

One early theorist who influenced modern anthropological research on these questions was Marcel Mauss, a French sociologist who argued that the concept of the "self" or "person" as separate from the "role" and "status" within society arose in relationship to modern capitalist society ([1938] 1985). Relying upon the ethnographic research of anthropologists such as Franz Boas, he theorized that the concept of the individual person had developed uniquely in the West through the evolution of Roman law, Christian ideas of morality, and modern philosophical thought.

For example, according to Mauss, during the medieval period in Europe, it would have been unheard of to think of an individual as completely separate from the larger social group. Medieval Christianity portrayed the individual as merely an element in God's creation, which was referred to as the "great chain of being." All elements in the universe were arranged in a hierarchy from God to angels, humans, animals, trees, rocks, and other inorganic materials. All these elements had distinct values, depending on their distance from God. To modern Westerners, these views appear strange and outmoded. However, according to some anthropologists, our view of ourselves as independent from groups and environments may be just as strange.

Influenced by Mauss, French anthropologist Louis Dumont (1970) argued that modern Western notions of individualism differ from those of other societies, such as India. In his book *Homo Hierarchicus*, he contrasted Western individualism with Indian Hindu conceptions that value social hierarchy. He pointed out that Hindu philosophy treats individuals as members of castes, which are linked to one another in a social hierarchy. Thus, from the Hindu vantage point, individuals cannot be thought of as separate from their social environment.

Francis Hsu, a Chinese-American anthropologist, maintained that the Chinese concept of self is radically different from that of the West (1981). Hsu argued that whereas individualism permeates all U.S. values and institutions, in China the individual is inclined to be socially and psychologically dependent on others. He contrasted the individual-centeredness of American society with the situation-centeredness of Chinese society. He concluded that the individual in China is strongly encouraged to conform to familistic and group norms.

Hsu argued that the situation-centeredness of Chinese society was partly responsible for its lack of economic and political development in the 1940s and 1950s. In contrast, he believed that the individualism of American society has encouraged capitalist enterprise and democratic institutions. However, he also believed that the American concern for self and individualism has led to rampant materialism and consumerism and to a lack of concern for the overall good of society.

Dorinne Kondo makes a similar argument regarding the Western notion of the self in comparison to the Japanese conception of the self (1990). Kondo refers to the Western notion of the autonomous, private self that moves across different social contexts, whereas the Japanese self is always viewed in a relational, socially bounded context. When the Japanese participate in workplace and neighborhood activities embedded within networks and hierarchies, they cannot conceive of their private "self." Even within their households, individuals are constrained by their neighbors. On the other hand, do Westerners or Americans, as students or workers feel they have complete control of their own self and their destiny (de Munck 2000)? Marilyn Strathern, an anthropologist who does research in New Guinea, posits that the Mt. Hagener populations she studies do not conceive of themselves as individuals or bounded units, but as "dividuals" or partible assemblages of the multiple social relations in which they participate (Strathern 1984, 1988). Diane Mines, who does research in India, uses the term 'dividuals' to refer to Indians who are members of hierarchical ranked castes (2009).

As we can see, psychological anthropologists differ over the degree to which culture influences the concept of the self. In some cases, these descriptions of different concepts of self may be exaggerations by anthropologists working in very different kinds of societies. Melford Spiro and some other psychological anthropologists think that humans everywhere have similar concepts regarding the self (Spiro 1993). These different understandings reflect various assumptions and conclusions based on philosophical commitments; they need to be evaluated and tested by anthropologists based on the most significant research findings available in biological, cross-cultural, and specific findings within ethnographic research.

Points to Ponder

1. To what extent are your views of yourself as a distinct individual influenced by prevailing social norms?
2. Do you think that people throughout the world hold similar views? Why or why not?
3. Do you agree with Hsu's analysis of the benefits and shortcomings of widespread individualism?
4. What would be the advantages and disadvantages of a system that emphasizes the overall society, rather than the individual?

The child is viewed as an active agent in this new conception of enculturation and learns to choose and design appropriate responses to specific social situations and contexts as he or she is exposed to them. Psychological anthropologists are contributing to a better understanding of how children acquire cultural knowledge through exposure and active participation in everyday social interaction.

Cognitive Anthropology

6.9 Discuss what cognitive anthropologists have learned about universals and human thought processes.

A number of anthropologists have been pursuing the understanding of human psychology through the fields of cognitive anthropology. As mentioned earlier in this chapter, cognitive anthropology is the study of cognition and cultural meanings through specific methodologies such as experiments, computer modeling, and other techniques to elicit underlying unconscious factors that structure human-thinking processes. Cognitive anthropology developed in the 1950s and 1960s through the systematic investigation of kinship terminologies within different cultures. However, more recently, cognitive anthropology has drawn on the findings within the field of cognitive science, the study of the human mind based upon computer modeling (D'Andrade 1995; de Munck 2000, Kronenfeld et al. 2011). Cognitive anthropologists have developed experimental methods and various cognitive tasks to use among people they study in their fieldwork so as to better comprehend human psychological processes and their relationship to culture. Through cognitive anthropology, we have learned that the human mind organizes and structures the natural and social worlds in distinctive ways.

For example, cognitive anthropologists have been doing research on how humans classify and perceive colors in the natural world. Color is a very complex phenomenon for scientists and anthropologists. To physicists, color is determined by wavelengths of light. To biologists, color involves the neural responses in the human eye and the brain and is related to the ability of humans to adapt and survive in nature. Color can also be symbolic and represent our feelings and emotions, and this symbolism varies from culture to culture. Early philosophers and scientists such as Aristotle, René Descartes, and Isaac Newton believed that there were seven basic colors. Later, anthropologists and linguists began to ask questions such as these: Do people classify and categorize colors in an arbitrary manner based on their language and culture? Or do people classify, categorize, and perceive colors in similar ways throughout the world? Cognitive anthropologists Brent Berlin and Paul Kay have been studying the basic color terms of different societies since the 1960s. They analyzed the color-naming practices of informants from 98 globally distributed language groups and found that societies differ dramatically in the number of basic color terms they possess, from two in some New Guinea tribes to eleven in English in the United States. They showed, however, that despite this difference, all color terms used by diverse societies follow a systematic pattern (1969).

A language with only two color terms will divide the color spectrum between white and black. If a language contains three terms, the spectrum will be black, red, and white. A language with four terms will have black, red, white, and then green, yellow, or blue. A language with six terms will have black, white, red, yellow, green, and blue. These become the focal colors that become universal (Kay, Regier, and Cook 2005).

Berlin and Kay suggested that this pattern indicates an evolutionary sequence common to all languages. Red is adopted after white and black. In general, a language does not adopt a term for brown unless it already has six color terms. English, most Western European languages, Russian, Japanese, and several others add four color terms—gray, pink, orange, and purple—after brown is classified. Berlin and Kay correlate the evolution of color terms with the evolution of society. Societies with only two color terms have a simple level of technology, whereas societies with eleven basic color terms have complex technology.

The evidence from Berlin and Kay's study suggests that color naming is not at all arbitrary. If color terms were selected randomly, there would be thousands of possible color systems. In fact, there are only 33 possible color-naming systems. Recently, Paul Kay and other colleagues reported that statistical tests from more than 100 languages in both industrial and nonindustrial societies demonstrated that there are strong universal tendencies in color classification and naming (Kay et al. 2005). In other words, to some extent, color perception transcends culture and language.

However, other anthropologists and psychologists have done some research that indicates that color is influenced by language and culture. British anthropologists and psychologists Debi Roberson, Ian Davies, and Jules Davidoff did research among members of the Berinomo tribe of Papua New Guinea and found that they do not distinguish blue from green, but they do distinguish between shades of green (*nul* and *wor*) that are not shared by Western peoples. Also, these researchers found some tribal members who, with training, could learn to distinguish blue from green, unlike other members of the tribe (Roberson, Davies, and Davidoff 2000, Roberson, Davidoff, and Shapiro 2005). This research tends to illustrate that color names do influence the perception of color in some cases. It appears that learning does play a role in how children perceive and categorize colors (Roberson 2010). Yet, these findings do not completely refute the empirical findings of Berlin, Kay, and other anthropologists.

Although much more research needs to be done on the perception and classification of colors, these findings do not support the conclusion that color classification is completely arbitrary. Instead, the vast majority of psychologists and anthropologists concur that the physiological basis of color vision is the same for all humans (and some primates) with normal color vision. Additionally, recent studies indicate that prelinguistic infants and toddlers within different language groups distinguish the same color categories (Franklin et al. 2005). On the other hand, anthropologists recognize that cognitive higher-order processing and linguistic learning may have an influence on color perception, and as is well known, the symbolic representation and meaning of colors do vary from society to society (Sahlins 1976a; Lucy and Shweder 1979).

In a cognitive anthropological study, James Boster concluded that as with colors, people from different societies classify birds in similar ways. Boster (1987) found that the South American Jivaro Indian population classified species of native birds in a manner corresponding to the way scientists classify these birds. To discover whether this pattern of classification was random, Boster had university students with no scientific training and no knowledge of South American birds classify those birds. The students did so with the exact criteria used by both the Jivaro Indians and the Western scientists. Most recently, two cognitive anthropologists working in Honduras found that insects were classified by Honduran farmers in the same way that scientists do worldwide (Bentley and Rodrigúez 2001). Despite variations in classifications found within groups and individuals within societies, cognitive anthropologists such as Scott Atran (1990, 1998, Atran and Medin 2008, Kronenfeld et al. 2011) have shown that plants and animals are categorized and classified in universally similar taxonomies. These taxonomies are ordered according to the distinctive morphological features of the various plants and animals in nature. Despite variant cultures in different regions of the world, the human mind appears to organize the natural world in nonarbitrary ways.

These findings in cognitive anthropology suggest that the human mind organizes reality in terms of **prototypes**, distinctive classifications that help us map and comprehend the world. If reality was inherently unorganized and could be perceived in any way, then color naming and animal and plant classification would be completely arbitrary. The results of this research support the notion that people the world over share certain cognitive abilities and that language and culture are as likely to reflect human cognition as they are to shape it. It suggests that evolution selected certain fundamental visual-processing and category-building abilities for humans everywhere (Lakoff 1987; Lakoff and Johnson 2000; D'Andrade 1995, Atran et al. 2002, Atran and Medin 2008).

Cognitive anthropologists have discovered that not only do humans think in prototypes, but also we use *schemas* to help us understand, organize, and interpret reality. **Schemas** are constructed out of language, images, and logical operations of the human mind in order to mediate and provide meaning to social and cultural reality. Thus, schemas are more complex than prototypes or taxonomic categories. And schemas may vary from one culture to the next. For example, the schemas *writing* in English and *kaku* in Japanese have some similarities, and these terms are usually translatable between the languages. They both refer to making some marks with an implement across a surface. The schema writing in English, however, always entails the act of writing in a language, whereas *kaku* can refer to writing or doodling or drawing a picture (D'Andrade 1995). Cognitive anthropologists find that like taxonomies, schemas are organized into hierarchies and aid in our adapting to, and coping with, cognitive and cultural complexities.

In addition to prototypes, taxonomies, and schemas, cognitive anthropologists investigate how *narratives* are used to coordinate thought processes. **Narratives** are stories or events that are represented within specific cultures. There are certain types of narratives, such as the story of Little Red Riding Hood, which are easily retained by an individual's memory and told over and over again within a society. Thus, certain forms of narrative have easily recognizable plots and can be distributed widely within a society (Sperber 1996). Other forms of narratives, such as a formal proof in mathematics or logic or an evolutionary biological explanation in science, are much more difficult to distribute widely. Cognitive anthropologists are studying religious mythologies, folktales, and other types of narratives to determine why some are effortlessly transmitted, spread quickly, and are used to produce cultural representations that endure for generations. Cognitive anthropological research has been fruitful in providing biocultural or interactionist models of the ways that humans everywhere classify, organize, understand, interpret, and narrate their natural social and cultural environment.

Enculturation and Emotions

6.10 Discuss what anthropologists have discovered about human emotions.

One significant question asked by psychological anthropologists is: To what degree does enculturation influence emotions? Obviously, different language groups have different terms for emotions, but do the feelings of anger, happiness, grief, and jealousy vary from society to society? Do some societies have unique emotions? For example, Catherine Lutz, in her book *Unnatural Emotions: Everyday Sentiments on a Micronesian Atoll and Their Challenge to Western Theory* (1988), suggested that many of the emotions exhibited by the Ifaluk people in the Pacific islands are not comparable to American or Western emotions. She noted that the Ifaluk emotion words *song* (justifiable anger) and *fago* (compassion/love/sadness) have no equivalent in English emotion terms and that anthropologists need to examine the linguistic and cultural context to interpret what emotions mean from culture to culture. Lutz does admit that there are some basic emotions that are universal based on biological and physiological factors (1988:210). However, she cautions anthropologists to comprehend these basic emotions in relationship to the cultural context of the society under study.

Psychological anthropologists have been conducting research on the topic of emotions since the early research of Benedict. As discussed earlier in this chapter, Benedict argued that each culture is unique and that people in various societies have different personalities and, consequently, different types of emotions. These different emotions are a result of the unique kind of enculturation that has shaped the individual's personality. In their view, the enculturation process is predominant in creating varying emotions among different societies. In other words, culture determines not only how people think and behave, but also how they feel emotionally.

In contrast, other early psychological anthropologists focused on universal biological processes that produce similar emotional developments and feelings in people throughout the world. According to this perspective, emotions are seen as instinctive behaviors that stimulate physiological processes involving hormones and other chemicals in the brain. In other words, if an individual feels "anger," this automatically raises his or her blood pressure and stimulates specific muscle movements. In this view, emotional developments are part of the biology of humans universally, and thus emotions are experienced in the same way everywhere.

Many psychological anthropologists have emphasized a biocultural or interactionist approach, taking both biology and culture into account in their studies of emotions (Hinton 1999). A study conducted by Karl Heider (1991) focused on three different ethnic groups in Indonesia: the Minangkabau in West Sumatra, the Minangkabau Indonesians, and the Javanese. Heider systematically described the vocabulary of emotions that each of these groups used to classify their feelings of sadness, anger, happiness, fear, surprise, love, contempt, shame, and disgust, along with other feelings. Through intensive interviews and observations, Heider determined whether the vocabulary of emotions is directly related to specific emotional behaviors.

Following his ethnographic study, Heider concluded that four of the emotions—sadness, anger, happiness, and surprise—tend to be what he classifies as basic cross-cultural emotions. In other words, these emotions appear to be universally understood and stable across cultures. Other emotions, however, such as love, fear, and disgust, appear to vary among these societies. For example, love among the Minangkabau and Minangkabau Indonesians is mixed with the feeling of pity and is close to sadness. Fear is also mixed with guilt, and feelings of disgust are difficult to translate across cultural boundaries. Heider emphasizes that his study is preliminary and needs much more analysis and reanalysis; nevertheless, it is an interesting use of the interactionist approach to the study of emotions.

Daniel Fessler also explored how both biology and culture contribute to the development of human emotions (1999). Fessler did ethnographic work among the Bengkulu, an ethnic group in Sumatra, a major island in Indonesia. He discusses the importance of two emotions, *malu* and *bangga*, exhibited in many situations by the Bengkulu. *Malu* appears to be quite similar to *shame* in English. Bengkulu who feel *malu* withdraw from social interaction, stoop, and avert their gaze. People who feel *malu* are described as those who have missed religious services, did not attend to the sick, did not send their children to school, drank alcohol, ate during times of fasting, or violated other norms. *Bangga* is the linguistic expression of the emotion that people feel when they do something well and have had success, such as doing well in baking cakes, winning an election, hosting a large feast, being skilled in oratory, or feeling good about their physical appearance or house and furnishings. *Bangga* seems to be most similar to the emotion term *pride* in English. Fessler notes that *malu* and *bangga* appear to be exact opposites of one another, and both emotions provide individuals with an assessment of their relationship to the rest of the group. He suggests that these two emotions are universal and that they have evolved in connection with attempts to coordinate one's mind and behavior for cooperation and competition within groups of people. Fessler emphasizes that though these emotions may be displayed and elaborated in different ways in various cultures, they reflect a universal, panhuman experience.

In *Thinking Through Cultures: Expeditions in Cultural Psychology* (1991), psychological anthropologist Richard Shweder emphasizes that ethnographic research on emotions has demonstrated the existence of both universals and culturally specific aspects of emotional functioning among people in different societies. He uses a piano keyboard as an analogy to discuss emotional development in children. Children have something like a universal emotional keyboard, with each key being a separate emotion: disgust, interest, distress, anger, fear, contempt, shame, shyness, guilt, and so forth. A key is struck whenever a situation such as loss, frustration, or novelty develops. All children recognize and can discriminate among basic emotions by a young age. However, as adults, the tunes that are played on the keyboard vary with experience. Some keys are not struck at all, whereas others are played frequently. Shweder concludes, "It is ludicrous to imagine that the emotional functioning of people in different cultures is basically the same. It is just as ludicrous to imagine that each culture's emotional life is unique" (1991:252). Psychological anthropologists recognize that a biocultural or interactionist approach that takes into account human biological factors and cultural variation is necessary to comprehend the enculturation process and emotional development.

The Limits of Enculturation

6.11 Discuss the limitations of enculturation in studying human behavior.

When we consider enculturation, we are confronted with this question: Are humans only robots who respond rigidly to the demands of their innate drives, their genes, and the norms of their culture? If our behavior depends so much upon the enculturation process, what becomes of human concepts such as freedom and free will? Do people in our society or others have any personal choice over their behavior, or is all behavior and thought shaped by innate drives and the norms of these societies?

Unique Biological Tendencies

In actuality, although enculturation plays a major role in producing personality and behavioral strategies within society, there are a number of reasons why enculturation is not completely determinative. First, people are born with different innate tendencies for responding to the environment in a variety of ways. Our individual behavior is partially a result of our own genetics and biological constitution, which influences our hormones, our metabolism, and other aspects of our physiology. All societies have people who differ with respect to temperament because of these innate tendencies. Enculturation cannot produce people who respond to environmental or cultural pressures in a uniform manner.

Individual Variation and Agency

Second, enculturation is never a completely uniform process. Enculturation experiences are blended and synthesized in unique ways by individuals. Even in the most isolated, small-scale societies, young people behave differently from their parents. Furthermore, not all people in a particular society are socialized or enculturated in exactly the same manner. As we have emphasized in the contemporary understanding of culture, anthropologists recognize that the vast amounts of information transmitted through enculturation often lead to variations in what children are taught in different families and institutions.

In addition, norms do not dictate behavior in any rigid manner. People in any society are always confronted with contradictory norms, and society is always changing, affecting the process of enculturation. Enculturation rarely provides people with a precise blueprint for the behavioral responses needed in the many situations they face.

Thus, enculturation is an imprecise process. People may internalize the general program for behavior—a series of ideal norms, rules, and cultural guidelines for action—but how these general principles apply in any specific set of concrete circumstances is difficult or impossible to specify. Anthropologists have been emphasizing the fact that human behavior involves "agency." **Agency** is the process of intentional conscious (self-aware) choices that humans make that may alter their social or cultural world (Bourdieu 1977, Smith 2013). Individuals have multiple motives and intentions related to their sociocultural environment that both constrains and enables opportunities for agency and action. In some cases, people obey social and cultural rules completely, whereas in others they violate or ignore them. Enculturation provides the historically developed cultural forms through which the members of society share meanings and symbols and relate to one another. But in reality, people maneuver within these cultural forms, choosing their actions to fulfill both their own needs and the demands of their society.

Summary and Review of Learning Objectives

6.1 Discuss the basic characteristics and components of *culture* as understood by anthropologists.

Culture consists of the material (technology, tools, weapons, etc.) and nonmaterial (values, beliefs, and norms) components that are distinct from our human biological inheritance or genetics.

6.2 Discuss how humans acquire their culture.

Humans acquire their culture through situational, social, and symbolic learning. Symbolic learning is the most important aspect of cultural transmission. Language and symbols enable humans to transmit culture across time and space. Children and adults learn and make inferences within the context of symbols and language to acquire their culture.

6.3 Discuss how anthropologists understand the sharing of culture.

Culture consists of the shared practices and understandings within a society. To some degree, culture is based on shared meanings that are, to some extent, "public" and thus, beyond the mind of any individual. However, culture is also carried within the mind of individuals. Through systematic ethnographic research, contemporary anthropologists have found that culture is not shared by everyone equally within a society, but is distributed among different individuals. This has led to less generalizations and stereotypes about various cultures throughout the world.

6.4 Discuss the components of nonmaterial culture studied by anthropologists.

Nonmaterial culture includes values, beliefs, and norms. Values are the standards by which members of a society define what is good or bad, holy or unholy, beautiful or ugly. They are assumptions that are widely shared within the society. Beliefs are specific cultural conventions that concern true or false assumptions, including specific descriptions of the nature of the universe and humanity's place in it. Norms are a society's rules of right and wrong behavior; another aspect of nonmaterial culture. Norms include folkways or etiquette rules and "'mores"' or specific rules regarding morality that are sanctioned within a society.

6.5 Describe how culture results in differences among people in various societies.

Ethnographic research by anthropologists on hundreds of societies on topics such as food and material and nonmaterial components of culture have shown that there is an enormous amount of cultural diversity throughout the world.

6.6 Describe how culture leads to universal similarities among people in widely separated societies.

While cultural diversity is obvious, anthropologists have also found many human universals that produce similarities for humans in widely separate societies. Language, cooking, norms, folklore, religion, and hundreds of other universals exist in the different cultures of the world. Thus, anthropologists have been engaged in exploring both the diversity and the similarity of human cultures throughout the world.

6.7 Discuss the relationship between biology and culture and how anthropologists regard the nature/nurture questions of humanity.

Psychological anthropologists attempt to understand similarities and differences in behavior, thought, and feelings among societies by focusing on the relationship between the individual and culture, or the process of enculturation. One question that psychological anthropologists focus on is the degree to which human behavior is influenced by biological tendencies versus learning. Today, most anthropologists have adopted a biocultural or interactionist approach that emphasizes both biology and culture as influences on enculturation and human behavior.

6.8 Describe how anthropologists study enculturation and its relationship to personality formation.

The early studies of enculturation, called culture-and-personality studies, focused on culture as if it was an integrated type of personality. These early studies by Ruth Benedict provided some important data regarding enculturation processes and these efforts led to a more systematic examination of enculturation and childhood training. These studies have refined our understanding of childhood training in many different types of societies.

6.9 Discuss what cognitive anthropologists have learned about universals and human thought processes.

The study of cognition has also been a field of study within psychological anthropology. Cognitive anthropologists have explored issues such as color classification, animal and plant taxonomies, and other issues to learn about some of the universals of human cultures. They have examined how humans everywhere use classifications, prototypes, schemas, and narratives in their thinking processes.

6.10 Discuss what anthropologists have discovered about human emotions.

Emotional development is another area of study in psychological anthropology. Researchers are trying to understand how emotions such as sadness, happiness, fear, anger, and contempt are similar and different from one society to another. Their findings indicate that there are both universal and specific cultural variations with respect to emotional development in different societies.

6.11 Discuss the limitations of enculturation in studying human behavior.

In actuality, although enculturation plays a major role in producing personality and behavioral strategies within society, there are a number of reasons why enculturation is not completely determinative. First, people are born with different innate tendencies for responding to the environment in a variety of ways. Our individual behavior is partially a result of our own genetics and biological constitution, which influences our hormones, our metabolism, and other aspects of our physiology. All societies have people who differ with respect to temperament because of these innate tendencies. Enculturation is never a completely uniform process. Enculturation experiences are blended and synthesized in unique ways by individuals. Even in the most isolated, small-scale societies, young people behave differently from their parents. Furthermore, not all people in a particular society are socialized or enculturated in exactly the same manner. In addition, norms do not dictate behavior in any rigid manner. People in any society are always confronted with contradictory norms, and society is always changing, affecting the process of enculturation. Enculturation rarely provides people with a precise blueprint for the behavioral responses needed in the many situations they face.

People may internalize the general program for behavior—a series of ideal norms, rules, and cultural guidelines for action—but how these general principles apply in any specific set of concrete circumstances is difficult or impossible to specify. Anthropologists have been emphasizing the fact that human behavior involves "agency." Agency is the process of intentional conscious (self-aware) choices that humans make that may alter their social or cultural world. Individuals have multiple motives and intentions related to their sociocultural environment that both constrains and enables opportunities for agency and action. In some cases, people obey social and cultural rules completely, whereas in others they violate or ignore them. Enculturation provides the historically developed cultural forms through which the members of society share meanings and symbols and relate to one another. But in reality, people maneuver within these cultural forms, choosing their actions to fulfill both their own needs and the demands of their society.

Key Terms

agency, p. 173
beliefs, p. 155
cognitive anthropology, p. 163
cultural hegemony, p. 156
cultural relativism, p. 159
cultural universals, p. 162
enculturation, p. 151
folkways, p. 156
ideal culture, p. 158
ideology, p. 155
mores, p. 157
narratives, p. 170
nonmaterial culture, p. 154
norms, p. 156
personality, p. 164
prototypes, p. 170
psychological anthropologists, p. 162
real culture, p. 158
schemas, p. 153
signs, p. 152
situational learning, p. 151
social learning, p. 151
society, p. 150
symbolic learning, p. 151
symbols, p. 151
values, p. 155

Chapter 7

Linguistic Anthropology

Chapter Outline

Learning Objectives

After reading this chapter you should be able to:

7.1 Compare and contrast how the laboratory studies of nonhuman animal communication differs from what is found in the studies of nonhuman animals in the wild.

7.2 Discuss what makes human languages unique in comparison with nonhuman animal communication.

7.3 Describe what anthropologists conclude about the evolution of language.

7.4 Discuss how linguistic anthropologists study language.

7.5 Explain how children acquire their languages.

7.6 Discuss the relationship between language and culture.

7.7 Describe how anthropologists study the history of languages.

7.8 Describe what the field of sociolinguistics tells us about language use.

7.9 Discuss other forms of communication humans use besides language.

In Chapter 6, we discussed how the capacity for culture enables humans to learn symbolically and to transmit symbols from generation to generation. **Language** is a system of *symbols* with standard meanings. Through language, members of a society are able to communicate with one another; it is an integral aspect of culture. Language allows humans to communicate what they are experiencing at any given moment, what they have experienced in the past, and what they are planning for in the future. Like culture, the language of any particular individual exists before the person's birth and is publicly shared *to some extent* by the members of a society. For example, people born in the United States are exposed to an English-speaking language community, whereas people in Russia learn the Russian language. These languages provide the context for symbolic understanding within these different societies. In this sense, language, as part of culture, transcends the individual. Without language, humans would have difficulty transmitting culture. Without culture, humans would lose their unique "humanity."

When linguists refer to language, they usually mean spoken language. Yet, spoken language is only one form of communication. **Communication** is the act of transferring information to others. As we will discover in this chapter, many nonhuman animals have basic communication skills. We will discuss current anthropologists' understanding of how animal communication has evolved into human language. We will also discover that humans communicate with one another in ways other than language.

Nonhuman Communication

7.1 Compare and contrast how the laboratory studies of nonhuman animal communication differs from what is found in the studies of nonhuman animals in the wild.

Teaching Apes to Sign

Psychologists and other scientists have conducted a considerable amount of research on animal communication. Some of the most interesting and controversial research has been done on chimpanzees and gorillas, animals that are close genetically, physiologically, and developmentally to humans. The study of nonhuman animal communication has implications for understanding how the ability to symbolize and language evolved. In 1966, psychologists Allen and Beatrice Gardner adopted a female chimpanzee named Washoe and began teaching her American Sign Language (ASL, or Ameslan), a nonvocal form of communication used by the deaf. The ASL used by deaf humans is not an "artificial language" for deaf people. ASL is a complex language that evolved over 150 years in the United States and is very similar to spoken language with complex grammar and abstract symbolic representations. After four years with the Gardners, Washoe was able to master over 150 signs. They reported that Washoe was able to combine signs to invent new signs. This was truly a remarkable feat for a chimpanzee, and it challenged the traditional assumption that only humans have the capacity for using symbols (Gardner and Gardner 1969; Gordon 2004).

At the Yerkes Regional Primate Research Center at Emory University in Atlanta, Georgia, in the 1970s, a chimpanzee named Lana was taught to communicate through a color-coded computer keyboard using *lexigrams* (graphic symbols). Researchers concluded that Lana was able to use and combine signs in the computer language. For example, she referred to a cucumber as a "green banana" and to an orange as an "apple that is orange" (Rumbaugh 1977). David and Ann Premack, psychologists at the University of California, Santa Barbara, taught a chimpanzee named Sarah to manipulate colored plastic discs and different shapes to form simple sentences and ask for objects (Gordon 2004). Eventually, primatologist Roger Fouts, who had been Allen Gardner's graduate student, took over the care of Washoe and spent some 30 years with her and other chimpanzees. During this period, Fouts observed Washoe communicating signs from the ASL with other chimpanzees. He has spent considerable time and research on chimpanzee communication abilities and linguistic capacities, recorded in his book *Next of Kin: What Chimpanzees Have Taught Me about Who We Are* (1997). He found that these chimps could produce category words for certain types of foods: Celery was "pipe food"; watermelon was "candy drink"; and radish, a food first tasted by Washoe, was "hurt cry food." Also, when he introduced Washoe to a newly adopted chimpanzee named Louis, Fouts signed in ASL, "I HAVE BABY FOR YOU." Washoe signed back "BABY, BABY, BABY!" and hooted for joy. In his book, Fouts argues that chimpanzee communication and linguistic capacities are very similar to human language capacities and differ only in *degree*.

In a widely publicized study in the 1970s, Francine Patterson taught Koko, a female gorilla, to use some 1,000 ASL words. Koko was billed as the world's first "talking" gorilla (Patterson and Cohn 1978; Patterson and Linden 1981). At the age of four, Koko was given an intelligence test based on the Stanford–Binet Intelligence Scale and scored an 85, only slightly below the score of an average human child. In addition, according to Patterson, Koko demonstrated the capacity to lie, deceive, swear, joke, and combine signs in new and creative ways. Koko also asked for, and received, a pet kitten to nurture (Gordon 2004).

Ape Sign Language Reexamined

These studies of ASL sign use by apes challenged traditional ideas regarding the gap between humans and other types of animals. They are not, however, without their critics. One source of criticism is based on work done at Columbia University by psychologist Herbert Terrace (1986). Terrace began examining the previous ape language studies by training a chimpanzee named Nim Chimpsky (named after the well-known linguist discussed later, Noam Chomsky). Videotapes of the learning sessions were used to carefully observe the cues that may have been emitted by the trainers. Terrace also viewed the videotapes of the other studies on chimpanzee communication.

Terrace's conclusions challenged some of the earlier studies. Videotape analysis revealed that Nim rarely initiated signing behaviors, signing only in response to gestures given by the instructors, and that 50 percent of his signs were simply imitative. Unlike humans, Nim did not learn the two-way nature of conversation. Nim also never signed without expecting some reward. In addition, Nim's phrases were random combinations of signs. And Nim never signed to another chimpanzee who knew ASL unless a teacher coached him. Finally, the videotapes of the other projects showed that prompters gave unconscious signals to the chimpanzees through their body gestures.

Terrace's overall conclusions indicate that chimpanzees are highly intelligent animals that can learn many signs. They cannot, however, understand syntax, the set of grammatical rules governing the way words combine to form sentences. An English-speaking child can systematically place a noun before a verb followed by an object without difficulty. A chimpanzee cannot use these types of grammatical rules to structure sentences. Terrace concludes that although chimpanzees have remarkable intellectual capacities and excellent memories, they do not have the syntactical abilities of humans to form sentences.

Joyce Butler and Nim

Terrace's work did not end the ape language debate. Sue Savage-Rumbaugh has tried to eliminate the methodological problem of giving ambiguous hand signs to train chimpanzees at the Yerkes laboratory at Emory University. Terrace had suggested that the researchers such as Patterson and Rumbaugh were cuing their subjects with their own signs to respond to specific signs. In her book *Ape Language: From Conditioned Response to Symbol* (1986), Savage-Rumbaugh reports on a 10-year-old *bonobo*, or "pygmy" chimpanzee (a different species of chimpanzee than the common chimpanzee) named Kanzi, who learned to communicate with lexigrams, the graphic, geometric word symbols that act as substitutes for human speech; 250 lexigrams are displayed on a large keyboard. At the age of two and a half Kanzi spontaneously reached for the keyboard, pointed to the lexigram for *chase*, and ran away. Savage-Rumbaugh observed him repeatedly touch the lexigram for *chase* and scamper off. By age 6, Kanzi had mastered a vocabulary of 90 symbols.

Ethological Research on Ape Communication

In addition to doing laboratory research on animal communication, *primatologists* study the behavior of primates in their natural environment and have conducted a number of impressive field studies. **Ethologists**, scientists who study animal behavior, find that many types of animals have *call systems*—certain sounds or vocalizations that produce specific meanings—that are used to communicate for adaptive purposes. Animals such as prairie dogs, chickens, various types of monkeys, and chimpanzees have call systems.

In a primatological study of gorillas in central Africa, George Schaller isolated 22 vocalizations used by these primates. This compares with 20 vocalizations used by howler monkeys, 30 used by Japanese macaque monkeys, and 9 used by gibbons (Schaller 1976). Like these other vocalizations, the gorilla sounds are associated with specific behaviors or emotional states, such as restful feeding, sexual behavior, play, anger, and warnings of approaching threats. Infant gorillas also emit certain sounds when their mothers venture off. Schaller admits that some vocalizations were not accompanied by any specific type of behavior or stimulus.

Chimpanzee Communication: Jane Goodall The most impressive long-term investigation of chimpanzees in their natural environment was carried out by Jane Goodall, a primatologist who studied the chimpanzees of the Gombe Game Reserve in Africa since 1960. Goodall has gathered a great deal of information on the vocalizations used by these chimps. Her observations demonstrated that the chimpanzees use a great variety of calls, which are tied directly to emotional states such as fear, annoyance, and sexual excitement. She concludes that "the production of a sound in the absence of the appropriate emotional state seems to be an almost impossible task for the chimpanzee" (Goodall 1986:125).

Goodall found that the chimps use "intraparty calls," communication within the group, and "distance calls," communication with other groups. Intraparty calls include pant-grunts directed to a higher-ranking individual within the group as a token of respect, and barks, whimpers, squeaks, screams, coughs, and other sounds directed toward other chimps in the immediate group. Distance calls serve a wider range of functions, including drawing attention to local food sources, announcing the precise location of individuals in the home territory, and, in times of distress, bringing

Jane Goodall with infant chimpanzee

help from distant allies. Other current primatological studies indicate that chimpanzee vocalization such as pant-hoots are context-specific and are not limited to predation or other behaviors (Crockford and Boesch 2003). Further research is needed to discover whether the chimps use these vocalizations to distinguish among different types of foods and dangers in the environment.

Although primate communication in the wild indicates that they do not use symbolic language or anything close to ASL, nevertheless the laboratory studies that have trained chimpanzees and gorillas to use ASL clearly demonstrate that the gap between primate communication and human language may be reduced. Whether they indicate that apes can use true human symbolic language remains undecided and controversial. Although recent neurological research on chimpanzees has shown that they have areas in their brains with linguistic capacities and potentialities similar to those of humans, more research needs to be done on primate communication to investigate this phenomenon (Gannon et al. 1998; Small 2001; Gordon 2004). Primatologist Michael Tomasello and colleagues have done studies that indicate that modern chimps lack the capacity for sharing and making inferences about the intentions of one another (2005). These primatologists suggest that this lack of capacity for sharing intentions and interest in cooperation with others for pursuing goals is a major difference between nonhuman primates and humans.

Most anthropologists and psychologists have concluded that apes show the ability to manipulate linguistic symbols when the symbols are hand gestures or plastic symbols. However, the fact that they do not have the capacity to transmit symbolic language beyond the level of a two year-old human child does not mean that they are *failed humans*. Chimps are perfectly good at being chimps. It would appear that humans have many different sorts of linguistic capacities. Whether they are different in *degree* or in *kind* is a topic that has divided the primatologists, linguistic anthropologists, and psychologists who assert differing claims based upon their evidence in the field or the laboratory. We will explore this aspect of linguistic capacities in humans later in this chapter.

Animal Communication and Human Language

7.2 Discuss what makes human languages unique in comparison with nonhuman animal communication.

Both laboratory and field studies of animal communication offer fascinating insights into the question of what distinguishes human communication from animal communication. Many Western philosophers such as Plato and René Descartes have identified speech and language as the major distinction between humans and other animals. Modern studies on animal communication, however, suggest that the language gap separating humans from other animals is not as wide as it once appeared. These studies also indicate that fundamental differences exist between animal communication and human languages. The question is not whether animals can communicate; we know that almost every animal can. The real question is: How does animal communication differ from human communication? In searching for an answer to this question, linguistic anthropologists have identified a number of distinctive characteristics of human languages. The four most important features are productivity, displacement, arbitrariness, and combining sounds (Hockett and Ascher 1964).

Productivity

Human languages are inherently flexible and creative. Users of human languages, even small children, can create sentences never heard before by anyone. There are no limits to our capability to produce messages that refer to the past, present, or future. We can express different thoughts, meanings, and experiences in infinite ways. In contrast, animal communication systems in natural settings are rigid and fixed. The sounds of animal communications do not vary and cannot be modified. The offspring of chimpanzees will always use the same pattern of vocalization as the parents. In contrast, the highly flexible nature of human languages allows for efficient and creative uses of symbolic communication. William von Humboldt, a nineteenth-century linguist, used the phrase "the infinite use of finite media" to suggest the idea of linguistic productivity (von Humboldt [1836] 1972; Pinker 1994).

Displacement

It is clear from field studies, and to some extent from laboratory studies, that the meaning of a sound or vocalization of a nonhuman animal is closely tied to a specific type of stimulus. For example, the chimpanzee's vocalization is associated with a particular emotional state and stimulus. Thus, a growl or scream as a warning to the group cannot be made in the absence of some perceived threat. Similarly, animals such as parrots and mynah birds can learn to imitate a wide variety of words, but they cannot substitute or displace one word for another. In contrast, the meanings of sounds in human languages can refer to people, things, or events that are not present, a feature called "displacement." We can discuss things that are not perceived by our visual or auditory capacities.

This capacity for displacement enables humans to communicate with one another using highly abstract concepts. Humans can express their objectives in reference to the past, present, and future. They can discuss spiritual or hypothetical phenomena that do not exist concretely. They can discuss past history through myth or specific genealogical relations. Humans can refer to what will happen after death through myth or theological concepts such as heaven or spiritual enlightenment. Displacement allows humans to plan for the future through the use of foresight. Obviously, this linguistic ability for displacement is interrelated with the general symbolic capacities that are shared by humans, providing the basis of culture, as discussed in Chapter 6. Symbolic capacities allow humans to manipulate abstract concepts to develop complex beliefs and worldviews.

Arbitrariness

The arbitrariness of sounds in a communication system is another distinctive feature of human languages. Words seldom have any necessary connection with the concrete objects or abstract symbols they represent. In English, we say one, two, and three to refer to the numbers, whereas the Chinese say *yi*, *er*, and *san*. Neither language has the "correct" word for the numbers because there is no correct word. "Ouch" is pronounced "*ay*" in Spanish and "*ishkatak*" in the Nootkan Indian language. A German shepherd dog does not have any difficulty understanding the bark of a French poodle. An English speaker, however, will have trouble understanding a Chinese speaker. A chimpanzee from West Africa will have no difficulty communicating with a chimpanzee from East Africa (although primatologists do find different behavior patterns, such as tool making and nut cracking, among chimpanzees residing in different locales in Africa) (Mercader, Panger, and Boesch 2002).

Combining Sounds to Produce Meanings

We have mentioned that various animals have sounds that indicate different meanings in specific contexts. Human languages, in addition, have units of sound that cannot be correlated with units of meaning. Every human language has between 12 and 60 of these sound units, called *phonemes*. A **phoneme** is a unit of sound that distinguishes

This cartoon illustrates the problems that animals have in communicating human language.

meaning in a particular language. For example, in English, the difference between "dime" and "dine" is distinguished by the sound difference or phonemic difference between /m/ and /n/. English has 45 phonemes, Italian has 27, and Hawaiian has 27 (Farb 1974).

Nonhuman animals cannot combine their sound units to communicate new meanings; one vocalization is given to indicate a specific response. In contrast, in human languages, the same sounds can be combined and recombined to form different meanings. As an illustration, the sounds usually represented by the English letters *p*, *t*, *c*, and *a* (the vowel sound in the word *bat*) have no meaning on their own. But they can be used to form words like *pat*, *tap*, *cat*, *apt*, *act*, *tact*, *pact*, and so on, which do have meanings. The Hawaiian language, with only 13 sound units, has almost 3,000 words consisting of different combinations of 3 sounds and many thousands of words formed by combinations of 6 sounds. Phonemes that may have no meaning alone can be combined and recombined to form literally as many meaningful units (words) as people need or want. Primates and other animals do not have this ability.

Having defined these features of human language, we can discern fundamental differences between human and animal communication. However, some researchers working with chimpanzees in laboratories are still not willing to label human languages as "true languages," as distinguished from "animal communication systems." They criticize what they refer to as the "anthropocentric" view of language—the view that takes human language as its standard. Because chimpanzees do not have the physical ability to form the sounds made by humans, it may be unfair to compare their language strictly in terms of vocal communication.

The Evolution of Language

7.3 Describe what anthropologists conclude about the evolution of language.

Throughout the centuries, linguists, philosophers, and physical anthropologists have developed theories concerning the origins of human language. One early theory, known as the "bowwow" theory, maintains that language arose when humans imitated the sounds of nature by the use of onomatopoeic words, such as *cock-a-doodle-doo*, or *sneeze*, or *mumble*. Another theory associated with the Greek philosopher Plato argues that language evolved as humans detected the natural sounds of objects in nature. Known as the "ding-dong" theory, this argument assumed that a relationship exists between a word and its meaning because nature gives off a harmonic ring. For example, all of nature, including rocks, streams, plants, and animals, was thought to emit a ringing sound that could be detected by humans. The harmonic ring of a rock supposedly sounded like the word *rock*. Both theories have been discredited, replaced by other scientific and linguistic anthropological hypotheses concerning the evolution of language. When anthropologists study the evolution of language, they draw on evidence from all four fields of anthropology: physical anthropology, archaeology, linguistic anthropology, and cultural anthropology, studies in genetics and psycholinguistics, as well as experiments in communication with animals and humans.

In Chapter 4 (pp. 112–113), we discussed the contemporary evidence for the evolution of language among hominins focusing on the requisites for anatomical and internal brain changes that would be required for the linguistic capacities, as well as the acquisition of the FOXP2 gene. In addition to these developments, a recent hypothesis regarding language evolution proposed by neuroscientist and anthropologist Michael A. Arbib, and his colleagues Katja Liebal and Simone Pika, suggests that human linguistic capacities may have evolved through the development of gestures rather than vocalization per se (2008). The data from current studies on primate vocalizations, facial expressions, and gestures used by primates and prelinguistic human children suggest that the use of gestures coupled with improved modes of imitation provided the foundations for the emergence of a protolanguage for ancestral creatures related to the human line. Prelinguistic human children communicate with gestures prior to spoken language. Nonhuman primates also communicate with some basic gestures. Arbib et al. propose that the growth of neurology for imitation and improved forms of pantomime associated with gestures may have been the important keys for the development of linguistic abilities within the ancestral human lineage (2008). Obviously, gestural communication would be supplemented with vocalization in the full development of human language capacities, but these researchers emphasize that language is multimodal with both gestures and vocalization, and this research has helped illuminate what may have been initially important in providing the basics of human language.

Additionally, another aspect of language evolution appears to be related to the development of "mirror neurons" in humans. Mirror neurons were discovered through experiments with macaque monkeys. Gallese and colleagues found that when measuring the activity of neurons in one specific area of the brain, these neurons discharged along with specific goal-directed manual activities of these monkeys, and also when the monkeys observed humans doing the same manual activities (1996). These mirror neurons provide a mechanism for linking the intentions of a sender of a message to a receiver, a necessary component of language. Many experiments have indicated that mirror neurons exist in humans. The mirror neuron network has been correlated with complex learning. The network appears to be related to both imitation (not found in monkeys) and the ability to understand the intentions and emotions of others, usually referred to as "Theory of Mind" or TOM, also prerequisites for complex language capacities. Some researchers hypothesize that Broca's area of the brain evolved atop of the mirror neuron circuits to create the capacity for language development involving manual, (tool use), facial, and vocal behaviors (Arbib 2011).

Some linguists and primatologists believe that the emergence of human language suggests that at some point in the expansion of the brain, a rewiring of the human brain developed that allowed for what is known as *recursion*, the linguistic capacity to build an infinite number of sentences within sentences (Hauser, Chomsky, and Fitch 2002). Other models emphasize the evolution of words and sounds, as well as motor control and other features of the language capacity as important as recursion (Lieberman 2007; Pinker 1994; Jackendoff and Pinker 2005). Anthropologist Dan Sperber and his colleague Deirdre Wilson suggest that fully modern human language involves making inferences about what people are saying to one another in particular contexts (1996). They point out that compared with humans, chimpanzees have only a very rudimentary capacity to make inferences about the beliefs and intentions of another chimpanzee. Thus, communication capacities for humans are connected with our cognitive capacities for developing inferences in particular cultural contexts. Whatever the precise determinants of the evolution of language, it is difficult to identify the critical stage in the evolution from a simple, sign-based communication system to a more advanced, symbolic form of language. It is, however, recognized that this capacity broadly expanded human capabilities for adaptation and creativity.

As stated in Chapter 4 in the discussion of hominin linguistic evolution, although anthropologists may disagree with one another regarding the actualities and purpose of language capacities in humans, this capacity for language was probably the last major step in our biological evolution. Since that time, human history has been dominated by *cultural* rather than *biological* evolution. This cultural evolution and the subsequent developments in adaptation and creativity could not have occurred before a fully evolved language capacity.

The Structure of Language

7.4 Discuss how linguistic anthropologists study language.

Linguistic anthropologists compare the structure of different languages. To do so, they study the sounds of a language (*phonology*), the words of a language (*morphology*), the *sentence structure* of a language (*syntax*), the meaning of a language (*semantics*), and the *rules* for the appropriate use of a language (*pragmatics*). More than 7,000 languages have existed throughout history, all of which have contained these five components, although the components vary considerably from one language to another.

Phonology

Phonology is the study of the sounds used in language. Although all human languages have both vowel and consonant sounds, no language makes use of all the sounds humans can make. The sounds of all languages are either oral or nasal. To study phonetic differences among languages, linguists have developed the International Phonetic Alphabet (IPA), which enables them to transcribe all the sounds produced in the world's languages. Each sound is used somewhere in the world, although no single language contains all of them. Each language has its own phonetic inventory, consisting of all the sounds normally produced by its speakers, and also its own phonemic inventory, consisting of the sound units that can produce word contrasts in the language. As we have already seen, human languages, which have only a limited number of sounds, can combine these sounds to produce complex meanings.

Linguists attempt to discover the phonemes, or contrasting sound units, of a language by looking for what are called minimal pairs: words that are identical except for one difference in sound. For example, the English words *lot* and *rot* form a minimal pair; they are identical except for their beginning sounds, spelled *l* and *r*. The fact that English speakers recognize *lot* and *rot* as different words establishes that /*l*/ and /*r*/ are contrasting sound units, or phonemes, in English. In contrast, when Japanese children acquire their native language, they do not make a sharp categorical distinction between the /*l*/ and /*r*/ sounds. Japanese adult speakers do not hear the distinction between /*l*/ and /*r*/, even when they listen very carefully to English speakers. Patricia Kuhl and her Japanese colleagues studied how Japanese infants attend to different sounds of their own language and why they do not make distinctions between /*l*/ and /*r*/ (1996). This research suggests that as we are exposed to our language environment, the initial sounds we detect as infants in our first language alter the neurological networks in our brains, resulting in enduring effects on our ability to distinguish particular sounds within a language.

When linguistic anthropologists analyze the phonological system of a language, they attempt to organize the sounds, or **phones**, of the language into a system of contrasting phonemes. For example, English speakers produce both a /*p*/ sound and the same sound accompanied by *aspiration*, a light puff of air, symbolized in the IPA as /*p*h/; compare the difference between the *p* sounds in *spy* and *pie*. Because in English the sounds /*p*/ and /*p*h/ never form a minimal pair and their pronunciation depends upon their position in a word, these sounds are allophones of the same phoneme. In other languages, such as Aymara (spoken in Bolivia, Peru, and Chile), the aspiration of consonants produces a phonemic contrast: Compare the Aymara words /*hupa*/, which means "they," and /*hup*h*a*/, which is a kind of cereal. In Aymara, then, the sounds /*p*/ and /*p*h/ belong to separate phonemes, just as /*l*/ and /*r*/ do in English, as we saw before. This illustrates the fact that the "same" sounds may be contrastive in one language and not contrastive in another. Also, what sounds like a /*b*/ to a native Spanish speaker sounds like a /*p*/ to a native English speaker. Obviously, neurological changes are occurring within the brain as a child acquires his or her native language.

In addition to aspiration, sounds may be modified in other ways, including nasality, pitch, stress, and length of time the sound is held. Many Asian languages, such as Chinese and Thai, are *tonal*; that is, a word's meaning is affected by the tones (contrasting pitches) of the sounds that make up the word. Put another way, the tones of the language have phonemic value. To an English speaker's ear, a Chinese or Thai speaker sounds musical. For example, in Thai, *may* can mean "new," "to burn," or "silk," depending upon the tone used.

Pueblo Indians use many nasalized sounds to produce phonemic differences. Arab speakers use the back of the tongue and the throat muscles, whereas Spanish speakers use the tip of the tongue. The !Kung San or Ju/'hoansi of southern Africa have a unique manner of producing phonemic differences. They use a sharp intake of air to make clicks that shape meaning for them. Their language also requires more use of the lips to produce smacks than most other languages. The Ju/'hoansi language has been referred to as a "clicking language."

Most people are unaware of the complex physiological and mental processes required to pronounce the sounds of their native tongue. Only through extensive phonetic and phonological analysis by linguists and anthropologists is this component of language understood.

Morphology

To study the words of human languages, anthropologists isolate the **morphemes**, the smallest units of a language that convey meaning. The study of morphemes is called **morphology**. Morphemes may be short, containing only a single phoneme, or they may include a combination of phonemes. They are the minimal building blocks of meaning and cannot be reduced further. *Bound morphemes* are those morphemes that cannot stand alone, such as suffixes and prefixes. For example, in English, *s* is a bound morpheme that indicates the plural, and the prefix *un* is a bound morpheme meaning "not." *Free morphemes*, in contrast, are independent units of meaning; they can stand alone, for example, as nouns, verbs, adjectives, or adverbs. Words such as *boy*, *girl*, *happy*, and *close* are free morphemes.

In any language, morphemes are limited in number, and languages differ in how these morphemes are used and combined. In contrast to many languages, English has complex rules governing the formation of plurals of certain words (for example, *geese*, *mice*, *children*, and *shrimp*). Some languages, such as Chinese, generally use one morpheme for each word. Other languages, such as the Eskimo (Inuit) languages, combine a large number of affixes to form words.

An important way in which languages differ is the extent to which they use morphology to convey meaning. For example, in English, we can say, "The girl sees the dog," or, "The dog sees the girl." The nouns *girl* and *dog* do not change form, and only their position in the sentence indicates which is subject and which is object. But in Russian, *dyevushka videt sobaku* means, "The girl sees the dog"; "The dog sees the girl" is *sobaka videt dyevushku*. Note that the endings on the nouns show which is subject and which is object, even if the word order is changed: *Sobaku videt dyevushka* still means, "The girl sees the dog."

Syntax

The **syntax** of a language is the collection of rules for the way phrases and sentences are made up out of words. For example, these rules determine whether a subject comes before or after a verb or whether an object follows a verb. Linguistic anthropologist Joseph Greenberg and colleagues (Greenberg, Denning, and Kemmer 1990) classified languages based on word order within sentences—that is, the location of the subject (S), the verb (V), and the object (O). They demonstrated that these components occur in six possible orders: VSO, SVO, SOV, VOS, OSV, and OVS. But, in fact,

Greenberg and his colleagues found in their cross-linguistic comparison that usually just three patterns of word order occur: VSO, SVO, and SOV. Since their study, other languages have been discovered with the VOS, OSV, and OVS forms, though the last two are extremely rare (Smith 1999).

Although most languages permit variation in syntax to allow for emphasis in expression, most linguists suggest that some innate universal capacities may influence word order. For example, the expression for the English sentence, "The boy drank the water," can be found in all languages. Notice the variations in syntactical order among six different languages:

	S	V	O
English:	the bóy	dránk	the wáter
	S	V	O
Russian:	mál'c_ik	vy'pil	vódu
	V	S	O
Arabic:	s_áraba	lwáladu	lma-a
	S	V	O
Hausa:	ya-ro-	yás_a-	ruwa-
	S	V	O
Thai:	dègchaaj	dyym	nàam
	S	O	V
Quechua:	wámbra	yakúta	upiárqan

(Hausa is a West African language. Quechua is a language of the ancient Incas and their modern descendants.)

The syntax of a language also includes rules for transforming one kind of sentence into another—for example, for forming questions from statements. To form questions from statements, English has a rule that moves the auxiliary verb from its normal position in the sentence to a position at the front of the sentence. This rule allows us to take the statement, "Mary will study for the exam." and, by moving *will* to the front, transform it into the question, "Will Mary study for the exam?"

Semantics

Semantics is the study of the meaning of the symbols, words, phrases, and sentences of a language. The field of semantics has led to important developments in linguistic anthropology. Linguistic anthropologists focus on the meaning of language as it relates to beliefs, concepts, and patterns of thought in different societies. A specialty has developed to account for the meaning of concepts and terms relating to kinship and other cultural phenomena. This specialty sometimes referred to as *ethnosemantics*, overlaps with the field of cognitive anthropology introduced in Chapter 6.

Kinship Terms The goal of ethnosemantics is to understand the meanings of words, phrases, and sentences and how members of other societies use language to organize things, events, and behaviors. For example, this type of analysis has been applied to the kinship terminologies of many societies. It became increasingly clear to many anthropologists that they could not understand the kinship terms of other societies by simply translating them into English. English terms such as *mother*, *father*, *brother*, *brother-in-law*, *cousin*, *aunt*, and *uncle* treat the meaning of kinship differently than do the kinship terms of other societies.

Some groups classify their kin with very precise terms for individuals, no matter how distantly they are related. English kin terms are fairly precise and distinct with respect to genealogical relatedness, yet English does not specify every kin relationship precisely. For example, English speakers do not distinguish between maternal and paternal uncles or aunts. Chinese kinship terminology, on the other hand, includes different terms for one's mother's brother and one's father's brother. There are separate terms for every sibling, as well as for different cousins. This is an example of a highly descriptive kinship terminology. Other forms of kinship terminology are highly generalized. In the Hawaiian kinship system, there is no specific term to parallel the English term *father*. Instead, the Hawaiians use one general term to classify their father and all male relatives in their father's generation. Some kinship terminologies, such as those of the Iroquois Indians, are intermediate between the descriptive and the generalized forms. The Iroquois have one single term for one's father and one's father's brother, but two separate terms for one's mother and one's mother's brother.

Ethnosemanticists or cognitive anthropologists have worked out systematic methods to understand the kinship terminologies of many different societies by focusing on the distinctive common features of these terminologies (D'Andrade 1995). For example, in English, there is a male and female contrast with every kin term except cousin. In addition, the feature of generation is designated in terms such as *uncle* and *nephew*, *aunt* and *niece*, and in these same terms, we distinguish between ascending and descending generations. There is also a contrast between direct (same generation) and collateral (different generation) relatives. Great-uncles and great-aunts are collateral relatives, whereas brothers and sisters are direct relatives. Ethnosemanticists use these methods to analyze other forms of kinship terminology in various societies.

A fascinating study by Larry Hirschfeld suggests that there are some universal aspects regarding the meaning of kinship terminology (1986, 1989). Hirschfeld found that children and adults assume that kinship terms refer to a "natural affinity" for their own genealogical relatives and families. Children appear to have an intuitive understanding of the relationship between kinship terms and their relatives and family. Kinship terms are used to refer to people who share a common descent and an internal "essence." The family is based upon a particular group of people and is different from a group of students in a class or other types of groups. Anthropologist Doug Jones has followed this model of linguistic research on kinship terms and also suggests that there is a "universal" aspect to kinship terminology found among all societies (2000, 2003, 2004). Other cognitive anthropologists continue to investigate kinship terminologies and other cultural phenomena to seek out both similarities and differences among human groups (Bloch and Sperber 2002).

Language Acquisition

7.5 Explain how children acquire their languages.

Although human infants are born with the ability to speak a language, they are not born preprogrammed to speak a particular language such as English. Just as infants are exposed to enculturation to absorb and learn about their culture, they must be exposed to the phonemes, morphemes, syntax, and semantics of the language within their culture. Linguistic anthropologists have examined this process, drawing on different hypotheses regarding language acquisition.

One of the earliest discussions in Western society of how humans learn their language came in the late fourth-century writings of the Catholic theologian Augustine in his famous book *Confessions* (1995). Augustine believed that as we hear our parents speak words and point to objects, we associate the words with the objects. Later, the empiricist philosopher John Locke (1632–1704) maintained a similar belief and suggested that the human mind at birth is like a blank tablet, a *tabula rasa*, and that infants learn language through habit formation. This hypothesis was further developed by twentieth-century behavioral psychologists such as B. F. Skinner, who maintained that infants learn language through conditioned responses and feedback from their

A teacher and young students acquiring language.

environment. This behaviorist approach to language became the dominant model of how language was acquired for many years. In the behaviorist view, an infant might babble a sound that resembles an acceptable word like *mama* or *daddy* and would then be rewarded for that response. Thus rewarded, the child would use the word *daddy* in certain contexts. According to Skinner, children learn their entire language through this type of social conditioning.

The Enlightenment philosopher René Descartes (1596–1650) advocated a contrasting view of language learning. He argued that innate ideas or structures in the human mind provide the basis for learning language. Until the late 1950s, most linguists and anthropologists working on language assumed that Locke's model—and, by extension, Skinner's—was correct. However, by about 1960, evidence began to accumulate that suggested that, in fact, humans come into the world especially equipped not only to acquire their own native language, but also to acquire any other human language.

Chomsky on Language Acquisition

The most influential modern proponent of a view that is somewhat similar to Descartes's hypothesis is linguist Noam Chomsky. Chomsky is interested in how people acquire *grammar*, the set of rules that determine how sentences are constructed to produce meaningful statements (2002). Most people cannot actually state the rules of their grammar, but they do use the rules to form understandable sentences. For example, in English, young children can easily transform the active sentence, "Bill loves Mary," into a passive sentence, "Mary is loved by Bill." This change requires much grammatical knowledge, but most English speakers carry out this operation without consciously thinking about it.

According to Chomsky, all children acquire these complex rules readily and do not seem to have difficulty producing meaningful statements, even when they have not been exposed to linguistic data that illustrate the rules in question. In other words, children acquire these complex rules with minimal exposure to the language. Furthermore, children are able to both produce and understand novel sentences they have never heard before. All this would be impossible, Chomsky claims, if acquiring language depended on trial-and-error learning and reinforcement, as the behaviorist psychologists led by Skinner had thought. In other words, Chomsky suggests that we are born with a brain *prewired* to enable us to acquire language easily; Chomsky often refers to this prewiring as *universal grammar*.

Universal grammar serves as a template, or model, against which a child matches and sorts out the patterns of morphemes and phonemes and the subtle distinctions that are needed to communicate in any language. According to Chomsky, a behavioristic understanding of language learning is too simplistic to account for the creativity and productivity of any human language. In his view, the universal grammar of the human mind enables the child to acquire language and produce sentences never heard before. In addition, Chomsky and others who study language acquisition propose a *critical period*, beginning with infancy and lasting through about the age of five and the onset of puberty, during which language acquisition must take place. If children are not exposed to language during that period, they may never be able to acquire it, or they may learn it only in a very rudimentary fashion. Chomsky believes that the human brain contains genetically programmed blueprints or *modules* for language learning, and he often refers to language acquisition as a part of children's "growth," not something they do but rather something that happens to them. In addition, Chomsky argues that there is a difference in *kind* between primate communication and human language capacities. He suggests in a well-known statement that "Olympic athlete broad-jumpers can *fly* some 30 feet in the air, but humans do not have the capacity to *fly* like chickens or other birds." The capacity for flying, like the "language capacity," has very different physical and anatomical requirements.

Another important contribution of Chomsky's is the realization that human languages, despite their apparently great diversity, are really more alike than they are different. Anthropologists had previously assumed that languages could vary infinitely and that there was no limit to what could be found in a human language. Chomsky and the researchers that followed him, in contrast, have cataloged many basic, underlying ways in which all languages are really the same. In this view, a hypothetical Martian linguist visiting Earth would probably decide that all humans speak dialects of one human language. Note that this is somewhat parallel to the search for *cultural universals* described in Chapter 6.

Noam Chomsky

Creole and Pidgin Languages One source of evidence for Chomsky's model of innate universal grammar is research on specific types of languages known as *creole* and *pidgin* languages. Linguist Derek Bickerton has compared these two types of languages from different areas of the world. Pidgin and creole languages develop from cross-cultural contact between speakers of mutually unintelligible languages. A *pidgin* form of communication emerges when people of different languages develop and use a simple grammatical structure and words to communicate with one another. For example, in the New Guinea highlands, where many different languages were spoken, a pidgin language developed between the indigenous peoples and the Westerners.

In some cases, the children of the pidgin speakers begin to speak a *creole* language. The vocabulary of the *creole* language is similar to that of the pidgin, but the grammar is much more complex. There are more than 100 known creole languages. Among them are the creole languages developed between African slaves and Europeans, leading to languages such as Haitian and Jamaican Creole. Hawaiian Creole emerged after contact between English-speaking Westerners and native Hawaiians.

What is remarkable, according to Bickerton, is that all these languages share similar grammatical patterns, despite the lack of contact among these diverse peoples. For example, Hawaiian Creole uses the English word *walk* in a different manner from standard English. The phrase *bin walk* means "had walked"; *stay walk* is continuing action, as in, "I am walking" or, "I was walking"; and *I bin stay walk* means, "I had been walking." Although this phrasing might sound unusual to a person from England or the United States, it does conform to a clear set of grammatical rules. Very similar tense systems are found in all other creole languages, whatever their vocabularies or geographic origins.

Bickerton suggests that the development of creole languages may parallel the evolution of early human languages. Because of an innate universal grammatical component of the human mind, languages emerged in uniform ways. The prehistoric languages would have had structures similar to those of the creole languages. As languages developed in various types of environments with different characteristics, different vocabularies and sentence structures evolved. Yet, when societies are uprooted by cultural contact, the innate rules for ordering language remain intact. Bickerton's thesis suggests that humans do have some sort of universal linguistic acquisition device, as hypothesized by Chomsky (Bickerton 1985, 1999, 2008).

Sign Language in Nicaragua: A Case for the Innateness of Language

An interesting study of deaf children in Nicaragua conducted by linguistic anthropologist Ann Senghas and her colleagues also supports the view that language has some innate characteristics, as Chomsky has indicated. This study demonstrates how language can develop from a gesture system to a full-fledged language with grammar, symbols, and meanings (Senghas, Kita, and Ozyurek 2004). Nicaragua's deaf schools were established in 1977 and had many hearing impaired children who interacted with one another. These children came from various backgrounds and regions of the country and had developed different means of communication with their parents. The school that was established focused on teaching the children to read lips and speak Spanish. Senghas and her colleagues studied three generations of deaf schoolchildren in Managua, Nicaragua, and found that they were actually constructing linguistic rules from various gestures that they were using with one another over the years. These gestures were different from any other communicative gestures found in other sign languages. The studies indicate that the preadolescent children are much more capable of learning the new deaf language than the older children, thus indicating that there is a "critical stage" in the capacity for learning grammar, syntax, and rules of language. This study demonstrated that this deaf language, invented by these Nicaraguan children, developed from a gestural sign system to a more structured linguistic system. This linguistic study provides more confirmation of Chomsky's views on language acquisition and also of the research on the transition from pidgin to creole languages previously described. It appears that children's brains are predisposed to learn the rules of complicated grammar and impose grammatical structure in innovative and productive ways. This study of deaf Nicaraguan children indicates that there is a biologically based language acquisition device that enables young children to learn and create extremely complex fundamental grammatical and linguistic systems with symbolic meanings understood by all of them.

It appears that language acquisition depends upon both biological readiness and learning. The ability to speak seems to be biologically programmed, whereas a specific language is learned from the society the child grows up in. Children who are not exposed to language during their "critical period" may not be able to learn to use language properly. Research such as Chomsky's provides for further advances in a biocultural or interactionist approach to test hypotheses regarding language, biology, mind, and thought.

Children using sign language

A recent book by linguist Andrea Moro discusses the use of new technologies in neuroimaging that has enabled a more comprehensive understanding of how language is integrated with our neurology (2008). The use of positron emission topography, or PET, and functional magnetic resonance imaging, or fMRI, has led to a biolinguistic revolution that has resulted in an enhanced understanding of language acquisition, genetics, neuroscience, and the universal grammar that Chomsky has been discussing for the last 50 years. The future of this research is bound to unlock more crucial areas of knowledge about the biological aspect of language for anthropological research.

Anthropologists At Work

RUSSELL BERNARD: Saving Languages

Native American children use computers to learn their native languages.

There are more than 7,000 languages distributed throughout a population of more than 7 billion people in the world. As many linguistic anthropologists have noted, however, tens of thousands of languages have become extinct through the years. In Western Europe, hundreds of languages disappeared with the expansion of agricultural empires that imposed their languages on conquered peoples. For example, during the expansion of the Roman Empire for approximately a thousand years, many tribal languages disappeared as they were replaced by Latin. Currently, only 45 native languages still exist in Western Europe.

When Columbus discovered the Americas, more than 2,000 languages existed among different Native American peoples. Yet, even in pre-Columbian America, before 1500 A.D., native languages were displaced by the expansion of peoples such as the Aztecs and Incas in Central and South America. As the Spanish and British empires expanded into these regions, the indigenous languages began to disappear even more rapidly. A similar process has been ongoing throughout Asia, Africa, and the Middle East.

The majority of people in the world speak one of the "large" groups of languages, such as Mandarin Chinese (with more than 1 billion speakers), Spanish, or English. Most of the more than 4,000 languages that exist are spoken in small-scale societies that have an average of 5,000 people or so. For example, Papua New Guinea alone has perhaps as many as a thousand different languages distributed among various ethnic groups (Diamond 1993). Other islands in countries such as Indonesia may have as many as 400 different languages. Yet, in all of the areas of the Pacific and Asia, the "large" languages are beginning to replace the "small" ones.

Some linguists estimate that if the present rate of the disappearance of languages remains constant, within a century or two our 4,000 languages could be reduced to just a few hundred. For example, as young people in the Pacific Islands begin to move from rural to urban regions, they usually abandon their traditional language and learn a majority tongue to be able to take advantage of educational and economic opportunities. As the media—television, radio, newspapers, and now the Internet—opt for a majority language, more people will elect to abandon their native languages. These are global processes that have resulted in linguistic homogeneity and the loss of traditional languages.

In North America and Alaska, there are some 200 languages ranging from Inuit and Yupik among the native Alaskans to Navajo, Hopi, Choctaw, Creek, Seminole, Chickasaw, and Cherokee in other areas. However, many of these languages are now on the verge of extinction. As Europeans began to expand and control North America and Alaska, they forced Native American children to speak the English language as a means of "civilizing" them. In many cases, Native American children were removed from their families and were forbidden to speak their native languages. In addition, most Native American peoples have had to learn English to adjust to circumstances in an English-language-dominated society. Thus, very few of the Native American languages are actively spoken today.

Some people say that this process of global and linguistic homogenization and the loss of traditional languages is a positive development. As people begin to speak a common language, communication is increased, leading to improvements in societies that formerly could not unify through language. For example, in India, hundreds of languages existed before the British colonized the area. As the educated class in India (a small minority at that time) began to learn and speak English, it helped provide a means of unifying India as a country. Many people say that for the purpose of developing commerce and political relationships, the abandonment of native languages is a good thing. Many businesspeople and politicians argue that multiple languages inhibit economic and political progress, and the elites of many countries have directly encouraged language loss.

A number of linguistic anthropologists, however, disagree with these policies. They may agree that people ought to have some common language to understand one another, to conduct business, and to pursue common political goals. But, they argue, this does not have to mean eliminating minority languages. It requires only that people become bilingual or multilingual. In most societies throughout the world, including Western Europe, people routinely learn two or more languages as children. The United States and Japan are exceptional in being monolingual societies. Linguistic anthropologists find from their studies that people who are forced to abandon their native languages and cultures begin to lose their self-esteem. Bilingualism would permit these people to retain their own language while simultaneously learning the majority language to be able to share in a common national culture.

The U.S. government is beginning to realize that bilingualism has a positive influence on community development among minority populations such as Native Americans. In the recent past, a number of educational programs were funded under the U.S. Bilingual Education Act. This act encouraged the development of English-speaking skills; however, it also offered instruction in the native languages. During the 1980s, there were more than 20 Title VII projects serving Native American students from 16 different language backgrounds. Through these government-sponsored programs, linguistic anthropologists have been actively engaged in both research and language renewal activities among the Native American population (Granadillo and Orcutt-Gachiri 2011). For example, the Cherokee communities of North Carolina have funded language revitalization through their casino revenue streams. They use toddler immersion programs, parent workshops, master-apprentice nests, emergent Cherokee literature, and online classes and podcasts. These kinds of activities have led many younger Native Americans to become interested in studying their traditional languages, which have improved classroom learning, thereby inhibiting high dropout rates among young students.

Anthropologist Russell Bernard has promoted the value of maintaining the native languages of people through the use of microcomputers (1992). Bernard received his Ph.D. from the University of Illinois and is professor emeritus of anthropology at the University of Florida. He has done research in Greece, Mexico, and the United States and has taught or done research at universities in the U.S., Greece, Japan, and Germany. Bernard's areas of research include technology and social change, language death, and social network analysis. Since 1987, Bernard has participated in summer courses, sponsored by the U.S. National Science Foundation, on research methods and research design. Bernard co-authored *Native Ethnography* with Jesús Salinas Pedraza, emphasizing collaboration between anthropologists and native peoples. Bernard was the 2003 recipient of the Franz Boas Award from the American Anthropological Association and is a member of the National Academy of Sciences.

Bernard assisted Native Americans with the development of writing systems and literature for native languages. Through computer technology, anthropologists can help native peoples produce literature in their own languages for future generations. Bernard emphasizes that this will enable all of humanity to profit from the ideas of these people. Bernard was able to establish a center in Mexico where the Indian population could learn to use computers to write in their native languages. Sixty Indian people have learned to write directly in languages such as Mixtec, Zapotec, Chatino, Amuzgo, Chinantec, and Mazataec. Since his pioneering innovations, people like the Cherokee have developed Tsalagi (Cherokee) computer keyboards to use in the modern classroom, which has enabled a vibrant Internet presence for the script as well as the spoken language (Granadillo and Orcutt-Gachiri 2011). Native authors will use these computers and texts to teach adults and children of their home regions to read. Projects such as these represent opportunities for anthropologists to apply their knowledge in solving important problems in U.S. society and beyond.

More recently, linguistic anthropologists have been contributing to the globally based Internet forum known as the Rosetta Project with a Web site http://rosettaproject.org. This Rosetta Project is a global collaboration between linguistic specialists and native speakers of the world's languages, including endangered languages. The Rosetta Project has thousands of essays and blog posts, and reports on different endangered languages throughout the world. For example, one report discusses the 275 endangered Australian Aboriginal languages and how the Australian government has a new program to help support the translation, teaching, and the saving of these Aboriginal languages. Another report by linguist Laura Welcher discusses the Navajo language, currently spoken by about 150,000 people who also speak English, and another several thousand who are monolingual and speak only Navajo (2009). However, many young Navajo are not learning the Navajo language and English is supplanting the traditional language of the community. This endangered Navajo language was important as a code used by the U.S. military during World War II. The Navajo code talkers were recruited by the U.S. military to send verbal messages by radio to provide support to troops in the field. At the time of World War II, there was not much knowledge of the Navajo language because their communities were physically and socially isolated. However, as Welcher suggests, linguistic anthropologists have learned much more about the grammatical structures and lexicon of most of the world's languages, therefore; it would be very difficult to have the "code talking" phenomenon in this era. The Rosetta Project is being used as a heuristic tool to bring together native speakers of languages and linguists to establish a foundation to save the endangered languages throughout the world.

Language, Thought, and Culture

7.6 Discuss the relationship between language and culture.

In the early part of the twentieth century, Edward Sapir and Benjamin Whorf carried out studies of language and culture. Sapir was a prodigious fieldworker who described many Native American languages and provided the basis for the comparative method in anthropological linguistics. Whorf, an insurance inspector by profession and a linguist and anthropologist by calling, conducted comparative research on a wide variety of languages. The research of Sapir and Whorf led their students to formulate a highly controversial hypothesis that differs dramatically from the theories of Chomsky and the ethnosemantics of cognitive anthropologists and linguists.

The Sapir–Whorf Hypothesis

The **Sapir–Whorf hypothesis** suggests that there is a close relationship between the properties or characteristics of a specific language and its associated culture, and that these features of specific languages define experiences for us. In other words, although humans everywhere have approximately the same set of physical organs for perceiving reality—eyes to see, ears to hear, noses to smell—the human nervous system is bombarded with sensations of all kinds, intensities, and durations. These sensations do not all reach our consciousness. Rather, humans have a filtering device that classifies reality. This filtering device, according to the Sapir–Whorf hypothesis, is based on the characteristics of a specific language. In this view, certain features of language, in effect, provide us with a special pair of glasses that heightens certain perceptions and dims others, determining what we perceive as reality.

A Case Study: The Hopi Language To understand this hypothesis, we look at some examples given by Whorf. He compared the grammar of English with that of the Native American Hopi language, spoken in the southwestern part of the United States. He found that the verb forms indicating tense differ in these two languages. English contains past, present, and future verb forms; the Hopi language does not. In English, we can say, "I came home," "I am coming home," or, "I will come home." The Hopi do not have a verb corresponding to the use of *come* (Whorf 1956). From this type of example, Whorf inferred that Hopi and English speakers think about time in fundamentally different ways.

English speakers conceptualize time in a measurable, linear form, speaking of a length of time or a point in time. We say that time is short, long, or great. We can save time, squander it, or spend it. To the Hopi, in contrast, time is connected to the cycles of nature. Because they were farmers, their lives revolved around the different seasons for planting and harvesting. The Hopi, Whorf argued, saw time not as a motion in space (that is, as time passing) but as a "getting later" of everything that has ever been done. Whorf concluded that the Hopi did not share the Western emphasis on history, calendars, and clocks. From evidence such as this, Sapir and Whorf developed their hypothesis that the specific aspects of a language provide a grid, or structure that influences how humans categorize space, time, and other aspects of reality into a worldview. The Sapir–Whorf hypothesis is an example of *linguistic relativism* because it maintains that the world is experienced differently among different language communities.

Hopi female child with traditional hairstyle

Universals of Time Expression Linguistic anthropologist Ekkehart Malotki (1983) investigated the Sapir–Whorf hypothesis by reexamining the Hopi language. His research, based on many interviews with Hopi speakers, showed that, in fact, the Hopi calculate time in units very similar to those used by native English speakers. He concluded that Whorf had exaggerated the extent to which specific linguistic features influence a people's perceptions of time and demonstrated that the Hopi do make linguistic distinctions between the past and the present based on tense form. In the Hopi language, tense is distinguished between future and nonfuture instead of between past and future.

Anthropologist Hoyt Alverson (1994) investigated four different unrelated languages to determine how time is conceptualized. Alverson studied the metaphors and symbolic usages of time in the Mandarin language of China, the Hindi language of India, the Sesotho language of Africa, and English. He looked at 150 different linguistic usages of time from native speakers and showed that there are basic metaphors that universally underlie the conceptualization of time in any language. However, in different languages, time may be conceptualized in one or more of five universal possibilities. For example, time is usually conceptualized as partible or divisible, or it can be expressed as being linear, circular, or oscillating or as being a causal force or is spatialized in relation to the human body. This study, along with that of Malotki (1983), suggested that all humans share a common cognitive framework when conceptualizing time. These findings undoubtedly have implications for humanity's biological heritage, a universal cognitive evolution, and a common identity as a species.

Weak Linguistic Relativity

Although these studies appear to have refuted the Sapir–Whorf hypothesis, most linguistic anthropologists agree that a relationship exists between language and thought. Rather than asserting that language determines thought, they maintain that language influences the speaker's thinking and concepts. Some experts refer to this approach as a "weak" version of the linguistic relativity hypothesis.

Some contemporary researchers have looked for ways to reformulate the Sapir–Whorf hypothesis in the form of a more precise, testable hypothesis about the relationship among language, thought, and behavior. For example, John Lucy (1992) compared speakers of English and Yucatec Maya to see if their languages led them to perform differently on tasks involving remembering and sorting objects. As predicted from the grammar of the languages, English speakers appeared to attend more closely to the number and also to the shape of the objects, while Mayan speakers paid less attention to the number and more attention to the material from which the objects were made.

It is also true that specific languages contain the vocabulary needed to cope in particular environments. The need for a specific vocabulary in a society does not necessarily mean that language determines our perception of reality. After all, when a need to express some unlabeled phenomenon arises, speakers easily manufacture new words. English-speaking skiers, like Eskimos (Inuit), distinguish among several types of snow, speaking of powder, corn, and so on.

Language may also influence social perception. For example, many people in English-speaking societies have long objected to the use of *man*, *men*, and *mankind* to refer to humanity and *he* to refer to any person, male or female. The word "man" developed in Old English to refer to "a human being," and there were several words for females, *wif*, and males *wer* or *carl* (Bonvillian 2010). "Man" was joined with these to designate genders, *wifman* and *werman* or *carlman*. Eventually *wifman* became "woman" and "man" referred to males. Contemporary experimental studies indicate that the use of the masculine terms such as man as in "Political Man," "Economic Man," or "Urban Man" reinforces the idea that humanity is male and women are outsiders, marginal, and the "second sex" (Bonvillian 2010). Other gender-biased language occurs when words such as *lady* and *girl* are used in a demeaning manner to refer to women. In addition, the tradition of addressing females by the title *Mrs.* or *Miss* reflects gender bias in English-speaking countries (Bonvillian 2010).

To help explain this presumed bias, another linguistic anthropologist, M. J. Hardman-de-Bautista (1978), has formulated the notion of linguistic postulates, distinctions that are made obligatorily in language and that also reflect distinctions central to culture. For example, in English, biological sex is marked on the third-person singular pronouns (*she*, *he*). This distinction between female and male permeates English-speaking culture in important ways—for example, in how children are socialized into appropriate behavior ("be a nice little girl," "act like a lady," "be a man," and the like). In the Aymara language of Peru and Bolivia, in contrast, the third-person pronoun is not marked for sex or number, so the Aymara word *jupa* means "she/

he/they." For Aymara, the relevant contrast is human versus nonhuman, and *jupa* cannot be used to refer to an animal, such as a dog or llama; instead, a different pronoun must be used. Aymara children are not taught to behave like "nice girls" or "good boys," but to behave "like human beings, not like animals." Linguistic anthropologists who study Chinese or the Bantu languages of Africa find that despite the gender inequalities associated with these societies, the languages do not distinguish sex or gender in their pronoun usage. So, the features of specific languages do not always reflect the social conditions and values of a particular society. Linguistic anthropologists continue to investigate these issues of gender and language in different societies.

Historical Linguistics

7.7 Describe how anthropologists study the history of languages.

Historical linguistics is the study of language change and the historical relationships among different languages in an effort to discover what kinds of changes occur in languages and why. Research on this subject began in the late eighteenth century when Sir William Jones, a British legal scholar, suggested that the linguistic similarities of Sanskrit, an ancient Indian tongue, to ancient Greek, Latin, German, and English indicate that these languages were descended from a common ancestral language. It was discovered that these languages are part of one family, the Indo-European family, and share certain words and grammar. For example, the English word *three* is *trayas* in Sanskrit, *tres* in Latin, *treis* in Greek, and *drei* in German (see Table 7.1). The similarity in Indo-European languages led some early anthropologists to conclude that all current languages could be traced to a single language family.

The Family-Tree Model

Modern historical linguists agree that they probably can never reconstruct the original language, but they still may be able to reach far back into history to reconstruct an early **protolanguage**, a parent language for many ancient and modern languages. Many linguists hold the view that all languages change in a regular, recognizable way and that similarities among languages are due to a historical relationship among these languages. In other words, the languages of people living in adjacent areas of

Table 7.1 Comparative Word Chart of Indo-European Languages

English	Sanskrit	Latin	Greek	German	Old English
To bear	Bhar	Ferre	Fero	Gebären	Beran
Father	Pitar	Pater	Patir	Vater	Fæder
Mother	Matar	Mater	Mitir	Mutter	Modor
Brother	Bhratar	Frater	Frater	Bruder	Brodor
Three	Trayas	Tres	Treis	Drei	Brie
Hundred	Sata	Centum	Ekaton	Hundert	Hund
Night	Nisitha	Noctis	Nikta	Nacht	Niht
Red	Rudhira	Ruber	Erithros	Rot	Read
Foot	Pada	Pedis	Podos	Fuss	Fot
Fish	Piska	Piscis	Ikhthis	Fisch	Fisc
Goose	Hamsa	Anser	Khin	Gans	Gos
What	Kwo	Quod	Ti	Was	Hwæt
Where	Kva	Quo	Pou	Wo	Hwær

Source: Table from *The Way of Language: An Introduction* by Fred West. Copyright ©1975. Reproduced by permission of Heinle & Heinle, a division of Thomson Learning. Fax 800–730–2215.

Figure 7.1 The family-tree model

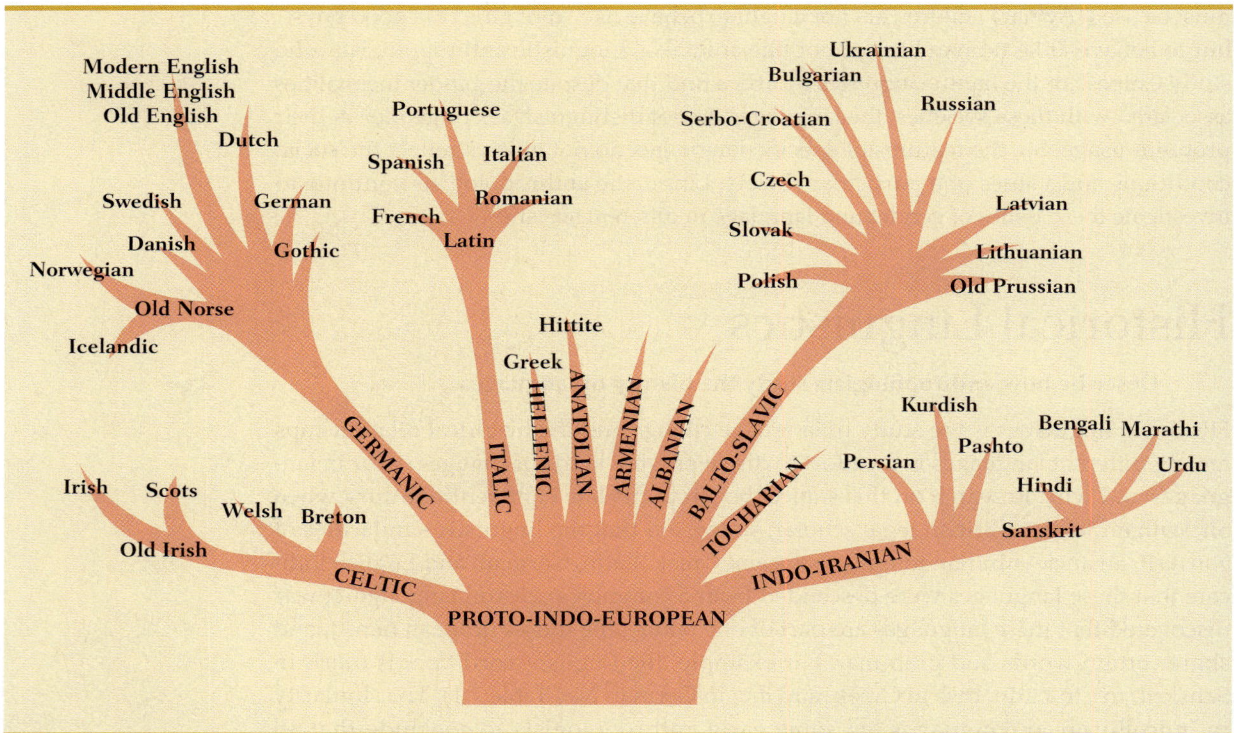

the world would tend to share similar phonological, syntactical, and semantic features. For example, the Romance languages of French, Spanish, Portuguese, Italian, and Romanian developed from Latin because of the historical relationship with one another through the influence of the Roman Empire. This view is known as the family-tree theory of language change (see Figure 7.1).

Most recently, historical linguists have been working with archaeologists to reconstruct the Proto-Indo-European language. They have found that the Indo-European languages did spread within distinctive regions for certain societies. British archaeologist Colin Renfrew (1989) hypothesizes that the spread of the Indo-European languages was linked to the spread of a particular technology and material culture. He suggests that the Indo-European languages spread throughout Europe from an original homeland in Anatolia, today part of Turkey, as early cultures adopted intensive agriculture. Similarly, English is currently promoted throughout the world as the language of television, computers, and other features of Western technology.

Assessing Language Change

To reconstruct a family tree of languages, the linguist compares the phonological characteristics (sounds) and morphological characteristics (words) of different languages. Linguistic anthropologist Morris Swadesh (1964) developed a systematic method of assessing historical language change. His goal was to date the separation of languages from one another using a statistical technique known as glottochronology (from the Greek *glotta*, meaning "tongue," and *chronos*, meaning "time"). Swadesh reasoned that the vocabulary of a language would remain stable at times, but would change rapidly at other times. Words for plants, animals, or technology would change quickly if the speakers migrated or came into contact with other groups. Swadesh thought, however, that a *core vocabulary* (pronouns and words for numbers or for the body, earth, wood, and stone) would remain immune to cultural change. He thought that if we could measure the rate of retention of this core vocabulary, then we could measure the separation of one language from another.

By comparing core vocabularies from different languages, linguists found that on average 19 percent of this core vocabulary would change in a language in approximately 1,000 years. In other words, about 81 percent of the core vocabulary would be retained. From this formula, linguistic anthropologists have reconstructed languages and produced "family trees" of languages from around the world.

Through the study of language change, linguistic anthropologists have put to rest the idea that all current languages in the world can be traced to a single language family. Language change has been swift in some circumstances and gradual in others. Multiple borrowings, or the spread of vocabulary and grammar throughout the world, have affected most languages. Linguistic researchers Sarah Thomason and Terrence Kaufman emphasize that many of the world's languages, including Russian, French, and English, have undergone radical change through language mixing. In their book (1988), Thomason and Kaufman claim that in the same way that many creole languages have emerged (discussed earlier in this chapter), other languages have developed through intensive culture contact. Instead of language developing from one source, there apparently are different centers and regions of language change.

Sociolinguistics

7.8 Describe what the field of sociolinguistics tells us about language use.

Linguistic anthropologists have researched the use of language in different social contexts, a field known as *sociolinguistics*. The sociolinguist takes the speech community as the framework for understanding the variation of speech in different social contexts. In general, linguistic anthropologists refer to this as the study of **pragmatics**, the rules for using language within a particular speech community.

The speech community is a social unit within which speakers share various ways of speaking. For example, in American society, certain patterns of English syntax and pronunciation are acceptable in specific contexts (American Standard English), whereas others are considered unacceptable. An American child may sometimes learn nonstandard words in the family environment, and if the family considers them cute, the child may continue to use them. Eventually, however, the child moves out of the family into the larger speech community, encountering speech habits that differ from those of the home. If the child uses those words in school or with others, he or she will be reprimanded or laughed at.

Through a process of enculturation and socialization into the speech community, the child learns the language used in a variety of social contexts. Language plays a prominent role in the process of enculturation. American children learn the regional pronunciation and grammatical usages within their speech community.

Dialectal Differences in Spoken Language

A speech community may consist of subgroups that share specific linguistic usages within a larger common language family. If the linguistic usages of these subgroups are different but mutually intelligible, their language variations are called dialects. **Dialects** are linguistic differences in pronunciation, vocabulary, or syntax that may differ within a single language. For example, dialectal differences in American Standard English exist in the Northeast, Midwest, South, and Southwest of the United States. In the southern United States, one might hear such grammatical constructions as, "It wan't [or weren't] me," and such pronunciations as *Miz* for *Mrs.* and the frequent loss of *r* except before vowels: *foah* for *four*, *heah* for *hear*, and *sulfuh* for *sulfur* (West 1975).

Certain dialects of English are looked on as more prestigious than others, reflecting educational, class, ethnic, race, and regional differences. When viewing language as a global phenomenon, however, all languages are dialects that have emerged in different locales and regions of the world. In actuality, the English language is not one standard language but consists of many different dialects. To say that British English is more "correct" than American Standard English simply because England is the homeland of English does not make sense to a linguist. The forms of English spoken in England, Australia, Canada, the United States, India, South Africa, and the West Indies have distinctive differences in pronunciation and vocabulary. The same generalization can be applied to many languages and dialects (Pinker 1994).

Some linguists studying speech communities in the United States have concluded that specific regional dialects are gradually disappearing. As people move from one region to another for jobs and education and as television and movies influence speech patterns, Americans are beginning to sound more alike. Many of the same processes are influencing different dialects and languages the world over (Pinker 1994).

African-American Vernacular English (AAVE) A number of linguists have been doing research on African-American Vernacular English (AAVE), a distinctive dialect of American English spoken by some African-Americans. Popularly, the term *Ebonics* is sometimes used for AAVE. Ebonics is derived from the words *ebony* and *phonics*, meaning "black sounds" (Rickford 1997, 1998). AAVE is also known as Black English Vernacular (BEV), Black English (BE), and African-American English (AAE). The majority of African-Americans do not speak AAVE or Ebonics; however, it is commonly spoken among working-class African-Americans and, in particular, among adolescent African-Americans. Linguistic anthropologists have suggested that Ebonics may have emerged as a creole language under the conditions of slavery in the United States. As slaves from Africa, captured from different areas and speaking an enormous variety of languages, were placed together on plantations in the American South, they developed a pidgin language to communicate. From this pidgin, the children may have created a systematic syntax and grammar, as they were at the critical stage of language learning. Just as Jamaican and Haitian Creole emerged in the Caribbean under the conditions of slavery, a variety of creole languages may have evolved in the United States.

One form of an early creole still exists among African-Americans on the Sea Islands off the coast of South Carolina and Georgia. This creole is known as Gullah and it is spoken by about 300,000 people. Gullah has some grammatical characteristics that are similar to West African languages; today it has been influenced strongly by standard English and southern regional dialects (Bonvillian 2010). Other forms of creole speech may have been introduced by the large numbers of slaves coming from Jamaica or Barbados into the American South, or they could have emerged within early communities of slaves within the United States. Ebonics may very well be a product of this early creolization.

Linguist John Rickford (1997, 1998) notes that Ebonics or the contemporary dialect AAVE is not just the use of slang. There are some slang terms in AAVE, such as *chillin* ("relaxing") and *homey* ("close friend"), but there is a systematic grammar and pronunciation within the language. Sentences within AAVE have standard usages, such as *He runnin* ("He is running"), *He be running* ("He is usually running"), and *He bin runnin* ("He has been running for a long time and still is"). Other rules, such as dropping consonants at the end of words such as *tes(t)* and *han(d)*, are evident in Ebonics. Rickford emphasizes that AAVE is not just a lazy form of English; AAVE is no more lazy English than Italian is a lazy form of Latin. These are different dialects within a language, just as Scottish is a dialect of English, with systematically ordered grammar and pronunciation usages.

A controversy regarding Ebonics or AAVE developed in Oakland, California, when the school board announced that it was going to recognize AAVE as a separate language. The school board was committed to teaching American Standard English to the African-American students. However, because of the prejudices and misunderstandings regarding AAVE as "a lazy form of English," the Oakland school board set off a controversy all over the United States. Linguistic anthropologist Ronald Kephart has commented on this Ebonics controversy based on his extensive research on the creoles in the Caribbean (Monaghan, Hinton, and Kephart 1997). Kephart studied creole English on the islands of Carriacou and Grenada. He did research on young students who were reading in the creole language as well as learning standard forms of English. The children who read in the creole language were able to learn the standard forms of English more readily, and they enjoyed the process. Kephart suggests that the recognition of AAVE by the school board in Oakland would help children learn American Standard English. These children would appreciate the fact that the language they brought with them into the school was to be respected as another form of English, and they would develop more positive attitudes about themselves and not be treated as "illiterate" or "lazy" children. This would help promote more effective learning strategies and enable these students to master American Standard English in a more humane manner.

The use of AAVE by some African-Americans also indicates what is referred to by linguistic anthropologists as "code-switching behavior." Some African-Americans use AAVE deliberately as a means of establishing rapport and solidarity with other African-Americans. They may switch to American Standard English in conversations with non-African-Americans, but move back to AAVE depending on the interactional context. This code switching has been documented by linguistic anthropologists in multiple studies (Bonvillian 2010).

Greeting Behaviors

The exchange of greetings is the most ordinary, everyday use of language and gesture found universally. Yet, sociolinguistic studies indicate that these routine greeting behaviors are considerably complex and produce different meanings in various social and cultural contexts. In many contexts, English speakers in the United States greet one another with the word *Hi* or *Hello*. (The word *hello* originated from the English phrase *healthy be thou*.) Members of U.S. society also greet one another with questions such as, "How are you?" or, "How's it going?" or, "What do you know?" or the somewhat popular, but fading, "Whassup?" In most contexts, these questions are not considered serious questions, and these exchanges of greetings are accompanied by a wave or a nod, a smile, or other gesture of recognition. They are familiar phrases that are used as exchanges in greetings. These greetings require little thought and seem almost mechanical.

Among Muslim populations around the world, the typical greeting between two males is the shaking of hands accompanied by the Arab utterance *As-salam ale-kum*, "May the peace of [Allah] be with you." This is the phrase used by Muslims even in non-Arabic-speaking societies. The Qur'an, the sacred religious text of Muslims, has an explicit requirement regarding this mode of greeting for the male Muslim community (Caton 1986). A similar greeting of *Scholem aleichem*, "May peace be with you," is found among the Jewish populace throughout the world. In some Southeast Asian societies such as Vietnam, the typical greeting translates into English as, "Have you eaten rice?"

All these greetings express a concern for another person's well-being. Although the English and Vietnamese greetings appear to be concerned with the physical condition of the person, whereas the Arab and Jewish phrases have a more spiritual connotation, they all essentially serve the same social purpose: They enable humans to interact in harmonious ways.

Yet, there is a great deal more social information contained in these brief greeting exchanges than appears on the surface. For example, an English-speaking person in the United States can usually identify the different types of social contexts for the following greeting exchanges:

1. "Hi, Mr. Thomas!"
   "Hello, Johnny. How are you?"
2. "Good morning, Monica."
   "Good morning, sir."
3. "Sarah! How are you? You look great!"
   "Bill! It's so good to see you!"
4. "Good evening, Congressman."
   "Hello there. Nice to see you."

In greeting 1, the speakers are a child and an adult; in 2, there is a difference in status, and the speakers may be an employer and employee; in 3, these speakers are close acquaintances; in 4, the second speaker does not remember or know the other person very well (Hickerson 1980).

One of the authors of this text did a systematic sociolinguistic study of greeting behaviors found among different ethnic and religious groups in Thailand (Scupin 1988). Precise cultural norms determine the forms of greetings given to people of different status levels and ethnic groups. The traditional greeting of Thai Buddhists on meeting one another is expressed by each raising both hands, palm to palm, and lightly touching the body between the face and chest. Simultaneously, the person utters a polite verbal phrase. This salutation, known as the *waaj* (pronounced "why"), varies in different social contexts. The person who is inferior in social status (determined by age and social class) initiates the *waaj*, and the higher the hands are raised, the greater the deference and politeness expressed. For example, a young child will *waaj* a superior by placing the fingertips above the eyebrows, whereas a superior returning a *waaj* will raise the fingertips only to the chest. A superior seldom performs a *waaj* when greeting someone of an inferior status. Other ethnic and religious groups such as the Muslims in Thailand use the *waaj* in formal interactions with Thai Buddhists, but among themselves, they use the traditional Muslim greeting described previously.

Another form of Thai greeting found among Buddhists includes the *kraab*, which involves kneeling down and bowing to the floor in conjunction with the *waaj* in expressing respect to a superior political or religious official. The *kraab* is used to greet a high-ranking member of the royal family, a Buddhist monk, a respected official, and, traditionally, one's parents Scupin 1988). These deferential forms of greeting are found in other societies that maintain social hierarchies based on royal authority or political or religious principles.

Although greeting behaviors differ from one society to another, anthropologists find that all peoples throughout the world have a means to greet one another to establish a basis for social interaction and demonstrate their concern for one another's welfare.

A Cambodian woman greeting Buddhist monks.

Arab males kissing one another in greeting

Nonverbal Communication

7.9 Discuss other forms of communication humans use besides language.

In interacting with other people, we use nonverbal cues, as well as speech. As with language, nonverbal communication varies in human populations in contrast to the nonverbal communication of nonhuman animals. Dogs, cats, and other animals have no difficulty communicating with one another in nonverbal ways. Human nonverbal communication, however, is extremely varied. It is often said that humans are the only creatures who can misunderstand one another.

Kinesics

Some anthropological linguists study gestures and other forms of body language. The study of **kinesics** is concerned with body motion and gestures used in nonverbal communication. Researchers estimate that humans use more than 250,000 facial expressions. Many of these expressions have different meanings in variouscircumstances. For example, the smile indicates pleasure, happiness, or friendliness in all parts of the world. Yet in certain contexts, a smile may signify an insult (Birdwhistle 1970). Thus, the movement of the head, eyes, eyebrows, and hands or the posture of the body may be associated with specific symbolic meanings that are culturally defined.

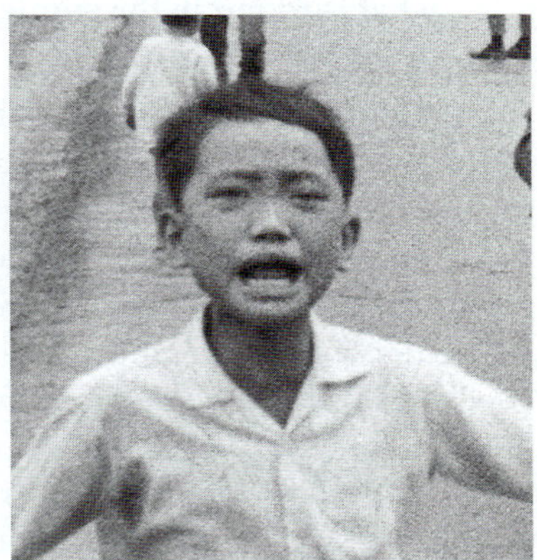

Many types of nonverbal communication differ from society to society. Americans point to things with their fingers, whereas other peoples point with only their eyes, their chins, or their heads. Shaking our heads up and down means "yes" and from side to side means "no," but in parts of India, Greece, and Turkey, the opposite is true. An "A–OK" sign in the United States or England means "you are all right," but it means "you are worth zero" in France or Belgium, and it is a very vulgar sign in Greece and Turkey (Ekman, Friesen, and Bear 1984). Pointing to your head means "he or she is smart" in the United States, whereas it means "stupid" in Europe. The "V" sign of the 1960s meant "peace"; in contrast, in World War II England, it meant "victory"; in Greece, it is an insult. Obviously, humans can easily misunderstand each other because of the specific cultural meanings of nonverbal gestures.

Despite all these differences, however, research has revealed certain universal features associated with some facial expressions. For example, research by psychologist Paul Ekman and his colleagues suggests that there are some basic uniformities regarding certain facial expressions. Peoples from various societies recognize facial expressions indicating emotional states such as happiness, grief, disgust, fear, surprise, and anger. Ekman studied peoples recently contacted by Western society, such as the Fore people of Papua New Guinea (Ekman 1973). When shown photos of facial expressions, the Fore had no difficulty determining the basic emotions that were being expressed. This research overlaps the psychological anthropology studies of emotions discussed in the previous chapter. Ekman has concluded that some universal emotional expressions are evident in certain facial displays of humans throughout the world.

Proxemics

Another nonverbal aspect of communication involves the use of space. **Proxemics** is the study of how people in different societies perceive and use space. Studies by Edward T. Hall (1981), the pioneering anthropologist in this area, indicate that no universal rules apply to the use of space. In American society, people maintain a different amount of "personal space" in different situations: We communicate with intimate acquaintances at a range of about 18 inches; however, with nonintimates, our space expands according to how well we know the person. In some other societies, people communicate at very close distances irrespective of the relationship among them.

Some human facial expressions are based on universally recognized emotions.

Nonverbal communication is an important aspect of social interaction. Obvious gestural movements, such as bowing in Japan and shaking hands in the United States, may have a deep symbolic significance in certain contexts. The study of nonverbal communication will enrich our understanding of human behavior and might even improve communication among different societies.

Summary and Review of Learning Objectives

7.1 Compare and contrast how the laboratory studies of nonhuman animal communication differs from what is found in the studies of nonhuman animals in the wild.

A number of researchers in laboratory studies were able to teach chimpanzees various signs through gesture use. In some cases these chimpanzees were able to combine these signs to communicate. A later study indicated that researchers may have been cuing chimpanzees to elicit particular signs or gestures. Sue Savage-Rumbaugh has tried to eliminate the methodological problem of giving ambiguous hand signs to train chimpanzees in her laboratory studies. She taught a 10-year-old *bonobo*, or "pygmy" chimpanzee named Kanzi to communicate with lexigrams, the graphic, geometric word-symbols that act as substitutes for human speech. By age six, Kanzi had mastered a vocabulary of ninety symbols. However, the chimpanzees or gorillas in laboratory settings do not progress beyond that of a human child of two and a half. In contrast to the laboratory studies, the field studies of chimpanzees and gorillas in their native habitats demonstrated that they used calls and gestures that were directly tied to their emotional states such as fear, annoyance, or sexual excitement.

7.2 Discuss what makes human languages unique in comparison with nonhuman animal communication.

Modern studies on animal communication suggest that the language gap separating humans from other animals is not as wide as it once appeared. These studies also indicate that fundamental differences exist between animal communication and human languages. The question is not whether animals can communicate; we know that almost every animal can. However, linguistic anthropologists have identified a number of distinctive characteristics of human languages that make it distinct from nonhuman animal communication. The four most important features are productivity, displacement, arbitrariness, and combining sounds. Productivity refers to how users of human languages, even small children, can create sentences never heard before by anyone. Displacement means that humans can discuss the past, present, future and many abstract phenomena. Arbitrariness refers to how the sounds of language and words rarely have a relationship or connection to the meaning of the objects or abstract notions they represent. And combining sounds is also a unique feature of human languages. Nonhuman animals are not able to combine sounds to create new meanings.

7.3 Describe what anthropologists conclude about the evolution of language.

Anthropologists have concluded that the earliest hominins did not have the language capacities of modern humans. However, new research indicates that the FOXP2 gene found in the DNA of both Neandertals and modern *Homo sapiens* that are associated with language and speech may have evolved as early as 300,000 years ago. Other aspects of language may have developed in relationship to gestural abilities of early hominins. Some linguists and primatologists believe that the emergence of human language suggests that at some point in the expansion of the brain, a rewiring of the human brain developed that allowed for what is known as *recursion*, the linguistic capacity to build an infinite number of sentences within sentences.

7.4 Discuss how linguistic anthropologists study language.

Linguistic anthropologists study the structure of language by examining sound patterns (phonology), the meaning of words (morphology), and how these meaningful units are put together in phrases and sentences (syntax). They also focus on the meaning (semantics) of different terms used to classify reality. Although there are many differences in how people in various societies use terms to describe kinship relations and physical phenomena, cognitive anthropologists have found some universals, such as the way people classify relatives. This suggests that humans have common biological capacities that determine how they perceive certain aspects of reality.

7.5 Explain how children acquire their languages.

Current research on language acquisition indicates that children are born with a brain *prewired* to enable humans to acquire language easily. This prewiring is associated with what Noam Chomsky calls a *universal grammar*.

Universal grammar serves as a template, or model, against which a child matches and sorts out the patterns of morphemes and phonemes and the subtle distinctions that are needed to communicate in any language. Thus, children are innately wired to be able to acquire any language that they are exposed to at an early age. The formation of creole languages found in many societies with multiple languages provides evidence for Chomsky's model of language acquisition.

7.6 Discuss the relationship between language and culture.

Early anthropologists such as Edward Sapir and Benjamin Whorf argued that the language that one acquires had a definitive influence on the perception of time, space, and other cultural phenomena. Current research indicates that the Sapir–Whorf hypothesis is limited in explaining how language determines culture; however, a weaker form of this hypothesis appears to be valid in demonstrating how language influences our perceptions and culture.

7.7 Describe how anthropologists study the history of languages.

Historical linguistics is the study of how languages are related to one another and how they have diverged from one another. Linguistic anthropologists have examined the historical relationships among languages by studying the phonology, words, syntax, and semantics through systematic methods such as glottochronology. This research has helped understand how languages change through time.

7.8 Describe what the field of sociolinguistics tells us about language use.

Sociolinguistics focuses on the relationship between language and society. It examines social interactions and the ways in which people use certain linguistic expressions that reflect the dialect patterns of their speech community. Researchers have found that many languages have nuances in linguistic usage such as greeting patterns or speech differences that vary according to age, gender, and status.

7.9 Discuss other forms of communication humans use besides language.

The study of nonverbal communication is also a rich field for linguistic anthropology. Although much nonverbal communication varies around the world, some forms can be understood universally. Anthropologists focus on the use of body language (kinesics) and the use of space (proxemics) to understand better how people supplement their spoken language skills with nonverbal communication.

Key Terms

communication, p. 177
dialects, p. 197
ethologists, p. 179
kinesics, p. 201
language, p. 177
morphemes, p. 185
morphology, p. 185
pragmatics, p. 197
phoneme, p. 181
phones, p. 184
phonology, p. 184
protolanguage, p. 195
proxemics, p. 201
Sapir–Whorf hypothesis, p. 193
semantics, p. 186
syntax, p. 185

Chapter 8
Anthropological Explanations

Chapter Outline

Learning Objectives

After you read this chapter you should be able to:

8.1 Explain the weaknesses of the nineteenth-century unilineal evolutionary approaches in anthropology.

8.2 Describe the basic strengths and weaknesses of the diffusionist approach in understanding different cultures.

8.3 Discuss historical particularism developed by Franz Boas.

8.4 Explain the differences between structural functionalism and psychological functionalism.

8.5 Discuss the twentieth-century neoevolutionary approaches, including cultural ecology and cultural materialism.

8.6 Describe the Marxist approach in anthropology that emerged in the 1970s.

8.7 Discuss the symbolic anthropology approach as a humanist method.

8.8 Discuss the approach of feminist anthropologists.

8.9 Discuss the strengths and weaknesses of the postmodern approach in anthropology.

In his conclusion to an excellent book titled *Culture, Self, and Meaning* (2000), anthropologist Victor de Munck writes about how anthropology needs to engage itself in an interdisciplinary effort to understand human behavior and culture. He refers to the ancient Hindu-Buddhist story regarding the blind men and the elephant. This story was popularized by the nineteenth-century poet John Godfrey Saxe in 1900 and begins:

It was six men of Indostan
To learning much inclined
Who went to see the Elephant
(Though all of them were blind),
That each by observation
Might satisfy his mind.
The First approached the Elephant,
And happening to fall
Against his broad and sturdy side,
At once began to bawl:
"God bless me! but the Elephant
Is very like a wall!"

In the poem, each of the blind men steps forward to examine the elephant. One feels the tusk and says the elephant is like a spear. Another grabs the trunk and likens the elephant to a snake. The poet concludes:

And so these men of Indostan
Disputed loud and long,
Each in his own opinion
Exceeding stiff and strong,
Though each was partly in the right
And all were in the wrong!

Thus, each of the blind men was mistaking his own limited understanding of the part of the elephant for the fuller reality of the whole. In this chapter on anthropological explanations, we need to keep this fable in mind. Anthropologists in every age have been attempting to understand humanity as a whole, but in reality, they had only partial understandings. Yet, each of these types of explanations has provided some limited perspectives on human behavior and culture. And, eventually, the knowledge accumulated from these partial perspectives has been probed and evaluated by anthropologists to offer a far more comprehensive picture of humanity in the twenty-first century than what we had in earlier centuries.

This photo of a Japanese woodblock print illustrates the story of the "Blind Men and the Elephant."

Another thing we need to keep in mind in this chapter is that anthropology consists of both the scientific and the humanistic orientations. In Chapter 1, we discussed the scientific method and its application to anthropology. In that discussion, we noted how anthropologists collect and classify data and then develop and test hypotheses. In the physical sciences, scientists use hypotheses to formulate theories from which they make predictions about natural phenomena. Chemists can rely on precise mathematical laws to help them deduce and predict what will happen when two chemical elements interact with one another. Physicists can predict from laws of gravity and motion what will happen when a spherical object is dropped from a building at a certain speed. These types of predictions allow engineers to produce aircraft that use certain fuels and withstand various physical pressures, enabling them to fly long distances.

Although anthropology relies on the scientific method, its major objective is to provide explanations of human society and behavior. Human behavior is extremely complicated. The product of many different, interacting variables, it can seldom, if ever, be predicted. Anthropologists cannot predict the outcome of interactions between two individuals or among small groups, let alone among large groups at the societal level. Consequently, anthropology as a discipline does not have any specific theories and laws that can be used to predict human action or thought. For the most part, anthropologists restrict their efforts to testing hypotheses and improving their explanations of human society and behavior.

We need to remember that anthropology also employs methods in the humanities to interpret human endeavors in religion, art, folklore, oral and written poetry, and other complex symbolic activities. This chapter will examine both the scientific and the humanistic attempts to comprehend the differences and similarities of human behavior and cultures.

Nineteenth-Century Evolutionism

8.1 Explain the weaknesses of the nineteenth-century unilineal evolutionary approaches in anthropology.

Although many philosophers and historians in Western society, including Aristotle and Herodotus in Greek society, and later Europeans such as John Locke, Immanuel Kant, and Johann Gottfried Herder, reflected on the concept of culture, it was nineteenth-century anthropologists who began to investigate the concept of "culture" as used today. Modern anthropology emerged from the intellectual atmosphere of the Enlightenment, an eighteenth- and nineteenth-century philosophical movement that stressed social progress based on human reason, and Darwin's theory of evolution based on naturalistic rather than supernatural explanations of humanity. The first professional anthropologist—that is, an individual appointed to an academic position in anthropology—was a nineteenth-century British scholar, Edward B. Tylor. In 1871, Tylor published a major work titled *Primitive Culture.* At that time, Great Britain was involved in imperialistic expansion all over the world. Tylor thus had access to descriptions of non-Western societies through his contacts with travelers, explorers, missionaries, traders, and government officials. He combined these descriptions with nineteenth-century philosophy and Charles Darwin's ideas to develop a theory of societal evolution.

Unilineal Evolution: Tylor

The major question addressed by early anthropologists was: Why are societies at similar or different levels of evolution and development? Many people ask the same kinds of questions today. Tylor tried to answer that question through an explanation known as unilineal evolution. **Unilineal evolution** is the view that societies evolve in a single direction toward complexity, progress, and civilization. Tylor's basic argument was that because all humans are bestowed with innate rational faculties, they are continuously improving their societies. Through this process of evolution, societies move toward "progress" and "civilization."

In arriving at this conclusion, Tylor used accounts from Western observers to compare certain cultural elements from different societies, including technology, family, economy, political organization, art, religion, and philosophy. He then organized this evidence into categories or stages, ranging from what he termed "savagery" to "barbarism" to "civilization" (see Figure 8.1). Theorists like Tylor assumed that hunter-gatherers and other non-Western societies were living at a lower level of existence than were the "civilized" societies of Europe. This was an ethnocentric view of societal development based on the belief that Western society is the center of the civilized world and that non-Western societies are inherently inferior.

Tylor and other nineteenth-century thinkers also claimed that "primitives" would eventually evolve through the stages of barbarism to become civilized like British gentlemen and ladies. However, Tylor believed that these societies would need some assistance from the civilized world to reach this stage.

Edward B. Tylor (1832–1917).

Figure 8.1 Edward Tylor's view of unilineal evolution.

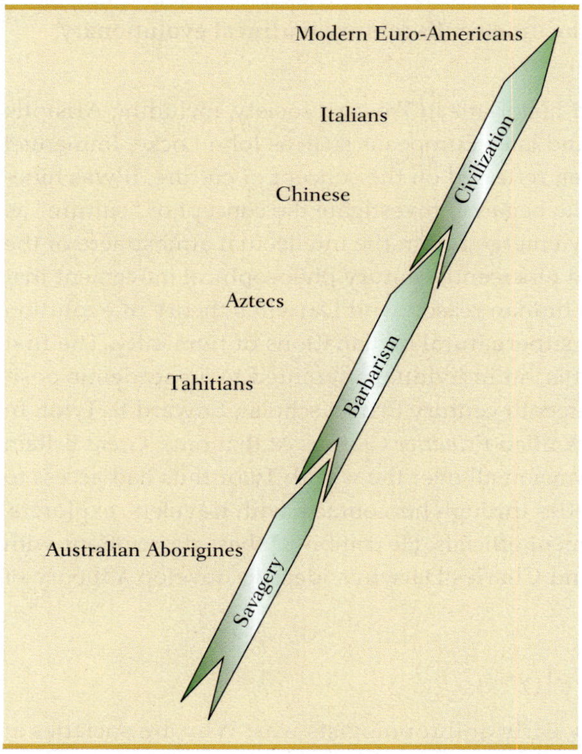

Unilineal Evolution: Morgan

Another nineteenth-century anthropologist who developed a unilineal scheme of evolution was an American, Lewis Henry Morgan (1818–1881). Morgan was a lawyer and banker who became fascinated with Native American Indian societies. He gathered information on the customs, language, and other cultural aspects of the Iroquois-speaking peoples of upstate New York. Eventually, under the auspices of the Smithsonian Institution, he distributed questionnaires to missionaries and travelers to collect information about many other non-Western societies.

Morgan and Kinship Theories Morgan was particularly interested in kinship terms used in different parts of the world. He observed that the Iroquois kinship terms were very different from those of English, Roman, Greek, and other European societies. He also noticed that these kinship terms were similar to those of the Ojibwa Indians, a group living in the midwestern United States. This led him to explore the relationship between the Iroquois and other peoples. Using the aforementioned questionnaires, he requested specific information on kinship terms from people all over the world.

From these data, Morgan began to conceive of the evolution of the family in a worldwide sense. He speculated that humans originally lived in "primitive hordes," in which sexual behavior was not regulated and individuals did not know who their fathers were. He based this assumption on the discovery that certain peoples, such as Hawaiians, use one general term to classify their father and all male relatives in their father's generation (see Chapter 7). He postulated that brother-sister marriage then developed, followed by group marriage, and eventually by a matriarchal family structure in which women held economic and political power. Morgan believed that the final stage of the evolution of the family began when males took control of the economy and politics, instituting a patriarchal system.

In addition to exploring the evolution of the family, Morgan, like Tylor, surveyed technological, economic, political, and religious conditions throughout the world. He compiled this evidence in his book *Ancient Society* ([1877] 1964), which presented his overall scheme of the evolution of society. Paralleling Tylor's views, Morgan believed in a hierarchy of evolutionary development from "savagery" to "civilization."

According to Morgan, one crucial distinction between civilized society and earlier societies is private property. He described the "savage" societies as "communistic," in contrast to "civilized" societies, whose institutions are based on private property.

Lewis Henry Morgan (1818–1881).

Unilineal Evolution: A Critique

Although these nineteenth-century thinkers shared the view that humanity was progressing through various stages of development, their views were ethnocentric, contradictory, and speculative, and their evidence secondhand, based on the accounts of biased Europeans. The unilineal scheme of evolution was much too simplistic to account for the development of different societies.

In general, the unilineal evolutionists relied on nineteenth-century racist views of human development and misunderstandings of biological evolution to explain societal differences. For example, both Morgan and Tylor believed that people in various societies have different levels of intelligence. They believed that the people in so-called "savage societies" were less intelligent than those in "civilized societies." As discussed in Chapter 5, this view of different levels of intelligence among different groups is no longer accepted by the scientific community or modern anthropologists. Nevertheless, despite their inadequate theories and speculations regarding the evolution of society, these early anthropologists provided the first systematic methods for thinking about and explaining the similarities and diversity of human societies. Like the blind men and the elephant, these anthropologists had only a limited perception and understanding of human behavior and culture.

Diffusionism

8.2 Describe the basic strengths and weaknesses of the diffusionist approach in understanding different cultures.

Another school of thought that used the comparative method to explain why different societies are at different levels of development is diffusionism. **Diffusionism**, which developed in the early part of the twentieth century, maintains that societal change occurs when societies *borrow* cultural traits from one another. Cultural knowledge regarding technology, economic ideas, religious views, or art forms spreads, or diffuses, from one society to another. There were two major schools of diffusionism: the British version associated with G. Elliot Smith and William J. Perry and the German version associated with Father Wilhelm Schmidt.

British Diffusionism

The British school of diffusionism derived its theory from research on ancient Egypt. Smith and Perry were specialists in Egyptian culture and had carried out research in Egyptology for a number of years. From this experience, they concluded that all aspects of civilizations, from technology to religion, originated in Egypt and diffused to other cultural areas. To explain the fact that some cultures no longer had cultural traits from Egypt, they resorted to an ethnocentric view, maintaining that some cultures had simply become "degenerate." That is, in contrast to the civilized world, the less-developed peoples had simply forgotten the original ideas borrowed from Egypt.

The Great Giza pyramid of Egypt. Some early anthropologists believed that all civilizations stemmed from ancient Egypt.

German Diffusionism

The German school of diffusionism differed somewhat from the British school. Schmidt and his followers argued that several early centers of civilization had existed and that from these early centers cultural traits diffused outward in circles to other regions and peoples. In German, this view is referred to as the *Kulturkreise* (culture circles) school of thought. In explaining why some primitive societies did not have the characteristics of civilization, the German school, like that of the British diffusionists, argued that these peoples had simply degenerated. Thus, diffusionist views, like the unilineal evolutionary views, represent ethnocentric perspectives of human societies outside the mainstream of Western civilization.

The Limitations and Strengths of Diffusionism

Early diffusionist views were based on erroneous assumptions regarding humankind's innovative capacities. Like the unilineal theorists, diffusionists maintained racist assumptions about the inherent inferiority of different non-Western peoples. They assumed that some people were not sufficiently innovative to develop their own cultural traits.

Another limitation of the diffusionist approach is its assumption that cultural traits in the same geographical vicinity will inevitably spread from one society to another. Anthropologists find that diffusion is not an inevitable process. Societies can adjoin one another without exchanging cultural traits. For example, some peoples have deliberately maintained their traditional ways despite being part of a nation in which modern technology is predominant.

However, diffusionism as a means of understanding societal development does have some validity. For instance, diffusionism helps explain the emergence of the classical civilizations of Egypt, Greece, Phoenicia, and Rome. These peoples maintained continuous contact through trade and travel, borrowing many cultural traits from one another, such as writing systems. Thus, these anthropologists, again like the blind men and the elephant, had some partial explanations to offer on human behavior and society.

Historical Particularism

8.3 Discuss historical particularism developed by Franz Boas.

An early twentieth-century movement that developed in response to the unilineal evolutionary theory was led by the U.S. anthropologist Franz Boas. This movement proposed an alternative answer to why societal similarities and differences exist. Boas was educated in Germany as a natural scientist. Eventually, he conducted fieldwork among the Eskimo (Inuit) in northern Canada and a Native American tribe known as the Kwakiutl or *Kwakwaka'wakw*, who lived on the northwest coast. He later solidified his position as the nation's foremost leader in anthropology at Columbia University in New York, where he trained many pioneers in the field until his retirement in 1937. Boas had a tremendous impact on the development of anthropology in the United States and internationally.

Boas versus the Unilineal Evolutionists

Boas became a vigorous opponent of the unilineal evolutionists. He criticized their attempts to propose stages of evolution through which all societies pass. He also criticized their use of the comparative method and the haphazard manner in which they organized the data to fit their theories of evolutionary stages. He maintained that these nineteenth-century schemes of evolution were based on insufficient empirical evidence. Boas called for an end to "armchair anthropology," in which scholars took data from travelers, traders, and missionaries and plugged them into a speculative model of evolution. He proposed that all anthropologists do rigorous, scientifically based fieldwork to collect basic ethnographic data.

Boas's fieldwork experience and his intellectual training in Germany led him to conclude that each society has its own unique historical development. This theory, known as **historical particularism**, maintains that each society must be understood as a product of its own history. This view led Boas to adopt the notion of cultural relativism, the belief that each society should be understood in terms of its own cultural practices and values (see Chapter 6). One aspect of this view is that no society evolved to a level higher or lower than that of another. Thus, we cannot rank any particular society above another in terms of degree of savagery, barbarity, or civility. Boas called for an end to the use of derogatory ethnocentric terms.

The Boasian view became the dominant theoretical trend in anthropology during the first half of the twentieth century. Anthropologists began to do rigorous ethnographic fieldwork in different societies to gather sound empirical evidence. Boas instituted the *participant observation method* as a basic research strategy of ethnographic fieldwork (see Chapter 9). This strategy enabled ethnographers to gather valid empirical data to explain human behavior. Boas also encouraged his students to develop their linguistic skills so that they could learn the languages of the peoples they studied.

Boas worked in all four subfields of anthropology: physical anthropology, archaeology, ethnology, and linguistics. Some of his most important work involved taking precise assessments of the physical characteristics, including brain size and cranial capacity, of people in different societies. Boas was one of the first scientists in the United States to demonstrate that the brain size and cranial capacity of modern humans are not linked directly to intelligence. Prior to his studies, many believed that different races had less intelligence than others based on brain size or cranial capacities. His research indicated that brain size and cranial capacity differ widely within all races. Boas's findings challenged the racist assumptions put forward by the unilineal evolutionists. They also repudiated the type of racism that characterized black-white relations in the United States, as well as Nazi theories of racial superiority.

Franz Boas (1858–1942).

A direct outgrowth of the Boasian approach was the emergence of *culture-and-personality theory* in American anthropology. For example, Ruth Benedict was a student of Boas whose research was described in Chapter 6. The anthropological school represented by Benedict led to the development of more careful research regarding personality and culture. The methods used in this field have been refined and tested by many anthropologists. As a result, we now have a better understanding of enculturation and personality formation in human societies. Boas's efforts set the stage for a sound scientific approach in anthropology that led to definite progress in our comprehension of race and other issues in explaining human behavior and culture.

Additionally, Boas pioneered the study of art, religion, folklore, music, dance, and oral literature, providing the humanistic aspect of the anthropological enterprise.

The contribution to anthropology of Boas and historical particularism was the recognition and importance of culture on the conscious and unconscious mind of individuals within specific regions of the world. Boas and his students emphasized the significance of cultural differences among peoples and criticized the earlier racialistic explanations for behavior and culture. The weakness of this historical particularism approach is that it tended to eschew any cross-cultural explanations for human behavior. Currently, most anthropologists agree that cross-cultural regularities, universals, and variations do exist.

Functionalism

8.4 Explain the differences between structural functionalism and psychological functionalism.

At approximately the same time that Boas and his U.S. students were questioning the claims of the unilineal evolutionists, British anthropologists were developing their own criticisms through the school of thought known as functionalism. **Functionalism** is the view that society consists of institutions that serve vital purposes for people. Instead of focusing on the origins and evolution of society, as the unilineal theorists did, the British functionalists explored the relationships among different institutions and how these institutions function to serve the society or the individual. The question of whether these institutions serve the interests of the society at large or the interests of the individual divided the school of functionalism into two camps, each associated with a prominent figure in British anthropology. These two figures were A. R. Radcliffe-Brown and Bronislaw Malinowski.

Structural Functionalism: Radcliffe-Brown

The type of functionalism associated with Radcliffe-Brown is sometimes referred to as *structural functionalism*. Radcliffe-Brown had done research in Africa and on the Andaman Islands in southeastern Asia. He focused on the social structure as reflected in the differing institutions that function to perpetuate the survival of *society*. He argued that a society's economic, social, political, and religious institutions serve to integrate the society as a whole. For example, he studied the social institutions that function to enhance group solidarity in small-scale societies. In some of his research, he emphasized how males had to marry outside their particular clan into another clan. Once the male marries, he establishes an important relationship with his wife's kin. Because he is an outsider, he has to show extreme respect to his new in-laws so that he does not produce hostility. The male may also establish a "joking relationship" with them, whereby hostility is reduced by playful teasing. Radcliffe-Brown suggested that all norms for specific behaviors and obligations among different people in kinship relationships promote order and stability. Thus, to Radcliffe-Brown, these social institutions serve society's needs.

Psychological Functionalism: Malinowski

Malinowski's functionalism differed from that of Radcliffe-Brown in that it focused on how society functions to serve the *individual's* interests or needs. This view is known as *psychological functionalism*. Malinowski did his major ethnographic study in the Trobriand Islands off the coast of Papua New Guinea. He tried to demonstrate how individuals use cultural norms to satisfy certain needs.

Malinowski's analysis of magic among the Trobriand Islanders illustrates his psychological functionalism. He observed that when the islanders went fishing in enclosed lagoons where fishing was reliable and safe, they depended on their technical

Bronislaw Malinowski among the Trobriands.

knowledge and skill alone. When they went fishing on the open sea, however, which was more dangerous and highly unpredictable, they employed extensive magical beliefs and techniques. Thus, Malinowski argued that the use of magic arises in situations in which humans have no control over circumstances, such as weather. Magical techniques are used to reduce internal anxieties and tensions for these individuals. In addition to magic, the Trobrianders have an elaborate system of beliefs concerning death, the afterlife, sickness, and health. These beliefs aid in serving the needs of individuals as they adapt to the circumstances and exigencies of life. In other words, the individual has needs, both physiological and psychological, and cultural institutions, customs, and traditions exist to satisfy them.

The Limitations of Functionalism

Like the other early developments in anthropology, functionalism has its theoretical weaknesses. It fails to explain why societies are different or similar. Why do some societies have different types of institutions, such as the extended family, when similar ones, such as the nuclear family, might be able to serve the same function? This weakness arose from the tendency of functionalists to ignore historical processes. They were not concerned with the historical development of differing institutions, but rather focused exclusively on how these institutions serve society and the individual. They could not explain, for example, why British society experienced rapid technological change, whereas other societies did not, when all of these societies had similar needs.

Functionalists were also unable to explain social and cultural change very well because they tended to view societies as static and unchanging. They could not explain why, if all institutions perform a particular function, these institutions would need to change.

Functionalism as a school of thought has influenced a great deal of research in anthropology. By focusing on the detailed, specific functions of institutions within existing societies, it encouraged the collection of valuable ethnographic data. As with Boas in U.S. anthropology, Radcliffe-Brown and Malinowski moved their field beyond the speculative theories of the "armchair anthropologists."

Twentieth-Century Evolutionism

8.5 Discuss the twentieth-century neoevolutionary approaches, including cultural ecology and cultural materialism.

After World War II, some anthropologists renewed their interest in evolutionary explanations of societal and cultural phenomena. Up until that time, most anthropologists had devoted themselves to criticizing the unilineal evolutionists. But some anthropologists, led by Leslie White of the University of Michigan, suggested a new twentieth-century perspective on the evolution of society, which is sometimes referred to as *neoevolutionism*.

White treated societies, or *sociocultural systems*, as entities that evolved in relation to the amount of energy captured and used by each member of society. This energy is directed toward the production of resources for their survival. In White's words, "Culture evolves as the amount of energy harnessed per capita per year is increased, or as the efficiency of the instrumental means of putting the energy to work is increased" ([1949] 1971: 368). In other words, the degree of societal development is measured by the amount of energy harnessed by these sociocultural systems. The greater energy resources available, the more highly evolved the sociocultural system.

White's hypothesis of cultural evolution explained the differences in levels of societal development by examining differences in technology and energy production. For example, he hypothesized that small-scale hunting-and-gathering societies had not developed complex sociocultural systems because they depended primarily on human energy for production. Because of a limited energy source for producing resources, their societies were simple, meager, and undeveloped. But following the agricultural revolution and the capture of energy through the domestication of plants and animals, sociocultural systems changed dramatically. The agricultural revolution represented an efficient use of human energy in harnessing new energy reserves, such as using draft animals to pull plows. In turn, these technological changes led to the emergence of cities, complex states, powerful political and religious elites, and new ideologies.

According to White, tracing the modern industrial age, as fossil-fuel technology developed, new forms of energy such as coal, oil, and natural gas were used, and sociocultural changes accelerated. Up until the Industrial Revolution, the changes in agricultural societies had been gradual, taking several thousand years. In contrast, the Industrial Revolution has taken less than 500 years to produce widespread global transformations. Because White focused on sociocultural change on the global level, rather than in particular societies, his approach has been called *general evolution*.

Steward and Cultural Ecology

At about the same period of time, anthropologist Julian Steward turned his attention to the evolution of society. Steward was instrumental in establishing the field of cultural ecology. Also called *ecological anthropology*, **cultural ecology** stresses the interrelationship among the natural conditions in the environment—rainfall, temperature, soils—and technology, social organization, and attitudes within a particular sociocultural system. Steward focused on how specific sociocultural systems adapt to environmental conditions.

Steward's cultural-ecology framework divides sociocultural systems into two different spheres: the culture core and secondary features. The *culture core* consists of those elements most closely related to subsistence: the environment, technology, and economic arrangements. The other characteristics, such as social organization, politics, and religion, constitute *secondary features* of society. Because Steward investigated the detailed characteristics of different environments, his approach is referred to as *specific evolution*, as opposed to White's general evolution. Steward emphasized that cultural evolution was not unilineal, but *multilineal*. **Multilineal evolution** is the view that societies and cultures have evolved and are evolving in many different directions. One of his most illustrative case studies involved the Shoshone Indians of the Great Basin of the western United States.

A Case Study: The Shoshone The Shoshone were hunter-gatherer groups whose society revolved around gathering seeds, pine nuts, roots and berries, and hunting rabbits and antelope. Steward discovered that these subsistence activities had definite effects on the organization of Shoshone kinship groups. Like all hunter-gatherer societies, the Shoshone were nomadic, moving from one location to another based on the availability of food. The Shoshone lived in a hot, dry desert environment that supported meager supplies of plants and animals. These people were forced to live in small, elementary family units and travel frequently in search of food. For a few months in the winter, however, they could live in larger social groups among interrelated family units because of the supply of pine nuts in the mountains. Thus, the environment and the availability of resources had a definite influence on the form of social organization during different seasons for these hunter-gatherer societies.

Through cases like this, Steward demonstrated how environmental influences (part of the culture core) affect the cultural developments in a sociocultural system. Steward used this approach to examine the agricultural civilizations of South America, Mesoamerica, the Near East, and the Far East. He found remarkable parallels in the evolution of these different civilizations. They all had irrigation systems, specialized occupations, centralized governments, and formalized state religions. Steward emphasized that many of these parallels were the result of similar environmental conditions, such as river valleys and alluvial plains that offered opportunities for the emergence of agricultural civilizations.

The Strengths of Neoevolutionism

The twentieth-century evolutionists differed from the nineteenth-century evolutionists in several ways. First, they did not assume a unilineal direction of society through formalized stages such as savagery, barbarism, and civilization. In later chapters, we will demonstrate how different forms of societies developed in relationship to variant geographical, prehistoric, and historical circumstances, a contribution that the neoevolutionists made to our current understanding of societal development. Second, they were not ethnocentrically biased or racist when it came to understanding why different societies are at various levels of development. They abandoned crude terms such as "savagery" and explored environment, technology, and energy resources in assessing levels of sociocultural development. Third, they did not assume that sociocultural evolution toward complexity (or "civilization") is always equated with "progress," as did the nineteenth-century theorists. The neoevolutionists held that some aspects of small-scale societies are, in fact, better than those of complex societies. For example, in some respects, family and social relationships tend to be more stable in small-scale societies than in large, complex societies.

Cultural ecology has become an extremely sophisticated area of research. It has been influenced by developments in biological ecology and theories derived from mathematics, computer modeling, and related sciences. Cultural ecologists do careful research on energy expenditures, use of resources, exchanges of nutrients, and population, as well as on the interrelations among these factors and with cultural values. As we shall see in later chapters, the research findings of ecological anthropology help to explain some basic sociocultural similarities and differences.

Criticisms of Cultural Ecology

A number of anthropologists have criticized the cultural ecology approach for a variety of reasons. Early critics claimed that in emphasizing the role of the environment, cultural ecologists do not take into account historical or political factors (Geertz 1963a; Friedman 1974; Hefner 1983). Thus, for example, cultural ecologists can explain how Shoshone culture represents an adaptation to a desert environment, but they cannot explain how or why the Shoshone came to reside in an environment with scarce resources. An explanation of this kind would require detailed historical research, examining local and global political factors.

Another criticism is that cultural ecology reduces human behavior to simple adaptations to the external environment. Because of the emphasis on adaptation, cultural ecologists tend to view every cultural element as the best of all possible solutions to the problems of subsistence and energy requirements. In fact, many sociocultural adaptations may involve compromises at the time that turn out later to be maladaptations.

For example, a number of early cultural ecologists have used their models to explain the development of warfare in different societies. Some hypothesize that warfare is associated with land ownership, population size, and resource shortages (Vayda 1961; Sweet 1965; Meggitt 1977). As populations expand in areas with scarce resources, societies resort to warfare to secure additional resources and thereby restore stability to the sociocultural system. Critics suggest that this explanation ignores various historical, political, and cultural factors that contribute to warfare, such as conflicting political or religious ideologies. Furthermore, they suggest that this is an extreme form of adaptationism. In most cases, warfare is definitely maladaptive.

Cultural Materialism

The late anthropologist Marvin Harris refined the neoevolutionary approach of White and Steward as a perspective he called cultural materialism. **Cultural materialism** is a research strategy that focuses on technology, environment, and economic factors as key determinants in sociocultural evolution. Cultural materialists divide all sociocultural systems into infrastructure, structure, and superstructure. The *infrastructure* includes the technology and practices used for expanding or limiting the production of basic resources such as food, clothing, and shelter. The *structure* consists of the domestic economy (family structure, domestic division of labor, age and gender roles) and the political economy (political organization, class, castes, police, and military). The *superstructure* includes philosophy, art, music, religion, ideas, literature, advertising, sports, games, science, and values (see Figure 8.2).

According to cultural materialist theory, the infrastructure largely determines the structure and superstructure of sociocultural systems. As the infrastructure changes, the structure and superstructure may change accordingly. Technology, energy, and environmental factors are crucial to the development of all aspects of society. All societies must devise ways to obtain food and shelter, and they must possess an adequate technology and energy to provide for the survival and continuity of the population. Although cultural materialists do not deny that superstructural and structural components of society may influence cultural evolution, they see infrastructural factors as being far more important. This theoretical perspective represents an extension of the foundations laid down by White and Steward.

Criticisms of Cultural Materialism

A variety of criticisms have been directed at Marvin Harris's theoretical paradigm of cultural materialism. One of the major criticisms is the same one directed at cultural ecology; that is, Harris focuses too exclusively on environmental factors and ignores social, political, and religious values and beliefs. In addition, cultural materialism tends to emphasize the infrastructural mechanisms that strictly "determine" the structure and superstructure of the society. This results in a form of technological determinism that is much too mechanistic in analyzing the social and cultural conditions within a society. As critics of technological determinists note, the level of technological development does not tell us anything about the complexity of religion, kinship, family and marriage systems, art, folklore, and so on. Finally, Harris's paradigm underplays the importance of symbolism and language and the influence these factors have upon people's beliefs and motivations.

Figure 8.2 The model for cultural materialism

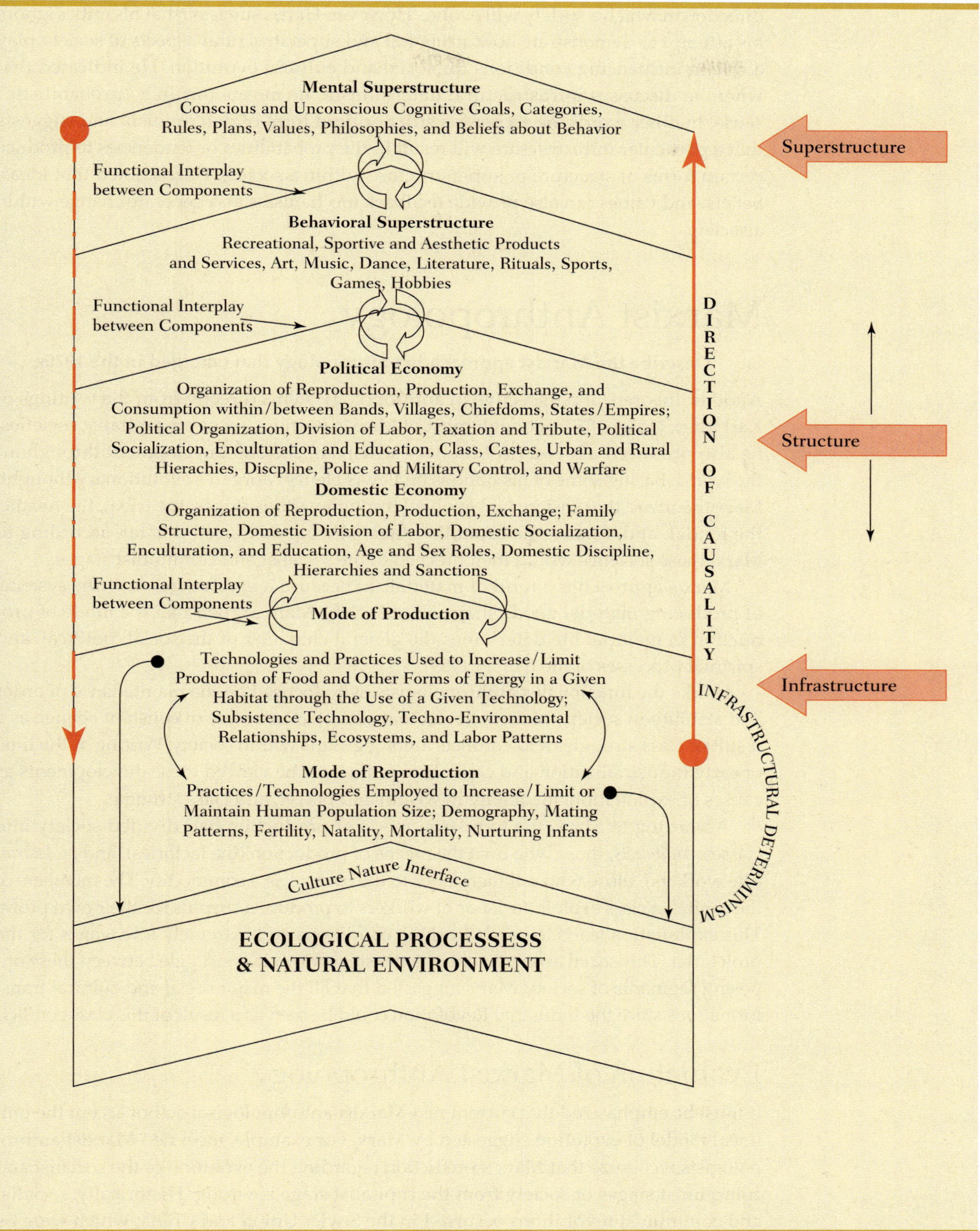

Harris replied to all of these criticisms in a number of texts (1979, 1988, 1999). He admitted that he does emphasize infrastructure as the major determinant of the direction in which a society will evolve. However, Harris suggests that his critics ignore his attempt to demonstrate how structural and superstructural aspects of society play a role in influencing conditions for social and cultural evolution. He indicated that when he discusses infrastructural determinism, he means this in a "probabilistic" sense. In other words, he eschews a strict or rigid form of determinism and suggests that a particular infrastructure will result in the probabilities or tendencies to produce certain forms of structure or superstructure within a society. Harris noted that ideas, beliefs, and values can also provide feedback mechanisms and generate change within a society.

Marxist Anthropology

8.6 Describe the Marxist approach in anthropology that emerged in the 1970s.

Another theoretical perspective in anthropology stems directly from the writings of Karl Marx (1818–1883). Though most of Marx's writings focus on capitalist societies, he also produced a broad evolutionary scheme of societal development throughout the world. Basing some of his notions on Lewis Henry Morgan's evolutionary thought, Marx theorized that society had evolved through various stages: the tribal, the Asiatic, the feudal, and, finally, the capitalist stage. Having advanced this far, according to Marx, these societies would then proceed to the socialist and communist stages.

Marx's approach is a form of materialism because it emphasizes how the systems of producing material goods shape all of society. Marx argued that the mode of production in material life determines the general character of the social, political, and spiritual processes of life ([1859] 1959).

Unlike the functionalist anthropologists, who focused on the maintenance of order and stability in society, Marx believed that society is in a state of constant change as a result of class struggles and conflicts among groups within society. Writing at the time of early industrialization and capitalism in Europe, he viewed these developments as causes of exploitation, inequality in wealth and power, and class struggle.

According to Marx, the industrial mode of production had divided society into classes: *capitalists*, those who own the means of production (the factories), and *proletariat* (the workers), those who sell their labor to the owners as a commodity. The members of the capitalist class exploit the labor of workers to produce a surplus for their own profit. This exploitation leads to harsh working conditions and extremely low wages for the proletariat. This social arrangement sets the stage for a class struggle between these opposing segments of society. Marx suggested that all the major social and cultural transformations since the Industrial Revolution could be seen as a result of this class conflict.

Evaluation of Marxist Anthropology

It must be emphasized that current neo-Marxist anthropologists do not accept the unilineal model of evolution suggested by Marx. For example, most neo-Marxist anthropologists recognize that Marx's prediction regarding the evolution of the socialist and communist stages of society from the capitalist stage is wrong. Historically, socialist and communist revolutions occurred in the Soviet Union and China, which were by no means industrial-capitalist societies. The industrial societies that Marx had focused on, such as Great Britain and Germany, did not develop into what Marx conceived of as socialist or communist societies.

Nevertheless, modern neo-Marxist anthropologists view as valid Marx's analytical approach to understanding societal development and some of the inherent problems of capitalist society. His critical perspective on the institutions of society, the modes of production, and the results of group conflict has inspired many fruitful hypotheses regarding social and cultural evolution and development. Unlike the functionalists, who assumed that society's institutions were balancing conflicting interests, the Marxist anthropologists have demonstrated that conflict is an inherent aspect of human behavior and culture.

An Indian farmer working in his fields. Marx believed that societies evolved through stages such as the Asiatic, in which land was cultivated by peasant farmers.

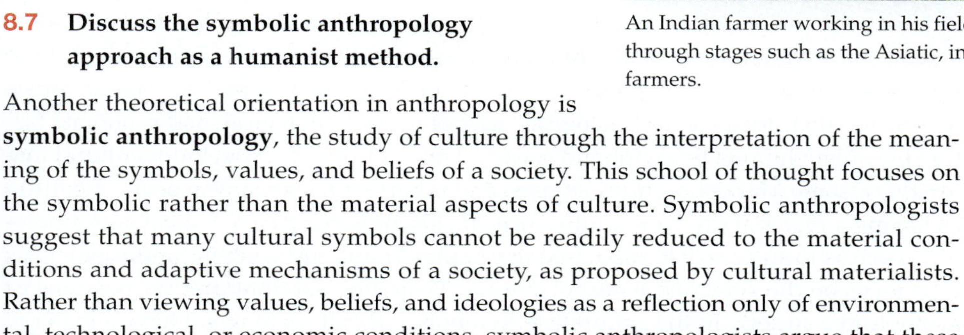

Symbolic Anthropology: A Humanistic Method of Inquiry

8.7 Discuss the symbolic anthropology approach as a humanist method.

Another theoretical orientation in anthropology is **symbolic anthropology**, the study of culture through the interpretation of the meaning of the symbols, values, and beliefs of a society. This school of thought focuses on the symbolic rather than the material aspects of culture. Symbolic anthropologists suggest that many cultural symbols cannot be readily reduced to the material conditions and adaptive mechanisms of a society, as proposed by cultural materialists. Rather than viewing values, beliefs, and ideologies as a reflection only of environmental, technological, or economic conditions, symbolic anthropologists argue that these cultural symbols may be completely autonomous from material factors.

From this standpoint, symbolic anthropologists reject the use of the scientific method as applied to human behavior. The goal of their research is instead to interpret the meaning of symbols within the worldviews of a particular society. For example, in Chapter 6 we discussed Mary Douglas's interpretation of the prohibition of different foods, including pork, among the ancient Israelites. She focused on the symbolic classification of various foods as being "clean" or "pure" and "unclean" or "polluted." The symbolic anthropologist tries to discern how such symbols help people produce meaning for themselves and their communities. A particular hairstyle or the classification of different foods may become a symbolic metaphor, communicating a message.

The methodology of symbolic anthropology focuses on the collection of data—especially data reflecting the point of view of the members of the society studied—on kinship, economy, ritual, myth, and values. Symbolic anthropologists describe this type of data collection as producing a *thick description*, the attempt to interpret the relationships among different symbols within a society. To do this, symbolic anthropologists must interpret the meanings of the symbolic beliefs and metaphors from the point of view of the people in a specific society. The aim of symbolic anthropologists is to show how other peoples' values, beliefs, and ideologies are meaningful and intelligible.

Criticisms of Symbolic Anthropology

A number of criticisms have been directed at symbolic anthropology. One major charge is that symbolic anthropologists focus exclusively upon cultural symbols at the expense of other variables that may influence human thought and behavior. Symbolic anthropologists may, therefore, neglect the conditions and processes that lead to the making of culture (Roseberry 1982; Fox 1985). For example, economic wealth and political power may be important factors in the development of cultural values and norms. Dominant groups may be responsible for the emergence of cultural hegemony in a society. Critics emphasize that culture cannot be treated as an autonomous phenomenon separate from historical, political, and economic processes and conditions that affect a society.

Another criticism is that symbolic anthropology substitutes one form of determinism for another. Instead of emphasizing technological or economic variables, symbolic anthropologists stress the meaning of cultural symbols. Despite their rejection of scientific causal explanations, they have been accused of reducing explanations of society and human activity to the "meanings" of cultural beliefs and symbols. Despite these criticisms, most anthropologists agree that symbolic anthropologists have contributed to our understanding of how humans have developed their symbolic cultures.

Materialism versus Culturalism

One major division in anthropology is between those anthropologists who prefer materialist explanations of society and those who prefer culturalist explanations. To some extent, this division reflects the differences between the scientific approach and the humanistic-interpretive perspective in anthropology (see Chapter 1). The scientists and materialists focus on technological, environmental, biological, and economic factors to explain human behavior and society. This group—which includes cultural materialists, some Marxist anthropologists, and others—views many aspects of culture as having a material purpose. Culturalists, including some psychological anthropologists such as Ruth Benedict (discussed in Chapter 6), and the symbolic anthropologists who focus on the symbolic aspect of culture. Their aim is to interpret the meaning of symbols in a society. To the culturalists, symbols and culture may not have a material purpose at all, but rather establish meaningfulness for the people in a society.

Anthropologist Richard Barrett (1984) notes that the difference between the materialist and culturalist approaches is related to the nature of society and human existence itself. As Barrett emphasizes, every society must confront the problem of adjusting to the practical circumstances of life. People need food, shelter, clothing, and the necessary technology and energy for survival. This is the material component of culture; it is related to survival. But there is also the nonmaterial aspect of culture: norms, values, beliefs, ideologies, and symbols. These cultural norms and symbols have emotional significance. Symbols may not be related at all to the practical circumstances of life; instead, they may indicate some aesthetic or moral values that are not related to the material conditions of society.

Thus, the distinction between the material and nonmaterial aspects of culture has led to different approaches to the analysis of human behavior and society. In later chapters, we learn how anthropologists have employed these approaches in explaining and interpreting human affairs.

Feminist Anthropology

8.8 Discuss the approach of feminist anthropologists.

One of the most important developments in anthropological theory was the emergence of a feminist orientation. After the beginning of the twentieth century, a number of female pioneers such as Ruth Benedict, Margaret Mead, Elsie Crews Parsons, Eleanor Leacock, and Phyllis Kaberry began to have a definite impact on the field of anthropology.

With the development of the feminist movement in U.S. society in the 1960s and 1970s, many female anthropologists initiated a *feminist perspective*. This feminist perspective challenged the tendency to concentrate on the male role and underestimate the position of women within different societies. Before the 1970s, most anthropologists were male, and for the most part, women were neglected in ethnographic research. And in some societies like the Middle East Islamic societies, it is very difficult for male anthropologists to interview women. As more women became involved in anthropology, they questioned the traditional emphasis on the male position and the invisibility of women in ethnographies. These feminist anthropologists emphasized that gender roles had to be taken into account in ethnographic research (Mascia-Lees and Black 2000). They also challenged essentialist or stereotypical portrayals of women. These feminist anthropologists have produced enormous insights regarding the role of women in societies throughout the world.

Feminist anthropologists directed their criticisms at a variety of targets that had become prevalent in the discipline. For example, they questioned the underlying assumptions made by sociobiologists regarding male and female behavioral tendencies. The feminist anthropologists argued that the view of men as sexually promiscuous and females as sexually conservative and desiring monogamy as a reproductive strategy was an overgeneralization and essentialist stereotype. They critiqued the view that males and females were radically different based on biological traits such as hormonal differences. In addition, they directed their criticisms at the physical anthropologists, who argued that females had become dependent on males for food and other resources, whereas males were developing tools and other strategies for hunting purposes. They suggested that the female role in human evolution had been overlooked. And feminist anthropologists criticized ethnographic descriptions that presented the male as the more active, aggressive agent within the family and the female as passive and inactive in terms of her behavior. These types of descriptions appeared in the ethnographies of the functionalists during the 1930s and 1940s (Mascia-Lees and Black 2000). Thus, feminist anthropologists provided new insightful hypotheses and created a more general awareness of gender and women's issues within the discipline.

One of the leading feminist anthropologists is Sherry Ortner, who wrote an important essay in 1974, "Is Female to Male as Nature Is to Culture?" In this essay, Ortner tackled the view regarding what appeared to be the universal subordination of women throughout the world. She tried to answer the question of why women were perceived and treated as inferior, second-class citizens in the vast majority of societies. In her analysis, Ortner drew on the structuralist approach in anthropology. Claude Lévi-Strauss, the pioneer of the structuralist approach in anthropology, had argued that the fundamental structural binary oppositions of the human mind were "nature" and "culture" (1966, 1969). Within this structuralist format, Ortner argued that since women gave birth to and cared for children, they were perceived as being "closer" to nature. In contrast, men were involved in political affairs and other more symbolic activities and were perceived to be "closer" to the "creative aspect" of culture and, therefore, cognitively "superior." According to Ortner, this nature/culture opposition of males and females had structural consequences for the social position of men and women within all societies. Women were regarded as inferior beings and were subjugated in societies worldwide.

This essay was a landmark piece in early feminist anthropology. More recently, Ortner returned to this early essay, which had received a lot of critical attention from other women in anthropology. On the basis of this critical attention, she reexamined her original essay in "So, Is Female to Male as Nature Is to Culture?" in a chapter in her book *Making Gender: The Politics and Erotics of Culture* (1996). In this chapter, she grants that in some societies the appearance of male superiority and female inferiority is fragmentary and very difficult to determine. She also concurs with her critics that the structuralist explanation regarding the distinction between nature and culture that resulted in the universal subordination of women was not very useful. However, she does think that this nature/culture distinction is something that all of humanity faces. But in different societies and historical conditions, men and women may articulate and respond to these distinctions in enormously variant ways. In general, Ortner suggests that the universal or near-universal male dominance and subordination of women is caused by a complex interaction of functional arrangements in society, power dynamics, and also biological differences between males and females. Ortner has offered some insightful hypotheses for further research on gender and women's issues in anthropology.

Criticisms of Feminist Anthropology

Although feminist anthropology has contributed substantially to the discipline in providing a critical awareness for male anthropologists, some anthropologists argue that this perspective has become too extreme and exaggerated. For example, some feminist anthropologists have put forth the view that biological factors have absolutely nothing to do with male and female differences (Collier and Yanagisako 1987). An enormous amount of data from various scientifically evaluated fields has demonstrated that both nature and nurture are important in shaping gender and male and female differences. Thus, the view that nature does not have anything to do with gender seems to be too extreme (Stone 2010).

In addition, some feminist anthropologists have argued that all of the scientific hypotheses and most of science are based on a Western cultural framework and an *androcentric* (male-centered) perspective. Consequently, male anthropologists cannot do research on women in other societies because of their androcentric biases; only women can conduct research on women and gender issues. These views also appear to be extreme. At present, most male anthropologists have been attuned to the feminist critique of anthropology and have adjusted to a more sensitive understanding of gender and women's issues. Many male anthropologists today consider themselves to be feminist anthropologists.

Also, as we have emphasized in this book, scientifically based hypotheses are tested by many individuals in both Western and non-Western societies, and as more women come into the field of anthropology, they will become actively involved in this type of testing. Thus, science and scientific hypotheses are not just products of a Western cultural framework and an androcentric perspective. The scientific method used correctly and precisely will weed out any erroneous biases or data and will result in a more comprehensive and refined understanding of the social and cultural worlds.

Postmodernism and Anthropology

8.9 Discuss the strengths and weaknesses of the postmodern approach in anthropology.

Although ethnographic fieldwork has long been a fundamental aspect of anthropology, one current school, **postmodernism**, is challenging basic ethnographic assumptions and methodologies. This group, known as postmodernist anthropologists, includes such figures as James Clifford, George Marcus, and Michael Fischer. The postmodernists suggest that traditional ethnographic research is based on a number of unsound assumptions. One such assumption is that the ethnographer is a detached, scientifically objective observer who is not influenced by the premises and biases of her or his own society. Clifford characterizes one of the models maintained by ethnographers such as Malinowski as that of the "scientific participant-observer" (1983). In his ethnographies, Malinowski eliminated any reference to himself and recorded data that were then written as the documentation of an "objective scientist." Malinowski produced his descriptions as if he did not have any involvement with the Trobriand people. It was as if he were some sort of computing machine without feelings, biases, or emotions, who was simply recording everything about native life.

According to postmodernist critics, ethnographies such as those compiled by Malinowski were intended as a type of scientific study in which the subjects behaved and the ethnographer simply recorded this behavior. From this standpoint, the postmodernists complain that the ethnographers assume they have a thoroughly scientific and objective view of reality, whereas the native view is highly subjective, based on traditional beliefs and cosmologies.

Postmodernists and Contemporary Research

One of the basic reasons for the postmodernist critiques is that the situation for ethnographic studies has changed substantially. Until recently, most subjects of ethnographic studies were illiterate peoples adjusting to the impact of the West. But as more people throughout the world become educated and familiar with the field of anthropology, Western ethnographers could no longer claim to be the sole authorities regarding anthropological knowledge. Many people in Latin America, Africa, the Middle East, and Asia can, and do, speak and write about their own cultures (some have become anthropologists themselves), and they are disseminating knowledge about their own societies. The world is no longer dependent on Western anthropologists to gather ethnographic data. Indigenous people are beginning to represent themselves and their societies to the world.

Postmodernists have recommended that ethnographers today adopt a different way of researching and writing. Instead of trying to distance themselves from their subjects, ethnographers should present themselves in dialogue with their subjects. Clifford (1983) argues that an ethnography should consist of many voices from the native population, rather than just those of the ethnographer and a few of his or her informants.

Reaction to this postmodernist critique has varied within the discipline. On the one hand, some ethnographers have charged the postmodernists with characterizing traditional ethnographic methodologies unjustly. Many ethnographers, they contend, were engaged in a form of dialogue with their informants and other members of the societies being studied. On the other hand, the postmodernist debate has stirred many anthropologists to rethink their roles. Currently, more ethnographers are writing about their actual interactions and relationships with the people they study. Ethnographers must take account of their own political position within the society under investigation. This type of data and personal reflection is no longer pushed into the background, but instead is presented as a vital ingredient of the ethnography. In the 1980s, a number of ethnographies appeared that reflected the postmodernist emphasis on interaction between ethnographers and their subjects. Some of these new ethnographies are based on the life histories of people within the studied population.

Following two periods of fieldwork among the !Kung San or Ju/'hoansi San, hunters and gatherers of the Kalahari Desert in southwestern Africa, the late Marjorie Shostak completed a life history, *Nisa: The Life and Words of A !Kung Woman* (1981). Shostak interviewed numerous !Kung women to gain a sense of their lives. She focused on the life history of Nisa, who discussed her family, sex life, marriage, pregnancies, experiences with !Kung men, and reaction to growing older. Shostak cautioned that Nisa does not represent a "typical" !Kung or Ju/'hoansi San female because her life experiences are unique (as are the experiences of all individuals in any society). In addition, Shostak exercised extreme care in discussing with Nisa the material that would go into the book to ensure a faithful representation of Nisa's life.

If we look back over years of ethnographic research, we find many accounts in which anthropologists were scrupulous in their representation of people in other societies. To this extent, the postmodernist critics have exaggerated the past mistakes of ethnographers. However, the postmodernists have alerted ethnographers to some unexamined assumptions concerning their work. Today, most anthropologists do not claim a completely "objective" viewpoint. Anthropologists generally want to maintain empathy with the people they study, yet they usually attempt some critical detachment as well. Otherwise, they could easily become merely the spokespersons for specific political interests and leaders in a community (Errington and Gewertz, 1987).

Collaborative fieldwork, with teams of ethnographers and informants working together to understand a society, is most likely the future direction for ethnographic study. The image of a solitary ethnographer such as Malinowski isolated on a Pacific island is outmoded (Salzman 1989). Collaborative research will lead to more systematic data collection and will offer opportunities to examine hypotheses of both ethnographers and subjects from a variety of perspectives.

Shifts in Anthropological Explanations

We began this chapter with the Hindu legend of the blind men and the elephant. The moral of that story was that we all have partial understandings of the world. As we have sketched a number of different anthropological explanations and critiques in this chapter, it is obvious that no one explanation provides a full understanding of human behavior and culture. In a recent essay assessing anthropological theory, British anthropologist Roy F. Ellen proposes that explanation and interpretation must be what he terms "conjunctural" (2010). In other words, anthropological explanations provide a framework within which to pose both general and comparative questions about human diversity and origins, whether biological, social, cultural, or (indeed) biocultural or biosocial. In other words, anthropological explanations and interpretations must be carefully structured into different levels, incorporating biological and ecological factors, individual decision making, and the historical, social and cultural factors that influence individuals. Ellen views anthropological theories as a pyramid with nested levels of explanations with the most general types of questions at the top and more local-level cultural interpretations at the bottom. This theoretical framework enables anthropologists to produce more synthetic and holistic explanations of human behavior in the past and present. After more than a century of anthropological research, we do have an improved and more comprehensive understanding of culture, society, and the role of individual behavior than we did in the nineteenth century. Through constant critical evaluation, hypothesis testing, and refinement of explanations and interpretations by anthropologists, we ought to know even more about these phenomena in the future.

Summary and Review of Learning Objectives

8.1 Explain the weaknesses of the nineteenth-century unilineal evolutionary approaches in anthropology.

The first professional anthropologists, notably E. B. Tylor and Lewis Henry Morgan, proposed a theory known as unilineal evolution to explain the differences and similarities in societal evolution. The unilineal evolutionists maintained that societies evolve in one direction from a stage of savagery to one of civilization. These unilineal views of evolution were based on ethnocentric and racist views of the nineteenth century.

8.2 Describe the basic strengths and weaknesses of the diffusionist approach in understanding different cultures.

In the early twentieth century, a theory of diffusionism was invoked as the best explanation of the differences and similarities among societies. The British diffusionists argued that all civilization emanated from Egypt, whereas the German diffusionists maintained that there were several original centers of civilization. Modern anthropologists have criticized these diffusionist approaches based on archaeological and cross-cultural research of many different societies. However, one strength of the diffusionist approach does remain, as it is well known that societies borrow ideas and technologies from one another.

8.3 Discuss historical particularism developed by Franz Boas.

Another early twentieth-century theory, historical particularism, was developed in the United States from the ideas of Franz Boas. Boas criticized the nineteenth-century unilineal view that societies could be ranked and compared with one another as "savage," "barbaric," or "civilized." Instead, he argued that each society is a unique product of its geographical and historical circumstances. This view of historical particularism is still important in modern anthropological explanations.

8.4 Explain the differences between structural functionalism and psychological functionalism.

The functionalist approaches developed in early twentieth-century British anthropology. Anthropologists such as A. R. Radcliffe-Brown were structural functionalists, viewing cultural institutions as satisfying societal needs such as maintaining order and stability. In contrast, Bronislaw Malinowski focused on cultural institutions as serving biological and psychological needs, such as reducing anxiety. Although functionalist explanations proved limited in explaining such matters as cultural change, they did provide valuable ethnographic data.

8.5 Discuss the twentieth-century neoevolutionary approaches, including cultural ecology and cultural materialism.

Following World War II, some anthropologists turned to new evolutionary theories. Anthropologists such as Leslie White and Julian Steward began to analyze how environment, technology, and energy requirements led to the evolution of societies. This neoevolutionism avoided the ethnocentric ideas of nineteenth-century unilineal evolution. Also, as an outgrowth of neoevolutionism, a school of thought known as cultural materialism developed through the writings of Marvin Harris. Harris systematized the analysis of sociocultural systems and maintained that the key determinant of sociocultural evolution is the infrastructure, including technology, environment, and material conditions.

8.6 Describe the Marxist approach in anthropology that emerged in the 1970s.

Another anthropological school of thought evolved from the writings of Karl Marx. In the 1970s, a number of anthropologists applied Marxist ideas about the mode of production to the analysis of preindustrial and industrial societies. Marxist anthropologists introduced a global view of societal evolution.

8.7 Discuss the symbolic anthropology approach as a humanist method.

Symbolic anthropology focuses on the study of the cultural symbols, beliefs, and ethos of a society. Symbolic anthropologists treat cultural traditions as texts that need to be interpreted by the ethnographer in the same way that humanists interpret literary texts. Symbolic anthropology represents a method of interpreting cultural traditions without reducing them to material conditions.

8.8 Discuss the approach of feminist anthropologists.

Feminist anthropology emerged in the 1970s to challenge some of the explanations that males were expressing about gender and women's issues. These feminist anthropologists have made an enormous contribution to ethnographic studies by refocusing attention on the significant role that women play in different societies.

8.9 Discuss the strengths and weaknesses of the postmodern approach in anthropology.

Postmodern anthropology developed as a critical program that suggested that traditional ethnographic research has a Western bias and was overly scientific. This postmodern program has produced a much more self-reflective type of ethnography that entails examining one's own political position within an ethnographic context. However, the postmodernists' tendency to reject the scientific method in anthropology has been a mistake that neglects a multiple array of data from biology and psychology that has contributed to better explanations of human similarities and differences throughout the world.

Key Terms

cultural ecology, p. 214
cultural materialism, p. 216
diffusionism, p. 209
functionalism, p. 212
historical particularism, p. 211
multilineal evolution, p. 214
postmodernism, p. 222
symbolic anthropology, p. 219
unilineal evolution, p. 207

Chapter 9

Analyzing Sociocultural Systems

Chapter Outline

Learning Objectives

After reading this chapter you should be able to:

9.1 Discuss how cultural anthropologists prepare to study society and culture.

9.2 Describe the actual research methods used for ethnographic studies.

9.3 Discuss some of the ethical dilemmas of ethnographic research.

9.4 How do cultural anthropologists analyze their ethnographic data?

9.5 Discuss how subsistence is influenced by the physical environment (biomes).

9.6 Describe how anthropologists study population with reference to fertility, mortality, and migration.

9.7 Discuss the anthropological explanations of technology.

9.8 Discuss how anthropologists study economics in different societies.

9.9 Discuss the general components of social structure, including status, the family, marriage, gender, and age.

9.10 Discuss how anthropologists understand politics, warfare, and law.

9.11 Discuss how anthropologists study religion, myth, ritual, and rites of passage.

9.12 Discuss the new developments by cognitive anthropologists and their understanding of religion.

9.13 Discuss how anthropologists study art and music in different societies.

9.14 Describe the strengths and limitations of the cross-cultural approach.

As we discussed in Chapter 6, at times anthropologists use the term *sociocultural system* as a combination of the terms *society* and *culture* in analyzing their data. We also saw that there are some basic cultural universals that are found in all societies (Brown 1991). This chapter provides insight on how anthropologists do research on the universal characteristics of sociocultural systems. Anthropologists approach universal features of sociocultural systems as *variables*. Immediately, this terminology suggests that these universals can *vary* within different sociocultural systems, and this is exactly what anthropologists have discovered in their research. There are basic universal similarities among all humans, but within different societies, these universal features exhibit tremendous variations. To account for patterned relationships within a sociocultural system anthropologists use *both* scientific causal *and* humanistic interpretations of cultural beliefs.

Anthropologists use the *holistic approach* to analyze sociocultural systems, which means demonstrating how all of these universals and variables interact and influence one another. Although anthropologists refer to *sociocultural systems*, the word *system* is used in a metaphorical manner. It does not suggest that sociocultural systems are somehow running "above," like some computer system in human affairs. Humans are not just automatons driven by some mechanical cultural system. Rather, humans as individuals are actively involved in managing, shaping, and modifying their culture from within these so-called systems. In this chapter, we discuss the research methods used in ethnographic research as well as the potential ethical dilemmas of this type of research.

In later chapters, we examine different types of universals and cultural variations found in different sociocultural systems to illustrate the interconnections of these variables.

Ethnographic Fieldwork

9.1 Discuss how cultural anthropologists prepare to study society and culture.

In Chapter 1, we introduced the subfield of anthropology known as cultural anthropology. This subfield focuses on the ethnographic study of contemporary societies all over the world. To prepare for ethnographic fieldwork, the anthropologist must be grounded in the different theoretical perspectives of anthropology that are discussed within different chapters of this text. This background knowledge is especially important for developing a research design for the fieldwork.

A *research design* is a strategy formulated to examine a particular topic and specifies the appropriate methods for gathering the richest possible data. The research design must take into account the types of data that will be collected and how those data relate to existing anthropological knowledge. In the research design, the cultural anthropologist specifies the types of methods that will be used in the investigation. Typically, the cultural anthropologist develops the research design, which is then reviewed by other anthropologists who recommend it for funding by various government or private research foundations.

Before going into the field for direct research, the cultural anthropologist analyzes available *archival data*, including photos, films, missionary reports, business and government surveys, musical recordings, journalistic accounts, diaries, court documents, medical records, birth, landholding documents, and death, marriage, and tax records. These help place the communities to be studied in a broad context. Historical material in the archives helps the cultural anthropologist evaluate the usefulness of the observations and interviews he or she will document. Archival data can enrich the sources of information that fieldworkers obtain once they get to the field. They must also read the published anthropological, historical, economic, sociological, and political science literature on the geographic region toward which they are heading.

Ethnographic Research and Strategies

9.2 Describe the actual research methods used for ethnographic studies.

After receiving funding and obtaining the proper research clearances from the country of destination, the cultural anthropologist takes up residence in that society to explore its institutions and values. This is the basis of the *participant observation* method, which involves learning the language and culture of the group being studied and participating in its daily activities. Language skills are the most important asset that a cultural anthropologist has in the field and the ability to communicate in the local language makes participant observation much easier and more enlightening. Anthropologist Victor de Munck views participant observation as a very powerful method and the "jewel on the crown of methodology" within cultural anthropology (2009). It involves collecting data within a specific cultural context and evaluating that data with rigorous techniques.

Participant observation includes making accurate descriptions of the physical locale and the daily activities of people in the society. This involves creating maps, or at least being able to read maps, to place the society's location in perspective. It may also involve intensive investigation into soil conditions, rates of precipitation, surveys of crops and livestock, and other environmental factors. Most importantly, participant observation involves the maintenance of accurate and reliable records of the cultural anthropologist's direct observations of human social interaction and behavior.

Some cultural anthropologists use what is called *time-allocation analysis* to record how much time the people in the society spend in various activities: work, leisure, recreation, religious ceremonies, and so on. For example, in a classic study, Allen Johnson (1975) did a systematic pioneering study of time allocation among the Machiguenga Indians, who live in the Andes Mountains of Peru. He found that men worked 4.6 hours per day and women worked 4.2 hours per day in the production and preparation of food. Women spent 2.1 hours and men spent 1.4 hours per day in craft production. Men were involved in trade and wage work, and women did housework and cared for children. The total amount of labor time allocated for this work was 7.6 hours for men and 7.4 hours for women. Johnson and other anthropologists sponsored a 10-year time-allocation studies program based at UCLA that eventually compared data from 14 different lowland Indian Amazonian societies (1987–1997). This project measured time allocation for males, females, and youth in these societies. These types of time-allocation studies can be useful in assessing how different societies use their time in various activities.

Cultural Anthropologist Sabah Rahmani interviewing a member of the Kayapo tribe in the Amazon.

Key Informants

Usually, cultural anthropologists learn about the society through trusted *key informants*, who offer insight into the culture's patterns (Powdermaker 1966; Wax 1971; Agar 1980). These informants become the initial source of information and help the cultural anthropologist identify major sources of data. Long-term collaboration with key informants is an integral part of quality ethnographic research.

The cultural anthropologist tries to choose key informants who have a deep knowledge of the community. These informants are usually "native cultural anthropologists" who are interested in their own society. They may serve as tutors or guides, answering general questions or identifying topics that could be of interest to the cultural anthropologist. They often help the cultural anthropologist establish rapport with the people in the community. In many situations, the people may not understand why the cultural anthropologist is interested in their society. The key informant can help explain the cultural anthropologist's role. In some cases, the key informant may become involved in interviewing other people in the community to assist the cultural anthropologist in collecting data. The relationship between the key informant and the cultural anthropologist is a close personal and professional one that often produces lifelong friendship and collaboration.

Interviews Cultural anthropologists use a number of *unstructured interviews*, which involve open-ended conversations with informants, to gain insights into a culture. These unstructured interviews may include the collecting of life histories, narratives, myths, and tales. Through these interviews, the cultural anthropologist may also find out information on dispute settlements, legal transactions, political conflicts, and religious and public events. Unstructured interviews sometimes involve on-the-spot questioning of informants.

The strength of this type of interviewing is that it gives informants tremendous freedom of expression in attempting to explain their culture (Bernard et al. 1986). The informant is not confined to answering a specific question that is designed by the cultural anthropologist. The informant may, for example, elaborate on connections between certain beliefs and political power in the community. Fredrik Barth (1975, 2002) discovered through his informant among the Baktaman people of New Guinea that when young males go through their initiation ceremonies, they are introduced to the secret lore and sacred knowledge of the males who are in authority. Thus, cultural beliefs are transmitted along with political authority. Barth found that this secretive sacred knowledge was often arcane and ambiguous. As these young Baktaman males went through each stage of the ritual, the knowledge became much more mysterious and ambiguous. It appeared that the most important feature of the ritual was the reinforcement of elder authority and group bonding. Without his informant's help, Barth might not have paid attention to this relationship between belief and the transmission of authority.

Following an unstructured interview, the cultural anthropologist focuses upon specific topics of interest related to the research project. In some cases, the cultural anthropologist then begins to develop *structured interviews*. Structured interviews can involve asking the same questions of every individual in a given sample. The cultural anthropologist must phrase the questions in a meaningful and sensitive manner, a task that requires knowledge of both the language and the cultural lifestyle of the people being studied.

By asking the same questions of every individual in a sample, the cultural anthropologist is able to obtain more accurate data. If the cultural anthropologist receives uniform answers to a particular question, then the data are more likely to be reliable. If a great deal of variation in responses is evident, then the data will be more unreliable or may indicate a complex issue with many facets. The structured interview helps assess the validity of the collected data. By asking people the same type of question, the cultural anthropologist attempts to gain more quality control over his or her findings (de Munck 2009). This type of data quality control must be a constant aspect of the cultural anthropologist's research strategy. However, as we discussed in Chapter 6, contemporary anthropologists concur that there is always a great deal of variation in cultural beliefs, values, and norms in every society. Thus, one cannot offer a simplistic account of "a culture" in the same way that anthropologists did in the 1930s, 1940s, and 1950s. Anthropologists want to avoid what is referred to as the "*reification*" of a culture. In the past, anthropologists tended to portray cultures and societies as if all the people within a society were sharing a homogeneous culture. As indicated in Chapter 6, this was a typical problem with the early culture and personality studies.

To develop an effective questionnaire, the cultural anthropologist must collaborate with her or his informants (de Munck 2009). This is tedious and difficult methodological work, but it is necessary if the cultural anthropologist is to understand the workings of the society. If the society is large, the cultural anthropologist must distribute the questionnaire to a random sample of the society. A **random sample** is a representative sample of people of different ages, genders, economic and political statuses, and other characteristics within the society. In a random sample, all the individuals in the society have an equal chance of being selected for the survey. If the cultural anthropologist draws information from only one sector of the population—for example, males or young people—the data may be biased. This shortcoming would limit the ability of the cultural anthropologist to develop a well-rounded portrait of the society.

Quantitative and Qualitative Data Through the structured interviews, the cultural anthropologist gathers basic **quantitative data**: census materials, dietary information, income and household-composition data, and other data that can be expressed as numbers. This information can be used as a database for developing a description of the variations in economic, social, political, and other patterns in the society. For example, dietary information can inform the cultural anthropologist about the basic health and nutritional problems that the society may have. Quantitative data provide background for the cultural anthropologist's direct and participant observations and further open-ended interviews with the individuals in the society. Sometimes, these objective quantitative data are referred to as an aspect of the *etic* perspective of the anthropologist. The **etic perspective** is the outsider's objective, quantifiable data that are used to scientifically analyze the culture of a society. *Etic* is derived from the term *phonetics* in linguistics, which are the sounds of a language.

Most of the data obtained through participant observation and interviewing are **qualitative data**, nonstatistical information that tends to be the most important aspect of ethnographic research. Qualitative data include descriptions of social organization, political activities, religious beliefs, and so on. These qualitative data are often referred to as part of the **emic perspective**, the insider's view of his or her own society and culture. The term *emic* is derived from the word *phonemics* in linguistics, which refers to the sound units of language that have "meaning" for the speakers of the language (see Chapter 7). For example, as we discussed in Chapter 6, the religious beliefs of some societies have influenced their cultural preferences for various foods. Islamic and Jewish cultural traditions prohibit the eating of pork, and orthodox Hindus encourage meatless vegetarian diets. The *emic*, qualitative data gathered about a society help cultural anthropologists understand the *etic*, quantitative data. Ordinarily, both the etic (quantitative) and emic (qualitative) data are integral to ethnographic research. Although there are considerable philosophical differences among anthropologists over the precise criteria on which emic knowledge and etic knowledge differ, most agree that the insider's emic understandings and perceptions of his or her culture differ from the outsider's etic views to some degree. Cultural anthropologists strive to understand the culture from both the outsider's and the insider's perspectives in their ethnographic descriptions.

Cultural anthropologists have a number of different methods for recording qualitative data. The best-known method is *field notes*, systematic recordings of observations or interviews in a field notebook. Cultural anthropologists should have some training in how to take useful field notes and how to manage them for more effective coding and recording of data. An increasing number of cultural anthropologists now use laptop computers as a means of constructing databases to manage their field notes. They select appropriate categories for classifying the data. For example, a cultural anthropologist may set up specific categories for kinship terms, religious taboos, plants, animals, colors, foods, and so on. These data can then easily be retrieved for analysis. Some cultural anthropologists rely on tape recorders for interviews, although they recognize the problems such devices present for producing valid accounts. Some people may feel self-conscious about having their personal thoughts recorded. Most ethnographic fieldworkers utilize photography to record and help document their findings. Cultural anthropologists must use extreme caution when using these technologies, however, for in some cultures people are very sensitive about being recorded or photographed.

Today, many anthropologists use video cameras when gathering primary data. Video recording is one of the most exciting recent developments in anthropology and has stimulated a new area of anthropological research known as *visual anthropology*. The visual documentation of economic, social, political, and ritual behavior sometimes reveals intricate patterns of interaction in a society—interaction that cannot otherwise be described thoroughly. One drawback to video recording, however, is that people who know they are being filmed frequently behave differently from the way they would normally. This may distort the cultural anthropologist's conclusions. On the other hand, the video can be shown to informants so they comment on the recorded behaviors. William Rittenberg, who did studies of Buddhist rituals in villages in central Thailand, often played back his video recordings of rituals for members of the community. The informants, including the Buddhist monks, viewed the recordings and offered more elaborate explanations of the meanings of the ritual. These strategies frequently help the cultural anthropologist gain a more comprehensive understanding of the culture.

Culture Shock Ethnographic fieldwork can be a demanding task. Cultural anthropologists sometimes experience **culture shock**, a severe psychological reaction that results from adjusting to the realities of a society radically different from one's own.

Cultural anthropologists may have to travel long distances in order to interview members of various societies.

A cultural anthropologist enculturated in the United States could experience culture shock when having to eat unfamiliar foods such as reptiles or insects, reside in uncomfortable huts in a rain forest, or observe practices that may not occur within his or her own society. Of course, the actual degree of culture shock may vary, depending upon the differences and similarities between the society studied and the anthropologist's own society. The symptoms may range from mild irritation to surprise or disgust.

Usually, after the cultural anthropologist learns the norms, beliefs, and practices of the community, the psychological disorientation of culture shock begins to diminish. Part of the challenge for anthropologists is adjusting to a different society and gaining a much better perspective on one's own society. In fact, most anthropologists report considerable culture shock upon returning home from another society. They will never again view their own society and culture in the same light. The adjustment process of culture shock out in the field and upon returning from the field enables cultural anthropologists to better understand themselves and their own society.

Ethics in Anthropological Research

9.3 Discuss some of the ethical dilemmas of ethnographic research.

Cultural anthropologists must not only be trained in appropriate research and analytical techniques, but also abide by the ethical guidelines of their discipline. In many instances, cultural anthropologists conduct research on politically powerless groups dominated by more powerful groups. When cultural anthropologists engage in participant observation, they usually become familiar with information that might, if made public, be harmful to the community or to individuals. For example, when researching isolated or rural communities, cultural anthropologists might come across economic or political behavior and information that could be used by government authorities. This information might include the specific sources of income for people in the community or the participation by people in the community in political opposition to the government. Whenever possible, cultural anthropologists attempt to keep such information confidential so as not to compromise their informants or other sources of data.

Most ethnographic reports do not include the real identities of informants or other people. Cultural anthropologists usually ensure their informants' anonymity, if at all possible (de Munck 2009). Sometimes, cultural anthropologists use pseudonyms (fictional names) to make identification difficult. In addition, cultural anthropologists ensure the confidentiality regarding their research to make sure that no one knows the identity of the participants who provided data. The data should not be traceable to individuals through name or residential, email, or IP addresses.

Cultural anthropologists also attempt to be frank and open with the population under study about the aims of the research. At times, this is difficult because the community does not understand the role of the cultural anthropologist. Out of courtesy, the cultural anthropologist should give the community a reasonable account of what he or she wants to do. The American Anthropological Association has developed a code of ethics that was last published in 2012 (American Anthropological Association 2012). The code provides anthropologists with ethical guidelines to help make decisions while in the field.

In general, cultural anthropologists do not accept research funding for projects that are supposed to be clandestine or secretive. This type of research was conducted by some anthropologists during World War II and the Cold War (Wax 2008). There has been a recent attempt by the U.S. military to recruit anthropologists during the wars in Afghanistan and Iraq, referred to as the Human Terrain System (HTS). Many contemporary anthropologists have grave reservations about undercover research in war zones (Price 2011). However, a recent discussion regarding the ethics for anthropologists considering participating in war zone research by Carolyn Fluehr-Lobban, who describes how ethnographic knowledge can contribute toward "doing no harm" in the complex settings that exist since 9/11 (2013). "Doing no harm" is promoted as the principal ethical guideline by the American Anthropological Association statement on ethics and professional responsibility (2012). Fluehr-Lobban notes that the HTS mission statement focuses on the prevention of harm to U.S. troops and local communities in combat zones, where saving lives is the intention of the mission (2013). She argues that many anthropologists who criticize the HTS overlook the benefits that accrue from ethnographic research and advice given to the military. Robert Rubinstein, Kerry Fisher, and Clementine Fujimoro have also contributed a nuanced understanding of the role of anthropologists who consult with the military since 9/11 (2012). They suggest that anthropologists can contribute some useful advice and assistance to the military. Anthropologist David Edwards, who is an Afghanistan specialist, believes that ethnographers ought to be doing research on the HTS itself (2010). This issue will likely remain a contested area of ethical responsibility among anthropologists for some time.

Analysis of Ethnographic Data

9.4 How do cultural anthropologists analyze their ethnographic data?

The results of ethnographic research are documented in a descriptive monograph referred to as an *ethnography*. In writing the ethnographic description, the cultural anthropologist must be extremely cautious. The accumulated field notes, photos, perhaps video or tape recordings, and quantitative data from survey sources must all be carefully managed to reduce bias, distortion, and error. The cultural anthropologist must analyze these data, making sure to cross-check the conclusions from a variety of sources, including informants, censuses, observations, and archival materials. In addition, the cultural anthropologist should plainly distinguish the views of the people being studied from his or her interpretation of those views.

Universals, Independent Variables, and Dependent Variables

Culture, society, and human behavior are not just a random array of occurrences that develop without rhyme or reason. They are the result of universal features and interacting variables that influence the human condition. In analyzing a sociocultural system, anthropologists frequently find that different universals and specific variables interact with one another. The interaction of two variables is called a **correlation**.

For example, a particular society may experience both population increases and a high incidence of warfare. This does not necessarily mean that the population growth causes the warfare or vice versa; it simply means that both conditions exist within the society. To determine whether a causal relationship exists between these variables would require further investigation, including, in many cases, comparisons with other societies. Further research may indicate that the relationship between population and warfare is a spurious correlation; that is, two variables occur together, but each is caused by some third variable.

Alternatively, research may indicate that in a certain society the rate of population growth does influence the frequency of warfare. In such cases, the anthropologist might hypothesize that population increases cause the high incidence of warfare. This hypothesis could then be tested and evaluated by other anthropologists.

In determining cause-and-effect relationships, anthropologists distinguish between independent and dependent variables. An **independent variable** is the causal variable that produces an effect on another variable, the **dependent variable**. That is, the dependent variable may *depend* upon or be explained, at least in part, by the independent variable. In the previous example, population growth is the independent variable because it determines the incidence of warfare, which is the dependent variable.

In actuality, this example of determining causal relationships is far too simplistic. Anthropologists recognize that no aspect of culture and society can be completely explained by any single cause or independent variable. They rely instead on hypotheses that are *multivariate* or *multidimensional*, in which many variables interact with one another. This multidimensional approach must be kept in mind when considering the specific variables explored by cultural anthropologists in their study of different societies. The multidimensional approach is linked with the holistic perspective in anthropology—that is, the attempt to demonstrate how sociocultural systems must be understood through the interconnections among universals and specific variables.

Universals and Variables Studied by Cultural Anthropologists The major variables and universal features of sociocultural systems include subsistence and the physical environment, demography, technology, the economy, the social structure, the political organization, religion, art, and music. Although this is not a complete list of the universals and specific variables studied by cultural anthropologists, it provides the general framework for understanding different societies.

Subsistence and the Physical Environment

9.5 Discuss how subsistence is influenced by the physical environment (biomes).

Living organisms, both plant and animal, do not live or evolve in a vacuum. The evolution and survival of a particular species are closely related to the type of physical environment in which it is located. The speed of a jackal has evolved in relationship to its predators and prey in East Africa, just as the arctic fox has evolved in relationship to the local ecology (the relationships between living things and their environment) of the Arctic. Of course, this relationship between organism and ecological context applies to plants as well as animals. For example, the physical characteristics of the orchid plant make it suited to a tropical environment. The environment affects organisms directly and, as Charles Darwin noted, affects the passing on the propagation of adaptive characteristics; those characteristics that enable individuals to survive and reproduce in their environment.

Biologists use the term *adaptation* to refer to the process in which an organism adjusts to environmental pressures. Organisms adapt to the environment through the physical traits that they inherit. Like other creatures, as we have seen in Chapter 5, humans have adapted to their respective environments through physical changes in body size and shape, blood groups, skin coloration, and biological traits. Humans, however, have adapted to their specific environments primarily through *culture*. By any measure, humans have been the most successful species in adapting to different types of environments. Like other species, humans exhibit physical and biological adaptation to the specific environments that they occupy. In addition, humans have the incredible capacity for symbolic and social learning, allowing for countless human cultural adaptations. Humans occupy an extraordinary range of environments, from the tropics to the Arctic, and have developed cultural solutions to the various challenges arising in these diverse regions. Anthropologists study these cultural solutions or adaptive strategies to explain both the similarities and the differences exhibited among societies.

Modern Cultural Ecology

The term *ecology* was coined by German biologist Ernest Haeckel in the nineteenth century from two Greek words (οίκος and -λογια) that mean "the study of the home." **Ecology** is the study of living organisms in relationship to their environment. Here we define environment broadly to include life-forms and the physical characteristics found in a particular geographical region. In biology, ecological studies focus on how plant and animal populations survive and reproduce in specific environmental niches. An **environmental niche** is a given set of ecological conditions that a life-form uses to make a living, survive, and adapt. From an anthropological perspective in particular, it is crucial to bear in mind that ecology encompasses all plants and animals in a given environment, *including humans*.

As discussed in Chapter 8, cultural ecology is the systematic study of the relationships between the environmental niche and culture. Anthropologists recognize that all humans can adjust in creative ways to different environments. Nevertheless, humans, like other organisms, are universally connected to the environment in a number of ways. Just as the environment has an impact on human behavior and society, humans have a major impact on their environment. Modern cultural ecologists examine these dynamic interrelationships as a means of understanding different societies.

Biomes

In their studies of different environments, cultural ecologists use the concept of a *biome*. A **biome** is an area distinguished by a particular climate and certain types of plants and animals. Biomes may be classified by certain attributes, such as mean rainfall, temperature, soil conditions, and vegetation that supports certain forms of animal life (Campbell 1983). Cultural ecologists investigate the relationship between specific biomes and human sociocultural systems. Some of the different biomes that will be encountered in this text are listed in Table 9.1.

Subsistence Patterns and Environments

In U.S. society, when we have the urge to satisfy our hunger drive, we have many options: We can go to a local fast-food restaurant, place money into a machine to select our choice of food, or obtain food for cooking from a grocery store or supermarket. These are just a handful of ways that humans obtain food. Cultural anthropologists study **subsistence patterns**—the means by which people in various societies acquire food. As we shall see, the amounts of sunlight and rainfall and the types of soil, forests, and mineral deposits all affect subsistence patterns. The specific biome and environmental conditions may limit the development of certain types of subsistence

Table 9.1 Various Biomes Discussed by Cultural Ecologists along with Their Major Characteristics

Biome	Principal Locations	Precipitation Range (mm/year)	Temperature Range (hr °C) (daily maximum and minimum)	Soils
Tropical rain forest	Central America (Atlantic coast) Amazon basin Brazilian coast West African coast Congo basin Malaya East Indies Philippines New Guinea Northeastern Australia Pacific islands	1,270–12,700 Equatorial type frequent torrential thunderstorms Tradewind type; steady, almost daily rains No dry period	Little annual variation Max. 29–35 Min. 18–27 No cold period	Mainly reddish laterites
Tropical savanna	Central America (Pacific coast) Orinoco basin Brazil, south of Amazon basin North Central Africa East Africa South Central Africa Madagascar India Southeast Asia Northern Australia	250–1,900 Warm-season thunderstorms Almost no rain in cool season Long dry period during low sun	Considerable annual variation; no really cold period *Rainy season (high sun)* Max. 24–32 Min. 18–27 *Dry season (low sun)* Max. 21–32 Min. 13–18 *Dry season (higher sun)* Max. 29–40 Min. 21–27	Some laterites; considerable variety
Temperate grasslands	Central North America Eastern Europe Central and Western Asia Argentina New Zealand	300–2,000; evenly distributed through the year or with a peak in summer; snow in winter	*Winter* Max. −18–29 Min. −28–10 *Summer* Max. −1–49 Min. −1–15	Black prairie soils Chestnut and brown soils almost all have a lime layer
Temperate deciduous forest	Eastern North America Western Europe Eastern Asia	630–2,300; evenly distributed through year; droughts rare; some snow	*Winter* Max. −12–21 Min. −29–7 *Summer* Max. 24–38 Min. 15–27	Gray-brown podzol Red and yellow podzols
Northern coniferous forest	Northern North America Northern Europe Northern Asia	400–1,000; evenly distributed; much snow	*Winter* Max. −37–1 Min. −54–9 *Summer* Max. 10–21 Min. 7–13	True podzols; bog soils; some permafrost at depth in places
Arctic tundra	Northern North America Greenland Northern Eurasia	250–750; considerable snow	*Winter* Max. −37–7 Min. −57–8 *Summer* Max. 2–15 Min. −1–7	Rocky or boggy Much patterned ground permafrost

SOURCE: Adapted from W. D. Billings, *Plants, Man, and the Ecosystem*, 2nd ed. ©1970. Reprinted by permission of Brooks/Cole, an imprint of the Wadsworth Group, a division of Thomson Learning.

patterns. For example, Arctic conditions are not conducive to agricultural activities, nor are arid regions suitable for rice production. These are the obvious limitations of biomes and environmental conditions on subsistence patterns.

The earliest type of subsistence pattern—known as foraging or hunting and gathering—goes back among early hominins to perhaps 2 million years ago. This pattern of subsistence, along with others such as horticulture, pastoralism, various types of intensive agriculture, and developments in agribusiness in industrial societies, is introduced below. As we shall see, these subsistence patterns not only are influenced by the environment, but also directly affect the environment. In other words, as humans transform their subsistence pattern to adapt to the environment, the environment is also transformed to varying degrees, depending upon the type of subsistence pattern developed. All humans alter their environment in some way. The result is called an *anthropogenic landscape*; these landscapes are created by foragers and by industrialists alike, though the degree and intensity of alteration may vary. The interaction between subsistence pattern and environment is an extremely important topic in anthropology and has a direct bearing on the future of human-environment relationships.

One other aspect of subsistence and the environment relates to the use of energy in different societies. In Chapter 8, we discussed Leslie White's attempt to explain sociocultural evolution in terms of energy use. He suggested that sociocultural evolution progressed in relationship to the harnessing of energy. A number of anthropologists, including John Bodley (1985), attempted to quantify White's ideas. Bodley suggested that sociocultural systems can be divided into *high-energy cultures* and *low-energy cultures* and that these categories have implications for the evolution of society. More recently, archaeologist Ian Morris has systematically measured energy capture by prehistoric peoples compared with modern contemporary societies (2010, 2013). By energy capture, Morris means that range of energy that includes food (whether consumed directly or fed to animals that are used for labor or consumption), fuel (whether for cooking, heating, cooling, firing kilns and furnaces, or powering machines, and including wind and water power, and wood, coal, oil, gas, and nuclear power), and raw materials (whether for construction, metalwork, potmaking, or any other purpose) (2013: 53). Food energy and nonfood energy, such as fuel, and raw materials can be measured in kilocalories per capita, per day. This is a broader measure of energy capture than expressed by White or Bodley, but Morris's model is more comprehensive and quantitatively more sophisticated. Morris is able to use archaeological evidence from different time periods, including the Paleolithic up to the present, to compare energy capture among various types of societies.

Demography

9.6 Describe how anthropologists study population with reference to fertility, mortality, and migration.

Human use of natural resources and energy, and the subsistence strategies employed to "make a living" in a given environment, relate to variables such as population size and growth rates. These variables are the basis of the field of **demography**, the study of the quantitative and statistical aspects of a population. Demographers study changes in the size, composition, and distribution of human populations. They also study the consequences of population increases and decreases for human societies. Demographic anthropology is an important specialty in anthropology.

Much of the research in demographic anthropology is concerned with the quantitative description of population. Demographic anthropologists design censuses and surveys to collect population statistics on the size, age and sex composition, and increasing or decreasing growth of the population of a society. After collecting these data, demographic anthropologists focus on three major variables in a population: fertility, mortality, and migration.

Fertility, Mortality, and Migration

To measure **fertility**—the number of births in a society—demographic anthropologists use the **crude birth rate**, that is, the number of live births in a given year for every thousand people in a population. They also measure **mortality**—the incidence of death in a society's population—by using the **crude death rate**, that is, the number of deaths in a given year for every thousand people in a population. In measuring the **migration rate**—the movement of people into and out of a specified territory—demographic anthropologists determine the number of in-migrants (people moving into the territory) and the number of out-migrants (people moving out of the territory). They then use these numbers to calculate the **net migration**, which indicates the general movement of the population in and out of the territory.

To assess overall population change, demographic anthropologists subtract the crude death rate from the crude birth rate to arrive at the *natural growth rate* of a population. The natural growth rate is usually the major indicator of population change in a society. Anthropologists calculate the total population change by adding the rate of migration to other measures of growth. A number of other variables also influence rates of fertility, mortality, and migration.

Fecundity—the potential number of children that women are capable of bearing—influences fertility rates. Fecundity varies, however, according to the age of females at puberty and menopause, nutrition, workload, and other conditions in the societies and individuals being studied.

Life expectancy is the number of years an average person can expect to live. A component of particular importance in determining the life expectancy of a given society is the **infant mortality rate**—the number of babies per thousand births in any year who die before reaching the age of 1. When the infant mortality rate is high, the life expectancy—a statistical average—decreases. In many countries throughout the world, the **childhood mortality rate**—the number of children per thousand per year who die before reaching the age of 5—is a major problem. Disease, nutrition, sanitation, warfare, the general standard of living, and medical care are some of the factors that influence mortality, life expectancy, and infant and child mortality rates.

Migration is related to a number of different factors. In many instances, migration is *involuntary*. For example, the Cajun people of Louisiana are descendants of French people who were forced out of Canada by the British in the 1700s. Migration can also be *voluntary*. This type of movement is influenced by what demographers refer to as *push-pull factors*. **Push factors** are those that lead people to leave specific territories; examples are poverty, warfare, and political instability. **Pull factors**, such as economic opportunity, peace, and political freedom, are powerful incentives for people to move to other societies.

Population and Environment Demographic anthropologists study the relationship between environments (specific biomes) and population. One variable they investigate is **carrying capacity**—the maximum population that a specific environment can support, as determined by the environment's potential energy and food resources. Some environments contain food and energy resources that allow for substantial population increases, whereas other environments contain only limited resources. For example, in the past, desert and Arctic biomes had carrying capacities that severely limited population increases. In contrast, various river valley regions containing water and fertile soils permitted opportunities for a larger population size. With the development of mechanized agriculture, fertilizers, and synthetic pesticides in industrial and postindustrial societies, the carrying capacity for larger populations has increased.

Population and Culture Demographic anthropologists examine the relationship between environment and population, as well as the cultural values, beliefs, and practices that affect fertility, mortality, and migration rates. In some societies, religious beliefs encourage high birth rates. In others, political authorities institute programs to increase or decrease population growth. Anthropologists gather data and develop hypotheses about individual and household decisions regarding the "costs and benefits" of having children as well as the fertility outcomes of these decisions. Anthropologists also investigate strategies of population regulation, such as birth control techniques.

An Italian couple with one child. The postindustrial societies of Europe have some of the lowest fertility rates in the world.

Technology

9.7 Discuss the anthropological explanations of technology.

The term *technology* is derived from the Greek word *techne*, which refers to "art" or "skill." When we hear this term, we usually think of tools, machines, clothing, shelter, and other such objects. As defined by modern anthropologists, however, **technology** consists of all the human techniques and methods of reaching a specific subsistence goal or of modifying or controlling the natural environment. Technology is cultural in that it includes methods for manipulating the environment. It consists of physical tools and of cultural knowledge that humans can apply in specific ways to help humans survive and thrive in changing environments in which they live and work. In societies in which people use technologies such as bows and arrows, canoes, plows, penicillin, or computers, the cultural knowledge needed to construct, design, and use these materials is extremely important.

To sustain life, human societies need to produce and allocate goods and services to provide food, clothing, shelter, tools, and transportation. **Goods** are elements of material culture produced from raw materials in the natural environment, ranging from the basic commodities for survival to luxury items. The commodities for survival may include axes and plows for clearing land and cultivating crops. Luxury commodities include such items as jewelry, decorative art, and musical instruments. **Services** are elements of nonmaterial culture in the form of specialized skills that benefit others, such as giving spiritual comfort or providing medical care. Goods and services are valued because they satisfy various human needs. To produce these goods and services, societies must have suitable technologies.

Anthropological Explanations of Technology

As we saw in Chapter 8, in the nineteenth century, anthropologists such as E. B. Tylor and Lewis Henry Morgan constructed a unilineal scheme of cultural evolution in which societies progressed from the simple, small-scale societies of "savages" to the more complex industrial technologies of modern civilizations. In the twentieth century, these simplistic views of technological evolution were rejected through detailed ethnographic research. Anthropologists in the 1950s and 1960s such as Leslie White and Julian Steward—who became known as *cultural materialists*—came to view technology as one of the primary factors of cultural evolution. White defined technology as an energy-capturing system made up of energy, tools, and products—that is, all the material means with which energy is harnessed, transformed, and

The laptop computer represents one of the most advanced technologies in postindustrial societies.

expended (1959). These anthropologists viewed technology as a basic and primary source of sociocultural change. They argued that we cannot explain different technological developments in society with reference to "cultural values." Instead, technology must be viewed as a method designed to cope with a particular environment. Therefore, variations in environment, or habitat, could account for the differences between, say, the Inuit (Eskimo) and the Australian Aborigine societies.

White's views on technology, as well as the views of other cultural materialists, have been criticized as a rigid form of "technological determinism." Although the cultural materialists see sociological, ideological, or emotional factors as conditioning or limiting the use or development of technology, these factors exert little influence on sociocultural systems compared to technology's dominant role. Anthropologists are currently evaluating this cultural materialist hypothesis to determine whether technology is a primary variable in societal development, or whether a number of factors work in conjunction with technology to condition societal developments and evolution. So far, anthropologists have concluded that technology alone does not result in cultural change and transformation, but rather cultural values, beliefs, and practices interact with technology to create changes. For example, some people reject modern technology because of their significant religious beliefs and cultural values. Technology has to be understood with respect to the cultural context in which it is accepted, rejected, or modified by human communities.

Economy

9.8 Discuss how anthropologists study economics in different societies.

Like other animals, humans universally require food and shelter. In addition, humans have special needs for other goods and services, ranging from hunting materials to spiritual guidance. As we have seen, these goods and services are produced through technology. The **economy** of a society consists of the social relationships that organize the production, exchange, and consumption of goods and services. **Production** is the organized system for the creation of goods and services. **Exchange** is the process whereby members of society transfer goods and services among themselves. **Consumption** is the use of goods and services to satisfy desires and needs. In this chapter, we are going to examine these three components of the economy in various forms of society.

Anthropologists have found that the economy is closely connected with the environment, subsistence base, demographic conditions, technology, and division of labor within the society. The **division of labor** consists of specialized economic roles (occupations) and activities. In small-scale societies, the division of labor is typically simple, and in large-scale societies, it is extremely complex. In the twentieth century, ethnographic descriptions of different types of societies generated two perspectives on economic systems: the *formalist* and *substantivist* approaches.

The Formalist Approach

The formalist approach maintains that all economic systems are fundamentally similar and can be compared with one another. Formalists assume that all people try to act "rationally," maximizing their individual self-interests and gains. In other words, all humans have a psychological inclination to calculate carefully their self-interest. Formalists hypothesize that people do not always choose the cheapest and most efficient strategies to carry out their economic decisions, but they do tend to look for the best rational strategy for economic decision making.

Formalists hold that the best method for studying any economy is to employ the same general theories developed by economists. Formalists collect quantitative data and interpret these data using sophisticated mathematical models developed by economists. They focus on such economic variables as production and consumption patterns, supply and demand, exchange, and investment decisions. One classic formalist study, by anthropologist Sol Tax (1953), focused on economic decision making in Guatemalan Indian communities. Tax analyzed the economic transactions in the traditional markets of these communities. He concluded that although the economy was undeveloped, the people made the same types of economic decisions as people in the developed world. Tax referred to these Indians as "penny capitalists."

The Substantivist Approach

The substantivist approach draws its supporting hypotheses from twentieth-century ethnographic studies. Substantivists maintain that the ways of allocating goods and services in small-scale societies differ fundamentally from those in large-scale Western economic systems. Thus, the social institutions found in small-scale societies or larger agricultural societies produce economic systems that are fundamentally different from the market economies of Western societies. According to substantivists, preindustrial economies are not driven by the motive of individual material gain or profit, as are industrial economies. They argue that the economy is *embedded* in the sociocultural system, including the kinship systems, values, beliefs, and norms of the society. They also argue that modern capitalist societies are *embedded* within an economy based on market exchange. In general, substantivists emphasize that precapitalist societies have different forms of logic and processes than do the market exchange economies of capitalist societies. These precapitalist societies also have other forms of exchange, such as reciprocity and redistribution. We focus on these other forms of exchange below.

Contemporary Economic Anthropology

Most anthropologists today do not identify exclusively with the formalist or the substantivist perspective; instead, they recognize the contributions of both perspectives to our knowledge of economic systems (Wilk 1996; Bloch and Parry 1989). Modern anthropologists investigate the different patterns of production, ownership, distribution, exchange, and consumption in relationship to ecological, demographic, and cultural factors, which influence economic choices, risk, and consumption preferences. They collect quantitative economic data along with more qualitative cultural data (*emic* or insider's understandings) to explain the workings of economic choices and systems. Most economic anthropologists are not as concerned with how precapitalist societies organize their economies; rather, they are more concerned with how precapitalist economies change as they are influenced by globalization and contact with the global market economy. In addition, many anthropologists are using psychological experiments based on game theory or other models to assess how people make their economic decisions (Henrich et al. 2004). These new psychological experiments tend to demonstrate that human economic decision making is not wholly based on rational calculations, but rather is influenced by "emotional" or "cultural" factors regarding choices and preferences. For example, Henrich et al. used economic games to collect data on exchange behaviors from 15 small-scale societies around the world, finding that in no society was behavior consistent with the "selfishness axiom" (that people seek to maximize their own gains and expect others to do the same), as predicted by the neoclassical economist perspective. In fact, the results of the study indicated that rather than focusing only on economic outcomes, people were also concerned with *how* a transaction took place, nonmaterial outcomes (e.g. reputation), and fairness. Research on these topics is important for understanding more than just behavior in economic games and experiments. This research is aimed at developing explanations for the origins of human cooperation. Humans rely on each other to survive, so explaining cooperation is of primary importance within anthropology and beyond.

One other area of new anthropological research on economic choices and preferences was inspired by anthropologist/sociologist Pierre Bourdieu. Bourdieu discussed three different forms of capital that individuals had in respect to their socioeconomic status or class background (1977, 1984). He distinguished *economic capital*, based on the wealth and assets of individuals, *social capital*, the social networks based on kinship, family ties, or political allies, and *cultural capital*, the tastes or aesthetic preferences for symbolic goods such as literature, art, foods, or music. These different forms of capital influenced economic choices and preferences for individuals within different socioeconomic strata or class background. Bourdieu argued that all three forms of capital gave individuals advantages or disadvantages for the accumulation of wealth, power, and status within different societies. Anthropologists have been investigating these different forms of capital in various societies and how they influence economic decisions regarding exchange and consumption.

Social Structure

9.9 Discuss the general components of social structure, including status, the family, marriage, gender, and age.

All inorganic and organic things, from planets to living cells, have a structure—they consist of interrelated parts in a particular arrangement. Anthropologists use the idea of structure when they analyze different societies. Societies are not just random, chaotic collections of people who interact with one another. Rather, social interaction in any society takes place in regular patterns. As we discussed in Chapter 6, people learn the norms, values, and behavioral patterns of their society through enculturation. In the absence of social patterns, people would find social life confusing. Anthropologists refer to this pattern of relationships in society as the **social structure**. Social structure provides the framework for all human societies, but it does not determine the decision making of individuals.

Components of Social Structure

One of the most important components of social structure is *status*. **Status** is a recognized position that a person occupies in society. A person's status determines where he or she fits in society in relationship to everyone else. Status may be based on or accompanied by wealth, power, prestige, or a combination of all of these. Many anthropologists use the term **socioeconomic status** (SES) to refer to how a specific position is related to the division of labor, the political system, and other cultural variables.

All societies recognize both *ascribed* and *achieved* statuses. An **ascribed status** is one that is attached to a person from birth or that a person assumes involuntarily later in life. The most prevalent ascribed statuses are based upon family and kinship relations (for example, daughter or son), sex (male or female), and age. In addition, in some societies, ascribed statuses are based on one's race or ethnicity. In contrast, an **achieved status** is one based, at least in part, on a person's voluntary actions. Examples of achieved statuses in the United States are one's profession and level of education. Of course, one's family and kinship connections may influence one's profession and level of education. George W. Bush's and John Kerry's educational level and status are interrelated to their families of birth. However, these individuals had to act voluntarily to achieve their status.

Closely related to status is the concept of social *roles*. A **role** is a set of expected behavior patterns, obligations, and norms attached to a particular status. The distinction between status and role is a simple one: You "occupy" a certain status, but you "play" a role (Linton 1936). For example, as a student, you occupy a certain status that differs from those of your professors, administrators, and other staff. As you occupy that status, you perform by attending lectures, taking notes, participating in class, and studying for examinations. This concept of role is derived from the theater and refers to the parts played by actors. If you are a husband, mother, son, daughter, teacher, lawyer, judge, male, or female, you are expected to behave in certain ways because of the norms associated with that particular status.

As mentioned, a society's social statuses usually correspond to wealth, power, and prestige. Anthropologists find that all societies have inequality in statuses, which are arranged in a hierarchy. This inequality of statuses is known as **social stratification**. The degree of social stratification varies from one society to another, depending on technological, economic, and political variables. Small-scale societies tend to be less stratified than large-scale societies; that is, they have fewer categories of status and fewer degrees of difference regarding wealth, power, and prestige.

In some societies, wealth, power, and prestige are linked with ownership of land or the number of animals acquired. In U.S. society, high status is strongly correlated with income and property. Exploring the causes of differing patterns of social stratification and how stratification relates to other facets of society is an important objective in ethnographic research.

The social structure of any society has several major components that anthropologists look at when analyzing a society. These components are discussed in the following sections on the family, marriage, gender, and age.

The Family

In a comprehensive cross-cultural study, George Murdock (1945) found that all societies recognize the family. Thus, the family is a *universal* feature of humans and may have its roots in our primate heritage (Chapais 2008). Anthropologists define the **family** as a social group of two or more people related by blood, marriage, or adoption who live or reside together for an extended period, sharing economic resources and caring for their young. Anthropologists differentiate between the *family of orientation*, the family into which people are born, and the *family of procreation*, the family within which people reproduce or adopt children of their own (Murdock 1949). The family is a social unit within a much wider group of relatives, or *kin*. Kinship relationships beyond the immediate nuclear family play a significant role in most societies throughout the world. Anthropologists study kinship relationships along with the family to fully comprehend how individual thought and behavior are influenced by these interacting aspects of human communities.

Although variations exist in types and forms, as mentioned before, George Murdock found that the family is a universal aspect of social organization. The reason for the universality of the family appears to be that it performs certain basic functions that serve human needs. The primary function of the family is the nurturing and enculturation of children. The basic norms, values, knowledge, and beliefs of the culture are transmitted to children through the family.

Another function of the family is the regulation of sexual activity. Every culture places some restrictions on sexual behavior. Sexual intercourse is the basis of human reproduction and inheritance; it is also a matter of considerable social importance. Regulating sexual behavior is, therefore, essential to the proper functioning of a society. For example, anthropologists find that the family prohibits sexual relations within the immediate family through incest avoidance behaviors.

Families also serve to protect and support their members physically, emotionally, and often economically from birth to death. In all societies, people need warmth, food, shelter, and care. Families provide a social environment in which these needs can be met. Additionally, humans have emotional needs for affection and intimacy that are most easily fulfilled within the family.

The two major types of families found throughout the world are the *nuclear* and *extended* families. A typical **nuclear family** is composed of two parents and their immediate biological offspring or adopted children. George Murdock believed that the nuclear family is a universal feature of all societies (1949). What he meant by this was that all societies have a male and female who reproduce children and are the core of the kinship unit. However, as we shall see below, the nuclear family is not the principal kinship unit in all societies. In many societies, the predominant form is the **extended family**, which is composed of parents, children, and other kin relations bound together as a social unit.

Marriage

In most societies, the family is a product of **marriage**, a social bond sanctioned by society between two or more people that involves economic cooperation, social obligations, rights, duties, and sometimes culturally approved sexual activity. Two general patterns of marriage exist: **endogamy**, which is marriage between people of the same social group or category, and **exogamy**, marriage between people of different social groups or categories.

A Hindu wedding ceremony

A marriage may include two or more partners. **Monogamy** generally involves two individuals in the marriage. Though this is the most familiar form of marriage in Western industrial societies, it is not the only type of marriage practiced in the world. Many societies practice some form of **polygamy**, or *plural marriage*, which involves a spouse of one sex and two or more spouses of the opposite sex. There are two forms of polygamy: **polygyny**, marriage between one husband and two or more wives, and **polyandry**, marriage between one wife and two or more husbands. Although the majority of the world's population currently practices monogamy, polygyny is a common form of marriage and is permitted in 80 percent of human societies, many of which have relatively small populations (Murdock 1981a, 1981b). Although polyandry is the rarest form of marriage, a new survey of polyandry indicates that it occurs in 81 different societies (Starkweather and Hames 2012). Although marriages typically involve the uniting of males and females, a number of societies have homosexual marriages that are recognized socially and legally (Stone 2010).

Gender

Gender relationships are another important component of the social structure of a society. When anthropologists discuss relationships between males and females in a society, they distinguish between *sex* and *gender*. **Sex** refers to the biological and anatomical differences between males and females. These differences include the primary sexual characteristics—the sex organs—and the secondary sexual characteristics, such as breasts and wider hips for females and more muscular development of the upper torso and extensive body hair for males. Note that these are general tendencies, to which many exceptions exist. That is, many males are smaller and lighter and have less body hair than many females. Nevertheless, in general, males and females are universally distinguished by physiological and anatomical differences (L Stone 2010).

In contrast to sex, most anthropologists view *gender* as cultural rather than biological. **Gender** refers to the specific human traits attached to each sex by a society. As members of a particular society, males and females occupy certain statuses, such as son, daughter, husband, wife, father, and mother. In assuming the gender roles that correspond to these different status positions, males are socialized to be "masculine," and females are socialized to be "feminine." Definitions of masculine and feminine vary among different societies (Yangisako and Collier 1990; Stone 2010).

Gender and Enculturation One major issue regarding gender is the degree to which enculturation influences male and female behavior. To study this issue, anthropologists focus on the values, beliefs, and norms that may influence gender roles. They also observe the types of activities associated with young boys and girls. In many societies, boys and girls play different games as an aspect of enculturation. For example, in U.S. society, boys in comparison with girls are traditionally encouraged to participate in aggressive, competitive team sports. Cultural values and beliefs that affect gender roles are found in other societies as well.

Sex and the Division of Labor A basic component of the division of labor in most societies is the assigning of different tasks to males and females. In studying this phenomenon, anthropologists focus on the issue of whether physical differences (sex differences) between males and females are responsible for these different roles. To address this issue, they ask a number of questions: Is there a universal division of labor based on sex? Does physical strength have anything to do with the work patterns associated with gender? Do childcare and pregnancy determine or influence economic specialization for females? To what degree do values and beliefs ascribed to masculine or feminine behavior affect work assignments?

Gender and Status Another important issue investigated by anthropologists is the social and political status of males and females in society. Some early anthropologists such as Lewis Henry Morgan believed that females at one time had a higher social and political status than males, but that through time this pattern was reversed. Anthropologists currently focus on how the status of males and females is related to biological factors, the division of labor, kinship relations, political systems, and values and beliefs.

Although sex characteristics are biologically determined, gender roles vary in accordance with the technological, economic, and sociocultural conditions of particular types of societies. Anthropologists have broadened our understanding of the variation of gender roles among a wide range of societies.

Age

Like kinship and gender, age is a universal principle used to prescribe social status in sociocultural systems. The biological processes of aging are an inevitable aspect of human life; from birth to death, our bodies are constantly changing. Definite biological changes occur for humans in their progress from infancy to childhood to adolescence to adulthood to old age. Hormonal and other physiological changes lead to maturation and the onset of the aging process. For example, as we approach old age, our sensory abilities begin to change: Our capacities for taste, eyesight, touch, smell, and hearing begin to diminish. Gray hair and wrinkles appear, and we experience a loss of height and weight and an overall decline in strength and vitality. Although these physical changes vary greatly from individual to individual and to some extent are influenced by societal and environmental factors, these processes are universal.

The biology of aging, however, is only one dimension of how age is related to the social structure of any specific culture. The human life cycle is the basis of social statuses and roles that have both a physical and a cultural dimension. The cultural meanings of these categories in the life cycle vary among different societies, as do the criteria people use to define age-related statuses. The definitions of the statuses and roles for specific ages have wide-ranging implications for those in these status positions.

Age and Enculturation As people move through the different phases of the human life cycle, they continually experience the process of enculturation. Because of the existence of different norms, values, and beliefs, people in various societies may be treated differently at each phase of the life cycle. For example, the period of enculturation during childhood varies among societies. In the United States and other postindustrial societies, childhood is associated with an extensive educational experience that continues for many years. In many preindustrial societies, however, childhood is a relatively short period of time, and children assume adult status and responsibilities at a fairly young age.

Another factor influenced by aging in a society is how individuals are viewed at different ages. How is *old age* defined? For example, in many societies, old age is not defined strictly in terms of the passage of time. More frequently, old age is defined in respect to changes in social status, work patterns, family status, or reproductive potential (Cowgill 1986). These factors influence how people are valued at different ages in a society.

Age and the Division of Labor The economic roles assumed by a person at different stages of the life cycle may also depend on age. Children everywhere are exposed to the technological skills they will need to survive in their environment. As they mature, they assume specific positions in the division of labor. Just as male and female roles differ, the roles for the young and old differ. For example, in some preindustrial societies, older people occupy central roles, whereas in others, they play no important role at all. In industrial and postindustrial societies, the elderly generally do not occupy important occupational roles.

Age and Status Age is one of the key determinants of social status. People are usually assigned a particular status associated with a phase of the life cycle. The result is **age stratification**, the unequal allocation of wealth, power, and prestige among people of different ages. Anthropologists find that age stratification varies in accordance with the level of technological development. For example, in many preindustrial societies, the elderly have a relatively high social status, whereas in most industrial societies, the elderly experience a loss of status.

One of the most common ways of allocating the status of people at different ages is through *age grades*. **Age grades** are statuses defined by age through which a person moves as he or she ages. For example, the age grades in most industrial societies correspond to the periods of infancy, preschool, kindergarten, elementary school, intermediate school, high school, young adulthood, middle age, young old, and old old (Cowgill 1986). Each of these grades conveys a particular social status.

Political Organization

9.10 Discuss how anthropologists understand politics, warfare, and law.

In the early twentieth century, German sociologist Max Weber introduced definitions of political power and authority that have since been adopted and modified by cultural anthropologists. Weber defined **political power** as the ability to achieve personal ends despite opposition. In this sense, political power can be based on physical or psychological *coercion*. Weber perceived this type of political power as *illegitimate*, in that it is unacceptable to most members of a society. According to Weber, the most effective and enduring form of political power is based on **authority**, power generally perceived by members of society as legitimate, rather than coercive.

A brief example will illustrate the difference between illegitimate and legitimate power. If a large country invades and conquers a smaller one, the occupied people generally will not consider their new rulers to be legitimate. Thus, the rulers must rely on coercion to enforce their laws and to collect payments in the form of taxes or tributes. In contrast, most U.S. citizens voluntarily comply with the tax laws. Although they may complain, they perceive their government as representing legitimate authority. Although physical coercion and force might be used to arrest some people who refuse to pay their taxes, in the majority of cases such actions are not necessary.

Types of Political Systems

The general categories used by anthropologists to describe political systems are *band*, *tribe*, *chiefdom*, and *state*. In Chapter 3, we discussed the Paleolithic period (Old Stone Age) and the emergence of hunting and gathering, which, as a means of subsistence, goes back to at least 1 million years ago. A **hunter-gatherer society** depends on hunting animals and gathering vegetation for subsistence. These hunter-gatherer societies are also known as **foraging societies**. Food production as a subsistence pattern developed relatively recently, about 12,000 to 10,000 years ago. Thus, for almost 99 percent of humanity's life span, humans lived as foragers. This lifestyle has been the most enduring and persistent adaptation humans have ever achieved. Therefore, band societies have been the basic type of sociocultural system for perhaps as long as 1 million years. When archaeologists do studies of the artifacts found during the Paleolithic to understand the human past, they often look to the ethnographic studies of modern hunter-gatherers. Most contemporary hunter-gatherer societies have relatively small groups, low population density, highly nomadic subsistence strategies, loosely defined territorial boundaries, social organizations that tie kin (related individuals) together, and foster unity within and among groups. Constant circulation of material goods in such societies not only enhances and maintains kin ties through mutual obligations, but also inhibits the accumulation of wealth by any individuals in the society. This enables these societies to remain **egalitarian**—to have very small differences in wealth among individuals. There are no rich or poor in most of these societies.

Also, the most common form of political organization among ethnographically documented hunter-gatherer societies is the band, a fairly small group of people tied together by close kinship relations. A **band** is the least complex form of political system—and most likely the oldest. Typically, each band is politically independent of the others and has its own internal leadership. Most of the leaders in the bands are males, but females also take on some important leadership roles. Leaders are chosen because of their skills in hunting, food collecting, communication, decision making, or other personal abilities. Political leaders, however, generally do not control the group's economic resources or exercise political power as they do in other societies, and there is little, if any, social stratification between political leaders and others in the band. In other words, band societies are highly *egalitarian*, with no major differences between those with and those without wealth or political power. Thus, leaders of bands must lead by persuasion and personal influence, rather than by coercing or withholding resources. Leaders do not maintain a military or police force and thus have no definitive authority.

Tribes are more complex societies with political institutions that unite larger groupings of people into a political system. Generally, tribal societies developed with food production such as small-scale agriculture, known as horticulture or pastoralism, domesticating animals for basic subsistence. Tribes do not have centralized, formal political institutions, but they do have **sodalities**, groups based upon kinship, age, or gender that provide for political organization. For example, in some tribal societies of Papua New Guinea, secret male societies function as political institutions.

Chiefdoms are more complex than tribal societies because they are formalized and centralized. Chiefdoms establish centralized, legitimate authority over many communities exercised through various complex economic, social, and religious institutions. However, despite their size and complexity, chiefdoms are still fundamentally organized by kinship principles. Although chiefdoms have different levels of status and political authority, people within these levels are related to one another through kinship ties.

States are political systems with centralized bureaucratic institutions to establish power and authority over large populations in defined territories. State systems are not based on kinship. Instead, state bureaucracies govern society on behalf of ruling authorities through procedures that plan, direct, and coordinate complex political processes. State political systems range from the early bureaucratic political units of agricultural societies, such as ancient Egypt and China, to the modern industrial and postindustrial societies of the United States, Japan, and numerous European nations.

Nevertheless, it must be emphasized that this classification does not represent a single scheme of political evolution for the entire world. We must emphasize that political evolution did not develop in a one-directional, unilineal type of evolution. The archaeological and ethnographic data demonstrate again and again that a stage-by-stage development or evolution from band to tribe to chiefdom to state did not occur in all areas. Contemporary anthropologists have demonstrated that political evolution is multilineal (see Chapter 8, p. 214). These classifications of band, tribe, chiefdom, and state are to be used only as categories to organize the vast amounts of data accumulated by anthropologists. As with all models, the boundaries separating the various categories are somewhat arbitrary and fuzzy.

Decision Making in a Political System

An important topic in the study of a society is the day-to-day, individual decision making and competition for power and authority. In studying this topic, anthropologists may focus on *fields* or *arenas* within a society. A field is an area in which political interaction and competition take place (Bourdieu 1977). It may involve a part of a society, or it may extend beyond the boundaries of a society. For example, a field could be a whole tribe, a chiefdom, a state, or several of these units. A political arena is a more local network specific in which individual actors or small groups compete for power and authority. An arena may be made up of factions, elites, or political parties in a society. Another aspect of political anthropology is the focus on how political succession occurs within different societies—in other words, who is appointed or elected to a position of political authority or who inherits such a position in a society.

Warfare and Feuds

The study of politics involves an understanding of political conflicts within and among societies. Two major forms of conflicts are warfare and feuds. Anthropologists define **warfare** as armed combat among territorial or political communities. They distinguish between *internal warfare,* which involves political communities within the same society, and *external warfare*, which occurs among different societal groups. A **feud** is a type of armed combat occurring within a political community, revenge seeking among kinship groups (Otterbein 1974; Kelly 2003). Anthropologists examine the different biological, environmental, demographic, economic, social, political, and other cultural variables that influence warfare and feuds.

Law and Social Control

Another aspect of political anthropology is the study of law and social control. As discussed in Chapter 6, one aspect of nonmaterial culture is the normative dimension, sometimes referred to as an *ethos*. All societies maintain an ethos that encourages certain behaviors and prohibits others. This ethos, along with the society's values, makes up the moral code that shapes human behavior. The particular ethos of a society represents an attempt to establish social control through various internal and external mechanisms. The internal mechanisms of social control are built into the enculturation process itself. Through enculturation, people learn the specific norms that make up society's expectations. Thereafter, those who violate these norms frequently experience emotional and cognitive discomfort in the form of guilt. Thus, internalized norms can shape and influence people's behavior, even in the absence of constraints from other people.

Despite these internal mechanisms, however, individuals frequently violate norms. For a variety of reasons, including biological influences on behavior, enculturation does not bring about perfect social control in a society. Hence, in addition to internal mechanisms, societies use external mechanisms to enforce norms. External mechanisms take the form of sanctions: rewards (positive sanctions) for appropriate behaviors and punishments (negative sanctions) for inappropriate behaviors.

Societies vary with respect to both the nature of their moral code and the types of external sanctions used to enforce the moral code. What one societal group considers deviant or unethical may be acceptable to another group. Divorce is an acceptable solution for severe marital conflicts in the United States. In Italy and Ireland, however, despite recent legislation that allows divorce, many still view it as an unethical pattern of behavior.

In large, complex social groups, sanctions are usually highly formalized. Rewards can take the form of public awards, parades, educational or professional degrees, and banquets. Negative sanctions include fines, imprisonment, expulsion, and sometimes death. In small-scale societies, sanctions tend to be informal. Examples of positive sanctions are smiles, handshakes, pats on the back, hugs, and compliments. Negative sanctions include restricted access to certain goods and services, gossip, frowns, impolite treatment, and ostracism.

Law as Formalized Norms and Sanctions Anthropologists describe *laws* as clearly defined norms, violations of which are punished through the application of formal sanctions by ruling authorities. In the 1960s, cultural anthropologist Leopold J. Pospisil attempted to distinguish law from other social norms, based on his research among the Kapaukan tribe of New Guinea. He specified four criteria that must be present for a norm to be considered a law: (1) authority, (2) intention of universal application, (3) obligation, and (4) sanction (1967). To institutionalize legal decisions, a society must have members who possess recognized authority and can, therefore, intervene to settle disputes. These authorities must be able to enforce a verdict by either persuasion or force. Their verdicts must have universal application; that is, these decisions must be applied in the same manner if a similar situation arises in the future. This distinguishes legal decisions from those based purely on political expediency.

Obligation refers to the status relationships among the people involved in the conflict. If status relationships are unequal, the rights, duties, and obligations of the different parties can vary. Legal decisions must attempt to define the rights and obligations of everyone involved and to restore or create an equitable solution for the community. Finally, punitive sanctions must be applied to carry out the legal decision. More recently in ethnographic studies, anthropologists have abandoned any simplistic, universalistic aspect that separates law from norms. Presently, anthropologists study the language, symbolism, and discourse used in society to distinguish legal sanctions along with historical and global developments that have an influence on legal processes. *PoLAR: The Political and Legal Anthropology Review* features many articles by anthropologists as they study legal processes in many different countries.

Religion

9.11 Discuss how anthropologists study religion, myth, ritual, and rites of passage.

As we saw in Chapter 4, archaeologists have discovered some limited evidence of religious beliefs and practices associated with archaic *Homo sapiens neanderthalensis*, or Neandertals, that date back to 100,000 years ago. Religion is a cultural universal, although specific beliefs and practices vary significantly from one society to another. For example, some religions are based on the worship of an all-knowing, all-powerful supreme being, whereas others have many deities, and some may have no deities at all. The term *religion* is derived from the Latin term *religio*, which has had different meanings in Western history. In some cases, it referred to a "transcendent" experience that individuals had beyond normal, everyday social life, but at other times it referred to "superstition" or "piety." It has been extremely difficult for anthropologists to define religion with a simple formula because it varies so much from one region and culture to another (Scupin 2008; Saler 1993; Boyer 2001).

Humans learn their religious traditions through enculturation. Religious convictions are, therefore, shaped by the historical and social situations in which a person lives. For example, a person enculturated in ancient Greece would most likely have believed in many deities, among whom Zeus was the most powerful.

In studying the anthropology of religion, a critical point must be understood: Anthropologists are not concerned with the "truth" or "falsity" of any particular religious belief. As anthropology is partially based on the scientific method, the field of anthropology is not competent or able to investigate supernatural or metaphysical questions that go beyond empirical data. Rather, anthropological research on religion focuses on the relationship of doctrines, beliefs, and other religious questions to aspects of cognition, emotions, and society. Most anthropologists recognize that religious faith is not a testable proposition that can be analyzed by science or logic. Faith is beyond empirical findings that can be uncovered by scientific investigation. The major questions posed by anthropologists are these: How do religious beliefs become established within a society? How do religious beliefs affect, relate to, and reflect the cognitive, emotional, and sociocultural conditions and concerns of a group of people?

In addition, anthropologists often use the humanistic-interpretive approach when analyzing religious beliefs, symbols, and myths. Clifford Geertz offered a definition of religion to use as a tool in this humanistic-interpretive mode of understanding religion:

> *A religion is a system of symbols which acts to establish powerful, pervasive, and long-lasting moods and motivations in men by formulating conceptions of a general order of existence and clothing these conceptions with such an aura of factuality that the moods and motivations seem uniquely realistic. (1973:90)*

Let us examine this definition more closely. Central to any religion is a "system of symbols," which includes all sacred objects, ranging from Christian crucifixes, Native American "medicine pouches," and Buddhist relics to sacred myths such as Genesis or the Ramayana of Hinduism. These symbols produce "moods," such as happiness and sadness, and "motivations" that provide direction or ethical goals in a person's life. Hence, religious symbols enhance particular feelings and dispositions, creating an intense 'sense of awe' in individuals. This sense of awe is induced through the use of sacred symbols in rituals and other religious performances to create an atmosphere of mystery going beyond everyday experience. But religious symbols also create and reaffirm a worldview by "formulating conceptions of a general order of existence." This worldview provides meaning or purpose to life and the universe. A religious worldview helps people discern the meaning of pain and suffering in the world. Sacred myths help people make sense of the world and also explain and justify cultural values and social rules. One problem with Geertz's definition of religion is that it does not recognize the diversity of cultural beliefs and symbolic meanings and the multiplicity of practices and variation within any religious tradition. In other words, as we emphasized in earlier chapters, presently anthropologists are more aware that the concept of a homogeneous culture as used in the past is not useful in understanding different religions or civilizations.

More recently, anthropologist David Parkin has reconstructed Geertz's definition of religion and combined it with a more current anthropological understanding of emotions and cognition in his studies of Muslims in Zanzibar, East Africa (2007). Parkin suggests that Geertz's definition tended to separate emotions and cognition in categorical ways, and today anthropologists recognize that emotions and cognition are inextricably combined. The ethnographic study of the Islamic tradition in Zanzibar by Parkin indicates that these people learn their religion through formal modes of cognition, but unconscious cognitive and emotional processes influence what they learn.

Myths

The study of religious traditions includes the analysis and interpretation of myths. **Myths** consist of a people's assumed knowledge about the universe and the natural and supernatural worlds and about humanity's place in these worlds. In Chapter 3, we presented some basic myths or cosmologies regarding the creation of the universe. All societies have such sacred myths. Anthropologists focus on a number of questions regarding myths: Why do myths of a particular type exist in different societies? What is the relationship between myths and other aspects of sociocultural systems? Are myths distortions of historical events? Or as Geertz suggested, do myths provide a blueprint for comprehending the natural and social worlds for a society? What are the functions of myths? How are myths interpreted and reinterpreted by different people within the society?

Rituals

The final portion of Geertz's definition—that these systems of symbols act to clothe those conceptions in "such an aura of factuality that the moods and motivations seem uniquely realistic"—attempts to deal with the question often asked about religious belief: How do humans come to believe in ideas about spirits, souls, revelations, and many unsupportable or untestable conceptions? Geertz's answer to this question is that religious rituals in which humans participate create an "aura of factuality." It is through ritual that deeper realities are reached. Religion is nonempirical and nonrational in its search for truth. It is not based on conclusions from scientific experience, but is "prior" to experience. Religious truth is not "inductive," providing evidence for metaphysical explanations. It symbolically and abstractly evokes the ultimate concerns of humans. Through ritual activities, these symbolic and abstract nonempirical truths are given meaning.

Religious **rituals** consist of repetitive behaviors that communicate sacred symbols to members of society. Examples of religious rituals are the Catholic Mass, Jewish Passover rites, and Native American sweat lodge rites, which include prayer, meditation, and other spiritual communication. Anthropologist Edmund Leach (1966) emphasized that religious rituals communicate these sacred symbols and information in a condensed manner. He noted that the verbal part of a ritual is not separable from the behavioral part and that rituals can have different symbolic meanings for people in a society. In other words, religious rituals convey a unique, personal, psychological experience for every individual who participates.

Recently, the anthropologist Harvey Whitehouse, using a cognitive-evolutionary approach suggests that there are two different modes of religiosity, the doctrinal and imagistic (Whitehouse 2004). The doctrinal mode is the formal scriptural or oral traditions that are associated with what children and adults learn from constant repetition within their religious tradition. In contrast, the imagistic mode is deeply emotional and results from an intense personal experience that an individual has with their religious tradition. In many cases, Whitehouse suggests, the imagistic mode of religiosity results from what he calls "flashbulb memories" from singular incidents that an individual has in ritual experiences. He has been doing ethnographic research on traumatic puberty life cycle initiation rituals in Melanesia and describes how these rituals create flashbulb memories that result in an imagistic mode of religiosity for these males. These flashbulb memories highlight the "trauma" of these ritual experiences and induce images that remain with individuals throughout their lives. This distinction between doctrinal and imagistic modes of religiosity has been an important means of understanding religious rituals for contemporary anthropologists.

Rites of Passage Anthropologists have done considerable research on the **rites of passage**, rituals associated with the life cycle and the movement of people between different age-status levels. Almost all cultures have rites of passage to demarcate these different stages of the life cycle. Arnold Van Gennep (1960), a Belgian anthropologist, wrote a classic study of different rites of passage throughout the world. He noted similarities among various rites connected with birth, puberty, marriage, and funerals. According to Van Gennep, these rites of passage are characterized by three interconnected stages: *separation*, *marginality*, and *aggregation*.

The first phase, *separation*, transforms people from one age status to another. In this phase, people leave behind the symbols, roles, and norms associated with their former position. The second phase, referred to as *marginality*, places people in a state of transition or a temporary period of ambiguity. This stage often involves separating individuals from the larger society to undergo traditional ordeals or indoctrination. The final phase is *aggregation*, or incorporation, when individuals assume their new status. Later the anthropologist Victor Turner refined the model of Van Gennep and referred to the three stages as *structure*, *antistructure* or *liminality*, and *communitas* (1969). *Structure* is the initial status of the individual. The period of *liminality* is the temporary period of ambiguity, marginality, and antistructure. Turner defined *communitas*, as also part of the antistructure phase, where the individual felt a strong bond and a sense of equality with others. The final phase of the rite of passage is reincorporation, marking a return to and reunion with society with a wholly new status.

The best-known examples of these rites of passage are various religious rituals associated with adolescence, such as the confirmation rituals associated with Catholicism and the *bar mitzvah* and *bat mitzvah* rituals in Judaism. However, college and university graduation ceremonies are a more secular form of a rite of passage for U.S. students.

Religious Specialists

One important area of research in the anthropology of religion is the study of religious specialists in different societies. Every society has certain individuals who possess specialized sacred knowledge. Such individuals officiate over rituals and interpret

Critical Perspectives

Graduation: A Rite of Passage in U.S. Society

As the United States continues to change from an industrial to a postindustrial society, more people are attending college to gain the skills and knowledge necessary to prepare them for careers. Consequently, one rite of passage that people increasingly look forward to is graduation. This rite of passage is similar to those in many other societies. Rites of passage, as mentioned above, are described by anthropologists as rituals that change the status of an individual within society. The late Victor Turner divided rites of passage into three distinctive stages: an initial structured phase (the original status of the individual); a liminal phase, wherein the individual is in a highly ambiguous and antistructured status called "communitas," where the student feels a strong emotional bond with others of equal status. In the final stage, the individual is reincorporated back into society with a new status (1969).

For most students, their undergraduate university or college education is a time of "liminality" or an ambiguous, transitional period of life. This liminal period is marked by an extensive four or five years of study, examinations, and research papers, as well as other social activities. During this liminal phase, students are neither children nor adults. If they reside on campus in dormitories or residence halls, they live separate from society. Like the initiates in rites of passage in small-scale societies, the students are exposed to former types of "secret knowledge," such as evolution or more controversial views of sexuality, gender, and religion. Students are often taken away from their local neighborhoods and locales and placed with other students from ethnic and class backgrounds different from their own. This liminal period is often a time of stress and uncertainty. The commencement ceremony marks the final stage of the rite of passage, as the graduates reenter society with a wholly new status.

The commencement ceremony dates back to the twelfth century at the University of Bologna in what is now Italy. Shortly thereafter, it spread to other European universities. The first U.S. graduates went through their commencement in 1642 at Harvard College. These first commencement ceremonies lasted several days and were accompanied by entertainment, wrestling matches, banquets, and dances.

The academic costumes worn by graduates come directly from the late Middle Ages and the Renaissance. The black gowns and square caps, called mortarboards, were donned to celebrate the change in status. A precise ritual dictates that the tassel that hangs off the cap should be moved from the right side to the left side when the degree is conferred.

Like rites of passage in other societies, graduation from college represents a transition in status. In Latin, *gradus* means "a step," and *degradus* means "a rung on a ladder." From the first, we get the word *graduation*; from the second, *degree*. Both words are connected to a stage in life, the end of one period of life and the beginning of another. To graduate means to change by degrees.

Typically, college graduates move from the status of a receiver to that of a giver. During the liminal period, many students are subsidized and nurtured by society and especially by parents. However, after graduation, and reincorporation back into society, they become givers in all sorts of ways. A degree qualifies graduates for jobs and careers to which they would not otherwise have access. Upon getting their jobs, former students will be givers and contribute to the workplace. In addition, degree holders will begin to subsidize others through taxes. Many will marry and accept such responsibilities as raising children and paying mortgages. This movement from receiver to giver represents a fundamental life-cycle transition for many U.S. students.

Points to Ponder

1. As you move toward your degree in college, do you believe that what you are learning has any relationship to what you will need after your change in status?
2. In what ways would you change the educational process so that it would help you develop your potential?
3. Do you think the grading system used by most colleges and universities is a fair means of assessing your acquisition of knowledge and skills?
4. What would you suggest as a better means of evaluating students?
5. What kinds of expectations do you have about your change in status after you receive your degree?

myths. The type of religious specialist varies with the form of sociocultural system. **Shamans** are usually part-time religious practitioners who are believed to have contact with supernatural beings and powers. They do not have a formalized official status as religious practitioners in their respective societies. Shamans are involved in various types of healing activities, treating both physical and psychological illnesses. Aside from their religious functions, they participate in the same subsistence activities and functions as anyone else in their society. Anthropologists also use terms such as *native healer*, *medicine man*, and *medicine woman* to refer to these practitioners.

The terms **priest** and **priestess** refer to full-time religious specialists who serve in an official capacity as a custodian of sacred knowledge. In contrast to shamans, priests and priestesses are usually trained through formal educational processes to maintain religious traditions and rituals. Priests and priestesses are usually associated with more complex sociocultural systems.

Religious Movements

Another topic of interest in the anthropology of religion is the analysis of religious movements. In early approaches within the social sciences, religion was viewed simply as an outcome of certain economic or political conditions in society. It was assumed that as society developed modern economic and political institutions, religious traditions would disappear. Religion was viewed as a peripheral element that served only to conserve society as a static system. Today, however, some anthropologists have begun to analyze religious beliefs and practices as major variables that induce societal change. For example, cultural anthropologists studying Islamic fundamentalist movements have concluded that, in the Middle East, religion is a major force for social change.

Cognition and Religion

9.12 Discuss the new developments by cognitive anthropologists and their understanding of religion.

In Chapter 6, we introduced the field of cognitive anthropology. A number of cognitive anthropologists such as Pascal Boyer, Scott Atran, Harvey Whitehouse, Stewart Guthrie, and Joseph Henrich have drawn on their research in order to explore religion. In Boyer's *Religion Explained: The Evolutionary Origins of Religious Thought* (2001) and Atran's *In Gods We Trust: The Evolutionary Landscape of Religion* (2002), these anthropologists recognize the importance of the humanistic-interpretive approach in understanding religion, but they also want to explore the scientific-causal aspects of religion and the universal aspects of religion everywhere. These anthropologists investigate questions such as these: Why does religion matter so much in people's lives everywhere? Are there any common features of religion? Why do certain types of religious beliefs develop rather than other types? Drawing upon a vast range of cross-cultural data, these anthropologists suggest that evolution and natural selection have designed the human mind to be "religious." Although there is a tremendous diversity of religious traditions throughout the world, some types of religious beliefs have more resilience and are retained and culturally transmitted by humans more than others. In all societies, children are exposed to various religious beliefs and practices. But as Atran and Boyer emphasize, because of specific predispositions and intuitions within our evolutionary-designed minds, certain forms of religious beliefs and concepts have exceptional relevance and meaning for humans.

In a related discussion regarding some of the most common features of religion, cognitive anthropologist Stewart Guthrie argues that human religious beliefs and concepts are based on the cognitive phenomena of anthropomorphism.

Anthropomorphism is the psychological disposition to project and perceive human characteristics in nonhuman phenomena. In his book *Faces in the Clouds: A New Theory of Religion,* Guthrie suggests that anthropomorphism is an inherent aspect of our cognitive and thinking processes (1993). As humans perceive the world, they tend to project human agency-like characteristics into the world. For example, when we look at clouds, we tend to perceive human "faces in the cloud." Guthrie draws on worldwide ethnographic data to indicate many similar phenomena reported by people. When humans project these human agency-like characteristics, in many cases they are attributed to unseen agents such as deities, spirits, or supernatural forces. Humans attribute agency to many types of nonhuman entities including clouds, computers, wind, or other phenomena. Guthrie asserts that as we grapple with complex phenomena, our cognitive processes use our understanding of persons and humans to interpret these complex phenomena. These cognitive processes are unconscious, but they have consequences for the emergence of religious thinking in all humans.

In contrast to the intuitive knowledge and inferences that become a reliable basis for comprehending the natural and social worlds, both Atran and Boyer emphasize that religious beliefs and knowledge are mostly counterintuitive. Religious spirits and gods have properties that normal people do not have. Although most humans treat religious spirits and gods as persons, they are radically different from what our intuitions tell us about persons. For the most part, they do not eat, grow old, or die; they can even fly through space, become invisible, change shape, and perceive our innermost thoughts. Gods and spirits become invisible partners and friends of people, but these spiritual beings are unlike normal persons. These spiritual agents can be at several places at one time and have full access to our innermost thoughts and specific behaviors and actions. Some societies have a concept of a god that knows everything. Children at an early age and adults understand that normal people do not have these capacities for knowledge.

These counterintuitive abilities of spirits and gods, including their full access to our thoughts and specific behaviors, are "attention-grabbing" for humans throughout the world. Spiritual agents who have this full access to knowledge become extremely relevant in understanding human social and moral conditions. Beings that can know our innermost thoughts and all of our behaviors resonate with our social and moral intuitions. Thus, religious beliefs and concepts become widespread and plausible in all societies because of the way human cognition is organized and designed. Beliefs in witches, ancestral spirits, and angry or beneficent gods become easily represented in all cultures because they are dependent on our human cognitive capacities and intuitive understanding of the natural and social worlds. These religious phenomena activate and trigger our human cognitive capacities and intuitive abilities, which results in the universal distribution of certain types of spiritual beliefs and concepts.

These cognitive anthropologists explain why religious beliefs have become so powerful throughout human prehistory and history. They do not suggest that there is a specialized area of the brain or "religious instinct" that is a religious center that handles god- or spiritual-related thoughts. In addition, they do not suggest that there are specific people who have exceptional religious abilities and were responsible for establishing religious beliefs and practices. Religion, like other everyday matters in our natural and social circumstances, does not require special capacities. Rather, religious beliefs and concepts become relevant to humans everywhere because they readily coincide with our cognitive capacities and our intuitive and inferential abilities. These religious beliefs and concepts are likely to have a direct effect on people's thoughts, emotions, and morality.

Additionally, many religious beliefs are different from our everyday commonsense beliefs and intuitions. Religious beliefs have commonalities such as spiritual agents that have full access to our innermost thoughts, concepts of life after death, and concepts of morality all over the world, and most likely have a long evolutionary history.

Other religious beliefs may have developed in the past, but they did not have the sustaining power of the ones known today, and they disappeared. The religious beliefs that still exist have a central relevance to many people, are extremely powerful, and converge with their cognitive capacities and abilities. In some cases, people may give up their lives or kill others based on their particular religious beliefs. These cognitive anthropological explorations of the interconnection between human cognition and religious expression have contributed to anthropological hypotheses about our cognitive capacities and about links between biological and psychological developments and our religious life.

Recently, a number of cognitive anthropologists have combined the cognitive approach to religion described above with an understanding of how religious beliefs and rituals induce both cooperation within groups and enmity between different groups (Atran 2010; Atran and Henrich 2010; Whitehouse 2004). Many small scale band, tribal, and chiefdom societies have "prosocial" norms based on reciprocity, sharing, and kinship for cooperation among individuals. **Prosocial norms** are cultural rules that encourage cooperation and altruistic behavior within society. However, how are "prosocial norms" for cooperation among people maintained in large-scale societies and interrelationships that are no longer based directly on reciprocity and kinship relations? Cognitive anthropologists suggest that as large-scale agricultural civilizations develop, major religious traditions and shared sacred values, beliefs, and rituals become the stabilizing "prosocial norms" for cooperation among people who no longer share kinship connections (Atran 2010; Atran and Henrich 2010; Whitehouse 2004; Whitehouse and Martin 2004). Building large-scale monuments (e.g. temples and pyramids) involved increasing commitments of labor to sustain particular religious beliefs and sacred values. These activities were costly to the individuals. The people who did not participate in these costly activities tended to be punished by members of their societies. Thus, most individuals tended to cooperate and participate in the costly activities. These costly activities produced cooperation and collective action among people of different family and socioeconomic backgrounds.

However, as these complex religious traditions and sacred values reinforced group solidarity and cooperation, economic and demographic expansion frequently resulted in conflict and warfare between different agricultural civilizations. This competition and conflict among civilizations led people to become more deeply committed to particular religious beliefs and practices within their own groups. Cooperation to defend one's own civilization and religious tradition became essential (Atran 2010; Atran and Henrich 2010; Whitehouse 2004; Whitehouse and Martin 2004). According to these cognitive anthropologists, this competition among agricultural civilizations and their religious traditions expanded the sphere of cooperation and solidarity within groups, but often created the potential for enmity and conflict between different groups.

Aesthetics: Art and Music

9.13 Discuss how anthropologists study art and music in different societies.

As described in Chapter 1, many anthropologists study the art and music of different societies throughout the world. Anthropologists define **art** as a diverse range of activities and skills, and the products of those activities that are used as expressions and representations of human emotions, intellect, and creativity. Art includes different modes of painting, sculpture, printmaking, photography, and other visual media. *Architecture* is also an art form that involves the practical applications of creative expression in its buildings and structures. **Music** is an art form that is based on the organization of sounds in combination and in temporal relationships to produce audible works for performance in various communities. The field of ethnomusicology is the study of music as it is connected with the cultural traditions in different societies. Ethnomusicologists study songs, dances, musical instruments and compositions, and other dramatic performances that accompany music.

Anthropologists and ethnomusicologists discuss how art and music have distinct functions for societies and individuals. Art and music help create social bonds through shared creative experiences and expressions of group identity. In addition, art and music enhances cognitive flexibility and reduces emotional anxiety for individuals. Art assists individuals and groups in extending their daily sensory and imaginary experiences outside of the present, into the future, and back to the past. Art and music can aid the construction of beliefs and patterns of morality as these creative processes interconnect with myths, legends, and collective narratives of their particular group. In all societies, art and music enter into childhood enculturation and help situate individuals within their environments. Often the major rites of passage and ceremonies regarding birth, initiation, coming of age, marriage, and death are accompanied by art and music. The symbolic imagery produced in art and music produce an imaginary world that assists in the cognitive and emotional development that are indispensable for human adaptations and are important sources of a meaningful life.

In Western societies for many years both art and music are usually associated with the fine arts or "high culture." Recall our discussion of anthropologist/sociologist Pierre Bourdieu's discussion of different forms of capital—economic capital, social capital, and cultural capital (see p. 242 above). Bourdieu described cultural capital as based on the *aesthetic* tastes and preferences for certain symbolic forms of literature, art, music, or foods that distinguished people with respect to their socioeconomic background (1984). For many centuries, the upper-class elites of Western societies determined and established the criteria for *aesthetic* tastes, or preferences for what was beautiful or inspirational in fine art and music. Elite expressions of Western culture fine art were usually contrasted with popular, folk, or "primitive" art or music. This folk, "primitive," or popular art or music was characterized as less refined or backward and less sophisticated than fine art. However, anthropologists take a much broader cross-cultural view of art and music than the Western elite. Although Franz Boas discussed the art in Northwest Coast American Indian cultures and titled his book *Primitive Art* (1927), this work challenged the assumptions of the earlier elite understandings of art. Boas stressed the principle of cultural relativism and debunked the categories of "savages," or "primitive," versus civilized peoples (see Chapter 6). Anthropologists emphasize that art and musical expression are universal and found in all societies (Brown 1991). Ethnomusicologists and anthropologists who study music and art find that what is considered beautiful or refined in art and music is dependent on the complex cultural context in different societies. Thus, they challenge the Western elite views of *aesthetics* regarding perceptions of beauty and tastes in art and music. This anthropological perspective entails a framework that includes the entire world's catalog of art and music that express and represent human emotions, intellect, and creativity.

A contemporary indigenous painting called "Honey Ant Dreaming" by Australian aborigine artist Marion Swift.

Cross-Cultural Research

9.14 Describe the strengths and limitations of the cross-cultural approach.

This chapter has focused on the fieldwork by cultural anthropologists and the different types of sociocultural systems they study. Although the primary objective of ethnographic research is to improve our understanding of a particular sociocultural system, another aim is to provide a basis for comparing different societies and to offer general explanations for human behavior. Specific ethnographies provide the necessary data for this type of cross-cultural research. This cross-cultural research is usually referred to as *ethnological research*. Anthropologists use ethnological research to explore the universal and specific cultural conditions that influence the development of societies throughout the world.

Cross-cultural research has been an ongoing project in anthropology for the past hundred years or so. Recently, a great deal of ethnographic data has been computerized in the Human Relations Area Files, commonly known as the HRAF. The HRAF contains descriptive ethnographic data on more than 300 societies. Initiated by George P. Murdock of Yale University, it is made up of original ethnographic descriptions classified for cross-cultural research purposes. Murdock incorporated data on 862 societies in his *Ethnographic Atlas* (1981b) and on 563 societies that cover the major geographic regions of the world in his *Atlas of World Cultures* (1981a). These ethnographic databases enable scholars to retrieve information quickly and can be used for statistical and computerized cross-cultural research. They are extremely valuable sources for assessing the differences and similarities among cultures. Cross-cultural studies allow anthropologists to make distinctions between behaviors that are culture specific and those that are universal. These distinctions help anthropologists provide general explanations for human behavior. In doing so, these studies help fulfill the major goals of anthropological research.

Cross-cultural methods have some limitations, however. One major weakness is that some cultural anthropologists in the past may not have taken historical circumstances into account when describing the particular conditions in a society. This omission may have led to a static, unchanging portrait of the society studied. For example, the description of the economic practices of people in Africa, Asia, or the Pacific Islands may not make sense outside of a specific historical context. These societies had historical relationships with other societies outside of their own cultural boundaries, and these relationships resulted in changes in the particular economic practices observed by the cultural anthropologist. Cultural anthropologists must understand the historical context of the different societies that they study so that they can fully comprehend the behavior being observed.

Another problem with cross-cultural studies lies with faulty ethnographic reporting, which can produce unreliable data, contributing, in turn, to a distorted image of the society being studied. Consequently, anthropologists approach cross-cultural research with caution. Contemporary anthropologists who use these data must review the work of their predecessors who gathered the basic information to assess its validity. Through careful examination of the original data in the HRAF and other cross-cultural databases, modern anthropologists will make further progress toward formulating sound generalizations regarding the cultures of humankind.

Summary and Review of Learning Objectives

9.1 Discuss how cultural anthropologists prepare to study society and culture.

Cultural anthropologists conduct fieldwork in different societies to examine people's lifestyles and behavior. They have to develop a research design to examine a particular topic that specifies the appropriate methods for gathering the richest possible data. Before going into the field for direct research, the cultural anthropologist analyzes available archival data, including photos, films, missionary reports, business and government surveys, musical recordings, journalistic accounts, diaries, court documents, medical records, birth, landholding documents, and death, marriage, and tax records. Historical material in the archives helps the cultural anthropologist evaluate the usefulness of the observations and interviews he or she will document. They must also read the published anthropological, historical, economic, sociological, and political science literature on the geographic region toward which they are heading.

9.2 Describe the actual research methods used for ethnographic studies.

Ethnographic studies are based on participant observation, the use of key informants, extensive interviewing, and the collection of both quantitative and qualitative data. They describe societies in written studies called ethnographies, which focus upon behavior and thought among the people studied. Cultural anthropologists must use systematic research methods and strategies in their examination of society.

9.3 Discuss some of the ethical dilemmas of ethnographic research.

In conducting ethnographic research, the cultural anthropologist may encounter some ethical dilemmas that may be harmful to the subjects of the studies. The American Anthropological Association has produced ethical guidelines that emphasize "doing no harm" among the people being studied. One recent ethical dilemma is whether anthropologists should participate in studies in war zones where they consult and advise the military.

9.4 How do cultural anthropologists analyze their ethnographic data?

In their analyses of sociocultural systems, anthropologists investigate cause-and-effect relationships among different independent and dependent variables. They use a multidimensional approach, examining the interaction among many variables to provide explanations for the similarities (universals) and differences among societies.

9.5 Discuss how subsistence is influenced by the physical environment (biomes).

A biome is an area distinguished by a particular climate and certain types of plants and animals. Biomes may be classified by certain attributes, such as mean rainfall, temperature, soil conditions, and vegetation that support certain forms of animal life. Cultural ecologists investigate the relationship between specific biomes and human sociocultural systems. Biomes influence the kind of subsistence patterns that humans develop primarily through cultural solutions. For example, deserts, tropical rain forests or Arctic environments demand different subsistence patterns.

9.6 Describe how anthropologists study population with reference to fertility, mortality, and migration.

To measure fertility—the number of births in a society—demographic anthropologists use the crude birth rate, that is, the number of live births in a given year for every thousand people in a population. They also measure mortality—the incidence of death in a society's population—by using the crude death rate, that is, the number of deaths in a given year for every thousand people in a population. In measuring the migration rate—the movement of people into and out of a specified territory—demographic anthropologists determine the number of in-migrants (people moving into the territory) and the number of out-migrants (people moving out of the territory). They then use these numbers to calculate the net migration, which indicates the general movement of the population in and out of the territory.

9.7 Discuss the anthropological explanations of technology.

Most anthropologists recognize that technology is one of the most important variables that impact a sociocultural system. However, anthropologists are cautious about technological determinism, the view that technology determines all aspects of society. Anthropologists have concluded that technology alone does not result in cultural change and transformation, but rather cultural values, beliefs, and practices interact with technology to create changes.

9.8 Discuss how anthropologists study economics in different societies.

Anthropologists have studied the economics of various societies by analysing the production, exchange, and consumption of goods and services. Contemporary anthropologists use both formalist and substantivist approaches in understanding different forms of economic systems.

9.9 Discuss the general components of social structure, including status, the family, marriage, gender, and age.

Status is a recognized position that a person occupies in society. A person's status determines where he or she fits into society in relationship to everyone else. Status may be based on or accompanied by wealth, power, prestige, or a combination of all of these. All societies recognize both *ascribed* and *achieved* statuses. When an individual occupies a particular status, they play a role based on the norms associated with the status. Anthropologists define the family as a social group of two or more people related by blood, marriage, or adoption who live or reside together for an extended period, sharing economic resources and caring for their young. The two main types of family found throughout the world are the nuclear family and the extended family. Marriage is a social bond sanctioned by society between two or more people that involves economic cooperation, social obligations, rights, duties, and sometimes culturally approved sexual activity. Anthropologists find different patterns of marriage including monogamy and polygamy. Forms of polygamy include polygyny and polyandry. Gender is the culturally based human traits that are assigned to individuals based on their sex (biological traits). Although sex characteristics are biologically determined, gender roles vary in accordance with the technological, economic, and sociocultural conditions of particular types of societies. Age is a universal principle used to prescribe social status in sociocultural systems.

9.10 Discuss how anthropologists understand politics, warfare, and law.

Anthropologists have been influenced by Max Weber's understanding of politics. Weber defined political power as the ability to achieve personal ends despite opposition. In this sense, political power can be based on physical or psychological *coercion*. Weber perceived this type of political power as *illegitimate*, in that it is unacceptable to most members of a society. Anthropologists analyze the basis of political power, authority, and decision making in different forms of sociocultural systems, bands, tribes, chiefdoms, and states. Anthropologists define warfare as armed combat among territorial or political communities. They distinguish between *internal warfare*, which involves political communities within the same society or culture, and *external warfare*, which occurs among different societal groups. A feud is a type of armed combat occurring within a political community and usually involving one kin group taking revenge against another kin group. Laws are understood as formalized norms with sanctions found in different societies. Four criteria must be present for a norm to be considered a law: (1) authority, (2) intention of universal application, (3) obligation, and (4) sanction.

9.11 Discuss how anthropologists study religion, myth, ritual, and rites of passage.

Clifford Geertz's definition of religion as *a system of symbols which acts to establish powerful, pervasive, and long-lasting moods and motivations in men by formulating conceptions of a general order of existence and clothing these conceptions with such an aura of factuality that the moods and motivations seem uniquely realistic* has been very influential in the interpretative-humanistic understanding of religion in different societies. Central to any religion is a "system of symbols," which includes all sacred objects such as Christian crucifixes, Islamic crescents, or Buddhist relics to sacred myths such as Genesis or the Ramayana of Hinduism. These symbols produce "moods," such as happiness and sadness, and "motivations" that provide direction or ethical goals in a person's life. Religious symbols enhance particular feelings and dispositions, creating an intense sense of awe in individuals. This sense of awe is induced through the use of sacred symbols in rituals and other religious performances to create an atmosphere of mystery going beyond everyday experience. But religious symbols also create and reaffirm a worldview by "formulating conceptions of a general order of existence." This worldview provides meaning or purpose to life and the universe. A religious worldview helps people discern the meaning of pain and suffering in the world. Sacred myths help people make sense of the world and also explain and justify cultural values and social rules. Despite some modern criticisms, this definition provided a means of studying religions in different societies.

Myths consist of a people's assumed knowledge about the universe and the natural and supernatural worlds and about humanity's place in these worlds. Religious rituals consist of repetitive behaviors that communicate sacred symbols to members of society. Anthropologists participate and describe rituals of many different cultures.

Anthropologists discuss three stages of rites of passage as (1) *structure*, (2) *antistructure* (or *liminality*, and *communitas*), and (3) *reincorporation*. *Structure* is the initial status of the individual. The period of *liminality* is the temporary period of ambiguity, marginality, and antistructure. *Communitas* is also part of the antistructural phase where the individual felt a strong bond and a sense of equality with others. The final phase of the rite of passage is reincorporation, marking a return to and reunion with society with a wholly new status.

9.12 Discuss the new developments by cognitive anthropologists and their understanding of religion.

Cognitive anthropologists assess the evidence from psychologists on how children learn their religious beliefs and concepts based upon some innate predispositions and "intuitive knowledge" that are an aspect of human nature. Anthropomorphism, the psychological disposition to project and perceive human characteristics in nonhuman phenomena, is found in all societies. Children and adults attribute human agency-like characteristics into the world, which appears to be an inherent aspect of our cognitive and thinking processes. Many of the beliefs about gods and spirits are counterintuitive, but many of the beliefs coincide with our cognitive capacities, intuitive knowledge, and human emotions. Cognitive anthropologists also explore how religion produces prosocial norms and group stability and cooperation within groups, but simultaneously increase the possibility of conflict with external groups.

9.13 Discuss how anthropologists study art and music in different societies.

Ethnomusicologists and anthropologists who study music and art find that what is considered beautiful or refined in art and music is dependent on the complex cultural context in different societies. Thus, they challenge the Western elite views of *aesthetics* regarding perceptions of beauty and tastes in art and music. The elite views were based on distinctions between "high culture" or "fine art," versus "folk" or "primitive art." Anthropologists introduced the concept of cultural relativism into the study of art and music.

9.14 Describe the strengths and limitations of the cross-cultural approach.

Many ethnographic data have been coded for computer use in cross-cultural studies. These cross-cultural studies can be employed to develop general explanations regarding human behavior in specific societies and across cultural boundaries. Yet, a major weakness is that some cultural anthropologists in the past may not have taken historical circumstances into account when describing the particular conditions in a society. This omission may have led to a static, unchanging portrait of the society studied. Another problem with cross-cultural studies lies with faulty ethnographic reporting, which can produce unreliable data, contributing, in turn, to a distorted image of the society being studied. Consequently, anthropologists approach cross-cultural research with caution. Contemporary anthropologists who use these data must review the work of their predecessors who gathered the basic information to assess its validity.

Key Terms

Chapter 10

Applied Anthropology

Chapter Outline

Learning Objectives

After reading this chapter you should be able to:

10.1 Describe the different roles of applied anthropologists.

10.2 Discuss the applied aspects of biological anthropology.

10.3 Define medical anthropology and discuss some of the research undertaken.

10.4 Define cultural resource management and discuss the role of archaeologists in the field.

10.5 Discuss the role of the NAGPRA legislation in the U.S.

10.6 Discuss the applied aspects of cultural anthropology.

10.7 Discuss how applied anthropologists are engaged in human rights research.

Anthropologists undertake wide-ranging research in the discipline's four basic subfields: biological anthropology, archaeology, linguistics, and cultural anthropology. Within these subfields, there are diverse specializations that focus on the spectrum of human societies and their behaviors in the past and present, as well as human origins and modern human variation. As mentioned in Chapter 1, however, one of the most important areas of the discipline is **applied anthropology**, the use of anthropological research to provide practical solutions to problems faced by modern societies. Applied anthropology embraces each of the discipline's four basic fields. Indeed, some anthropologists have suggested that *all* anthropological research has the potential of practical application: It may be "applied." This chapter examines some of the areas of biological anthropology, archaeology, linguistics, and cultural anthropology that deal with the application of anthropological information in solving practical problems in the modern world.

The Roles of the Applied Anthropologist

10.1 Describe the different roles of applied anthropologists.

The popular, if not accurate, images of anthropologists vary from the adventurous explorer in search of lost treasure to the absent-minded professor working away in the dusty halls of a museum. These perspectives, however entertaining, do not represent the modern anthropologist. Anthropologists are increasingly engaged in activities that have direct relevance to the modern world. Rather than being confined to the halls of the university, an increasing number of anthropologists have become practitioners of anthropology, actively engaging with the communities that they study and solving problems. These concerns range from assisting in murder investigations and protecting cultural resources, to assisting in development projects and medical treatment in different cultural settings.

Distinguishing applied anthropology from the other subdisciplines of anthropology in many respects presents a false dichotomy. Methodological, as well as theoretical, concerns are shared by all; the difference lies in perceptions of the anthropologists' objectives, an arbitrary division based on the practicality of the intended outcomes. As the renowned cultural anthropologist Bronislaw Malinowski observed more than 60 years ago: "Unfortunately, there is still a strong but erroneous opinion in some circles that practical anthropology is fundamentally different from theoretical or academic anthropology. The truth is that science begins with application. . . . What is application in science and when does 'theory' become practical? When it first allows us a definite grip on empirical reality" (1945:5).

Much of anthropological research can be seen as applied in some sense. Reviewing applied anthropology, Erve Chambers (1985) classified the different roles of applied anthropologists. Although he was primarily concerned with the applied aspects of cultural anthropology, his observations are equally relevant to the field's other subdisciplines. Chambers considered the varied roles of the anthropologist as: representative, facilitator, informant, analyst, and mediator. As a *representative*, the anthropologist becomes the spokesperson for the particular group being studied. Anthropologists have, for example, represented Native American communities in negotiations with state and federal authorities, mining companies, and development organizations. Anthropologists can also be seen as *facilitators*. In this capacity, anthropologists actively help bring about change or development in the community being researched. They may take a proactive, participatory role in economic or social change to improve medical care, education, or public facilities.

An alternative position is the *informant role*, in which the applied anthropologist transfers cultural knowledge obtained from anthropological research to federal, state, or international agencies that are working to promote change in particular areas. The U.S. government, for example, has long employed anthropologists as on-site researchers to provide data on how local-level service clients and delivery agencies respond to government policy. Informally, many archaeologists and anthropologists become involved in local activities and educational programs that present anthropological findings to the public.

Yet another role of applied anthropologists is that of *analyst*. Rather than being just a provider of data, the practicing anthropologist sometimes becomes engaged in the actual formulation of policy. In the United States, this has become an important area for archaeologists with the passage of the National Historic Preservation Act in 1966, the Native American Graves Repatriation Act of 1990, and other related cultural resources legislation. These laws provide increased protection for some archaeological resources by mandating the consideration of archaeological resources in planning development, and also insure the recognition of Native American concerns. Archaeologists have increasingly found employment in federal, state, or local governments, reviewing proposals for development and construction projects that impact cultural resources and archaeological sites.

Another role Chambers identified is that of *mediator*, which involves the anthropologist as an intermediary among different interest groups that are participating in a development project. This may include private developers, government officials, and the people who will be affected by the project. As mediator, the anthropologist must try to reconcile differences among these groups, facilitating compromises that ideally will benefit all parties involved in the project. The following discussions highlight some of the applied work that biological anthropologists, archaeologists, and cultural anthropologists are engaged in.

Biological Anthropology

10.2 Discuss the applied aspects of biological anthropology.

As seen in the preceding chapters, biological anthropologists deal with humans as a biological species, studying biological aspects of humans in the past and the present. Some of the basic information they gather focuses on human variation, and includes the measurement, observation, and explanation of various physical characteristics. Anthropometry, for example, concerns the measurement of human body parts, while osteometry is the measurement of skeletal elements. This information is basic to the interpretation of fossil hominins, as well as human remains recovered from archaeological sites. However, some of this information also has immediate relevance to the present. Such information may be used in combination with engineering data to design ergonomically efficient airplane cockpits, work environments, or equipment. Such data may also provide important assistance to the police in murder investigations or the identification of disaster victims. Physical anthropological study of the causes of diseases, when combined with knowledge of cultural anthropology, offers important insight into perceptions of medical treatment in different cultural settings. Some of these examples of practicing anthropologists are considered in this section.

Forensic Anthropology

A fragmentary skeleton is accidentally found in a desolate part of the desert. Through a series of twists and turns, an enterprising detective pieces together clues to a 20-year-old murder and brings a fugitive to justice. Such a scenario is the stuff of mystery novels, but real-life criminal investigations often do depend upon the identification of fragmentary skeletal remains. **Forensic anthropology** can be defined as the application of biological anthropological data to law (Byers 2008). Biological anthropologists in this area of specialization are often called to assist police when unidentified human remains are found. Whereas human biologists and medical doctors focus on the body's soft tissues, forensic anthropologists study the hard tissues—the skeletal remains (Reichs 1998; Steadman 2009). Analysis of such material begins by reconstructing the skeleton and joining together the often fragmentary and broken remains. Missing pieces might be reconstructed or estimated. The materials are then carefully measured and compared to anthropological data. This information may yield clues regarding the sex, approximate age, height, and physical characteristics of an individual.

Skeletal remains also provide a record of medical problems, illnesses, and the overall health of a person. The bones may preserve information about a person's health at the time of death, as well as the living conditions and health problems the individual faced during his or her lifetime. For example, broken bones, although healed, still leave a trace on the skeleton. Arthritis, certain infections, dietary stress, and nutrition may also be in evidence. This kind of information may provide insight into living conditions in the distant human past, as, for example, when considering health and nutrition in ancient societies, but it also provides details that may be helpful to the police in identifying victims. Unidentified skeletal remains from a white female, 5'4" to 5'6", 40 to 45 years of age, with a healed fracture of the left leg and traces of arthritis in the hands, would dramatically reduce the number of potential fits with reported missing person files.

Forensic Facial Reconstruction A very specialized area within forensic anthropology deals with the reconstruction of faces (Prag and Neave 1997; Wilkinson 2004). Using average skin depths, muscle patterns, and knowledge derived from the skull, the researcher creates an image of what a person looked like when alive. This interdisciplinary work draws on information from anatomy, facial surgery, pathology, dentistry, and biological anthropology, as well as the skills of the artist.

A variety of different approaches have been used, including two-dimensional sketches by artists, computer reconstructions, or even detailed models based on reconstructed skulls. In the latter case, underlying muscles of clay are sculpted over the skull, or a model of it, and then covered with additional clay that represents the overlying tissues. The thickness of the skin is based on average thickness at different points of the skull, estimated for individuals of different ages, sexes, body builds, and ethnic groups—information that is inferred from the skeletal remains. A final model is prepared using plaster of Paris, which is colored and given hair and eyes.

Forensic facial reconstruction is not without its limitations. As discussed in Chapter 5, humans vary tremendously in terms of their physical attributes, even within populations. While average tissue thicknesses may be calculated, there is not

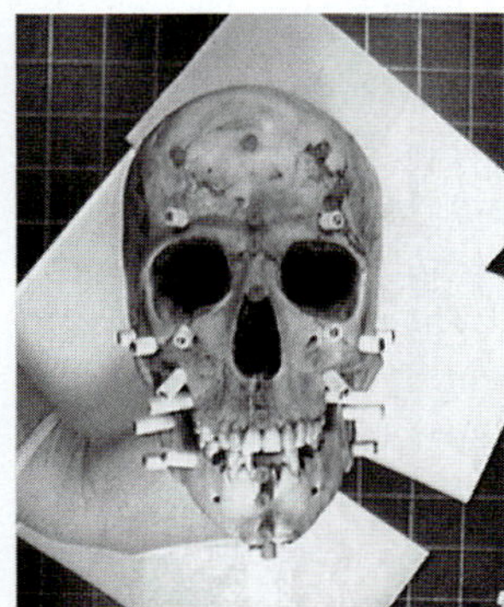
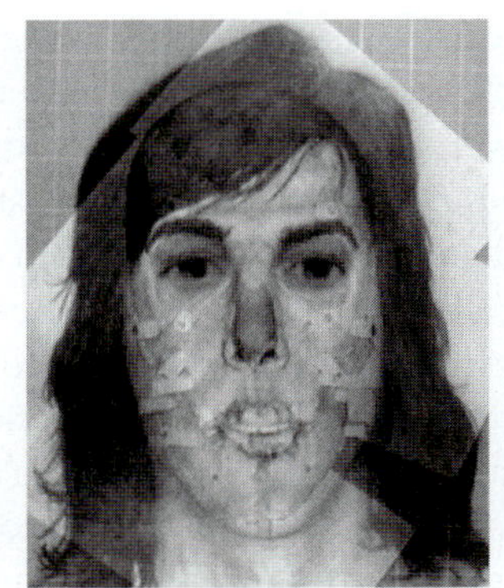
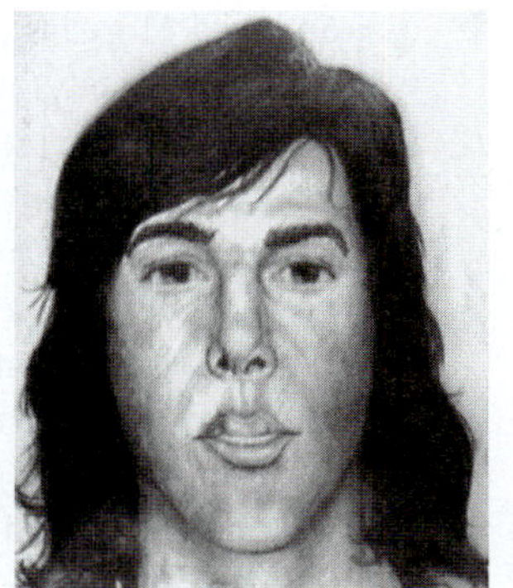
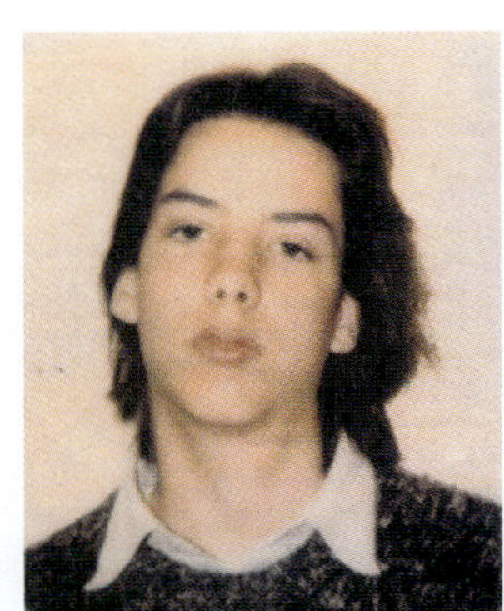

A specialized area of forensic anthropology deals with the reconstruction of facial features. The photographs illustrate (from left) the victim's skull, a reconstruction of the face, a sketch based on the reconstruction, and a photograph of how the victim actually appeared in life.
Source: Courtesy of Gene O'Donnell, FBI.

unanimous agreement on the most appropriate methods to use and the characteristics present in specific individuals may vary widely (Iscan and Helmer 1993). In many instances, researchers may also have very limited information to infer things such as hair or skin color. Interpretations can, therefore, be quite subjective. Nevertheless, techniques such as these, whether using a pen and ink, a computer, or plaster models, help police put flesh on the bones and can be invaluable in investigations. Although the final products may not always be exact portraits, in some instances the resemblance to the living individual has proven remarkable.

Determining the Cause of Death Forensic anthropology may also offer important clues about the actual circumstances of a person's death, as well as the treatment of the body after death (Byers 2008; Haglund and Sorg 1997; Steadman 2009). Damage or trauma to the bones may provide a primary indicator of the cause of death. For example, bullet wounds, stabbings, and blunt-force trauma may be identified in skeletal remains. Careful study of the skeleton may also indicate whether an individual was killed where the body was found, or at another location and then transported to the burial site. Forensic anthropologists may also be able to determine whether the body was disturbed or moved after burial. Such information may be extremely important in determining the cause of death. However, it may be equally important in reconstructing the events surrounding it. As in the case of archaeological and paleontological investigations, the *context* of the findings is very important. Hence, biological anthropologists with archaeological training can help ensure that all of the remains are recovered.

Because the cause of death may be central to a murder investigation and trial, the forensic anthropologist is often called upon to testify as an expert witness. In such cases, the researcher impartially presents his or her findings that may prove or disprove the identity or cause of death of the victim. The ultimate concern of the forensic anthropologist is not the outcome of the trial, but the evidence provided by the skeletal remains.

The amount of information extracted from skeletal remains can be surprising. For example, fractures of the hyoid bone, a small bone attached to the thyroid cartilage of the throat, may indicate strangulation. The location and kind of breaks may offer clues to the type of weapon used, as well as the position of the attacker relative to the victim. In the vein of a Sherlock Holmes novel, it may actually be possible to determine that a fatal blow was struck from behind by a right-handed assailant. Many illustrations from actual criminal cases can be recounted (Rathbun and Buikstra 1984; Sauer et al. 2003; Steadman 2009; Manhein 2013).

The key roles of both archaeology and forensic anthropology in determining the cause of death are illustrated by the John McRae murder case (Sauer et al. 2003). In 1997, police in northern Michigan were called when a farmworker uncovered human skeletal remains while excavating a refuse pit with a backhoe. On the basis of dental records, the police identified the victim as Randy Laufer, a 15-year-old boy who had disappeared 11 years previously. The principal suspect in the case was John McRae, who had previously owned the land where the bones were recovered. At the time of their discovery, the bones were fragmentary and devoid of flesh. More significantly, they had not been recovered under ideal conditions; structures that had been on the property had been removed and the remains had been disturbed by a backhoe. However, the archaeological and physical anthropological evidence proved crucial in bringing McRae to justice. Archaeologists were able to recover the remaining bones, locate the original burial pit, and reconstruct the location of structures that had been on the property when McRae owned the property. The archaeological information established that the body had likely been buried no more than 15 feet from the front door of McRae's trailer, beneath a gravel driveway or just inside an adjacent barn. The skeletal evidence established Laufer's identity and also that he had been mutilated at the time of death. Study of the cut marks on the bones indicated that the boy had been stabbed or hacked in the left shoulder and his body cut in half.

Excavation of the burial site of civilians who were killed by government troops in Poland. Forensic anthropologists often play an important role in the identification of victims of natural disasters, airplane crashes, wars, and genocide.
Source: Courtesy of **Marek E. Jasinski**, Institute of Historical Studies; Archaeology Programme Norwegian University of Science and Technology.

Identifying Victims of War and Genocide Forensic anthropologists have also played important roles in the identification of victims of natural disasters, airplane crashes, bombings, war, and genocide (Stewart 1970; Stover 1981, 1992; Snow et al. 1989; Snow and Bihurriet 1992; Steadman 2009). Forensic anthropologists and archaeologists have assisted in the documentation of human rights abuses and recovery of victims from mass graves in Argentina, Brazil, Croatia, El Salvador, Haiti, Iraq, Poland, Rwanda, and many other areas. For example, the *Polish Genetic Base of Totalitarianism Victims* has undertaken the excavation of mass graves and burials of individuals executed in Poland during the country's authoritarian regime between 1944 and 1956. Researchers draw on DNA recovered from the remains, as well as material culture and forensic data, to identify the victims.

Many of the methods and techniques used by modern forensic anthropologists were needed during and after World War II to assist with the identification and repatriation of the remains of soldiers killed in battle. This remained an important role for forensic anthropologists during the Korean and Vietnam wars (Stewart 1970; Mann et al. 2003). Identification of the remains has often been dependent on matching the physical remains recovered with life histories provided by medical and dental records. In such cases, positive identification may be dependent on relatively minor variation in bony structures.

Biological anthropologists and forensic archaeologists continue to play important roles today in locating and identifying American soldiers killed or missing in past conflicts (Mather 1994). The Joint POW/MIA Accounting Command (referred to as JPAC) is a U.S. Department of Defense task force whose mission it is to account for all Americans who are listed as prisoners of war, or missing in action, from all past wars and conflicts. JPAC's missions span the globe and the recovery of a single individual's remains, involving both documentary research and fieldwork, may take years. Researchers are now able to bring much more sophisticated techniques to identify human remains. These methods include the extraction of DNA from small fragments of bone, which may be matched with the DNA of the soldier's surviving relatives.

Anthropologist at Work

CLYDE COLLINS SNOW: Forensic Anthropologist

Clyde Collins Snow

Clyde Collins Snow obtained a master's degree in zoology from Texas Tech University and planned to pursue a doctorate in physiology, but his career plans were interrupted by military service. While stationed at Lackland Air Force Base near San Antonio, he was introduced to the field of archaeology and became fascinated with the ancient artifacts discovered in the surrounding area.

After leaving the military, Snow attended the University of Arizona, where his zoological training and archaeology interests led him to a doctorate in physical anthropology. He became skilled at identifying old bones, as well as artifacts. With his doctoral degree completed, he joined the Federal Aviation Administration as a consulting forensic anthropologist, providing technical assistance in the identification of victims of aircraft accidents. Snow also lent his expertise to the design of safety equipment to prevent injuries in aircraft accidents.

As word of Snow's extraordinary skill in forensic anthropology spread, he was called to consult on and provide expert testimony in many criminal cases. His testimony was crucial at the sensational murder trial of John Wayne Gacy, accused of murdering more than thirty teenagers in the Chicago area. Snow also collaborated with experts in the reinvestigation of President John F. Kennedy's assassination. These experts built a full-scale model of Kennedy's head to determine whether Lee Harvey Oswald could have inflicted all of Kennedy's wounds. They did not uncover any scientific evidence to contradict the Warren Commission's conclusion that Oswald was the sole assassin.

More recently, Snow and his team have been recognized for their contributions to human rights issues. Snow served as a consultant to the Argentine government's National Commission on Disappeared Persons in its efforts to determine the fate of thousands of Argentineans who were abducted and murdered by military death squads between 1976 and 1983, when the country was under the rule of a military dictatorship. As a result of his investigations, Snow was asked to testify as an expert witness in the trial of the nine junta members who ruled Argentina during the period of military repression. He also assisted people in locating their dead relatives.

Snow stressed that in his human rights investigative work he is functioning as an expert, not necessarily as an advocate. He must maintain an objective viewpoint in interpreting his findings. The evidence he finds may then be presented by lawyers (as advocates) in the interests of justice. Snow's and other forensic anthropological human rights work was supported by various agencies, such as the American Association for the Advancement of Science, the Ford Foundation, the J. Roderick MacArthur Foundation, Amnesty International, Physicians for Human Rights, and Human Rights Watch (Mann and Holland 2004). Clyde Collins Snow died on May 16, 2014. He was a pioneer who made considerable contributions to the field of forensic anthropology.

Medical Anthropology

10.3 Define medical anthropology and discuss some of the research undertaken.

Another subfield of applied anthropology, **medical anthropology**, represents the intersection of cultural anthropology and the other four fields of anthropology, including biological anthropology (Brown and Barrett 2010; McElroy and Townsend 2009). Medical anthropologists study disease, health care systems, medical practices, curing, and mental illness with a cross-cultural perspective. Medical anthropologists work with physicians, nurses, and other public health care workers to apply their knowledge about cultural practices in different settings to provide more effective health care. One of the key issues that medical anthropologists focus on is the comparison between Western-based biomedical scientific techniques and theories with other nonscientific beliefs and models of disease, illness and medicine. From a Western biomedical perspective, disease is the result of natural causes, either genetic disabilities, autoimmune factors, or external sources such as infectious microbes, injuries, or syndromes that impair the normal function of the body. Illness is the feeling of pain or sickness by individuals or populations. Health care provided by the Western biomedical model to diagnose and treat disease and illness involves physicians and nurses with advanced technologies such as X-rays, MRIs, CT scans, surgery, and pharmaceutical medicines that are tested and developed through scientific methods.

Ethnomedicine

In other cultural settings, disease, illness, or injuries may be attributed to a variety of other reasons other than physical causation, including religious or spiritual beliefs. The beliefs may dramatically influence how medical treatment is viewed. Medical anthropologists developed the field of **ethnomedicine**, the study and comparison of traditional, spiritually based medical practices by different ethnic groups. Ethnomedicine reveals that concepts of disease and illness are not universally defined. The local culture deeply influences the understanding and meaning of disease and illness and the techniques used for healing. For example, medical anthropologists investigate the practices of acupuncture as developed in traditional Chinese medicine and the Ayurvedic beliefs about disease, illness, and healing maintained in the Hindu religious tradition. Both the Chinese and Ayurvedic Hindu medical beliefs are based on restoring balance and equilibrium within the body that might be caused by injuries or illnesses induced by the ingestion of inappropriate foods or exposure to climate changes or diseases.

Ethnomedicine in Thailand A classic example of medical anthropology and ethnomedicine is the work of Louis Golomb (1985), who conducted ethnographic research on curing practices in Thailand. Golomb did research on Buddhist and Muslim medical practitioners who rely on native spiritualistic beliefs to diagnose and cure diseases. These practices are based on earlier Hindu, magical, and animistic beliefs that had been syncretized with Buddhist and Muslim traditions. Practitioners draw on astrology, faith healing, massage, folk psychotherapy, exorcism, herbs, and charms and amulets to treat patients. The most traditional practitioners are curer-magicians, or shamans, who diagnose and treat every illness as an instance of spirit possession or spirit attack. Other practitioners are more skeptical of the supernatural causation of illness and diagnose health problems in reference to natural or organic causes. They frequently use herbal medicines to treat illnesses.

Golomb discovered that although Western-based scientific forms of medicine may be available, many Thais still rely on traditional practitioners. He found that even urban-educated elite, including those who had studied in the United States and other Western countries, adhered to both supernatural and scientific views. Golomb referred to this as *therapeutic pluralism*. He observed that patients did not rely on any single therapeutic approach, but rather used a combination of therapies that include elements of ritual, magic, and modern scientific medications. Parasites or germs are rarely seen as the only explanations of disease; a sick person may go to a clinic to receive medication to relieve symptoms, but may then seek out a traditional curer for a more complete treatment. Golomb emphasized that the multiplicity of alternative therapies encourages people to play an active role in preserving their health, something that has therapeutic benefits.

In Thailand, as in many other countries undergoing modernization and globalization, modern medical facilities have been established based on the scientific treatment of disease. Golomb found that personnel in these facilities are critical of traditional medical practices. He also found that while the people in the villages often respected the modern doctor's ability to diagnose diseases and prescribe medications to relieve symptoms, in most cases they did not accept the scientific explanation of the disease. In addition, villagers felt that modern medical methods are brusque and impersonal because doctors did not offer any psychological or spiritual consolation. Doctors also do not make house calls and rarely spend much time with patients. This impersonality in the doctor–patient relationship is also due to social status differences based on wealth, education, and power. Golomb found that many public health personnel expected deference from their rural clientele. For these reasons, many people preferred to rely upon traditional curers.

Through his study of traditional medical techniques and beliefs, Golomb isolated some of the strengths and weaknesses of modern medical treatment in Thailand. His work contributed to a better understanding of how to deliver health care services to rural and urban Thais. For example, the Thai Ministry of Public Health began to experiment with ways of coordinating the efforts of modern and traditional medical practitioners. Village midwives and traditional herbalists were called on to dispense modern medications and pass out information about nutrition and hygiene. Some Thai hospitals have established training sessions for traditional practitioners to learn modern medical techniques. Golomb's studies in medical anthropology offer a model for practical applications in the health field for other developing societies.

Chinese Acupuncture Another example of the intersection of local cultural knowledge and Western medical practices is provided by Chinese medicine and the practice of acupuncture, which are based on cosmological beliefs derived from Daoist, Confucianist, and Buddhist beliefs. According to these beliefs, spiritual forces and energy known as *qi*, usually translated as "air" or "breath," inhabits all living things. As in other living things, *qi* flows through the human body along various channels or meridians. It is believed that injuries, illness, or disease may obstruct the flow of *qi* to create dysfunctions within the body. The acupuncturist attempts to control the flow of *qi* that might be obstructed by inserting needles to harmonize and restore equilibrium to bodily functions.

The Western model of biomedicine does not recognize the spiritual energy force *qi* or meridian channels within a scientific framework. However, Chinese acupuncture treatment has been accepted by many patients with illnesses as an alternative therapy within the U.S. Medical anthropologist Linda Barnes has been studying Chinese acupuncture as it exists in the very cosmopolitan city of Boston, Massachusetts (2005). Through extensive interviewing of acupuncturists and patients and observing acupuncture treatment sessions for over two years, Barnes examined the meaning of efficacy or effectiveness of acupuncture treatment. She notes that acupuncture, as derived from traditional Chinese medicine, has been the basis of licensure and government regulations in the U.S. Barnes describes five different forms of acupuncture traditions in the Boston area: the Worsley Five Elements school, Japanese acupuncture, and limited instances of Korean, Vietnamese, and French schools. Some practitioners within these different schools have trained with Chinese Daoist priests to learn how to harmonize the flow of *qi*. Some of the practitioners are Chinese-Americans, Asian-Americans, but many are Americans of European descent.

Barnes describes the variation of practices and beliefs about the efficacy of acupuncture within the different schools. Many of the patients select acupuncture as only one of many nonscientific therapies in tandem with other Western biomedical scientific therapies. Some of the practitioners view their acupuncture treatments as a form of religious healing, whereas others, mainly European American practitioners, view it as embedded with "spirit." Some of the practitioners view the efficacy of acupuncture as "empowerment" for the individual. Barnes discusses how acupuncture has crossed the boundaries of Western biomedical practices, as it is accepted and regulated by the National Institutes of Health (NIH) as a Complementary and Alternative Medicine (CAM). Since 1997, NIH has accepted the efficacy of acupuncture as an adjunct treatment for postoperative and chemotherapy nausea and vomiting, stroke rehabilitation, headache, low back pain, asthma, and some other injuries or illnesses. Barnes describes how some practitioners agree that a patient's symptoms of illness may not always change, but nevertheless healing does occur. Some patients that use acupuncture for drug addiction withdrawal or chronic pain feel their anxiety has been reduced. Barnes concludes her essay by discussing therapeutic pluralism and the multiple meanings regarding the efficacy of acupuncture as it is embedded within the medical care and health system in U.S. society.

Tanya Luhrmann provides insight into the dynamics of religious healing and prayer that has a bearing on what medical anthropologists discover in their research on therapeutic pluralism (2013). In her studies of prayer and religious experience among Christians in Chicago and San Francisco, Luhrmann found that some individuals experienced prayer and healing differently than others. As part of her ethnographic research, Luhrmann used a survey instrument that measured the degree of "absorption," or hypnotic susceptibility and imaginative involvement in narratives, myths, or other sensations. Absorption is the capacity to focus one's attention on the mind's object while neglecting the distractions of everyday life. The degree of absorption varies between individuals and at different times of the day for individuals. Through extensive interviews, meditation and prayer experiments, and surveys, Luhrmann found that those individuals who were more susceptible to prayer and healing experienced mystical states, out-of-body feelings, and lucid visions. She suggests that absorption is central to spirituality and religious experience. Universally, medical anthropologists find that some individuals experience religious and spiritual healing in different degrees based on this capacity for absorption.

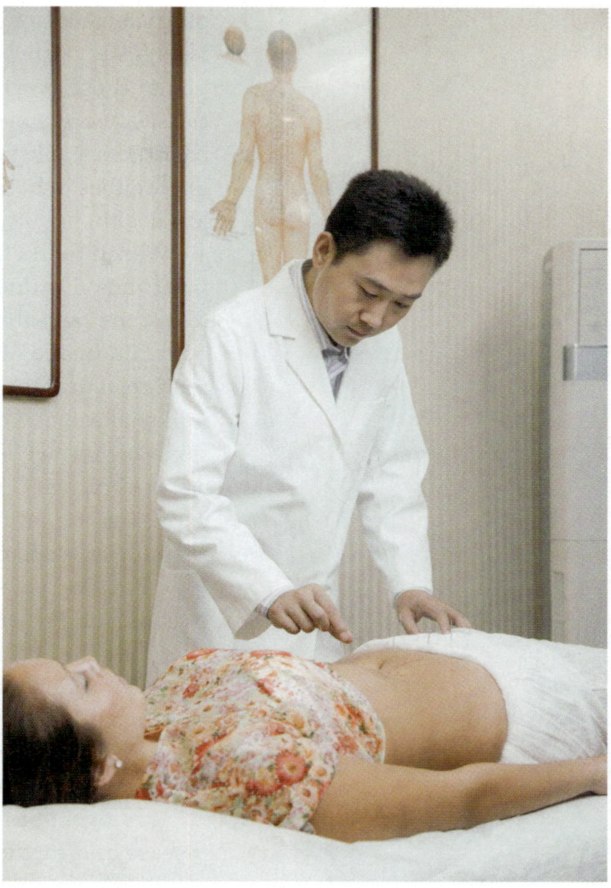

Chinese acupuncture treatments are readily available in U.S. society.

Cultural Patterns and Epidemiology Other medical anthropologists focus specifically on **epidemiology**, which examines the spread and distribution of diseases and how they are influenced by cultural patterns. For example, these anthropologists may be able to determine whether coronary (heart) disease or cancer is related to particular cultural or social dietary habits, such as the consumption of foods high in sodium or saturated fats. These studies can often help health providers design more effective means for delivering health care and formulating health care policies (Schell and Denham 2003). Thus, applied medical anthropology deals with intervention, prevention, and policy issues in public health care. In addition, medical anthropologists also demonstrate the linkages between socioeconomic status, illness, and access to health care.

Medical anthropologist Caroline Wilson has been doing research on cardiac disease in the state of Kerala in South India (2010). Globalization has increased heart disease in India with diets richer in fats and sugar, reduced physical activity, increases in smoking, alcohol use, stress, and inequality. Kerala has high rates of cardiac disease, type 2 diabetes, high blood pressure, cholesterol, and obesity for both men and women from their late 20s onward. Thus, these medical problems are not due to aging. Wilson studied consumer practices, specifically eating and feasting activities, levels of physical activity, and the lifestyle among Hindus and Muslims in the city of Malabar in Kerala. She observed medical practices in outpatient clinics that were staffed by cardiologists and general

Tanya Luhrmann

physicians where patients were treated for hypertension, high cholesterol, and diabetes. Wilson participated in the social and cultural practices in various settings, in particular those practices that involved feasting and eating, such as weddings, cooking classes, and many other rituals and events. As in many other societies, food becomes a means of establishing and maintaining social networks among these Hindu and Muslim families in Kerala. In Kerala, a "good appetite" indicates both emotional and physical health, vitality, and well-being.

Wilson found that in the middle-class Hindu households, home-cooking used less meat and oil, affluent Muslim households served meat-based curries three times a day, and some households added fish on a regular basis. However, outside of the home, both Hindu and Muslim men and women consumed more meat and fried foods. Fast-food restaurants and bakeries that serve fried chicken or biscuits, sweet cakes, and milkshakes have developed with increasing globalization in Kerala. At ritual functions such as wedding feasts, both Hindus and Muslims serve abundant portions of a spicy chicken cooked with oil and rice, *biriyani*. In these communities concerns are expressed regarding the increase of heart attacks and its relationship to nutrition. Yet, pressures to consume large amounts of food at feasting rituals are prevalent. Refusing to accept food is a sign of anger or annoyance. Wilson says "breaking out of the culture of eating and feasting requires cognitive intent, to resist the flow of food and love in everyday life" (2010:270). Dietary restrictions that inhibit participation in new forms of consumption among the affluent people of Kerala are signs of emotional ill-being. Wilson has identified this culture of overeating and feasting that relates to increases in cardiac disease in order to assist public health authorities in preventing these health problems in Kerala.

Ethnographic studies such as these that combine scientific understanding of disease and medicine with in-depth local cultural knowledge have proven to be an effective combination in many other settings. They provide excellent illustration of the relevance of anthropological research in solving important social and medical problems.

Cultural Resource Management: Applied Archaeology

10.4 Define cultural resource management and discuss the role of archaeologists in the field.

One of the problems that humanity faces is how to safeguard the cultural heritage preserved in the archaeological record. Although archaeology may address questions of general interest to all of humanity, it is also important in promoting national heritage, cultural identity, and ethnic pride. Museums the world over offer displays documenting diverse local populations, regional histories, important events, and cultural traditions. The number of specialized museums focusing on particular peoples, regions, or historic periods has become increasingly important. Archaeologists must be concerned with the preservation of archaeological sites and the recovery of information from sites threatened with destruction, as well as the interpretation and presentation of their findings to the more general public (Jameson 2004; Little 2007). As a result of these concerns, a very important area of specialization within archaeology is **Cultural Resource Management**. Cultural resource management (often referred to as CRM) focuses on the evaluation, protection, and supervision of cultural resources, including the archaeological record, as well as the arts, historic sites and cultural property. Many archaeologists now find employment as applied archaeologists, doing CRM evaluating, salvaging, and protecting archaeological resources that are threatened with destruction.

Preservation of the past and effective cultural resource management are challenges to archaeologists, government officials, and the concerned public alike, as archaeological sites are being destroyed at an alarming rate. Archaeological materials naturally decay in the ground, and sites are constantly destroyed through geological processes, erosion, and animal burrowing (see Chapter 3). Yet, while natural processes contribute to the disappearance of archaeological sites, by far the greatest threat to the archaeological record is human activity. Construction projects such as dams, roads, buildings, and pipelines all disturb the ground and can destroy archaeological sites in the process. In many instances, archaeologists work only a few feet ahead of construction equipment, trying to salvage any information they can before a site disappears forever.

Some archaeological sites are intentionally destroyed by collectors searching for artifacts that have value in the antiquities market, such as arrowheads and pottery. Statues from ancient Egypt, Mayan terra cotta figurines, and Native American pottery may be worth thousands of dollars on the antiques market. To fulfill the demands, archaeological sites in many areas are looted by pot hunters, who dig to retrieve artifacts for collectors, ignoring the traces of ancient housing, burials, and cooking hearths. Removed from their context, with no record of where they came from, such artifacts are of limited value to archaeologists. The rate of destruction of North American archaeological sites is such that some researchers have estimated that 98 percent of sites predating the year 2000 will be destroyed by the middle of the twenty-first century (Herscher 1989; Knudson 1989).

The rate at which archaeological sites are being destroyed is particularly distressing because the archaeological record is an irreplaceable, *nonrenewable* resource. That is, after sites are destroyed, they are gone forever, along with the unique information about the past that they contained. In many parts of the world, recognition of this fact has led to legislation aimed at protecting archaeological sites (see Table 10.1). The rational for this legislation is that the past has value to the present and, hence, should be protected and interpreted for the benefit of the public.

Preserving the Past

Recognition of the value and nonrenewable nature of archaeological resources is the first step in the planning process. Archaeological resources can then be systematically identified and evaluated. Steps can be taken to preserve them by limiting development or designing projects in a way that will preserve the resource. For example, the projected path of a new road might be moved to avoid an archaeological site or a building might be planned so that the foundations do not extend into a historic burial ground (see the photos of the African burial ground on page 275). Alternatively, if a site must be destroyed, effective planning can ensure that information about the site is recovered by archaeologists prior to its destruction.

One of the most spectacular examples of salvage archaeology arose as a result of the construction of a dam across the Nile River at Aswan, Egypt, in the 1960s (Abu-Zeid and El-Shibini 1997; Stock 1993). The project offered many benefits, including water for irrigation and the generation of electricity. However, the rising water behind the dam threatened thousands of archaeological sites that had lain undisturbed and safely buried by desert sand for thousands of years. The Egyptian government appealed to the international community and archaeologists from around the world to mount projects to locate and excavate the threatened sites.

Among the sites that were to be flooded by the dam was the temple of Pharaoh Ramses II at Abu Simbel, a huge monument consisting of four colossal figures carved from a cliff face on the banks of the Nile River. With help from the United Nations Educational, Scientific, and Cultural Organization (UNESCO), the Egyptian government was able to cut the monument into more than a thousand pieces, some weighing as much as 33 tons, and reassemble them above the floodwater. Today, the temple of Ramses can be seen completely restored only a few hundred feet from its original location. Numerous other archaeological sites threatened by the flooding of the Nile were partly salvaged or recorded. Unfortunately, countless other sites could not be recorded or even identified before they were flooded.

Cultural Resource Management in the United States The first legislation in the United States designed to protect historic sites was the Antiquities Act of 1906, which safeguarded archaeological sites on federal land (see Table 10.1). Other, more recent legislation, such as the National Historic Preservation Act passed in 1966, has extended protection to sites threatened by projects that are funded or regulated by the government. The federal Abandoned Shipwreck Act of 1988 gives states jurisdiction over shipwreck sites (King 2000, 2007, 2013). This legislation has had a dramatic impact on the number of archaeologists in the United States. Whereas most archaeologists had traditionally found employment teaching or working in museums, today a large proportion find employment in cultural resource management, and are employed by federal, state, and local agencies, and private companies. Applied archaeologists conduct surveys before construction begins to determine if any sites will be affected. Government agencies such as the United States Forest Service have developed comprehensive programs to discover, record, protect, and interpret archaeological resources on their land (Johnson and Schene 1987).

Unfortunately, current legislation in the United States leaves many archaeological resources unprotected. In many countries, excavated artifacts, even those located on privately owned land, become the property of the government. This is not the case in the United States. One example of the limitations of the existing legislation is provided by the case of Slack Farm, located near Uniontown, Kentucky (Arden 1989). Archaeologists had long known that an undisturbed Native American site of the Late Mississippian period was on the property. Dating roughly to between 1450 and 1650, the site was particularly important because it was the only surviving Mississippian site from the period of first contact with Europeans. The Slack family, who had owned the land for many years, protected the site and prevented people from digging (Arden

Table 10.1 Major Federal Legislation for the Protection of Archaeological Resources in the U.S.

Antiquities Act of 1906	Protects sites on federal land
Historic Sites Act of 1935	Provides authority for designating National Historic Landmarks and for conducting archaeological surveys before destruction by development programs
National Historic Preservation Act of 1966 (amended 1976 and 1980)	Strengthens protection of sites via the National Register and integrates state and local agencies into a national program for site preservation
National Environmental Policy Act of 1969	Requires all federal agencies to specify the impact of development programs on cultural resources
Archaeological Resources Protection Act of 1979	Provides criminal and civil penalties for looting or damaging sites on public and Native American land
Convention on Cultural Property of 1982	Authorizes U.S. participation in the 1970 UNESCO conventions to prevent illegal international trade in cultural property
Cultural Property Act of 1983	Provides sanctions against the U.S. import or export of illicit antiquities
National Museum of the American Indian Act of 1989	Established the National Museum of the American Indian as part of the Smithsonian Institution; required the Smithsonian to inventory Indian and Native Hawaiian human remains and funerary objects in its collections, and to consider the repatriation of these items
Native American Graves Protection and Repatriation Act (NAGPRA) of 1990	Requires federal agencies and institutions that receive federal funding to return Native American cultural items to lineal descendants and culturally affiliated Indian tribes and Native Hawaiian organizations

SOURCE: From *Discovering Our Past: A Brief Introduction to Archaeology* by Wendy Ashmore and Robert J. Sharer. Copyright ©1988 by Mayfield Publishing Company. Reprinted by permission of the publisher.

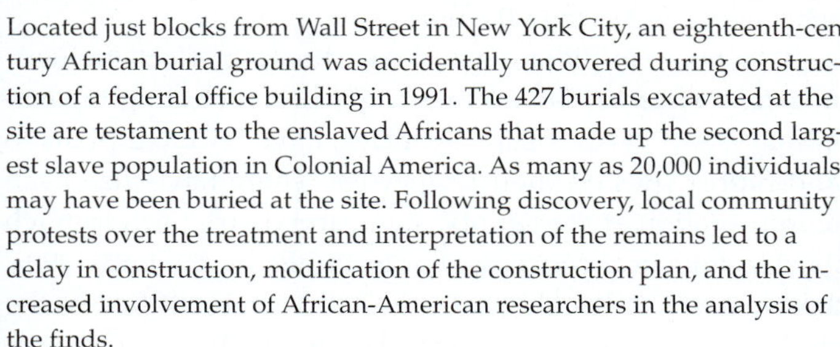

Located just blocks from Wall Street in New York City, an eighteenth-century African burial ground was accidentally uncovered during construction of a federal office building in 1991. The 427 burials excavated at the site are testament to the enslaved Africans that made up the second largest slave population in Colonial America. As many as 20,000 individuals may have been buried at the site. Following discovery, local community protests over the treatment and interpretation of the remains led to a delay in construction, modification of the construction plan, and the increased involvement of African-American researchers in the analysis of the finds.

Source: Courtesy of the General Services Administration.

1989). When the property was sold in 1988, however, conditions changed. Anthropologist Brian Fagan described the results:

> *Ten pot hunters from Kentucky, Indiana, and Illinois paid the new owner of the land $10,000 for the right to "excavate" the site. They rented a tractor and began bulldozing their way through the village midden to reach graves. They pushed heaps of bones aside and dug through dwellings and potsherds, hearths, and stone tools associated with them. Along the way, they left detritus of their own—empty pop-top beer and soda cans—scattered on the ground alongside Late Mississippian pottery fragments. Today Slack Farm looks like a battlefield—a morass of crude shovel holes and gaping trenches. Broken human bones litter the ground, and fractured artifacts crunch underfoot. (1988:15)*

The looting at the site was eventually stopped by the Kentucky State Police, using a state law that prohibits the desecration of human graves. Archaeologists went to the site attempting to salvage what information was left, but there is no way of knowing how many artifacts were removed. The record of America's prehistoric past was irrevocably damaged.

Regrettably, the events at Slack Farm are not unique. Many states lack adequate legislation protecting archaeological sites on private land. For example, Arkansas had no laws protecting unmarked burial sites until 1991. As a result, Native American burial grounds were systematically mined for artifacts. In fact, one article written about the problem was titled "The Looting of Arkansas" (Harrington 1991a). Although Arkansas now has legislation prohibiting the unauthorized excavation of burial grounds, the professional archaeologists of the Arkansas Archaeological Survey face the impossible job of trying to locate and monitor all of the state's archaeological sites. This problem is not unique. Even on federal land, the protection of sites is dependent on a relatively small number of park rangers and personnel to police large areas. Even in national parks, such as Mesa Verde or Yellowstone, archaeological sites are sometimes vandalized or looted for artifacts. Much of the success that there has been in protecting sites is largely due to the active involvement of amateur archaeologists and concerned citizens who bring archaeological remains to the attention of professionals.

The preservation of the past needs to be everyone's concern. Unfortunately, however well intentioned the legislation and efforts to provide protection for archaeological sites may be, they are rarely integrated into comprehensive management plans. For example, a particular county or city area might have a variety of sites and resources of historic significance identified using a variety of different criteria and presented in different lists and directories. These might include National Historic sites, designated through the National Historic Preservation office; state files of archaeological sites; data held by avocational archaeological organizations and clubs; and a variety of locations of historical importance identified by county or city historical societies. Other sites of potential historical significance might be identified through documentary research or oral traditions. Ideally, all of these sources of information should be integrated and used to plan development. Such comprehensive approaches to cultural resource management plans are rare rather than the norm.

Important strides have been taken in planning and coordinating efforts to identify and manage archaeological resources. Government agencies, including the National Park Service, the military, and various state agencies, have initiated plans to systematically identify and report sites on their properties. There have also been notable efforts to compile information at the county, state, and district levels. Such efforts are faced with imposing logistical concerns. For example, by the mid-1990s, over 180,000 historic and prehistoric archaeological sites had been identified in the American Southeast (including the states of Alabama, Arkansas, Florida, Georgia, Kentucky, Louisiana, Mississippi, North Carolina, South Carolina, and Tennessee). In addition, an estimated 10,000 new sites are discovered each year (Anderson and Horak 1995). A map of these resources reveals a great deal of variation in their concentration. On one hand, this diversity reflects the actual distribution of sites; on the other, it reflects the areas where archaeological research has and has not been undertaken. Incorporating the thousands of new site reports into the database requires substantial commitment of staff resources. What information should be recorded for each site? What computer resources are needed? The volume of information is difficult to process with available staff, and massive backlogs of reports waiting to be incorporated into the files often exist. Nevertheless, this kind of holistic perspective is needed to ensure effective site management and the compliance of developers with laws protecting archaeological sites. It also provides a holistic view of past land use that is of great use to archaeologists.

Cultural Resource Management in Global Perspective Cultural resource management is a worldwide concern, particularly in developing countries that often lack legislation and resources to protect archaeological sites, but similar problems are faced in industrialized countries (Serageldin and Taboroff 1994; Schmidt and McIntosh 1996; Kankpeyeng and DeCorse 2004). On one hand, archaeological sites are looted for artifacts to be sold on the antiquities market. On the other hand, the priority given to development—including the construction of new housing, roads, and dams—often results in the destruction of archaeological sites. These facts are all the more troubling because some countries lack well-developed archaeological traditions, and the archaeological past will be gone before anyone has the opportunity to study it. To address these concerns, UNESCO launched the "World Decade for Cultural Development" in 1988, which emphasized the need to consider cultural resources planning in development (Serageldin and Taboroff 1994).

Development and the management of archaeological resources can go hand in hand. While the material traces of the past—including archaeological resources, historic buildings, and cultural sites—may be important in promoting cultural heritage and national identity, many governments have also started to realize the potential economic worth of effective cultural resource management. Cultural tourism, arising out of the human fascination with the past, has become a major revenue source for some nations. The treatment of cultural heritage as a commodity is most obvious in Western Europe and the United States, but many countries in Asia, South America, and Mesoamerica have also capitalized on their cultural patrimony (Layton 1989; Ekechukwu 1990; Bruner 1996a, b).

A number of archaeologists throughout the world are using their skills to both preserve archaeological sites and improve the lives of modern inhabitants of the communities where the sites are located. In countries such as Guatemala, the location of a number of spectacular Mayan ruins, archaeologists are increasingly integrating economic development and environmental preservation into their research programs. The ancient Mayan sites pose special conservation concerns because of their size. For example, Chocolá, the focus of research by American archaeologist Jonathan Kaplan, has more than 60 mounds, large irrigation systems, and numerous monuments (Bawaya 2005). Information from the site has shed insight into the origins of Mayan civilization. Yet the farmers of modern Chocolá, descendants of the ancient Maya, face poverty and disease. In the face of such modern needs, the preservation of ancient monuments and the surrounding environment is of limited concern.

The past cannot be preserved without addressing the concerns of the present. To address these problems, Kaplan has established a trash removal service, worked with an environmental scientist to improve drinking water, and developed plans for museums that might attract tourists and so stimulate economic development. He is also working with the local government officials on a plan that would allow farmers to swap land of no archaeological value with areas that include Mayan ruins. At El Pilar, another Mayan site, archaeologist Anabel Ford not only does archaeological excavations, but also directs efforts to help conserve the archaeological sites and the surrounding forest. Straddling the Belize and Guatemalan border, the site of El Pilar is also one of the richest forest areas in the world. Ford hopes the archaeological field research and the data recorded on the tropical forest will heighten the awareness of local officials, tourism directors, and others in the region to improve conservation methods.

Another important series of archaeological projects in the Amazon area in South America has studied human impact on the environment. Archaeologists Thomas Neumann, Anna C. Roosevelt, Clark Erickson, and Peter Stahl, as well as anthropological botanist Charles R. Clement, discovered that the early Native American societies in this region not only had very large settlements—overturning earlier archaeological assessments that the Amazon did not support large civilizations—but contributed new methods that may help conserve this fragile environment (Mann 2002). These early civilizations had extensive agricultural systems that were crippled since the advent of European colonialism. Research may provide insight into how to restore the productivity of the land and more efficient land use in the future. Thus, applied archaeology can provide new knowledge that will enhance the conservation and preservation of different environments throughout the world. A broad holistic perspective involving teams of archaeologists and other scientists is needed to ensure effective site management and the compliance of developers with laws protecting archaeological sites. It also provides a holistic view of past land use that is of great use to archaeologists. Called "community" or "action" archaeology by some, engagement with local peoples' needs has become an increasing concern of archaeologists worldwide.

The Study of Garbage

The majority of archaeological research deals with the interpretation of past societies. Whether the focus is on the Stone Age inhabitants of Australia or the archaeology of nineteenth-century mining communities in the American West, the people being examined lived at a time somewhat removed from the present. There are, however, some archaeologists who are concerned with the study of the refuse of modern society and the application of archaeological methods and techniques to concerns of the present—and the future. The focus for these researchers is not the interpretation of past societies, but the immediate application of archaeological methods and techniques to the modern world. The topics examined range from the use of archaeological data in marketing strategies to the best methods for marking nuclear waste sites. Archaeologists who routinely examine artifacts thousands of years old can, for example, provide important perspectives of the suitability of different materials and burial strategies that can be used to bury nuclear waste (Kaplan and Mendel 1982).

Le Projet du Garbage One of the more interesting examples of this kind of applied archaeology is *Le Projet du Garbage*, or the Garbage Project, that grew out of an archaeological method and theory class at the University of Arizona in 1971 (Rathje and Ritenbaugh 1984; Rathje 1992). Archaeologists William L. Rathje and Fred Gorman were so intrigued by the results of the student projects that they established the Garbage Project the following year, and the project is still going. The researchers gather trash from households with the help of the city of Tucson sanitation foremen, who tag the waste with identification numbers that allow the trash bags to be identified with specific census tracts within the city. The trash bags are not identified with particular households, and personal items and photographs are not examined. Over the years, research has been broadened to the study of trash from other communities, including Milwaukee, Marin County, and Mexico City, and also to the excavation of modern landfills in Chicago, San Francisco, and Phoenix using archaeological methods.

The Garbage Project has provided a surprising amount of information on a diversity of topics. On one hand, the study provides data that are extremely useful in monitoring trash disposal programs. As Rathje observed, study of waste allows the effective evaluation of current conditions, the anticipation of changing directions in waste disposal, and, therefore, more effective planning and policymaking (1984:10). Reviewing data on the project, Rathje noted a number of areas in which this archaeological research dispelled some common notions about trash disposal and landfills. Despite common perceptions, items such as fast-food packaging, polystyrene foam, and disposable diapers do not account for a substantial percentage of landfills. Rathje observed:

Archaeological study of modern garbage has provided important insights into waste management procedures, marketing, food waste, and recycling.

> *Of the 14 tons of garbage from nine municipal landfills that the Garbage Project has excavated and sorted in the past five years, there was less than a hundred pounds of fast-food packaging—that is, containers or wrappers for hamburgers, pizzas, chicken, fish and convenience-store sandwiches, as well as the accessories most of us deplore, such as cups, lids, straws, sauce containers, and so on. (Rathje 1992:115)*

Hence, fast-food packaging makes up less than one-half of 1 percent of the weight of landfills. The percentage by volume is even lower. Rathje further noted that despite the burgeoning of materials made from plastic, the amount of plastic in landfills has remained fairly constant since the 1960s, or even decreased. The reason for this, he believes, is that while more things are made of plastic, many objects are now made with less plastic. A plastic milk bottle that weighed 120 grams in the 1960s weighs 65 grams today.

Rathje found that the real culprit in landfills remains plain old paper. A year's subscription to *The New York Times* is roughly equivalent to the volume of 18,660 crushed aluminum cans or 14,969 flattened Big Mac containers. While some predicted that computers would bring about a paperless office, the photocopier and millions of personal printers ensure that millions of pounds of paper are discarded each year: "Where the creation of paper waste is concerned, technology is proving to be not so much a contraceptive as a fertility drug" (Rathje 1992:116). He also observed that despite popular perception, much of the paper in landfills is not biodegrading. Because of the limited amount of moisture, air, and biological activity in the middle of a landfill, much of the nation's newsprint is being preserved for posterity.

The Garbage Project has also provided information on a diversity of issues connected with food waste, marketing, and the disposal of hazardous materials. In these studies, archaeology has provided a unique perspective. Much of the available data on such topics has typically been provided by questionnaires, interviews, and data collection methods that rely on the cooperation of informants. The problem is that informants often present biased responses, consistently providing lower estimates of the alcohol, snack food, or hazardous waste that they dispose of than is actually the case. Archaeology, on the other hand, presents a fairly impartial material record. While there are sampling problems in archaeological data—some material may be sent down the garbage disposal and not preserved in a landfill—the material record can provide a fairly unambiguous record of some activities.

The Garbage Project has examined the discarding of food and food waste for the U.S. Department of Agriculture; the recycling of paper and aluminum cans for the Environmental Protection Agency; studies of candy and snack food consumption for dental associations and manufacturers; and the impact of a new liquor store on alcohol consumption in a Los Angeles neighborhood. In the latter case, researchers conducted both interviews and garbage analysis before and after the liquor store opened. The interview data suggested no change in consumption patterns before and after the store's opening. Study of the trash, however, showed a marked increase in the discarding of beer, wine, and liquor cans and bottles. Studies such as these have wide applications both for marketing and policymakers.

Who Owns the Past?

10.5 Discuss the role of the NAGPRA legislation in the U.S.

A critical issue for modern archaeologists and physical anthropologists is **cultural patrimony**, that is, who owns the human remains, artifacts, and associated cultural materials that are recovered in the course of research projects. Are they the property of the scientists who collected or excavated them? The descendants of the peoples discovered archaeologically? The owners of the land on which the materials were recovered? Or the public as a whole? Resolution of this issue has at times been contentious, and the position taken by anthropologists has not always been the best. Prior to the twentieth century, laws governing the deposition of antiquities were nonexistent or unclear at best, and the "owner" often became the person, institution, or country with the most money or the strongest political clout. Colonial governments amassed tremendous collections from their territories throughout the world; the spoils of war belonged to the victors. Such a position remained the norm until after the turn of the century. Rights of conquest were only outlawed by the Hague Convention of 1907 (Shaw 1986; Fagan 1992).

Prior to the twentieth century, there was also little or no legislation governing human remains. Researchers appropriated excavated skeletal material, medical samples, and even cadavers of the recently deceased (Blakely and Harrington 1997). Native American remains from archaeological sites were displayed to the public, despite the fact that some of the descendant communities found such displays inappropriate or sacrilegious. Scientific value was the underlying rationale for ownership, though until the latter half of the twentieth century there was little discussion of this issue. As in the case of antiquities, value and ownership were vested in the politically stronger, whether a colonial government or the politically enfranchised within a country. Such remains had scientific value, and this was viewed as more important than the interests of other groups or cultural values.

Ironically, such views would seem to fly in the face of some of the basic tenets of modern anthropology, which underscore sensitivity and openness to other cultural perspectives and beliefs. In fact, archaeological resources and human remains at times do provide unique, irreplaceable information that cannot be obtained through any other source. Archaeologists and physical anthropologists have provided information extremely important in documenting the past of Native Americans and indigenous peoples throughout the world, at times serving to underscore their ties to the land and revealing cultural practices forgotten from memory. But what is the cost of such information if the treatment and methods of obtaining the artifacts and remains are abhorrent to the populations whose history is represented? Researchers of the present cannot afford to ignore the views and concerns of the focus of their research.

Recognition of the validity of different concerns and perspectives of cultural patrimony has not made resolution of debate easier. Artifacts now in museums were, in some instances, obtained hundreds of years ago in ways that were consistent with the moral and legal norms of that time (see the box "The Elgin Marbles"). Many antiquities have legitimately changed ownership numerous times. Not infrequently, information about the original origins may be unclear, and there are differences of opinion or uncertainty about the cultural associations of some artifacts or cultural remains. These issues aside, there remain fundamentally different perspectives about the role of the descendant population.

Critical Perspectives

THE ELGIN MARBLES

The story of the Parthenon sculptures—or Elgin marbles as they came to be called—is a twisted tale of the nineteenth-century quest for antiquities, international politics, and the complexities of cultural heritage. The Parthenon, perched on a hilltop overlooking Athens, is a striking symbol of both ancient Greece and the modern Greek nation-state. It was built by the Greek ruler Pericles to commemorate the Greek victory over the Persians at Plataea in 479 B.C. A temple to Athena, the patron goddess of Athens, the Parthenon was deemed by Pericles to be one of the most striking edifices in the city. The Parthenon is clearly the most impressive of the buildings in the Acropolis, the cluster of classical structures that cover Mount Athena. It is regarded by some to be one of the world's most perfect buildings. The Parthenon was distinguished by a full surrounding colonnade, and the exterior walls were decorated with a processional frieze. The pediments, or peaked eaves, in the east and west also had exquisitely detailed sculptures.

The structure has endured for millennia, and it has come to embody classical civilization to the world. In recent years, the Parthenon has been the focus of several restoration efforts that have stabilized the structure, removed more recent additions, and replaced some of the fallen masonry.

The Parthenon still overlooks Athens and it hopefully will for years to come. But while the Parthenon is an architectural treasure, today only traces of the magnificent art that once adorned it remain. Fragments of its frieze and sculptures are scattered in museums around the world. The largest collection is in the British Museum in London, where large portions of the Parthenon's frieze are displayed in a specially designed room. To understand why statuary of such clear cultural significance to Greece is to be found in England, one has to go back to the early nineteenth century and the exploits of Thomas Bruce, the seventh Earl of Elgin (Jackson 1992).

By the early nineteenth century, Britain was in the midst of a classical revival. The country's well-to-do traveled to Europe to visit the historic ruins of ancient Greece and Rome. The wealthier purchased statuary and antiquities for their estates. Patterns and illustrations from classical Greek and Roman motifs were reproduced and incorporated into architectural features, jewelry, and ceramic designs. Within this setting, Lord Elgin, a Scottish nobleman, set out to obtain sketches and casts of classical sculptures that might be used at his estate, then being built near the Firth of Forth.

In 1799, Elgin was appointed British ambassador to the Ottoman Empire, which extended over much of the eastern Mediterranean from Western Europe to Egypt. By the late eighteenth century, the Ottomans had ruled Greece for 350 years. A major military power and one-time master of the Mediterranean, the Ottomans have been viewed by historians in a variety of ways, but one thing is certain: They were not overly concerned with the glories of ancient Greece. During their rule, the Parthenon was used as a mosque, then as an ammunition dump; also, various Turkish structures were built on the site. Much of the north colonnade was destroyed in the

Venetian bombardment of 1687. Some of the Parthenon marble was ground to make lime, and bits of statuary were broken off (Jackson 1992). In 1800, one of the world's most perfect buildings was in a sorry state.

Elgin initially proposed that the British government finance a survey of the art of the Acropolis as a resource for British art. When this initiative was turned down, Elgin made his own plans and contracted laborers. Initially, his workers were to make copies of the Parthenon sculptures. In 1801, however, Britain defeated Napoleon's forces in Egypt, saving the Ottoman Empire. Coincidentally, Elgin soon obtained a permit from the Ottomans not only to copy and make molds of the Parthenon art, but also to "take away any pieces of stone with old inscriptions or sculptures thereon" (Jackson 1992:137). During 1801 and 1802, scaffolding was erected, and hundreds of laborers went to work on the Parthenon with blocks and tackles and marble saws. Some sculptures broke or crashed to the ground. Twenty-two ships conveyed the marbles, loaded in hundreds of crates, back to England.

The marbles hardly proved to be good fortune for Elgin. The expense of obtaining them ruined his credit, and he discarded the idea of installing them at his estate. Totaling all of his expenses, Elgin estimated that he had spent over £60,000. To recoup his costs, he began negotiations for sale of the marbles to the government for display in the British Museum. After long parliamentary debate, they were sold for £35,000 in 1816. More than half of this amount went to clear Elgin's debt.

Elgin's treatment of the Parthenon's marbles had its contemporary critics. Among the most vocal opponents was none other than the Romantic poet and celebrator of Greek art and culture, Lord Byron, who immortalized the story of the Elgin marbles in the poems "Childe Harold's Pilgrimage" and "Curse of Minerva." Disgusted by what he saw as the desecration of the Parthenon, Byron asked by what right Elgin had removed these treasures of national cultural significance.

Greece gained independence from Turkey in 1830, and the Parthenon became integrally tied to the new nation's identity. The first restoration efforts began soon after independence. In the years since their installation in the British Museum, the ownership of the Parthenon's marbles and demands for their return have periodically been raised by Greeks and Britons alike, but to no avail. In the 1980s, then Greek Minister of Culture Melina Mercouri charged the British with vandalism and argued that the continued possession of the marbles by the British Museum was provocative. Although garnering substantial international support from ministers of culture from around the world, these efforts also proved unsuccessful.

In his defense of his actions, Elgin pointed to the poor conditions of the Parthenon and the ill treatment that the sculptures had received. If left in place they would surely have continued to deteriorate. Why not remove them and have them cared for and appreciated by those who could afford to preserve them? Despite criticism, Elgin believed he was saving the sculptures from the ravages of time and neglect. Time has proven Elgin at least somewhat correct. The Parthenon continues to present a complex and continuous preservation problem. Time has ravaged the remains of the sculptures that were not removed, and deterioration of the monument accelerated rather than diminished throughout the twentieth century. Stonework and architectural detail have been eaten away by erosion, pollution, and acid rain, as well as by early and poorly conceived restoration efforts. As recently as 1971, a UNESCO report stated that the building itself was so weakened that it was in danger of collapse. Recent supporters of retaining the Elgin marbles argue that the marbles were obtained honestly with the permission of the government then in power. Other ancient Greek treasures, such as the Venus de Milo (currently on display in the Louvre in Paris), have also been removed from the country. Are these to be returned as well? For the time being it seems that the Elgin marbles remain in London.

Two young horsemen join a procession of sculpted figures on the Parthenon frieze. The marbles were taken from Greece in the early nineteenth century and are now on display in the British Museum, London.

Points to Ponder

1. Do you feel Elgin was right or wrong to remove the marbles?
2. Should the Elgin marbles be returned to Greece? On what basis did you make your decision?
3. The conservation of the Parthenon and the preservation of the sculptures are valid concerns. How can these concerns be reconciled with the question of ownership?

Native American Graves Protection and Repatriation Act

The most important legislation affecting the treatment and protection of archaeological and physical anthropological resources in the United States is the Native American Graves Protection and Repatriation Act (NAGPRA), passed on November 16, 1990 (McKeown 1998). This legislation is the most comprehensive of a series of recent laws dealing with the deposition of Native American burials and cultural properties.

NAGPRA and related legislation require that federal institutions consult with the lineal descendants of Native American groups and Native Hawaiians prior to the initial excavation of Native American human remains and associated artifacts on federal or tribal lands. Under this legislation, federal agencies and institutions receiving federal funding are also required to **repatriate**—or return—human remains and cultural items in their collections at the request of the descendant populations of the relevant Native American group. NAGPRA also dictates criminal penalties for trade in Native American human remains and cultural properties.

The impact of NAGPRA has been profound, not only on the way in which many archaeological projects are conducted, but also on the way in which museums and institutions inventory, curate, and manage their collections. The law has, at times, placed very different worldviews in opposition. For many Native Americans, the past is intricately connected to the present, and the natural world—animals, rocks, and trees, as well as cultural objects—may have spiritual meaning (Bataille et al. 2000; Rose et al. 1996). This perspective is fundamentally different from that of most museums, where both human remains and cultural artifacts are treated as nonliving entities, and the continuing spiritual links with the present are, at least at times, unrecognized. Museums are traditionally concerned with the collection and exhibition of objects. Reburial or repatriation of collections is the antithesis of their mission. As one scholar noted: "No museum curator will gladly and happily relinquish anything which he has enjoyed having in his museum, of which he is proud, which he has developed an affection for, and which is one of the principal attractions of his museum" (Shaw 1986:46). In a similar vein, reburial and repatriation may conflict with researchers' desire for complete analysis and study. The intersection of these varied interests is highlighted by ongoing debate about the treatment of skeletal remains (Bruning 2006).

NAGPRA and repatriation also raise pragmatic concerns. Return of objects or remains is dependent on a complete and accurate inventory of all of a museum's holdings. Yet, often museums have amassed collections over many decades, and detailed information on all of their collections may not exist or be readily assessable. A case in point is the collection of the Peabody Museum of Archaeology and Ethnology at Harvard University. Founded in 1866, the Peabody has a massive collection from all over the world, including substantial Native American and ancient Mesoamerican holdings. In the 1970s and 1980s, before the passage of NAGPRA, the museum repatriated several burials, collections, and objects at the request of various constituencies. NAGPRA spurred the museum to complete a detailed inventory. They found that the estimated 7,000 human remains in the collections grew to an inventory of about 10,000, while the amount of archaeological objects grew from 800,000 to 8 million (Isaac 1995). Following NAGPRA guidelines, the Peabody sent out summaries of collections to the 756 recognized tribal groups in the United States. Determining the cultural affiliations, the relevant descendant communities, and the need for repatriation of all of these items is a daunting task.

Many museums have undertaken major inventories, revamped storage facilities, and hired additional staff specifically to deal with the issue of repatriation. Impending repatriation of collections and human remains has also spurred many institutions and researchers to reexamine old collections. Such study is necessary to ensure that the presumed age and cultural attribution of individual remains are correct. Of course, all of these concerns have serious budgetary considerations.

While NAGPRA has produced conflicts, it has also both vastly increased the tempo of work on skeletal collections and provided an avenue for new cooperation between Native Americans and researchers. Many of the collections now analyzed would not have been examined if not for NAGPRA. Native claims will, in some instances, necessitate additional research on poorly documented groups. Indeed, anthropological or archaeological research may be critical to assessing the association and ownership of cultural materials and human remains. On the other hand, anthropologists are given the opportunity to share their discoveries with those populations for whom the knowledge is most relevant.

Applied Cultural Anthropology

10.6 Discuss the applied aspects of cultural anthropology.

Planning Change

Over the years, many applied cultural anthropologists have worked in helping to improve societies through planned change. To assist governments, private developers, or other agencies, applied anthropologists are hired because of their ethnographic studies of particular societies. Government and private agencies often employ applied anthropologists to prepare **social-impact studies**, research on the possible consequences that change will have for a community. Social-impact studies involve in-depth interviews and ethnological studies in local communities to determine how various policies and developments will affect social life in those communities.

One classic social-impact study was carried out by Thayer Scudder and Elizabeth Colson (1979) in the African country of Zambia. Scudder and Colson had conducted long-term ethnographic research for about 30 years in the Gwembe Valley in Zambia. In the mid-1950s, the Zambian government subsidized the development of a large-scale dam, which would provide for more efficient agricultural activities and electrification. Because of the location of the dam, however, the people in the Gwembe Valley would be forced to relocate. Scudder and Colson used their knowledge from their long-term research and subsequent interviews to study the potential impact of this project on the community.

From their social-impact study, Scudder and Colson concluded that the forced relocation of this rural community would create extreme stresses that would result in people clinging to familiar traditions and institutions during the period of relocation. Scudder did social-impact studies of other societies in Africa experiencing forced relocation due to dams, highways, and other developments. These studies enabled Scudder and Colson to offer advice to the various African government officials, who could then assess the costs and benefits of resettling these populations and could plan their development projects, taking into consideration the impact on the people involved.

Applied anthropologists often serve as consultants to government organizations, such as the U.S. Agency for International Development (USAID), that formulate policies involving foreign aid. For example, anthropologist Patrick Fleuret (1988), a full-time employee of USAID, studied the problems of farmers in Uganda after the downfall of Idi Amin in 1979. Fleuret and other USAID anthropologists discovered that on the heels of the political turmoil in Uganda, many of the peasants had retreated into subsistence production, rather than participating in the market economy. They also found that subsistence production was affected by a technological problem—a scarcity of hoes for preparing the land for cultivation. In response, USAID anthropologists helped design and implement a system to distribute hoes through local cooperative organizations.

This plan for the distribution of hoes reflects the development of new strategies on the part of USAID and the facilitator role for applied anthropologists. Most of the development work sponsored by USAID and applied anthropology in the 1950s and 1960s was aimed at large-scale development projects such as hydroelectric dams and other forms of mechanized agriculture and industrialism. Many of these large-scale projects, however, have resulted in unintended negative consequences. Often these large-scale projects were devised in terms of the modernization views proposed by economists such as Walt Rostow and were designed to shift an underdeveloped country to industrialism very rapidly.

Most recently, USAID and applied anthropologists have modified their policies on development projects in many less-developed countries. They now focus on projects that involve small-scale economic change with an emphasis on the development of appropriate technologies. Rather than relying upon large-scale projects to have "trickle-down" influences on local populations, applied anthropologists have begun to focus more realistically on determining where basic needs must be fulfilled. After assessing the needs of the local population, the applied anthropologist can help facilitate change by helping people learn new skills.

The Vicos Project One early project that placed applied anthropologists in decision making and analytical roles was run by Allan Holmberg of Cornell University. In the 1950s and 1960s, Holmberg and Mario Vasquez, a Peruvian anthropologist, developed what is known as the Vicos Project in the Andean highlands. Vicos is the name of a *hacienda* that was leased by Cornell in 1952 as part of a program to increase education and literacy, improve sanitation and health care, and teach new agricultural methods to the Andean Indians. Prior to the Vicos Project, the 1,700 Quechua-speaking Indians were peasant farmers who were not able to feed themselves. Their land on the *hacienda* was broken into small plots that were insufficient to raise potato crops. The Indians were indebted to the *hacendado* (owners of the *haciendas*) and were required to work on the *hacendado's* fields without pay to service their debts.

Although the applied anthropologists took on the role of a new patron to the Indians, the overall aim was to dissolve historical patterns of exploitation and to guide the Indians toward self-sufficiency (Holmberg 1962; Chambers 1985, Isbell 2013). The Indians were paid for their labor and were also introduced to new varieties of potatoes, fertilizers, and pesticides. New crops, such as leafy vegetables, and foods, such as eggs and fruit, were introduced into their diet.

Through an educational program, the Indians became acquainted with forms of representative democratic organization. Developing more independence, they eventually overturned the traditional authority structure of the *hacienda*. In 1962, the Indians purchased the land of the *hacienda* from its former owners, which gave the Indians a measure of self-sufficiency. Overall, the Vicos Project led to basic improvements in housing, nutrition, clothing, and health conditions for the Indians. The most significant achievement of the project was to improve the education of the Indian peasants. Currently over 30 percent of the Vicos people are studying in postsecondary institutions (Isbell 2013). This educational background enabled the Vicos people to negotiate with outside agencies and to clearly articulate their needs and demands. It has enhanced their sense of empowerment and self-sufficiency. One of the other major contributions of the Vicos project was to make the subjugation of the Indian peasants by the *hacienda* system widely known (Isbell 2013).

Engaged Anthropology Problems sometimes arise between applied anthropologists and private developers or government officials. Many developers and governments want to induce modernization and social change as rapidly as possible with capital-intensive projects, hydroelectric dams, and manufacturing facilities. In many cases, anthropologists have recommended against these innovations because of their expense and inefficient use of labor resources and the heavy cost to communities.

The consequences of globalization have been tragic for many indigenous societies. In 1972, the late David Maybury-Lewis established an advocacy organization called Cultural Survival, which is actively engaged in trying to reduce the costs imposed by globalization on small-scale societies. Driven by trade deficits and gigantic foreign debts, many governments in developing countries want to extract as much wealth as possible from their national territories. Highway expansion, mining operations, giant hydroelectric projects, lumbering, mechanized agriculture, and other industrial developments all intrude on the traditional lifestyle and territory of small-scale societies. Applied anthropologists connected with groups such as Cultural Survival try to obtain input from the people themselves and help them represent their interests to the government or private developers.

Many cultural anthropologists are applying their knowledge of culture to assist people and solve problems throughout the world.

Maybury-Lewis (1985) admitted that the advocacy role in anthropology was extremely difficult, and requires great sensitivity and complex moral and political judgments. Most recently, many small-scale societies and minority groups in developing countries are organizing themselves to represent their own interests. This has diminished the role of the applied anthropologist as advocate or representative. Generally, anthropologists are pleased when their role as advocate or representative is diminished because this role is called for only when native people are dominated by forces from globalization that are beyond their control.

In a new volume titled *Toward Engaged Anthropology*, a number of anthropologists are advocating applied approaches that involve using the theories and methods within anthropology to partner with the people studied to reduce inequities and other injustices (Beck and Maida 2013). The authors of this book promote "a kind of anthropology . . . in which partnerships, collaborations, and mutuality are central to the work, and local stake holders co-produce knowledge by providing their wisdom and expertise, even in co-authorship." (Beck and Maida 2013:8). In the volume, Thomas Hylland Eriksen indicates how Norwegian anthropologists who do studies on the ethnic minority Sami, nomadic pastoralists who herd reindeer, have resulted in an indigenous rights movement, legislation on land tenure, and the formation of a Sami parliament with some political autonomy in their regions (2013). Partnerships among anthropologists and the people studied to improve environmental, economic, social, and political conditions is the major goal of applied anthropology.

Applied Anthropology and Human Rights

10.7 Discuss how applied anthropologists are engaged in human rights research.

Cultural Relativism and Human Rights

A recent development that has had wide-ranging consequences for applied anthropology and ethnographic research involves the ways in which anthropologists assess and respond to the values and norms of other societies. Recall our discussion of *cultural relativism*, the method used by anthropologists to understand another society through their own cultural values, beliefs, norms, and behaviors. In order to understand an indigenous culture, the anthropologist must strive to temporarily suspend judgment of that culture's practices (Maybury-Lewis 2002). Anthropologists refer to this as *methodological relativism* (Brown 2008). While difficult, this procedure does help the anthropologist gain insights into that culture. However, some critics have charged that anthropologists (and other people) who adopt this position cannot (or will not) make value judgments concerning the values, norms, and practices of any society. If this is the case, then how can anthropologists encourage any conception of human rights that would be valid for all of humanity? Must anthropologists accept such practices as infanticide, caste and class inequalities, slavery, torture, and female subordination out of fear of forcing their own values on other people?

Relativism Reconsidered These criticisms have led some anthropologists to re-evaluate the basic assumptions regarding cultural relativism. In his 1983 book *Culture and Morality: The Relativity of Values in Anthropology*, Elvin Hatch recounted the historical acceptance of the cultural relativist view. As we saw in Chapter 8, this was the approach of Franz Boas, who challenged the unilineal evolutionary models of nineteenth-century anthropologists like E. B. Tylor, with their underlying assumptions of Western cultural superiority. Boas's approach, with its emphasis on tolerance and equality, appealed to many liberal-minded Western scholars. For example, the earlier nineteenth-century ethnocentric and racist assumptions held within anthropology were used at the 1904 World's Fair in St. Louis to display other peoples as barbaric, uncivilized, and savage to the "civilized" citizens who viewed them. These "pygmies" from Central Africa were given machetes to show how they "beheaded" one another in their local regions and the Igorot tribal people of the Philippines were given a dog to cook and eat daily in front of the "civilized" citizens of the United States in order to portray them as inferior races and cultures (Breitbart 1997). Such displays of these peoples during that period both distorted their cultural practices and allowed *anthropologists* of the time to treat them in an inhumane and unethical manner; they also resulted in harmful practices toward these native peoples in different regions. Thus, the criticisms of these racist and ethnocentric views and the endorsement of cultural relativism were important human rights innovations by twentieth-century anthropologists. In addition, many Westerners were stunned by the horrific events of World War I and the devastation and massive casualties for people within Western societies that were supposedly morally and culturally superior to other non-Western societies. Cultural relativism appealed to many people in the West as a correction to the earlier racist and ethnocentric views (Hatch 1983; Brown 2008).

Ethical Relativism However, belief in cultural relativism led to the acceptance by some early twentieth-century anthropologists of moral or **ethical relativism**, the notion that we cannot impose the values or morality of one society on other societies. Ethical relativists argued that because anthropologists had not discovered any universal moral values, each society's values were valid with respect to that society's circumstances and conditions. No society could claim any superior position over another regarding ethics and morality.

As many philosophers and anthropologists have noted, the argument of ethical relativism is a circular one that itself assumes a particular moral position. It is, in fact, a moral theory that encourages people to be tolerant toward all cultural values, norms, and practices. Hatch notes that in the history of anthropology, many who accepted the premises of ethical relativism could not maintain these assumptions in light of their data. Ethical relativists would have to tolerate practices such as homicide, child abuse, human sacrifice, torture, warfare, racial discrimination, and even genocide. In fact, even anthropologists who held the ethical relativist position in the early period of the twentieth century condemned many cultural practices. For example, Ruth Benedict condemned the practice of the Plains Indians to cut off the nose of an adulterous wife. Boas himself condemned racism, anti-Semitism, and other forms of bigotry. Thus, these anthropologists did not consistently adhere to the ethical relativist paradigm.

Photo from 1904 World's Fair in St. Louis showing "pygmies" beheading one another. This was never an aspect of "pygmy" culture.

The horrors associated with World War II eventually led most scholars to reject ethical relativism. The argument that Nazi Germany could not be condemned because of its unique moral and ethical standards appeared ludicrous to most people. In the 1950s, some anthropologists such as Robert Redfield suggested that general standards of judgment could be applied to most societies. However, these anthropologists were reluctant to impose Western standards on pre-state indigenous societies. In essence, they suggested a *double standard* in which they could criticize large-scale, industrial state societies but not pre-state indigenous societies.

This double standard of morality poses problems, however. Can anthropologists make value judgments about homicide, child abuse, warfare, torture, rape, and other acts of violence in a small-scale society? Why should they adopt different standards in evaluating such behaviors in pre-state indigenous societies as compared with industrial state societies? In both types of societies, human beings are harmed. Don't all humans in all societies have equal value?

A Resolution to the Problem of Relativism Is there a resolution to these philosophical and moral dilemmas? First, we need to distinguish between *cultural relativism* (or *methodological relativism*) and *ethical relativism*. In other words, to understand the values, the reasoning and logic, and the worldviews of another people does not mean to accept all of their practices and standards (Salmon 1997). Second, we need to realize that the culture of a society is not completely homogeneous or unified. In Chapter 6, we noted how culture was distributed differentially within any society. People do not all share the same culture within any society. For example, men and women do not share exactly the same "culture" in a society. Ethnographic experience tells anthropologists that there are always people who may not agree with the content of the moral and ethical values of a society. Treating cultures as "uniform united wholes" is a conceptual mistake. For one thing, it ignores the *power relationships* within a society. Elites within a society can maintain cultural hegemony or dominance and can use harmful practices against their own members to produce conformity. In some cases, governments use the concept of relativism to justify their repressive policies and deflect criticism of these practices by the international community. In Asia, many political leaders argue that their specific culture does not have the same notion of human rights that is accepted in Western society. Therefore, in China or Singapore, human rights may be restricted by political rulers who draw on their cultural tradition to support repressive and totalitarian political policies (Ong 2006; Brown 2008). Those who impose these harmful practices upon others may be the beneficiaries of those practices.

To get beyond the problem of ethical relativism, we ought to adopt a humanitarian standard that would be recognized by all people throughout the world. This standard would not be derived from any particular cultural values—such as the U.S. Declaration of Independence—but rather would involve the basic principle that every individual is entitled to a certain standard of "well-being." No individual ought to be subjected to bodily harm through violence or starvation.

Of course, we recognize certain problems with this solution. Perhaps, the key problem is that people in many societies accept—or at least appear to accept—behaviors that Westerners would condemn as inhumane. For example, what about the Aztec practice of human sacrifice? The Aztecs firmly believed that they would be destroyed if they did not sacrifice victims to the sun deity. Would an outside group have been justified in condemning and abolishing this practice? A more recent case involves the West Irian tribe known as the Dani, who engaged in constant warfare with neighboring tribes. They believed that through revenge they had to placate the ghosts of their kin who had been killed in warfare because unavenged ghosts bring sickness and disaster to the tribe. Another way of placating the ghosts was to bring two or three young girls related to the deceased victim to the funeral site and chop two fingers off their hands. Until recently, all Dani women lost from two to six fingers in this way (Heider 1979; Bagish 1981). Apparently, these practices were accepted by many Dani males and females.

In some Islamic countries, women have been accused of sexual misconduct and then executed by male members in what are called "honor killings." The practice of honor killings, which victimizes women, has been defended in some of these societies as a means to restore harmony to the society. The males argue that the shedding of blood washes away the shame of sexual dishonor. There have been a number of "honor killings" among immigrant Middle Eastern families within the United States. In both Africa and the Middle East, young girls are subjected to female circumcision, a polite term for the removal of the clitoris and other areas of the vagina. These practices, referred to by most human rights advocates as female genital mutilation/cutting (FGM or FGC), range from the cutting out of the clitoris to a more severe practice known as pharaonic infibulation, which involves stitching the cut labia to cover the vagina of the woman. One of the purposes of these procedures is to reduce the pleasure related to sexual intercourse and thereby induce more fidelity from women in marriage. Chronic infections are a common result of this practice. Sexual intercourse is painful, and childbirth is much more difficult for many of these women. However, the cultural ideology may maintain that an uncircumcised woman is not respectable, and few families want to risk their daughter's chances of marriage by not having her circumcised (Fluehr-Lobban 2003, 2013).

The right of males to discipline, hit, or beat their wives is often maintained in a male-dominated culture (Tapper and Tapper 1992, 1993). Other examples of these types of practices, such as head-hunting, slavery, female subordination, torture, and unnecessarily dangerous child labor, also fall into this category. According to a universal humanitarian standard suggested here, all of these practices could be condemned as harmful behaviors.

The Problem of Intervention

The condemnation of harmful cultural practices with reference to a universal standard is fairly easy. The abolition of such practices, however, is not. Anthropologists recommend that one should take a pragmatic approach in reducing these practices. Sometimes intervention in the cultures in which practices such as genocide are occurring would be a moral imperative. This intervention would proceed not from the standpoint of specific Western values, but from the commonly recognized universal standards of humanitarianism.

Such intervention, however, must proceed cautiously and be based on a thorough knowledge of the society. Ethnographers must gather empirical knowledge, studying the history, local conditions, social life, and various institutions, and assess carefully whether the cultural practice is shown to clearly create pain and suffering for people. For example, in Thailand, many young women are incorporated into the prostitution and sex tourist industry to help increase their parents' income (Barmé 2002). This prostitution and sex tourist industry must be thoroughly understood within the historical, economic, and cultural context of Thai society prior to endorsing a human rights intervention that would abolish these practices. When such understanding is present, intervention should take place by engaging in a form of dialogue, rather than by preaching human rights in a monolithic manner to various people in the community. In a recent ethnographic study of the attempt to abolish FGM in the Darfur region of the Sudan, anthropologist Ellen Gruenbaum focused on seven different communities to investigate how the UN agencies, the nongovernment organizations, and other human rights agencies are influencing these practices (2004). Gruenbaum found that, at times, women were participating in the FGM practices, such as pharaonic infibulation, because they "perceived" them as a means of protection against rape and illicit premarital intercourse within their communities. Rape is often used in these communities as a means of warfare. Thus, the historical and cultural context of these practices needs to be investigated cautiously by anthropologists prior to advocating a rapid enforcement of human rights that may result in outright rejection of the dedicated human rights workers (Shweder 2003, 2013).

As is obvious, these suggestions are based on the highly idealistic standards of a universal humanitarianism. In many cases, intervention to stamp out a particular cultural practice may not be possible, and in some cases, it may cause even greater problems. Communal riots, group violence, or social chaos may result from the dislocation of certain cultural practices. Thus, caution, understanding, and dialogue are critical to successful intervention. We need to be sensitive to cultural differences, but not allow them to produce severe harm to individuals within a society.

Universal Human Rights

The espousal of universally recognized standards to eradicate harmful practices is a worthwhile, albeit idealistic goal. Since the time of the Enlightenment, Western societies have prided themselves on extending human rights. Many Western theorists emphasize that human rights have spread to other parts of the world through globalization, thus providing the catalyst for social change, reform, and political liberation. At the same time, as people from non-Western societies can testify, the West has also promoted intolerance, racism, and genocide. Western society has not always lived up to the ideals of its own tradition.

The Role of Applied Anthropology in Human Rights Cultural anthropologists and applied anthropologists have a role in helping to define the universal standards for human rights in all societies. By systematically studying community standards, applied anthropologists can determine whether practices are harmful and then help provide solutions for reducing these harmful practices. This may involve consultation with local government officials and dialogue with members of the community to resolve the complex issues surrounding the identified harmful practices. The exchange of ideas across cultures through anthropological research is beginning to foster acceptance of the universal nature of some human rights regardless of cultural differences.

A good illustration of this type of research and effort by applied anthropologists is the work of John Van Willigen and V. C. Channa (1991), who have done research on the harmful consequences of the dowry in India. India, like some other primarily agricultural societies, has the cultural institution known as the *dowry*, in which the bride's family gives a certain amount of cash or other goods to the groom's family upon marriage. Recently, the traditions of the dowry have led to increasing cases of what has been referred to as "dowry death" or "bride burning." Some husbands or their families have been dissatisfied with the amount of the dowry that the new wife brings into the family. Following marriage, the family of the groom begins to make additional demands for more money and goods from the wife's family. These demands result in harassment and abuse of the wife, culminating in her murder. The woman is typically doused with kerosene and burned to death, hence the use of the term *bride burning*.

Dowry deaths have increased in recent years. In 1986, 1,319 cases were reported nationally in India. There are many other cases in which the evidence is more ambiguous, however, and the deaths of these women might be reported as kitchen accidents or suicides (Van Willigen and Channa 1991). In addition, the burdens imposed by the dowry tradition have led many pregnant women to pay for amniocentesis (a medical procedure to determine the health status of the fetus) as a means to determine the sex of the fetus. If the fetus is female, in many cases Indians have an abortion partly because of the increasing burden and expense of raising a daughter and developing a substantial dowry for her marriage. Thus, male children are preferred and female fetuses are selectively aborted.

Van Willigen, an American anthropologist, and Channa, an Indian anthropologist, studied the dowry problem together. They found that the national law established against the institution of the dowry (the Dowry Prohibition Act of 1961, amended in 1984 and 1986) is very tough. The law makes it illegal to give or take a dowry, but the law is ineffective in restraining the practice. In addition, a number of public education groups have been organized in India. Using slogans such as "Say No to Dowry," they have been advertising and campaigning against the dowry practices. Yet, the problem continues to plague India.

After carefully studying the dowry practices of different regions and local areas of India, Van Willigen and Channa concluded that the increase in dowry deaths was partially the result of the rapid inflationary pressures of the Indian economy, as well as the demands of a consumer-oriented economy. Consumer price increases have resulted in increasing demands for more dowry money to buy consumer goods. It has become more and more difficult to save resources for a dowry for a daughter or sister that is substantial enough to satisfy the groom's family. Van Willigen and Channa found that aside from wealth, family "prestige" that comes with wealth expenditures is sought by the groom's family.

From the perspective of the bride's family, dowry payments provide for present consumption and future earning power for their daughter through acquiring a husband with better connections and future earning potential. In a developing society such as India, with extremely high unemployment rates and rapid inflation, the importance of investing in a husband with high future earning potential is emphasized. When asked why they give a dowry when their daughters are being married, people respond, "Because we love them." The decision by the groom's family to forgo the dowry would also be very difficult.

There appears to be a very positive commitment to the institution of the dowry in India. Most people have given and received a dowry. Thus, declaring dowry a crime technically makes many people criminals. Van Willigen and Channa recommended that to be effective, the antidowry practices must be displaced by other, less problematic practices and that the apparent causes of the practice must be attacked. Women's property rights must be examined so as to increase their economic access. Traditional Hindu cultural norms regarding inheritance, which give sons the right from birth to claim the so-called ancestral properties, must be reformed. At present, male descendants inherit property, but females must pay for marriage expenses and dowry gifts. Van Willigen and Channa assert that a gender-neutral inheritance law in which women and men receive equal shares ought to be established to help reduce the discrepancy between males and females in India.

In addition, Van Willigen and Channa recommended the establishment of universal marriage registration and licensing throughout India. This may enable the government to monitor dowry abuses so that antidowry legislation could be more effective. These anthropologists concluded that a broad program to increase the social and economic status of women, along with more rigorous control of marriage registration and licensing, would be more effective in solving the dowry death problem in Indian society.

The use of applied anthropology, based on collaboration among Western and non-Western anthropologists, government and military officials, economic consultants and advisers, and local and national government leaders, to help solve fundamental human rights issues represents a commendable strategy for applied anthropologists in the future. It is hoped that through better cross-cultural understanding aided by ethnographic research, and through applied anthropology, universally recognized humanitarian standards will be widely adopted throughout the world. Many anthropologists are promoting advocacy anthropology, the use of anthropological knowledge to further human rights. Universal human rights would include the right to life and freedom from physical and psychological abuse, including torture;

freedom from arbitrary arrest and imprisonment; freedom from slavery and genocide; the right to nationality; freedom of movement and departure from one's country; the right to seek asylum in other countries because of persecution in one's own country; the rights to privacy, ownership of property, and freedom of speech, religion, and assembly; the right of self-determination; and the right to adequate food, shelter, health care, and education (Sponsel 1996). Obviously, not all these rights exist in any society at present. However, most people will probably agree that these rights ought to be part of any society's obligations to its people.

As people everywhere are brought closer together with the expansion of the global village, different societies will experience greater pressures to treat one another in sensitive and humane ways. We live in a world in which our destinies are intertwined more closely than they have ever been. Yet, it is a world containing many different societies with varied norms and practices. Sometimes, this leads to mutual distrust and dangerous confrontations, such as the 9/11 tragedy in the United States.

Anthropologists may be able to play a role in bringing about mutual understanding of others' rights to existence. Perhaps through this understanding, we may be able to develop a worldwide, pluralistic **metaculture**, a global system emphasizing fundamental human rights, with a sense of political and global responsibility. This cross-cultural understanding and mutual respect for human rights may be the most important aspect of anthropological research today.

Rural East Indian women often face human rights problems.

Summary and Review of Learning Objectives

10.1 Describe the different roles of applied anthropologists.

Rather than being confined to the halls of the university, an increasing number of anthropologists have become practitioners of anthropology, actively engaging with the communities that they study and solving problems in the modern world. Applied anthropologists may be in a *representative* role in which the anthropologist becomes the spokesperson for the particular group being studied. They can also be seen as *facilitators*. In this capacity, anthropologists actively help bring about change or development in the community being researched. An alternative position is the *informant role*, in which the applied anthropologist transfers cultural knowledge obtained from anthropological research to the government or other agency that wants to promote change in a particular area. Another role of applied anthropologists is that of *analyst*. Rather than being just a provider of data, the practicing anthropologist sometimes becomes engaged in the actual formulation of policy. Another role of the applied anthropologist is that of *mediator*, which involves the anthropologist as an intermediary among different interest groups that are participating in a development project.

10.2 Discuss the applied aspects of biological anthropology.

Biological anthropologists study the biological aspects of humans in the past and the present. This includes the measurement, observation, and explanation of various physical characteristics. Anthropometry, for example, concerns the measurement of human body parts, while osteometry is the measurement of skeletal elements. This information is important in studying human evolution and modern human variation. However, some of this research also has immediate relevance to the present. For example, biological anthropological data may be used by engineers to design ergonomically efficient work environments, airplane cockpits, or equipment. A specialized field within biological anthropology is forensic anthropology, which can be defined as the application of biological anthropological data to law. Researchers in this area of specialization assist police when unidentified human remains are found, including murder investigations and the identification of disaster victims. Biological anthropological study of the causes of diseases, when combined with knowledge of cultural anthropology, offers important insight into perceptions of medical treatment in different cultural settings.

10.3 Define medical anthropology and discuss some of the research undertaken.

The field of medical anthropology draws on cultural and biological anthropology, as well as the other subfields of anthropology and other disciplines. Medical anthropologists study disease, health care systems, medical practices, curing, and mental illness with a cross-cultural perspective. They often work with physicians and other public health care workers to apply their knowledge about cultural practices in different setting to provide more effective health care. Medical anthropologists study ethnomedicine, which examines traditionally based medical practices of different ethnic groups. These studies reveal that beliefs about disease and illness and medical treatment vary in different societies throughout the world. The study of these beliefs and medical treatments can enable medical anthropologists to help deliver more effective health care. Medical anthropologists also do epidemiological studies to determine the links between social and cultural factors and specific diseases such as cardiovascular problems, diabetes, AIDS, and other illnesses.

10.4 Define cultural resource management and discuss the role of archaeologists in the field.

Cultural resource management (often referred to as CRM) focuses on the evaluation, protection, and supervision of cultural resources, including the archaeological record, as well as the arts, historic sites and cultural property. One of the problems that humanity faces is how to safeguard the cultural heritage preserved in the archaeological record. Although archaeology may address questions of general interest to all of humanity, it is also important in promoting national heritage, cultural identity, and ethnic pride. Museums the world over offer displays documenting diverse local populations, regional histories, important events, and cultural traditions. The number of specialized museums focusing on particular peoples, regions, or historic periods has become increasingly important. Yet, the archaeological record is being destroyed at an alarming rate. In many parts of the world, recognition of this fact has led to legislation aimed at protecting archaeological sites. Archaeologists must be concerned with the preservation of archaeological sites and the recovery of information from sites threatened with destruction, as well as the interpretation and presentation of their findings to the more general public. Many archaeologists now find employment as applied archaeologists, doing CRM evaluating, salvaging, and protecting archaeological resources that are threatened with destruction.

10.5 Discuss the role of the NAGPRA legislation in the U.S.

The most important legislation affecting the treatment and protection of archaeological and physical anthropological resources in the United States is the Native American Graves Protection and Repatriation Act (NAGPRA), passed on November 16, 1990. This legislation is the most comprehensive of a series of laws dealing with the deposition of Native American burials and cultural properties. NAGPRA and related legislation require that federal institutions consult with the lineal descendants of Native American groups and Native Hawaiians prior to the initial excavation of Native American human remains and associated artifacts on federal or tribal lands. Under this legislation, federal agencies and institutions receiving federal funding are also required to repatriate—or return—human remains and cultural items in their collections at the request of the descendant populations of the relevant Native American group. NAGPRA also dictates criminal penalties for trade in Native American human remains and cultural properties.

10.6 Discuss the applied aspects of cultural anthropology.

To assist governments, private developers, or other agencies, applied anthropologists are hired because of their ethnographic studies of particular societies. Government and private agencies often employ applied anthropologists to prepare social-impact studies, research on the possible consequences that change will have for a community. Rather than relying upon large-scale projects to have "trickle-down" influences on local populations, applied anthropologists have begun to focus more realistically on determining where basic needs must be fulfilled. After assessing the needs of the local population, the applied anthropologist can help facilitate change by helping people learn new skills. Partnerships among anthropologists and the people studied to improve environmental, economic, social, and political conditions is the major goal of applied anthropology.

10.7 Discuss how applied anthropologists are engaged in human rights research.

Early cultural anthropologists who accepted the tenets of cultural relativism sometimes also embraced ethical relativism, the idea that a person could not make value judgments about other societies. Although most anthropologists reject ethical relativism, the issue of universal standards to evaluate values and harmful cultural practices is still problematic. Many applied anthropologists are engaged in research on harmful practices to help promote their prevention. Proposing universal standards by which to make value judgments and help reduce harmful cultural practices remains one of the most important tasks for applied anthropology and future ethnographic research.

Key Terms

applied anthropology, p. 263
cultural patrimony, p. 279
cultural resource management, p. 272
epidemiology, p. 271
ethical relativism, p. 286
ethnomedicine, p. 269
forensic anthropology, p. 264
medical anthropology, p. 268
metaculture, p. 291
repatriate, p. 282
social-impact studies, p. 283

Glossary

acclimatization The physiological process of being or becoming accustomed to a new physical environment.

achieved status Status that results, at least in part, from a person's voluntary actions.

adaptation The process in which an organism makes a successful adjustment to a specific environment.

adaptive radiation The relatively rapid evolution of a species in a new environmental niche.

aerial photography Photographs taken from the air of archaeological sites and the landscape. Helpful to archaeologists in mapping and locating sites.

age grades Statuses defined by age through which a person moves in the course of his or her lifetime.

age stratification The unequal allocation of wealth, power, and prestige among people of different ages.

agency The process of intentional conscious (self-aware) choices that humans make that may alter their social or cultural worlds.

alleles The alternate forms of a gene.

analogy Similarities in organisms that have no genetic relatedness.

anatomically modern *Homo sapiens* The most recent form of human, distinguished by a unique anatomy that differs from that of earlier, archaic *Homo sapiens*.

antiquaries Collectors whose interest lies in the object itself, not in where the fossils might have come from or what the artifact and associated materials might tell about the people that produced them. Collectors of this kind characterized the early history of archaeology.

anthropology The systematic study of humankind.

anthropomorphism A psychological disposition to project and attribute human characteristics to nonhuman phenomena.

applied anthropology The use of data gathered from the other subfields of anthropology to find practical solutions to problems in a society.

archaeology The subfield of anthropology that focuses on the study of the artifacts from past societies to determine the lifestyles, history, and evolution of those societies.

archaeological sites Places of past human activity that are preserved in the ground.

archaic *Homo sapiens* The earliest form of *Homo sapiens*, dating back more than 200,000 years.

art A diverse range of activities and skills and the products of those activities that are used as expressions and representations of human emotions, intellect, and creativity.

artifacts The material products of past societies.

ascribed status Status that is attached to a person from birth—for example, sex, caste, and race.

authority Power generally perceived by members of society as legitimate, rather than coercive.

balanced polymorphism The mixture of homozygous and heterozygous genes of a population in a state of equilibrium.

band The least complex and, most likely, the oldest form of a political system.

beliefs Specific cultural conventions concerning true or false assumptions shared by a particular group.

biological anthropology (Also referred to as physical anthropology) The subfield that studies the biological characteristics of humanity in the past and present.

biome An area distinguished by a particular climate and certain types of plants and animals.

bipedalism The ability to walk erect on two hind legs.

carrying capacity The maximum population that a specific environment can support.

catastrophism A theory that suggests that many species have disappeared since the time of creation because of major catastrophes such as floods, earthquakes, and other major geological disasters.

chief A person who owns, manages, and controls the basic productive factors of the economy and has privileged access to strategic and luxury goods.

chiefdom A political system with a formalized and centralized leadership, headed by a chief.

childhood mortality rate The number of children who die before reaching the age of 5.

clinal distribution Plotting the varying distribution of physical traits in various populations on maps by clines, or zones.

clines The zones on a map used to plot physical traits of populations.

cognitive anthropology The study of human psychological thought processes based on computer modeling.

communication The act of transferring information.

consumption The use of goods and services to satisfy desires and needs.

context The specific location in the ground of an artifact or fossil and all associated materials.

continental drift The separation of continents that occurred over millions of years as a result of the geological process of plate tectonics.

continuous variation A phenomenon whereby variation in a particular trait or characteristic cannot be divided into discrete, readily definable groups, but varies continuously from one end of the spectrum to the other.

cosmologies Ideas that present the universe as an orderly system, including answers to basic questions about the place of humankind.

correlation The simultaneous occurrence of two variables.

crude birth rate The number of live births in a given year for every thousand people in a population.

crude death rate The number of deaths in a given year for every thousand people in a population.

cultural anthropology The subfield of anthropology that focuses on the study of contemporary societies.

cultural ecology The systematic study of the relationships between the environment and society.

cultural hegemony The control over beliefs, values, and norms exercised by the dominant group in a society.

cultural materialism A research strategy that focuses on technology, environment, and economic factors as key determinants in sociocultural evolution.

cultural patrimony The ownership of cultural properties such as human remains, artifacts, monuments, sacred sites, and associated cultural materials.

cultural relativism The view that cultural traditions must be understood within the context of a particular society's responses to problems, cultural practices, and values.

culture shock A severe psychological reaction that results from adjusting to the realities of a society radically different from one's own.

cultural universals Essential behavioral characteristics of humans found in all societies.

cultural resource management The attempt to protect and conserve artifacts and archaeological resources for the future.

culture A shared way of life that includes material products, values, beliefs, and norms that are transmitted within a particular society from generation to generation.

datum point A reference point in an archaeological excavation, often some permanent feature or marker, from which all measurements of contour, level, and location are taken.

deductive method A method of investigation in which a scientist begins with a general theory, develops specific hypotheses, and tests them.

dendrochronology A numerical dating technique based on the varying pattern of environmental conditions preserved in the annual growth rings of trees.

demography The study of population and its relationship to society.

Denisovans, or the Denisova hominins A previously unknown species or subspecies of hominin identified on the basis of genetic material recovered from hominin bones discovered in Denasova cave in Siberia, Russia. Mitochondrial DNA and genomic data from bones dating between 30,000 and 48,000 years ago revealed a genetic pattern unlike that found in either modern humans or Neandertals. Additional study of the nuclear genome suggests that the Denisovans share a common origin with Neandertals, and that they interbred with the ancestors of modern-day Melanesians and Australian Aborigines. Additional study of the genomic data suggests interbreeding with another, unknown human lineage distinct from the Neandertals and modern humans.

deoxyribonucleic acid (DNA) A chain of chemicals contained in each chromosome that produces physical traits that are transmitted to the offspring during reproduction.

dependent variable A variable whose value changes in response to changes in the independent variable.

developmental acclimatization Permanent or nonreversible adaptation to specialized environmental conditions such as high altitude.

dialect A linguistic pattern involving differences in pronunciation, vocabulary, or syntax that occurs within a common language family.

diffusionism The spread of cultural traits from one society to another.

division of labor The specialized economic roles and activities within a society.

dominant The form of a gene that is expressed in a heterozygous pair.

ecofacts Archaeological finds that have cultural significance but that are not artifacts manufactured or produced by humans. Examples of ecofacts would be botanical, faunal, and shell remains recovered from an archaeological site.

ecology The study of living organisms in relationship to their environment.

ecological niche The specific environmental setting to which an organism is adapted.

economy The social relationships that organize the production, exchange, and consumption of goods and services.

egalitarian A type of social structure that emphasizes equality among different statuses.

emic perspective The study of a culture from an insider's point of view.

enculturation The process of social interaction through which people learn their culture.

endogamy Marriage between people of the same social group or category.

environmental niche A locale that contains various plants, animals, and other ecological conditions to which a species must adjust.

epidemiology The study of disease patterns in a society.

ethical relativism The belief that the values of one society should never be imposed on another society.

ethnoarchaeology The study of material artifacts of the past along with the observation of modern peoples who have knowledge of the use and symbolic meaning of those artifacts.

ethnocentrism The practice of judging another society by the values and standards of one's own.

ethnography A description of a society written by an anthropologist who conducted field research in that society.

ethnohistory The study of the history of a particular ethnic group based on written documents or oral narratives.

ethnology The subfield of anthropology that focuses on the cross-cultural aspects of ethnographic studies.

ethnomedicine The study and comparison of traditional spiritually based medical practices by different ethnic groups.

ethnomusicology The study of musical traditions in different societies.

ethnopoetics The study of the poetry traditions and practices in different societies.

ethologist A scientist who studies the behaviors of animals in their natural setting.

etic perspective The study of a culture from an outsider's point of view.

evolution Process of change within the genetic makeup of a species over time.

exchange The transfer of goods and services from one member of society to another.

exogamy Marriage between people of different social groups or categories.

extended family A family that is made up of parents, children, and other kin relations bound together as a social unit.

family A social group of two or more people related by blood, marriage, or adoption who live or reside together for an extended period, sharing economic resources and caring for their young.

faunal correlation The dating of fossils through the comparison of similar fossils from better-dated sequences.

faunal succession Literally, "animal" succession; recognizes that life-forms change through time. First noted by the English geologist William Smith.

features Nonmovable artifacts or traces of past human activity such as an ancient fire hearth, a pit dug in the ground, or a wall.

fecundity The potential number of children that women in a society are capable of bearing.

fertility The number of births in a society.

feud A type of armed combat within a political community.

fission-track dating A numerical dating method based on the decay of an unstable isotope of uranium. Used to date volcanic rocks.

folkways Norms guiding ordinary usages and conventions of everyday life.

foraging society Another classification used for a hunting-and-gathering society.

foramen magnum The opening in the base of the skull through which the spinal cord passes.

forensic anthropology The identification of human skeletal remains for legal purposes.

fossil The remains of bones and living materials preserved from earlier periods.

fossil localities Places where fossils are found. These may be locations where predators dropped animals they killed, places where creatures were naturally covered by sediments, or sites where early humans or primates actually lived.

founder effect A type of genetic drift resulting from the randomly determined genetic complement present in the founders of an isolated population.

functionalism An anthropological perspective based upon the assumption that society consists of institutions that serve vital purposes for people.

gametes Sex cells (such as egg and sperm in humans). They contain only half of the chromosomes found in ordinary body, or somatic, cells.

gene Discrete units of hereditary information that determine specific physical characteristics of organisms.

gene flow The exchange of genes between populations as a result of interbreeding.

gene pool The total collection of all the alleles within a particular population.

genetic drift Change in allele frequencies within a population as a result of random processes of selection.

gender Specific human traits defined by culture and attached to each sex by a society.

genotype The specific genetic constitution of an organism.

goods Elements of material culture produced from raw materials in the natural environment, ranging from the basic commodities for survival to luxury items.

Hardy-Weinberg theory of genetic equilibrium An idealized mathematical model that sets hypothetical conditions under which no evolution is taking place. Developed independently by G. H. Hardy and W. Weinberg, the model is used to evaluate evolutionary processes operating on a population.

heterozygous Having two different alleles in a gene pair.

historical linguistics The comparison and classification of different languages to discern the historical links among them.

historical particularism An approach to studying human societies in which each society has to be understood as a unique product of its own history.

holistic A broad, comprehensive approach to the study of humankind drawing on the four subfields of anthropology and integrating both biological and cultural phenomena.

hominids In taxonomic classification, hominids (members of family Hominidae) is a term that was traditionally used to refer to bipedal apes, a group that represents humans and their immediate ancestors. This classification was revised on the basis of the genetic study of modern primates. Family *Hominidae* now includes subfamilies *Ponginae* and *Homininae*, while hominins (members of the tribe *Homininae*) is used to refer to humans and their immediate ancestors.

hominins In taxonomic classification, hominins refers to members of the Hominini tribe of subfamily *Homininae*, which includes humans and their immediate ancestors. Hominins share a number of distinctive characteristics, particularly bipedalism.

homology Traits that have a common genetic origin, but may differ in form and function.

homozygous Having the same alleles in a gene pair.

hybridization and assimilation models Models of the evolution of anatomically modern humans that allow for varying degrees of gene flow between *Homo sapiens* and earlier populations of archaic *H. sapiens* via gene flow or genetic admixture.

hypothesis A testable proposition concerning the relationship between different sets of variables within the collected data.

ideal culture What people say they do or should do.

ideology Cultural symbols and beliefs that reflect and support the interests of specific groups within a society.

independent variable A causal variable that produces an effect on another variable, the dependent variable.

inductive method A method of investigation in which a scientist first makes observations and collects data and then formulates a hypothesis.

infant mortality rate The number of babies per thousand births in any year who die before reaching the age of 1.

intelligence The capacity to process information and adapt to the world.

kinesics The study of body motion and gestures used in nonverbal communication.

knowledge The storage and recall of learned information based on experience.

lactase deficiency The inability to digest lactose, the sugar found in milk.

language A system of symbols with standard meanings through which members of a society communicate with one another.

law of supraposition States that in any succession of rock layers, the lowest rocks were deposited first and the upper rocks have been in place for progressively shorter periods. This assumption forms the basis of stratigraphic dating.

life expectancy The number of years as average person can expect to live.

linguistic anthropology The subfield of anthropology that focuses on the study of language.

linguistics The study of language.

marriage A social bond sanctioned by society between two or more people that involves economic cooperation, social obligations, and culturally approved sexual activity.

material culture Tangible products of human society.

medical anthropology The study of disease, health care systems, and theories of disease and curing in different societies.

meiosis The process by which gametes, which contain only half the number of chromosomes present in the original cell, are formed.

metaculture A global system of values that transcends any particular culture.

middens Ancient dumps or trash heaps.

migration rate The rate at which people move into and out of a specific territory.

mitosis The process by which somatic cells divide to produce new cells with the full number of chromosomes present in the original cell.

monogamy A form of marriage that involves two individuals.

mores Stronger norms than folkways; violators are usually punished severely.

morphemes The smallest units of a language that convey meaning.

morphology The study of morphemes.

mortality The incidence of death in a society's population.

multilineal evolution The view that societies and cultures have evolved and are evolving in many different directions.

multiregional evolutionary model The view that *Homo sapiens* evolved from *Homo erectus* concurrently in different regions of the world.

multivariate analysis A complex form of analysis that examines the distributions and interrelations among multiple variables or characteristics as, for example, patterns of disease, blood groups, and demographics in human populations.

music An art form that is based on the organization of sounds in combination and in temporal relationships to produce audible works for performance in various communities.

mutations A change in the genotype of an individual through the alteration of the chromosomes or DNA.

myth Assumed knowledge about the universe and the natural and supernatural worlds and about humanity's place therein.

narrative The oral or written representation of an event or a story.

natural selection A theory presented by Darwin and Wallace that nature or environmental circumstances determine which characteristics are essential for survival. Individuals with these characteristics survive and pass them on to their offspring.

net migration The total movement of a population into and out of a territory.

nonmaterial culture Intangible products of human society, including values, beliefs, and norms.

norms Shared rules that define how people are supposed to behave under certain circumstances.

nuclear family A family that is composed of two parents and their immediate biological offspring or adopted children.

obsidian hydration A relative dating method used on stone tools made from obsidian. Obsidian, sometimes referred to as volcanic glass, is a naturally occurring stone that is common in some world areas. When an obsidian artifact is made, the old weathered surface is flaked off, exposing the unweathered interior of the stone. Obsidian hydration dating is based on the rate at which hydration layers accumulate on the newly exposed surfaces of the tools. It is a relative dating method because the rate at which the hydration layers form is influenced by the local environmental conditions in which the obsidian artifacts are found.

paleoanthropology The study of human evolution through the analysis of fossil remains.

paleoecology *Paleo*, meaning "old," and *ecology*, meaning "study of environment." The area of research focusing on the reconstruction and interpretation of ancient environments.

palynology The study of pollen grains, the minute male reproductive part of plants. It may provide a means of reconstructing past environments and of relative dating.

participant observation The method used by the ethnographer who learns the culture of the group being studied by participating in the group's daily activities.

personality Stable patterns of thought, feeling, and action associated with a specific person.

phenotype The external, observable physical characteristics of an organism that result from the interaction of the organism's genetic makeup (the genotype) and its distinctive life history.

phonology The study of the sounds made in speech.

phoneme A basic unit of sound that distinguishes meaning in a language.

phones Units of sound in a language.

phyletic gradualism The theory that speciation is a gradual process of evolution that occurs very slowly as different populations become isolated. It was originally proposed by Charles Darwin.

plate tectonics The gradual movement of plates on the Earth's surface as a result of geological processes, one consequence of which is the movement of continents or continental drift.

political power The ability to achieve personal ends despite opposition.

polyandry Marriage between one wife and two or more husbands.

polygamy Marriage involving a spouse of one sex and two or more spouses of the opposite sex.

polygyny Marriage between one husband and two or more wives.

polymorphism A trait that exhibits variation within a species.

polytypic A species exhibiting physical variation in different regional populations.

population A group of organisms that interbreeds and occupies a given territory at the same time.

postmodernism A viewpoint that is critical of modern scientific and philosophical perspectives.

postorbital constriction A feature of *Homo erectus* in which the front portion of the skull is narrow and the forehead is low.

potassium-argon dating A numerical dating method based on the decay of an unstable isotope of potassium into the inert gas argon. It is used by paleoanthropologists to date volcanic rocks.

pragmatics The rules for using language within a particular speech community.

priest A full-time, formally trained, male religious specialist.

priestess A full-time, formally trained, female religious specialist.

primates A diverse order of mammals, including humans, monkeys, and apes, that share similar characteristics.

primatology The study of primates.

production The organized system for the creation of goods and services.

protolanguage The parent language for many ancient and modern languages.

proton magnetometer A sensor that can detect differences in the soil's magnetic field caused by buried features and artifacts.

prototypes Initial classifications of the world that help the human mind organize external reality.

proxemics The study of how people in different societies perceive and use space.

psychological anthropologist An anthropologist who studies the interrelationship between the individual and culture, or the process of enculturation.

pull factors The incentives that lead people to move to other societies.

punctuated equilibrium The theory of evolution that species remain relatively stable for long periods, with major changes (punctuations) and new species arising very rapidly as a result of mutations or changes in selective pressures.

push factors The conditions that lead people to leave specific territories.

qualitative data Nonstatistical information that tends to be the most important aspect of ethnographic research.

quantitative data Data that can be expressed as numbers, including census materials, dietary information, and income and household-composition data.

racism Beliefs and practices that advocate the superiority of certain races and the inferiority of others.

radiocarbon dating A numerical dating technique based on the decay of the unstable isotope carbon-14. Can be used to date organic material such as charcoal, wood fragments, or skeletal material as much as 80,000 years old.

random sample A representative sample of people of various ages or statuses in a society.

real culture People's actual behaviors, as opposed to ideal culture.

recessive Designating a gene that is unexpressed when occurring in a heterozygous pair with a dominant form.

relative dating A variety of dating methods that can be used to establish the age of a fossil, artifact, or geological feature relative to another.

repatriation The return of human remains or cultural property to a descendant community or interest group.

replacement model The paleoanthropological theory that *Homo sapiens* evolved in one world area and then expanded, replacing regional populations of earlier hominids.

research design A proposal in which the objectives of a project are set out and the strategy for recovering the relevant data is outlined.

resistivity A subsurface detection method that identifies buried archaeological features. Measurement of variation in the electrical current passing between electrodes placed in the ground indicates variation in conductivity, which in turn is an indication of buried ditches, foundations, or walls that retain moisture to varying degrees and have varying degrees of conductivity.

rites of passage Rituals associated with the life cycle and the movement of people between different age-status levels.

rituals Repetitive behaviors that communicate sacred symbols to members of society.

role A set of expected behavior patterns, obligations, and norms attached to a particular status.

sagittal crest A bony ridge along the top of the skull.

Sapir–Whorf hypothesis A hypothesis that assumes a close relationship between language and culture, claiming that language defines people's experiences.

schema The mental codification of experience that includes a particular organized way of perceiving cognitively and responding to a complex situation or set of stimuli.

scientific method A method used to investigate the natural and social worlds involving critical thinking, logical reasoning, and skeptical thought.

semantics The meaning of words, phrases, and sentences.

seriation A relative dating method based on the assumption that any particular artifact, attribute, or style will appear, gradually increase in popularity until it reaches a peak, and then progressively decrease.

services Elements of nonmaterial culture derived from cultural knowledge in the form of specialized skills that benefit others, such as giving spiritual comfort or providing medical care.

sex Biological differences between males and females.

shamans Part-time religious specialists who are believed to be linked with supernatural beings and powers.

signs Units of meaning that are directly associated with concrete physical phenomena.

situational learning A type of learning in which an organism adjusts its behavior in response to direct experience.

social learning A type of learning in which an organism observes another organism's response to a stimulus and then adds that response to its own collection of behaviors.

social stratification The inequality of statuses in a society.

social structure The pattern of relationships in a society.

social impact studies Research on the possible consequences of change in a society.

society A group of people who reside within a specific territory and share a common culture.

socioeconomic status A specific position determined by economic circumstances and other cultural variables within a society.

sociolinguistics The systematic study of language use in various social settings to discern the links between language and social behavior.

sodalities Groups based on kinship, age, gender, or other principles that provide for political organization.

somatic cells Body cells; unlike gametes (sex cells), they have the full number of chromosomes.

speciation The development of new species.

species Groups of organisms with similar physical characteristics that can potentially interbreed successfully.

state A form of political system with centralized bureaucratic institutions to establish power and authority over large populations in clearly defined territories.

status A recognized position that a person occupies in a society.

stratigraphic dating A relative dating method based on the law of supraposition, which states that in any succession of rock strata or soil layers, the oldest layers are located at the bottom with each of the upper layers being successively younger.

structural linguistics An area of research that investigates the structure of language patterns as they presently exist.

subsistence patterns The means by which people obtain their food supply.

survey An examination of a particular area, region, or country to locate archaeological sites or fossil localities.

symbolic anthropology The study of culture through the interpretation of a society's symbols, values, beliefs, and ethos.

symbolic learning The ability to use and understand symbols.

symbols Arbitrary units of meaning that can stand for different concrete or abstract phenomena.

syntax Rules for phrase and sentence construction in a language.

taphonomy The study of the variety of natural and behavioral processes that led to the formation of a fossil locality. This may include traces of the activities of early human ancestors, as well as natural agencies such as erosion, decay, and animal activities.

technology All the human techniques and methods of reaching a specific subsistence goal or of modifying or controlling the natural environment.

theories Interconnected hypotheses that offer general explanations of natural or social phenomena.

thermoluminescence dating Dating method based on the amount of electrons trapped in crystalline minerals as a consequence of radioactive decay.

transitional forms The hominin fossils that are either advanced *Homo erectus* or early *Homo sapiens*.

tribes Complex societies having political institutions that unite horticulturalist or pastoralist groups into a political system.

uniformitarianism The geological view that the Earth's geological features are the result of gradual, natural processes that can still be observed.

unilineal evolution The belief, widespread during the nineteenth century, that societies were evolving in a single direction toward complexity and industrial progress.

values Standards by which a society defines what is desirable and undesirable.

variable A datum that varies from case to case.

warfare Armed combat among territorial or political communities.

zygote A cell formed by the combination of a male and female sex cell that has the potential of developing into a new organism.

References

Abu-Lughod, Lila. 1987. *Veiled Sentiments: Honor and Poetry in a Bedouin Society*. Berkeley: University of California Press.

Abu-Zeid, M.A. and **F. Z. El-Shibini.** 1997. "Egypt's High Aswan Dam." *Water Resources Development*, Vol. 13, No. 2, pp. 209–217.

Adovasio, James M., and **Jake Page.** 2002. *The First Americans: In Pursuit of Archaeology's Greatest Mystery*. New York: Random House.

Agar, Michael. 1980. *The Professional Stranger: An Informal Introduction to Ethnography*. New York: Academic Press.

Aiken, M. J. 1990. *Science Based Dating in Archaeology*. New York: Longman.

Alemseged, Zeresenay, Fred Spoor, William H. Kimbel, René Bobe, Denis Geraads, Denné Reed, and **Jonathan G. Wynn.** 2006. "A Juvenile Early Hominin Skeleton from Dikika, Ethiopia." *Nature* 443: 296–301.

Alverson, Hoyt. 1994. *Semantics and Experience: Universal Metaphors of Time in English, Mandarin, Hindi, and Sesotho*. Baltimore, MD: Johns Hopkins University Press.

American Anthropological Association 2012. *Statement-on-Ethics-Principles-of-Professional-Responsibility*.pdf. http://www.aaanet.org/profdev/ethics/upload/. Washington, DC: American Anthropological Association.

Anderson, David G., and **Virginia Horak, eds.** 1995. *Archaeological Site File Management: A Southeastern Perspective*. Readings in Archaeological Resource Protection Series No. 3. Atlanta, GA: Interagency Archaeological Service Division.

Andrews, Peter, and **Lawrence Martin.** 1987. "Cladistic Relationships of Extant and Fossil Hominoid Primates." *Journal of Human Evolution* 16: 101–18.

Appadurai Arjun. 1981. "Gastro-politics in Hindu South Asia." *American Ethnologist*, 8: 494–511.

Arbib, Michael A. 2011. "From mirror neurons to complex imitation in the evolution of language and tool use." *Annual Review of Anthropology* 40, 257–273.

Arbib, Michael, Katja Liebal, and **Simone Pika.** 2008. "Primate Vocalization, Gesture, and the Evolution of Human Language." *Current Anthropology* 49 (6): 1053–1076.

Arden, Harvey. 1989. "Who Owns Our Past?" *National Geographic* 75 (3): 378.

Armelagous, George, and **Dennis van Gerven.** 2003. "A century of skeletal biology and paleopathology: contrasts, contradictions, and conflicts."*American Anthropologist* 105: 53–64.

Atran, Scott. 1990. *Cognitive Foundations of Natural History*. Cambridge: Cambridge University Press.

———. 1998. "Folk Biology and the Anthropology of Science: Cognitive Universals and Cultural Particulars." *Behavioral and Brain Sciences* 21 (4): 547–609.

———. 2002. *In Gods We Trust: The Evolutionary Landscape of Religion*. Oxford, England: Oxford University Press.

———. 2010. *Talking to the Enemy: Faith, Brotherhood, and the (Un)Making of Terrorists*. New York: Ecco, HarperCollins.

Atran, Scott and **Joseph Henrich.** 2010. "The Evolution of Religion: How Cognitive By-Products, Adaptive Learning Heuristics, Ritual **Displays,** and **Group Competition.** Generate Deep Commitments to Prosocial Religions *Biological Theory* 5 (1): 18–30.

Atran, Scott and **Douglas Medin**. 2008. *The Native Mind and the Cultural Construction of Nature*. Cambridge, MA: MIT Press.

Auel, Jean M. 1981. *The Clan of the Cave Bear*. New York: Bantam.

Ayala, F. J. 1995. "The Myth of Eve: Molecular Biology and Human Origins." *Science* 270: 1930–36.

Bagish, Henry H. 1981. *Confessions of a Former Cultural Relativist*. Santa Barbara, CA: Santa Barbara City College Publications.

Balter, Michael, and **Ann Gibbons.** 2000. "A Glimpse of Humans' First Journey Out of Africa." *Science* 288: 948–50.

Banton, Michael. 1998. *Racial Theories*. Cambridge: Cambridge University Press.

Barmè, Scott. 2002. *Woman, Man, Bangkok: Love, Sex and Popular Culture in Thailand*. Lanham, MD: Rowman and Littlefield.

Barnes, Linda L. 2005. "American Acupuncture and Efficacy: Meanings and Their Points of Insertion." *Medical Anthropology Quarterly* 19 (3): 239–266.

Barrett, Richard A. 1984. *Culture and Conduct: An Excursion in Anthropology*. Belmont, CA: Wadsworth.

Barth, Fredrik. 1975. *Ritual and Knowledge Among the Baktaman of New Guinea*. Oslo: Universitets Forlaget; New Haven, CT: Yale University Press.

———. 2002. "Toward a Richer Description and Analysis of Cultural Phenomena." In *Anthropology beyond Culture*, edited by Richard Fox and Barbara J. King. Oxford, England: Berg.

Bass, George Fletcher. 1963. "Underwater Archaeology: Key to History's Warehouse." *National Geographic* 124 (1): 138–56.

———. 1973. *Archaeology Beneath the Sea*. New York: Harper & Row.

Bass, George (ed). 2005. *Beneath the Seven Seas: Adventures with the Institute of Nautical Archaeology*. New York: Thames and Hudson.

Bass, George, Sheila D. Matthews, J. Richard Steffy, and **Frederick H. van Doornink, Jr. (eds).** 2004. *Serce Limani: An Eleventh-Century Shipwreck, Vol. 1, The Ship and Its Anchorage, Crew, and Passengers*. College Station: Texas A&M University.

Bataille, Gretchen, David M. Gradwohl, and **Charles L. P. Silet.** 2000. *The Worlds between Two Rivers: Perspectives on American Indians in Iowa*. Iowa City: University of Iowa Press.

Bawaya, Michael. 2005. "Maya Archaeologists Turn to the Living to Help Save the Dead." *Science* 309: 1317–18.

Beall, Cynthia M. 2007. "Two routes to functional adaptation: Tibetan and Andean high-altitude natives." *Proceeding of the National Academy of Sciences*, U S A. 104, Supplement 1: 8655–60.

Beall, C., K. Song, R. Elston, and **M. Goldstein.** 2004. "Higher Offspring Survival among Tibetan Women with High Oxygen Saturation Genotypes Residing at 4,000 m." PDF.

Proceedings of National Academy of Sciences, PNAS, September 7, 10.1073/pnas 0405949101 (Anthropology-Social Sciences).

Beals, Kenneth L. Courtland L. Smith, and **Stephen M. Dodd.** 1984. Brain Size, Cranial Morphology, Climate, and Time Machines *Current Anthropology* 25 (3): 301–330.

Beck, Sam and **Carl Maida., eds.** 2013. *Toward Engaged Anthropology*. New York and Oxford: Berghahn Books.

Bednarik, R. G. 2011. *The Human Condition*. New York: Springer.

Beeman, William O. 1986. *Language, Status, and Power in Iran*. Bloomington: Indiana University Press.

Begun, David R. Ed. 2012 "The African Origin of Homo Sapiens". *A Companion to Paleoanthropology*. John Wiley & Sons.

Behe, Michael J. 1996.*Darwin's Black Box: The Biochemical Challenge to Evolution*. New York: Free Press.

Beja-Pereira, Albano, Gordon Luikart, Phillip R. England, Daniel G. Bradley, Oliver C. Jann, Giorgio Bertorelle, Andrew T. Chamberlain, Telmo P. Nunes, Stoitcho Metodiev, Nuno Ferrand, and **Georg Erhardt.** 2003. "Gene-culture coevolution between cattle milk protein genes and human lactase genes."*Nature Genetics* 35 (4): 311–312.

Bellah, R., R. Madsen, W. Sullivan, A. Swidler, and **S. M. Tipton.** 1985. *Habits of the Heart: Individualism and Commitment in American Life*. New York: Harper & Row.

———. 1998. "Is There a Common American Culture?" *Journal of the American Academy of Religion* 66 (3): 613–26. Reprinted in Barbara Mori, ed. 2000. *Stand! Contending Ideas and Opinions: Race and Ethnicity*. Bellevue, WA: Coursewise Publishing.

Benedict, Ruth. 1928. "Psychological Types in the Cultures of the Southwest." Reprinted in Margaret Mead, ed., *An Anthropologist at Work: Writings of Ruth Benedict*. Boston: Houghton Mifflin.

———. 1934. *Patterns of Culture*. Boston: Houghton Mifflin.

Benedict, Ruth, and **Gene Weltfish.** 1943. "The Races of Mankind," Public Affairs Pamphlet No. 85. New York: Public Affairs Committee, Inc.

Bentley, Jeffery W., and **Gonzalo Rodrigúez.** 2001. "Honduran Folk Entomology." *Current Anthropology* 42 (2): 285–300.

Berlin, Brent, and **Paul Kay.** 1969. *Basic Color Terms: Their Universality and Evolution*. Berkeley: University of California Press.

Bermúdez de Castro, J. M., M. Matinón-Torres, E. Carbonell, S. Sarmiento, A. Rosas, J. Van der Made, and **M. Lozano.** 2004. "The Atapuerca Sites and Their Contribution to the Knowledge of Human Evolution in Europe." *Evolutionary Anthropology* 13 (1): 25–41.

Bernard, R. H., Pertti Pelto, O. Werner, J. Boster, K. A. Romney, A. Johnson, C. Ember, and **A. Kasakott.** 1986. "The Construction of Primary Data in Cultural Anthropology." *Current Anthropology* 27 (4): 382–96.

Bernard, Russell H. 1992. "Preserving Language Diversity." *Human Organization* 51 (1): 82–89.

Bickerton, Derek. 1985. *Roots of Language*. Ann Arbor, MI: Karoma Publishing.

———. 1999. *Language and Human Behavior*. Seattle: University of Washington Press.

———. 2008. *Bastard Tongue: A Trailblazing Linguist Finds Clues to Our Common Humanity in the World's Lowliest Languages*. New York: Hill and Wang.

Birdsell, Joseph B. 1981. *Human Evolution*, 3rd ed. Boston: Houghton Mifflin.

Birdwhistle, Ray. 1970. *Kinesics and Context*. Philadelphia: University of Pennsylvania Press.

Blakely, Robert L., and **Judith M. Harrington.** 1997. *Bones in the Basement: Postmortem Racism in Nineteenth-Century Medical Training*. Washington, DC: Smithsonian Institution Press.

Blinderman, C. 1986. *The Piltdown Inquest*. Buffalo, NY: Prometheus Books.

Bloch, Maurice. 2012. *Anthropology and the Cognitive Challenge*. Cambridge: Cambridge University Press.

Bloch, M., and **J. Parry.** 1989. *Money and the Morality of Exchange*. Cambridge: Cambridge University Press.

Bloch, Maurice, and **Dan Sperber.** 2002. "Kinship and Evolved Psychological Dispositions: The Mother's Brother Controversy Reconsidered." *Current Anthropology* 43 (5): 723–48.

Blumenschine, Robert J. 1995. "Percussion Marks, Tooth Marks, and Experimental Determinations of the Timing of Hominid and Carnivore Access to Long Bones at FLK Zinjanthropus, Olduvai Gorge, Tanzania." *Journal of Human Evolution* 29: 21–51.

Boas, Franz. 1927. *Primitive Art*. New York: Dover.

———. [1940] 1966. *Race, Language, and Culture*. New York: Free Press.

Bodley, John H. 1985. *Anthropology and Contemporary Human Problems*, 2nd ed. Mountain View, CA: Mayfield.

Bogin, B. A. 1978. "Seasonal Pattern in the Rate of Growth in Height of Children Living in Guatemala." *American Journal of Physical Anthropology* 49: 205–10.

Bonvillian, Nancy. 2010. *Language, Culture, and Communication: The Meaning of Messages*. 6th ed. Upper Saddle River, NJ: Pearson Prentice Hall.

Boster, James. 1987. "Agreement Between Biological Classification Systems Is Not Dependent on Cultural Transmission." *American Anthropologist* 89 (4): 914–19.

Bourdieu, Pierre. 1977. *Outline of a Theory of Practice*. Cambridge: Cambridge University Press.

———. 1984. *Distinction: A Social Critique of the Judgement of Taste*. London: Routledge.

Bower, Bruce. 1990. "Biographies Etched in Bone." *Science News* 138: 106–8.

Bown, T. M., and **K. D. Rose.** 1987. "*Patterns of Dental Evolution in Early Eocene Anaptomorphine Commomyodael from the Bighorn Basin, Wyoming*." *Journal of Paleontology* 61: 1–62.

Boyer, Pascal. 2001. *Religion Explained: The Evolutionary Origins of Religious Thought*. New York: Basic Books.

Brace, C. L. 1964. "The Fate of the 'Classic' Neanderthals: A Consideration of Hominid Catastrophism." *Current Anthropology* 5: 3–43.

———. 1967. *The Stages of Human Evolution: Human and Cultural Origins*. Englewood Cliffs, NJ: Prentice Hall.

———. 1989. "Medieval Thinking and the Paradigms of Paleoanthropology." *American Anthropologist* 91 (2): 442–46.

Brace, C. L., and **M. F. A. Montagu.** 1965. *Man's Evolution: An Introduction to Physical Evolution*. New York: Macmillan.

Bramble, D.M. and **D. E. Lieberman.** 2004. "Endurance Running and the Evolution of *Homo*." *Nature* 432: 345–352.

Braude, Benjamin. 1997. "The Sons of Noah and the Construction of Ethnic and Geographical Identities in the Medieval and Early Modern Periods."*The William and Mary Quarterly: A Magazine of Early American History and Culture* 54 (1): 103–42.

Breitbart, Eric. 1997. *A World on Display: Photographs from the St. Louis World's Fair, 1904*. Albuquerque: University of New Mexico Press.

Briller, Sheryln, H. and **Amy Goldmacher.** 2008. *Designing an Anthropology Career: Professional Development Exercises*. Walnut Creek, CA: Altamira Press.

Britten, Roy J. 2002. "Divergence between samples of chimpanzee and human DNA sequences is 5%, counting indels," *Proceedings of the National Academy of Science* 99 (21): 13633–13635.

Brooks, Alison, Fatimah L. C. Jackson, and **Roy Richard Grinker.** 2004. "Race and Ethnicity." In Ruth Osterweiss Selig, Marilyn R. London, and P. Ann Kaupp, eds., *Anthropology Explored: Revised and Expanded: The Best of Smithsonian Anthronotes*. Washington, DC: Smithsonian Books.

Broom, Robert. 1938. "The Pleistocene Anthropoid Apes of South Africa." *Nature* 142: 377–79.

———. 1949. "Another New Type of Fossil Ape Man." *Nature* 163: 57.

Brophy, K. and **Cowley, D., eds.** 2005. *From the Air: Understanding Aerial Archaeology*. London: The History Press Ltd.

Brothwell, D. R. and **A. M. Pollard.** 2001. *A Handbook of Archaeological Science*. Chicester: Willey.

Brown, Donald E. 1991. *Human Universals*. New York: McGraw-Hill.

Brown, Michael F. 2008. "Cultural Relativism 2.0" *Current Anthropology* 49 (3): 363–383.

Brown, P., and **R. Barrett. (Eds.).** 2010. *Understanding and Applying Medical Anthropology*. 2nd edition. New York: McGraw-Hill.

Brumfiel, Elizabeth. 1991. "Weaving and Cooking: Women's Production in Aztec Mexico." In Joan M. Gero and Margaret Conkey, eds., *Engendering Archaeology: Women and Prehistory*, pp. 224–51. Cambridge: Blackwell.

———. ed. 2005. "Production and Power at Postclassic Xaltocan." *Arqueología de México*, No. 6, published by University of Pittsburgh Latin American Archaeology Publications and Instituto Nacional de Antropología e Historia (México, D.F.).

Bruner, Edward M. 1996a. "Tourism in the Balinese Borderzone." In Smadar Lavie and Ted Swedenburg, eds., *Displacement, Diaspora, and Geographic Identity*, pp. 157–79. Durham: Duke University Press.

———. 1996b. "Tourism in Ghana: The Representation of Slavery and the Return of the Black Diaspora." *American Anthropologist* 98 (2): 290–304.

Brunet, Michel, Franck Guy, David Pilbeam, Hassane Taisso Mackaye, Andossa Likius, Djimdoumalbaye Ahounta, Alain Beauvilain, Cécile Blondel et al. 2002. "A New Hominid from the Upper Miocene of Chad, Central Africa." *Nature* 418: 145–51.

Bruning, Susan B., 2006. "Complex Legal Legacies: The Native American Graves Protection and Repatriation Act, Scientific Study, and Kennewick Man." *American Antiquity* 71(3): 501–521.

Byers, S. N. 2008. *Forensic Anthropology*. Boston: Pearson Education

Cain, Chester R. 2006. "Human Activity Suggested by the Taphonomy of 60 ka and 50 ka Faunal Remains From Sibudu Cave." *Southern African Humanities* 18(1):241–260.

Campbell, Anne, and **Patricia C. Rice.** 2003. "Why Do Anthropological Experts Disagree?" In Philip Carl Salzman and Patricia Rice, eds., *Thinking Anthropologically: A Practical Guide for Students*. Upper Saddle River, NJ: Prentice Hall.

Campbell, Bernard G. 1983. *Human Ecology: The Story of Our Place in Nature from Prehistory to the Present*. Chicago: Aldine.

Camps, M. and **Chauhan, P.R. (Eds.).** 2009. *Sourcebook of Paleolithic Transitions: Methods, Theories and Interpretations*. New York: Springer Press.

Cann, R. L., W. M. Brown, and **A. C. Wilson.** 1987. "Mitochondrial DNA and Human Evolution." *Nature* 325: 31–36.

Castro, A. Peter. 1995. *Facing Kirinyaga: A Social History of Forest Commons in Southern Mount Kenya*. Indigenous Knowledge Series. London: Intermediate Technology Publications.

———, ed. 1998a. "Special Section on Historical Consciousness and Development Planning." *World Development* 26 (9): 1695–1784.

———. 1998b. "Sustainable Agriculture or Sustained Error? The Case of Cotton in Kirinyaga, Kenya." *World Development* 26 (9): 1719–31.

Castro, A. Peter, ed. 1998. "Special Section on Historical Consciousness and Development Planning." *World Development* 26 (9): 1695–784.

Castro, A. Peter, and **Erik Nielsen.** 2001. "Indigenous People and Co-Management: Implications for Conflict Management." *Environmental Science and Policy* 4 (4–5): 229–39.

Castro, A. Peter, Dan Taylor, and **David Brokensha, eds.** 2012. *Climate Change and Threatened Communities: Vulnerability, Capacity and Action*. London: Practical Action Publishing.

Caton, Steven C. 1986. "Salam Tahiyah: Greetings from the Highlands of Yemen." *American Ethnologist* 13 (2): 290–308.

Cavalli-Sforza, L., P. Menozzi, and **A. Piazza.** 1994. *The History and Geography of Human Genes*. Princeton: Princeton University Press.

Chambers, Erve. 1985. *Applied Anthropology: A Practical Guide*. Englewood Cliffs, NJ: Prentice Hall.

Chapais, Bernard. 2008. *Primeval Kinship: How Pair-Bonding Gave Birth to Human Society*. Cambridge, MA: Harvard University Press.

Chomsky, Noam. 2002. *On Nature and Language*, edited by A. Belletti and Luigi Rizzi. Cambridge: Cambridge University Press.

Clapp, Nicholas. 1998. *The Road to Ubar: Finding the Atlantis of the Sands*. NY: Houghton Mifflin.

Clegg, Margaret. 2004. "Modern Approaches to the Evolution of Speech and Language." *General Anthropology* 10 (2): 8–12.

Clifford, James. 1983. "On Ethnographic Authority." *Representations* 1: 118–46.

Collier, Jane Fishburne, and **Sylvia Junko Yanagisako (eds.).** 1987. *Gender and Kinship: Towards a Unified Analysis*. Stanford: Stanford University Press.

Comaroff, Jean, and **John L. Comaroff.** 1991. *Of revelation and revolution: Christianity, colonialism, and consciousness in South Africa*. Vol. 1. Chicago: University of Chicago Press.

Coolidge, Frederick L., and **Thomas Wynn.** 2009. *The Rise of Homo sapiens*. Chichester: Wiley.

Cowgill, Donald O. 1986. *Aging Around the World*. Belmont, CA: Wadsworth.

Crockford, C. and **C. Boesch.** 2003. "Context-specific calls in wild chimpanzees, *Pan troglodytes verus*: Analysis of barks. *Animal Behaviour* 66: 115–25.

Cyran K. A., Kimmel M. 2010 "Alternatives to the Wright-Fisher model: the robustness of mitochondrial Eve dating". *Theor Popul Biol* 78 (3): 165–172.

D'Andrade, Roy G. 1989. "Cultural Cognition." In M. Posner, ed., *Foundations of Cognitive Science*. Cambridge, MA: MIT Press.

———. 1995. *The Development of Cognitive Anthropology*. Cambridge: Cambridge University Press.

Dalton, Rex. 2010. "Fossil finger points to new human species. DNA analysis reveals lost relative from 40,000 years ago." *Nature* 464: 472–473

Daniel, Glyn. 1981. *A Short History of Archaeology*. New York: Thames and Hudson.

Dart, Raymond A. 1925. "*Australopithecus africanus*: The Man-Ape of South Africa." *Nature* 115: 195–99.

———. 1967. *Adventures with the Missing Link*. Philadelphia: Institutes Press.

Darwin, Charles, and **E. Mayr. [1859]** 1966. *The Origin of Species* (Facsimile of the 1st ed.). Cambridge, MA: Harvard University Press.

Davies, Paul. 2000. *The Fifth Miracle: The Search for the Origin and Meaning of Life*. New York: Simon and Schuster.

Davis, David Brion. 1997. "Constructing Race: A Reflection." *The William and Mary Quarterly: A Magazine of Early American History and Culture*. 54 (1): 7–18.

Day, Michael H. 1986. *Guide to Fossil Man*, 4th ed. Chicago: University of Chicago Press.

Deacon, T. 1997. *The Symbolic Species: The Co-evolution of Language and the Brain*. New York: W.W. Norton.

DeCorse, Christopher. 2001. *An Archaeology of Elmina: Africans and Europeans on the Gold Coast, 1400–1900*. Washington, DC: Smithsonian Institution Press.

Deetz, James. 1996. *In Small Things Forgotten: An Archaeology of Early American Life*. New York: Anchor Books.

Degler, Carl N. 1991. *In Search of Human Nature: The Decline and Revival of Darwinism in American Social Thought*. New York: Oxford University Press.

de Heinzelin J, J. D. Clark, T. White, W. Hart, P. Renne, G. WoldeGabriel, Y. Beyene, and **E. Vrba.** 1999. "Environment and behavior of 2.5-million-year-old Bouri hominids." *Science* 284 (5414): 625–9.

Dembski, William A. 1999. *Intelligent Design: The Bridge Between Science and Theology*. Dallas: Intervarsity Press.

de Munck, Victor. 2000. *Culture, Self, and Meaning*. Prospect Heights, IL: Waveland Press.

———. 2009. *Research Design and Methods for Studying Cultures*. Lanham, MD: AltaMira Press.

Desmond, Adrian, and **James Moore.** 1991. *Darwin: The Life of a Tormented Evolutionist*. New York: Warner Books, Inc.

Deshpande, Omkar, Serafim Batzoglou, Marcus W. Feldman, and **L. Luca Cavalli-Sforza,** 2009. "A serial founder effect model for human settlement out of Africa." *Proceedings of the Royal Society B* 276, 291–300.

Diamond, Jared. 1993. "Speaking with a Single Tongue." *Discover* (February): 78–85.

Douglas, Mary. 1966. *Purity and Danger: An Analysis of the Concepts of Pollution and Taboo*. London: Routledge and Kegan Paul.

Duarte C., Maurício J., Pettitt P. B., Souto P., Trinkaus E., van der Plicht H., and **J. Zilhão.** 1999. "The early Upper Paleolithic human skeleton from the Abrigo do Lagar Velho (Portugal) and modern human emergence in Iberia." *Proceedings of the National Academy of Sciences* 96 (13): 7604–9.

Dubois, E. 1894. "*Pithecanthropus erectus*, Transitional Form Between Man and the Apes." *Scientific Transactions of the Royal Dublin Society* 6: 1–18.

Dumont, Louis. 1970. *Homo Hierarchicus: An Essay on the Caste System*, trans. Mark Sainsburg. Chicago: University of Chicago Press.

Edwards, David. 2010. "Counterinsurgency as a cultural system." *Small Wars Journal*. December 27.

Ekechukwu, L. C. 1990. "Encouraging National Development through the Promotion of Tourism: The Place of Archaeology." *Cultural Resource Management* 20: 120–25.

Ekman, Paul. 1973. "Cross-Cultural Studies of Facial Expressions." In P. Ekman, ed., *Darwin and Facial Expression: A Century of Research in Review*. New York: Academic Press.

Ekman, Paul, Wallace V. Friesen, and **John Bear.** 1984. "The International Language of Gestures." *Psychology Today*, May 1984. pp. 64–69.

Ellen, Roy F. 2010. "Theories in anthropology and anthropological theory." *Journal of the Royal Anthropological Institute (N.S.)* 16: 387–404.

Eriksen, Thomas Hylland. 2013. "Norwegian Anthropologists Study Minorities at Home: Political and Academic Agendas." In *Toward Engaged Anthropology*, edited by Sam Beck and Carl Maida. New York and Oxford: Berghahn Books.

Errington, Frederick, and **Deborah Gewertz.** 1987. "Of Unfinished Dialogues and Paper Pigs." *American Ethnologist* 14 (2): 367–76.

Evans-Pritchard, E. E. 1937. *Witchcraft, Oracles and Magic Among the Azande*. Oxford: Clarendon Press.

Fagan, Brian. 1988. "Black Day at Slack Farm." *Archaeology* 41 (4): 15–16, 73.

———. 1992. *Rape of the Nile*. Providence, RI: Moyer-Bell.

Farb, Peter. 1974. *Word Play: What Happens When People Talk*. New York: Knopf/Bantam.

Ferguson, Leland G. 1992. *Uncommon Ground: Archaeology and Colonial African America 1650–1800*. Smithsonian Institution Press, Washington, DC.

Fessler, Daniel M. T. 1999. "Toward an Understanding of the Universality of Second Order Emotions." In Alexander Laban Hinton, ed., *Biocultural Approaches to the Emotions*. Cambridge: Cambridge University Press.

Fessler, Daniel M. T., and **C. D. Naverette.** 2003. "Meat is good to taboo: dietary proscriptions as a product of the interaction of psychological mechanisms and social processes." *Journal of Cognition & Culture* 3: 1–40.

Fleuret, Patrick. 1988. "Farmers, Cooperatives, and Development Assistance in Uganda: An Anthropological Perspective." In David Brokensha and Peter D. Little, eds., *Anthropology of Development and Change in East Africa*. Boulder, CO: Westview Press.

Fluehr-Lobban, Carolyn. 2006. *Race and Racism: An Introduction*. Lanham, MD: AltaMira Press.

———. 2013. *Ethics and Anthropology: Ideas and Practices*. Lanham, MD: AltaMira Press.

Fouts, R. S. 1997. *Next of Kin: What Chimpanzees Have Taught Me about Who We Are*. New York: William Morrow and Company.

Fowler, Brenda. 2000. *Iceman: Uncovering the Life and Times of a Prehistoric Man Found in an Alpine Glacier*. Chicago: Chicago University Press.

Fox, Richard G. 1985. *Lions of the Punjab: Culture in the Making*. Berkeley: University of California Press.

Fox, Richard G., and **Barbara King, eds.** 2002. *Anthropology beyond Culture*. Oxford, England: Berg.

Franklin, A. Clifford, E. Williamson, and **I. R. L. Davies.** 2005. "The nature of infant color categorization: evidence from eye movements on a target detection task." *Journal of Experimental. Child Psychology*. 91, 227–248.

Frayer, David W., Milford H., Wolposs, Alan G., Thorne, Fred H., Smith, and **Geoffrey G. Pope.** 1993. "Theories of Modern Human Origins: The Paleontological Test." *American Anthropologist* 95 (1): 14–50.

Friedman, Jonathan. 1974. "Marxism, Structuralism, and Vulgar Materialism." *Man* 9: 444–69.

Frisancho, A. R. 1979. *Human Adaptation: A Functional Interpretation*. St. Louis, MO: C. V. Mosby.

Gallese Vittorio, Luciano Fadiga, Leonardo Fogassi, Giacommo Rizzolatti. 1996. "Action recognition in the premotor cortex." *Brain* 119, 593–609.

Gannon, J., R. L. Holloway, D. C. Broadfield, and **A. R. Braun.** 1998. "Asymmetry of Chimpanzee Planum Temporale: Humanlike Pattern of Wernicke's Brain Language Area Homolog." *Science* 279: 220–22.

Gardner, Howard. 2004. *Frames of Mind: The Theory of Multiple Intelligences*. New York: Basic Books.

Gardner, R. A., and **B. T. Gardner.** 1969. "Teaching Sign Language to a Chimpanzee." *Science* 16: 664–72.

Garn, Stanley. 1971. *Human Races*, 3rd ed. Springfield, IL: Chas. C Thomas.

Geertz, Clifford. 1963a. *Agricultural Involution: The Processes of Ecological Change in Indonesia*. Berkeley and Los Angeles: University of California Press.

———. 1973. *The Interpretation of Cultures: Selected Essays by Clifford Geertz*. New York: Basic Books.

Gibbons, A. 2011. "A new view of the birth of *Homo sapiens*." *Science* **331,** 392–394.

Gingerich, P. D. 1984. "Punctuated Equilibrium—Where is the Evidence?" *Systematic Zoology*, 33 (3): 335–38.

Gobineau, Joseph-Arthur. [1966] 1854. *Essays on the Inequality of Human Races*. Adrian Collins, trans. Los Angeles: Noontide Press.

Golding, William G. 1981. *The Inheritors*. New York: Harcourt Brace Jovanovich.

Golomb, Louis. 1985. *An Anthropology of Curing in Multiethnic Thailand*. Urbana: University of Illinois Press.

———. 1986. *The Chimpanzees of Gombe*. Cambridge, MA: Harvard University Press.

Goodman, M., M. L. Baba, and **L. L. Darga.** 1983. "The Bearings of Molecular Data on the Cladogenesis and Times of Divergence of Hominoid Lineages." In R. L. Ciochon and R. Corruccini, eds., *New Interpretations of Ape and Human Ancestry*, pp. 67–86. New York: Plenum Press.

Gordon, Alison. 2004. "Ape-ing Language: Communicating with Our Closest Relatives." In *Anthropology Explored: The Best of Smithsonian Anthronotes*. Washington, DC: Smithsonian Books.

Gould, S. J., and **Niles Eldredge.** 1972. "Punctuated Equilibrium: The Tempo and Mode of Evolution Reconsidered." *Paleobiology* 3: 115–51.

Granadillo, Tania and **Heidi A. Orcutt-Gachiri, eds.** 2011. *Ethnographic Contributions to the Study of Endangered Languages*. Tucson: University of Arizona Press.

Grant, P. R. 1999. *Ecology and Evolution of Darwin's Finches*. Princeton, NJ: Princeton University Press.

Green, Richard E., Johannes Krause, Adrian W. Briggs, Tomislav Maricic, Udo Stenzel, Martin Kircher, Nick Patterson, Heng Li, Weiwei Zhai, Markus Hsi-Yang Fritz, Nancy F. Hansen, Eric Y. Durand, Anna-Sapfo Malaspinas, Jeffrey D. Jensen, Tomas Marques-Bonet, Can Alkan, Kay Prüfer, Matthias Meyer, Hernán A. Burbano, Jeffrey M. Good, Rigo Schultz, Ayinuer Aximu-Petri, Anne Butthof, Barbara Höber, Barbara Höffner, Madlen Siegemund, Antje Weihmann, Chad Nusbaum, Eric S. Lander, Carsten Russ, Nathaniel Novod, Jason Affourtit, Michael Egholm, Christine Verna, Pavao Rudan, Dejana Brajkovic, Željko Kucan, Ivan Gušic, Vladimir B. Doronichev, Liubov V. Golovanova, Carles Lalueza-Fox, Marco de la Rasilla, Javier Fortea, Antonio Rosas, Ralf W. Schmitz, Philip L. F. Johnson, Evan E. Eichler, Daniel Falush, Ewan Birney, James C. Mullikin, Montgomery Slatkin, Rasmus Nielsen, Janet Kelso, Michael Lachmann, David Reich, and **Svante Pääbo.** 2010. "A Draft Sequence of the Neandertal Genome." *Science* 328 (5979): 710–722.

Greenberg, Joseph H., Keith Denning, and **Suzanne Kemmer, eds.** 1990. *On Language: Selected Writings of Joseph H. Greenberg*. Palo Alto, CA: Stanford University Press.

Gross, Paul and **Barbara Forest.** 2004. *Creationism's Trojan Horse: The Wedge of Intelligent Design*. New York: Oxford University Press.

Gruenbaum, Ellen. 2004. "Humanitarian Aid to Women and the Children of Darfur." *Anthropology News*, October: 8–11.

Gunz, Philip, Fred L. Bookstein, Philipp Mitteroecker, Andrea Stadlmayr, Horst Seidler and **Gerhard W. Weber.** 2009. "Early modern human diversity suggests subdivided population structure and a complex out-of-Africa scenario". *Proceedings of the National Academy of Sciences of the United States of America* 106 (15): 6094–6098.

Guthrie, Stewart. 1993. *Faces in the Clouds: A New Theory of Religion*. New York: Oxford University Press.

Haglund, K., and **M. H. Sorg.** 1997. *Forensic Taphonomy: The Postmortem Fate of Human Remains*. Boca Raton, FL: CRC Press.

Haile-Selassie, Yohannes; Suwa, Gen; White, Tim D. 2004. "Late Miocene Teeth from Middle Awash, Ethiopia, and Early Hominid Dental Evolution". *Science* 303 (5663): 1503–1505.

Hall, Edward T. 1981. *The Silent Language*. New York: Anchor Press.

Hall, Martin. 1988. "Archaeology Under Apartheid." *Archaeology* 41 (6): 62–64.

Halverson, John. 1987. "Art for Art's Sake in the Paleolithic." *Current Anthropology* 28: 63–89.

Hamilton, D. L., and **Robyn Woodward.** 1984. "A Sunken 17th Century City: Port Royal, Jamaica." *Archaeology* 37 (1): 38–45.

Hammer, M. F., T. Karafet, A. Rasnayagam, E. T. Wood, T. K. Alteide, T. Jenkins, R. C. Griffiths, A. R. Templeton, and **S. L. Zegura.** 1998. "Out of Africa and Back Again: Nested Cladistic Analysis of Human Y Chromosome Variation." *Molecular Biology and Evolution* 15: 427–41.

Hammer, Michael F., and **Stephen L. Zegura.** 2002. "The Human Y Chromosome Haplogroup Tree." *Annual Review of Anthropology* 31: 303–21.

Harding, R. M., S. M. Fullerton, R. C. Griffiths, J. Bond, M. J. Cox, J. A. Schneider, D. S. Moulin, and **J. B. Clegg.** 1997. "Archaic African and Asian Lineages in the Genetic Ancestry of Modern Humans." *American Journal of Human Genetics* 60: 772–89.

Hardman-de-Bautista, M. 1978. "Linguistic Postulates and Applied Anthropological Linguistics." In V. Honsa and M. Hardmande-Bautista, eds., *Papers on Linguistics and Child Language*. The Hague: Mouton.

Harrington, Spencer P. M. 1991a. "The Looting of Arkansas." *Archaeology* 44 (3): 22–30.

Harris, E. E., and **J. Hey.** 1999. "X Chromosome Evidence for Ancient Human Histories." *Proceedings of the National Academy of Sciences, USA* 96: 3320–24.

Harris, Marvin. 1977. *Cannibals and Kings: The Origins of Cultures*. New York: Random House.

———. 1979. *Cultural Materialism: The Struggle for a Science of Culture*. New York: Random House.

———. 1985. *The Sacred Cow and the Abominable Pig: Riddles of Food and Culture*. New York: Simon & Schuster.

———. 1988. *Culture, People, Nature: An Introduction to General Anthropology*, 5th ed. New York: Harper & Row.

———. 1999. *Theories of Culture in Postmodern Times*. Walnut Creek, CA: Altamira Press.

Hatch, Elvin. 1983. *Culture and Morality: The Relativity of Values in Anthropology*. New York: Columbia University Press.

Hauser, M. D., Chomsky, N., and **W. T. Fitch.** 2002. "The faculty of language: What is it, who has it, and how did it evolve?" *Science* 298: 1569–79.

Hawks, John D. 2013. Significance of Neandertal and Denisovan Genomes in Human Evolution." *Annual Review of Anthropology* 42: 433–49.

Hawks, John, Eric T. Wang, Gregory M. Cochran, Henry C. Harpending, and **Robert C. Moyzis.** 2007. "Recent acceleration of human adaptive evolution." *Proceedings of the National Science Academy* 26; 104 (52): 20753–20758.

Hays-Gilpin, Kelley. 2004. *Ambiguous Images: Gender and Rock Art*. Lanham Maryland. AltaMira Press.

Hays-Gilpin, Kelley, Ann Cordy Deegan, and **Elizabeth Ann Morris.** 1998. *Prehistoric Sandals from Northeastern Arizona: The Earl H. and Ann Axtell Morris Research*. University of Arizona Papers in Anthropology 62, Tucson.

Hays-Gilpin, Kelley, and **David S. Whitley, eds.** 1998. *Reader in Gender Archaeology*. London: Routledge.

Hefner, Robert W. 1983. "The Culture Problem in Human Ecology: A Review Article." *Comparative Studies in Society and History* 25 (3): 547–56.

Heider, Karl. 1979. *Grand Valley Dani: Peaceful Warriors*. New York: Holt, Rinehart and Winston.

———. 1991. *Landscapes of Emotion: Mapping Three Cultures of Emotion in Indonesia*. Cambridge: Cambridge University Press.

Hellenthal, Garrett, George B.J. Busby, Gavin Band, James F. Wilson, Cristian Capelli, Daniel Falush, Simon Myers. 2014. "A Genetic Atlas of Human Admixture History." *Science* 343 (6172): 747–751

Hendry, Joy. 2013. *Understanding Japanese Society*. 4th ed. New York: Routledge.

———. 1992. "Introduction and Individuality: Entry into a Social World." In Roger Goodman and Kirsten Refsing, eds., *Ideology and Practice in Modern Japan*. London: Routledge Press.

Henn, B. M.; Gignoux, C. R.; Feldman, M. W.; Mountain, J. L. 2009. "Characterizing the Time Dependency of Human Mitochondrial DNA Mutation Rate Estimates", *Molecular Biology and Evolution* 26 (1): 217–230

Henrich, Joseph, Steven Heine, and **Ara Norenzayan.** 2010. "The weirdest people in the world." *Behavioral and Brain Sciences* 33 (2/3): 1–75.

Henrich, Joseph, Robert Boyd, Samuel Bowles, Colin Camerer, Ernst Fehr, and **Herbert Gintis (eds.)** 2004. *Foundations of Human Sociality: Economic Experiments and Ethnographic Evidence from Fifteen Small-Scale Societies*. Oxford: Oxford University Press.

Henry, John. 2002. *The Scientific Revolution and the Origins of Modern Science*. New York: Palgrave.

Herrnstein, Richard J., and **Charles Murray.** 1994. *The Bell Curve: Intelligence and Class Structure in American Life*. New York: Free Press.

Herscher, Ellen. 1989. "A Future in Ruins." *Archaeology* 42 (1): 67–70.

Hewes, Gordon W., 1961. "Food Transport and the Origin of Hominid Bipedalism." *American Anthropologist*, 63, 687–710, (1961).

Hickerson, Nancy Parrott. 1980. *Linguistic Anthropology*. New York: Harper & Row.

Hinton, Alexander Laban, ed. 1999. *Biocultural Approaches to the Emotions*. Cambridge: Cambridge University Press.

Hirschfeld, Lawrence. 1986. "Kinship and Cognition: Geneology and the Meaning of Kinship Terms." *Current Anthropology* 27: 217–42.

———. 1989. "Rethinking the Acquisition of Kinship Terms." *International Journal of Behavioral Development* 12: 541–68.

Ho, S. Y., Phillips, M.J., Cooper, A., Drummond, A J. 2005. "Time Dependency of Molecular Rate Estimates and Systematic Overestimation of Recent Divergence Times", *Molecular Biology and Evolution* 22 (7): 1561–8.

Hockett, Charles F., and **R. Ascher.** 1964. "The Human Revolution." *Current Anthropology* 5: 135–68.

Hodgson, J. A., Bergey, C. M. & Disotell, T. R. 2010. "Neanderthal genome: The ins and outs of African genetic diversity." *Current Biology* 20, R517-R519.

Holloway, R. L. 1985. "The Poor Brain of *Homo sapiens neanderthalensis*: See What You Please." In E. Delson, ed., *Ancestors: The Hard Evidence*, pp. 319–24. New York: Alan R. Liss.

Hollox, Edward. 2005. "Evolutionary Genetics: Genetics of lactase persistence – fresh lessons in the history of milk drinking." *European Journal of Human Genetics*, 13, 267–269.

Holmberg, Allan R. 1962. "Community and Regional Development: The Joint Cornell-Peru Experiment." *Human Organization* 17: 12–16.

Howell, N; Smejkal, CB; MacKey, DA; Chinnery, PF; Turnbull, DM; Herrnstadt, C. 2003."The Pedigree Rate of Sequence Divergence in the Human Mitochondrial Genome: There Is a Difference Between Phylogenetic and Pedigree Rates", *American Journal of Human Genetics* 72 (3): 659–70.

Hsu, Francis. 1981. *Americans and Chinese: Passage to Differences*, 3rd ed. Honolulu: University of Hawaii Press.

Isaac, Barbara. 1995. "An Epimethean View of the Future at the Peabody Museum of Archaeology and Ethnology at Harvard University." *Federal Archaeology*. Offprint Series, Fall/Winter, pp. 18–22.

Isaac, G. L. 1978a. "The Food-Sharing Behavior of Protohuman Hominids." *Scientific American* 238 (4): 90–108.

Isaak, Mark. 2007. *The Counter-Creationism Handbook*. Westport: Greenwood Press.

Isbell, Billie Jean. 2013. "Lessons from Vicos." In *Toward Engaged Anthropology*, edited by Sam Beck and Carl Maida. New York and Oxford: Berghahn Books.

Iscan, Mehmet Yasar, and **Richard Helmer eds.** 1993. *Forensic Analysis of the Skull: Craniofacial Analysis, Reconstruction, and Identification*. New York: Wiley-Liss.

Işçan, M. Y. S., and **K. A. R. Kennedy.** 1989. *Reconstruction of Life from the Skeleton*. New York: Alan R. Liss.

Jablonka, E. and **M. J. Lamb.** 2006. *Evolution in Four Dimensions: Genetic, Epigenetic, Behavioral, and Symbolic in the History of Life*. Cambridge: MIT Press.

Jablonski, Nina G. 2012. *Living color: The biological and social meaning of skin color*. Berkeley: University of California Press.

Jablonski, Nina, and **George Chaplin.** 2010. "The Evolution of Skin Color." *Journal of Human Evolution* 39 (1): 57–106.

Jackendoff, R., and **S. Pinker.** 2005. The nature of the language faculty and its implications for evolution of language (reply to Fitch, Hauser, and Chomsky). *Cognition* 9 (7): 211–25.

Jackson, Donald Dale. 1992. "How Lord Elgin First Won—and Lost—His Marbles." *Smithsonian* 23 (9): 135–46.

Jameson, John H. 2004. *Reconstructed past: Reconstructions in the Public Interpretation of Archaeology and History*. Walnut Creek, CA: Altamira Press.

Jeong, Choongwon, Gorka Alkorta-Aranburu,Buddha Basnyat, Maniraj Neupane, David B. Witonsky, Jonathan K. Pritchard, Cynthia M. Beall, & Anna Di Rienzo. 2013. "Admixture facilitates genetic adaptations to high altitude in Tibet." *Nature Communications* 5 (3281).

Johanson, Donald C., and **James Shreeve.** 1989. *Lucy's Child: The Discovery of a Human Ancestor*. New York: Avon Books.

Johanson, Donald, and **Timothy White.** 1979. "A Systematic Assessment of Early African Hominids." *Science* 203: 321–30.

Johanson, Donald C., M. Taieb, and **Y. Coppens.** 1982. "Pliocene Hominid Fossils from Hadar, Ethiopia." *American Journal of Physical Anthropology* 57 (4): 1973–77.

Johnson, Allen W. 1975. "Time Allocation in a Machiguenga Community." *Ethnology* 14: 301–10.

Johnson, Ronald W., and **Michael G. Schene.** 1987. *Cultural Resources Management*. Malabar, FL: Robert E. Krieger.

Jones, Doug. 2000. "Group Nepotism and Human Kinship." *Current Anthropology* 41 (5): 779–809.

———. 2003. "Kinship and Deep History: Exploring Connections between Culture Areas, Genes, and Language." *American Anthropologist* 105 (3): 501–14.

———. 2004. "The Universal Psychology of Kinship: Evidence from Language." *Trends in Cognitive Sciences* 8 (5): 211–15.

Jorde, Lynn B. and **Stephen P. Wooding.** 2004. "Genetic Variation, Classification and 'Race'." *Nature Genetics* 36 (11): S28–S33.

Jurmain, Robert, L. Kilgore, W. Trevathan, and **R.L. Ciochon.** 2014. *Introduction to Physical Anthropology*. (2013–2014 ed.). Belmont, CA: Wadsworth. Cengage Learning.

Kankpeyeng, B. W., and **C. R. DeCorse.** 2004. "Ghana's Vanishing Past: Development, Antiquities and the Destruction of the Archaeological Record." *African Archaeological Review* 21 (2): 89–128.

Kaplan, Maureen F., and **John E. Mendel.** 1982. "Ancient Glass and the Disposal of Nuclear Waste." *Archaeology* 35 (4): 22–29.

Kay, Paul, Regier, T., and **Cook, S.** 2005. "Focal colors are universal after all." *Proceedings of the National Academy of Science, USA,* 102: 8386–8391.

Kelly, Raymond C. 2003. *Warless Societies and the Origin of War*. Ann Arbor: University of Michigan Press.

King, Thomas F. 2000. *Federal Planning and Historic Places: The Section 106 Process*. Walnut Creek, CA: Alta Mira Press.

———.2007. *Saving Places that Matter: A Citizen's Guide to the National Historic Preservation Act*. Walnut Creek, CA: Left-Coast Press.

———.2013. *Cultural Resource Laws and Practice*. Walnut Creek, CA: Alta Mira Press.

Klein, Richard. 2002. *The Dawn of Human Culture* with Blake Edgar. New York: John Wiley and Sons.

Kluckhohn, Clyde. 1967. *Navajo Witchcraft*. Boston: Beacon Press.

Knudson, Ruthann. 1989. "North America's Threatened Heritage." *Archaeology* 42 (1): 71–75.

Kondo, Dorinne. 1990. *Crafting Selves: Power, Gender, and Discourses of Identity in a Japanese Workplace*. Chicago: University of Chicago Press.

Konner, Melvin. 2002. *The Tangled Wing: Biological Constraints on the Human Spirit*, 2nd ed. New York: Holt, Rinehart and Winston.

———. 2010. *The Evolution of Childhood: Relationships, Emotion, Mind*. Cambridge, MASS: Belknap Press of Harvard University Press.

Krause, Johannes, Carles Lalueza-Fox, Ludovic Orlando, Wolfgang Enard, Richard E. Green, Hernán A. Burbano, Jean-Jacques Hublin, Catherine Hänni, Javier Fortea, Marco de la Rasilla, Jaume Bertranpetit, Antonio Rosas, Svante Pääbo. 2007. "The Derived *FOXP2* Variant of Modern Humans Was Shared with Neandertals" *Current Biology* 17(21): 1908–1912.

Krause, Johannes; Fu, Qiaomei; Good, Jeffrey M.; Viola, Bence; Shunkov, Michael V.; Derevianko, Anatoli P. & Pääbo, Svante. 2010. "The complete mitochondrial DNA genome of an unknown hominin from southern Siberia", *Nature* 464 (7290): 894–897

Krings, M., A. Stone, R. W. Schmitz, H. Krainitski, M. Stoneking, and **S. Paabo.** 1997. "Neandertal DNA Sequences and the Origins of Modern Humans." *Cell* 90: 19–30.

Kronenfeld, David B., Giovanni Bennardo, Victor C. de Munck, and **Michael D. Fischer (eds.)** 2011. *A Companion to Cognitive Anthropology*. Malden, Mass: Wiley-Blackwell

Kruckman, L. 1987. "The Role of Remote Sensing in Ethnohistorical Research." *Journal of Field Archaeology* 14: 343–51.

Kuhl, P. K., and **A. N. Meltzoff.** 1996. "Infant vocalizations in response to speech: Vocal imitation and developmental change." *Journal of the Acoustical Society of America*. 100: 2425–38.

Kumar, S., A. Filipski, V. Swarna, A. Walker, and **S. B. Hedges.** 2005. "Placing confidence limits on the molecular age of the human-chimpanzee divergence." *Proceedings of the National Academy of Sciences*, 102: 18842–18847.

Lahr, Marta Mirazon, and **Robert Foley.** 1994. "Multiple Dispersals and Modern Human Origins." *Evolutionary Anthropology* 3 (2): 48–60.

Kuper, Adam. 1988. *The Invention of Primitive Society*. London: Routledge Press.

Lakoff, George. 1987. *Women, Fire, and Dangerous Things*. Chicago: University of Chicago Press.

Lakoff, George, and **Mark Johnson.** 2000. *Philosophy in the Flesh: The Embodied Mind and Its Challenge to Western Thought*. New York: Basic Books.

Laland, Kevin N., and **Bennett G. Galef.** 2009. *The Question of Animal Culture*. Cambridge: Harvard University Press.

Lamason, Rebecca L., Manzoor-Ali P. K. Mohideen, Jason R. Mest, Andrew C. Wong, Heather L. Norton, Michele C. Aros, Michael J. Jurynec, Xianyun Mao, Vanessa R. Humphreville, Jasper E. Humbert, Soniya Sinha, Jessica L. Moore, Pudur Jagadeeswaran, Wei Zhao, Gang Ning,

Izabela Makalowska, Paul M. McKeigue, David O'Donnell, Rick Kittles, Esteban J. Parra, Nancy J. Mangini, David J. Grunwald, Mark D. Shriver, Victor A. Canfield, and **Keith C. Cheng.** 2005. "SLC24A5, a Putative Cation Exchanger, Affects Pigmentation in Zebrafish and Humans." Science 310 (5755): 1782–1786.

Lamberg-Karlovsky, C. C. 1989. *Archaeological Thought in America*. Cambridge: Cambridge University Press.

Langergraber, Kevin E., Kay Prüfer, Carolyn Rowney, Christophe Boesch, Catherine Crockford, Katie Fawcett, Eiji Inoue, Miho Inoue-Muruyama, John C. Mitani, Martin N. Muller, Martha M. Robbins, Grit Schubert, Tara S. Stoinski, Bence Viola, David Watts, Roman M. Wittig, Richard W. Wrangham, Klaus Zuberbühler, Svante Pääbo, and **Linda Vigilant.** 2012. "Generation times in wild chimpanzees and gorillas suggest earlier divergence times in great ape and human evolution." *Proceedings of the National Academy of the United States of America* 109 (39): 15716–15721.

Layton, R., ed. 1989. *Who Needs the Past? Indigenous Values and Archaeology*. London: Unwin Hyman Ltd.

Leach, Edmund. 1966. "Ritualization in Man in Relation to Conceptual and Social Development." *Philosophical Transactions of the Royal Society of London*, Series B 251 (772): 403–8.

———. 1988. "Noah's Second Son." *Anthropology Today* 4 (4): 2–5.

Leakey, L. S. B. 1959. "A New Fossil Skull from Olduvai." *Nature* 201: 967–70.

———. 1961. "Exploring 1,750,000 Years into Man's Past." *National Geographic* 120 (4): 564–89.

Leakey, M. D., and **R. L. Hay.** 1979. "Pliocene Footprints in Laetoli Beds at Laetoli, Northern Tanzania." *Nature* 278: 317–23.

Leakey, Meave G., C. S. Feibel, I. McDougall, and **A. Walker.** 1995. "New Four-Million-Year-Old Hominid Species from Kanapoi and Allia Bay, Kenya." *Nature* 376: 565–71.

Leakey, Meave; Spoor, Fred; Dean, M. Christopher; Feibel, Craig S., Antón, Susan C.; Kiarie, Christopher; Leakey, Louise N.2012 "New fossils from Koobi Fora in northern Kenya confirm taxonomic diversity in early Homo". *Nature* 488 (7410): 201–4.

Levinton, Jeffrey. 1988. *Genetics, Paleontology, and Macroevolution*. New York: Cambridge University Press.

Levi-Strauss, Claude. 1966. *The Savage Mind*, trans. George Weidenfeld and Nicholson, Ltd. Chicago: University of Chicago Press.

———. 1969. *The Elementary Structures of Kinship*, rev. ed., trans. J. H. Bell. Boston: Beacon Press.

Lewontin, R. 1972. "The Apportionment of Human Diversity." In Theodore Dobzhansky and William C. Steere, eds., *Evolutionary Biology*, Vol. 6, pp. 381–98. New York: Plenum Press.

Li, Wen-Hsiung, and **Masako Tanimura.** 1987. "The Molecular Clock Runs More Slowly in Man Than in Apes and Monkeys." *Nature* 326: 93–96.

Liebenberg, L. 2006. "Persistence hunting by Modern Hunter-Gatherers", *Current Anthropology* 47(6): 1017–1025.

Lieberman, Daniel E., Dennis M. Bramble, David A. Raichlen, and **John J. Shea.** 2007. "The evolution of endurance running and the tyranny of ethnography: A reply to Pickering and Bunn (2007)". *Journal of Human Evolution* 53: 434–437.

Lieberman, Leonard, and **Scupin, Raymond.** 2012. "A History of 'Scientific' Racialism." In *Race and Ethnicity: The United States and the World*, edited by Raymond Scupin. 2nd ed. Upper Saddle River, NJ: Prentice Hall.

Lieberman, Philip. 2007. "The Evolution of Human Speech: Its Anatomical and Neural Basis." *Current Anthropology* 48 (1): 39–66.

Lightfoot, K. G. 2005. *Indians, Missionaries, and Merchants: The Legacy of Colonial Encounters on the Colonial Frontiers*. University of California Press, Berkeley.

Linton, Ralph. 1936. *The Study of Man*. New York: Appleton-Century-Crofts.

Little, Barbara J. 2008 *Historical Archaeology: Why the Past Matters*. Walnut Creek, CA: LeftCoast Press.

Liu, Hua, Franck Prugnolle, Andrea Manica, and **François Balloux,** 2006. "A Geographically Explicit Genetic Model of Worldwide Human-Settlement History." *American Journal of Human Genetics* 79(2), 230–237.

Lovejoy, Owen C. 1981. "The Origin of Man." *Science* 211: 341–50.

———. 1984. "The Natural Detective." *Natural History* 93 (10): 24–28.

———. 1988. "Evolution of Human Walking." *Scientific American* 259 (5): 118–25.

Lovejoy, Owen C., Gen Suwa, Scott W. Simpson, Jay H. Matternes, and **Tim D. White.** 2009. "The Great Divides: *Ardipithecus ramidus* Reveals the Postcrania of Our Last Common Ancestors with African Apes." *Science* Vol. 326 (5949): 73, 100–106.

Lovejoy, Owen C., and **R. S. Meindl.** 1972. "Eukaryote Mutation and the Protein Clock." *Yearbook of Physical Anthropology* 16: 18–30.

Lucas, Gavin. 2012. *Understanding the Archaeological Record*. New York: Cambridge University Press.

Lucy, J., and **R. Shweder.** 1979. "Whorf and His Critics: Linguistic and Nonlinguistic Influences on Color Memory." *American Anthropologist* 81: 581–615.

Lucy, John. 1992. *Grammatical Categories and Cognition: A Case Study of the Linguistic Relativity Hypothesis*. Cambridge: Cambridge University Press.

Luhrmann, Tanya. 2013. "Building on William James: The role of learning in religious experience." In *Mental Culture: Classical Social Theory and the Cognitive Science of Religion* edited by Dimitris Xygalatas and William W. McCorkle Jr. Bristol, CT: Acumen Publishing Limited.

Lutz, Catherine. 1988. *Unnatural Emotions: Everyday Sentiments on a Micronesian Atoll and Their Challenge to Western Theory*. Chicago: University of Chicago Press.

Lyman, R. L. 2002. "Taphonomic Agents and Taphonomic Signatures." *American Antiquity* 67(2): 361–366.

MacEachern, Scott. 2012. "Race." In *Race and Ethnicity: The United States and the World*, edited by Raymond Scupin. 2nd ed. Upper Saddle River, NJ: Pearson Prentice Hall.

Madry, Scott. 2003. "Introduction to Remote Sensing: 15–3 to 15–14" in *Keys to Space, An Interdisciplinary Approach to Space Studies*, pages 15–3 to 15–14, edited by A. Houston and M. Rycroft, New York: McGraw-Hill.

———. 2007. "An Evaluation of Google Earth for Archaeological Aerial Prospection and Site Survey." In *Digital Discovery: Exploring New Frontiers in Human Heritage. CAA 2006—Computer Applications and Quantitative Methods in Archaeology*, Proceedings of the 34th Conference, Fargo, United States, April 2006. Jeffrey T. Clark and Emily M. Hagemeister, Editors. Budapest: Archaeolingua.

Madry, S., J. Sellers, and **M. Rycroft.** 2003. "Space in our Lives," in *Keys to Space, An Interdisciplinary Approach to Space Studies*, pages 1–1 to 1–9, edited by A. Houston and M. Rycroft, New York: McGraw-Hill.

Malinowski, Bronislaw. 1945. Foreword. In P. Kaberry, ed., *The Dynamics of Culture Change: An Inquiry into Race Relations in Africa*. New Haven, CT: Yale University Press.

Malotki, Ekkehart. 1983. *Hopi Time: A Linguistic Analysis of the Temporal Concepts in the Hopi Language*. Berlin: Mouton.

Manhein, Mary H. 2013. *Bone Remains: Cold Cases in Forensic Anthropology*. Baton Rouge: Louisiana State University Press.

Mann, Charles. 2002. "1491." *Atlantic Monthly*, March.

Mann, Robert W., Bruce E. Anderson, Thomas Holland, David R. Rankin, and **Johnny E. Webb, Jr.** 2003. "Unusual 'Crime' Scenes: The Role of Forensic Anthropology in Recovering and Identifying American MIAs." In Dawnie Wolfe Steadman, ed., *Hard Evidence: Case Studies in Forensic Anthropology*, pp, 108–16. Upper Saddle River, NJ: Prentice Hall.

Mann, Robert W., and **Thomas D. Holland.** 2004. "America's MIAs: Forensic Anthropology in Action." In Ruth Osterweiss Selig, Marilyn R. London, and P. Ann Kaupp, eds., *Anthropology Explored: Revised and Expanded: The Best of Smithsonian Anthronotes*. Washington, DC: Smithsonian Books.

Maricic, Tomislav, Viola Günther, Oleg Georgiev, Sabine Gehre, Marija Ćurlin, Christiane Schreiweis, Ronald Naumann, Herna´n A. Burbano, Matthias Meyer, Carles Lalueza-Fox, Marco de la Rasilla, Antonio Rosas, Srec´ko Gajovic´, Janet Kelso, Wolfgang Enard, Walter Schaffner, and **Svante Pääbo.** 2012. A Recent Evolutionary Change Affects a Regulatory Element in the Human FOXP2 Gene. *Molecular Biology and Evolution* 30 (4):844–852.

Marsden, Peter. 2003. *Sealed by Time: The Loss and Recovery of the Mary Rose*. Portsmouth: The Mary Rose Trust Ltd.

———. 2009. *Your Noblest Shippe: Anatomy of a Tudor Warship*. Portsmouth: The Mary Rose Trust Ltd.

Martin, R.D. 1990. *Primate Origins and Evolution: A Phylogenetic Reconstruction*. Princeton: Princeton University Press.

Martinez, I., Arsuaga J.L., Quam R., Carretero J.M., Gracia A., Rodrigues L. 2008. "Human hyoid bones from the middle Pleistocene site of the Sima de los Huesos (Sierra de Atapuerca, Spain. *Journal of Human Evolution* 54: 118–124.

Marx, Karl. [1859] 1959. *A Contribution of the Critique of Political Economy*. New York: International Publishers.

Mascia-Lees, Frances, and **Nancy Johnson Black.** 2000. *Gender and Anthropology*. Prospect Heights, IL: Waveland Press.

Mather, Paul D. 1994. *M.I.A.: accounting for the missing in Southeast Asia*. National Defense University Press.

Mauss, Marcel. 1985. "A Category of the Human Mind: The Notion of Person; the Notion of Self," trans. W. D. Halls. In Michael Carrithers, Steven Collins, and Steven Lukes, eds., *The Category of the Person: Anthropology, Philosophy, History*. Cambridge: Cambridge University Press.

Maybury-Lewis, David. 1985. "A Special Sort of Pleading: Anthropology at the Service of Ethnic Groups." In R. Paine, ed., *Advocacy and Anthropology*. St. John's: Institute of Social and Economic Research, Memorial University of Newfoundland.

———. 2002. *Indigenous Peoples, Ethnic Groups, and the State*. 2nd ed. Boston: Pearson Education, Allyn & Bacon.

Mayr, E. 1982. *The Growth of Biological Thought: Diversity, Evolution, and Inheritance*. Cambridge, MA: Belnap Press.

McBrearty, Sally and **Alison S. Brooks.** 2000. "The revolution that wasn't: a new interpretation of the origin of modern human behavior." *Journal of Human Evolution* 39(5):453–563

McDougall, Ian and **T. Mark Harrison,** 1999, *Geochronology and thermochronology by the $^{40}Ar/^{39}Ar$ method*. Oxford: Oxford University Press.

McDougall, Ian; Brown, Francis H.; Fleagle, John G. 2005. "Stratigraphic placement and age of modern humans from Kibish, Ethiopia". *Nature* 433 (7027): 733–736.

McElroy, A. and **P. Townsend**. 2009. *Medical Anthropology in Ecological Perspective*, 5th edition. Philadelphia: Westview.

McHenry, Henry M. 1982. "The Pattern of Human Evolution Studies on Bipedalism, Mastication, and Encephalization." *Annual Review of Anthropology* 11: 151–73.

———. 1988. "New Estimates of Body Weight in Early Hominids and Their Significance to Encephalization and Megadentia in Robust Australopithecines." In F. E. Grine, ed., *Evolutionary History of the Robust Australopithecines*, pp. 133–48. Hawthorne, NJ: Aldine.

McKeown, C. Timothy. 1998. "Ethical and Legal Issues, Complying with NAGPRA." In Rebecca A. Buck, Amanda Murphy, and Jennifer Schansberg, eds.,*The New Museums Registration Methods*. Washington, D.C.: American Association of Museums.

McPherron, Shannon P., Zeresenay Alemseged, Curtis W. Marean, Jonathan G. Wynn, Denné Reed, Denis Geraads, René Bobe, and **Hamdallah A. Béarat,** 2010. "Evidence for stone-tool-assisted consumption of animal tissues before 3.39 million years ago at Dikika, Ethiopia." *Nature* 466: 857–860.

Meggitt, Mervyn. 1977. *Blood Is Their Argument: Warfare Among the Mae Enga Tribesmen of the New Guinea Highlands*. Palo Alto, CA: Mayfield.

Mellars, Paul. 2006. "Why did modern human populations disperse from Africa ca. 60,000 years ago?" *Proceedings of the National Academy of Sciences* 103(25):9381–6.

Menotti, Francesco. 2004. *Living on the Lake in Prehistoric Europe: 150 Years of Lake-Dwelling Research*. New York: Routledge.

Mercader, Julio, Melissa Panger, and **Christophe Boesch.** 2002. "Excavation of a Chimpanzee Stone Tool Site in the African Rainforest." *Science* 296: 1452–55.

Miller, Kenneth R. 2000. *Finding Darwin's God: A Scientist's Search for Common Ground Between God and Evolution*. New York: HarperCollins.

Mines, Diane P. 2009. *Caste in India*. Key Studies in Asian Studies No. 4. Ann Arbor: Association for Asian Studies.

Mintz, Sidney, and **Christine M. Dubois.** 2002. "The Anthropology of Food and Eating." *Annual Reviews in Anthropology*. 31: 99–119.

Mithen, Steven. 1996. *The Prehistory of the Mind*. London: Thames and Hudson.

Molnar, Stephen. 2006. *Human Variation: Races, Types, and Ethnic Groups*, 6th ed. Upper Saddle River, NJ: Prentice Hall.

Monaghan, L., L. Hinton, and **R. Kephart.** 1997. "Can't Teach a Dog to Be a Cat?: A Dialogue on Ebonics." *Anthropology Newsletter* 38 (3): 1, 8, 9.

Montagu, Ashley. 1997. *Man's Most Dangerous Myth: The Fallacy of Race*, 6th ed. Walnut Creek, CA: Altamira Press.

Morgan, Lewis Henry. [1877] 1964. *Ancient Society*. Cambridge, MA: Harvard University Press.

Moro, Andrea. 2008. *The Boundaries of Babel: The Brain and the Enigma of Impossible Languages*. (Current Studies in Linguistics). Cambridge: MIT Press.

Morris, Ian. 2010. *Why the West Rules – For Now: The Patterns of History, and What They Reveal about the Future*. New York: Farrar, Straus and Giroux.

———. 2013. *The Measure of Civilization: How Social Development Decides the Fate of Nations*. Princeton: Princeton University Press.

Morton, D. Holmes; Morton, Caroline S.; Strauss, Kevin A.; Robinson, Donna L.; Puffenberger, Erik G; Hendrickson, Christine; Kelley, Richard I. 2003. "Pediatric medicine and the genetic disorders of the Amish and Mennonite people of Pennsylvania". *American Journal of Medical Genetics* 121C (1): 5 (June).

Motulsky, Arno. 1971. "Metabolic Polymorphisms and the Role of Infectious Diseases in Human Evolution." In Laura Newell Morris, ed., *Human Populations, Genetic Variation, and Evolution*. San Francisco: Chandler.

Mountain, Joanna L. 1998. "Molecular Evolution and Modern Human Origins." *Evolutionary Anthropology* 7 (1): 21–38.

Mukhopadhyay, Carol C., Rosemary Henze, and **Yolanda T. Moses. 2014.** *How Real Is Race: A Sourcebook on Race, Culture, and Biology*. Lanham and Boulder: Altamira Press.

Murdock, George. 1945. "The Common Denominator of Cultures." In Ralph Linton, ed., *The Science of Man in the World Crisis*, pp. 123–42. New York: Columbia University Press.

———. 1949. *Social Structure*. New York: Macmillan.

———. 1981a. *Atlas of World Cultures*. Pittsburgh: University of Pittsburgh Press.

———. 1981b. *Ethnographic Atlas*. Pittsburgh: University of Pittsburgh Press.

Myers, David G. 2012. *Exploring Psychology*, 9th ed. New York: Worth Publishers.

Newman, R. W., and **E. H. Munro.** 1955. "The Relation of Climate and Body Size in U.S. Males." *American Journal of Physical Anthropology* 13: 1–17.

Nisbett, Richard. 2009. *Intelligence and How to Get It: Why Schools and Culture Count*. New York: W.W. Norton & Co.

Noel Hume, Ivor. 1983. *Historical Archaeology: A Comprehensive Guide*. New York: Knopf.

Noonan, James P., Graham Coop, Sridhar Kdaravalli, Doug Smith, Johannes Krause, Joe Alessi, Feng Chen, Darren Platt, Svante Pääbo, Jonathan K. Pritchard, and **Edward M. Rubin.** 2006. "Sequencing and Analysis of Neanderthal Genomic DNA." *Science* 314 (5802): 1113–1118.

Norton, Heather L., Rick A. Kittles, Esteban Parra, Paul Mckiegue, Xianyun Mao, Keith Cheng, Victor A. Canfield, Daniel G. Bradley, Briand Mccoy, and **Mark D. Shriver.** 2007. "Genetic Evidence for the Convergent Evolution of Light Skin in Europeans and East Asians." *Molecular Biology and Evolution* 24(3): 710–722.

Olsen, Dale. 2004. *The Chrysanthemum and the Song: Music, Memory and Identity in the South American Japanese Diaspora*. Gainesville: University of Florida Press.

Omohundro, John. 1998. *Careers in Anthropology*. Mountain View, CA: Mayfield.

Ong, Aihwa. 2006. *Neoliberalism as Exception: Mutations in Citizenship and Sovereignty*. Durham, NC: Duke University Press.

Orlando L., Ludovic Orlando, Pierre Darlu, Michel Toussaint, Dominique Bonjean, Marcel Otte, and **Catherine Hänni.** 2006. "Revisiting Neandertal Diversity with a 100,000 Year Old mtDNA Sequence." *Current Biology* 16: 400–02.

Orser, Charles E. 2004. *Historical Archaeology*. Upper Saddle River, NJ: Pearson Education.

Ortner, Sherry. 1974. "Is Female to Male as Nature Is to Culture?" In Michelle Zimbalist Rosaldo and Louise Lamphere, eds., *Woman, Culture, and Society*, pp. 67–87. Stanford, CA: Stanford University Press.

———. 1996. *Making Gender: The Politics and Erotics of Culture*. Boston: Beacon Press.

Otterbein, Keith. 1974. "The Anthropology of War." In John Honigmann, ed., *Handbook of Social and Cultural Anthropology*. Chicago: Rand McNally.

Paigen, B., L. R. Goldman, J. H. Magnant, J. H. Highland, and **A. T. Steegman.** 1987. "Growth and Children Living Near the Hazardous Waste Site, Love Canal." *Human Biology* 59: 489–508.

Parkin, David. 2007. "The Accidental in Religious Instruction: Ideas and Convictions." In Berliner, David, and Ramon Sarr´o (eds.): *Learning Religion. Anthropological Approaches*. New York: Berghahn Books.

Parra, Esteban J. 2007. "Human Pigmentation Variation: Evolution, Genetic Basis, and Implications for Public Health." *Yearbook of Physical Anthropology* 50: 85–105.

Passingham, R. E. 1982. *The Human Primate*. San Francisco: W. H. Freeman.

Patterson, Francine, and **Donald Cohn.** 1978. "Conversations with a Gorilla." *National Geographic* 154: 454–62.

Patterson, Francine, and **Eugene Linden.** 1981. *The Education of Koko*. New York: Holt, Rinehart and Winston.

Peacock, James. 1986. *The Anthropological Lens: Harsh Light, Soft Focus*. Cambridge: Cambridge University Press.

Pennisi, Elizabeth. 2013 "More Genomes from Denisova Cave Show Mixing of Early Human Groups", *Science* 340: 799.

Pennock, Robert T. 2003. "Creationism and Intelligent Design." *Annual Review of Genomics and Human Genetics* 4: 143–63.

Petto, Andrew J., and **Laurie R. Godfrey, (eds.)** 2007. *Scientists Confront Intelligent Design and Creationism*. New York: W.W. Norton & Company.

Pilbeam, David. 1972. *The Ascent of Man*. New York: Macmillan.

Pinker, Steven. 1994. *The Language Instinct: How the Mind Creates Language*. New York: HarperCollins.

Plastino, W., L. Kaihola, P. Bartolomei, and **F. Bella.** 2001. "Cosmic Background Reduction in the Radiocarbon Measurement by Scintillation Spectrometry at the Underground Laboratory Of Gran Sasso." *Radiocarbon* 43 (2A): 157–161.

Pospisil, Leonard. 1967. "The Attributes of Law." In Paul Bohannon, ed., *Law and Warfare: Studies in the Anthropology of Conflict*. Garden City, NY: Natural History Press.

Potts, Richard. 1991. "Why the Oldowan? Plio-Pleistocene Toolmaking and the Transport of Resources." *Journal of Anthropological Research* 47: 153–76.

———. 1993. "Archaeological Interpretations of Early Hominid Behavior and Ecology." In D. Tab Rasmussen, ed., *The Origins and Evolution of Humans and Humanness*, pp. 49–74. Boston: Jones and Barlett.

Powdermaker, Hortense. 1966. *Stranger and Friend: The Way of an Anthropologist*. New York: W. W. Norton.

Poznik, G. David , Brenna M. Henn, Muh-Ching Yee, Elzbieta Sliwerska, Ghia M. Euskirchen, Alice A. Lin, Michael Snyder, Lluis Quintana-Murci, Jeffrey M. Kidd, Peter A. Underhill, Carlos D. Bustamante. 2013 "Sequencing Y Chromosomes Resolves Discrepancy in Time to Common Ancestor of Males Versus Females." *Science* 341(6145): 562–565

Prag, John, and **Richard Neave.** 1997. *Making Faces*. College Station: Texas A&M University Press.

Price, David, H. 2011. *Weaponizing Anthropology: Social Service of the Militarized State.* Oakland, CA: AK Press.

Pringle, Heather. 2006. *Master Plan: Himmler's Scholars and the Holocaust* (Paperback edition). *New York*: HarperCollins.

Prothero, Donald R. 1989. *Interpreting the Stratigraphic Record*. New York: W. H. Freeman.

Quinn, Naomi, and **Dorothy Holland.** 1987. "Culture and Cognition." In D. Holland and N. Quinn, eds., *Cultural Models in Language and Thought*. Cambridge: Cambridge University Press.

Quintyn, C. 2009 "The naming of new species in hominin evolution: A radical proposal—A temporary cessation in assigning new names." *HOMO: Journal of Comparative Human Biology* 60: 307–341

Rathbun, T. A., and **J. E. Buikstra.** 1984. *Human Identification: Case Studies in Forensic Anthropology*. Springfield, IL: Charles C. Thomas.

Rathje, William. 1984. "The Garbage Decade." *American Behavioral Scientist* 28 (1): 9–29.

———. 1992. "Five Major Myths about Garbage, and Why They Are Wrong." *Smithsonian* 23 (4): 113–22.

Rathje, William L., and **Cheryl K. Ritenbaugh.** 1984. "Household Refuse Analysis: Theory, Method, and Applications in Social Science." *American Behavioral Scientist* 28 (1): 5–153.

Reichs, Kathleen J. 1998. *Forensic Osteology: Advances in the Identification of Human Remains*, 2nd ed. Springfield, IL: Charles C. Thomas.

Relethford, John H. 2003. *Reflections of Our Past*. Boulder: Westview Press.

———. 2013. *The Human Species: An Introduction to Biological Anthropology*, 9th ed. Boston: McGraw-Hill.

Rendell, L., R. Boyd, D. Cownden, M. Enquist, K. Eriksson, M. W. Feldman, L. Fogarty, S. Ghirlanda, T. Lillicrap, and **K. N. Laland.** 2010. "Why Copy Others? Insights from the Social Learning Tournament." *Science9*: 328 (5975): 208–213.

Renfrew, Colin. 1989. *Archaeology and Language: The Puzzle of Indo-European Origins*. Cambridge: Cambridge University Press.

Renfrew, Colin, and **Paul Bahn.** 2012. *Archaeology: Theories, Methods and Practice*, 3rd ed. New York: Thames & Hudson.

Rennie, John. 2002. "Answers to Creationist Nonsense." *Scientific American*, July, pp. 78–85.

Repcheck, Jack. 2003. *The Man Who Found Time: James Hutton and the Discovery of the Earth's Antiquity*. New York: Perseus Books.

Rice, Prudence M. 1987. *Pottery Analysis: A Sourcebook*. Chicago: University of Chicago Press.

Richmond, D. G., D. R. Begu, and **D. S. Strait.** 2001. "Origin of Human Bipedalism." *Yearbook of Physical Anthropology* 44 (S33): 70–105.

Rickford, John R. 1997. "Suite for Ebony and Phonics." *Discovery* 18 (2): 82–87.

———. 1998. "The Creole Origins of African American Vernacular English: Evidence from *copula absence*." In Salikoko S. Mufwene, John R. Rickford, Guy Bailey and John Baugh, (eds). *African American English*, London: Routledge

Riesenfeld, Alphonse. 1973. "The Effect of Extreme Temperatures and Starvation on the Body Proportions of the Rat." *American Journal of Physical Anthropology* 39: 427–59.

Rightmire, G. P. 1993. *The Evolution of Homo Erectus: Comparative Anatomical Studies of an Extinct Human Species*. New York: Cambridge University Press.

———. 1997. "Human Evolution in the Middle Pleistocene: The Role of *Homo heidelbergensis*." *Evolutionary Anthropology* 6: 218–27.

Roberson, Debi. 2010. "Color in Mind, Culture, and Language." In Schaller, Mark, Ara Norenzayan, Steven J. Heine, Toshio Yamagishi, and Tatsuya Kameda (eds.) *Evolution, Culture, and the Human Mind*. New York: Psychology Press.

Roberson, Debi, Ian Davies, and **Jules Davidoff.** 2000. "Colour Categories Are Not Universal: Replications and New Evidence from Stone Age Culture." *Journal of Experimental Psychology* 129 (3): 369–98.

Roberson, Debi, J. Davidoff, and **I. Shapiro.** 2002. "Squaring the circle: the cultural relativity of good shape." *Journal of Culture and Cognition* 2: 29–52.

Rose, Jerome C., Thomas J. Green, and **Victoria D. Green.** 1996. "NAGPRA is Forever: Osteology and the Repatriation of Skeletons." *Annual Review of Anthropology* 25(1): 81–103

Roseberry, William. 1982. "Balinese Cockfights and the Seduction of Anthropology." *Social Research* 49: 1013–38.

Ross, Norbert. 2004. *Culture and cognition: implications for theory and method*. Thousand Oaks, CA, Sage.

Rossano, Matt, J. 2010. "Making Friends, Making Tools, and Making Symbols." *Current Anthropology* 51 (Supplement 1): S89–S98.

Royal, Charmaine D. M., and **Georgia M. Dunston.** 2004. "Changing the Paradigm from 'Race' to Human Genome Variation." *Nature Genetics* 36 (11): S5–S7.

Rozin, Paul. 2010. "Towards a Cultural/Evolutionary Psychology." In Schaller, Mark, Ara Norenzayan, Steven J. Heine, Toshio Yamagishi, and Tatsuya Kameda (eds.) *Evolution, Culture, and the Human Mind*. New York: Psychology Press.

Rubenstein, Robert A., Kerry Fisher, and **Clementine Fujimoro, eds.** 2012. *Practicing Military Anthropology: Beyond Expectations and Traditional Boundaries*. Sterling, VA: Kumarian Press.

Rudwick, Martin J. S. 1997. *Georges Cuvier, Fossil Bones, and Geological Catastrophes: New Translations and Interpretations of the Primary Texts*. Chicago: University of Chicago Press.

Rumbaugh, D. M. 1977. *Language Learning by a Chimpanzee: The Lana Project*. New York: Academic Press.

Sahlins, Marshall. 1976. *Culture and Practical Reason*. Chicago: University of Chicago Press.

Saler, Benson. 1993. *Conceptualizing Religion: Immanent Anthropologists, Transcendent Natives, and Unbound Categories*. Leiden: E. J. Brill.

Salmon, Merrilee H. 1997. "Ethical Considerations in Anthropology and Archaeology, or Relativism and Justice for All." *Journal of Anthropological Research* 53: 47–63.

Salzman, Philip. 1989. "The Lone Stranger and the Solitary Quest." *Anthropology Newsletter* 30 (5): 16, 44.

Sapolsky, Robert. 2006. "Social Culture Among Nonhuman Primates" *Current Anthropology* 47 (4): 641–656.

Sarich, V. M., and **A. C. Wilson.** 1967. "Rates of Albumen Evolution in Primates." *Proceedings of the National Academy of Sciences* 58: 142–48.

Sauer, Norman J., William A. Lovis, Mark E. Blumer, and **Jennifer Fillion.** 2003. "The Contributions of Archaeology and Physical Anthropology to the John McRae Case." In Dawnie Wolfe Steadman, ed., *Hard Evidence: Case Studies in Forensic Anthropology*, pp. 117–26. Upper Saddle River, NJ: Prentice Hall.

Savage-Rumbaugh, Sue E. 1986. *Ape Language: From Conditioned Response to Symbol*. New York: Columbia University Press.

Scarr, S., and **R. A. Weinberg.** 1978. "Attitudes, Interests, and IQ." *Human Nature* 1 (4): 29–36.

Schaller, George. 1976. *The Mountain Gorilla—Ecology and Behavior*. Chicago: University of Chicago Press.

Schell, Lawrence M., and **Melinda Denham.** 2003. "Environmental Pollution in Urban Environments and Human Biology." *Annual Review of Anthropology* 32: 111–34.

Schiffer, Michael B. 1987. *Formation Processes of the Archaeological Record*. Albuquerque: University of New Mexico Press.

Schmidt, Peter R., and **McIntosh, Roderick J., eds.** 1996. *Plundering Africa's Past*. Bloomington: Indiana University Press.

Scott, Eugenie C. 2004. *Evolution vs. Creationism: An Introduction*. Westport, CT: Greenwood Press.

Scudder, Thayer, and **Elizabeth Colson.** 1979. "Long-Term Research in Gwembe Valley, Zambia." In G. Foster, ed., *Long Term Field Research in Social Anthropology*. New York: Academic Press.

Scupin, Raymond. 1988. "Language, Hierarchy and Hegemony: Thai Muslim Discourse Strategies." *Language Sciences* 10 (2): 331–51.

———, ed. 2008a. *Religion and Culture: An Anthropological Focus*, 2nd ed. Upper Saddle River, NJ: Prentice Hall.

Sedley, D. N. 2007. *Creationism and Its Critics in Antiquity*. Berkeley: University of California Press.

Semaw, S.; Rogers, M. J.; Quade, J.; Renne, P. R.; Butler, R. F.; Domínguez-Rodrigo, M.; Stout, D.; Hart, W. S.; Pickering, T. et al. 2003. "2.6-Million-year-old stone tools and associated bones from OGS-6 and OGS-7, Gona, Afar, Ethiopia". *Journal of Human Evolution* 45 (2): 169–177.

Senghas, Kita S., and **A. Ozyurek.** 2004. "Children Creating Core Properties of Language: Evidence from an Emerging Sign Language in Nicaragua." *Science* 305 (5691): 1779–95.

Serageldin, Ismail, and **June Taboroff, eds.** 1994. "Culture and Development in Africa," *Environmentally Sustainable Development Proceedings Series* No. 1. Washington, DC: International Bank for Reconstruction and Development.

Serrat, M.A., King D., Lovejoy CO. 2008. "Temperature regulates limb length in homeotherms by directly modulating cartilage growth". *Proceeding of the National Academy of Sciences of the United States of America* 105 (49): 19348–19353

Shanks, Niall. 2004. *God, the Devil, and Darwin: A Critique of Intelligent Design Theory*. New York: Oxford University Press.

Shanks, Niall, and **Karl Joplin.**1999. "Redundant Complexity: A Critical Analysis of Intelligent Design in Biochemistry." *Philosophy of Science* 66: 268–82.

Shaw, Thurstan. 1986. "Whose Heritage?" *Museum* 149: 46–48.

Shea, B. T., and **A. M. Gomez.** 1988. "Tooth Scaling and Evolutionary Dwarfism: An Investigation of Allometry in Human Pygmies." *American Journal of Physical Anthropology* 77: 117–32.

Shipman, Pat. 1984. "Scavenger Hunt." *Natural History* 4 (84): 20–27.

———. 1986a. "Baffling Limb on the Family Tree." *Discover* 7 (9): 86–93.

———. 1994. *The Evolution of Racism*. New York, Simon and Schuster.

Shostak, Marjorie. 1981. *Nisa: The Life and Words of a !Kung Woman*. New York: Vintage Books, Random House.

Shweder, Richard. 1991. *Thinking Through Cultures: Expeditions in Cultural Psychology*. Cambridge, MA: Harvard University Press.

———. 2003. *Why Do Men Barbeque?: Recipes for Cultural Psychology*. Cambridge, MA: Harvard University Press.

———. 2013. "The goose and the gander: the genital wars." *Global Discourse: An Interdisciplinary Journal of Current Affairs and Applied Contemporary Thought* 3 (2): 348–366.

Simons, Elwyn L. 1989b. "Human Origins." *Science* 245: 1343–50.

Singleton, Theresa A. 1999. "I, Too, Am America." *Archaeological Studies in African American Life*. Charlottesville: University of Virginia Press.

Small, Meredith. 1998. *Our Babies, Ourselves: How Biology and Culture Shape the Way We Parent*. New York: Anchor Books.

———. 2001. *Kids: How Biology and Culture Shape the Way We Raise Our Children*. New York: Doubleday.

Smith, Eric Alden. 2013. "Agency and Adaptation: New Directions in Evolutionary Anthropology." *Annual Review of Anthropology* 42: 103–20.

Smith, F. H. 1984. "Fossil Hominids from the Upper Pleistocene of Central Europe and the Origin of Modern Europeans." In F. H. Smith and F. Spencer, eds., *The Origins of Modern Humans: A World Survey of Fossil Evidence*, pp. 137–210. New York: Alan R. Liss.

Smith, Neil. 1999. *Chomsky: Ideas and Ideals*. Cambridge: Cambridge University Press.

Snow, C. C., E. Stover, and **K. Hannibal.** 1989. "Scientists as Detectives Investigating Human Rights." *Technology Review* 92:2.

Snow, C. C., and **M. J. Bihurriet.** 1992. "An Epidemiology of Homicide: Ning'n Nombre Burials in the Province of Buenos Aires from 1970 to 1984." In T. B. Jabine and R. P. Claude, eds., *Human Rights and Statistics: Getting the Record Straight*. Philadelphia: University of Pennsylvania Press.

Soares P, Ermini L, Thomson N, et al. 2009. "Correcting for purifying selection: an improved human mitochondrial molecular clock", *American Journal of Human Genetics* 84 (6): 740–59

Soficaru, A., Doboş, A. and **Trinkaus, E.** 2006. "Early modern humans from the Peştera Muierii, Baia de Fier, Romania." *Proceedings of the National Academy of Sciences of the United States* 103 (46): 17196–17201.

Sperber, Dan. 1996. *Explaining Culture: A Naturalistic Approach*. Oxford: Blackwell Publishers.

Sperber, Dan, and **Deirdre Wilson.** 1996. *Relevance: Communication and Cognition*. Hoboken, NJ: Wiley-Blackwell.

Sperber, Dan, and **Lawrence Hirschfeld.** 1999. "Culture, Cognition, and Evolution." In Robert Wilson & Frank Keil (eds.) *MIT Encyclopedia of the Cognitive Sciences* (Cambridge, Mass. MIT Press, 1999), pp.cxi–cxxxii.

Spiro, Melford. 1993. *Culture and Human Nature*. New Brunswick: Transaction Publishers.

Sponsel, Leslie. 1996. "Human Rights and Advocacy Anthropology." In M. Ember and D. Levinson, eds., *Encyclopedia of Cultural Anthropology*, Vol. 2. New York: Henry Holt and Company.

Stanford, Craig B. 2012. "Chimpanzees and the Behavior of *Ardipithecus ramidus*." *Annual Review of Anthropology*, Vol. 41: 139–149

Starkweather, Katherine and **Raymond Hames**. 2012. "A Survey of Non-Classical Polyandry." *Human Nature* 23 (2): 149–172.

Steadman, Dawnie W. 2009. *Hard Evidence: Case Studies in Forensic Anthropology*. New York: Pearson.

Steudel, K. L. 1994. "Locomotor Energetics and Hominid Evolution." *Evolutionary Anthropology* 3: 40–48.

Stewart, T. D., ed. 1970. *Personal Identification in Mass Disasters*. Washington, DC: Smithsonian Institution Press.

Stiebing, William H. 1994. *Uncovering the Past: A History of Archaeology*. New York: Oxford University Press.

Stock, Jill Kamil. 1993. *Aswan and Abu Simbel: history and guide*. Cairo: American University in Cairo Press. pp. 141–142.

Stone, Linda. 2010. *Kinship and Gender: An Introduction*. 4th ed. Boulder, CO: Westview Press.

Stoneking, M., K. Bhatia, and **A. C. Wilson.** 1987. "Rate of Sequence Divergence Estimated from Restricted Maps of Mitochondrial DNAs from Papua, New Guinea." *Cold Spring Harbor Symposia on Quantitative Biology* 51: 433–39.

Stover, E. 1981. "Scientists Aid Search for Argentina's 'Desaparacidos.'" *Science* 211 (4486): 6.

———. 1992. "Unquiet Graves: The Search for the Disappeared in Iraqi Kurdistan." A report published by Middle East Watch and Physicians for Human Rights.

Strathern, Marilyn. 1984. "Subject or object? Women and the circulation of valuables in Highland New Guinea." In Renée Hirschon (ed.) *Women and property, women as property*. New York: St. Martins.

———. 1988. *The gender of the gift: Problems with women and problems with society in Melanesia*. Berkeley: University of California Press.

Stringer, C. B. 1985. "Middle Pleistocene Hominid Variability and the Origin of Late Pleistocene Humans." In E. Delson, ed., *Ancestors: The Hard Evidence*, pp. 289–95. New York: Alan R. Liss.

Stringer, C. B. 2001. "Modern human origins—distinguishing the models." *African Archaeological Review* 18(2): 67–75.

Stringer, C. B., and **P. Andrews.** 2005. *The Complete World of Human Evolution*. New York: Thames and Hudson Inc.

Sussman R. L. 1994. Fossil evidence for early hominid tool use. *Science* 265: 1570–1573.

Swadesh, Morris. 1964. "Linguistics as an Instrument of Prehistory." In Dell H. Hymes, ed., *Language and Society*. New York: Harper & Row.

Sweet, Louise. 1965. "Camel Raiding of North Arabian Bedouin: A Mechanism of Ecological Adaptation." *American Anthropologist* 67: 1132–50.

Szabo, G. 1967. "The Regional Anatomy of the Human Integument with Special Reference to the Distribution of Hair Follicles, Sweat Glands and Melanocytes." *Philosophical Transactions of the Royal Society of London* 252B: 447–85.

Tapper, Richard, and **Nancy Tapper.** 1992, 1993. "Marriage, Honor, and Responsibility: Islamic and Local Models in the Mediterranean and Middle East." *Cambridge Anthropology* 16 (2): 3–21.

Tattersall, Ian. 1986. "Species Recognition in Human Paleontology." *Journal of Human Evolution* 15: 165–75.

———. 1998. *Becoming Human*. New York: Harcourt Brace and Company.

Tax, Sol. 1953. *Penny Capitalism: A Guatemalan Indian Economy*. Smithsonian Institution, Institute of Social Anthropology, Publication No. 16. Washington, DC: U.S. Government Printing Office.

Taylor R. E and **J. Southon,** 2007. "Use of natural diamonds to monitor 14C AMS instrument backgrounds." *Nuclear Instruments and Methods in Physics Research B 259*: 282–28.

Templeton, Alan R. 1993. "The 'Eve' Hypothesis: A Genetic Critique and Reanalysis." *American Anthropologist* 95 (1): 51–72.

———. 2002. "Out of Africa Again and Again." *Nature* 416: 45–51.

Terrace, Herbert S. 1986. *Nim: A Chimpanzee Who Learned Sign Language*. New York: Columbia University Press.

Thomason, Sarah G., and **Terrence Kaufman.** 1988. *Language Contact, Creolization, and Genetic Linguistics*. Berkeley: University of California Press.

Thorne, A., and **M. H. Wolpoff.** 1992. "The Multiregional Evolution of Humans." *Scientific American* 266: 76–83.

Throckmorton, Peter. 1962. "Oldest Known Shipwreck Yields Bronze Age Cargo." *National Geographic* 121 (5): 697–711.

Tobias, P. V. 1998. "Evidence for the early beginnings of spoken language." *Cambridge Archaeological Journal* 1: 72–78.

Tomasello, M., Carpenter, M., Call J., Behne, T., and **Moll, H.** 2005. "Understanding and sharing intentions: The origins of cultural cognition." *Behavioral and Brain Sciences* 28: 675–691.

Toth, Nicholas, and **Kathy Schick, eds.** 2004. *The Oldowan: Case Studies into the Earliest Stone Age*. Bloomington, IN: Stone Age Institute Press.

Trigger, Bruce. 1993. *Early Civilizations: Ancient Egypt in Context*. Cairo: American University in Cairo Press.

———.2006. *A History of Archaeological Thought. 2nd ed.* Cambridge: Cambridge University Press.

Trinkaus, Erik. 2006. Modern Human versus Neandertal Evolutionary Distinctiveness. *Current Anthropology* 47(4): 597–620.

Trinkaus, Erik and **Shipman, Pat.** 1993. *The Neandertals: Changing the Image of Mankind*. New York: Alfred A. Knopf Pub.

Tripcevich, Nicholas and **Steven A. Wernke.** 2010. "On-Site Recording of Excavation Data Using Mobile GIS." *Journal of Field Archaeology* 35(4): 380–397.

Turner, Victor. 1969. *The Ritual Process: Structure and Anti-Structure*. Ithaca, NY: Cornell University Press.

Tylor, Edward B. 1871. *Primitive Culture*. London: J. Murray.

Urciuoli, Bonnie. 1996. *Exposing Prejudice: Puerto Rican Experiences of Language, Race, and Class*. Boulder: Westview Press.

———. 2003. "Boundaries, Language, and the Self: Issues faced by Puerto Ricans and other Latina/o College Students." *The Journal of Latin American Anthropology* 8 (2): 152–173.

Van Gennep, Arnold. 1960. *The Rites of Passage*. Chicago: University of Chicago Press.

Van Willigen, John, and **V. C. Channa.** 1991. "Law, Custom, and Crimes Against Women: The Problem of Dowry Death in India." *Human Organization* 50 (4): 369–77.

Vayda, Andrew P. 1961. "Expansion and Warfare Among Swidden Agriculturalists." *American Anthropologist* 63: 346–58.

Vekua, Abesalom, David Lordkipanidze, G. Philip Rightmire, Jordi Agusti, Reid Ferring, Givi Maisuradze, Alexander Mouskhelishvili, Medea Nioradze, Marcia Ponce de Leon, Martha Tappen, Merab Tvalchrelidze, and **Christoph Zollikofer.** 2002. "A New Skull of Early *Homo* from Dmanisi, Georgia." *Science* 297: 85–89.

Vianna, N. J., and **A. K. Polan.** 1984. "Incidence of Low Birth Weight Among Love Canal Residents." *Science* 226: 1217–19.

von Humboldt, W. [1836] 1972. *Linguistic Variability and Intellectual Development*, trans. C. G. Buck and F. Raven. Philadelphia: University of Pennsylvania Press.

Walker, A. R., E. Leakey, J. M. Harris, and **F. H. Brown.** 1986. "2.5 MYR *Australopithecus boisei* from West of Lake Turkana, Kenya." *Nature* 322: 517–22.

Washburn, Sherwood. 1960. "Tools and Human Evolution." *Scientific American* 203 (3): 67–75.

Wax, Dustin. 2008. *Anthropology at the Dawn of the Cold War*. London: Pluto.

Wax, Rosalie. 1971. *Doing Fieldwork: Warnings and Advice*. Chicago: University of Chicago Press.

Weiner, J. 1994. *The Beak of the Finch*. New York: Knopf.

Weiner, J. S. 1955. *The Piltdown Forgery*. London: Oxford University Press.

Welcher, Laura. 2009. "Human Language as a Secret Weapon." *Rosetta Project* http://rosettaproject.org/blog/02009/nov/25/human-language-secret-weapon/.

West, Fred. 1975. *The Way of Language: An Introduction*. New York: Harcourt Brace Jovanovich.

Wheeler, P.E. 1991. "The thermoregulatory advantage of hominid bipedalism in open equatorial environments: The contribution of increased convective heat loss and cutaneous evaluative cooling." *Journal of Human Evolution* 21: 117–136.

———. 1992. "The influence of the loss of functional body hair on the water budgets of early hominids." *Journal of Human Evolution* 23, 379–388.

———. 1994. "The thermoregulatory advantages of heat storage and shade-seeking behavior to hominids foraging in equatorial savannah environments." *Journal of Human Evolution* 26, 339–350.

White, Leslie. [1949] 1971. "The Symbol: The Origin and Basis of Human Behavior." In Leslie White, ed., *The Science of Culture: A Study of Man and Civilization*. New York: Farrar, Straus & Giroux.

———. 1959. *The Evolution of Culture*. New York: McGraw-Hill.

White, T. D. 1995. "Early Hominids—Diversity or Distortion?" *Science* 299: 1994–97.

White, T. D., B. Asfaw, D. DeGusta, H. Gilbert, G. D. Richards, G. Suwa, and **F. C. Howell.** 2003. "Pleistocene Homo sapiens from Middle Awash, Ethiopia." *Nature* 423: 742–47.

White, Tim D.; Asfaw, Berhane; Beyene, Yonas; Haile-Selassie, Yohannes; Lovejoy, C. Owen; Suwa, Gen; Wolde-Gabriel, Giday. 2009. "Ardipithecus ramidus and the Paleobiology of Early Hominids". *Science* 326 (5949): 75–86.

Whitehouse, Harvey. 2004. *Modes of Religiosity: A Cognitive Theory of Religious Transmission*. Walnut Creek, CA: AltaMira Press.

Whitehouse, Harvey and **Luther H. Martin.** 2004. *Theorizing Religions Past: Archaeology, History, and Cognition*. Walnut Creek, CA: Altamira Press.

Whorf, Benjamin. 1956. *Language, Thought, and Reality: The Selected Writings of Benjamin Lee Whorf*. Cambridge, MA: MIT Press.

Wilk, Richard R. 1996. *Economies and Cultures: Foundations of Economic Anthropology*. Boulder, CO: Westview Press.

Wilkinson, Caroline D. 2004. *Forensic Facial Reconstruction*. Cambridge University Press.

Williams, Robin M., Jr. 1970. *American Society: A Sociological Interpretation*, 3rd ed. New York: Knopf.

Williams-Blangero, S., and **J. Blangero.** 1992. "Quantitative Genetic Analysis of Skin Reflectance: A Multivariate Approach." *Human Biology* 64: 35–49.

Wilson, A. C., and **R. L. Cann.** 1992. "The Recent African Genesis of Humans." *Scientific American* 266 (4): 68–73.

Wilson, Caroline. 2010. "'Eating, eating is always there, food consumerism and cardiovascular disease: Some evidence from Kerala south India." *Anthropology and Medicine* 17 (3): 261–275.

Winchester, Simon. 2002. *The Map That Changed the World: William Smith and the Birth of Modern Geology*. New York: HarperCollins.

Wolpoff, M., and **R. Caspari.** 1997. *Race and Human Evolution*. West view Press, Boulder, CO.

Wolpoff, M., and **R. Caspari.** 2002. *Race and Human Evolution: A Fatal Attraction*. New York: Simon and Schuster.

Wolpoff, M. H., Hawks J., Senut B., Pickford M., and **J. Ahern.** 2006. "An Ape or *the* Ape: Is the Toumaï Cranium TM 266 a Hominid?" *PaleoAnthropology*, 2006: 36–50.

Wood, B. A. 2002. "Palaeoanthropology: Hominid revelations from Chad." *Nature* 418, 133–135.

Workman, P. L., B. S. Blumberg, and **A. J. Cooper.** 1963. "Selection, Gene Migration and Polymorphic Stability in a U.S. White and Negro Population." *American Journal of Human Genetics* 15: 71–84.

Wynn, T. 1995. "Handaxe enigmas." *World Archaeology* 27: 10–24.

———. 1998. "Did *Homo erectus* speak?" *Cambridge Archaeological Journal* 1: 78–81.

Yang, Z. 2002. "Likelihood and Bayes estimation of ancestral population sizes in hominoids using data from multiple loci."*Genetics* 162: 1811–1823.

Yangisako, Sylvia J., and **Jane F. Collier.** 1990. "The Mode of Reproduction in Anthropology." In *Theoretical Perspectives on Sexual Difference*, edited by Deborah Rhode. New Haven, CT: Yale University Press.

Yengoyan, Aram A. 1986. "Theory in Anthropology: On the Demise of the Concept of Culture." *Comparative Studies in Society and History* 28 (2): 357–74.

Yokoyama Y, Falguères C, Sémah F, Jacob T, Grün R. 2008."Gamma-ray spectrometric dating of late Homo erectus skulls from Ngandong and Sambungmacan, Central Java, Indonesia." *Journal of Human Evolution* 55(2):274–7.

Young, Christian C., and **Mark A. Largent.** 2007. *Evolution and Creationism: A Documentary and Reference Guide*. Westport: Greenwood Press.

Photo Credits

Chapter 1 Dr. Raymond B. Hames, 1; dtopal/Shutterstock.com, 4 (tl); Education Images/Universal Images Group Limited/Alamy, 4 (bl); John Hawks, 5 (tl); Christopher DeCorse, 6 (t); Kelley Hays-Gilpin at the Museum of Northern Arizona front entrance, Photo by Michele Mountain, © 2006 Museum of Northern Arizona, 7 (tl); Courtesy of Christina Dames, 8 (tl); Nancy L. Ford Photography, 9 (tl); Courtesy of Scott Atran, 11 (tl); Courtesy of A.H. Peter Castro, 12 (tl); Christopher DeCorse, 18 (tl).

Chapter 2 Bob Ainsworth/Getty Images, 21; Erich Lessing / Art Resource, NY, 23 (t); bpk, Berlin/ Art Resource, NY, 27 (tr); akg-images/Newscom, 27 (br); Courtesy of Rodney Livingston, 28 (tl); Christopher DeCorse, 28 (tc); sbarabu/ Shutterstock, 28 (tr); AKG/Science Source, 30 (bl); U.S. Department of Agriculture, 39 (br).

Chapter 3 Christopher Ricciardi, 54; Christopher R. DeCorse, 57 (tl); Merrick Posnansky, 62 (cl); Institute of Nautical Archaeology, 64 (tl); AP Photo/Jae C. Hong, 65 (tl); Reuters/ Corbis, 65 (tr); Press Association / AP Images, 66 (tl); Courtesy of Matthew Johnson, 67 (br); Courtesy of Laurence Kruckman, Indiana University of Pennsylvania, 68 (bl); Courtesy of Laurence Kruckman, Indiana University of Pennsylvania, 68 (br); NASA, 69 (tl); Courtesy of Douglas V. Armstrong, Syracuse University, 70 (tl); J.D. Dallet/AGE Fotostock, 71 (tl); Courtesy of Marek E. Jasinski, Institute of Historical Studies, Archaeology Programme Norwegian University of Science and Technology, 71 (br); Christopher R. DeCorse, 78 (br); Denny Ellis / Alamy, 78 (cl); Pics/Fotolia, 78 (tl).

Chapter 4 John Reader / Science Source, 82; Christophe Boisvieux/Eureka/Corbis, 92 (tl); Pearson Education/PH College, 93 (tr); Christopher DeCorse, 94 (bl); Christopher DeCorse, 96 (bl).

Chapter 5 Rawpixel/Shutterstock, 121; John Moss/Science Source, 128 (bl); Cindy Hopkins/Alamy, 128 (br); Jackie Lewin, Royal Free Hospital / Science Source, 131 (tr); John Warburton-Lee/Getty Images, 133 (bl); H. Mark Weidman Photography / Alamy, 134 (bl); George Holton/Science Source, 136 (tl); Peter Menzel / Science Source, 137 (tl); National Archives and Records Administration, 141 (tl).

Chapter 6 Jon Bower Thailand / Alamy, 149; Courtesy: CSU Archives / Everett Collection / Alamy, 151 (tl); Tom McHugh / Science Source, 151 (cr); Lawrence Migdale/Science Source, 151 (br); Ali Mubarak/Grapheast / Alamy, 157 (bl); Cartoonresource/Shutterstock, 157 (tr); Connie Bransilver / Science source, 160 (bl); Donald E. Brown, 162 (tl); Vassar College Art Gallery/Library, 165 (tr); Creativa/Fotolia, 166 (t); Raymond Scupin, 167 (tl).

Chapter 7 Michael DeFreitas Middle East / Alamy, 176; Susan Kuklin/Science Source, 179 (tr); Kay & Karl Ammann/ BRUCE COLEMAN INC./Alamy, 180 (tl); Cartoonresource/ Shutterstock, 182 (tl); Goodluz/Shutterstock, 188 (tl); Anette Selmer-Andresen / Alamy, 189 (tr); Angela Hampton Picture Library/Alamy, 190 (bl); Ed Kashi/ Encyclopedia / Corbis, 191 (tl); Edward S. Curtis/Corbis, 193 (br); Pawel Bienkowski / Alamy, 200 (br); Robin Laurance / Alamy, 200 (br); Hoang Van Danh/Bettmann/Corbis, 201 (tc); JackF/Fotolia, 201 (cr); Platslee/Shutterstock, 201 (br); Rob/Fotolia, 201 (tr).

Chapter 8 Morandi Bruno/Hemis.fr/Alamy, 204; Library of Congress Prints and Photographs Division[LC-USZC4-8725], 206 (tl); Time & Life Pictures/Getty Images, 207 (br); North Wind Picture Archives / Alamy, 209 (tr); Ian Stewart/ Shutterstock, 210 (tl); SPL / Science Source, 211 (br); Mary Evans Picture Library / Alamy, 213 (t); Stefan Ember/123RF, 219 (tr).

Chapter 9 Karl Johaentges/Alamy, 226; Haytham Pictures/Alamy, 229 (tr); Cartoonresource/Shutterstock, 232 (t); Vasina Nazarenko/Fotolia, 239 (tr); Yulia Nikulyasha Nikitina/Shutterstock, 240 (tl); FotoFlirt/Alamy, 244 (bl); Andres Rodriguez/Fotolia, 253 (tl); Nancy L. Bridges, 257 (br).

Chapter 10 Hamilton Wright/Photo Researchers Inc., 262; Courtesy of Gene O'Donnell, FBI, 265 (bl); Courtesy of Federal Bureau of Investigation, 265 (lc); Federal Bureau of Investigation, 265 (rc); Federal Bureau of Investigation, 265 (br); Jacinski, 267 (tl); AP Images/Victor Ruiz C, 268 (tl); xixinxing/Fotolia, 271 (tr); CASBS Archives, 271 (br); Courtesy of the General Services Administration, 275 (cr); Jacinski, 275 (tr); Rick Shupper /Ambient Images Inc. / Alamy, 275 (tl); Christopher R. DeCorse, 278 (bl); The Trustees of The British Museum / Art Resource, NY, 281 (tr); Design Pics / Alberto Arzoz/Alberto Arzoz/Newscom, 285 (tr); Library of Congress, 286 (tl); Adam Kazmierski/Getty Images, 291 (tr).

Index